NORFOLK: THE FIRST FOUR CENTURIES

≈

NORFOLK

The First Four Centuries

THOMAS C. PARRAMORE

with Peter C. Stewart
and Tommy L. Bogger

University Press of Virginia
Charlottesville and London

THE UNIVERSITY PRESS OF VIRGINIA
Copyright © 1994 by the Rector and Visitors
of the University of Virginia

First published 1994

Library of Congress Cataloging-in-Publication Data
Parramore, Thomas C.
    Norfolk : the first four centuries / by Thomas C. Parramore with Peter C. Stewart
    and Tommy L. Bogger.
p.   cm.
  ISBN 0-8139-1557-0
  1. Norfolk (Va.)—History.   I. Stewart, Peter C.   II. Bogger, Tommy.   III. Title.
  F234.N8P375   1994
975.5'521—dc20   94–9457
                                                 CIP

Printed in the United States of America

CONTENTS

CONTENTS

CONTENTS

ILLUSTRATIONS

ILLUSTRATIONS

Cover (in color): From Nauticus to Harber Park: A New Vision
for an Old City (Bill Tiernan); The Elizabeth River (Latrobe),
Maryland Historical Society, Baltimore.

ACKNOWLEDGMENTS

OUR WORK in preparing this volume has been facilitated and encouraged by many individuals. We owe a special debt of gratitude to Dr. John Foster, city councilman and pastor of Shiloh Baptist Church in Norfolk, for conceiving the plan to publish a history of Norfolk and for his guidance and help throughout the course of the project.

Dr. Linda C. Davis, Norfolk parking administrator, has served as the project's coordinator from the beginning and has enabled us to surmount innumerable difficulties. Her constant support and her uncanny ability to resolve problems have kept us on track when matters threatened to go awry.

General oversight of the Norfolk History Project was undertaken by an advisory committee appointed in 1988 by the Norfolk city council. The members of this committee were Dr. Mason C. Andrews, now the mayor of Norfolk, Richard Barry, president of Landmark Communications, Staige Blackford, editor of the *Virginia Quarterly*, Dr. Tommy Bogger, archivist of Norfolk State University, Dr. Marion Capps, professor emerita of Norfolk State, Dr. Gene Carter, former superintendent of Norfolk public schools, Dr. John Foster, Dr. Alf J. Mapp Jr., eminent professor of English of Old Dominion University, Dr. Herbert Marshall, professor emeritus of Norfolk State University, Robert Mason, former editor of the *Virginian-Pilot*, and George Tucker, columnist and historian of the *Virginian-Pilot*.

Especially helpful was the diligence of Dr. John Selby of the department of history at the College of William and Mary and Richard Barry, members of a supervisory subcommittee of the advisory committee. Both read various drafts of the manuscript and offered many suggestions and corrections that have much improved the book. Drs. Capps and Mapp also provided helpful suggestions. Another subcommittee member, City Manager James B. Oliver, has been a source of assistance in many ways, including arrangements to keep the citizens of Norfolk abreast of the project's progress. Dr. Peter Wallenstein, associate professor of history of the Virginia Polytechnical Institute, also read the manuscript and offered copious criticisms and suggestions, which have much improved the work.

Important historical materials were furnished by Dr. Andrews, Rick

ACKNOWLEDGMENTS

Nowitzky, Irwin Berent, and Albert Doumar, among others. Vital aid in locating sources and illustrations was provided by the staff of the Norfolk Public Library. Miss Peggy Haile, head of the Library's Sargeant Room, and her predecessor, Cynthia Seay, were infinitely patient and resourceful in tracking down hard-to-find items and directing us to helpful sources. We also acknowledge the courtesy and cooperation of the library's director, Mrs. Sue Darden Williams.

Former Mayor Joseph B. Leafe was instrumental in giving the project a proper start and supporting it in its early phases. Much of the labor of locating illustrations was efficiently performed by Mrs. Laurie Cecil. Assistant City Manager Darlene L. Burcham was indispensable in her handling of the finances of the Norfolk History Project. Others who furnished helpful services have included Brenda Andrews, publisher of the Norfolk *Journal and Guide*, Mrs. Margaret Gordon, former mayor Roy B. Martin, and the staffs of the Swem Library of the College of William and Mary, the Portsmouth Public Library, Chrysler Museum, and Hampton Roads Maritime Museum. Dr. Barbara M. Parramore of North Carolina State University has been of extraordinary technical, intellectual, and emotional aid to the main author throughout the life of the project.

Also helpful in the research were the following, to whom we offer our appreciation: Mrs. Myrtle Crawford, Herbert Collins, Joseph T. Fitzpatrick, Father Joseph Green, Mrs. Edythe C. Harrison, Julian Hirst, Judge Walter Hoffman, Ms. Annette Montgomery, Mrs. Celestyne Porter, Dr. Samuel D. Proctor, Dr. Marvin Schlegel, Mrs. Zelda Silverman, Judge Lydia C. Taylor, Herman Valentine, Mr. and Mrs. Forest White, Dr. Lucy Wilson, and Mrs. Mattie Roane and her staff at the Lyman Beecher Brooks Library, Norfolk State University.

Finally we were greatly aided by the work of the late Carroll Walker, whose extensive collection of photographs and illustrations of the old Norfolk and the new, published and unpublished, are the finest and most extensive source of pictorial materials relating to the city.

INTRODUCTION

NORFOLK'S harbor has provided mariners with one of the world's best and safest ports for over three centuries. The city has developed into the principal home of the United States Navy and America's largest maritime shipper.

In contrast, however, with its well-deserved reputation as a haven from the storms and other dangers of the North Atlantic, Norfolk's metropolitan history has been one of fierce contention between the city, on one hand, and outside forces and its own inner demons on the other. Inhabitants of this great refuge from the sea have rarely enjoyed the blessings of tranquility.

Even its aboriginal Chesapeake Indians were victims of a mysterious fate, first, possibly, by carnage at the hands of Chief Powhatan, then, more certainly, by white forces from the Jamestown settlement. The Indian town of Skicoak, on the site of the present Norfolk, disappeared, like the tribe itself, without a trace before some of their remains were unearthed in the twentieth century.

The history of Norfolk is that of continuing challenges and the quest for effective responses. Conceived in the late seventeenth century, it emerged in 1682 out of a demoralizing tide of adverse circumstances. These included wars between England and Holland, which several times came to Norfolk's doorstep, and hurricanes that visited with unremitting regularity, on one occasion destroying virtually every manmade structure in Virginia. Then came social explosions, climaxed by Bacon's Rebellion in the 1670s, which set the classes in opposition to one another and wrought civil chaos—in Norfolk as elsewhere in Virginia.

But that was not all. In its earliest years, Norfolk was plagued by pirates, Blackbeard and Captain Kidd among them, who ravaged the Virginia coast and all but interdicted the port's commerce. Then came devastating eighteenth-century plagues, notably a smallpox epidemic that carried off a high percentage of the city's population. In the Revolutionary War, Norfolk, several times a scene of British occupation and bloody military encounters, was burned to the ground, mostly at the hands of Patriot forces aiming to keep it out of the hands of the British.

INTRODUCTION

Malevolent forces struck early in the nineteenth century in the form of a prolonged sea-war, culminating in the War of 1812 and British blockade of the Chesapeake Bay. This was followed by the scourge of epidemic cholera and a yellow fever plague that carried off a third of the population and caused many of the survivors to abandon the city for good. All races suffered in these calamities, but the Afro-American population, slave and free, endured, in addition, its own peculiar categories of day-to-day desperation.

Norfolk rallied from each disaster, but they were only rehearsals for the trials of the Civil War, which saw the city occupied by an enemy army in the war's first year and made captive for the duration. Afro-Americans gained a temporary respite of freedom at the war's end, only to see it largely snatched away in the postwar years.

Alien forces—war, storm, disease, and more—have continued to threaten Norfolk in the past century. But modern Norfolk has had less to fear from these crises, severe though they have sometimes been, than from its inner struggles. Politics and race, the Janus faces of the unresolved war for the emancipation of slaves, have sustained Norfolk's heritage of struggle. Maelstroms of reform and reaction, progress and retrenchment, have afflicted the past four or five generations more than any enemy from beyond the city limits.

Norfolk has been a focus of judicial struggles for and against mandated school-busing for integration, equal pay for black and white teachers, the treatment of blacks by labor unions, discriminatory housing and election machinery, and other legal battles of the past seven decades. For lengthy epochs of its modern history, it has been held in thralldom to ill-intentioned forces within and beyond. Sometimes this thralldom has been to the dominance of rival cities or to the machinations of state and federal politicians. But often enough it has been to Norfolk's own dynamic energies, which, for good and ill, have been all but impossible to channel or control.

A city with so much turbulence marking its history would seem to have been destined to be physically stunted and emotionally frustrated. But Norfolk has fought its way back from ruin in each of its first three centuries and continues doing so in its fourth. Gifts of nature and circumstance, in the form of a magnificent harbor, a gentle climate, a curiously effective ethnic amalgam, and a generally progressive partnership of elites and ordinary citizens, have worn down every adversary, outwrestled the inner demons. Long a "Navy Town," thriving on America's foreign wars, it has in recent decades managed to diversify its economy and weaken the negative impact of post— Cold War military reductions. A creature of the Chesapeake Bay, it now struggles to arrest the great bay's deterioration. Its history provides encouragement that it will succeed.

Norfolk's haven has given it opportunity to serve the nation and the world in invaluable ways; its storms have added drama and character to the undertaking. As harsh as the consequences have so often been, the city's citizens may do well to pray that challenges of the sort they have mastered will not cease. Conflicts of wartime and peace have built this great city and with their recurrence its future rests.

NORFOLK: THE FIRST FOUR CENTURIES

CHAPTER 1

Mission to Ajacán

JUNE 1561. The great canoe sat almost motionless, its white wings somehow tucked away, its hairy-faced people waving their arms and shouting obscure words of encouragement toward the land. As news of the visitation spread, other Indians joined those on the beach and there was talk of someone paddling out to test whether the visitors were inclined to do some trading.

Such strangers had appeared before from time to time along Ajacán's shores and were known to carry exotic wares. It was said by some that such boat-people could be seduced with an armful of deerhides or martenskins into parting with such priceless articles as copper vessels or iron tomahawks. It was axiomatic that no such goose should pass unplucked.

Presently a party of the Chiskiack men embarked in canoes, boarded the vessel, and greeted its company. With clear indications of the friendly disposition of the visitors, the *weroance* himself, his son Paquiquino, and others of distinction were taken out to the vessel in a dugout heavy with furs and fresh provisions. It was a rare commercial opportunity that beckoned, one that might not present itself again for years to come. The waiting ship, the *Santa Catalina*, like a sister vessel farther out in the bay, was commanded by Pedro Menéndez de Avilés and had left Havana some weeks before to explore the North American coast.[1]

Menéndez perhaps had put in here in the southern part of what his charts called Bahía de Santa Maria (Chesapeake Bay) only for refuge from a winter storm. But it was to be a memorable occasion in the history of colonial enterprise. From this brief encounter came Spain's northernmost attempt at American colonization and one of the most extraordinary adventures to befall an American Indian in the course of European colonial experience.

The circumstance destined to ignite the remarkable chain of events of the next dozen years was the agreeable impression the Indian chief's son made on Menéndez. Paquiquino in 1561 was probably about seventeen years of age, reputedly a tall, well-made, and intelligent young man.[2] To Menéndez and others he seemed the very embodiment of the sort of native American Spain needed in order to convert these Indians one day to Christianity and unlock the secrets of their mysterious continent.

In Spanish versions of the tale, Menéndez proposed to the weroance that the splendid son be permitted, with a servant of his, to accompany the ship to Spain and remain some time as a guest. The Spaniard is said to have "pledged his word to return him with much wealth and many garments." Whether the chief actually assented to this proposition or the two Indians were simply kidnapped cannot be known, but the young man was soon en route to Europe. The *Santa Catalina* reached Seville on September 29, 1561.[3]

The voyage may have given Paquiquino opportunity to gain a working knowledge of the Spanish tongue and some appreciation of the purposes of the light-skinned men. They talked to him a good deal about their religion and questioned him as to whether there might be another great sea not far west of Bahía de Santa Maria. They spoke of their king, Philip II, and of rival kings with similar interests who might send ships to harm the people of Ajacán, as Paquiquino called his homeland. But the astonishing relations of the mariners and the wonders of their ships were soon overwhelmed by Paquiquino's experiences in Spain itself.

Paquiquino's introduction to the Spanish court and royal family in October 1561 was for Pedro Menéndez de Avilés more than the exhibition of a human trophy from the New World. Old men still lived who had accompanied Columbus abroad in the previous century, but the years since had revealed no passage through America to storied India and China. Much of the North American coast, however, was still unexplored and might yet reveal a water passage to the Pacific. It was Menéndez's belief from his investigations that Bahía de Santa Maria was connected by an inland waterway north to the Gulf of St. Lawrence. From the latter, he felt, one might sail westward to the Pacific.[4] Thus, Bahía de Santa Maria was a door to the Orient and Paquiquino the key to opening it.

Bahía de Santa Maria had been dimly known and more dimly charted by Europeans for almost half a century. The French under Verrazzano and the Spanish under Estevan Gomes sailed past it in 1524. Pedro de Quejo first placed it on a map in 1525 when, arriving there on July 2, the feast day of St. Mary, he gave the bay its name. Englishman John Rut in 1527 and another French ship in 1546 were among those known to have passed or entered the bay. By 1560 there were reports of shipwrecks and other European contacts with the region.[5] But no one had scouted the bay for an opening to the west, and Menéndez, an aristocrat of wealth and enterprise, was determined to see that it was done.

Only Spanish settlement could achieve both the conversion of the natives to the religion of Christ and extended inquiry into the geography of the hinterland. In addition, a Spanish presence on the bay might deny its use to English and French privateers and pirates who preyed on Spanish treasure fleets. Shipments of silver and gold from the Gulf of Mexico, using the Gulf Stream as far north as Hatteras, were vulnerable to enemies operating from the Bahía de Santa Maria. Moreover, a Spanish outpost there might help thwart the French, who were already trying to settle in Canada, from encroaching into the American heartland.[6]

While Menéndez sought help for a settlement on Bahía de Santa Maria, Paquiquino won favor with Philip II and a royal allowance to outfit himself in the clothing and gear of a man of high rank. It was arranged that he would be placed with friars of the Dominican order in Seville for studies in religion and Spanish to ready him for possible service among the American Indians.[7]

As the training and acculturation of Paquiquino proceeded, he gained insight into the nature of European society and the workings of the Western mind. But his great hope was to return to Ajacán, and he represented himself as a champion of the colonization scheme and an optimist regarding the prospect of converting his own and other tribes.[8] Clearly, as the son and heir of a chief as well as a fluent interpreter, he would be indispensable to such an effort.

In May 1562 Paquiquino and his servant left Spain with the redoubtable Menéndez for Mexico, royal and ecclesiastical support for a mission in Ajacán all but assured. But Menéndez, hoping for early realization of his project, was baffled by accidents and delays. The two Indians fell gravely ill in Mexico City. Then there was interference from the archbishop of New Spain, who suspected Paquiquino, a pagan, of disloyalty to the Catholic cause. (A colony on the Carolina coast in 1526 had been ruined by a native interpreter-guide who, trained much as Paquiquino was, betrayed the colonists.) Recovering his health, Paquiquino applied for and was granted Christian baptism, allaying suspicions against him. So pleased was the Mexican viceroy with this that he bestowed his own name, Luis de Velasco, on Paquiquino, and the Spanish thereafter referred to him by that name.[9]

When Paquiquino finally set out by ship in August 1566 with a party of Dominicans and soldiers, their captain, Pedro de Coronas, missed Bahía de

Santa Maria heading north and again after doubling back. After a fruitless search of the Currituck Sound area south of the bay for something Luis might recognize, and a storm-ravaged effort to land at Chincoteague Island, the expedition headed for Spain. They reached Cadiz in late October.[10]

The disappointed Paquiquino, trusting in Menéndez to find means to renew the project, resumed his studies in Seville. This time, however, he resided with the Jesuits, now the foremost backers of colonization and an object of courtship by the energetic Menéndez. During three years with the Jesuits, Paquiquino was reported as "advancing in the Spanish language, both in reading and writing, together with other branches of knowledge which they taught him." He also gained a reputation as something of a "big talker," a "self-styled 'big chief,'" whose tales of himself and his homeland might not be wholly reliable. Around 1567 the Jesuits administered to Paquiquino "the holy sacraments and confirmation" as a Roman Catholic.[11]

In the end it was Paquiquino rather than Menéndez who set the plan in motion again. He persuaded the Jesuits that he could convert "his parents, relations, and countrymen" to Christianity. The Jesuits so far had had little success with their *La Florida* missions but blamed it on the small and declining Indian populations in this southeastern region. Perhaps a mission in more populous areas to the north would fare better. The order applied to both Philip II and Pope Paul V for permission, and Menéndez again provided financial backing. In early 1570 a new expedition, headed by Father Juan Baptista de Segura (and including Paquiquino and other Jesuits), set sail for St. Augustine.[12]

This time things went more smoothly. The missionaries convened at Santa Elena (Parris Island, S.C.) in August 1570 and set sail for Ajacán. With Segura and Paquiquino went six other Jesuits, including Father Luis de Quirós and three boys. Captain Vicente Gómez put them ashore on Paquiquino's native soil on September 10, fulfilling the nine-year-old promise of Pedro Menéndez de Avilés. They landed on the north bank of what the English later called the James River, probably at what is now College Creek, about five miles east of the future Jamestown. Segura and Quirós were delighted when the Ajacán Indians received them joyfully, greeting Paquiquino as having "risen from the dead and come down from heaven."[13]

Probably at Paquiquino's urging, the Spanish moved north across the peninsula to the York River. Trunks of vestments, ornaments, clothing, and so on were carried to a new location at the mouth of Kings Creek where it met the river. The site was near a sprawling village of a tribe later known as the Chiskiacks, ruled by a brother of Paquiquino. It was a walk of a day and a half—perhaps twenty miles—from Paquiquino's native village.[14]

Paquiquino's joy at homecoming was impaired by the stupefying blight that had enveloped Ajacán in the preceding six years. His father and older brother were dead, a younger brother at the point of death. Yet another younger brother had assumed the office of weroance. He at once offered to step aside so that Paquiquino might become weroance. But the latter declined, a decision that did not seem to suit some of his people.[15]

The main concern of the moment was the famine throughout the region, where little rain had fallen since 1564. Father Segura wrote in a letter dispatched on a returning ship that many natives had died and others had moved away in search of a better food supply. Maize, wild roots, and fruit, the staples of both human and animal diets, were extremely scarce, and the Indians would part with food only upon adequate reimbursement. Meat was also in short supply, though fish were presumably abundant. Segura dispatched to New Spain a plea that grain be sent at least by early April for planting by both Indians and whites. Because the Indians were too poor even to have large canoes, the missionaries appropriated a whaleboat from Gómez's ship for their own needs.[16]

The mission itself, its food supply reduced to a small amount of flour and biscuits after feeding the ship's crew from its rations, could expect lean times until relief supplies arrived some months later. Nevertheless, Father Quirós added that "Don Luis has turned out well as was hoped, he is most obedient to the wishes of Father [Segura] and shows deep respect for him, as also the rest of us here."[17] No doubt the Spaniards had entertained suspicions as to Paquiquino's loyalty once he was back on his native soil.

Paquiquino was obviously crucial to the welfare of the mission, particularly since he was entitled to a position on the council of the weroance. His tribe was only one of two dozen or more between the lower Potomac River and Lynnhaven Bay, but the favor of a weroance would be decisive in procuring food and molding the attitude of members of the tribe.[18]

With Indian help, the Jesuits soon built a log "cottage" or "cabin," with a "small apartment" to one side for holding Mass until a chapel could be erected. The structure must have contrasted strongly with the irregular scattering of barrel-roofed cabins that comprised the surrounding village. The Indians made cabins by bending and lashing together the tops of sapling poles and covering them with bark or reed mats. Each cabin normally housed six to twenty persons; a small entrance and a smoke-hole at the top were the only openings. The Jesuits probably desired more durable struc-

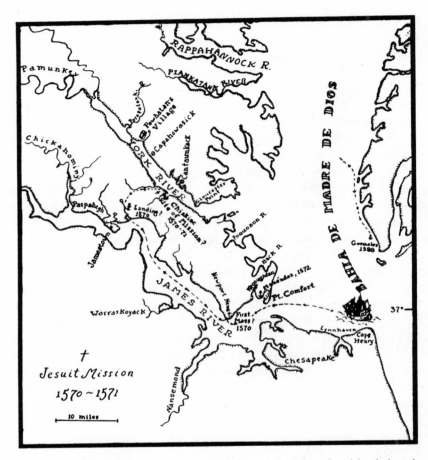

Location on the James River (near what became Jamestown) where Spanish missionaries are thought to have landed in 1570 and their supposed York River mission. (Reprinted from *The Spanish Jesuit Mission in Virginia,* by Lewis and Loomie. Copyright © 1953 by The University of North Carolina Press)

tures than those of the Indians, who were used to moving whole villages every few years as gardens and fields became unproductive.[19]

Ajacán's people, normally accustomed to a better diet than most Europeans and robust from their lives as hunters and warriors, were generally taller and more erect than the Spaniards. Women built the Indian cabins; made all houseware such as mats, baskets, pots, utensils, and cordage; planted and harvested corn; and performed all household and child-rearing duties.[20]

This busy regimen freed the men for hunting and fighting, both of which were demanding professional occupations requiring long training and experience for proficiency. Skill in the hunt and war was the avenue to wealth and status; the cultivation of requisite talents and attitudes was the key determinant of Indian character.[21]

Paquiquino's character had been formed by those experiences far more than the Spaniards could hope to influence him. In his Ajacán boyhood he would have received no breakfast until he performed well in a test of his archery skills. Approaching manhood, he was subjected to the grueling *husquenaw* ritual, in which groups of boys were taken to an isolated area, fed root poison that induced raging madness, and confined for weeks in cages. Those evincing any recollection of their former lives were forced to undergo the whole ritual again and not infrequently died from it.[22]

Thus transformed or "reborn," a young man's primary loyalty abruptly shifted from family to tribe. The ritual helped foster individual traits of endurance, aggression, and pride that were the guarantee of personal and tribal survival. A man captured in war was routinely subjected to death by torture and was obliged to endure the procedure not only with stoic patience but also with expressions of mocking contempt for his torturers. Such was the ideal and quite often the reality of Indian manhood.[23]

An implicit question, then, concerning the success of the Jesuit mission, was whether nine years of European socialization had counteracted in Paquiquino the lessons of seventeen years of Indian upbringing. First indications gave the Jesuits confidence that he would remain true to his European attainments. But Paquiquino, about three days after reaching the York River, announced that he was going to a place some twelve miles distant to look "for chestnuts and nuts of other varieties" and would be gone for several days.[24]

Paquiquino's failure to return from this expedition was a matter of acute concern for the Jesuits, who depended utterly on him as translator and negotiator. Counting on aid from converted natives, as was their practice elsewhere, they had brought few supplies.[25] (It was a curious manifestation of Spanish colonial attitudes that they had hosted Paquiquino for nine years without any apparent attempt to master his native tongue.)

Word came that Paquiquino was living with an uncle, the chief of a tribe some distance away. Moreover, he had taken several wives, a shocking departure from moral principles taught by the Jesuits and Dominicans, though perfectly compatible with Indian practice. Outraged, Father Segura sent Paquiquino a reprimand, reminding him that missionaries must set an example of "cleanliness of life" for the natives if there was to be any hope of their ultimate conversion. This and other appeals to Paquiquino went unanswered. October passed with no word from him, as did an anxious fall and a desolate Christmas. Their own supplies exhausted, the Jesuits by now had traded many of their tools and other articles to the Chiskiacks for food.[26]

Not long after Christmas, Segura sent Quirós with two other Jesuits to look for Paquiquino and try to persuade him to return. The party found him and were relieved to hear his promise to return shortly. Quirós and his companions set off for the mission, but Paquiquino, according to a later report, followed with a party of his own. On February 4 the Indians overtook the Spaniards and, with a "shower of arrows," killed all three, stripped them of their traveling clothes and gear, and burned the bodies.[27]

Paquiquino and his men continued to the mission and, upon arriving, said that Quirós and the others, accompanied by Indians bringing a supply of nuts, would arrive the next morning. Further, he meant for all the Indians the next day to join in cutting wood to build a chapel and for that purpose asked Segura for "hatchets and other tools." With the mission thus disarmed, Paquiquino and his party spent the night at the village, whose chief, Paquiquino's brother, was party to the plot.[28]

The next morning, February 9, Paquiquino led his men to the mission cabin where the Jesuits were at Mass. Paquiquino split Segura's head "with a cutlass" and wounded and killed others in the ensuing melee. Within minutes, all the Jesuits were dead except a boy named Alonso de los Olmos, who had spent the night at the cabin of Paquiquino's brother and who, owing to the Indian custom of adopting captive children, was spared. Paquiquino argued that they should also kill Alonso to prevent him from revealing the fate of the mission to other Spanish ships, but two chiefs overruled him.[29]

The destruction of the mission—and of Spanish hopes for a colony far enough north to discourage French or English settlements in North America—probably resulted from the situation in which Paquiquino found himself once he began testing his residual influence among his tribe's leaders. His refusal to accept the transfer of authority from his younger brother may have generated Indian ill-will toward both men, one now perceived as a pretender, the other as a scoffer at tradition.

In this state of affairs, Paquiquino must have found that he could be of no great service to the Jesuits nor claim any special regard among the Indians. There was no role in Indian society for a man who lacked either a warrior-hunter's skills or the arcane learning of a priest. Trained for the former

P.Ioañes Bapt: de Segura, Gabriel Gomez. Petrus de Linarez, Sancti, Sauelli,
Christoph. Rotundᵍ Hisp S.I. in Florida pro Christi fide trucidati Aᴼ.1571. 8. Febr
C.Screta del .   Melch. Küsell f .

Chiskiack Indians of the York River, led by Paquiquino, slay Father Segura, head of the
Jesuit mission there, on February 9, 1571.

role, Paquiquino must choose it if forced to decide. The only way to recover credibility would be to ally himself with native society and make some irrefutable display of loyalty and manly attributes. For the sake of tribal unity and his own ambition, the mission must be sacrificed. The first Virginian to enter history's annals was evidently a thoroughly political animal.

The Spaniards later had it on good authority that Paquiquino took pains to hedge his bets on the possibility of having offended the Christian God. A chest with sacred relics and a crucifix were spared from the ransacking of mission goods, and Paquiquino, with Alonso de los Olmos's help, stored it in a *garita,* or Indian granary. A show of respect for the sacred articles might be construed as an act of compensatory merit in the next life. It was later said that the Indians still revered the old chest some forty years afterward.[30]

Whatever the political situation created by Paquiquino's return to Ajacán, one should reflect that he had spent years in Mexico. His opportunity there to assess the effects of Hispanic rule on native peoples perhaps suggested that Ajacán would be unwise to follow a parallel path. The Spanish may at first have seemed to the Indians godlike in their peculiar arts, but experience showed them to be as weak and mortal as any men. In any event, the Ajacán Algonquians, perhaps made as fiercely ethnocentric by wars with Siouan tribes to the west as Spain by its struggles with the Moors, rejected Jesuit intentions to remake their society.[31]

Vicente Gonzalez, hurrying north from Florida in the spring of 1571 with relief supplies, anchored in the James within sight of the mission village. He was greeted by people on the beach, outfitted reassuringly in Jesuit robes and cassocks. Several Indians came aboard the ship, but Gonzalez, puzzled as to why no Jesuits came, sent to shore a written inquiry. When there was no reply, he grew suspicious and seized two of the messengers; the rest leaped overboard.[32]

The subsequent approach of a large number of Indians in war canoes persuaded Gonzalez that it was not safe to remain. Firing artillery and hurling ballast stones at the attackers, Gonzalez and his crew sailed out of the river and back to Cuba. He soon learned from his captives (one of whom jumped overboard and drowned en route to Havana) that the missionaries had been slaughtered, though Alonso de los Olmos remained alive.[33]

Pedro Menéndez de Avilés, informed of the massacre, left St. Augustine in July 1572 with a fleet bound for Spain but intent on searching for Alonso de los Olmos in Ajacán and taking revenge on Paquiquino and his people. Arriving at Bahía de Santa Maria in August, Menéndez anchored, evidently in Hampton Roads, and sent an armed boat with thirty soldiers sixty miles up the James and Chickahominy rivers. An Indian captured the year before was bound and taken along as interpreter.[34]

Over the preceding three-quarters of a century, the Spaniards had evolved crude but effective techniques for manipulating native peoples, and these were employed with ruthless skill in the days that followed. The Spanish party at length "anchored in the middle of a small stream" (probably College Creek on the James) and made signs of friendship to the Indians on shore.

Several came out to the boat and were rewarded with gifts and hospitality. They returned to shore and another group arrived to a similar reception. Then a larger party, including the local weroance, Luis's uncle, along with some of his chief men, arrived. One wore a breastplate fashioned from a silver paten, a bread plate used in the Mass. The Spaniards treated this group to honey cakes and biscuits. During the meal soldiers hiding below deck rushed up and attacked the guests. More than twenty of the Indians were killed and thirteen were captured. The Spaniards then sailed back to the river, exchanging gunfire for arrows as they went.[35]

Anchoring again, the Spanish permitted a small body of Indian negotiators to board their vessel. It was learned that Alonso de los Olmos was with a weroance two days distant and could be fetched if the Spaniards would wait quietly. The proposition was accepted, and the negotiators were given trinkets to present to Alonso's captors. When the negotiators left, a considerable force of Indians in two large canoes tried to ambush the ship but were driven off. When the time limit expired without news of Alonso, the ship proceeded to the mouth of the river, again firing into parties of Indians along the banks.[36]

Menéndez made a further effort of his own. Some Indians contacted near the river's mouth were told that Menéndez was Alonso's father, who wished to send gifts to Alonso's captor to effect his release. Two days later a force of two hundred Indians arrived with Alonso and handed him over to Menéndez—among whose complement were Alonso's father and brother Juan.[37]

Still not satisfied, Menéndez had his thirteen captives canvassed for a volunteer to bring Paquiquino to him dead or alive; the other twelve were to be executed if he failed. An Indian agreed to the proposal, was granted five days to complete the mission, and departed. When the man did not return on the fifth day, Menéndez let five of his captives go but had the rest hanged from the yardarms of his ship where they might make a salutary impression along the shore. The Ajacán project ended, Menéndez sailed for Spain and died there two years later.[38]

The Spanish government did not abandon hope for a Chesapeake Bay colony for almost half a century. Some Ajacán inhabitants had spoken encouragingly of a great salt sea not far west of the bay and deposits of precious metals near at hand. Pedro Menéndez Marqués, a nephew of Paquiquino's sponsor, conducted a careful exploration of the Chesapeake in 1573 but offered no additional hope for the tantalizing possibilities so long nourished in his uncle's breast.[39]

The Spanish appear to have learned valuable lessons from their bitter trials in Ajacán. The experience demonstrated the folly of heavy reliance on native informants and interpreters. In Mexico the Jesuits made it a practice thereafter to master the native tongues before attempting missions. They also used food and other allurements to cause Indians to settle within the periphery of mission stations, thus creating a dependency on the Spaniards that interrupted the patterns and cohesion of native life.[40]

Perhaps the only direct legacy of Spanish encroachment on Ajacán was their introduction of the poisonous Latin American thorn apple, later dubbed "Jamestown weed" by the English and better known as Jimsonweed. In return, the Indians introduced the Spaniards to the hemp dogbane plant from which the natives spun a thread. The Ajacán word for the plant— *pemmenau*—was soon an entry in Spanish lexicons.[41]

Spanish records suggest that the famine conditions encountered by the Jesuits in 1570 had largely disappeared by mid-1572.[42] Very likely those Indians who had dispersed to other regions were by this time drifting back as food sources improved. Paquiquino and his people might now begin to treat the injuries imposed on them by man and nature over the past eight years.

But Ajacán never recovered its prehistoric ambience. Even as the last Spaniards departed, heavy pressures were exerted on it by other enemies, other circumstances. And from the bloody crucible of foreign intervention, a new native vision was emerging of an Indian empire capable of warding off the threats of enemies and coping more effectively with the recurrent blight of famine.

CHAPTER 2

The Chesapeians

CHOWAN River, April 1586. Old Menatonon sat patiently and heavy-eyed as the young Indian, Manteo, struggled to frame the questions:

What is the number of your people?
How far do they go, do they extend?
Who are your neighbors?
How big are they—no, strong—how strong?
Which are your enemies and friends?
Do any of them have yellow or silver *wassador*, bright stones?
Do you know of a great salt water to the west?

The questions flowed on and on. Each time the old man answered with measured deliberation, searching his recollections from a long life's experience, a rich accumulation of hearsay, to respond as judiciously as he could.

The Englishman would pause now and then, groping for new lines of inquiry and, finding them, press on Manteo, his interpreter, a new battery of questions. Now and then the old weroance dozed off, and a period of quiet ensued until his catnap was over. But each time the questions began anew: who, where, what, how much, how far? Many questions Menatonon could not answer. Some seemed foolish, and he told the interpreter so; but he did not think these comments were translated for the Englishman.

Ralph Lane's pulse pounded harder as the interrogation progressed. In eight months in the New World, from the summer of 1585, he had met no Indian so well-informed, so forthcoming with useful information. Old Menatonon was a treasure, the key to a hundred mysteries. He knew things about the country and its people that would have taken Lane years to discover. The trip from Roanoke Island up the Chowanoke River was worth every minute, though it left the remnant of his island colony dangerously exposed. Menatonon was "a man impotent in his lims, but otherwise for a savage," Lane would tell Walter Raleigh, "a very grave and wise man and of singular good discourse, not onely of his owne Countrey . . . , but also of his neighbors . . . as well farre as neere, and of the commodities that each Countrey yeeldeth."[1]

The interview by Lane, leader of the Roanoke Colony, with the old weroance of the Chowanoke Indians, was a dramatic turning point in English interest in North America. For eight months he and his hundred or so men had scoured the outer islands and adjacent mainland without any encouraging discoveries. Bits of gold and silver some Indians wore in their ears, the scrawny pearls, were painful evidence of the seeming failure of Lane's quest. Nor had there been credible testimony of a passage to the South Sea or sign of valuable products that might become payloads for English ships.

Old Menatonon, Lane's prisoner for two days in March 1586, had finally given him reason for excitement. Perhaps it would be possible, after all, to report to Sir Walter something of real importance. Maybe there was still reality in the vision of riches that Lane and his men nourished on leaving home.

As Menatonon divined from questions of his own, the English had come up the river to circumvent a raid they thought he was planning against the Roanoke Colony. Wingina, hot-headed chief of the Secotan, had told Lane foolish tales to make him leave the island: that the Chowanoke had formed an improbable league with the hated Tuscarora; that the two tribes, for no particular reason, would risk facing the English death-sticks. So Lane, fearing a surprise assault, had gathered part of his force and rushed to head it off. He had brought with him Manteo, a Croatoan youth who had spent some months in Lane's country, as his interpreter.[2]

One question in particular spurred Lane's eager interest. The chief and some of his people wore ornaments of a delicate orange color that appeared to be a natural alloy of copper and silver. The source, said the chief, was the Tuscarora mines on the Moratoc (Roanoke) River. The Tuscarora had "so great store" of the metal, "that they beautifie their houses with great plates of the same." At the head of their river, moreover, was "a Sea . . . the waves whereof are beaten into the fresh streame, so that" it "groweth salt and brackish."[3]

Lane's mind raced ahead to practical questions of logistics. Mines of valuable ore would require a route to convey heavy loads safely through wilderness country. There had to be a deep harbor on the coast. So far the English were unaware of such a harbor. Did Menatonon know of a place of deep water? He did! If one traveled up the Chowanoke by canoe for three days, then northeast by land for four more, he would find "a certain King's countrey, whose Province lyeth upon the Sea, but his place of greatest strength is an Iland situate . . . in a Bay, the water round about the Iland very deepe."[4]

A deepwater bay within a few days' journey! If this were true, a grand design fell neatly into place: great English ore ships anchored in this bay under the protection of a fort, a fortified land route from there to the Chowanoke River, then on to Moratoc and its mines, fleets of English treasure ships like those of the Spanish, a revolution in the fierce rivalry of European powers.[5]

Could Menatonon provide guides for a reconnaissance of these routes? Yes. Could the Tuscarora's mineral wealth be verified? Yes. Menatonon's son Skiko had been a prisoner of the Tuscarora. He could show Lane how to get to a place on the Moratoc (Roanoke) River where some of the metal could be obtained.[6]

(We should observe in passing that Lane's preparation for leading Raleigh's colony included no hint of the great bay so near Roanoke Island.[7] The English to this point knew nothing of the bay save its appearance on Spanish maps as Quejo's middling indentation in the North American coastline. The Spaniards had kept the English in ignorance of the data collected from their visits to the bay in 1561, 1570, 1571, 1572, and 1573. The Elizabethans were plunging into the colonization of North America with only the scantiest conception of what they would find.)

Ralph Lane promptly released Menatonan, took Skiko as a guide and hostage for the Chowanokes' good behavior, and set off in two double-wherries (large rowboats) down the Chowanoke toward its confluence with the Moratoc. He would get samples of the Tuscarora wassador for assay, send a party of his men up the coast to find the bay Menatonon revealed, then move his colony from Roanoke Island to the bay and prepare his great ore-shipping project.[8]

The forty English soldiers pushed down the Chowanoke and swung northwest into the Moratoc. But the struggle against the strong current of the Moratoc proved to be a grinding ordeal. When Tuscarora country was reached, they were met by a rain of arrows from unseen forces on the west bank. The English food supply was by now reduced to sassafras porridge prepared for their two mastiff hounds and there was no friendly source to provide anything better. Even Ralph Lane's fierce resolution failed and the English, relinquishing the search for now, turned back toward the fish weirs of Nomopana (in Albemarle Sound).[9]

Reaching Roanoke Island, Lane quickly dispatched some men north by boat to find the deepwater bay. If Menatonon spoke rightly, it ought to be not far north or northwest from Roanoke Island. But with Wingina and the Secotan now maliciously holding back food he depended on, Lane instructed the party to camp for the present in the vicinity of the bay and feed themselves there. Other parties had to move off in other directions to live on whatever land and sea could provide until a relief expedition, daily expected from England, arrived. But Lane meant to try again soon to procure Tuscarora wassador and, once he had it, abandon Roanoke and his inhospitable Secotan neighbors.[10]

April was dismal for the English, and May was even worse. Relief ships failed to arrive and Wingina made thinly disguised excuses for not supplying the English with food. By late May rumors arose that Wingina was quietly building an army with his own people as well as mercenary forces. The existence of Menatonon's bay was by now confirmed, but the "Chesapioc" Indians, among whom Lane's search party sojourned, were said to be among Wingina's allies and the party had to be summoned back. The dispersal of his men had left Lane's strength considerably reduced, and his men were fearful and discouraged. Before daylight on June 1, Lane led a preemptive strike on Wingina's mainland village and killed a number of the Secotan, including the weroance himself. There would be no more peace for the English.[11]

The unexpected arrival on June 8 of Sir Francis Drake's fleet, checking on the Roanoke Colony after a West Indian foray, was a godsend. Drake provided badly needed provisions, gave Lane a ship and boats to move his people to the northern bay, and offered whatever else Lane might need for his enterprise. But the morning of June 13 brought a raging four-day Atlantic storm, a mauling of Drake's fleet, damage to the ship assigned to Lane, and general agreement by June 16 that Roanoke's colony was finished.[12]

Lane's men packed their gear and headed home with Drake. They had done what they could, but too many circumstances had worked against them. Lane's epitaph on the experience to Raleigh conveyed his disappointment: "the discovery of a good mine, by the goodnesse of God, or a passage to the Southsea, . . . and nothing else can bring this country in request to be inhabited by our nation."[13]

For Walter Raleigh, the collapse of his colony was not so discouraging that it banished hope for another near the sea lanes of Spanish treasure fleets. Roanoke Island had been a poor choice, but the enigmatic Bahía de Santa Maria beckoned as a far more favorable site. Lane's report to Raleigh fairly sang of the territory "of the Chesepians (being distant fifteen miles from the shoare)," perhaps meaning fifteen miles west of Cape Henry or near the mouth of the Elizabeth River. The area, "for pleasantnes of seate, for temperature of Climate, for fertilitie of soyle, and for commoditie of the Sea, besides the multitude of beares (being excellent good victual, with great woods of Sassafras, and Wall nut trees) is not to be excelled by any other whatsoever." On its south shore, the bay had a splendid harbor.[14]

Raleigh solicited help for another try. Lane had brought Manteo back from Roanoke Island, and the Indian might be of great service as an interpreter of the Algonquian tongue for a second colony. Some veterans of the Lane colony volunteered for another try. By May 1587 Raleigh had procured the requisite funds, supplies, and ships and a miscellaneous company of 110 farmers, merchants, and artisans, including women and children. Their "governor" was to be watercolorist John White, who had accompanied Lane abroad and brought back excellent maps and pictures. The second colony set out from Plymouth in three ships on May 8, 1587, for Chesapeake Bay.[15]

Taking the usual transatlantic route southeast on prevailing winds to the Florida gulf stream, then north along the American coast, the expedition came abreast of Roanoke Island in July. White and others boarded a boat to look for a party of fifteen men who had been left to hold the island by the previous summer's tardy relief expedition. But the master of White's ship abruptly insisted that the colonists all must land here or "in no other place." The summer, he observed, "was farre spent"—perhaps owing to the approach of hurricane season—and the Chesapeake still lay well to the north. (It was actually within a day's easy sail, as John White well knew.)[16]

This rationalization was accepted meekly by White, who conducted his people to the deserted island. There remained, at least, some huts and the ruins of a fort from the previous year, but the situation with the local Secotan made the colony's survival problematic from the start. There were early signs that the Secotan remained irreconcilably hostile. Worse, an inventory of supplies and provisions brought ashore for the colonists revealed alarming shortages. Someone must return to England with the ships and purchase more goods without delay.[17]

Curiously for the offspring of a hierarchical society, the colonists insisted that White himself undertake the mission; he left on August 27. It was decided that the colony would move to a new site "50 miles further up into the maine," leaving at Roanoke Island signs showing where they had relocated.[18]

The sequel is a story often told. White, delayed by the intrusion of the Spanish armada and other problems, returned to Roanoke Island in August

1590. The colonists had vanished, leaving signs carved with the words "CRO" and "Croatoan." The signs lacked the accompanying Maltese cross that was to indicate that they were in danger when they left. A severe storm the next day damaged White's ship and kept him from sailing south to Croatoan (Manteo's Hatteras) Island. Instead, the ship limped back to England and White was unable to make another search.[19]

Had the "lost colonists," perhaps after a brief sojourn with the Croatoans, moved on to Chesapeake Bay, their original destination? Their intention to move fifty miles into the mainland suggests a nearer site, possibly among the friendly Weapemeoc tribe to the north of Albemarle Sound. Lane estimated in 1586 that the "Chesepians" lived some 130 miles north of Roanoke Island (it was actually about seventy).[20] But recent studies argue that the colony did find its way to the Chesapeake's shores. To this evidence we will come shortly.

Spanish officials, through agents in England and the Caribbean, kept as closely in touch as they could with the English activities. Philip II, still claiming exclusive dominion over North America, in 1587 ordered Pedro Menéndez Marqués, former Chesapeake explorer and now governor of Florida, to have Bahía de Santa Maria investigated in regard to a rumored English settlement there. In June 1588 Vicente Gonzalez was sent north from St. Augustine. He made a careful search up the west side and down the east side of the bay. He found nothing to indicate a European presence, but he happened to touch at Roanoke Island in July. There he found traces of the English settlers but no colonists.[21]

It was some years after the armada of 1588 and the ensuing Spanish war before England was prepared to make further efforts at planting an American colony. Adventurers in these years looked to the plunder of Spanish ships and outposts as a more tempting route to wealth. Only a few, such as Walter Raleigh and Christopher Newport, kept alive the prospect of lucrative Indian trade and permanent English settlement as legitimate enterprises.[22]

Raleigh sponsored occasional trading voyages, instructing captains sent out for American payloads of sassafras (valued for its medicinal properties) and other products to be alert for news of his missing colony. Historian David B. Quinn has reconstructed evidence that one of these voyages, by Samuel Mace in 1603, may have entered the Chesapeake and made the reconnaissance necessary for the Jamestown expedition of 1607. Mace seems to have brought back to England two or more Ajacán Indians and a canoe in which they sometimes gave demonstrations on the Thames.[23]

Eiakintamino, a Virginia Indian, was taken by English explorers to England. His portrait was rendered by Dutch artist Michael van Meer. (Courtesy of Edinburgh University Library, The University of Edinburgh)

The years immediately after the death of Elizabeth I in 1603 witnessed a growing English interest in North America in general and "the bay of the Chesepians" in particular. The new English monarch, James I, sought an end to the Spanish war and in 1604 signed the Treaty of London. Spain maintained theoretical rights to North America but granted trade concessions that could not help but energize England's colonial impulse. Raleigh, imprisoned in 1603 to appease Spain, played no further active role in colonization. But King James, feeling his way cautiously toward a new Spanish policy, agreed in 1606 to the first English colonization scheme in almost twenty years.[24]

A royal charter of 1606 granted mercantile interests in Plymouth license to plant a settlement between thirty-eight and forty-five degrees north latitude (northern Chesapeake Bay to Maine). A London group won similar permission for a colony between latitudes thirty-four and forty-one (Cape Fear to Long Island). The effort of the first group was aborted on the coast of Maine in the same year; that of "the Virginia Company of London" succeeded—though not on terms envisioned by its sponsors.[25]

Close links between backers of the Roanoke settlements and that of 1606 meant that Chesapeake Bay would be the scene of the renewed project. Christopher Newport, a former associate of Raleigh and John White, led the London Company's first expedition. He had lost an arm fighting Spaniards in the Gulf of Mexico, and was evidently familiar with Chesapeake Bay. Three ships with over a hundred colonists in Newport's charge left the Thames five days before Christmas 1606, reaching Chesapeake Bay on April 26, 1607. By May 14 the expedition had selected an island in the river they called the James as the site for their settlement.[26]

By this time, the English had visited the shore west of Cape Henry (the bay's southern headland) to Lynnhaven Bay and encountered some "Chesepian" Indians. John White's splendid map of the coastal region indicated the site of their "City of Skicoake" (almost certainly on the present Ghent waterfront), said to be "above a daies journey about."[27] (Given the loose sprawl of "plantation" settlements, the size is not unthinkable.) There was already an air of mystery and danger surrounding this people. Neither the tribe's role in Indian affairs nor its fate as a nation is satisfactorily accounted for, and they remain among the least known of the tribes encountered by the Jamestown settlers.

On the day of his arrival in Chesapeake Bay, Newport and a party of men went ashore at a point just west of Cape Henry, then apparently a high promontory—the English appear to have called it "the mountain." There was a prospect of the expedition going no farther but settling here on the south shore of the bay.[28]

Reaching land in an area later known as "The Desert," Newport's party, in George Percy's words, found "nothing worth speaking of" except tall trees, fair meadows, and a stream or two of fresh water. Returning to the landing place after dark, the explorers were about to start back to the ships when they were attacked by a group of Indians armed with bows and arrows. The attackers, "creeping on all four . . . like bears, with their bows in their mouths," wounded Captain Gabriel Archer and gave a sailor two dangerous cuts. But the English fired their guns, forcing the Indians to flee "into the woods with a great noise."[29]

Concluding that the vicinity warranted further search, the next morning the English set some men to work assembling parts of a portable boat they had for shallow-water exploration. The rest of the party set out on a trek that carried them some eight miles (probably around the Broad Bay neighborhood) but with no further sight of natives. At one point they came upon a place where some Indians had been roasting oysters, which proved to be "very large and delicate." But there was no other signs of life so the English, after camping overnight on the shore, the next day set off in their small boat for a more extended search.[30]

A short trip south along the shoreline brought them to the mouth of "a river," evidently the Lynnhaven River, "running into the main." This stream proved to be disappointingly shallow, so the explorers ran back into the bay and farther southeast, landing at a point probably just east of Little Creek. Here they found "a plain plot of ground . . . five mile in compass, without either bush or tree." Nearby sat an unattended forty-five-foot canoe. The visitors took time to gather mussels and oysters, "which lay on the ground as thick as stones."[31]

Marching three or four miles into the woods, they saw in the distance some large fires, perhaps used as signals. When the English reached the fires, once again they found no Indians. Of interest to the mariners was a large and colorful expanse of wildflowers, a patch of magnificent strawberries ("four times bigger and better than ours in England"), and some tall cedars, cypresses, and other trees. But "all this march" they "could neither see savage nor town." (This is puzzling since White's map of 1590 shows the village of Apasus on what seems to be the Lynnhaven River.)[32]

It was now clear that the waters in all this vicinity were too shoal to facilitate settlement, and the explorers departed in some disappointment. Gabriel Archer later wrote that the hostility of the Indians was also instrumental in the decision not to settle here,[33] but a close reading of Ralph Lane's report of 1586 might have warned them to expect an unfriendly Chesapeake reception.

Lane, it will be recalled, sent a group of his men to live for a time in or near the village of "Chesipeoc," and warmly praised the fertility and abundance of the country roundabout. Neighboring "Mandoages, Tripanicks, and Opposians"—the latter evidently from Apasus—had visited the English encampment during these weeks. But Lane later learned that the Chesapeake were allied in Wingina's conspiracy against the Roanoke Island English. This was reason enough for Newport to be wary, though a Spanish tale of how the "Cacho Peos" (Chesapeake) Indians of this region in 1584 killed and ate thirty-eight English sailors was no doubt overdrawn.[34]

John Smith, probing six or seven miles by boat up the Elizabeth River in 1608, saw a few cabins and garden plots along his route—"the shores overgrown with the greatest fir trees we ever saw in this country"—but no people. (His failure, like Newport's, to find any hint of the fabled City of Skicoak is remarkable.) He estimated Chesapeake fighting strength in 1612 at about a hundred men, signifying perhaps from three hundred to five hundred inhabitants. But a son of Powhatan told the English that the Chesapeake were "an enemy generally to all these kingdoms."[35] They appear to have been the only tribe of the Virginia coastal plain not yet dominated by the ambitious Powhatan.

So far, these observations on the Chesapeake tribe provide a reasonably coherent picture: a people perhaps initially disposed to friendship with Lane's colonists but soon turning against them; a tribe modest in scope but still holding out in the early seventeenth century against Powhatan's machinations to absorb them; a solitary society that might either avoid or strike at interlopers but who sought no trade or contact with them.

What shall we make, then, of comments by William Strachey, secretary of the Jamestown Colony from 1610 to 1612 and historian of the colony's early years? Strachey was firm in declaring that the Chesapeake were "extinct," having been slaughtered by Powhatan before the arrival of the English in 1607.[36] The evident disappearance of what must have been important villages on and near the site of Norfolk tends to verify Strachey's view. The Chesapeake Indians, then, raise intriguing questions.

For light on the aboriginal denizens of the tidewater country, we may turn to the historical role and record of Powhatan himself. Some reputable scholars hold that Powhatan was either a son or younger brother of Paquiquino, the nemesis of the Jesuit mission on the James River in the 1570s. A few would have it that Opechancanough, represented in Jamestown as brother to Powhatan and scourge of the English in the Indian uprisings of 1622 and 1644, was none other than Paquiquino himself.[37] But the identifications are painfully elusive and need not clutter our inquiry.

What is certain is that Powhatan, partly by inheritance and partly by warfare and intimidation, succeeded in bringing under his control an impressive list of tribes, some thirty in all. His empire—confederacy is too weak a word for the grip of his authority—reached from the Potomac to Hampton Roads and across the bay to the eastern shore. The Paspahegh tribe, among whom the Jamestown settlers resided, were subject to his will. This brought the pioneer colonists almost immediately into contact with the emperor, "a tall well proportioned man, with a sower looke."[38]

As to why so powerful a monarch would allow English settlement in his dominion, it may be that he benefited from their presence. The weapons and trade goods of the colonists must have been of service to Powhatan in cementing relationships and harassing enemies, especially those arrayed along his Piedmont frontier. Powhatan remained doubtful to the last—he

John White, later governor of Sir Walter Raleigh's "lost colony," evidently visited the vicinity of what is now Norfolk in the spring of 1586. His watercolor of Indians fishing with spears, weirs, and other means, depicts an important aspect of the life of sixteenth-century Chesapeake Indians. (From *America 1585: The Complete Drawings of John White*, by Paul Hulton. Color plates © The British Museum of Art. © 1984 The University of North Carolina Press. Reprinted by permission.)

died in 1618—as to whether the time had come to dispose of the colony as some of his counselors insisted he should.[39]

Powhatan's power over subject tribes was generally unchallenged by those nearest his own tribe and capital on the Pamunkey River but less effective as far north as the Potomac and as far south as the Nansemond River. The Chesapeake tribe lay— had lain—on his empire's southeastern fringe, prime candidates for absorption at some stage of the empire's expansion.[40]

It was William Strachey's understanding that some of Powhatan's priests came to him prior to 1607 with a prophecy that an unnamed people "from the Chesapeake Bay should arise, which would dissolve and give end to his Empier." To minimize such a prospect, Powhatan was said to have "destroyed and put to the sword, all such" as might fit the prophecy. It was for this reason, claimed Strachey, that the Chesapeake were extinct by 1607.[41]

Who was it, then, that attacked Newport and his party near Lynnhaven Bay in April 1607? Who were the "Chesapeake" warriors enumerated by John Smith in 1612? Strachey again is our source, but his answers tend to raise even more questions. The Chesapeake, he states, having been slaughtered, were superseded in their territory by new peoples transplanted there at Powhatan's command. It was the newcomers, the new "Chesapeake" perhaps, who attacked Newport in 1607 and were mentioned by Smith in 1612.[42]

Strachey has another surprise. He alleges that Powhatan also ordered the extermination of Raleigh's Roanoke colonists for the same reason he destroyed the Chesapeake. David Quinn extrapolates from this, though Strachey does not say it, that the lost colonists of 1587 made their way north to their original destination, settled among the Chesapeake, and shared their fate at Powhatan's hands. Strachey declares that the colonists "for twenty and odd years lived peaceably with those savages [the Chesapeake?] and were off" Powhatan's territory when the slayings took place. This suggests to Quinn that the slaughter might have occurred in the Elizabeth River area not earlier than 1607, almost simultaneously with the arrival of the Jamestown colonists.[43] Thus the bones of the lost colonists may lie somewhere along Hampton Boulevard.

This interpretation of Strachey's obscure argument is seductive but flawed. So recent an assault on Europeans as well as Indians would have been a sensation on the lower James, and would not have escaped the attention of chronicler John Smith and others, who give no hint of it. One imagines a traffic in confiscated European goods sufficient to attract attention at

Jamestown in 1607 and to lead to public exposure of Powhatan's crime. We are asked by Quinn to accept a destruction so complete, with bows and tomahawks—sticks and stones after all—as to eliminate all intended victims, security so tight as to prevent whisperings by a multitude of witnesses, except to the favored Strachey. One must imagine a coverup so efficient as to destroy all physical evidence at the site, which was soon thoroughly familiar to the English.

We have it on the authority of Strachey's contemporary, Samuel Purchas, that Powhatan boasted of having directed the massacre of the lost colonists, but the need to overawe Jamestown's settlers may account for his assertion. His "evidence," a few pieces of iron, is unimpressive. There is also Strachey's fragile authority for the massacre occurring "at Roanoke," the common Virginia expression for the Albemarle Sound area, which places the scene well south of Chesapeake country.[44]

On balance, it seems more likely that a destruction of whites, if it occurred, took place in the Weapemeoc country on Albemarle Sound and that Powhatan was not involved. His destruction of the Chesapeake tribe, however, is easier to conceive and may have occurred between the arrival of the Jamestown colonists and John Smith's visit to the Elizabeth River in 1608. Jamestown colonists, nevertheless, were still waging battles with people they designated as the "Chesapeake" long after Strachey rendered them extinct.[45] Meanwhile, archaeologists continue to probe the shrinking Chesapeake Indian territory still open to them and are, perhaps, the best hope for shedding more light on the subject.

Interestingly, as it was an Ajacán Indian, Paquiquino, who instigated Spanish settlement on the Chesapeake in the 1570s, so it was a Chowanoke Indian, Menatonon, who later directed the English to the Chesapeake. But Jamestown settlers were unable to verify Ralph Lane's reports—or Menéndez's hopes—of rich Tuscarora mines to the south or a great ocean not far west. Hampton Roads would be no great portal leading to sudden wealth or Far Eastern trade, but an escape route from the confines of Europe and a gaping wound to the lifeblood of Indian culture.

CHAPTER 3

Adam's Rib

THE COURT of Lower Norfolk County issued its order of March 12, 1641, with its accustomed magisterial aplomb. High Sheriff Francis Mason must go to the widow's home and instruct her to render at the next court, as required by law, her accounts as guardian of her children by the late Adam Thorowgood. Owing, however, to "the great distance of her residence" from the Elizabeth River, a rare judicial courtesy was extended. Magistrate Thomas Willoughby would send two agents to her plantation to make the necessary appraisals. The lady would thus be spared the arduous twelve-mile journey from Lynnhaven to the Elizabeth River.[1]

Even casual observers might have noticed something curiously amiss in the dry condescension of the court's order. An attached memorandum noted that Captain Willoughby, on behalf of himself and Henry Sewell, overseers (assistants to the executrix) of the Thorowgood estate, "disclaimed" responsibility in the matter; hence the two agents.[2] Not only would the lady not appear in court, but neither of the Thorowgood overseers would help settle the accounts. The record thus bespeaks pertinent circumstances that the court chose not to clarify. But there were few in Lower Norfolk County without some idea of what the circumstances were.

From its vaguely mysterious beginning, the issue of the Thorowgood estate followed a sinuous and fascinating path. One court order followed another over the next five and a half years, during which the widow was remarried to John Gookin. All of the court's politely phrased orders were ignored by her and no accounts were rendered. If there was initially a question of the court's authority to demand her accounts, it was resolved at Jamestown in 1642 when the assembly decreed that overseers and guardians must give "an exact account" each year to "the Commissioners of the . . . county courts." The justices hopefully cited the statute in a new order of November 1646 to Mrs. Gookin, but it availed nothing;[3] she remained deaf to the court's entreaty.

The irritation of the king's magistrates was abundantly obvious by July 1647: "Mrs. Sarah Gookin," complain the minutes, "hath been oftentymes by severall orders of this court . . . summoned," but she "utterly refuseth."[4] Moreover, the lady, on the most recent occasion, had sent the court a letter citing why it should expect no accounts to be forthcoming. It was an astonishing declaration: "Yor. letter received with a copy of an order of the last court," Mrs. Gookin begins. "Please to take for answere that my resolutions are from this inferior court to appeal to the Grand Court of the Governor and Counsell, at James Citty, there to give up such accoumpts . . . in case the lawe may compell an executrix and mother of her children, left . . . sole guardian to theire full age to give up accoumpts, to any but her children."[5]

What was wanting, continued Mrs. Gookin, was a precedent "eyther in the Realm of England or in these parts . . . where an executrix in my condition was ever called to accopt. before the full age of theire children." She was "confident that none but my children may call me to accoumpt, nor they till full age." She desired "not to be molested" further about it. "I must wonder that my self, of all others, should be . . . troubled in this kynd, I being able to showe many precedents to confirme these my resolutions." The judges should understand, finally, that she was "not solely under the power of this court," the greater part of her estate being in England, "and I conceive I should doe wrong" to the English court to "register any accoumpts here."[6]

Almost equally galling as the rebuff were the postscripted fond wishes of the writer to William Claiborne, the embattled commander of the court and his wife, "to whom I have sent a small basket of apples per the bearer."[7] Apples, yes; accounts, no.

The Lower Norfolk county court was ruefully aware of a serious challenge. To retreat must be to renounce authority over persons of wealth and standing who refused its commands. Accordingly, the justices now produced an instrument they had so far forborne to use. High Sheriff Mason, owing to her "contempt," should go within ten days to Lynnhaven and "levy by distresse" on Mrs. Gookin's estate "the full value" of five hundred pounds of tobacco, "to be disposed of as shall . . . be thought fitt." If she failed to appear at the next (August) court, further punishment would be ordered.[8]

August came but Mrs. Gookin did not. Inquiry revealed that Sheriff Mason, for reasons unstated, had not performed the "distresse" order. He was fined two hundred pounds of tobacco, to be increased if action against Sarah were not taken within ten days. But the magistrates seemed unsure of themselves, as though, in spite of everything, they might be vulnerable to accusations of persecuting the lady: "This court doth thinke fitt," muses an afterthought, to give Mrs. Gookin "respite till the next court to bring in an accopt. and inventory," the fine to be one thousand pounds of tobacco if she declined.[9]

It had now been over six years since the first confident order to Sarah Gookin, and over seven years since Thorowgood's death. During those years civil war erupted in England, Charles I was deposed, chaotic social, religious, and political revolution began, and Indian uprisings devastated much of the Virginia colony. Only Sarah Gookin's disdain stood as a talisman of stable times, assurance that the surface of things was more altered by the tide of events than the substance. High Sheriff Mason having submitted a tactical resignation,[10] there seemed to be no county officer empowered to execute its orders had the court been clear how to proceed.

September 1647 passed into October with no response from Mrs. Gookin. But on November 15 came a petition from her for additional time in the matter. The justices, evidently flattered by the unexpected token of cooperation, not only granted her an extension to the December session but declared that "all orders allready passed in the said businesse as well as orders for her fygures . . . bee revoked and made voyd."[11]

The issue of Mrs. Gookin's accounts now stood just where it had when Adam Thorowgood died. December, in fact, did not bring Sarah to court. But on December 15 Captain Francis Yeardley of Lynnhaven brought the court a petition reciting his recent marriage to the now twice-widowed Sarah. He appealed, unnecessarily it seems, that the fine of five hundred pounds of tobacco assessed against her in August be rescinded and that he be allowed to undertake by April 1648 to submit the delinquent Thorowgood accounts.[12]

Through the faded scrawl of three and half centuries breathes the collective sigh of judicial relief. In effect, the justices were foiled again, but the matter might now be pursued through a husband rather than directly through the imperious Sarah. The intention of the law might at last be fulfilled, the dignity of the court—arguably—preserved. Wisely, no one chose to raise the new question of the late John Gookin's accounts and thereby risk thrusting the whole annoying matter back into limbo.

Perhaps there would ultimately be an account of Thorowgood's estate and perhaps not. But it is time to ask who this daunting woman was who could twit the magistrates with occupying an "inferior" tribunal, instruct them on the law's meaning, and hold them coolly at bay for seven years. Clearly, Sarah Offley Thorowgood Gookin Yeardley was a woman to match the men of her own time—or any other.

Leading citizens of Lower Norfolk County in the 1640s were probably aware that the great lady of Lynnhaven was a daughter of Robert Offley, eminent Turkey merchant and former lord mayor of London, and granddaughter of another lord mayor of the city, Sir William Hewitt. Sir William had held the office in 1585 when the English made their first attempt to establish a colony in North America. Sarah was eighteen when, in July 1627, she married Adam Thorowgood at St. Anne's Church, Blackfriars.[13]

The Thorowgoods were a respectable family of Grimston, County Norfolk, England, where Adam's father had for many years been rector. But Adam, at age eighteen, had gone to Virginia as an indentured servant in 1621 to learn the business of growing tobacco. Five years at Kecoughtan on Chesapeake Bay gave him the tools he needed to become a man of wealth and position. By 1627, when he visited England, he had acquired his own modest holdings.[14]

When Adam left London aboard the *Hopewell* for Virginia in 1628, he had with him his new wife and thirty-five passengers he had recruited for emigration. Each passenger, including Sarah and himself, represented fifty acres of choice Virginia land he might claim. A dozen more emigrants were contracted to follow as soon as shipping allowed.[15]

It was to no log cabin in forest primeval that Sarah committed her fate. In her baggage, with other wedding accoutrements and gifts suitable to her lifestyle, were two dozen silver spoons and a pair of silver bowls from Adam's brothers, Thomas and John, the latter a thriving merchant at King's Lynn, Lincolnshire.[16] Some of the emigrants were Adam's indentured servants, so there would be no want of proper staff in Virginia.

The career of the youthful Thorowgood was a brief but brilliant foregone conclusion. Adam served as an Elizabeth City County court commissioner, and in the House of Burgesses in 1629, 1630, and 1632. He sailed to England in 1633 to recruit more "headright" emigrants; more than thirty were sent promptly to Virginia, Adam himself accompanying the remaining two dozen or so aboard the *John and Dorothy* in 1634.[17] He was now eligible to select over five thousand acres of land as the foundation for the estate he and Sarah meant to build. So much activity on behalf of Virginia settlement did not go unnoticed by Charles I's Privy Council, and Adam returned to Virginia confident of high favor on both sides of the Atlantic.

Adam was attracted to the unsettled region on the south shore of Chesa-

Artist Joshua Shaw did this painting of Lynnhaven Bay about 1819. It depicts the bay as it probably had appeared to the English explorers in 1607. (Courtesy of the Museum of Early Southern Decorative Arts, Winston-Salem, N.C.)

peake Bay where Christopher Newport first set foot in the spring of 1607. In the colony's first years the "Chesapeian" country was a wilderness filled with hostile Indians, but by the early 1630s it was all but void of human life. The Jamestown government, still trembling from a terrible Indian uprising in 1622, had sent a militia force headed by Ensign Thomas Willoughby against the Chesapeake Indians in 1627.[18] This raid apparently wiped out or permanently routed the Chesapeake from their homeland. (Not Powhatan, then, but, more likely, Tom Willoughby was the cause of the "extinction" of the Chesapeake.)

On June 24, 1635, taking note of "special recommendation . . . from their lordships & others his Majesties most Honble. privie councell," the Virginia government awarded Adam a grant of 5,320 acres on the west side of the mouth of the Lynnhaven River.[19] It was by far the largest private grant in the colony's history and vaulted the Thorowgoods at once into the tight fraternity of Virginia's leading landholders.

Adam and his laborers, in anticipation of the award, may already have been preparing a manor house and other buildings at Lynnhaven when the grant was confirmed. Pregnancy perhaps kept Sarah on the Kecoughtan shore until late 1635, when her son Adam was born, but the Thorowgoods were apparently well established in their new home by the beginning of 1636.[20]

Lynnhaven land produced tobacco of indifferent quality, but the area had promise as the seat of a thriving livestock industry. The confluence of small waterways with larger ones made possible huge pastures at the cost of a fence from one stream to the other enclosing triangles of hundreds or even thousands of acres. Stock maintained itself on natural growth, and a ready market in the West Indies offered in cattle, sheep, and hogs a promise already losing its early luster in tobacco. Coasting vessels could anchor virtually at the doorstep of Lynnhaven cattlemen and entrepreneurs in naval stores. Archaeological evidence suggests that the Thorowgoods built a summer house by a small lake, shown on later maps at the north end of what is now Pleasure House Road.[21]

Adam acquired other lands in the bay country, but it was at Lynnhaven that he hoped to make his mark. The stream itself, heretofore known to the English as the "Chesopean River," was renamed by Adam in honor of his birthplace, King's Lynn, by now well identified with his family. (Brother Robert in the 1650s became King's Lynn's mayor.)[22]

The Thorowgoods were among the first colonists—if not *the* first—to settle on the bay's south shore. Almost simultaneously, however, others, including Thomas Willoughby and Francis Mason, were crossing from the lower James River to stake out claims on the Lynnhaven and Elizabeth. The region was still a part of Elizabeth City County in 1635, but an influx of settlers brought the erection of New Norfolk County in 1636, followed quickly by its division into Upper (Nansemond River) and Lower Norfolk (Lynnhaven and Elizabeth rivers) counties in 1637.[23]

Most leading families among these earliest settlers had been neighbors at "Bass's Choice" on the James River. They included Willoughby, Mason, John Sibsey, and Daniel Tanner, all of whom took up land on or near the Elizabeth River. Willoughby, like Adam Thorowgood, was a leading man on the James River, burgess from 1629 to 1632 and, in the latter year, a member of the governor's council. Only thirty-five years old in 1635, he was the son of an important English and West Indian merchant and had inherited property on both rivers. These included lands at the north side of the Elizabeth River's mouth (which yet bear his name) and at what became Town

Point in Norfolk. The latter land was probably on or near the former site of Skicoak, the Chesapeake Indian village.[24]

A neighbor of the Thorowgoods was young William Wilkinson, an Oxford-educated priest of the Church of England, who perhaps arrived under Adam's patronage. Court records cite divine services at the Thorowgood home in 1637 and Adam's donation two years later of land for a church and parsonage at a site still known as Church Point. The Thorowgoods, despite Adam's Puritan background, seem to have been orthodox Anglicans, perhaps shaped by Sarah's preference more than his. But Upper and Lower Norfolk almost from the start attracted colonists of Puritan leanings who sought physical as well as spiritual distance from Jamestown's implacable conservatives.[25]

Nonconformists of various sorts may have seized the opportunity when, in 1640, Elizabeth River parish's first minister, Thomas Wilson, died and Rev. Wilkinson abandoned Lynnhaven. The first church in the former parish was just being completed at Sewell's Point, and Adam's will that year left his Lynnhaven church one thousand pounds of tobacco to purchase "some necessary and decent" ornament.[26] At any rate, Jamestown soon manifested concern over growing radicalism on the south shore, notably in the Sewell's Point neighborhood.

Fundamental to the role of leadership in Virginia was the safeguarding of family reputation from aspersions of the less fortunate. It is not surprising, then, to see Adam Thorowgood's name frequently in the court minutes through the agency of his attorneys. At the first session of Lower Norfolk's court in May 1637 Mrs. Anne Fowler was ordered to receive twenty lashes for scandalous remarks about Captain (of militia) Thorowgood. She had also addressed Adam's servant, Thomas Keeling, unbecomingly as "Jackanapes, Newgate rogue and brigand and told him if he did not get out of doors she would break his head."[27]

Within a year, Jeoffrey Wight, Adam's cowkeeper, was awarded forty lashes for slandering him after being admonished for using bars from the cowpen to beat goats "from the cow pen on the further side of the pond to the tobacco house . . . in Capt. Thorowgood's yard." In most cases, as in this one, convicted persons had to stand at Sunday church services in a white cloth and beg forgiveness from the injured party. But remarks against Adam by Francis Land in 1639 were such as only to require that he perform church penance without the stripes.[28]

Reputations had to be defended in death as in life, and this is what first brought Sarah Thorowgood's name before the county court in the summer of 1640. A neighbor, in conversation with Sarah at the Thorowgood house shortly after Adam's death, remarked that he had paid his bills "slowly or paid not at all." "Why Goody Layton," replied Sarah, "could you never get yours?" Goody admitted that she had had no such problem with him.[29]

Pressing the point, Sarah demanded whether Goody could name anyone Adam had ill-used in money matters. Goody, according to witnesses, now "turns her[self] about in a scornful manner and cried pish!" "Goody Layton," retorted the widow, "you must not think to put it off with a pish! for if you have wronged him you must answer for it, for though he be dead, I am here in his behalf to right him." Goody was lucky to get off with church penance and an apology given on her knees.[30]

Wealthy widows were unlikely to remain single in Virginia, and Sarah was only thirty-one when Adam died in the spring of 1640. His will left her, "as a memorial of my love," not only a life estate in the manor plantation, orchard, and certain cattle, but her widow's division with the surviving children as well. The children—Adam, Sarah, and Elizabeth—were to be reared "in virtue & training." Besides neighbors Willoughby and Sewell as overseers of the Virginia properties, Adam named Sir John Thorowgood (his brother) of Kensington, and Alexander Harris of London, Sarah's uncle, to oversee his inherited estate in England. A division at Jamestown in 1642 left Sarah with silverware, sundry other household articles, cattle, servants, crops, and other goods.[31]

Sarah was not yet entangled with the Lower Norfolk court over the accounts when, in January 1641, she married John Gookin of Nansemond River, four years her junior. Gookin, like Adam, was the scion of a gentle English family. He came to Virginia, probably with his older brother Daniel, in 1631 to manage property previously acquired by their father. He also patented fifty acres of his own on the lower Nansemond in 1636 and was named burgess for Upper Norfolk County three years later.[32]

Each party to the union entered unaware into circumstances that made for a tumultuous thirty-two months of married life. Sarah began her odyssey with the county court over Adam's estate, and John struggled to respond tactfully to the unpleasant situation between his brother Daniel and Jamestown authorities.

The Gookin family was nonconformist in religion and Daniel represented the radical wing of Puritanism as manifested in the civil war that engulfed England in 1642. In that year Daniel, late burgess for the county, and two like-minded residents of Nansemond, sent an agent and written appeals to Boston for Puritan ministers. They appealed that the three parishes of Upper Norfolk were in miserable condition for want of preachers of the true faith. Three New England ministers promptly arrived and began making scores of converts on the south shore.[33]

Governor Berkeley and his administration cracked down furiously on Puritan ministers and congregations with acts intended to curtail their meetings and force them to conform to Church of England doctrine. Persecution became so intense that Daniel and others in 1644 bought a ship and fled to Maryland. Later settling in Massachusetts, Daniel became a leading Puritan official and noted writer before his death in 1687.[34]

The virus in Upper Norfolk spread to Lower Norfolk County. Rev. Thomas Harrison, former chaplain to Governor Berkeley, was employed by the Elizabeth River vestry in 1640. By 1645 he had gone over to Puritanism, evidently the only established minister in Virginia ever to do so. He refused to teach the Book of Common Prayer in church, officiate at baptisms, or give religious instruction on Sunday afternoons. He resigned under pressure. His successor, Rev. Sampson Calvert, was convicted of adultery in 1649. Meanwhile, William Durand began serving a nonconformist congregation on the Elizabeth River; his followers included High Sheriff Richard Conquest, county commissioners Cornelius and Edward Lloyd, and other worthy citizens. Durand, like Thomas Harrison, was banished from the colony.[35] Ironically, Puritanism gained full sway over England by the late 1640s, but Virginia's leaders, royalist and Anglican to the core, still battled against it.

Religious turbulence in Lower Norfolk was made more critical by the Indian uprising of 1644, a last desperate effort by the centenarian Opechancanough to recover Tsenecomoco for its aboriginal people. Even the fringes of Lower Norfolk County appear to have experienced Indian raids. A court record in 1647 refers to John Webb, Lower Norfolk planter and former servant of Adam Thorowgood, as having been killed and his house burned "in the tyme of the Massacre of the Indians."[36]

Captain William Claiborne, placed by Berkeley in charge of Virginia's defenses, summoned militia from seven counties, including forty from Norfolk. They rendezvoused in June 1644 with others of Claiborne's "Pamunkey army" and went up the York River, where they attacked Opechancanough and drove him into the interior after destroying villages and cornfields. John Moye, described in Lower Norfolk records as having been "killed by the last massacre of the Indians," may have been a casualty of this expedition.[37]

In 1645 Upper and Lower Norfolk, with Isle of Wight County, appointed a "Council of War," including old Indian fighter Thomas Willoughby, to head joint operations against Indians to the south. A company of eighty men was recruited for a march into the Chowan and Roanoke river valleys. A tax of twenty-eight pounds of tobacco on every titheable person in the three counties defrayed the expedition's considerable cost of 38,000 pounds—tobacco and cattle being the universal media of exchange on the south shore. Opechancanough was crushed and killed, but strife between Indians and whites continued intermittently for many years.[38]

Anglicans attributed the 1644 massacre of whites to the wrath of God for Virginia's harboring of nonconformists. Puritans were equally sure that God had punished the colony for persecuting dissidents.[39]

John Gookin seems to have been unencumbered by his brother's religious embroilments, though his lands on the exposed Nansemond frontier drew his close attention to Indian affairs. In 1642 he gave James City forewarning of the impending Indian attack by complaining of the Nansemond tribe's forays into Lower Norfolk for the purpose of theft. The Indian "outrages," he proposed, should be countered with "condigne punishment."[40]

Although active in the public affairs of Upper Norfolk and Accomac counties, Gookin evidently moved in with Sarah at Lynnhaven, where he and Thomas Willoughby contracted in 1641 to build a public warehouse. In the following year he was named commander of the court of Lower Norfolk County while yet under the age of thirty. His death in November 1643 left Sarah once again a young widow. She now had an infant daughter named Mary in addition to three young children by Adam Thorowgood.[41]

Sarah's second widowhood was made memorable by her frequent business with the county court. It included suits for debts owing to the Thorowgood and Gookin estates and attachments of debtors' property. She prosecuted complaints against Bathsheba Lovett and others for slandering her and her daughters, against John Williamson for consorting with one of her servant girls (twenty lashes), and various other causes. She had the court re-register Adam Thorowgood's land patents as a precaution against the loss of invaluable records; she even permitted the county to take inventory of her cattle, apparently the only concession won by the court in the long struggle over Thorowgood's estate.[42]

By about 1644 Sarah had a new neighbor, Francis Yeardley, son of former Governor George Yeardley. She seems to have been on intimate terms with the young man in the spring of 1647 when a touching incident unfolded at her plantation. A company of gentlemen, including Yeardley, spent the night of June 10 there. At breakfast, they "fedd hartily," according to Francis, passing the time "healthfully and cheerefully." The occasion was brightened when two of the guests, Richard Eyers of Elizabeth River (a member of the House of Burgesses) and Peregrine Bland, found that they were cousins. The time slipped by "in Divers Discourses drinking . . . moderately a dramm and a cupp of sack" (white wine). One suspects, in fact, that all were soon quite drunk.

After breakfast, Bland agreed to accompany Eyres and Dr. Edward Hall on foot to Eyres' home on the eastern branch of the Elizabeth River. Yeardley suggested that he postpone his trek "till the heate of the day was over." Bland, however, set out rather rashly ahead of his companions. Eyres, by now unsure of the route home himself, solicited Edward Windham to accompany them as far as the path to Little Creek. (One hears little of roads and bridges in these first years; it was boat country.)

The trio proceeded only a short distance when, passing Mrs. Gookin's "barne fort" (possibly a stockade against Indian attack), they spied Bland dozing in its shade. Awakened, Bland apologized that he must rest, asked Eyres to wait for him, and bade the others continue their journey. Eyres, concluding mellowly that he might as well have a nap himself, lay down "feet to feet" with Bland. He awoke in half an hour to find Bland dead, "purging at the mouth bloody froth." A coroner's inquest concluded laconically that death was owing to Bland "having finished the course which God had appointed him in this life."[43]

Sarah married Francis Yeardley that fall, entrusting to him the vexed issue of Thorowgood's estate. Francis, like John Gookin, appears to have moved in with her. Sarah's accounts for the year show new roofing and work on the malt house, and the purchase from John Murray of a male servant for two thousand pounds of tobacco and a young female for five hundred pounds. The girl was diseased; Francis and his brother Argoll paid her medical expenses pending the outcome of Sarah's suit against Murray for selling her "an unsound wench." Inquiry revealed that Murray "had undone her for by him she had gott . . . the poxe" (syphilis).[44]

Sarah's new husband, fifteen years her junior, represented the same breed of enterprising, public-minded men as her first two—perhaps even more so. Born in Jamestown in 1624 between his father's two terms as governor, he was only three years old in 1627 when George Yeardley died (and Sarah wed Adam Thorowgood). The governor's widow, Temperance Yeardley, soon remarried; her three children (the eldest, Argoll, only seven years old) were in 1628 packed off to London to the care of an uncle, Ralph Yeardley.[45]

The Yeardley brothers returned to Virginia in 1638, Argoll now married, and settled in Northampton County on the Chesapeake's eastern shore. Francis was just eighteen when, in 1642, Governor Berkeley appointed him "captain over the Inhabitants" between Hungar's Creek and King's Creek;[46] he was not yet twenty when he became involved in the colony's tempestuous politics.

The brothers were on an English ship on the Northampton shore in August 1643 when Francis began arguing with Richard Ingle, the ship's captain, over "Roundheads and Rattleheads." The former term signified Parliament's side in England's ongoing civil war; the latter was Ingle's term for allies of King Charles I. Francis, a decided royalist like most Virginia gentry, bridled at being called a "Rattlehead." Ingle went below and returned with a cutlass and pole axe, pointing the former at Francis's breast to underscore the aptness of his own terminology. Argoll tried to get Francis ashore, but hot words continued to fly. A magistrate, Argoll at length announced to Ingle that he was arrested "in his Majesty's name." The captain replied that he recognized no right of arrest except in the name of both king and Parliament and ordered both men off his ship. They left.[47]

Ingle sailed on to Maryland, where he boasted of having thrown "the commander of Northampton and his brother over the side of the ship." Later, however, he was brought back to Northampton and compelled to apologize to both.[48]

Francis ran in rough company during these years and often had to defend himself from such allegations as that he "was on the bedd with Alice . . . Travellor with his hands under [her] coates," that his father once "worked upon a Taylor Stall in Burchin Lane in London," or that "his mother had been a midwife . . . to bye blowes" (bastard offspring). But Argoll, formerly a burgess, was more recently a member of the governor's council[49] and Francis was eager, when he moved to Lower Norfolk around 1644, to follow in his brother's steps.

By marrying Sarah, Francis came into control of a handsome estate in Virginia and England, including properties inherited by the Thorowgood and Gookin children but not deliverable until the girls reached sixteen and their brother turned twenty-one. (The eldest was twelve when Sarah wed Francis.) A prenuptial contract safeguarded Sarah's property from inheritance by Francis should she die first. A priority in the first months of marriage was a sprucing-up at Lynnhaven, including new brickwork, plastering, liming, and whitewashing "the dining room, yellow room, kitchen and chamber over the kitchen," and repairs to other rooms.[50]

Like his most prosperous Lower Norfolk neighbors, Francis, first and foremost, was a planter and cattleman, dealing in livestock with Governor Berkeley, among others. But the most active and successful were shipowners or associates of merchant exporters. Increasingly in the seventeenth century, it was to Dutch shipping merchants that Virginians turned, and numbers of Dutchmen settled on the Chesapeake in behalf of personal interests or those of Holland's great mercantile houses. The Dutch paid higher prices for tobacco than did English traders, used ships better suited to the trade, and took advantage of civil chaos in England in the 1640s to insinuate themselves into Chesapeake commerce. Parliament's efforts to restrict Dutch trade helped start a sea war with Holland in 1652, but Virginians circumvented the laws to protect their profitable Dutch connections.[51]

Francis Yeardley dealt with Dutch traders while living on the eastern shore and continued doing so in Lower Norfolk. In 1650 he became partner to Simon Overzee, son of a Rotterdam tobacco trader, and they jointly bought a Dutch ship, *Het Witte Pard*. Francis also acquired a pinnace, or light sailing vessel, from the Gookin estate, which could be useful in the Indian trade. Overzee married Francis's Thorowgood stepdaughter Sarah and, after her death in childbirth, Captain Tom Willoughby's daughter Elizabeth.[52]

It was through the Dutch connection that Sarah Yeardley gained her most prized possession, an elegant set of jewels. In 1649 Elizabeth River merchant William Moseley was residing in The Hague when his wife Susan acquired some custom-made jewelry from a Rotterdam goldsmith and jeweler. The principal piece was a hatband with gold "buckle and tipp . . . sett with Diamonds and in part Enamelled att five hundred gilders." There were also a gold ring set with a diamond, ruby, sapphire, and emerald, and a jewel (probably a pendant) of gold "Enameled and sett with Diamonds."

In July 1650, having settled on the eastern branch of the Elizabeth River, Moseley found himself in need of breeding stock and short of cash. He arranged with Francis Yeardley to exchange the jewelry for nine head of cattle—"two draft oxen, two steeres and five cowes." Susan, whose son William later married Sarah's daughter Mary Gookin, may have suffered tortures at the loss of her jewels, but her letter to Sarah graciously wished her the "health and prosperity to weare them in . . . and commit you all to god, and remain your frend and servant."[53]

Francis Yeardley by 1653 began to realize his political ambitions. He was either serving, or had lately served, as a burgess for Lower Norfolk County, colonel of county militia, collector for the western shore of the Lynnhaven River, and county court commissioner. He was also appointed in 1652 to the governor's council in Maryland.[54] But political office alone did not satisfy his aspirations.

In the fall of 1653 he conceived a project that seized control of his imagination. He was perhaps ruminating on it when, in September, a young fur trader named Nathaniel Batts came to him to request the use of a small vessel. Batts had intended to sail south with a fur-trading expedition but, by accident, the sloop left without him. He hoped to find the ship at Roanoke Island if he had transportation to that point.[55]

As Francis tells it, he furnished a boat and proposed that a member of his family (perhaps his eighteen-year-old stepson Adam Thorowgood II) and two neighbors (probably Thomas Willoughby and Francis Mason) accompany Batts. One of the group knew enough of the Indian languages to serve as interpreter. The party sailed around Cape Henry and through Currituck Inlet into Currituck and Albemarle sounds, in what was then known as "the south part of Virginia." An Indian chief, probably Kiscatanewh of the Pasquotank River Yeopim, evidently represented himself as "the great commander in these parts" and escorted them to Roanoke Island.[56]

Batts apparently did not find his sloop, but his party made a reconnoissance of the mainland near Roanoke Island. Something like a state of war had existed between Virginia and Indians in this area from 1644 or earlier; the visitors thus proposed that leaders of several area tribes "come in and make their peace with the English, which they willingly condescended unto."[57] Representatives of one or more tribes accompanied the party to Lynnhaven and spent a week at Yeardley's, showing "much civility of behavior." One of the chiefs saw the Thorowgood and Gookin children reading and proposed that Francis take "his only son . . . and teach him to do as our children, namely . . . to speak out of a book, and to make a writing." Yeardley, with visions of buying Indian land, agreed to take charge of the boy's English education; the chief said he would bring his son to Lynnhaven within a month. Yeardley acceded as well to the chief's request to have an English house built for him in the Albemarle country. There was also an apparent understanding that Francis could later buy Albemarle lands.[58]

Francis was on business in Maryland in early December when the Indian "came once himself, and sent twice to know, if I was returned, that he might bring his child." But the chief's brief presence at Yeardley's home raised a local stir, some supposing that Francis "had great gains by commerce with him." Others worried that the comings and goings of Indians compromised local security; they "murmured, and carried themselves uncivilly towards" the chief, warning him to stay away.[59]

With her husband's plans at risk, Sarah took the chief under her wing, even escorting him to Sunday worship services. The result, in Francis's words, was "over-busy justices" threatening to whip the Indian and run him off. Sarah had Francis's power of attorney and used it to defuse the situation. She took the Indian "in her hand by her side, and confidently and constantly on [Francis's] behalf resisted their threatenings, . . . she worthily engaged [his] whole fortunes for any damage should arise by or from them, till [his] return." Sarah's April suit against Alice Spencer for scandalous abuse of Francis may have arisen from this imbroglio.[60]

Francis returned by March from Maryland, having enlisted Argoll in his schemes. At Lynnhaven he promptly dispatched a boat with six men, one of them carpenter Robert Bodnam, to Albemarle Sound to build the chief's English house. He also sent a note for two hundred pounds sterling to buy lands and was pleased when his agents came back with "a turf of the earth with an arrow shot into it," signifying his purchase of "three great rivers, and also all such others" as he might wish to buy. On a second trip to Albemarle a little later, Bodnam and his crew built a fur-trading cabin for Batts on Salmon Creek. This building is recognized as the home of the first permanent settler in what is now North Carolina.[61]

Just what land Yeardley purchased is not known, but the understanding was evidently garbled in translation. There was no Indian in that region of small tribes with "three great rivers" to sell, even had the English notion of simple tenure coincided with Indian ideas of possession. Nevertheless, it was Yeardley's information that the Indians "totally left the [purchased] lands and rivers, retiring to a new habitation, where our people built the great commander a fair house, the which I am to furnish with English utensils and chattels."[62]

By now Yeardley was on fire with a plan to develop plantations and trading facilities in the sounds region. On May 1 the Albemarle chief showed up at Lynnhaven with his wife and son and some great men of the Roanoke River Tuscarora. Two days later the chief "presented his child to the minister before the congregation to be baptized, which was solemnly performed in presence of all the Indians, and the child left with [Francis] to be bred up a Christian." Before the chief left, he agreed that Francis would come south in July for further discoveries "by sea and land."[63]

On May 8 Francis summarized these extraordinary proceedings and posted them to Virginia-born geographer John Farrar of Little Gidding, Huntingdonshire. He did not know Farrar, but Argoll did and suggested that Farrar had influence with gentry who might aid in extending English settlement south toward the Spanish outposts. Francis sent Farrar "an arrow that came from Indians inhabiting on the South-sea" (the Pacific Ocean), which he was assured lay not far from Albemarle and which he meant, "God willing, to see this summer, *non obstante periculo*."[64]

Francis closed his epistle by noting that he had spent over three hundred pounds sterling on the project and hinting that English funds would be welcome. He meant to try winemaking in the south and applied to Farrar for olive trees, material for silkmaking, silkworm eggs, "and what other good fruits, or roots, or plants, may be proper for such a country." He finished with a ringing challenge: "God guide us to his glory and England's and Virginia's honor!"[65]

Francis Yeardley did not carry out his planned expedition in the summer of 1654. He was probably ill by the beginning of July, and he died later that year. Argoll Yeardley, whose daughter had married Sarah's son Adam, may have continued for a time to keep alive the dream of a southern settlement; following his own death in the fall of 1655, his estate inventory mentioned a "small boate to the Southward," possibly engaged in the Indian trade.[66]

The enterprise of the Yeardleys initiated settlement of what soon became the Carolina colony. Willoughby and Mason bought a tract of Pasquotank River land from the obliging Kiskatanewh, as did Nathaniel Batts. In 1657 Batts, in consideration of his "discovery of an Inlett to the southward, which is likely to be of mutch advantage to . . . this Colony," was awarded by the Lower Norfolk Court a year's relief from his creditors. By 1659 the first permanent settlers from Virginia were establishing plantations on the west bank of Albemarle Sound.[67] This was the beginning of a settlement destined to be of critical importance to the development of the community emerging on the east bank of the Elizabeth River and soon to take the name Norfolk.

In August 1657 Sarah Yeardley, Lower Norfolk's grande dame for over two decades, followed her third husband to the grave. Her will directed that her "best diamond necklace and jewell" (probably Susan Moseley's Dutch pendant) be sold in England to buy six diamond rings for her heirs and "two black tombstones." Her executor, Colonel John Sibsey, forwarded the necklace and jewel to London merchant Nicholas Trott, who made the exchanges. Sarah was buried in the Lynnhaven parish church graveyard on Church Point beside her second husband, John Gookin. Her headstone, long since lost underwater, was still visible in 1819 when its inscription was recorded: "Here lieth the body of Capt. Gooking and also ye body of Mrs. Sarah Yardley, who was wife to Capt. Adam Thorowgood first, Capt. John Gooking & Francis Yardley who Deceased August 1657."[68]

Sarah Yeardley's independent spirit was uncommon to women of her time. More typical was Anne Bennet, in 1661 ordered by the Lower Norfolk court to live with her husband, Thomas Bennet. If she refused, she was "to be whipt & Sent from constable to constable to her husband's place of Abode."[69] No court would have dared tax Sarah Yeardley with such an obligation.

In her two decades in Lower Norfolk County, Sarah gave determined support and, we may suppose, inspiration to a trio of prominent and progressive husbands. Each of the three made important contributions to the evolution of the settlement and the civilization of the southern shore and its hinterland. A vexation to magistrates and a terror to traducers of her family, her independent spirit and dogged defense of what she conceived as her right was as close to the essence of Anglo-American self-government as the seventeenth century was to come. Sarah is as entitled as any man to be considered a founder of Norfolk society and its special character.

CHAPTER 4

The Foundling

TO SOME of the tobacco gentry, there was something subversive about the very idea of a town: no person of refinement would wish to live in one, no sober artisan would want to be employed in one. A town of sorts might accommodate legislators attending the assembly, but Virginia already had such a site—and Jamestown obligingly shrank to a shell of a place between sessions.[1] Beyond this, towns could offer no service or amenity that honest men might covet.

Towns, said their detractors, were the invention of faceless bureaucrats, agents of tyranny whose minds turned remorselessly upon ways to arrange, to organize, to control. Such persons aimed to divert plantation trade from a thousand river wharves to a few administrative centers. Here might dwell collectors of customs, weighers and measurers of produce, parasitical regulators engaged in a secret war against personal liberty and private enterprise.[2]

Other Virginians were as sure that the colony's greatest fault was its "failure to develop compact settlements," "orderly villages." Towns, it was held by most, together with forts, would discourage invaders and tendencies toward civil discord. They would induce more regular attendance at worship services and in other ways facilitate civilized order.[3]

So it was with ambiguity that the assembly in 1655 greeted a proposal for "Regulating Trade and Establishing Places for Ports and Markets." To some, it was clearly a scheme born in London and it had the support of the "court party," the governor and his lackeys. Among sites proposed for towns were William Shipp's land on the north side of the lower Elizabeth River and "Mistress Yardley's" on the Lynnhaven River. Each site was to have a courthouse, clerk's and sheriff's offices, a prison, a meeting place, a church, and "ordinaries for entertainment and lodging." The bill was muscled through the 1655 session, though sound judgment soon returned and it was repealed in 1656 before any damage was done.[4]

But the demon was not exorcised. Restoration of royal authority in England in 1660 was echoed in Virginia by the return of royalist William Berkeley as governor after eight years in retirement. In the interim, Berkeley and other leaders had persuaded themselves that Virginia must be emancipated from the sinking fortunes of a tobacco economy and diversify its commerce. Only towns could guarantee the growth of shipbuilding, as well as the erection of looms and iron foundries. Towns and cities, Berkeley dared claim, would foster the arts, surround gifted artisans with appreciative clientele, and protect settlers from Indian and foreign invasion.[5] Only freedom, as it seemed to some, must suffer.

Berkeley's view coincided with that of the new royal government and England's influential merchant class. Importing English merchants would find cargoes more quickly in towns than by soliciting at innumerable river wharves—and time was money. The royal government could better rely on customs collected in towns than from furtive exchanges at remote plantations. Returning from a mission to England in 1661, Berkeley brought with him royal orders to build a town on every important river.[6] His personal dynamism would carry most lawmakers with him into an era of town-building and urban civilization—and collectivistic order.

It was a grandiose vision, but fate decreed that every force of man and nature would conspire against it. Far into the eighteenth century, wizened old settlers would rehearse in whispered awe events of the terrible decade that began in the mid-1660s. Younger generations would grow wearily accustomed to having the grandeur of any fresh calamity diminished by some geriatric one-upman who could recall the "Great Storm of '67," or the Dutch Wars, or Bacon's Rebellion, or some other overripe horror of the Time of Troubles.

A signal of the coming decade of disaster was the outbreak of bubonic plague in London in 1665, which kept the tobacco fleet from sailing to the colonies. With the 1665 crop still in warehouses, the following year brought an immense crop that promised to shatter prices on the English market. On Berkeley's initiative, agents from Virginia, Maryland, and Carolina met at Jamestown in July 1666 and agreed to the suspension of planting for the year 1667. Vessels could be found to ship only about half of Virginia's huge accumulation; its arrival in London was greeted by the Great Fire of September 1666, further disrupting the market. Meanwhile, Lord Baltimore, fearing a rebellion of small farmers, vetoed the restriction on planting, thus assuring low tobacco prices for the next twenty years.[7]

Virginia's travail was increased by new conflict between whites and Indians in the region of the Potomac River. Settlers south of the James were harassed in the summer of 1667 by incursions of the Tuscarora Indians from Carolina. Carolina's governor called out his militia and was reported to be drafting even outlying Lower Norfolk County men for service against the Indians.[8]

While the economy stumbled and Indian troubles persisted, an April storm, with hailstones the size of turkey eggs, ruined much of the 1667 tobacco crop. It beat down fruit trees and crops, broke windows and roof-tiles, and killed hogs and cattle. This was followed by forty summer days of rain that destroyed the remaining grains.[9]

Foreign troubles redoubled the severity of domestic ones. To exclude the Dutch from the tobacco trade of the English colonies, Parliament in 1660 had passed the first of the so-called Navigation Acts. One result was to be a succession of three wars with the Dutch in the next few years and a new menace to Virginia's shores.[10]

The bad weather impeded the building of a fort at Point Comfort against the possibility of a Dutch attack but failed to deter four Dutch warships that entered Chesapeake Bay in June 1667. A twenty-ship tobacco fleet lay at the James River's mouth awaiting departure to England, its safety en-trusted to a leaky man-of-war frigate, the *Elizabeth*, anchored at Newport News for repairs. Flying English colors as a ruse, the Dutch came broadside of the *Elizabeth* on June 4 and opened fire. Driving off the crew, the Dutch boarded and burned the ship. The intruders then conducted an unhurried six-day roundup of tobacco ships, burning five and taking thirteen as prizes.[11] Many Norfolk County farmers watched from shore as their finan-cial hopes were blasted.

Torrential summer rains ended in late August only after a monstrous hurricane damaged practically every building in Carolina and Virginia. A Carolina planter, within fifty miles of Hampton Roads, lamented that the storm destroyed his corn and tobacco, "blew downe the roof of the great hogg howse . . . [and] caried away the frame & boards of two howses." In Virginia the hurricane lasted twenty-four hours, knocked down from ten to fifteen thousand houses, flooded river valleys, and broke down fences so that cattle strayed into the fields and ate whatever was left standing. Many boats and ships were sunk or driven onto high land; people living far from any stream were forced to take to rooftops for safety from rising waters. At least two-thirds of Virginia's crops were destroyed by the howling tempest. It would take years to clear the colony's roads of fallen timbers.[12]

The dance of death tripped on. The year 1668 was distinguished by an August hurricane, which followed heavy rains that began on July 30 after a three-month drought. There was another hurricane in August 1669 (report-edly a poor tobacco year) and two more, less severe, in August and September 1670. Southeastern Virginia bore the brunt of such storms and experienced the heaviest losses. To all these calamities was added a harsh winter in 1672–73, during which epidemic diseases struck humans and cattle alike. Disease and bad weather were said to have destroyed half of Virginia's livestock that winter.[13]

In March 1673 a new Anglo–Dutch war broke out and Virginia was an early victim of the hostilities. A tobacco fleet of some forty ships was about to sail when, on July 12, eight Dutch men-of-war anchored in Lynnhaven Bay. They were challenged by two English warships accompanied by some hastily converted merchant vessels. The ensuing battle cost several merchantmen, which were run ashore, but the invaders were foiled from penetrating the James River. The Dutch prowled close by for a few days, capturing or destroying eleven merchant ships before finally sailing for New York. But most of the tobacco fleet was saved through the gallant defense of Virginia's tiny naval force.[14]

If the era of misfortune temporarily silenced townmongers, it may have exaggerated an evil that might prove more destructive than the pommelings of nature and alien enemies: growing numbers of rootless and impoverished men, some of them criminals and ne'er-do-wells dumped on Virginia by the English government. Still more alarming were former indentured servants who, freed from obligations of service, were unable to find steady work or remained as hirelings to their former masters. Such men, a chronic source of civic anxiety, infested every county. Groups of them would occasionally take up arms and hurl themselves heedlessly at authority and property.[15] The multiple crises of the epoch rendered them more wretched and may have sapped the establishment's ability to maintain order.

The bolder misfits and unfortunates might be drawn toward the Indian frontier in search of whatever scraps of free or cheap land were available. But eastern counties retained a full share; Lower Norfolk's population was as heterogeneous, as afflicted with disasters, as any others. Here mingled a restless miscellany drawn from four continents. Most were Englishmen, but Asia's representatives included Simon, a Turkish servant to Francis Yeardley, and a shadowy Near Eastern pair, Hamet Masselon and Abdola Martin, the first dying in 1650 and leaving his scant belongings to the second.[16]

Representatives of European nationalities included Yeardley's French servant, Captain John Sibsey's Portuguese man, Tawney, and Saville Gaskin's Scottish hand, James. There were numerous Dutchmen in Lower Norfolk, some of them unidentifiable owing to a tendency to anglicize their names. These might be persons of substance, such as Simon Overzee and Edward Kooken, but were as likely to be the dregs of the Rotterdam wharf district.[17]

There were still a few Indians in Lower Norfolk, but they seem to have been culturally assimilated individuals like the one who lived with Christopher Burroughs of Lynnhaven as a servant artisan. Remnants of organized tribes—Yeopim, Pasquotank, Nansemond, Chowan—lived on the fringes of the Great Dismal Swamp, from which they traded with whites or engaged in acts of theft and vandalism and were bullied and jostled in turn. Travel between Hampton Roads and Albemarle Sound was still unsafe in the 1670s owing to the death struggles of the Chowan against white encroachment.[18]

Still a small element in the 1660s and 1670s were blacks, some of them sailors on foreign and domestic ships. Francis Yeardley and other entrepreneurs brought some in on terms probably identical to those of white servants and bondsmen. Some could expect freedom after a term of years, but black labor was deteriorating into permanent slavery. A few were doubtless from Africa but most were West Indians, like a trio Yeardley brought from Barbados named Francisco, Antonio, and Maria, who had presumably resided in the Spanish Caribbean.[19] Slaves were still too few in number for collective resistance but might opt to flee to the ubiquitous swamps and forests and commit their fate to an outlaw's existence.

With the institution of slavery taking shape, it was hard for Virginia's few free blacks to maintain their fragile status. In 1667 "Ferdinando a negro" sued a Captain Warren for his freedom, partly on grounds that he was a Christian and, arguably, exempt from permanent servitude. He produced "papers in Portugell or some other language wch the Court could not understand" as proof that he had lived free under several governments, including England's. Unswayed either by faith or documentation, the court ruled that he was "a slave for his life time."[20]

Racial lines were as yet drawn little, if any, more strictly than social lines. Francis Stripes, white, of Lower Norfolk, was ordered matter-of-factly by the court in 1671 to pay required taxes for his wife, "(shee being a negro)." William Watts, white, and Cornelius Lloyd's black woman, like William Bennett's black William and his white paramour, Mary Williamson, were sentenced for fornication to the same penance as any white couple. In William's case, thirty lashes were added for his alleged arrogance "in Lynnhaven Church in the face of the Congregation."[21]

The danger of such a population came less from its diverse origins and creeds than from the circumstances of the lives of the poor. There was the prospect of early death from "seasoning" fevers that attacked all new arrivals. Lower Norfolk's water came mainly from shallow wells that induced a high incidence of typhoid and other fevers. The development of orchards provided fermented drinks but probably not before the late seventeenth century. Medical treatment, consequently, was in high demand. Lower Norfolk records yield the names of some sixteen physicians between 1637 and 1660 for a population never exceeding eight hundred. Most lives were short and old age came early. Thus, Bartholomew Hoskins won relief from county taxes because, at forty-seven, he was old and infirm, Samuel Turbey for being "ancient, poor and decrepit" at fifty-three, Rowland Morgan because he was "a poor ancient man" at fifty-four. The county was reputed to be "an unhealthy place."[22]

Possibly a destabilizing element in Upper and Lower Norfolk counties by the late 1650s was a group of newly converted and stiff-necked Quakers. London's Elizabeth Harris in 1656 was the first of a succession of Quaker missionaries who planted a small but earnest following in the fertile soils of dissidence south of the James. These Quakers incurred the same official antagonism that earlier threatened the Puritans. Many continued to meet furtively even after the colony in 1658 demanded expulsion of all Quakers; some fled south into what became Carolina.[23]

Governor Berkeley wrote bitterly to Lower Norfolk's high sheriff in 1661 for failing to evict this "pestilential sect." Berkeley considered women especially susceptible, and ordered that Quaker females be required publicly to confess error and take prescribed oaths or else be imprisoned. Seven women were among a group arrested in Lower Norfolk in December 1662. Each of twenty-three persons convicted of attending a Quaker meeting in November 1663 and fined two hundred pounds of tobacco were excused after a rare recantation. The governor's anger was matched by lesser Anglicans such as Lower Norfolk's Henry Beecher, who declared of a dissenter that "[i]t would be better for that Quaker dog to go stark naked into a red hot oven than to put his foot on my plantation." The Quakers may have included elements of the despairing poor but some prominent local families were also represented among them.[24]

Repression, it has been argued, only inspired many Quakers to persist more ardently in their doctrine. At any rate, their number declined significantly in Lower Norfolk after the advent of William and Mary to England's throne in 1689 and a new policy of toleration toward religious dissidents, Puritan as well as Quaker.[25]

Not only dissenters faced repression. Even hunting unmarked cattle, a source of livelihood for the downtrodden ("Idle persons," the court called them), was punished by a fine of two hundred pounds of tobacco and loss of the privilege of carrying a gun into the woods. (As early as 1638 the Lower Norfolk court convicted Captain Sibsey's servants of "mutiny" and sentenced each to receive a hundred stripes as a warning to others.) Moreover, the drop in tobacco prices fell more harshly on small farmers and laborers, of which Lower Norfolk had large numbers, than on men of wealth. Governor Berkeley, forced to raise taxes to pay the costs of defense against the Dutch, was roundly criticized.[26]

Thousands of demoralized men, lacking property and family, may thus have been ripe for an orgy of random vengeance when Bacon's Rebellion broke over Virginia in 1676. There were also men of property and high repute who had their own scores to settle, including Berkeley's thirty-year policy of enforcing strict limits on the colony's growth to preserve peace with the Indians. Savage attacks by frontier colonists against both hostile and friendly Indians was a quick means of access to good lands, but ruined Berkeley's pacific policy.[27]

The early scenes of war were confined mainly to the frontier, but Nathaniel Bacon in the summer of 1676 led his ragtag army east to Jamestown to overturn Berkeley's government. When the governor fled to the eastern shore, Captain William Carver, a rebellious Lower Norfolk landholder and shipowner, took charge of Bacon's tiny navy and sought to blockade Berkeley on the far side of the Chesapeake so that Bacon might take control of the colony. But, when Bacon fell ill and died in September, the rebellion quickly collapsed and Carver was hanged for his role.[28] Had Bacon reached Lower Norfolk he could no doubt have recruited a large number of landless or otherwise disaffected men to his ranks.

Berkeley's policies also had the effect of confining the Carolina colony, of which he was a lord proprietor, to the east of the Chowan-Blackwater river line. Bacon's rebels had scarcely disintegrated when one of them, John Culpeper, helped raise a rebellion in Carolina that threw out the governor and other Berkeley confederates. In late 1677 the Carolina rebels closed their border with Lower Norfolk to thwart a march by Berkeley into the colony. But the expansionist faction soon collapsed and Virginia was spared the need for a costly intervention.[29]

The shockwaves wore themselves out in the late 1670s; exhausted Virginians took stock of the extent of injury and possible remedies. Permitted to list their grievances for the king's consideration, Lower Norfolk residents in 1677 cited their losses during the rebellion and expressed the wish to be exempted from its costs. They complained that strangers like Bacon too often received positions of public trust, that there was no accounting for the expenditure of the latest poll tax, that it should be legal to ship tobacco to any English port without paying duty, that it should be unlawful to sell ammunition to Indians.[30] The list failed to address some of the leading causes of the uprising, perhaps because those with the most to complain about could not participate.

One result of meditation on the Age of Affliction was that many more colonists questioned whether towns were really the menace to freedom and profit that some claimed. Impoverished Virginia was willing to consider anything that promised to create jobs and lift the economy back to its feet. Towns, one now heard, might stimulate manufacturers and so help Virginia reduce its dependency on costly English goods. They might provide work for the poor.[31] Besides, there was every indication that Charles II's government meant to inflict towns on Virginia, come what may.

A step fostering the emergence of towns was the acts passed by the assembly between 1667 and 1673 to erect forts, mainly for protection from Dutch warships. Forts might induce storekeepers to settle nearby, and merchants and planters to build warehouses in the vicinity. A fort was built around 1673 on the north side of the confluence of the Elizabeth River's eastern and southern branches. The site was called Four Farthing Point (later Town Point at the west end of Norfolk's Main Street). In the shape of a half-moon, it cost the county a burdensome 35,000 pounds of tobacco.[32]

The new fort guarded no isolated outpost but the epicenter of Lower Norfolk County's busiest public and private enterprise. The Elizabeth River parish church, moved from Sewell's Point to a site between Tanner's Creek and Town Point (approximately Atlantic City) around 1660, stood about half a mile west of the fort. The county courthouse, erected under the aborted Ports and Markets Act of 1655, was near the church. Court had been held at private homes in the vicinity for many years, and William Shipp had conducted a tavern from the 1640s. The busy life of the neighborhood is suggested by the fact that Shipp's tavern accounts in 1648 numbered some eighty men when the county's male population over fifteen years of age was only 334.[33]

Just east of the fort, at the point crossed in modern times by the Norfolk–

Portsmouth ferry, was a ferry established in 1636 by Adam Thorowgood. Taken over by the county soon after it opened, the flat connected what became Norfolk, points on the western branch of the Elizabeth River, and Lynnhaven River. Most travel was still by water although a network of roads or pathways was developing. From the ferry, a road seems to have snaked north and west through the woods and across fords or "wading places" to another ferry over Tanner's Creek (Lafayette River), then on to a third across the western branch of the Lynnhaven River. Another road probably forked north from this one and wound past branches of Tanner's and Mason's creeks to Sewell's Point.[34] Cart paths connected the roads with leading farms and plantations.

Along these paths and cartways, often impassable in bad weather, but more especially along the small waterways that crinkled Lower Norfolk's topography like the grizzled face of an old sailor, flowed the lifeblood of the local economy. Notably in the fall, Elizabeth River wharves and pens at Four Farthing Point or Dun-in-the-Mire Creek, or Wise's, or Sibsey's, or Lambert's and Sewell's points, strained under the burden of nature's bounty—shingles and planks of oak and cypress, casks of pine tar and pitch, livestock and salted meat, hides and furs, tobacco, wheat and corn, beans and peas, butter and cheese. The produce went chiefly to the West Indies but also to Europe and the northern colonies in exchange for rum, sugar, and the manufactures that a rural society must buy abroad or live without.[35]

If Lower Norfolk's belly seemed great with the embryo of a town, the London government stood as an impatient midwife at its bedside. Berkeley turned over the governorship to Lord Thomas Culpeper in 1677; the new executive brought orders to create the long-delayed towns. As was feared, the town scheme proved to be part of a greater imperial plot to reduce Virginia and the other colonies to more unquestioning obedience to the Crown.[36]

By leading burgesses to expect that townsmen would be exempt from customs duties for a year, Culpeper in June 1680 got his act for "the Encouragement of Trade and Manufactures." The towns the act created would ship all the colony's tobacco and other exports and receive all its imports. But it was a clumsy dinosaur of a statute. In calling for a town in each of Virginia's twenty counties, it made little economic sense—perhaps deliberately so in order to undermine it. Under the act, each county court would appoint agents to buy fifty acres of land and have it surveyed and laid off in half-acre lots. The lots would be sold to anyone agreeing to build dwellings or warehouses and settle on them within three months. Carpenters, brickmakers, and other "mechanicks," laborers, and traders resident in towns would be exempt from arrest and seizure for the first year.[37]

The town act had numerous defects, not least its premise that residents need not pay customs duties. Even Charles II recognized that it was impractical and suspended it (permanently as it turned out) in December 1681. But Lower Norfolk was among those counties that rushed to get its town going quickly, hoping to seize whatever benefit there might be in customs exemptions. Thus the death of the act found a townsite laid off beside the fort at Four Farthing Point and at least one cruelly deluded family already resident there.[38]

Lower Norfolk's town, then, owed its creation to acts of 1655 and 1680, both of which were set aside within months after they were passed. Under any terms to which all parties would consent, no one, neither county, colony, nor Crown, wanted a town here or anywhere else. The townsite on the Elizabeth River, despite the many reasons that might be argued in its behalf, was something of an accident, an unintended consequence of the game of imperial and colonial politics.

Lower Norfolk, however, bustled with anticlimactic momentum. On August 18, 1680, the county court ordered its surveyor, John Ferebee, to survey fifty acres of shipwright Nicholas Wise's land as designated by the act of assembly. It lay on a narrow east-west peninsula of woods and old fields stretching about three-quarters of a mile along the north side of the Elizabeth River and connected to the shoreline by a slender isthmus. Ferebee carried out his commission in October, but it was a year before he finished laying off the streets and fifty-one adjoining lots.[39]

Ferebee's dog-leg Main Street reached from end to end along the peninsula, with one diagonal street leading south "down to the waterside" (approximately at the present Omni Hotel) and another north "into the woods" (now St. Paul's Boulevard). A lot at the head of the latter street was apparently set aside for a church, with a school lot opposite, while one on Main Street was designated for a courthouse.[40]

Despite the king's suspension of the town act, the county court in 1682 assigned Colonel Anthony Lawson and Captain William Robinson to close the purchase for ten thousand pounds of tobacco and its casks and to begin selling lots. Mariner Peter Smith promptly bought three waterfront lots and was evidently living on them by late 1681 or early 1682. Several others had spoken for town lots by 1683, but it appears that for about five years the Smiths were the only family in residence.[41] The whole business no doubt appeared to some to be an exercise in bureaucratic futility, an aborted fetus of a town with little prospect of survival.

But political, religious, and business life in Lower Norfolk gravitated toward the fork of the Elizabeth River for reasons that had little to do with governments. If the emergence of a town there could not be rushed by legislative fiat, neither could it be long delayed. As the seventeenth century neared its close, the population of this southeastern corner of Virginia required a market center, a convenient port of entry. The Elizabeth and Lynnhaven rivers now served not only the commerce of the contiguous countryside but a considerable Carolina region that was effectively landlocked by its own shallow waters and treacherous outer banks.

Moreover, some of Virginia's problems were yielding to solutions that favored towns. By 1660 English and northern ships no longer arrived in summer, when passengers and crews were likely to develop fevers and when shipworms played most havoc with wooden hulls. They came, instead, mainly in the fall or early winter. The fourteen doctors in Lower Norfolk records between 1661 and 1700 were far fewer in proportion to the population than those of the preceding era. This suggests that the health of the area had improved, that doctors found less business than in former times.[42]

Lower Norfolk had also gained a reputation as a producer of pork, especially for the West Indian sugar islands where land was too valuable to permit much hog raising. Increasingly large droves of cattle and hogs were brought up the mirey Carolina road that passed along the eastern side of the Great Dismal Swamp. A cattleman like Henry Woodhouse by the 1680s was likely to own over a hundred head of livestock, despite the county's infestation with wolves. The estate of merchant Robert Hodges listed 11,620 pounds of pork owed to him by various clients.[43]

Lower Norfolk's town probably had no more than five families living in it as the final decade of the seventeenth century opened. Peter Smith now had neighbors in the households of veteran County Clerk William Porten; mariner William Knott, who served as the keeper of the public ferry; Captain William Robinson, formerly of Lynnhaven and lately a member of the House of Burgesses; and Mrs. Jane Sawcer, widow.[44]

The Elizabeth River town would have emerged eventually as a place of commercial significance, but events of the year 1691 provided a more decisive impetus. In April the assembly decreed the division of Lower Norfolk into the counties of Norfolk and Princess Anne. They were divided at approximately the boundaries between the Lynnhaven and Elizabeth River parishes. Anticipating this action, the Lower Norfolk court in September 1689 ordered the building of two courthouses, one of them on "the towne land in Elizabeth River." The 1691 assembly also passed a new act (soon suspended, of course) to create "Ports and Markets." It aimed to establish twenty towns, fifteen of them ports of entry, including ten at sites where the beginnings of towns already existed. The one in Lower Norfolk was described in the act as having "several dwelling houses and warehouses already built."[45]

The courthouse was started in 1691 at the head of the street "down to the waterside," fronting its intersection with Main Street to form the public marketplace. Completed in 1694, the courthouse was a thirty-five by twenty feet brick rectangle with a cellar, two ground floor rooms, and an upstairs jury room. A brick prison ordered to be built on the same lot may have been postponed indefinitely. For the convenience of courtgoers, a bridge was built in 1691, apparently over an arm of Dun-in-the-Mire (Newton's) Creek (corner of the present Church and Charlotte streets).[46]

The events of 1691 engendered a fresh interest in Norfolk Town; most of its lots seem to have been occupied by 1696. From its inception in 1655, it had required four decades to bring the idea to fruition. For the first thirty years, town-building was a pawn in the struggles of colony against Crown, gentry against common people, planter against merchant. But the final decade of the period witnessed a profound upheaval in English government. The bloodless expulsion of James II and the "Glorious Revolution" of 1689 ended "divine-right" monarchy and spawned a Parliament with primary power under England's constitution. The new era of flexibility this brought to colonial administration helped remove some of the obstacles that for so long had thwarted towns.

But towns remained alien presences in a colony not yet fully persuaded of their value. Norfolk Town in particular was suspect because it lay in an area only marginal to Virginia's main commercial interests. It was a region of exotic religious enthusiasms, witchcraft and conjuration, "bad water and bad air," the resort, in the eyes of upcountry aristocrats, of the same species of scofflaw and scapegrace who lurked in the adjacent wilds of Carolina. It challenged the imagination to foresee how a town in such circumstances might benefit a tobacco colony.

CHAPTER 5

The Exorcism

IT WAS not only in and around Norfolk Town in the spring of 1691 that people were uncommonly jumpy and irritable. The same could be said of nearly everyone up and down both sides of the Chesapeake Bay from Cape Henry to the Susquehanna and beyond. The chief source of the tension was that the danger of pirates, as much a threat to landsmen as to mariners, was once more emerging after several years of blessed abatement.

England's Privy Council in 1683 had adopted Governor Lord Effingham's proposal that the way to control piracy in the bay and along the capes was to post a warship of the Royal Navy in those waters. The latest of these men-of-war, HMS *Dumbarton*, had proved effective for a time in protecting Virginia and Maryland shipping, but the vessel was now a rotting hulk, a victim of shipworms and hard usage. Its replacement, HMS *Wolf,* arrived in mid–March but was scheduled to leave with the tobacco ships in June, having accomplished nothing more remarkable than grounding itself for a week on a bar between the York and Rappahannock rivers still known as Wolftrap Shoal. For the first time in seven years, the Chesapeake would be without a guardship.[1]

Captain John Jennings, "Commodore of the Virginia and Maryland ships" for the year's tobacco fleet, was more irritable than most. His office was bothered with a thousand vexations, including delays in his scheduled departure for England and keeping impatient shipmasters from leaving illegally ahead of the fleet. The cause of his particular annoyance with John Porter Jr. of Norfolk County is unknown, but may have been related to an issue pending in 1691 over the seizure four years earlier of the ship *Society of Bristol.* It involved the fate of some "Elephant's Teeth" (ivory tusks), black slaves, and other cargo, part of which was sold unlawfully by the ship's master, John Skeetch, an associate of Porter.[2]

Magistrates of Norfolk's county court called a special session to hear an indictment by Captain Christopher Thruston, owner of the Elizabeth River

ship *Little John,* against John Porter for debt and injury to Thruston's repu-
tation. As the case was being heard in the courthouse (still downriver from
Norfolk Town) on May 7, Commodore Jennings arrived from his ship,
HMS *Elizabeth,* at "the courthouse landing." Accompanied by seven armed
men, he headed straight for the courthouse. Encountering Norfolk County
Sheriff George Newton in his path, the petulant captain shook his cane at
Newton, called him "a 'rascall,'" and declared that he "'had it in his heart
to break his pate.'" Newton, noting anxiously that Jennings' men carried
guns, swords, bayonets, and clubs, prudently stood aside while the invaders
swept past and into the courthouse.[3]

Porter at that moment was pleading his case before the bar. Jennings and
his men stormed into the courtroom. The commodore seized Porter by the
hair, pulled him to the center of the room, threw him to the floor, and began
kicking him. Subsheriff Anthony Jackson moved to challenge Jennings but
was stopped by the latter pulling his sword halfway out of its scabbard.[4]

The prisoner secured, Jennings and his men left the building and
marched Porter to the landing, where he was placed in the commodore's
boat. Magistrate William Crafford, hurrying from the courthouse, pled with
Jennings to return Porter to county officials, but Jennings "layd his hand on
his Sword & Swore a great Oath ["God Dam him or such like Expressions"
and] that they were all a parcell of Rogues." So swearing, the commodore
pushed off, taking Porter to the *Elizabeth* and placing him in irons.[5]

The peace and order of the Norfolk court had not been so rudely
breeched in more than half a century of the county's existence. The royal
officer, having usurped authority without warrant or mitigation, had to be
held answerable. Norfolk court officials at once sent witness depositions to
Jamestown's House of Burgesses with a request that Jennings "should not
go unpunished." The assembly forwarded these depositions to the governor
and council for action. The commodore meanwhile claimed that he had
found the Norfolk County magistrates at the courthouse "sitting about a
table drinking strong Drinke" when he took Porter into custody.[6]

The outraged Virginia government issued warrants for the apprehension
of Jennings and the release of Porter, but the commodore ignored both.
Since the tobacco fleet was ready to sail and Jennings must not be prevented
from protecting it, Governor Francis Nicholson and his council sent word
to London that the captain was in contempt in Virginia and ought to be
dealt with accordingly.[7]

John Porter Jr., evidently spirited away with the 1691 tobacco fleet, was
the second of a remarkable Norfolk County trio of his name. In some re-

spects, the three John Porters were representative men of the county, but it seems unlikely that such men could have flourished elsewhere in Virginia. Their lives point up some of the features that distinguished society in the colony's southeastern corner from patterns established elsewhere.

John Porter Jr. was the younger of two brothers of the same name, the elder styling himself "Sr." to avoid confusion. They came to Lower Norfolk in the 1640s, possibly from Somersetshire, England, and were soon men of property and prominence. They were married to two of the county's most eligible women, the elder to Thomas Willoughby's daughter Sarah, the younger to Colonel John Sibsey's daughter Mary. Both became commissioners of the county court and, in that role, contributed an important service to the community.[8]

In 1655 John Sr. sat with the court to hear a charge of witchcraft brought against several women. The court not only exonerated the defendants, but ordered that anyone thereafter bringing such charges and unable to prove them would be fined a thousand pounds of tobacco and be liable to further punishment.[9] This official attitude was notably in contrast with that in New England and elsewhere in the English-speaking world, where charges of witchcraft were routinely accepted at face value.

Four years later, this enlightened resolution was put to a test when Mrs. Anne Godby accused a Mrs. Robinson of witchcraft. The court, including John Porter Jr., fined Thomas Godby, the accuser's husband, three hundred pounds of tobacco and costs. It was perhaps partly in consequence of this no-nonsense attitude that Norfolk County was spared the scandalous eruption of witch mania that later enveloped neighboring Virginia and North Carolina counties. In 1679 Mrs. Alice Cartwright was examined by several women at the instance of Norfolk's court but was found to have none of the marks that might identify her as a witch.[10]

The Porters, however, were better known for their religious views and activities than their intolerance of witchmongers. Both men were stout defenders of Lower Norfolk's beleaguered Quakers, though apparently neither was a member of the sect. John Jr. was fined in 1662 for attending a Quaker meeting and almost expelled from the colony. Both men were elected to the House of Burgesses, but the elder brother was expelled from it in 1663 for being "very loveing to the Quakers," a charge he freely admitted. Nine years later, an unrepentant John Sr. entertained George Fox, founder of the Society of Friends, at his Elizabeth River plantation and hosted a Quaker meeting extolled in Fox's journal as "precious and glorious."[11]

The elder Porter died in 1675, the younger, after returning from his abduction to England, in Princess Anne some years later. John Porter Jr. had a son with his name who moved as a young man to North Carolina where he became the most famous (or infamous) of the three. The latter John became North Carolina's attorney general in 1694 and a staunch ally of the colony's then-dominant Quakers, though he built North Carolina's first Anglican chapel. His Quaker sympathies cast him in the role of "kingmaker" in Carolina's "Cary Rebellion" in the first years of the eighteenth century. Arrested for treason by Virginia Governor Alexander Spotswood and sent to England for trial, Porter was acquitted for want of evidence against him and died in 1712 in Bridgewater, Somersetshire.[12]

The Porters, then, were all distinguished as champions of religious toleration and foes of superstition and what they considered unwarranted interference by government in the lives and consciences of individuals. If Norfolk County could be said to have a more lenient disposition toward Protestant minorities than was true elsewhere, less patience with superstitious nonsense, and a greater tendency to defy royal intrusion, a measure of the credit must be ascribed to the three John Porters.

The menace of pirates had waxed and waned for decades. In 1665 Governor Berkeley had complained to London that Virginia's waters were "so full of pirates that it is impossible for any ships to go home [to England] safely."[13] But the Crown, in almost constant conflict with European neighbors, felt hard-pressed to send even a single warship. With William III at the century's end sweeping England into Holland's long struggle against France, the prospects for protecting Virginia's trade did not brighten, despite huge profits the English government derived from that commerce.

Another guardship, the *Henry Prize,* arrived in the fall of 1691 but proved to be ill-constructed and a vexation to captain and crew. Moreover, conditions on the ship were so miserable in the winter of 1691–92 that many sailors deserted to Norfolk and Princess Anne counties. Inhabitants harbored the deserters and helped some flee into Carolina beyond pursuit. By early 1693 the *Henry Prize* was laid up and short of cables and anchors—as well as sailors—for sea duty.[14]

Word of the Chesapeake's undefended condition spread quickly along the coast, beckoning irresistibly to pirate bands, including some who had found hospitality among the innumerable coves and backwaters of the Carolina sounds. There, as in certain other regions, local populations embraced pirates as a source of scarce goods not available through legitimate channels of trade.[15] Still, piracy was little more than a recurring nuisance in the Chesapeake for several more years. The most celebrated episode of the period was one that occasioned more hilarity than consternation.

In June 1688 a small shallop was stopped by naval officers near the mouth of the James River and searched. It was manned by a crew of four and, surprisingly, was found to contain a fortune in bags of Spanish pieces-of-eight, silver dishes and lace, broken silver plates, and other articles. The shallop's crew, claiming to be law-abiding citizens en route from the head of Chesapeake Bay to Lynnhaven to settle, were arrested and sent to James-town for trial on suspicion of piracy. (Part of the treasure was said to belong to a certain William Grinton of Lynnhaven.)[16]

Three of the prisoners gave creative explanations of how they came by their booty, but the fourth, a black named Peter Cloise, slave to one of his white companions, admitted that they made their fortune as West Indian pirates. The case dragged on for years but was ultimately settled by their agreement to yield a quarter of what remained of the treasure to founding a Virginia school, the College of William and Mary.[17] (Rarely has pirates' gold served a more noble purpose; less deserving patrons have had residence halls dedicated in their names.)

The Chesapeake had been fortunate to avoid serious pirate intrusion, but its vulnerability was emphatically exposed in the spring and summer of 1699. A small guardship, the *Essex Prize*, had been on patrol for over a year when, in April, Governor Francis Nicholson learned that the pirate ship *Adventure Galley*, under Captain William Kidd, might soon arrive on the Virginia coast. Within a short time Kidd, fresh from a successful cruise in the Indian Ocean, showed up on the Virginia and Delaware coasts. Nichol-son dispatched the *Essex Prize* to search for the buccaneer, but it was discovered that he had sailed for Boston. He was apprehended there, sent to England, and, on May 23, 1701, hanged.[18]

In the meantime, Captain John James, a pock-marked brute almost as much feared as Kidd, entered the Chesapeake in July 1699 and ascertained that his ship, the *Providence Galley*, was substantially larger, faster, and better armed than the English guardship.

James searched for the *Essex Prize* and, in the early hours of July 26, spotted the tobacco ship *Maryland Merchant* crossing Lynnhaven Bay toward open sea. The pirate gave chase but soon found himself being over-taken by the *Essex Prize* under Captain John Aldred. When the guardship drew abreast of the pirate, James unleashed a broadside and Aldred realized that it was an unequal fight, with his sixteen guns against the pirate's twenty-six. As the pirate turned in pursuit, Aldred made for shallow water near Cape Henry, causing James to break off the chase and return to his prey. The *Maryland Merchant,* having turned west toward refuge in the James River, was quickly overtaken and subjected to a leisurely sacking. It later drifted aground at Willoughby Point.[19]

The next day, with the *Essex Prize* anchored under the guns of a fort near Hampton, the *Providence Galley* encountered the *Roanoke Merchant* just entering Lynnhaven Bay from Barbados. James ran up royal colors and managed to get within hailing distance without arousing the trader's suspicion. There followed an easy capture and looting of the prize for provisions and tackle, the pirates recognizing that such a ship must have nothing of real value on board. In fact, the pirates voted that evening to leave the Chesapeake in search of more promising booty.[20]

The visit of the *Providence Galley* was an embarrassment to Governor Nicholson and other Virginia leaders. The *Essex Prize* was clearly of no use except against the smallest pirate raiders. When Captain Aldred announced that she must be taken into the Elizabeth River for refitting, Nicholson sent orders to militia commanders in Norfolk, Princess Anne, and other exposed counties to keep watch along their shores; a guard should be appointed to patrol the beaches between the Lynnhaven River and Cape Henry, another between Cape Henry and Currituck Inlet. Virginia's best hope now was the approach of the end of September and a season when adverse weather and rough seas might discourage pirates until spring.[21]

The benefits of a county town able to summon and marshall large forces at short notice had grown more obvious as the pirate menace increased. Pirates and enemy warships might penetrate the James or York rivers but they stayed clear of the Elizabeth and its inhospitable town. In times of real or imagined danger, the Virginia government ordered ships in this part of the bay to move upriver beyond Norfolk Town for safety. Royal guardships could be refitted or careened in security along the river, especially at Powder Point (now Berkley), just opposite Norfolk Town at the fork of the eastern and southern branches.[22] Thus the town, spurred by war and piracy, drew to itself scores of unemployed sailors, ship carpenters, caulkers, riggers, and brokers in naval stores and ship supplies required by its expanding role.

Norfolk Town, in the absence of a charter of incorporation, was governed by the county court and had no municipal ordinances or officers. But the variety of its public facilities steadily increased after the early 1690s. County records indicate the existence of a "publique spring" and designated "public laving" area (for washing clothes) at the eastern end of town as early as 1696.

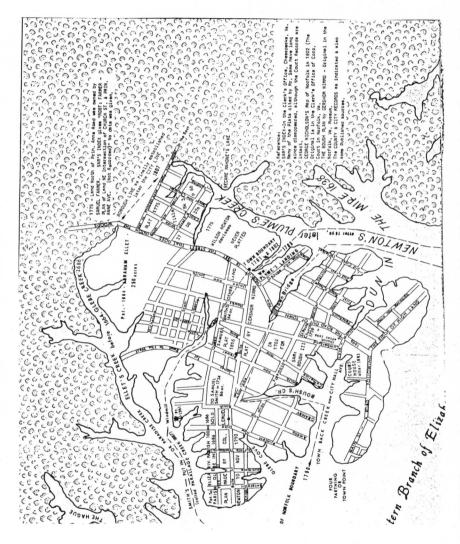

By 1736, when Norfolk became a borough town, it had grown beyond its original site on the peninsula (lower center of the map) north and east to Smith's Creek. (Courtesy of Alice Granbery Walker)

Construction of a brick church was begun in 1698 and finished two years later (on the lot assigned for it in 1680). A ferry from town to Lovett's plantation at the mouth of the western branch was established in 1702 (in addition to the old Thorowgood ferry), and, three years later, a county ferry from Sewell's Point over to Hampton.[23]

Apart from the new courthouse and church, the most important town institutions were undoubtedly its taverns, where one might not only find solace from the cares of life, celebrate its joys, and share convivial society, but learn the news of the county and the world. John Redmond, who later conducted a popular Williamsburg tavern, was a Norfolk resident and, perhaps, kept a tavern in Norfolk as early as 1693. By June 1717, when all the town's tavern keepers were wrongly accused of false measure in their drinks, Norfolk Town had eight "ordinaries," and James Toomoth, late jailer, court cryer, constable, and barbershop proprietor (between courthouse and jail), was prosecuted as "a common Drunkard."[24]

Taverns also provided an arena for games, horseplay, and, sometimes, settling differences. Thus Sam Rogers, merchant Nathaniel Newton, James Hastins, and Captain Henry Jenkins were delighted on the evening of June 19, 1716, to welcome Irishman William Finiken to their table at Richard Josslin's tavern. Finiken was reputed to be a fine dancer and, when a violin was produced, performed several jigs for the company. Finiken and Rogers next engaged in half an hour of a card game called "All Fours" for bowls of sangaree—a sugared and spiced wine drink. Finiken at length grew tired of the game and declined playing further. A jocular tap on the head from Rogers brought on a mock "[t]umbling upon the floor," a push from Newton, and a violent fall by Finiken, from which he died the next morning.[25]

Norfolk Town's trade by the early eighteenth century embraced ports in the British Isles, New England, the West Indies, and Africa. But it was a trade unlike that of other Virginia ports. Tobacco grown in Norfolk County was said to be "of the worst Esteem, and soe little Value, that it discourages the Inhabitants to plant." This forced people "to Cloathe & Maintaine themselves by Manufacturing Wool & Leather, and raisinge Stocks of Cattle & Hoggs." The county also had some fifty thousand acres of piney woodland, from which, with Princess Anne, were produced around three thousand barrels of tar a year. Norfolk residents used tar "for their houses Boats &c.," but shipped most of it to Barbados, Jamaica, and the Leeward Islands. Pirates disdained such bulk cargo, generally preferring ships inward-bound to those engaged in export.[26]

In any case, Norfolk's residents, for the most part, profitted only indirectly from their produce. Since the earliest days of commerce in the region, much of the carrying trade had been in the hands of New England mariners. Virginians built and owned few ships, yet they complained often about northerners because of the low prices they offered and their penchant for illicit trafficking in slaves. Only in the 1740s did Virginians, taking advantage of their shorter distances to West Indian markets, begin to seize control of the trade.[27]

Norfolk County's poor reputation was highlighted when English promoters proposed to plant several hundred French Huguenots along both sides of the Carolina–Norfolk county line in 1701. James River grandee William Byrd argued that the region was low and swampy, "unfit for planting and Improvement, and ye air of it very moist and unhealthy, so that to send Frenchmen [there] from a dry and Serene Clymate were to send 'em to their Graves." They would be beset in "that Fog end" by "Criminals and Servants [who] wou'd run away thither" for the protection of Carolina laws, by "the Entertainment and Protection" pirates would demand of them, and other annoyances.[28]

The Huguenots were shunted off to Manakin Town on the upper James, but Norfolk's reputation as a haven for exotic creeds was not at risk. In 1692 the colony's first Presbyterian congregations were founded after Norfolk County justices authorized persons of that persuasion to hold public meetings in three places, two of them on branches of the Elizabeth River. The pastor for all three was Rev. Josias Mackie of Norfolk County, an Anglican who was ultimately dismissed by Governor Nicholson for deviations from Church of England orthodoxy. He continued to serve congregations on the Lynnhaven and Elizabeth rivers until his death in 1716.[29]

But there were locals who did well for themselves and none more than Colonel Samuel Boush of Norfolk Town. Boush was a native of Lynnhaven parish and a Norfolk lot-owner by 1696. He became a leading Elizabeth River merchant and was often employed by the government to supervise the repair and provisioning of royal guardships. He operated both of the Norfolk Town ferries and owned large tracts of land at the northern edge of town. As a public servant, Boush held numerous offices, including militia commander, high sheriff, magistrate, and, probably, churchwarden and vestryman. (A silver chalice he gave the church in March 1700 is still held by the Chrysler Museum.) In 1714 he was granted authority to erect a public warehouse and wharf adjacent to Captain William Robinson's store in Norfolk Town "at the common landing."[30]

Colonel Boush's brother Maximilian in 1706 was prosecuting attorney in a Princess Anne case involving Grace Sherwood, the subject of Virginia's most sensational witch trial and a further source (or perhaps result) of the corroding disquiet of the period. Mrs. Sherwood was first accused of witchcraft by neighbors in 1698 for hexing a farmer's pigs and blighting his corn. She successfully prosecuted a Mrs. Hill in 1705 for assault, but the Hills brought a second charge of witchcraft against her the following year. In July 1706 she received a "trial by water" at a Lynnhaven Bay site still known as "Witchduck Point."

A large Princess Anne and Norfolk crowd gathered to see Grace bound and thrown into the water. She floated—proof of her guilt—and was then examined by five "ancient and knowing" women, who reported finding unnatural marks on her body. Clapped briefly in irons but soon released, she lived another thirty-five years in Princess Anne, the focus of a hundred stories of mysterious powers and witchly shenanigans. The Princess Anne contagion spread during the years 1704 to 1706 into adjacent North Carolina counties, where there were several more witchcraft trials.[31]

Norfolk County's atmosphere in the pirate and witchcraft years was perhaps a cause of role model Samuel Boush being accused of piracy in the summer of 1700. Leave was granted to his accuser, Simon Alderson, to take testimony from witnesses in Norfolk and Princess Anne counties, but he found too little to warrant prosecution. As rumors of piracy accumulated, it was soon bruited about that a notorious flat-nosed Maryland buccaneer, Richard Clarke, alias Robert Garrett, was frequenting Peter Cartwright's "Rose and Crown" tavern in Norfolk. Clarke was under indictment in Maryland for blowing up the powder magazine at Annapolis.[32]

In late April 1700 French pirate Lewis Guittar in his ship *La Paix* ran down an Irish merchantman off Cape Henry and learned that the Chesapeake's only guardship, the *Essex Prize*, was out at sea. His water casks nearly empty and rigging badly in need of replacement, Guittar headed around the cape, and on April 28 took the tobacco ship *Nicholson* in Lynnhaven Bay. A cargo of some 110 hogsheads of tobacco was contemptuously thrown overboard by the pirates, but they helped themselves to the prize's water, sails, and rigging to replenish their own.[33]

Lewis Guittar, however, had arrived in the Chesapeake at an inopportune time and with inaccurate information. The *Essex Prize*, assigned to accompany the tobacco fleet to England, was not far distant and its replacement, the thirty-two-gun *Shoreham*, lay at anchor in the lower James. News of the pirate reached Captain William Passenger of the *Shoreham* on the evening of April 28, and by 3:00 A.M. the next morning, with Governor Nicholson on board, the big guardship was en route to Lynnhaven.[34]

Dawn had not yet broken when the *Shoreham* picked up the dark outline of the pirate ship. It was an especially awkward moment for Guittar; some of his men were still drunk from the looting of the *Nicholson*'s rum. Shots were exchanged with the first light of dawn and the fight, witnessed by a gathering crowd on shore, developed into an all-day battle. Although the two ships, sometimes within pistol-shot of one another, poured out round after round, it was the pirate ship that suffered the most damage. Around 4:00 P.M., its rudder, bowlines, sheets, and braces all shot away and its crew cowering below deck, *La Paix* signaled surrender.[35]

Guittar still had one time-honored ploy. Holding fifty prisoners below deck, he spread a trail of gunpowder about his ship and sent one of the captives swimming to inform Captain Passenger that he would blow up ship, crew, and captives unless his own life were spared. Passenger, content that Guittar should face royal justice, agreed and accepted the surrender of 124 pirates; some two dozen pirates had been killed in the battle, along with four of the *Shoreham*'s company. Three pirate officers, tried and convicted in Virginia, were sent to Princess Anne County and hanged by the sheriff, Major John Thorowgood. Guittar, with many of his men, was swung off in November after trials in London.[36]

Lewis Guittar's capture did not end the immediate danger of pirates. The *Baltimore*, also part of Guittar's company, still lurked near the entrance to the Chesapeake and on April 30, one day after *La Paix*'s capture, seized a trader off Cape Henry. Some of the crew of the prize reached Princess Anne on May 3 and reported the pirate to Sheriff Thorowgood. The *Shoreham* and *Essex Prize* were put on patrol, but the pirate as abruptly vanished as he had appeared. Hereafter, a combination of guardships and shore patrols kept the Chesapeake relatively safe for several years.[37]

A final period of serious pirate activity in the bay began in early 1708. French privateers, driven from the West Indies by the Royal Navy, began to lurk about the Virginia capes. When the Chesapeake guardship, HMS *Garland*, was wrecked at Currituck Inlet in November 1709, privateers were soon loose in the bay itself. In May 1710 parties of them plundered homes in Lynnhaven, even carrying off a white man and several slaves. Fortunately, the new governor, Alexander Spotswood, reached Virginia in June with the HMS *Deptford* and took vigorous measures to secure the bay once again. When the Treaty of Utrecht ended England's war with France in 1713, the peril appeared to be over as well.[38]

It was, but only for a while. Hundreds of mariners, released from the naval services, turned to piracy, particularly against the rich galleons of the West Indies. Eventually, the Crown sent Captain Woodes Rogers with enough force to clear pirates out of the British Caribbean. In addition, buccaneers were offered pardon by the English government for crimes committed before January 5, 1718, on condition that they obtain their pardons prior to September 5 of that year.[39]

Meanwhile, the most feared pirate of all, "Blackbeard," with his erstwhile partner Stede Bonnet, left the Caribbean to plunder on the American coast. They appeared along the Virginia shore in the fall of 1717, returned briefly to the West Indies, and were operating off the Carolinas by the next summer. Here Bonnet and Blackbeard separated, the latter moving on to the Virginia capes in July in his ship, the *Queen Anne's Revenge*. After seizing several ships, Blackbeard returned to his refuge on the Carolina coast. Because North Carolina's government could not or would not act, residents of that colony appealed to Spotswood, who decided to terminate the great pirate's career.[40]

In November Spotswood sent the guardships *Jane* and *Lyme* in search of the pirate's lair. The former vessel, under Lieutenant Robert Maynard, found the *Queen Anne's Revenge* at Ocracoke Inlet, and on November 22 engaged the pirates in a battle that resulted in the death of Blackbeard and seizure of his ship and crew. Maynard returned to the Chesapeake in January with the head of the fabled marauder dangling from his ship's bowsprit. Trials in Virginia resulted in the execution of thirteen of Blackbeard's men and a welcome respite for Chesapeake traders. Stede Bonnet, meanwhile, was captured and executed by South Carolinians.[41]

The pirate affliction did not entirely end with the deaths of Blackbeard and Bonnet, but the danger diminished and, before the end of the 1720s, disappeared.[42] In these fading years of "the Golden Age of Piracy," Norfolk Town began to realize its promise as a Chesapeake port. When Virginia and North Carolina in 1728 sent commissioners to the Currituck shore to begin surveying the long-disputed dividing line between the colonies, William Byrd, a Virginia commissioner, had occasion to spend a few days in Norfolk. His diary description is the best we have for the years prior to Norfolk being elevated to new dignity as a borough town in 1736.

Approaching Norfolk with his retinue from west of the Elizabeth River on March 1, 1728, Byrd left his fifteen-man team of woodsmen quartered at Major Crafford's plantation (now Portsmouth) to avoid overwhelming Norfolk's limited accommodations. Crossing the river, he was spared the indignity of putting up at an ordinary by an invitation from Colonel George Newton, a leading merchant, whose waterfront home was at the ferry landing.

Mrs. Aphia Newton, who "appear'd to be one of the fine Lady's of the

Town," provided Byrd with a plain but satisfying dinner. The next morning
he was visited at Newton's by "Old Colo. [Samuel] Boush." Byrd and others
returned the favor two days later by spending an evening with Boush, "who
stir'd his Old Bones very cheerfully in our Service." On the preceding evening, Byrd had shared oysters and punch with Norfolk's Samuel Smith, "a
plain Man worth 20000 Pounds," a mercantile nest egg that appeared to
impress the prince of Westover.[43]

In the meantime Byrd had formed a favorable impression of Norfolk, a
place of almost a thousand inhabitants, as having "most the ayr of a Town
of any in Virginia." It was "the Mart for most of the Commodoties in the
Adjacent Parts of North Carolina," receiving large quantities of boards and
shingles from the Great Dismal Swamp region and shipping, mainly to the
West Indies, an "abundance of Beef, Pork, Flour and Lumber." Byrd
counted twenty sloops and brigantines lying in the harbor or at town
wharves and was told that there were often more. "The Town," he observed,

is built on a level Spot of Ground upon Elizabeth River, the Banks
whereof are neither so high as to make the landing of Goods troublesome,
or so low as to be in Danger of over-flowing. The Streets are Straight and
adorned with several Good Houses [many of them brick], which Encrease
every Day. It is not a Town of Ordinarys [!] and Publick Houses, like most
others in this Country, but the Inhabitants consist of Merchants, Ship-
Carpenters and other useful Artisans, with Sailors enough to manage
their Navigation.[44]

The wharves were built by setting long pine logs from the shore to the
edge of the river channel and joining them with notched cross-pieces. This
produced a structure that would "stand Several Years, in spight of the
Worm, which bites here very much, but may be soon repaired in a Place
where so many Pines grow in the Neighbourhood."[45]

Although Byrd felt that Norfolk Town suffered from the drawback of
"having neither good Air nor good Water," and despite its contribution toward "debauching the Country" with imported rum, the future seemed
promising: "The two Cardinal Vertues that make a Place thrive, Industry
and Frugality, are seen here in Perfection; and so long as they can banish
Luxury and Idleness, the Town will remain in a happy and flourishing Condition." It had, moreover, "all the advantages of Situation requisite for
Trade and Navigation," including "a Secure Harbour for a good Number of
Ships of any Burthen."[46]

On Sunday, March 3, Byrd and some of his party attended services at the town's Anglican chapel, where the congregation gawked at the upcountry dignitaries "as if we had come from China and Japan." The sermon, a good one in the diarist's view, was delivered by Rev. John Marsden, a gentlemen with the irreverent gall to flee Virginia in the following year, leaving behind debts of more than four hundred pounds sterling.[47]

Byrd arranged for his expedition's supplies of wine, rum, bread, and other provisions at Norfolk, but could find no one there willing to serve as a guide into the storied Great Dismal region nor even any townsmen who could give directions to Currituck. At last encountering a countryman who could provide a sketch-map, Byrd and his party left on March 4. They were accompanied to Great Bridge by "Several of the Grandees of the Town" and by Captain Willis Wilson's troop all the way to the Northwest River, where boats awaited to take them to Currituck.[48]

The failure of the dividing-line commissioners to find Norfolk residents familiar with the route to Currituck was apparently a disconcerting surprise. By this time there were roads leading into Virginia from Edenton along both sides of the Great Dismal Swamp. One route skirted the swamp to the west, through Suffolk, and around the head of western branch to enter town from the north by Church Street. The other passed eastward by the swamp and joined the first road at Great Bridge.[49] But the Currituck shore lay about twenty-five miles east of this road across a ghastly wilderness of bogs and swamps, as Byrd soon discovered.

By the time of Byrd's visit, as many as fifty thousand live hogs and nearly as many cattle reached Virginia annually along the Edenton routes, most of them bound for Norfolk Town. The animals were slaughtered in or near Norfolk and salted for export. Drovers complained bitterly of butchers who paid only for meat and took for themselves the hide, tallow, and other by-products. Tobacco, deerskins and beaverskins, wax, tallow, butter, and cheese were also brought in considerable quantity from Carolina.[50]

Byrd evidently took no notice of Norfolk's new brick courthouse, authorized in 1726 and built soon thereafter. Nor did he find worthy of comment the court's impressive array of punitive devices—its pre-1717 jail, its whipping post dating from 1719, its ducking stool (a chair at the end of a long shaft projecting over the water from Boush's wharf at the upper end of town) from 1716, or its pillory and stocks from 1703.[51] The great James River slaveowner took no particular notice of the growing black population, which provided so many laborers for Norfolk's waterfront business and subjects for the varied instrumentalities of judicial torture.

The pirates and witches were gone, yet the slave population was much more a source of Norfolk's pervasive uneasiness than can be discerned in Byrd's journals. This condition was evident in the increasing severity of Norfolk County courts in dealing with criminal charges against blacks. When John Chichester's slave Jack was accused in August 1714 of stealing seventeen yards of cloth from his master, the defendant pled benefit of clergy but failed the test of ability "to read as a clerk" (or parson). He escaped jail in Norfolk, was recaptured, and was sentenced to hang. In 1720 Martha Thruston's Luke was executed for the burglary of Samuel Smith's house. White and free black women alike were routinely sentenced to thirty-nine lashes for bearing bastard children, but unwed mulatto mother Mary Sparrow, servant to Mrs. Ann Furlong, also had her term of service extended and her children assigned to others.[52]

Governor William Gooch, complaining to the bishop of London in 1731 of masters who "use their Negros no better than their Cattle," sketched the latest panic over slave conspiracy. In Norfolk and Princess Anne counties, some two hundred blacks were said to have assembled on a Sunday "whilst the People were at Church." They reportedly chose officers "to command their intended Insurrection, which was to have been put in execution very soon after." The plot was "happily discovered," its ringleaders were tried, and four were executed. Gooch ordered militia in those counties to carry arms to church, a precaution not likely to dispel a chronic sense of unease.[53] Here was a nervous affliction that Norfolk, its other chief terrors by now exorcised, had to bear for another 130 years.

Norfolk's enduring experience with the communal shakes perhaps resulted from the nightmare years of the 1660s and 1670s. Neither pirates, witches, nor, at this early stage, slave revolts, represented as direct and palpable a danger as the storms and abrasions of earlier years. If anything, the nervous palpitations of the era after 1690 were evidence of developing strength, a concern for the possibility of being deprived of hard-won gains. For all the fear created by pirates, their presence helped Norfolk more than they hurt. By the 1730s Norfolk Town, its West Indian trade now conducted more on its own terms than on those of New England shippers, stood at the threshold of an age of burgeoning growth and prosperity for many of its inhabitants.

CHAPTER 6

Red Horse, Pale Horse

IT WOULD have been easy to conclude that the Common Council of Norfolk Borough was called into being in 1736 to address just two primary issues. There were, of course, routine concerns—fire prevention, water procurement, regulation of the market—which often filled the council's agenda, but these problems yielded readily to rational solutions. It was not so with civic disorder and smallpox. If the white and black horses of the Apocalypse—war and famine—were rarely seen in the borough's streets, the terrible clatter of the red and pale steeds of strife and pestilence was never far from Norfolk's ears.

The issue of civic disorder confronted the council at its first meeting on November 18, 1736. Smallpox came to the fore the following June. The council took two initial steps to minimize disorder. It forbade tavern keepers from allowing day-laborers, apprentices, or minors from gaming "in their Houses," and instituted measures for "discovering . . . all vagrants and Idle Persons and the better restraining them." The opening sally against smallpox was to fine any who entertained or received goods from "any Family where the Small Pox is," especially from the town of Hampton, where an epidemic erupted in the spring of 1737.[1]

Such measures gave council members and other citizens confidence that disorder and disease were being resolutely resisted, but the policies dealt with only marginal aspects of the basic challenges. Norfolk's trade by 1736–37 had reached a point where both vagrants and lethal microorganisms had to be considered ever-present facts of life. Ships arriving at any season from the West Indies might carry deadly cargoes of either.

The Common Council pursued the question of disorder in 1737 by decreeing that only licensed tavern keepers could sell liquor in amounts of less than a gallon to "the meaner Sort of People Servants and Slaves." A session later it created a town watch whose duties included enforcing a 10:00 P.M. curfew on blacks and whipping any taken up.[2]

The results were not encouraging. In July 1741 the council had to order that "for the future the Inhabitants . . . shall (to prevent any Invasion or Insurrection) be Armed at the Church on Sunday" or other days of worship. It received complaints that "the Negro's are become incorrigable," held "unlawful and Tumultuous meeting . . . upon Sundays, Holydays &c.," and offered citizens "frequent Insults and Abuses." In September 1744 the town watch was enhanced; the constable was directed to break up "tumultuous" assemblies of blacks and assess their owners for the service.[3]

The year 1744, in fact, was discouraging for the cause of law and order. Borough fathers prosecuted John Cook for "ill behaviour in the late Tumult" and, two months later, Archibald McNeil "for Assaulting and breeding a very great Disturbance" as well as "several Crimes of the like Nature." The constable was reminded to break up "tumultuous" Sunday assemblies of blacks and that crew members of Royal Navy vessels were among "Disorderly Persons" for whom he and borough militia must be responsible.[4]

If the red horse rested, the pale horse rampaged. Smallpox was reported at Norfolk in October 1738. Ships arriving in early 1744 brought a number of victims, some of whom were sent for treatment "in the most Populous part of this Town whereby the said Distemper must unavoidably Spread." The council ordered sufferers to be removed either to their ships or to more remote places ashore. "In case of obstinacy," they were to be removed by force and could not "approach this Town" without permission from proper authorities.[5]

Steps were taken to erect an infirmary for any cases as "shall hereafter occur." Nurses and attendants were to receive fifteen shillings each time they reported unauthorized visitors to patients; the visitors were to be fined if white or to receive thirty-nine lashes if black. No infirmary was built at this time, so that, when a West Indian ship brought in more smallpox in late 1746, the glebe house of Rev. Charles Smith was appropriated for the purpose. Shipmasters were warned "at their peril [not] to Land any infected Person" within the borough's limits.[6] Still, the fever reappeared in 1751, 1752 ("intirely ruining several families"), and 1753.[7]

So far, strife and pestilence had made their visitations separately, and the borough was required to face only one crisis at a time. But what if both the wild horses of disease and disorder appeared at once? What if a riot erupted while the pale horse ran rampant in the streets? It was a threat not yet reckoned with in Norfolk's civic imagination, an evil too doleful to contemplate.

The commerce that sired the red and pale stallions was a result of changes in North Atlantic trading patterns that proved highly favorable to

Norfolk. Increases in the size of ocean-going vessels denied many ships access to shallow Chesapeake tributaries long accustomed to their visits. Norfolk's deep, safe, and capacious harbor was one of the few—and by far the most convenient—on the bay for large ships. By the middle decades of the eighteenth century, many Tidewater planters were sending their produce by small craft to Norfolk for transfer to larger ones. This meant a much greater region of backcountry resources to Norfolk's business.[8]

Another changing pattern of benefit to the town was a shift in Virginia's export trade to grain and other foodstuffs. As Tidewater tobacco fields wore out, they were often replanted with corn or wheat. Wheat production, invigorated by Caribbean, Spanish, and Portuguese demand, also spread into Maryland, North Carolina, and the Virginia Piedmont. Norfolk became a major center of the grain trade, and Scottish merchant Neil Jamieson, factor for a big Glasgow house, began his rise as one of Virginia's leading grain-dealers. Tobacco remained the colony's richest export, but Virginia by the 1770s would be the largest colonial exporter of corn and the third largest exporter of wheat.[9]

As Glasgow emerged as Britain's premier tobacco port, Scottish merchants swarmed to the Chesapeake country. Glasgow was not only the closest British port to reach from Virginia, but it furnished the goods most wanted in the tobacco trade and enjoyed the advantages of ample labor, low-cost refitting, and extensive financial facilities. By the 1730s surnames such as Campbell, McPherson, and Taylor (of County Stirling) were both common and prominent in Norfolk's affairs. (Some who opposed the rebellion of their countrymen probably joined the town's celebration in July 1746 of England's recent victory over rebel Scots at Culloden.)[10]

Early effects of the new commercial forces led Norfolk to petition the House of Burgesses in the summer of 1736 for a charter of incorporation and enlargement. (Williamsburg and Jamestown were still the colony's only incorporated cities.) Enlargement was needed because the last of the original 1680 survey lands was taken up by 1729, and Colonel Boush was now selling lots from his tract at the northern edge of town.[11] Incorporation would allow Norfolk an administration separate from that of the overburdened county.

The charter of September 23, 1736, authorized a municipal government composed of a mayor, recorder, eight aldermen, and sixteen common councilmen. The aldermen met annually on June 24 (the feast of St. John the Baptist) to select a mayor from their ranks and to fill other vacancies in the "Common Hall," as the whole body was known. The Common Hall, or

Council, met periodically to choose constables, surveyors, and other officials, supervise buildings and streets, regulate trade, build prisons, and inflict penalties for breaking municipal regulations. The town could hold a Court of Hustings for common and land pleas, and property owners could elect a borough delegate to the House of Burgesses.[12]

Enlargement was allowed north to the Town Bridge (up Church Street to present Charlotte Street), and Samuel Boush was named by Governor William Gooch as Norfolk's first mayor. But the "old Colonel," who had done so much to foster the town's growth, died shortly before the first council meeting. His office was filled by merchant George Newton. (A further extension of boundaries—northwest along Charlotte to near the present Boush Street—came in 1750).[13]

Among the duties of the Common Council was regulating the two yearly market-fairs the borough was entitled to hold on the first Mondays of April and October. There were also weekly markets on Tuesday, Thursday, and Saturday (daily except Sunday beginning in 1757), but it was the fairs that became Norfolk's most popular attraction, enhanced as they were by exemption on those days of all persons from arrest or attachment. An accompaniment of fair-day was the "pie-powder" court for settling small issues that were considered beneath the dignity of regular courts.[14]

Fairs were held in Market Square (where old Commercial Place intersected with Main Street) amid displays of fancy merchandise, sporting competitions, and general merriment. Young men essayed a greased pole in the middle of the square in quest of a gold-laced cap at the top. Others contested in sack-races or through a row of open-ended sugar casks that rolled around as they were entered. Girls might sprint for the right to "a fine holland chemise" or other prize. A highlight of the day came when greased pigs, turned loose in the crowd, set off a scramble to see who could catch one and hold it up by its tail. This event quickly dissolved into a "scuffling and jostling, and upsetting," reported a participant, "and the fun . . . created among the spectators of the melee, may easily be imagined."[15]

As on court days, militia musters, and other public occasions, fairs usually generated a few "rough-and-tumble" fights, in which eye-gouging and mayhem of other sorts were not uncommon. Order of a sort might be restored with a contest to determine who could eat a hot kettle of hasty pudding the fastest. "The wry faces of the candidates . . . , while enduring the pain of scalded mouths, constituted the amusement of the multitude." The climax might come with a raucous bull-baiting that sent children scrambling to rooftops to watch in safety. (The recreations of townspeople reflected the coarse reality of their lives.) The county court in 1750 paid Charles Sweeney and Captain John Hutchings to build a wheeled ducking stool; it was put to use the next year to duck Mary Moore, a "Common Disturber," several times at the foot of Commercial Street.[16]

A more genteel form of convivial setting was offered by the town's Masonic Lodge, one of Virginia's earliest, probably founded in the 1730s. Masons were much given to the pleasures of the wassail bowl, but demanded upright conduct of their members in business and other professions. They were regularly in evidence at ceremonial functions, especially the funerals of members, whose widows and orphans might qualify for the fraternity's charity. Masons subscribed to a vaguely rationalistic creed but were often the pillars of community churches. An exchange lodge was founded in Norfolk in 1763.[17]

Less frequently, news from abroad provided the inspiration for Norfolk revelry. When "Bonnie Prince Charlie" Stuart's bid to seize the Scottish throne was foiled by the English in 1746, the town put together a procession of three drummers followed by a piper and three violins. Then came six figures with sashes bearing patriotic mottoes, a man in female dress signifying the Pretender's disguise when fleeing the English, a nurse with a warming pan and baby peeking out connoting an old tale of Charles' illegitimacy, and Charles' full-sized effigy in Highland dress in an armchair drawn on a cart. An escort of six men with drawn cutlasses followed, trailed by a shouting host of townsmen and rural brethren.[18]

The procession halted where three main streets intersected (probably Market Square) to hang the effigy from a gibbet while all were treated with liquor to drink to the health of George II, the governor, and others. A twenty-one-gun salute from batteries on shore was answered by the cannon of ships in the harbor. Town fathers enjoyed a banquet at the courthouse until, in early evening, with windows all over town brightly illuminated, a fire was set around the gibbet and the effigy was burned. Gentlemen then escorted their ladies to a dress ball.[19]

Between celebrations, the serendipity of daily existence provided its own invoice of droll or notable events. Thomas Seale, Norfolk's thief-in-residence, was sent to the Williamsburg general court several times before his arrest for burglary in 1749. While in the Norfolk jail, he contrived to escape via the chimney, rob the same house, and return to his cell, his object being to divert suspicion from himself. Facing a death sentence for horse-stealing in 1751, he petitioned the court that, "tho' a Brother should sin Seventy Times Seven, yet, on his repentence, Christianity obliged us to forgive him." At the unlikely solicitation of "several Gentlemen of Distinction," he won the governor's pardon. The Common Council in 1753 drew the necessary inference from Seale's adventure and voted to build a new jail.[20]

Common skylarking was also rife among the younger people, though the council's tolerance of it was minimal. On municipal election day in 1755 a youthful company convened at Richard Scott's tavern and held its own mock election. Will, a slave of the proprietor, was elected "mayor," ceremoniously seated, and toasted. The council's choice for mayor, Richard Kelsick, called the whole company before him on June 26 for "an Indignity and a great Insult." They included future mayor Lewis Hansford, future councilmen Daniel Hutchings, John Hunter, Robert Waller, and William Aitchison, and eight others, one of them a namesake of former New York governor Peter Stuyvesant. Upon humble affirmation that they intended no indignity or insult, all were dismissed.[21]

Kelsick's term as mayor was brightened by a visit from America's international celebrity, Benjamin Franklin. After receiving the College of William and Mary's first honorary degree on April 2, 1756, Franklin reached Norfolk on April 10. Borough fathers presented him with a certificate as honorary burgess and citizen of the town. By this time events of high ceremony could be enhanced by the use of Norfolk's mace, forty-one inches long and containing 104 ounces of pure silver. It was presented to the borough on April 1, 1754, by Robert Dinwiddie, then lieutenant-governor of Virginia. The mace was the work of well-known London silversmith Fuller White.[22]

England engaged in almost constant war with French and other enemies during the 1740s and 1750s. The War of Jenkins' Ear and the French and Indian War passed without much effect on Norfolk and its business. Now and then a Norfolk merchantman was lost to enemy depredations, but a French privateer that came into the bay in 1760 was apparently routed by a group of young Norfolk men who hurriedly fitted out their own privateer and gave chase. Of more immediate concern was a hurricane on October 19, 1749, which washed up an eight hundred-acre sandspit just west of what is now Ocean View. With additional sand washed up in 1806, it became Willoughby Spit, after the seventeenth-century Indian-fighter and pioneer settler.[23]

An anonymous French visitor in April 1765 left a description of Georgian Norfolk as "the most Considerable town for trade and shiping in virginia" and "the only part . . . where they build . . . ships." The outlying country furnished masts aplenty while sending "great quantitys" abroad,

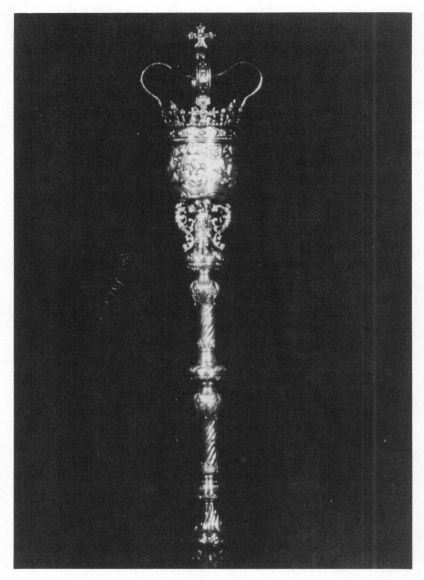

This forty-one-inch mace of solid silver was presented to Norfolk by Lieutenant-Governor Robert Dinwiddie in 1751. It is kept in The Chrysler Museum; a replica is used on Norfolk's ceremonial occasions. (Used by permission of R. Breckenridge Daughtrey, City Clerk, Norfolk, Va.)

especially to the West Indies. There was "a fine ropery" besides warehouses holding lumber and naval stores and even iron shipped down from Maryland. Both Norfolk and the new town of Portsmouth were by now "Chiefly Inhabited by scotch, all presbyterians and altho they are the most bigoted set of people in the world, they have no house of worship of their own." Each town, however, had an Anglican chapel.[24]

Architecturally, Norfolk was a place of unassuming one-, sometimes two-story buildings. The homes of the merchants and professional upper class usually had a central hall separating the "withdrawing" room from the dining room, where a walnut or mahogany table and chairs were the nearest approach to finery. Still less pretentious were the abodes of the artisan middle class, the laboring white and free black lower class, and the floorless huts of slaves. Ubiquitous were taverns, all with tables battered by long nights of gambling with dice in one chamber and "carousing and drinking" Madeira and Jamaican rum punch in another.[25]

Norfolk's "Borough Church" had been completed on the site of the original one in 1739, with a parish house in 1750, and a new courthouse on the future Commercial Place in 1755. Elizabeth River parish, because of unspecified "illegal practices oppressing its inhabitants," was subdivided into three parishes in 1761, the name being retained by the parish north of the river and its eastern branch. The church supported various charitable activities, including a workhouse for the poor on its property.[26]

Anglicans enjoyed a religious monopoly until 1772, when Rev. Robert Williams, an Englishman, delivered Norfolk's first Wesleyan sermon from the courthouse steps. "This was a strange sight in the old Borough," says one account. "The people assembled and thinking him a madman, were very disorderly, talking, walking, and laughing." Williams preached, prayed, and cried, using the terms "hell" and "devil" so much he was thought to be swearing at the gawkers. He returned the next day for a repetition, at length persuaded listeners of his sanity, and was invited to visit the homes of some. "This," says the account, "may be considered the beginning of Methodism in Virginia, and it was not long before a Methodist Society was formed" in Norfolk.[27]

The Frenchman in 1765 had lodged at Portsmouth, where the water was better, but dined with leading citizens of Norfolk, including Colonel Richard Tucker ("a very Clever old Gentleman"), John Gilchrist, Dr. Archibald Campbell, the enterprising Neil Jamieson, and Messrs. Hutchinson [Hutchins?] and Muter, all of whom were "gentlemen . . . In trade." He joined a company of gentlemen and ladies who went down to bayside to watch a seine haul in "a great quantity of fish." Norfolk's exports at this time included "a Smart trade" in pork, pork fat, candles and tallow, ham and bacon, corn and flour, butter and cheese, lumber and naval stores. The Frenchman judged the place "one of the properest on the Continent for a King's [or naval] port." A royal frigate, the *Hornet,* was stationed in Norfolk to scare off French and Spanish privateers and interdict strenuous efforts by Chesapeake merchants to trade outside the Navigation Acts with French islands in the Caribbean.[28]

The frigate's injury to Norfolk's business was partially repaired, however, through the efforts of the town's "crimps." These brokers in maritime labor harbored deserters from British ships and saw to their needs and entertainment until they exhausted their wages and were ready to reship to another vessel—a simple matter at a busy port.[29]

The visitor failed to note the new grammar school, the first such institution in the town's history. It is likely that courses of instruction had been offered from time to time in Norfolk by Church of England ministers and others. A school across from the chapel was contemplated in 1728, when trustees were named to build a schoolhouse and hire a teacher. But no school was erected and no teacher was mentioned in early records prior to parish clerk James Pasteur assuming the position in 1750.[30]

Son of a Williamsburg barber, Pasteur was authorized by the Elizabeth River parish vestry in 1750 to use bricks and timbers from the old chapel to build a school. Authority was obtained from the assembly in 1752 to hire a schoolmaster certified by the College of William and Mary and able to teach both Greek and Latin, qualifications that Pasteur may have met. Still, it was 1761 or 1762 before Norfolk had its schoolhouse, a boys' institution managed by the borough council. Girls received such learning as was considered proper at the private school of the aptly named Mrs. Drudge, a Mrs. Gardner (at Point Pleasant), or elsewhere. A school was opened at the head of Cumberland Street "over against the Church" by John Bruce in 1771 for students of Greek, Latin, English, navigation, bookkeeping, and mathematics.[31]

It was still early for indigenous theater, literature, or fine arts in a town of merchants and seamen, but the first awkward stirrings of artistic sensibility were seen in the 1760s and 1770s. A troupe advertised as the American Company of Comedians played in Norfolk in 1772, probably a rare offering. Public celebration of England's repeal of the Stamp Act in 1766 featured a panoramic painting, evidently by a local artist. It showed George III, to whom prostrate America offered gratitude, while figures representing Manufacture, Agriculture, and Commerce smiled from the right and Tyranny, Slavery, and Oppression drooped from the left.[32]

Where the muse of turgid painting skulked, that of fulsome verse probably lurked as well. In late 1767 Norfolk found itself the subject of a grandiloquent canto contributed anonymously to the *Virginia Gazette* by Dr. Thomas Burke, an Irishman who later became North Carolina's governor. The lines extolled the "sturdy oaks, by sweating labor fell'd," "stubborn pelts by skillful artists drest," "commerce spreading sails for distant climes," and much else of the sort. Burke moved in 1769 from the eastern shore to Norfolk, practiced law, and, on one occasion, engaged in a fight with Joseph Calvert, the borough's rowdy sergeant of the watch. In 1770 Burke married Norfolk County's Mary "Polly" Freeman.[33]

Norfolk's chronic concern for civic order, manifested from the borough's creation in 1736, had focused for several decades on the intimidation of blacks and containment of barroom brawls. By the 1760s, however, there existed a mix of combustibles in the town's makeup sufficient to generate a different order of violence. The mix was stirred by outside influences—the late stages of the French and Indian War and the first signs of serious conflict with the Mother Country—which plunged Norfolk into the most raucous epoch in its history.

The epoch was introduced by what one historian has termed "one of the most lethal riots in the history of colonial America." In November 1762, with Spain an ally of France against Britain, a ship from Havana put into the Elizabeth River for provisions. On November 16 rumors spread through Portsmouth that Spanish sailors were murdering inhabitants. The tale came to the ears of sailors from HMS *Arundel*, anchored nearby, and a party of them set out in quest of Spaniards. Finding some in Portsmouth's streets, they herded them into a building and, firing on them, killed three.[34]

In the meantime a Spanish official and his retinue from the Havana ship were beaten and robbed, and an attempt was made to blow up the lodgings where he stayed. Local people tried to quell the riot, but five Spaniards were dead before Norfolk militia arrived to restore order. Locals apparently took no part in the riot, though they may have helped cause it by giving uncritical countenance to baseless rumors. Norfolk alderman Maximilian Calvert won a measure of celebrity when, ordering the Spaniards back to their ship, he reportedly styled himself "Don Maximilian de Calverto, Grand Magistrate de Norfolco Boro." He became mayor three years later, though not necessarily for that reason.[35]

An alien presence was also the culprit in a brutal affair in March 1766.

Captain William Smith, suspected of informing against smugglers, was seized by John and Matthew Phripp, James Campbell, John Gilchrist, and a Captain Fleming. He was tied behind a cart, led to the county wharf, his face tarred and feathered, put in the ducking stool, pelted with rotten eggs and stones, paraded through the streets, and, finally, thrown "headlong over the wharf" into the Elizabeth River. Smith barely escaped drowning before he was rescued by a passing boat. A leading assailant was Mayor Calvert, who "encouraged" others and even stoned the victim.[36]

It was therefore ill-advised of Captain Jeremiah Morgan of the guardship *Hornet* to enter Norfolk in September 1767 at the head of a press gang in search of deserters or involuntary replacements. Impressment was deemed a notoriously odious form of servitude, especially under the tyrannical discipline of Royal Navy officers.

Morgan and his men rowed to the town wharf on the night of September 5 and went "to that part of town where seamen resorted to." Several inns and bawdy houses were raided, and prospective sailors were subdued and dragged off. When the night watch gave alarm, an armed and enraged crowd of blacks and whites, led by Mayor George Abyvon, forced the captain, sword in hand, back to his boat. Morgan, deprived of all his captives and even some of his own men, assured Governor Francis Fauquier that, if all rioters were prosecuted, "there would not be twenty left unhang'd" in the town.[37]

When next the red horse of strife appeared in Norfolk, in the spring of 1768, it was accompanied by the pale horse of pestilence, a dire concurrence Norfolk had so far had the good fortune to avoid. In June of the previous year, a traveling man in Norfolk had been found to have smallpox. Dr. John Dalgleish, a Scottish physician with considerable experience coping with the disease, sent the victim to the pesthouse outside town. He also gave an inoculation, apparently the first ever administered in Norfolk, to his apprentice, Robert Bell, who soon died. It was this occurrence that lay in the background of the trouble that broke out the following year.[38]

In February a West Indian ship arrived with some smallpox victims on board. Several gentlemen asked Dalgleish for inoculations for themselves and their families. He agreed but, encountering some community resistance, then changed his mind. In June, with more shipborne cases coming in, merchant-physician Archibald Campbell decided to inoculate his own family. He meant to keep them at his Tanner's Creek plantation, three miles from town, until the inoculation-induced fevers ran their course. Merchant

Cornelius Calvert and others asked Campbell and Dalgleish to treat their families and the doctors agreed.[39]

Strenuous objection to inoculation was voiced by parties in town and the Tanner's Creek vicinity. Some opponents appreciated the value of inoculation but disapproved of the plantation house being near town. Others threatened to inoculate their families in town if Campbell went through with his purpose, and rumors arose that his plantation would be attacked. Campbell agreed to confine treatment to his family and twenty-six others already promised inoculation, including six blacks.[40]

On the day scheduled for the families to go to Tanner's Creek, a group of opponents applied to several Norfolk magistrates for an order to forbid the project. The magistrates declined, citing lack of legal authority to intervene, but the families delayed leaving. With tempers flaring, Maximilian Calvert, brother of Cornelius, proposed to Campbell a meeting of leaders on both sides of the issue. This was accepted and the meeting convened at Mrs. Ross's tavern to try to find a compromise.[41]

The conferring "antis" included Samuel Boush Jr., Mayor George Abyvon, Dr. John Ramsay and his partner Dr. James Taylor, Paul Loyall, and Maximilian Calvert. Those supporting inoculation were Cornelius Calvert, James Archdeacon, James Parker, Lewis Hansford, and Neil Jamieson. A plan that won unanimous approval was to seek a new site for the inoculations while many on both sides were absent in Williamsburg for the June Court of Oyer and Terminer. If no better place were found before the court session ended, Campbell's plantation must suffice. The doctors would join together to perform the inoculations.[42]

The plan quickly fell apart. No other house was found to be suitable to all parties; Drs. Ramsay and Taylor then dissociated themselves from the project. On June 23 opponents of inoculation went to Campbell's plantation, where they broke out windows and doors. Two days later, however, the families seeking inoculation took up quarters there anyhow. Signs were posted promising due care in undertaking the treatment and warning people to stay clear of the place.[43]

Mob violence was now a greater threat than smallpox. On June 26 Alderman Paul Loyall visited Campbell in Norfolk and suggested that the inoculated families be moved to the pesthouse, then occupied by several smallpox patients. Campbell assented, provided that the pesthouse were cleared, whitewashed, and otherwise put in order, which would entail three or four days' delay. But delay proved unacceptable to the opponents. "Such is the spirit of rioting and licentiousness here," wrote a Scottish merchant to a friend, "that the most . . . inoffensive persons are not secure from outrage and we . . . displace our families and convert our houses into garrisons, where [we] watch every night under arms . . . to prevent the demolition of our houses and abuse of our persons."[44]

On June 27 Joseph Calvert, another of the numerous brothers of that family and sergeant of the watch, led a mob of some two hundred, preceded by a flag and drummers, to Tanner's Creek. Application was made to several magistrates to halt the march, but neither borough nor county militia was summoned. Calvert, who had already engaged the doctor in an affray, reached Campbell's with his mob in mid-afternoon and demanded that the inmates leave at once for the pesthouse. Neither Paul Loyall nor any of the four or more justices of the peace in the mob could be prevailed upon to use their influence to disperse it, in spite of Calvert's role as a funtionary of the Common Council. Assured of violence if they refused, the families in early evening set out on foot toward the pesthouse, five miles distant.[45]

The Pesthouse March was a hideous indiscretion on the part of Calvert's mob, one that left festering scars for years to come. The families included those of sisters Margaret Ellegood (Mrs. James) Parker and Rebecca Ellegood (Mrs. William) Aitchison, whose husbands were mercantile partners. Other families were those of Ann Taylor (Mrs. Lewis) Hansford, wife of an alderman and former mayor; Elizabeth Thorowgood (Mrs. Cornelius) Calvert, wife of the new mayor (as of June 24) and daughter of late Sheriff John Thorowgood (also sister-in-law of her main persecutor); and her daughters. There were members of the Archibald Campbell and Robert Tucker families (including "pretty Miss Beckie Tucker"), and, possibly, those of James Archdeacon and Neil Jamieson, with several slaves. One of the children was a suckling infant.[46]

The hurried exodus from the house around 7:00 P.M. was urged along by members of the mob with what a witness called "amazing barbarity." With a violent thunderstorm beginning, some of the mob headed home while others escorted the marchers, exultantly firing guns over their heads. Some marchers became disoriented in the driving rain and spent hours wandering the woods in search of the road to the pesthouse. Although a few procured horses along the way, it was 11:00 P.M. before the first of them began to arrive at the facility. The last straggled in past midnight.[47]

The work of cleaning and outfitting the pesthouse for the new arrivals was sorely incomplete. Bedraggled marchers found the floor strewn with workmen's tools and materials. No fires were laid; there were no candles or refreshments. Though the marchers were soaked to the bone and the night air was cold, the doctors felt obligated to insist that all windows and doors remain open. The chilled air was considered preferable to the "putrid steams with which the house was filled" from recent cases of smallpox, dysentery, and other diseases. A few days later, Campbell's plantation house was burned down.[48]

Under the circumstances, it seemed just that poet Thomas Burke should rail in the *Virginia Gazette* against "[u]nfeeling monsters!" through whose bosoms "[n]o beam of pity" stole. No doubt many others shared his sympathy for "beauteous Aitcheson," "lovely Nancy," "enchanting Tucker," and others, and hailed with the author "Intrepid Campbell" for discharging his promises under great difficulty. But the poet concluded with assurance that all were now "freed from harms," regaining "their vigour and uninjur'd charms / That mothers clasp in health and safety blesst / The smiling infant to the joyful breast."[49]

Charges and countercharges in newspapers, suits and countersuits in the courts, occupied the Norfolk gentry throughout the fall of 1768. (Thomas Jefferson, inoculated in 1766, was one of the attorneys retained by inoculationists.) Most of the suits were still pending in April 1769, when Norfolk erupted again. This time the unrest was touched off by Dalgleish's inoculation of an apprentice and three slaves of Cornelius Calvert. Within a day after this information was made public, a mob attacked Calvert's house and Dalgleish was arrested and jailed.[50]

Soon afterward, workmen on one of Calvert's ships, some of them veterans of the 1768 riot, assaulted a ropemaker associated with inoculationist James Parker. Calvert, still mayor, remonstrated with them to no effect. A small mob formed and visited, in turn, the homes of Calvert, Campbell, and Parker, demanding at each to be furnished with drinks and that the suits of the inoculationists be dropped. Some forty panes of Calvert's glass were broken and other minor damage wrought, but the mob broke up on meeting armed resistance at Parker's. Joseph Calvert was again a principal agitator. Although Cornelius Calvert, Campbell, and Parker now kept their homes under guard, there were further riots at intervals throughout the summer, including the hanging of effigies.[51]

The flurry of indictments and suits arising from the 1768 and 1769 troubles occupied Virginia courts for much of the next four years. At Williamsburg, the general court heard argument that Dr. Dalgleish "maliciously intended to spread the infection all around to make a fortune," a theory the judges rejected out of hand. When Judge William Nelson remarked that he would hang "every man that would inoculate even in his own house," Governor Botetourt responded archly that inoculation was "the greatest addition that ever was made to physical knowledge." [52]

On the whole, the courts found in inoculation mitigating grounds for the mob activity and gave out mild punishments or none. In November 1769 the general assembly rejected a Norfolk petition to ban inoculation but endorsed another calling for regulation of the practice. An act of June 1770 allowed those wanting inoculation to apply to magistrates, who might grant or deny it under any restrictions they judged necessary. After this, inoculation virtually ceased in the colony. It was probably Jefferson who in 1777 proposed a policy, soon enacted, to allow inoculation if a majority of neighbors within two miles agreed. [53]

A feature of the Norfolk trouble that gave it a vehemence perhaps greater than inoculation warranted was that the "pro" faction were mostly Scots, while the "antis" were English. The difference was already politically institutionalized as a rivalry of Scottish "Orange" and native "Blue" or "Buckskin." Leaders of both provided voters with ginger cakes and hogsheads of rum on voting days and awaited results over bowls of "hot arrack punch and jolly." But the colors seem to have functioned in harmony on the Common Council and in regard to the vexed imperial issues of the day, a sign that the difference was more cultural than political. [54]

Scots like Parker and Aitchison had won a measure of acceptance but were resented by some for their business success and the debts owed to them by many natives. Hence, the riots and judicial proceedings to some extent pitted "foreigner" against "native" and kept both sides in concern over the supposed biases of the judges. Some Scots tried unsuccessfully to have their cases removed to Britain, where their chances might be better. [55]

The widening gulf between colonial and Old World values was also reflected in the celebrated Somerset case of 1772. James was a trusted slave of Norfolk merchant Charles Somerset. Somerset, on a business trip to England in 1769, took James along and was enraged when the slave ran off to the protection of a group of abolitionists. Somerset recovered James and revealed his intention to sell him in Jamaica, whereupon the abolitionists sued to prevent it. Chief Justice Mansfield of the King's Bench found that a slave became free as soon as he set foot on English soil, a decision immediately construed by some as an argument for freeing all slaves throughout the British Empire. [56]

In Norfolk, the maverick carouse of the red and pale horses had reduced society to a state of virtual anomie, borough fathers setting the masses a wretched example of civic responsibility. The common pesthouse, focus of so much official and popular concern, was only slightly farther from town than the Campbell plantation and, of course, not a whit safer or more dangerous. Inoculation had been in use in Virginia for fifteen or twenty years, and even George III had undergone immunization in this way.[57] In neither mob nor disease control did municipal leaders show courage or enlightenment.

In particular, evidence weighed heavily against chiefs of the "Blue" or native faction, who often channeled or exploited mobs rather than preventing or dispersing them. George Abyvon, Paul Loyall, and Maximilian Calvert were experienced rioters, the latter having had a leading role in previous disturbances.[58] After decades of struggling to maintain civic discipline among "the meaner sort," they showed themselves to be the graver danger.

A full accounting for the inoculation riots might also include the perceived religious and political insensitivity of the Scots. Their attitudes, observed by the French visitor in 1765, contrasted profoundly with the easy tolerance that had been the Norfolk area's heritage since the founding of the county. It may not have been so much the Scots' goal of inoculation that fueled discord as their failure to insure community approval before undertaking it. The borough's history of mob violence might have forewarned the Scots that the campaign of Drs. Dalgleish and Campbell must be preceded by a public-relations effort.

Common Council minutes in the early 1770s, not surprisingly, evince obsessive concern for the town watch—how to fund, staff, conduct, and supervise it. They worried over "the great risque the Inhabitants run by the large Importation of Gunpowder, . . . lodged in private warehouses."[59] There was no obvious answer to the smoldering passions whipped up by the inoculation riots, though a solution of sorts was in the offing. It was perhaps the only feasible one: a thorough purging by the white horse of war of the society that had been thrown into turmoil by its brother stallions.

CHAPTER 7

The Tempering of Nellie
and Margaret

SCOTTISH Orange and native Blue in Norfolk, so bitterly divided by inoculation up to 1773, were reunited, after a fashion, in the latter year through the unlikely agency of cheap tea. Parliament's new Tea Act designated agents to sell tea, eliminated smugglers and middlemen, and promised a cheaper brew. A modest duty on tea imports would go to shore up the sagging fortunes of the East India Company, thereby fostering enlightened economic policy as well as more flavorful interludes in the humdrum day.

Orangemen, possibly under duress, joined Blue to flay the Tea Act as a vicious, perhaps fatal, blow to Britain's constitution. Colonists, who sent no representative to Parliament, were required by that far-off body to pay a tax. If the principle were conceded by buying tea, the gates of Hell itself would fly open to vomit more duties and strangle the ancient heritage, dear-won at Runnymede, of English liberty. When the first cargo of subversive brown leaves was thrown into Boston Harbor in the fall of 1773, the "Boston Tea Party," Orange joined Blue to celebrate the deed.[1]

News of the British crackdown on Boston and the Massachusetts Colony, the "Intolerable Acts," brought resentful rumblings among Orange and Blue factions alike. In May 1774 the Virginia assembly declared a day of fasting in support of Boston, and the governor, Lord Dunmore, dismissed the body. When the legislators defied the governor by forming an association against British imports, Norfolk's leaders established a committee of public safety to rally support for the association and maintain contact with other communities. Chaired by Matthew Phripp of the Blue and including Neil Jamieson and others of the Orange, the committee promised Boston to "support you to the limit of our ability."[2] In August a Boston invitation for other colonies to boycott British exports as well as imports won support from the new Virginia Convention.

Throughout the rest of 1774 and early 1775 Norfolk was alive with public meetings resolving against "the tyrannick exercise of unlawful power" and turning back cargoes of boycotted goods. In March 1775 the public safety committee censured merchant John Brown for importing Jamaican slaves and a Captain Sampson for selling salt he had agreed to keep off the market while refitting his ship. The boycott had begun to hurt Norfolk's importers, especially the Scots. James Parker groused that the committee managed everything, including the price of goods, "and forcing some to sign scandalous concessions . . . to bring the Government to their own terms." By summer, even native merchants felt persecuted by the association. Recent restrictions had caught merchants with contracts already signed and perishable produce on the wharves. Meanwhile, fighting erupted in New England between colonial and British troops.[3]

Virginia's relations with England took a decisive turn for the worse when, in early June 1775, Dunmore fled seething Williamsburg and established the seat of his crumbling authority aboard the frigate *Otter* in the Elizabeth River. He also collected a small flotilla of vessels, impressing and arming several merchantmen. From here he could disrupt Chesapeake trade as a way of bringing pressure on patriot elements. At the end of July he was reinforced by sixty Redcoats from Florida represented as his bodyguard.[4]

Norfolk seemed to be on the verge of open combat when, in mid-August, Mayor Paul Loyall received a letter from Captain John McCartney of HMS *Mercury* in the Elizabeth River. McCartney complained of recent treatment of certain loyalists, including merchant Andrew Sprowle, charged by the committee of public safety with having harbored royal troops at Gosport. Merchant John Schaw was mobbed and paraded to the tune of "Yankey Doodle" at Norfolk on August 11 for causing a citizen to be imprisoned by Dunmore as a minuteman. McCartney warned that he would meet violence against loyal subjects and their property by placing his ship abreast of town and using "the utmost coercive measures in my power."[5]

Almost any untoward incident might hurl Virginia into the vortex of war: it happened to be an early September hurricane. A tender of the *Otter* plowed ashore near Hampton and patriots seized it. When they refused to return even certain equipment from the prize unless Dunmore gave up slave Joseph Harris, the *Otter*'s pilot, the British declared a blockade of Hampton Roads. Captain Matthew Squire of the *Otter,* earlier lauded by whigs for refusing to harbor escaped slaves, became an object of patriot invective over this and other incidents. Especially galling to Squire was the sniping of John Hunter Holt, editor of Norfolk's weekly *Virginia Gazette, or Norfolk Intelligencer.*[6]

On September 14 Captain Squire sent Holt a note promising, if again insulted by the paper, to seize both editor and press. Holt failed to oblige. On September 30 seventeen soldiers and marines reached the county wharf about 2:00 P.M. The marines marched to the Market Street printing office and seized the press, types, papers, and two journeymen printers. (Holt was absent). Another party returned a few days later for ink and more paper.[7]

Reports of the incident put Norfolk in a bad light from which it did not emerge during the war. A group of Norfolk citizens was said to have watched from a distance without trying to interfere; a drum-call summoning militia got no response. (Nothing in Norfolk could match the guns of a large warship.) No previous episode had so emphatically demonstrated the small support patriots could hope for from the Norfolk area.[8] In the first display of British armed force, the coiling patriot serpent of earlier weeks was found to have slithered into the undergrowth.

The curse of the Blue, so earnest and daring in defiance in previous months, was perhaps only a loss of nerve. On September 19 Maximilian Calvert, bending to the strains of office, resigned as borough alderman.[9] The appalling apathy of the town at the loss of its newspaper was perhaps for him the last straw. Yet here was the veteran incendiary who had often called out the street-rabble in lesser causes. How could he, of all people, desert freedom's call at this critical moment in Virginia's history?

The Calverts were in many ways representative of the Blue faction. Nellie Calvert was fifteen when her father stoned customs-snitch William Smith and, days later, hosted the meeting that launched Norfolk toward revolution. To an adoring daughter, he was "a fine, portly man, of a handsome ruddy face, . . . and sociable disposition," well beloved of neighbors and friends. But to the captain of a Chesapeake guardship he was a firebrand who, on March 29, 1766, led thirty hooligans from a tavern and "brought day on" plotting mischief against the Stamp Act. Patriots called the Stamp Act an internal duty that only the colony's own legislature might impose.[10]

Maximilian Calvert was, in truth, an exasperating contradiction of a man. He was at once a fond father "naturally disposed to wink" at his wife's indulgences of the children and the likeliest fuse to every sort of civic combustion. Bred to the sea—like nine of his ten brothers—he embraced gentility as a wholesale merchant in "a fine, old-fashioned coat with large cuffs and ruffles." He still emptied his three-pint silver tankard twice or thrice daily, but named his Tanner's Creek country place "Pomfret" for a seventeenth-century poet.[11]

The sea may have lost its enchantment for Calvert on a snow-blown winter's day in the 1760s when his brother Jonathan's ship returned from the

West Indies. Its "sails set and frozen," as Nellie recalled, "and steering about in a wild manner . . . made those who saw her think all was not right on board." Boarders found Jonathan dead, others frozen to death or ill with smallpox, and a family slave at the helm. But Maximilian and his wife, Mary Savage Calvert, a native Bermudian "of a more prudent and saving turn," recovered to build a tidy fortune. Their townhouse was Norfolk's finest; the Tanner's Creek farm boasted an imported Scottish gardener "to plant and dress the ground in taste."[12]

Nellie, like her brothers and sisters, was exposed to the best schooling Norfolk offered. After an obligatory sojourn with old Mrs. Drudge to learn spelling and reading, she passed an interval with Mrs. Johnson, "a very large fat woman, . . . a monstrous woman, indeed," who taught "needle-work, and marking on the sampler." There was even talk of sending Nellie, an apt pupil, to an elite boarding school at Williamsburg, an idea that faded with the arrival in Norfolk of one Buchan from Scotland who offered French and Spanish as well as English. But Nellie's truly memorable early experience was a 1763 sermon in Portsmouth by George Whitefield, which drew great crowds from the whole region.[13]

The brief excitement over the Stamp Act ended in May 1766 with Britain's revocation of it and Norfolk's noisy celebration. But the royal government turned promptly to new sources of colonial revenue, and there was soon trouble over tea, a beverage perhaps more important on principle than on palates. With Parliament's passage of the Tea Act in 1773, Calvert came home one night in high spirits, saying: "'Well, now, take notice, one and all of you, that I have joined the Association'" against tea. His decree that the household consume no more was circumvented by Mrs. Calvert's expedient of serving it in a coffee pot, a device her lord and master accepted without comment.[14] A levy on arrack punch would have been a far graver offense to the old captain.

A consignment of tea for Jamieson and others was returned to its point of origin in mid-1774, but sly winking at the ban on tea was probably widespread. "Penelope Housewife" reminded the *Norfolk Intelligencer* in August that tea was not only soothing but that "the civilization of the world is owing, in great measure, to Tea-drinking." She called on wives to resist "domestic tyranny" over tea as stoutly as the men did "state tyranny."[15]

In 1767 Nellie married Norfolk merchant James Maxwell, to whom her father gave a house and lot next to his own and a half-interest in the ship *Two Sisters* (named for Nellie and her sister Polly). When her new husband took her on a wedding voyage to Barbados, Nellie spent giddy weeks among the island's social elite before returning home. Maxwell was frequently abroad but could be excused since he "was making money every voyage." Their first child was born in 1770 and another a year later.[16]

Scarcely anyone imagined that the dispute with England would rupture imperial relations. Maximilian Calvert continued to entertain officers from royal ships lying off Sewell's Point as well as all "strangers of any note." This society meant not only agreeable discourse but opportunities for his unmarried daughters to meet eligible midshipmen, including a few "sprigs of nobility." It was also a chance to display the culinary magic of "old Quashabee," a venerable black cook who "made the best soups, sauces, gravies, and all such things, in the world."[17]

If the political situation deteriorated drastically toward the end of the summer of 1775, it offered splendid chances for the Norfolk gentry to exercise in the name of patriotism the leadership it had often displayed for less lofty purposes. The urban masses might be summoned once again to parade the streets and shout defiance at kings. The Scots, yoked by interest and inclination to royalism, no longer participated. But there remained a practiced vanguard of patriot Blue to carry rebellion into the open, and no doubt hundreds, as ever, awaiting their call.

Maximilian Calvert gave no public accounting for his resignation from the Common Council, but his motives seem clear. All he had achieved in a third of a century of hard work lay open under the mouths of British cannon. Not for him the flinty truculence of the Puritan Bostonian; if the material emblems of his success were lost, then his life must have little meaning. So he removed himself from the fray and retired for the duration at Pomfret farm. Like many of the crowd-brave Blue, he would sip the tea of submission if he must—and call it coffee, too.

Easy suppression of the local whig organ encouraged the Scots and other loyalists more than it should have. Dunmore began to publish his own shipboard paper, a decided advantage in molding local opinion. James Parker, reflecting the renewed dissonance of Orange and Blue, wrote a friend on October 10 that "My *good friend* Mayor Mr. Judas [Paul Loyall] is almost the only Rebel left in Town." Tories who had so far held back now furnished provisions for Dunmore's forces, information on patriot activities, and proffers of enrollment in royal service.[18]

Hearing of patriot militia forming at Williamsburg to march on Norfolk, Dunmore began clearing out local opposition before it could be reinforced. On October 12 and 17 he sent men up the southern and eastern branches after cannon taken from the Norfolk wharves by militia. His intelligence proved sound, and the marchers destroyed or seized nineteen cannon besides small arms and other equipment. Tories gave out that militia at

Kemp's Landing on October 17 were ordered by Colonel Joseph Hutchings, who "made rather too free with the bottle," to run away, he himself escaping capture when a butcher "covered him with trash" after finding him lying in a woods. On October 19 some British landing at Norfolk found twenty more cannon. Dunmore was sure by November that the seventy-two cannon taken or destroyed so far had crippled local resistance.[19]

Dunmore could now proceed to more formal and long-term arrangements. On November 7 he issued a proclamation of martial law. He summoned to his standard all who would defend the king and made a further offer that bade fair to work some advantage for the king's men: a promise of freedom to slaves who fled to the British from patriot masters. In this the governor struck the one note the most likely to bring wavering white Virginians to the patriot side. Dunmore, in dire need of reinforcements, promptly formed an "Ethiopian Regiment" of former slaves.[20]

It was also useful to break up small militia groups trying to protect the road over which the Williamsburg forces must come. On November 15 Dunmore led some two hundred regulars and black and white tories (Captain James Parker among them) to Great Bridge, which crossed the southern branch eight miles southeast of Norfolk. He learned there of three or four hundred patriots under Joseph Hutchings and Anthony Lawson ten miles away at Kemp's Landing. Arriving there, the British were fired on from a thicket a mile short of the village but routed the assailants, killing several, wounding more, and capturing eighteen. Hutchings, pursued by black troops, saw that one was his former slave and fired at him. He sustained a saber slash across his face and was captured by the soldier.[21]

The next day Dunmore marched in triumph to Norfolk and took control of the borough. Mayor Loyall and the aldermen were among two hundred who took the governor's oath of allegiance and pinned on red badges of loyalty to the Crown. Within weeks, some three thousand more from the borough and surrounding areas were reported to have done likewise. Lieutenant Colonel Jacob Ellegood of the local militia brought six hundred of his men over to Dunmore and was appointed colonel of the "Queen's Own" regiment.[22]

Other loyalists served Dunmore in key roles. His defenses were supervised by business partners Thomas McKnight and James Parker, the latter designated chief engineer for the British. Andrew Sprowle built barracks for royal troops and Neil Jamieson served as the British supply agent. With the chief port in hand and Chesapeake traffic under his control, Dunmore had reason to feel that the reconquest of Virginia was well launched.[23]

Residents in and around Norfolk accommodated themselves as best they could to fluctuating fortunes. Scots and other tories who could do so sought safety on ships in the river or left for the eastern shore and elsewhere. Many patriots fled upcountry or hid in swampy areas—even among Cape Henry's sand dunes—in hope of early recovery by patriot forces. Others of either persuasion or none, hoping to protect their property and livelihoods, stayed and adapted their conduct to whatever norm seemed most expedient at a given time. They had sometimes to endure ravagement of their farms, "wives and children stripped to nakedness, and our very bed chambers invaded by midnight ruffians with drawn daggers and bayonets."[24] It made little difference to such people in the next six years which side happened to be in control.

The Calvert and Maxwell families, among others, were buffeted willy-nilly about the region by the events of late fall. Maximilian Calvert in November sent his wife to Max Herbert's home at Sewell's Point and fled town himself before dawn on December 11. His daughter Nellie Maxwell and her children were installed at Billy White's boarding house at Kemp's Landing, but fled almost at once as Dunmore approached in mid-November.[25]

Nellie and her sister, Polly Marsden, lodged at the home of Charles Sawyer, a friend near Kemp's Landing, where they were visited by "an ugly looking negro man, dressed up in a full suit of British regimentals, and armed with a gun." The intruder inquired for "dirty-shirts," meaning militia, poked around a bit, and left, an encounter deemed by Nellie "a provoking piece of insolence" and prompting her immediate removal back to Billie White's, where Dunmore now ruled securely. This move also soon proved unsuitable. One night when Maxwell, a patriot who needed to avoid Dunmore, was secretly visiting Nellie, two grenadiers invaded their room but ran off when challenged by Maxwell. New quarters were found for Nellie in adjacent Pasquotank County, North Carolina, but within weeks she had to move yet again.[26]

Dunmore understood that the key to Norfolk was the passage through Great Bridge, which must be defended if the borough was to be held. He had a small fortification erected to cover the bridge and causeway and garrisoned it with about a hundred men, white and black. But he unwisely held the remainder of his men in the Norfolk entrenchments, which would be of no use if the Great Bridge fell. On November 28 an advanced guard from Williamsburg took a position on the opposite (southern) side of the river, and four days later the main force under Colonel William Woodford arrived. A breastwork was thrown up on the south bank while Dunmore rushed more men from Norfolk to prevent a crossing.[27]

Although the patriots referred contemptuously to Dunmore's jerry-built fort as "the Hogpen," it kept Woodford off the bridge. Swamps on either side of the causeway meant that the bridge, its planks removed from the runners, had to be crossed in order to strike effectively. Action for several days consisted of desultory firing, light probes across the river, and attempts by each side to gain control of a ford five or six miles downstream. Though Dunmore hoped to be reinforced soon, Woodford could count on a body of Carolinians coming north under General Robert Howe. Dunmore, perhaps informed of Howe's approach, decided on the night of December 8 to risk all in an effort to force his way over the bridge. Experience, after all, suggested that patriot militia were easily discouraged.[28]

Dunmore's plan called for two companies of black troops to circle behind the rebel barricade before daylight and force them out at sunrise. Simultaneously, the Hogpen garrison would storm over the bridge. Unhappily, Captain Samuel Leslie, arriving at the Hogpen in the night from Norfolk to lead the charge, found that the black units had been sent to guard the ford downriver.[29]

Leslie ordered his three hundred or so troops out of the fort just after daylight, quickly laid planks across the bridge, and sent an impetuous charge toward the rebel barricade. It was as brave and criminally imbecile an attack as Lord Cardigan's subsequent "Charge of the Light Brigade" in the Crimean War and had the same outcome. Captain Charles Fordyce, leading the British regulars, was cut down as he reached the patriot breastwork; bodies behind him bore as many as a dozen bullet holes. The charge broke, and the dismayed attackers fell back to their fort in crippled confusion.[30]

Among those said to have earned special commendation on the patriot side was William Flora, a free black from Portsmouth who was with a group in front of his own breastworks when the British attacked. Flora "kept firing at the attacking British when all his comrades had retired to their breastwork" and helped break the charge. One patriot was wounded in a finger; the royalists had seventeen killed and forty-eight wounded in the half-hour action. The British abandoned the Hogpen on the night of December 9. Nellie Maxwell, visiting her mother at Sewell's Point, witnessed the return of Dunmore's men to Norfolk on December 10, "the poor creatures . . . crying water, water, and I and the young women . . . went out and carried them pitchers."[31]

It was clear that Dunmore could not hold Norfolk since patriot forces could cut off access by land and hinder provisions from reaching his ships or land forces. The next three days witnessed an evacuation of troops and tory civilians, including many of Norfolk's thirty-five merchants, to British ships or their own. On the night of December 14 Woodford, reinforced by Carolina troops to 1,600 or more men, reached Norfolk to find it abandoned except by a few civilians anxious to be regarded as patriots.[32]

Woodford and Howe concluded that Norfolk was not worth holding since it was subject to control by whoever commanded Hampton Roads navigation, a goal well beyond patriot means. Any sizable British reinforcements could cut off American forces east of the Elizabeth River. The commanders felt that the place ought to be abandoned but that it should first be rendered useless to the British. These views were conveyed to the Convention, which had to decide Norfolk's fate. For his own part, Dunmore seems to have had no clear idea what to do next, while conditions on his crowded ships rapidly deteriorated. Provisions and water were hard to procure and smallpox broke out.[33]

Nellie Maxwell by late December had moved again, this time from Pasquotank to her father's farm at Tanner's Creek. The site was exposed but she soon joined her husband, lately placed in charge of the rebels' York River shipyard. British officers continued to visit Pomfret, even in the tense days around Christmas, and one, named Lane, promised the Calverts and Maxwells that he would get word to them if a bombardment was imminent. Patriot troops, in fact, were daily goading the British to lay the town in ruins and spare them the trouble.[34]

Nellie recalled the sequel many years later: "Accordingly a few days after, [Lane] told us it was time for us to be moving, and we set about sending all our valuable articles of furniture &c. over to Max Herbert's at the point, where we took a room." Pomfret was abandoned except for a slave named Sarah, who stayed to look after the property as well as "a sow and pigs which she was raising for herself." At Norfolk, Dunmore was informed on the morning of January 1 that patriot troops were parading the streets with "Hats fixed on to their Bayonets." The governor, apparently viewing this as an impertinence, ordered the place to be bombarded. His men-of-war now drew up abreast of the wharves and, about 3:15 P.M., opened a heavy cannonade.[35]

Annoyed by snipers from waterfront buildings, Dunmore in the early evening sent parties ashore to burn warehouses and other buildings used by the snipers. There had been a surgical clearing of this sort on November 30, involving destruction of some thirty-two buildings, to make room for Dunmore's fortifications, and now nineteen more were razed. But the withdrawal of the British parties, together with the late-night end of the covering

Artist-architect Benjamin Latrobe in March 1796 found Norfolk still only partially rebuilt from the conflagration that had destroyed it in January 1776. (Courtesy of Maryland Historical Society, Baltimore)

bombardment, was followed by what amounted to a rampage by patriot
troops.[36]

Soldiers, perhaps embittered by long tours of duty, bad food, and miserable weather, moved from street to street plundering and setting one house
after another on fire as the last residents fled in panic. Adding to the chaos,
Dunmore sent more landing parties, several with cannon, to capitalize on
patriot confusion. There was intermittent fighting in lower parts of town as
the flames grew steadily into an inferno. Both sides eventually had to with-
draw. With the countryside lit brightly for miles, Nellie Maxwell at Sewell's
Point saw a small boat put off from Pomfret and head in her direction. A
British barge cut off the boat but soon permitted the refugee to resume her
flight; it proved to be "Old Sarah," Maximilian Calvert's cook, who was
fleeing to Sewell's Point with her treasured sow and pigs.[37]

Norfolk burned furiously through the night. Pillaging and destruction
resumed the next day and continued until Howe and Woodford regained
control of their men on January 3. When the flames died, some 863 buildings had been consumed besides the handful burned by Dunmore. Over
four hundred others still stood but these the Convention in February or-

dered to be burned. The Convention also decreed destruction of Archibald Campbell's and Neil Jamieson's Thistle Distillery at Norfolk and Andrew Sprowle's store at Gosport, both of which had supplied the British. Thomas Newton alone lost ten warehouses, nine tenements, both his "elegantly furnished" residences, and a well-stocked store. There was a widespread assumption elsewhere that Dunmore did all the burning—an error neither Howe nor Woodford troubled themselves to correct.[38]

The burning of Norfolk has been called "the end of rebellion and the beginning of revolution" in Virginia. More than Tom Paine's call to arms in *Common Sense,* the events at Norfolk appear to have persuaded Virginians that there could be no reconciliation, no papering over of the fierce animosities that corroded attitudes on both sides. Both Virginia's constitution and Jefferson's Declaration of Independence in July cited Norfolk's destruction as a reason for breaking America's bonds with England. No longer must a change in British policy be the goal, but independence.[39]

Dunmore took over a few acres at Tucker's Point on the river's Portsmouth side, but raging smallpox and increasing problems in finding supplies wore down his resolution. Amid rumors that the rebels planned to send fireships downriver into his fleet, the governor in May spent three days demolishing his Tucker's Point buildings. In June his fleet sailed out of the river, throwing off the bodies of many blacks who had died from smallpox. The motley array of some ninety vessels swung northward and made for Gwynn's Island, a safer Chesapeake haven offshore from Mathews County. In August they left for New York.[40]

Lord Dunmore's defeat at Great Bridge and the burning of Norfolk were disasters almost beyond comprehension for embattled loyalists. James Parker and his brother-in-law Jacob Ellegood were among the first to commit themselves to Dunmore, secure in the expectation that the rebellion would soon self-destruct. The governor's shortcomings as a military man, the want of timely reinforcement by royal forces, and the unexpected determination of the patriots all came as astonishing revelations. The immediate result for Parker and Ellegood was a fortune lost in real estate and goods, including their homes, stores, warehouses, ropewalk, and other properties.[41] Few of the Orangemen, however, doubted that the king would eventually reclaim his own.

Ellegood represented an old and respected Princess Anne family. Parker was a native of Port Glasgow, Scotland, who had come to Virginia as a lad of eighteen in 1747. He was then employed by the great Glasgow house of Alexander Spiers, but within a decade he began his own business as partner to William Aitchison, an older Scot, who, like himself, wed one of Ellegood's sisters. In 1763 Parker was elected to the first of several terms on the Common Council, serving with Maximilian Calvert and others to manage the borough's throbbing growth. He took the patriot side in the Stamp Act crisis of 1766 and was for some years Norfolk's postmaster. Aitchison from 1758 to 1761 was the borough's assembly delegate.[42]

Married to Margaret Ellegood in 1760, Parker built his bride a handsome two-story, eight-room Granby Street house with cellar and garret, marble chimneys, kitchen and stables, brick boundary wall, and what was soon the finest garden in the area. He and some associates also erected what he regarded as "the largest rope and tan works in America," with fourteen buildings and a shoe factory on the premises. He became involved in a large exporting concern on the Pasquotank River and purchased tracts in Currituck County and in Northampton County on the eastern shore. By 1775 he was one of the richest men in the Norfolk area.[43]

James Parker resolved the labored political choice in 1775 when he declined to sign the association against trade with Britain. Trade was not his sole means of livelihood, but he felt strongly that the agitators were constitutionally and morally bankrupt.[44] Nor was it coincidence that Maximilian Calvert and other associationists were his persecutors during the inoculation riots and his antagonists in court for years after that.

As Norfolk and Princess Anne counties became a theater of war in late 1775, Parker, Ellegood, and Aitchison moved their families from town and, when patriots seized control, to eastern shore farms. Both Aitchison and Ellegood were soon seized by patriots, the former to be released and to die of ague in a few months, the latter to spend over five years as an exile or parolee.[45]

Parker was commissioned captain and chief engineer by Dunmore. He was shipwrecked and captured on the eastern shore in mid-1776, escaped, and taken again at sea by the French in 1781. In the early months of the fighting he could write to his wife, but his letters soon grew less frequent and, for two years while he was imprisoned and then paroled by the French, ceased entirely.[46]

If Nellie Maxwell eventually found security with her husband on the York River, Margaret Parker, like so many tory wives and their children, never had a moment of it in the course of the war. She had borne well her ordeal at the hands of anti-inoculationists in 1768, writing to a friend only that she and her young son had been "never drove from place to place so ill." But she would go to her grave despising her tormenters.[47]

By early 1777 the Princess Anne refugees had moved back from North-ampton County, the Ellegoods to their plantation at "Rose Hall," the Par-kers and Aitchisons to "Eastwood," their farm nearby. In the meantime James Parker wrote to Margaret of a glimpse he had at Norfolk of "the wreck of our little Eden." The surrounding brick wall was "greatly battered with canon shot, . . . the flowering hedge, the few trees I collected . . . de-stroyed & the clover Walks all rooted up."[48]

The four-room cottage at "Eastwood" was pressed into service as a home for Margaret, her widowed sister Rebecca Aitchison, their four youngest children, and two young female wards. (Their three older sons were sent before the war to England for schooling.) There was also a bookkeeper, who recorded the steady erosion of the families' remaining properties through confiscation and other causes. Margaret was able to salvage from her Nor-folk house only enough furniture for about one room, though Rebecca had done better and could furnish the rest of the house.[49]

In a letter of 1778, Margaret described their life in these narrow quarters:

> we spin our own cloaths, Nitt, Sew, raise Poultry, and everything we are capable of doing to maintain ourselves. Everything has got to such prices here that we buy nothing that we can do without. Our girls are all dressed in their Spining even little Molly A assists and . . . Jenny is as Notable at this Country Work as if she had been brought up to it. . . . I am sorry our present circumstances prevent them from improving themselves by reading, Writing, keeping polite Company etc.[50]

The war that went away with Dunmore's departure in 1776 insisted on returning with dismal frequency. Failing to subdue New England, the Brit-ish turned in 1779 to the reconquest of their former southern colonies. In May a British expedition surprised Norfolk, briefly seizing the town and outlying regions, burning Gosport and Suffolk, and capturing a vast amount of supplies. These included naval stores, vessels building on the Elizabeth and other rivers, and merchant craft of various types numbering some 137 in all. It was years before Virginia's shipping recovered. James Parker seized the occasion for a hurried visit with his wife, but it was agreed that she should stay on in the hope that what remained of the families' properties might not be confiscated.[51]

Patriots and tories meanwhile engaged in incessant guerrilla warfare. Mi-litia Colonel Thomas Newton Jr. wrote in 1781 that "Princess Anne has neither civil or military law in it. Murder is committed and no notice is taken of it. . . . A few desperate fellows go about on the sea coasts and large swamps, and do mischiefs in the night." During 1777 and 1778 a gang led by Josiah Phillips, formerly a landless Lynnhaven laborer, plundered parts of Norfolk and Princess Anne counties, at first with a commission from Dunmore but later as desperadoes. Besides murders, including that of Norfolk militia Captain Josiah Wilson, the gang was charged with "burning houses, wasting farms and doing other acts of hostility." [52]

Phillips and some of his gang of fifty were seized and executed in 1778, but others, including runaway slaves, remained at large. In particular, Levi Sikes and Robert Stewart preyed on farms and families, the former subsisting in this way for five years. Those who were captured often escaped to resume their criminal careers. Colonel Newton complained loudly to the Convention in 1781 that outlaw "Tories and Refugees . . . live in affluence while those . . . engaged in their Country's service are ruin'd." [53]

From this form of injury the inmates of Eastwood cottage were spared, except for losing some cattle. But they bore a series of calamities of other sorts and their Ellegood sister-in-law was at one point "plunder'd of every thing." Several of the children died during the war, some of illness, Mrs. Aitchison's son Walter after being struck by a cannonball in Chesapeake Bay. A few of the slaves remained but most were confiscated or ran off to the British. Meanwhile, everything cost "at least double the price they used to be," as Margaret wrote a friend. [54]

Jacob Ellegood in 1781 was able to visit Princess Anne and found Margaret and Rebecca in good spirits. To a friend he wrote:

> When I reflect on the behaviour of these two ladys I sometimes think it impossible that human nature can be capable of so much fortitude. . . . You may believe me if you was at the little smiling cottage . . . you would see as much cheerfulness (at least the appearance of it) as you ever saw in any house whatever, they seem to try to make what few friends comes to see them perfectly happy. . . . You never hear one of them mention any misfortune that they have met with. [55]

Twice more before the war's end the Norfolk area came briefly under British control. An expedition that arrived at Portsmouth in October 1780 was designed to relieve Lord Cornwallis of some of the patriot forces opposing him in South Carolina. The setback dealt royal forces at King's Mountain meant the abandonment of this idea and withdrawal of the invaders to Charleston. [56]

Two months later Hampton Roads again hosted British invaders, this time under the traitor Benedict Arnold, whose designs on Virginia were more far-reaching. After surprising Virginia's government by sailing up the James and attacking Richmond, Arnold pulled back to the Elizabeth River and in January 1781 established winter quarters at Portsmouth. From here his men conducted raids and foraging expeditions into adjacent counties. Loyalists had a final chance to savor the hope of ultimate success, patriots faded into the shadows, and Washington's army was denied many provisions the region might have supplied to it.[57]

Tory renegades such as Adam Lovett and Aquilla Jones led gangs through Norfolk and other counties plundering patriots or pointing them out to the British. Patriot groups retaliated where they could and a state of virtual civil war existed south of the James. There were others as willing to serve under one flag as the other if it meant license to work their will on the defenseless. Arnold kept his army in the area until April 1781 when he joined Cornwallis, who, after marching across North Carolina, later that year made his winter quarters near Yorktown. But the attacks by gangs against civilians and each other persisted well into 1782.[58]

Cornwallis was bottled up at Yorktown and forced to surrender in October 1781, but it was almost two years before peace terms were concluded between England and its former colonies. In no part of America had the devastation been more total than in the Norfolk–Portsmouth vicinity. In 1781 a visitor described the towns as "mere heaps of rubbish," but that was not strictly accurate. Two years earlier a visitor to Norfolk had been shocked by the devastation of "that once agreeable place," but noted "a great many small huts built up in it" by those who professed that they could not "be happy anywhere else." Some had begun rebuilding as early as the fall of 1776, and the British expedition in 1779 bore witness to the flourishing revival of trade on the Elizabeth River and throughout the region. The Norfolk county court, authorized by the Convention to meet wherever it could in the absence of a courthouse, was convening regularly in private homes by mid-1777.[59]

Tory merchants, still anticipating British victory, did much to foster rebuilding in Norfolk in the late stages of the war. Neil Jamieson's son and namesake by the summer of 1783 had seven storehouses, two dwellings, and smaller structures there; Jonathan Eilbeck owned a brick house on Main Street; William Chisholm owned three more dwellings at Town Bridge and on Church Street. In January of that year James Parker heard from his son Patrick, clerk in a Norfolk store, that "The Town is rebuilding pretty fast again" and that provisions were abundant.[60]

There was reason to hope that whig and tory might suppress their mutual hatred and live again as neighbors, even friends. Patrick Parker in 1783 told his father of dining with Paul Loyall, though "from what I heard you & he were no great friends." Patrick felt that Loyall's hospitality showed "that the people here dont carry their resentment to the second generation as you used to say sometimes you were afraid of." But James Parker, in London pursuing claims against the British government for his losses, resolved never again to set foot in America. He wrote his wife to sell his remaining American estate and rejoin him in Britain.[61]

The war gave blacks unprecedented opportunity to prove their right to equality with whites, and they had reason to feel that they had done so. Those on both the British and patriot sides showed their fighting qualities many times over. Many from Norfolk, such as James Thomas and the former slave Pluto, served with valor on American warships. Pluto, a seaman on the *Patriot*, displayed conspicuous courage in an encounter with a British privateer. William Flora, the hero of Great Bridge, remained for many years a respected Portsmouth resident and, though by then an elderly man, was an eager volunteer for service in the War of 1812. Such efforts were unrewarded by any weakening of slavery's bonds, though a law of 1782 gave freedom to black veterans still in bondage and another wartime statute allowed masters to free their slaves.[62]

Nellie Maxwell came down from York River after Cornwallis's surrender. She and her husband could find no Norfolk lodgings and took a house of William Plume's at what is now Fort Norfolk. James Maxwell soon bought part of Neil Jamieson's confiscated estate and a residence at the head of "little Water Street." He also became owner of several boats and one of the town's ferries. By now James, in the words of Maximilian Calvert's daughter, was "making money rapidly."[63]

The fortunes of peace often made for finer discrimination than those of war, which brought destruction impartially to Orange and Blue. For Margaret Parker, the war years took the lives of so many friends that, as she wrote one who survived, it left "such a blank in our Society that we can never be so happy again." Her husband's order that she leave the home of her birth was as hurtful as any deprivation of war. She pled that she had been "treated with great respect by every body & friendship by some" and would suffer to lose her sister's companionship. Though quite unwell, she sailed dutifully for England in late 1784. She died the next summer.[64]

CHAPTER 8

Les Miserables

THE EDITORS of Norfolk's *Virginia Chronicle* had finished setting type for their July 6, 1793 issue when the startling notice was brought up from the wharf. A few lines shoehorned in hurriedly across the bottom of page 3 gave the facts as they knew them.

"Just as this paper was going to press," they wrote,

> intelligence came to hand from Hampton Road, of the arrival of . . . a fleet of near 300 . . . vessels . . . from Cap François; we learn that an action had taken place between the whites and mulattoes on the 20th June; that the town was reduced to ashes, and a great number of the inhabitants . . . obliged to retire on board the shipping. . . . they sent a request to be admitted in this place. We have not been able to obtain further particulars.[1]

It was a thunderclap of an announcement, copied in the days following by newspapers across the new Republic. Apart from its revelation of a great victory by Santo Domingo's (or St. Domingue's) rebel slaves over their masters, it signaled that a mass of burnt-out refugees was descending on American shores without warning. There would necessarily be thousands (ten thousand in fact) on so many ships, many with only the clothes on their backs and all in need of immediate relief.[2] Their care would tax the mercy and resources of the new nation beyond any emergency in its history.

As the fleets of lighters and small boats began coming ashore along the waterfront, townspeople peered at them in appalled sympathy and dismay. First to arrive were the sick and injured, their misery intensified by having fled without requisite supplies of food, clothing, and medicine. They would require prolonged attendance by every available physician and ship's surgeon in the region. Then came the pathetic hordes of women and children, many newly widowed or orphaned, pleading for food and shelter from a community not fully recovered from its own recent devastation. And, finally, came the dazed and desperate men, most of them in recent days witnesses to the destruction of all they possessed, the slaughter of loved ones, the collapse of their opulent world.

Some sailed on in a few days to Baltimore, Philadelphia, and other places, but little Norfolk had to accommodate the largest proportionate share of any town on the continent. A population of scarcely three thousand, living in some five hundred small or modest houses, had to try to furnish shelter for over two thousand refugees, including four hundred ill and wounded. "At Norfolk," as one of them wrote, "the French . . . wandered every where relating their misfortunes to sympathetic Americans. Those who had saved some money crowded the inns; others sought out canopies of the market places, which gave some shelter against the inclemencies of night."[3]

There were suffocating strains on every kind of facility and resource, frantic appeals for help from all directions. Former Mayor Thomas Newton Jr., who claimed to have visited all of the refugees personally, sent an express to Governor Henry Lee alerting him that "Husbands, wives, parents, & children are distributed in such a manner that they Know not where to find each other." Twelve thousand were said to have been slain in the islands; "many were taken out of the water & thrown on board the vessels without cloathes or any subsistence whatever. I beg you to do what you can." On July 13 new Mayor Robert Taylor added that Norfolk was providing rations for up to 350 but that new refugees came ashore daily. In fact, ships were still arriving from the distressed island and would continue to do so for months.[4]

A subscription was opened at the post office and others at Portsmouth, Petersburg, Richmond, Williamsburg, Yorktown, Hampton, and elsewhere; over $1,000 was raised in a week. The state opened the new Marine Hospital at Washington Point (now Berkley) upriver and sent emergency funds of $2,000. On July 9 the Common Council sent Councilman John Nivison (a William and Mary graduate and a founder of Phi Beta Kappa) to assure the French that Norfolk was using all the money it had "to releive the Nescessities of Sufferers." The *Chronicle*, carrying vivid accounts of ruin at Cap François, urged Americans to "view with compassion the accumulated distress of those . . . nurtured in the lap of ease, affluence & plenty, now reduced almost to . . . penury, and observe what their conscience will dictate." A notice pleaded for "all the Rags" readers could send to Mr. Lynam on Loyall's Wharf or M. Grandiden in Church Street for the wounded and sick.[5]

Even at the height of the crisis there were moments of joy—reunions of family members who thought each other dead—and of mirth. A Frenchman later related being assigned a bed at "a respectable inn" by its landlady.

Staying out late his first night to visit "those of my friends who had escaped the carnage," he went quietly to his room, undressed, and fell wearily into a designated bed. A piercing scream catapulted him to his feet, and he found himself in the midst of "twenty candles," the bearers of which all thought "that the house was afire." Clad in his smallclothes, the Frenchman stammered to two furious women, his unintended bedmates, that his aim was not "robbery or rape." His and the landlady's apologies finally accepted, "the ladies kept their bed; and I . . . gravely gathered up my scattered clothing and went to sleep on one of the kitchen tables."[6]

Emergency funds, including a small sum voted by Congress, were almost gone when managers of Norfolk's theater held a benefit concert of vocal and instrumental music, with "some of the most approved French airs." The performers included several refugees. The Marine Hospital was packed with some eight hundred patients. The slaughter of a single head of cattle that had heretofore supplied Norfolk's daily beef was raised to two or three. In accord with state law, the legislature voted to return to the West Indies the slaves some of the French had managed to bring out, but a petition from slaveowners got the law rescinded.[7]

In the meantime the presence of so many Frenchmen was having a pleasantly pronounced impact on Norfolk's character. McKinney and Pusey's brewery advertised as the "Brasserie de Norfolk" offering "Bierre Forte," "Bonne Bierre de Table," and "de la Petite Bierre." M. Delavoix in October opened a French school and Louis Roussel not long afterward a dancing school. A "throng of young girls" turned out to hear Moreau de St. Mery's niece perform on the harp, evidently a novel instrument in Norfolk. The New Theatre offered authentically Gallic entertainments, including a French troupe performing "a scene, lyric, of the celebrated Jean James [Jean Jacques] Rousseau," with Mme. Val on the hornpipe. Something in the way of a French Quarter emerged along the west side of Market Square.[8]

As the weeks passed in the summer and fall of 1793, the refugee colony at Norfolk thinned out but problems associated with their presence remained. There was praise for the "prudent, polite and decent conduct of every class" of fugitives, but their enemies circulated rumors that a French cruiser had pursued a British brig to sea from Hampton Roads.[9] Issues of politics and ideology began to complicate the relationship between some of the Americans and their guests. Norfolk had been a town of decidedly pro–French sentiments since the arrival of Count DeGrasse's fleet in Chesapeake Bay in the summer of 1781 and, more especially, since the outbreak of the French Revolution in 1789.

In January, six months before the refugee fleet's arrival, Norfolk greeted the victory of France's revolutionary army at Valmy with a clamoring celebration. Light infantry volunteers paraded to Town Point, fired a salute, and were answered from the old fort there by fifteen cannons. Celebrants at the Borough Tavern passed the evening "in harmony and hilarity," toasting "The Republic of France," "the Rights of Man," and so on. In June Norfolk citizens formed a "Republican Society" to foster awareness that the threat was not confined to France but menaced all who cherished republican "sentiments, manners, morals, and affections."[10]

If many saw the advent of the refugees mainly as a chance to pay off old debts and strengthen bonds with France's republicans, they were soon disabused of their error. The Santo Domingans were mostly implacable royalists bitterly hostile to Robespierre and his radicalism, especially since Louis XVI's execution in January. They blamed the Revolution's National Convention for igniting the West Indian slave revolt. France might be at war with England, but most refugees harbored hope for a British victory that would restore the French monarchy.[11]

For the time being, pity and need prevailed over ideology, but many people despised French (or any other) republicanism. For one thing, the schemes of French agent "Citizen Genet" to undercut the neutrality of Washington's government were at full tide. Resentment over this and shock at the king's death were widespread. Both the refugees and English residents were harassed by "menacing gestures by Frenchmen in red caps" and "nocturnal parades of armed Frenchmen." A late July report that sailors on the French warship *Jupiter* had "taken off the head of the Admiral" brought a curious crowd to the waterfront, "expecting to see the decapitated trunk of the Admiral hanging to one of the yardarms."[12]

Even so, the town's pro-Revolution sentiments remained marked as the French minister and naval commandant conveyed earnest thanks for kindnesses rendered to the refugees. There was an outpouring of solicitude in late October after the tragic loss of *l'Amiable société*. This French brig, one of the last from Cape François, entered Lynnhaven Bay on October 27. The next day a storm dragged it from its anchorage. The brig was driven aground off Princess Anne and "went to pieces," losing all hands, "though not 60 fathoms from shore." Victims included the crew and some eighty refugees. A Norfolk paper reported that those sent to take up bodies washed ashore found mostly heads, arms, and legs, "mangled and torn by the surf"; they buried about fifty corpses.[13]

It was perhaps the presence of cultivated newcomers that led to Norfolk's belated concern for its health and physical appearance. A sarcastic "Peter Police" in 1794 proposed in the *Chronicle* that "a few more loads of filth . . . be distributed, in the [town's] most frequented parts," that fish "(if sufficiently stale) will be preferred." He hoped inhabitants would "fling every thing of this nature in front of their houses," especially in August. A more somber critic urged that kitchen slops be taken to the river rather than tossed into streets and alleys, that "stagnant ditches and marshes" be filled in. Many Norfolk creeks held water only at high tide and were otherwise "receptacles of the filth of all privies, and the nurseries of muskitoes," as well as obstacles to traffic.[14]

In the rebuilding years after 1776, Norfolk had earned a reputation of altogether legendary proportions for ugliness and nastiness. A visitor saw "Void and Waste" in the fall of 1776, and another three years later wrote that Norfolk "shocks me exceedingly when ever I see it." Even when a transient in 1784 saw "nothing but ruins," people housed in "sheds and outhouses," or one the next year saw only "a vast heap of ruins and Devastation," no one blamed anything but the awful fire of 1776.[15]

But the war was a distant memory in 1796 when a traveler saw Norfolk as "ill-built and unhealthy," its streets "irregular, unpaved, dusty or dirty according to the weather, crooked [and] too narrow," with "an innumerable retinue of . . . filthy alleys." Ruins of houses were still almost as numerous as newly built ones, all "intermingled in every street." (Norfolk's reputation as a "Chimney Town" owed something to the durability of shell-lime mortar, widely used in the colonial era.)[16]

Another wayfarer about the same time noted more charitably that the streets were narrow and irregular toward the harbor, wider in the upper portions. New streets since the fire included Wide water (1782), Commerce (1792), and Bank (1796). But none were paved, "and all are filthy; indeed, in the hot months of summer, the stench . . . from some of them is horrid." One in six residents died of smallpox in 1795, but inhabitants remained quite "inattentive to cleanliness."[17]

The refugees were gallantly silent as to their impressions of Norfolk, but a pair of travel books by emigré French writers soon offered unvarnished assessments. The duke de la Rochefoucault Liancourt, who was in Norfolk for a while in 1796, called it "one of the ugliest, most irregular, and most filthy towns that can any-where be found." Its houses were "low and unsightly," almost all built "without any attention to make them regularly line with each other." Swamps on all sides gave off a "nastiness and stench which

. . . are excessive." A year earlier, Moreau de St. Mery had written that the streets were laid out "helter-skelter," the sewage ditches open, and "one crosses them on little narrow bridges made of short lengths of plank nailed on crosspieces."[18]

It was late to blame the war or fire for such conditions. More culpable was the Common Council, still guided by laissez-faire administrative precepts. The council groped haltingly toward a democratic idea of government, but remained transfixed by matters relating to the town watch and regulation of the market. Popular election of common councilmen, mandated by the state, after 1787 gave this body an infusion of a few artisans but did not much alter its conservative bias. Men of more modest wealth and fewer blood-ties than in the colonial era managed city affairs but, typical of communities of the era, did not at first prove more imaginative in conducting municipal business.[19] Streets remained stinking refuse pits until the emergent "fourth estate" began in 1794 to evince stirrings of civic conscience.

In September 1788 the Common Council adopted a regulation "preventing the throwing of Filth & Garbage in the Streets and Lanes"—and then dropped the subject for nearly six years. It did not arise again until May 1794, when amendments were proposed to strengthen the old law, and a new ordinance did not result until September. The regulation, covering "dead Animals . . . stinking fish, dirty Waters, or any other kind of filth," was backed by fearful punishments and enforceable by overseers of streets. Only time would show whether old habits could be changed by some lines in the city code, but the council had learned a lesson in democratic governance: the full text of the law was ordered to be published in the *Chronicle.*[20]

In intervals of civic initiative, the council fostered postwar revival by rebuilding the city market, its "irregular position," a visitor wrote, "in harmoney with its filth and deformity." The council had also acquired fire engines, opened new wells, built a town hall and prison, and erected several bridges. But nearly all else was left to private enterprise, and property owners did little to improve Norfolk's noxious unsightliness. Merchants and carpenters, indeed, often piled goods and materials in the streets, forcing traffic to find its way around as best it could.[21]

For a while after the war, one might argue that Norfolk could not afford enough inspectors and overseers to guarantee minimum standards of cleanliness and order. Its mercantile wealth had been largely shattered by the war and the new Norfolk was conspicuously a town of carpenters, plasterers, joiners, shipbuilders, and common laborers. Merchants and shippers used what funds they had for wharves, warehouses, ships, and stores, with little left for life's amenities. Tax revenue was scanty.

Norfolk's trade, however, rebounded smartly with the peace of 1783 and was flourishing as early as 1784. The English government offered a gratuitous slap by closing its West Indian islands to all but a short list of American imports and these in British ships, but the deficit was made up in other ways. St. Eustatius and other non–British islands remained open to Chesapeake trade, and British island governors found ways to permit smuggling. Coastwise trade and American commerce with Europe soon surpassed pre-war levels. Merchants complained that the Articles of Confederation left the government too weak to negotiate satisfactory terms with foreign powers, but trade figures belied the argument.[22]

Amid elaborate festivities at Norfolk and elsewhere, Virginia adopted the new federal Constitution in 1788, but English regulations of the previous year banned American trade with the British West Indies. This helped induce an economic slump as the new Constitution went into effect. It required the outbreak of war in Europe in 1792 to stimulate another revival. With the coming of war, the Caribbean became a great emporium for American trade, and Norfolk cashed in as never before. "Six years ago," wrote La Rochefoucault in 1796, "there were not ten large vessels belonging to Norfolk; to-day there are fifty, to say nothing of fifty more smaller ones, engaged chiefly in the West Indian trade."[23]

The Norfolk known to French refugees and expatriates was, for all its jarring squalor, a place of vibrant life. The Free School, in operation since 1786 at the old school site opposite the Episcopal church, provided an academic regimen for boys only, though grammatical and other training deemed suitable for girls was available from private sources. An Englishman named Hunter had a book store and book-rental service, and in 1802 a Bostonian named Mirick opened a subscription library of "several thousand volumes in every branch of useful and polite literature." The same gentleman soon advertised the opening of a "new and singular academy," the precise character of which is unknown.[24]

But Norfolk aspired now beyond mere literacy and even appeared to celebrate somewhat prematurely its artistic arrival. (A Norfolk surgeon had, after a fashion, broken into literary ranks in 1788 with "A Treatise on Gonorrhoea.") An advertisement in the *Norfolk and Portsmouth Chronicle* in July 1790 solicited for the Norfolk Theatre "well studied comedians to join a Company just arrived from London" and "several Instrumental

Performers to complete a Band." The "Old Theatre" opened in a Calvert's Lane warehouse in 1793, but was replaced two years later with the brick "New Theatre" at Main and Fenchurch. The latter was Norfolk's pride and joy. The Old Theatre was perhaps the one advertised in 1786 by Messrs. Heard and Villiers as large and elegant; a tragedy, *The Fair Penitent*, was performed there that December. A theater had also stood before the Revolution just south of Main Street's junction with the old road leading out of town.[25]

Norfolk revealed its attitude toward the New Theatre when, on July 4, 1792, Freemasons of three lodges conducted the laying of its cornerstone. Lodge masters led more than sixty brethren, accompanied by the volunteer company, to the theater ground and, afterward, to the Battery for a salute of fifteen cannons and three rounds of small arms. In the afternoon, actor-proprietors Thomas Wade West and John Bignall, recent arrivals from the English stage, feted the Masons with a "cold collation."[26]

In West and Bignall and their wives, Norfolk by 1790 had a distinguished and versatile group of performers. They were inaugurating similar ventures in Richmond, Charleston, and elsewhere to create a circuit that would keep them occupied virtually year-round. Bignall scored a rousing Norfolk success in June in a tragedy called *The Dramatist*. The performer, trumpeted the *Chronicle*, received a "flattering burst of applause which was enhanced by his performance of Vapid . . . , in such a masterly style, that we imagine that Dramatic excellence at its zenith, can be but little above him."[27]

When a Mr. Edgar appeared in the comic-opera *No Song, No Supper*, his American debut, it was soon after his run at "the Theatre Royal in Covent Garden." Stage scenery for this and other productions was by M. Anthony Audin, "Painter at the Opera House, Cadiz upwards of seven years." A Mr. Brooks executed portrait miniatures at Mrs. Byrne's boarding house at the head of Maxwell's Wharf. Awash in both the performing and bozarts, Norfolk appeared to imagine itself at the crossroads of Occidental high culture. The theater suffered a setback when Bignall died in 1794, and other problems eventually sapped the strength and popularity of the Norfolk stage. But residents of 1802 could still applaud performances at Vauxhall Gardens, besides *Blue Beard, Pizarro*, and other offerings of the New Theatre.[28]

Those of less exquisite taste thronged to twice-yearly races across the eastern branch at Washington Point, with four-mile heats the first day, three-mile heats the second. There was also racing at the Thorowgood farm on Pollard's Point west of Newton's Creek. Off-season, money was made to disappear as readily at any of a dozen billiard rooms or several faro dens.

(Nicholas Booze was issued a tavern license in 1792.) Phineas Parker's balloon offered pastoral landscapes and grand vistas of the town from a basket carrying up to eight people. The "restoration of health" he advertised came presumably from spending some moments beyond the reeking vapors of Norfolk street-life. A lot behind the Old Theatre was used in 1794 for an equestrian show; young Ricketts hung from a saddle at full gallop by a foot, with hands sweeping the ground, while his father danced on horseback to a hornpipe.[29]

A popular gathering place was Lindsey's Gardens, opened in 1800 by Thomas Crossley. Here congregated the Irish on St. Patrick's Day and, in the spring, "great numbers of people of all ages, ranks and colours, sporting away the day—some playing ball, some riding wooden horses (a sort of fandango) others drinking, smoking &c." Others consorted at the Exchange Coffee House or Borough Tavern, Vauxhall Gardens on Dameron's (Yaxley's) Lane, or, on Sundays, "took the air" in coaches, "some playing at ball, at nine pins, marbles, and every kind of game." An enterprising tavern keeper in 1793 lured clients with a live Goree lion.[30]

When not soaring in the physical or cultural empyrean, the Norfolkian escorted his French guests to a variety of social and fraternal clubs. The Mechanical Club catered to skilled artisans as the Freemasons (Lodge No. 1 and Lodge No. 56 of Naphtali, with a combined total in 1800 of 329 members) looked to commerce and the professions. Republicans had a Democratic Society and Federalists a Society of Constitutional and Governmental Support. The Debating Society allocated a Saturday night in 1794 to "Whether a man is more happy in a married or a single state," and, still more ominously, the next Monday to "Whether it is better for Europe in general for France to remain as a Republic, or be annihilated."[31]

Norfolk found any number of excuses for communal celebration, especially on patriotic occasions such as July 4 and Washington's Birthday. The first of May was welcomed by a tuft of deer's tail in the hat and green branches suspended from yardarms of ships, besides "may poles & pine & other trees set up at many doors, decorated with ribbons, bottles of wine, & c." This was also the day for the annual militia review, featuring a ragamuffin assortment of arms and uniforms and an open-air barbecue of "animals roasted whole on crisscrossed pieces of wood over a great fire."[32]

From its single colonial chapel, Norfolk's religious life at the turn of the century revolved around six congregations. The Episcopalians had acrimoniously split, one group using the shell of St. Paul's (the old Borough Church), though "uncieled, unplaistered and unpewed," its "miserable fourlegged turret . . . tumbling down," the second erecting Christ Church in 1800. By 1801 there were also a Methodist congregation (formed in 1793 but housed in 1802 in a new building) on Cumberland Street with slave and free black as well as white members, a Baptist church, and a Roman Catholic body formed in 1791 by French emigrés. Catholic services were led by an Irish priest in a chapel built in 1794 at Holt and what was later known as Chapel streets. In 1802 the Presbyterians also had a new church, with Rev. Conrad Speece as pastor.[33]

From some downtown areas one could not see the waterfront, so crowded together were the warehouses, most of them on pilings and up to three stories high. Log wharves (there were twenty-three between Main Street's east and west ends in 1802) stretched in "every direction of obliquity," rarely surviving the worms for as much as eight years. Six boats of a private company took six to eight passengers a trip (up to fifteen when boatmen could get away with it) between Norfolk and Portsmouth, with three scows for horses and wheeled vehicles. Private homes were almost all of wood, the better having a central hall, open at each end, where inhabitants lived in warm months. Rich merchants, like ropewalk entrepreneur William Plume or partners Moses Myers and William Pennock, had fine townhouses in East Main or the upper parts of town, but most houses lacked either plate glass or carpeting.[34]

Norfolk's diet required a piece of salt pork, be it ham, bacon, or otherwise—"as necessary at the head of the table," observed a visitor, "as the Lady of the house." It also demanded a concoction of corn, whether hominy, hoecake (dough baked or toasted on a hoe over a fire), or Johnny cake (dough baked on a board). The Eagle Tavern kept a popular table, where breakfast comprised "beefsteaks, sausages, stewed veal, fried ham, eggs, coffee and tea"—and hoecake. The French commented favorably on the fish, oysters, geese, strawberries and cherries, asparagus, peas, and sweet potatoes. Cider, peach brandy, Madeira wine, and West Indian rum were among the most approved libations. (The French avoided drinking Norfolk's water.)[35]

Shipbuilding, especially after the start of the European war, was the major industry of the area, with as many as eighty or ninety great and small craft a year built on the Elizabeth River and its tributaries. Plume's ropewalk (north of what became Wood Street) furnished much of Norfolk's cordage, procuring its hemp not only from Virginia sources but from Russia, where a stronger, more easily wrought type was grown. A smaller ropewalk, Newton's, stood about where High Street was later located, between branches of Smith's Creek. Plume also had a tannery that made leather for export.

Confidence was high that a canal joining the Elizabeth and Pasquotank rivers would soon give immense stimulus to the town's burgeoning trade. Sponsored by a joint-stock company formed in 1787, some eleven miles were excavated by the mid-1790s and work was expected to be finished before the decade's end.[36]

The canal work was done by crews of slaves, many from Norfolk and its vicinity, under harsh conditions that cost many lives. Norfolk's black population by 1795 stood at about 1,500 slaves and two hundred free persons. The latter were often little better off materially, but careful exploitation of slender opportunities could occasionally yield considerable benefits. Francis Drake, freed by his master in 1791, became proprietor of a Water Street barbershop. He and Lemuel Bailey, a free black shoemaker in Commerce Street, managed to buy the freedom of several slaves.[37]

Blacks performed much of Norfolk's chimney sweeping, using bundles of brush pulled up and down inside chimneys to remove soot. Both Moreau de St. Mery and La Rouchefoucault were much impressed with an Elizabeth River ferryman named Semes (or Sem), who had taught himself reading and writing, conversed with "solid good sense," and seemed earnest in his "desire for instruction." Black men appeared in public on Sundays in boots and knickerbockers and women in their prettiest dresses, some for Methodist or Baptist services, more for evening dances.[38]

Slaves as well as free blacks turned out on Christmas and five subsequent "negro's holidays" to fill the streets, "drest in their best, playing, dancing, shaking hands &c (some crying shoe black, shoe black while brushing boots.)" This was a sort of "Mardi Gras" before the January 1 "hiring day" when slaves were "sold like the herds in the stalls."[39]

The French were not to be spared one of Norfolk's periodic epidemics of smallpox, when a sailor from the schooner *Antelope* brought the disease ashore in 1795. Some five hundred deaths that summer and fall were attributed to the outbreak, the principal victims being "unseasoned" mechanics lately arrived from England. One result was an extreme labor shortage, "especially for joiners and carpenters." Newspapers were inclined to blame these outbreaks on the victims for living "on made land, the houses occupied by people of discordant habits and different countries, for the most part much crowded, and [with] little regard for personal or household cleanliness."[40]

A big downtown fire in 1799 swept away most of the flimsy structures south of Main Street from Market Square to Town Point, and yellow fever epidemics in the autumns of 1800 and 1801 carried off some four hundred people, "nearly all said to be strangers." A "Potter's Field" burial ground for strangers and the impoverished was opened half a mile north of town in 1802. A workhouse for the poor sat near where Queen Street was later intersected by Granby.[41]

Norfolk's enthusiasm for revolutionary France weathered the coming of the Santo Domingans, some of them as antiroyalist as any American, and for a time even increased. Early 1794 witnessed a veritable binational love feast, with the two groups trying to outdo one another in displays of mutual regard. The arrival of the French frigate *Normandie* in January was the occasion of cannon salutes and a dinner by the Americans for their French guests at the Eagle Tavern. The French reciprocated at the Borough Tavern, and a Portsmouth delegation was boomed noisily across to the county wharf by all the French ships in the river. French guests joined Americans to celebrate Washington's Birthday in February with toasts and songs in both languages.[42]

Republicans held a meeting to drum up concern over British ships using local facilities and allegedly encroaching on the terms of American neutrality. The British minister to the United States was moved to reply with complaints of the Norfolk people refusing water for English ships and encouraging their sailors to desert. The *Chronicle* responded testily that private citizens sold no water to foreign ships because of the scarcity of that commodity in Norfolk and that the public well was as open to the British as to any other nationality. In March, Norfolk and Portsmouth residents met under the chairmanship of Thomas Mathews to draft a petition to Congress complaining of the activity of British privateers. John and Wills Cowper, Willis Wilson, George Kelly, Moses Myers, Thomas Newton Jr., and Baylor Hill were among its signers.[43]

Moreau de St. Mery was glad that "large numbers" in Norfolk wore tricolored flags, and he passed along other illustrations of prevailing sentiment. In May 1794, for example, someone fired three shots at the anchored British frigate *Daedalus,* one of them embedding itself in a plank at the waterline. It may have been at this time that the bursting of a cannon killed a well-known Norfolkian named Morfit. When a Scotsman named Logan expressed pleasure that it left Norfolk with one less republican, some sailors poured warm tar over him and took him on a dray to Marsden's Lane, off Market Square, where bed feathers were dumped on him from an upstairs window. He was then taken to Town Point and "bound to the blade of a large oar," ducked repeatedly into the river, and set adrift in a small boat without oars.[44]

In April an American who spoke disrespectfully of the French was made to "ride an entire day through the streets in a cart." When some Santo Domingans were about to leave in convoy for France, it was rumored that Norfolk pilot boats were to be sent to Nova Scotia to warn the British: "That very evening, every pilot boat in Norfolk had its rigging destroyed." In fact, nowhere in America did the French receive "so many signs of affection as in Norfolk, nor such a cordial reception."[45] No doubt the strains of *La Marseillaise* often broke the downtown's midnight quiet and floated lingeringly off toward the nether shore.

Republicans had so far ignored the vicious turn by the French Revolution and the fact that French privateers were as guilty as the British of seizing American ships bound for ports of the other. By 1796 the strain showed. French opinion bridled at the Jay Treaty for concessions to the British. French interference with American trade reached the dimensions of a "quasi-war" and was exacerbated by the "X. Y. Z. Affair" of 1798, when French agents tried to extort bribes from American diplomats before talks even began. The Adams administration passed the Alien and Sedition Acts allowing the president to expel aliens he thought dangerous and criminalizing various kinds of antigovernment criticism. The exodus of French refugees from America gained momentum, and the United States plunged into a McCarthyite era of neighbor-bashing.[46]

The ferocity of antirepublican attitudes is seen in remarks by Cornelius Calvert to visiting architect Benjamin Latrobe. Cornelius, brother of the late Maximilian Calvert, unblushingly told Latrobe that he could not "bear to hear of the *will of the people*. In the first place the people have no will. In the second if they had a will, it cannot be collected, and in the third, if it could be collected it ought never to regulate the measures of government." He approved "those two excellent bills the Alien and Sedition [Acts], the first to drive unruly foreigners away, and the other to keep in order the unruly mob."[47]

It was even suspected in some Federalist circles that a quasi-Masonic Portsmouth organization, the "Lodge of Wisdom," was an outpost of the Society of the Illuminati, a European secret order opposed to all religious dogma and revelation. When Boston clergyman-geographer Jedidiah Morse learned in 1799 that the Portsmouth group included numerous Frenchmen and other native Europeans, he delivered and printed a paranoid sermon claiming that "the professed design" of such chapters was "to subvert and overthrow our holy religion and our free . . . government."[48] (Morse's son,

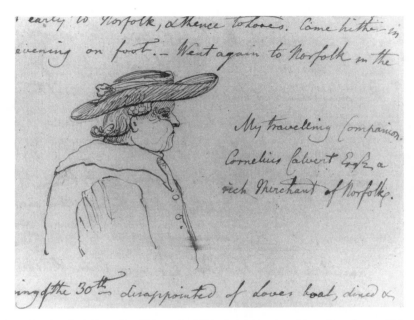

early to Norfolk, & thence to loores. Came hither in evening on foot. — Went again to Norfolk in the

My travelling Companion. Cornelius Calvert Esq. a rich Merchant of Norfolk.

ing of the 30th disappointed of Loves boat, dined &

Latrobe sketched Cornelius Calvert in 1796. A merchant and member of one of Norfolk's leading families, Calvert impressed the artist with the vehemence of his antirepublican political sentiments. (Courtesy of Maryland Historical Society, Baltimore)

telegraph inventor Samuel F. B. Morse, later proved to be as virulently anti-immigrant as his father.)

The presiding officer at Portsmouth was Peter Valentin Davezac, a Santo Domingan, with Norfolk's Jean Antoine Gieu as secretary. But members included Princess Anne's William Ward, a tailor, John Smith of Norfolk, and others of non-French extraction. The "Lodge of Truth," founded in Norfolk in 1801 with a mostly French membership, was evidently of the same order, though cited in the newspapers as simply another Masonic lodge.[49] The designs of both groups appear to have been essentially social and recreational.

So far, then, were American political sympathies swayed that the French, so warmly embraced in 1793, often found themselves shunned at the decade's end even in normally francophile Norfolk. Jefferson's presidential victory in 1800 insured the continuing strength of republicanism, but it did not sway public opinion back toward the French. More often now, newspapers carried such items as the one in April 1798 about "a tall, lank, ill-looking fellow" who spent a Saturday night strutting up and down the Norfolk wharves. He was said to have declared repeatedly that he would soon have command of a French privateer, "with which he would set the Borough of Norfolk in a blaze!!!"[50]

The effective end of *l'Affaire francaise* for Norfolk came perhaps with the *Magicienne* incident. A french frigate of that name had spent several months in 1801 blockaded in Norfolk harbor by an English warship. On a Sunday night, sailors from the French vessel were downtown when they encountered a group of English and Irish seamen. Threatened by their counterparts, the Frenchmen drew swords but threw them down and fled when some American sailors sided with the English. The pursuers battled their prey up Main to Water Street, where the fray could be witnessed from the French frigate, anchored in midriver. When armed French boats started for shore, anxious citizens, many of whom had collected on the wharves to enjoy a donnybrook, realized that a disastrous fight might erupt. A quick end was made to the skirmish.[51]

Fortunately, officers in the approaching French boats recognized on the wharf Jewish merchant Moses Myers, an agent for the French in outfitting their ships. The officers were told that there had been a tiff among the seamen, now concluded, and that there would be no need for the armed men to land. This explanation was accepted by the French who, waiting until their terrorized sailors were rounded up, returned peaceably to their ship.

English merchant Charles W. Janson, a witness to the episode, blamed it on the propensity of the common class of Frenchmen to be "ferociously insulting" to others "since the adoption of liberty and equality." It was his understanding that French sailors had on occasion "conducted themselves with insult towards some of their own body, as well as to the inhabitants." He heard a rumor that a Frenchman was killed in the affray, but this fact was not publicly acknowledged.[52] Janson's, of course, was a biased account, but it was clear that the French had worn out their welcome; Norfolk's romance with its revolutionary allies was over.

Postwar Norfolk, by all accounts an aesthetic and hygienic disaster, was in important respects a better place than its predecessor. Its inhabitants, perhaps reassured by modest gains in self-government, no longer looked to riot as a solution to communal problems. Gone were the hatreds that threatened to tear the old town apart. On the other hand, Norfolk had not yet imbibed the notion that such matters as the health and appearance of the town were the legitimate concern of a corporate body any more than they

Latrobe's March 1796 sketch shows that Norfolk's maritime commerce had recovered from the Revolutionary War and that the city was prospering once more. (Courtesy of Maryland Historical Society, Baltimore)

were the responsibility of individual citizens. (Such was the case, in fact, throughout urban America.) These matters were still resigned to the mysterious workings of fate.

So English Baron Thomas Fairfax, visiting Norfolk in August 1799, found accommodations at Lindsey's Hotel "at the corner of two narrow alleys, in a very dirty part of Town and contiguous to several sink holes full of stagnant water." It was near the river and "much infested" by mosquitoes. "A very offensive smell is emitted . . . when the tide is out, especially at the ferry wharf . . . the rendezvous of provision boats bringing meats, fruits and vegetables to market." Here were consumed hundreds of melons "every day at this season, and the rinds cast into the dock." Uptown Norfolk, however, where the bay breezes could circulate, was cool and pleasant.[53]

The role of the French in shaping the character of the new Norfolk must remain imponderable, though some of the emigrés and refugees became citizens and stayed on. The black Catholic congregation formed in 1860 in the former St. Patrick's Catholic Church on Holt Street may have had its roots among the refugees of 1793. A Norfolk woman's diary in 1801 and 1802 speaks often of French visitors in her home, a fire in the Church Street house of another, a French baker, "Sophia, a French negro girl," "Mr Forde a Frenchman," and others. Many "opened little shops of different kinds," but no E. I. DuPont lingered to found an industrial empire on the Elizabeth River; no Fevret de Saint-Memin engraved a brilliant panoply of portraits of Norfolk's leading citizens.[54]

"Forty years ago," wrote a Norfolk editor in 1866, when only "two or three" of the emigrés were left alive, "the French language was heard spoken all about the streets of Norfolk. There were many families who had escaped the massacre of Santo Domingo and settled in Norfolk and they were among the very best of our citizens."[55]

The French presence almost certainly contributed to the first stirrings of community conscience in the new Norfolk, to a livelier sense of Enlightenment thought, perhaps to an enhanced aestheticism and sensitivity to manners. And, maybe most of all, the French sojourn provided Norfolk with an opportunity to delve into the wellsprings of its humanity. The community's readiness to come to the aid of *les miserables* was to remain a marked characteristic of the borough into the distant future.

If, however, the issue of the Norfolk's white refugees had been resolved by 1801, that of its black refugees was about to explode.

CHAPTER 9

O Jeremiah

Run to and fro through the streets of Jerusalem . . .
Search her squares to see if you can find a man,
One who does justice and seeks truth
that I may pardon her.

JEREMIAH 5:1

IT BEGAN with an encounter on a Princess Anne road about five miles from Norfolk. On Thursday, April 15, 1802, Norfolk merchant Caleb Boush and a Mr. Jarvis were riding on the road when they met a slave named Will, the property of John Floyd. Jarvis, finding that Will had no pass giving him permission to be abroad, accused him of running away. The white men took Will to a nearby house, where he was interrogated, especially in regard to recent rumors of an insurrection plot. Jarvis accused Will of being one of "sixty or seventy such sons of bitches as him" said to have met lately in secret at a field on Town Point. The accuser had elicited only denials when Boush left after about twenty minutes.[1]

Jarvis bound Will and took him to Floyd, proposing that Will receive "a severe correction." He added that Will might provide information "that will be of service to us," in which case he might be forgiven for running off. Will, tied to a tree, at length confessed that he knew of a plot among the slaves. He said that about noon the previous Sunday (April 11) he had met William Walke's Ned and the late John Cornick's Jeremiah near Town Bridge. The pair invited him to join a plot to burn Norfolk on Easter Monday night, April 19. Aware of rumors of a slave uprising, Will assumed that this was part of the same plan, replied that he "would have nothing to do with it," and left immediately.[2]

Jarvis had Will committed next morning to the Kempsville jail and took his information to Norfolk Mayor John Cowper. Cowper sent Alderman

John K. Read to examine Will; Reed returned within hours to confirm Jarvis's intelligence. Ned and Jeremiah were jailed at Norfolk. Several others, including one white man, were picked up on various suspicions on April 16 and five or six more blacks on April 20, but all were soon released for want of evidence. The town guard was increased "to defend . . . against the blacks."[3]

Jeremiah and Ned were tried on April 26 in a tense borough courtroom packed with some three hundred spectators. Mayor Cowper, Recorder Thomas Newton, Aldermen Read, Samuel Moseley, and William Vaughan comprised the court. Based on Will's testimony, Ned and Jeremiah were convicted and sentenced to hang on May 14. The mayor wrote Governor James Monroe that the evidence of guilt "was such as to remove all doubt"; Norfolk now had "nothing to apprehend."[4]

Disappointingly, the trial produced no evidence of the alleged plot's scope, manpower, leadership, or other details. A quick hanging of the two blacks, however, was deemed likely to discourage other plotters and insure Norfolk's safety. In the meantime, all available white men were called out for militia duty, and guards were posted around town night and day.[5]

Norfolk merchant George McIntosh, a Scotsman in whose kitchen near the Market House Jeremiah lived, was uneasy. McIntosh had married into the prominent Cornick and Walke families, and had hired Jeremiah from John Cornick's estate. Will's wife was a slave of Mrs. McIntosh, who insisted that Will was untrustworthy. On April 27, the day after Ned and Jeremiah's trial, the pregnant wife of the latter asked Mrs. McIntosh for a pen and some paper for Jeremiah. Supposing that he wished to make a confession, McIntosh, with Alderman Read, went to the jail to hear it.[6]

What Jeremiah confessed, and now wrote, was his "innocence in the charge . . . , and this he pens down as his last dying words. . . . Such words as I stand charged with was never by me spoken as I expect to appear at the Great tribunal of Heaven and false witness has been born against me." (There were other Virginia cases of the sort in 1802 where such literary fluency was held to be evidence of the defendant's capacity for insurrection.)[7]

Did Jeremiah have an alibi? Yes, he left his quarters at McIntosh's early on the morning in question to buy fish. Returning soon with the fish, he went back to bed, rose for breakfast, returned to bed owing to indisposition, and arose for a midday meal, taken with McIntosh's cook, Edney. In early afternoon he spoke with a Mr. Chambers on the lot, went to preaching with slaves of Messrs. Lamb and Vanholt, sat during the service on a tombstone, attended a baptism, and came home about sunset.[8]

On May 3 McIntosh interviewed Will at the jail. When had he last seen Jeremiah before being solicited by him to join the plot? At Tucker's kitchen with Kitty, Peggy, George, Bob, and Agey. Next day Alderman Moseley, with James Bennett and Mr. Tucker, visited Tucker's kitchen. Kitty, Peggy, and George (the others being absent) were examined separately, each alleging that Jeremiah and Will were never known to be there at the same time.[9]

By now, George McIntosh was convinced that Will was a liar by whose unsupported testimony no one should be convicted of a crime. He took Alderman Moseley home for separate examinations of his own slave Sam and cook Edney. Both affirmed Jeremiah's testimony as to his whereabouts in the midday hours of the Sunday in question.

Later, McIntosh quizzed the wife of Ned, Jeremiah's convicted co-conspirator. He was told that she and Ned spent most of that Sunday at George Sugg's house, cooked the midday meal, and stayed until at least 3:00 P.M. (Sugg testified at the trial that he was absent that day from home for several hours, long enough for Ned to have gone to Town Bridge.) It seemed to McIntosh that neither of the convicted blacks could have had the meeting at Town Bridge described by Will.[10]

In the midst of his investigation, McIntosh received a note from the re-signed Jeremiah attesting to the slave's remarkable eloquence, perhaps a reason for McIntosh's single-minded crusade: "As I expect shortly", he wrote,

> to enter into an endless Eternity, I have only to imploy my time . . . endeavouring to make peace with my God whom I call this day to witness my innocence in the Charge against me. Perhaps I may never see you more therefore Gratitude bids me to return to you and your Lady my most sincere thanks for the many favours received at your hands - pray Sir take care of my wife [Mary] and the dear little Ones while they remain with you - I hope you and yours may be happy here and hereafter is the sincere wish of the innocent but unfortunate Jeremiah.[11]

On May 5, with the execution of Jeremiah and Ned nine days off, McIntosh sent Governor James Monroe a packet of his findings. (Mrs. McIntosh was the niece of Cornelius Calvert, a member of the Governor's Council.) He enclosed Caleb Boush's deposition charging that Jarvis was "much in liquor" when he interviewed Will, recounting Will's denials while Boush was present, and stating that Jarvis promised "after many threats" to release him "if he would tell him any thing about the conspiracy." It appeared that Will's confession was made after Jarvis and John Floyd discussed what punishment he deserved for running away.[12]

Former Mayor Thomas Newton, a member of the convicting court, on May 7 wrote Monroe that, though he was persuaded at the trial of the defendants' guilt, he now felt Will to be unreliable. Could not the governor alter the sentence to transportation out of the state? Ned was all the more deserving of mercy owing to the fact that he was "almost an idiot."[13]

Monroe promptly sent an express inquiry to Mayor Cowper in regard to the fairness of the slaves' trial. Cowper replied with a ringing endorsement of the verdict. The defendants were represented by "able Council, who made a most ingenious defense," none of the capacity crowd was heard to disagree with the sentence, and even defense attorney Robert B. Taylor acknowledged that the verdict was warranted. Even so, Cowper recommended Ned to executive mercy because the prisoner was "of the simple cast" and no doubt was led into mischief by "artful and wicked" men.[14]

Meanwhile, the Governor's Council had come upon a problem in the Norfolk trial transcript: it bore no evidence of the commission of a felony. The defendants were charged with conspiracy to commit rebellion or insurrection but convicted for a plot to burn Norfolk, an aim not defined in law as felonious. The council wanted time to inquire of William Sharp, Norfolk's borough clerk, if anything were omitted from the transcript. For this purpose, Monroe granted a stay of execution until May 28.[15]

Monroe found himself faced with an officeholder's nightmare. Virginia had been plagued by rumors of slave plots since the traumatic Gabriel Plot near Richmond in 1800 and the ensuing execution of thirty-five slaves. The latest rumors began in Dinwiddie County in late 1801 and soon spread to "nearly every county" in the state. Nottoway and Brunswick counties set a precedent in January by holding quick trials, executing two suspects in each county and whipping others, but some slaveholders worried that this might be the onset of a bloodbath by panicky whites.[16]

Monroe had been receiving calls since January to intervene and restrain the tendency toward drumhead justice and patrol brutality but had so far resisted.[17] He was a man of humane sensitivity and high political aspiration, but Norfolk was in a perfect uproar. His motives in stark conflict, he agonized over the situation but could see no clear direction for himself.

Norfolk, its population over 40 percent black, was as susceptible to rumor as any place in Virginia. It had been awash in tales of black plots since Santo

Domingo's revolt in 1791 and felt itself highly vulnerable to influences from that quarter. An eastern shore report in 1792 told how six hundred blacks were to cross to Norfolk, join rebels there, blow up the powder magazine, and massacre whites. A few Norfolk and Portsmouth blacks were arrested and a cache of "English muskets" reportedly was found concealed, but the incident blew over without serious repercussions. Up to 150 Norfolk and Suffolk-area blacks were said to have been ready to rebel if Gabriel's Plot succeeded, and it was at Norfolk that Gabriel and henchman John Scott were apprehended.[18]

As elsewhere in Virginia, the policy of Norfolk's leaders was to counter rumors and incidents of slave trouble with admonitory examples of condign punishment to discourage others. Thus, when Benjamin Baker and William Snail were executed for robbery in 1788, the *Norfolk and Portsmouth Journal* voiced hope that the fate of the defendants would "prove a warning to the Aethiope colour to keep within doors at untimely hours of the night." The town's environs furnished fugitive slaves numerous hideaways that made the problem seem more troublesome. A gang of runaway slaves was found to have constructed a "room under ground," supported by beams and well provisioned.[19]

A further Norfolk complication was the presence of slaves brought by French owners from Santo Domingo and who might be affected by the rhetoric of the French Revolution. (They might also be moved by more than ideology; an ad in a Norfolk newspaper in 1793 offered a reward for the return of M. Chaigneau's runaway slave Matthew, on whose breast was branded the word "Chaigneau.") Councilman Thomas Newton had complained repeatedly that "we have too many of the blacks from the islands among us."[20]

The *Norfolk Herald* in early 1801 carried a letter from a reader who discerned republican radicalism at the bottom of it all:

> Santo Domingo is a beacon, which might warn Virginia. . . . They had their *Les Amis des Noirs*, . . . their free people of colour, . . . their slaves also. Into the minds of these, poison was daily infused by Jacobins, and party spirit [was] equally active in Paris and Cape Francois. . . . The *Amis des Noirs* here . . . are playing the same . . . game . . . , and, unless we repel their machinations, will exhibit the same scenes of woe and tragedy. I know not a place more exposed to danger than Norfolk; its harbour, its situation, its circumstances of paucity of whites compared to blacks . . . point it out as a chosen spot for servile insurrection.[21]

Mayor Cowper wrote Monroe in March 1802 to complain that both Norfolk and Virginia in 1793 winked at a law banning foreign slaves from being domiciled in Virginia; might not their expulsion yet be achieved? Monroe, sidestepping the presence of many such slaves with jealous and sophisticated owners, replied that existing law allowed magistrates to deport foreign blacks. But with panic sweeping Virginia, Norfolk was almost certain to succumb. On April 12, three days before the apprehension of the voluble Will, Ruth Henshaw, a visitor from New England, wrote in her Norfolk diary of having just "heard of an intended insurrection among the blacks."[22] The self-fulfilling prophecy was realized on April 15.

The great majority of Norfolk whites, convinced that immediate hangings were essential to thwarting a greater plot, was stunned by Monroe's action. Federalists were sure that francophile Republicans were behind it all; Republicans were certain what "English muskets" in slave hands meant; and both wanted quick and decisive executive action. Panic had been building since the first dim rumors from Dinwiddie County. By early March the town had its own tales of "frequent meetings" by local blacks and correspondence with cohorts in North Carolina.[23]

Cowper wrote Monroe that he was "mortified to be compelled to state that the governor's indulgence" was the source of much discontent in Norfolk. He could "never remember to have witnessed as much anxiety"; public safety demanded that an example be made. A May 19 petition bore 227 Norfolk names attesting the fairness of Ned and Jeremiah's trial. Monroe's interference was clearly a political blunder; he must be made to see that the narrow judicial issue was a secondary consideration.[24]

Later generations would find it hard to see how Norfolk could have gotten itself into such a state in the spring of 1802. But for the political conflict swirling across the Republic, panicky reaction might have been avoided. Evidence of mass action by slaves was absurdly shallow, means to accomplish it almost totally absent. It was a fear communicated to Norfolk from elsewhere but supported by nothing tangible in the town itself. Surely the danger of arson was real; such a deed required only a handful, at most, of willful people. Norfolk had, in fact, suffered a disastrous fire in 1799, when over 260 buildings from Commerce Street to Woodside's Lane were razed. Arson could yield a measure of vengeance but would surely harm black residents greatly while achieving no political goal. The capacity of whites to react with genocidal brutality was obvious to both races.[25]

Intelligent people of both races, on the other hand, understood both the heightened black aspiration and white determination to thwart it. An act of

1782 allowed masters voluntarily to free slaves; by 1803 perhaps a hundred had been manumitted. One of these, James Twopence, won his freedom by "uncommon fidelity and extraordinary exertion" in suppressing a mutiny on the brig *Martha Johnston* en route to Norfolk from Jamaica. The town's economic success in the 1790s drew free blacks from neighboring areas, with the result that the black population had grown from sixty-one in 1790 to over 350 by 1800. Free blacks were attracted to Norfolk by the availability of work, fugitive slaves by urban anonymity and opportunity to abscond on outgoing ships.[26]

Many local slaves were allowed to hire themselves out, sometimes earning enough to buy freedom. Slavemasters from Maryland to North Carolina, aware that the town was a magnet for blacks, often advertised in Norfolk papers for their runaways.[27]

Blacks were heavily represented in certain occupations and even monopolized some. Draymen who hauled most of goods and baggage to and from wharves, operators of ferries to Portsmouth and Hampton, and the town's barbers were exclusively black. Proudly aware of the need for their services, draymen were acquiring a reputation for insolence in dealing with whites. A prudent barber, such as Francis Drake or Thomas Knight, could amass respectable property. Knight was said to be Norfolk's wealthiest black, owner of six lots including his Main Street home; carpenter Benjamin Payne in 1799 owned seven lots. An inventory of Drake's estate showed thirteen Windsor chairs, twenty prints, mantlepiece ornaments, dining table, and other signs of wealth.[28]

Both slaves and free blacks were well represented in carpentry, coopering, stonecutting, plastering, painting, and blacksmithing. They were widely employed as pilots, sailors and stevedores, riggers and sailmakers, oystermen and fishermen. Black women, who outnumbered men, were in demand as domestic servants, cooks, seamstresses, cloakmakers, nurses, and laundresses. Anna Tyra was listed in town records in 1801 as a free black midwife. Porters, waiters, and housekeepers at taverns and boarding houses were generally black. Some operated small shoemaking and barber shops, and at least one ran a livery stable. A great many were used at ropewalks, in Dismal Swamp lumber camps, on the aborning Dismal Swamp Canal, and at bay fisheries.[29]

Many blacks lived in the homes of their masters and employers, enjoying a material lifestyle in some respects not far below that of their white families. But a free black community had arisen in cheap tenements along the Water Street docks and up a midtown corridor running north between Catherine

Latrobe's March 4, 1797 sketch portrays young black boys dressing for what they expect to be a pleasant day. Sunday was a welcome day of rest and recreation for most Norfolk blacks. (Courtesy of Maryland Historical Society, Baltimore)

and Church streets to the town limit at Queen Street. Success stories included that of slave-dentist Sam Nixon, who learned the profession from his master, Dr. C. F. Martin, kept Martin's books, and made housecalls for him.[30] Indications are that free blacks had developed a stable and mutually supportive community, steadily enlarging and offering possibilities of a limited upward mobility.

While all churches accommodated blacks in special galleries or on back benches, the Baptists and Methodists welcomed them as members. Portsmouth had a Baptist church attended by many Norfolk blacks and presided over in the 1790s by Norfolk's Joshua Bishop, a licensed minister from Northampton County. Norfolk's first Methodist Episcopal church was organized on Cumberland Street in 1793; by 1800 the Methodist Norfolk and Portsmouth Circuit had 692 black members. The city's first Baptist church, on Bute Street, was formed in July 1800 and became virtually all-black in 1816 when white members built a new church. A split in the Bute Street congregation around 1840 led to the founding of a second black Baptist church on Bank Street.[31]

For slaves, urban life held few of the terrors of plantations. Whippings were perhaps as frequent but probably tempered in town by public opinion.

Town life was vastly more interesting than that of rural areas, its social and recreational opportunities imcomparably superior. It seems certain that urban slaves, on the whole, were less closely supervised, better informed, and more sophisticated than those confined to plantations.

Norfolk blacks of whatever circumstances were, at the opening of the nineteenth century, daily victims of racial prejudice and mistreatment. Riffaud's Gardens, a popular entertainment site, regularly advertised that "No People of Colour or Women of the Town can be admitted."[32] Even so, Norfolk held out prospects that a fortunate few might find quite agreeable and a great many at least tolerable. Some had lately gained freedom, others could hope soon to do so. The free status of some was earned by participation in patriot armies and navies of the Revolutionary War; others had been manumitted generations before.

But the State of Virginia and the slaveholding South had surrendered any pretension they might once have entertained about suppressing slavery. Apart from Quakers, religious groups who had shown antislavery impulses in the eighteenth century were now in retreat from them. The hope that the grand theories of the revolutionary era might somehow benefit blacks soon vanished. Moreover, enveloping fear among the whites since the start of slave rebellion in the West Indies had brought a cascade of additional restrictions for both free blacks and slaves.

After 1792 slaves could not leave their owners' premises without a pass, engage in trade, or practice medicine. (The requirement of passes was an argument against teaching slaves to read or write.) After 1793 free blacks had to register yearly with town clerks and keep on their persons the clerk's certificate. No free blacks could migrate legally into Virginia after 1793. After 1798 it was a crime for whites to entertain slaves without consent of their masters, or for a free black to give a slave his papers. Blacks were required to register proof of free status with a magistrate before boarding a ship.[33]

An act of 1802 forbade blacks from acquiring new licenses as pilots, a business in which Henry Jackson and other Norfolk blacks had acquired stature and long experience. Other restrictions soon enacted included more limits on manumission and a ban on teaching black apprentices to read, write, or cipher. After 1806 all freed blacks were expelled from the state, a measure that virtually repealed manumission.[34]

A matter of acute concern to free blacks was their inability to testify against whites in court. It meant that white fraud against black businessmen, nonpayment of wages or fees, taking goods from black shelves, reneging on promises, and so on were all but impossible to prove. In 1809 thirteen Norfolk free black artisans petitioned the legislature that, though they had nothing to fear from the better class, many "wanton and malignant" whites took advantage of them. A black could be bodily punished on "[t]he oath of the complainant alone"; their own oaths attesting the legitimacy of their business accounts had no legal standing.[35]

Norfolk blacks were also subject to increasing economic pressures that no legal remedy could address. By the early nineteenth century they were being legally barred from piloting, their most lucrative trade. In the following decades, they faced increasing competition from European immigrants in barbering, drayage, and other occupations. They could be denied the right to serve as masters of merchant ships on the grounds that they were not citizens. In addition, neighborhoods where most blacks lived were the likeliest to be affected by fire and epidemics, except yellow fever. After 1793 it had been fashionable among whites to assert that native blacks were made more "impertinent" by association with those from the West Indies.[36]

In 1802 both races could discern that the slim prospects of freedom and well-being for blacks were rapidly eroding. Norfolk blacks had lived through a decade of unremitting legal assault that was taking a toll on the few prospects they had for a decent livelihood and a measure of personal autonomy. Every session of the legislature added new restrictions and greater burdens. As white competition pushed blacks from traditional occupations, it was easy to believe that black hopes were giving way to desperation.

In late April 1802 news reached Philadelphia that Norfolk had foiled a black plot to seize "the Bank, magazine, and another point," that it was being "fired in all parts . . . as a signal for a general massacre!" Norfolk's terror as it awaited word of Jeremiah's fate was seen in the case of the stoppered jug. On May 14 militia Colonel Thomas Newton sent Monroe suspicious papers found used as a stopper in a jug on a Petersburg riverboat just arrived at Norfolk. Norfolk authorities arrested the free black shipmaster and an Irish passenger, owner of the jug. The wording of the papers was judged by some to be a message from plotters in the interior to Norfolk cohorts, though Newton thought them more in the nature of a "Collector's memo." Petersburg's mayor, after examining the papers, assured Monroe that they were harmless.[37]

James Monroe's consternation over Jeremiah's fate was heightened by late developments as the prisoner awaited his May 28 execution. Another trial in Norfolk County concerned a third slave accused by Will, this one known as John Ingram's Ned. At the May 17 trial, Will claimed to have met

Ned about sunrise on April 11, the day he allegedly met Jeremiah and Walke's Ned. Ingram's Ned was said to have invited Will to join an Easter Monday torching of Norfolk in precisely the same words and word-order used by the others. Four judges favored conviction, one initially abstained, and a fifth, James Holt, feeling that Will's testimony sounded memorized, voted for acquittal; the defendant went free.[38]

If Will's testimony could not convict Ingram's Ned, how could the same testimony condemn the other two? George McIntosh had used Monroe's stay of Jeremiah's execution to get an affidavit from Holt and depositions from blacks as to the whereabouts of Walke's Ned on the day he allegedly asked Will to join the plot. He attended the trial of Ingram's Ned and got Caleb Boush's deposition that, having known Will twenty-five years, he could attest that Will was "the greatest Villian" and "most *notorious* Lyar" Boush ever knew.[39]

McIntosh, forwarding his new data to Monroe, added that Will, a runaway for nine of the past twelve months, had been been hired out of jail by John Floyd, and had "a very bad Character" in Princess Anne County where he was reared. Princess Anne High Sheriff Dennis Dawley, with whom Will once lived, felt that if Will told the truth in this instance, "he never knew him to *tell it before.*" Jarvis, McIntosh contended, was "drunk every day before breakfast if he can find *Rum.*" The presiding magistrate at the trial of Ingram's Ned had whispered that he thought Will a liar.[40]

Monroe on May 25 dictated for Mayor Cowper an order that Jeremiah's execution be carried out but that Ned's be delayed pending receipt of more information. (The council presumably dropped its objection to Jeremiah's conviction for a crime with which he was not charged.) Cowper received the order at the "old fields" outside Norfolk on May 28 as Jeremiah, who had just bade farewell of his wife and children, fell through the gallows trap and minutes before Walke's Ned was to follow. Cowper informed Monroe that Jeremiah, taking "leave of his wife and two children," maintained his innocence to the gallows, then fell silent, "and nothing could extract an answer."[41]

Ned's sentence was later reduced to transportation. Two other suspects in the alleged plot to burn Norfolk, James Haynes' Jonas and Joel Cornick's Moody, won acquittal in Princess Anne on April 30 and May 4, respectively. At least ten Virginia executions of blacks in 1802 resulted from conspiracy trials, besides incidents of vigilante terror, court-ordered whippings, and transportations. Another two dozen or more hangings in conspiracy cases occurred in northeastern North Carolina in the year's first six months.[42]

None of the testimony in the Norfolk-area trials implicated, directly or indirectly, any West Indian blacks. The fear that they were especially dangerous proved groundless. Neither were there any free black suspects, though a letter in the *Norfolk Herald* in 1801 had called for their expulsion from the borough as Boston had done in the previous year.[43] Although there were many reasons why blacks, free as well as slave, might yearn for a new social order, the forces arrayed against them were far too powerful to be overcome, a fact most blacks knew only too well.

George McIntosh, an old man in 1856, still maintained Jeremiah's innocence of criminal intent. He thought the blacks in and around Norfolk "too intelligent to enter into a combination to effect any measure by force." He had suffered, nonetheless, "universal obloquy" for his efforts on Jeremiah's behalf. Yet the *Petersburg Intelligencer* on August 25, 1802, had carried a Norfolk dispatch that "reports respecting the negroes have entirely subsided. The prevalent opinion is, that they have been propagated by negro purchasers from southern states."[44]

Governor Monroe's hesitation in Jeremiah's case may have cost him political influence in Norfolk. Not long after the hanging, the *Norfolk Herald* groused of "the coolness with which the magisterial exertion and judicial decision of this place has been treated by the executive." The governor's actions stood in sharp contrast, the editor felt, to his energy at the time of the Gabriel Plot, "self-preservation" being "the first law of nature." It seemed to the editor requisite that each citizen "stand centinel at his own door, and have a rallying-place, to which, in alarm, he may repair. We see no other remedy—an executive cloud darkens our safety."[45] But the necessary judicial example had been delivered and Monroe's political future was essentially undimmed.

George McIntosh paid a price for his unpopular stand. He complained to Monroe of unspecified "unbecoming treatment" accorded him in Norfolk and of the means "used to irritate and alarm the Public mind." It was surely relevant that McIntosh, like Monroe, was a "firm and ardent" Republican, that many Federalists found their political rivals to be overfond of reckless rhetoric and irresponsible designs regarding slavery.[46]

Cornick's Jeremiah was hanged for an act not defined as a crime and with which, in any case, he was not charged. He was convicted by uncorroborated testimony that was immediately discredited, in spite of a formidable alibi, and as punishment for aims neither he nor anyone else is likely to have harbored. It was his misfortune that public policy called for at least one prompt execution to intimidate potential malefactors. A few voices cried out for justice above the roar of the mob; they were, in fact, six in number: Mr. and Mrs. George McIntosh, Caleb Boush, Thomas Newton, James Holt, and Dennis Dawley.

Tranquility, at least, restored? Jeremiah's body was not cold in his grave when Norfolk's General Thomas Mathews alerted Richmond of a newly found letter warning whites of "a plan now forming . . . to be put in execution this harvest time."[47] *Plus ça change.*

CHAPTER 10

Duel of the Damned

ARLY on Monday morning, June 22, 1807, with a southwesterly breeze wafting across Hampton Roads, Commodore James Barron ordered his flagship to put to sea. The USS *Chesapeake* had waited several days for a favorable wind and could now begin its cruise to the Mediterranean. "At 1/4 past 7," says the ship's log, "weighed anchor, made sail with a pleasant Breeze . . . and stood out for sea."[1] It was to be one of the briefest and most memorable cruises an American warship ever took.

Around 9:00 A.M. the *Chesapeake,* a thirty-eight-gun frigate, glided past two British warships at anchor in Lynnhaven Bay. The British had kept a vigil for months to blockade French men-of-war in the Chesapeake, one of them anchored off Craney Island. The British ships seemed friendly enough and the *Chesapeake* sailed on toward Cape Henry, clearing the capes before noon.[2]

In early afternoon, the frigate paused to drop her pilot and then began adding sail for her ocean voyage. Curiously, a British ship could be discerned at some distance back to the west and apparently closing. The distance narrowed gradually, slowed at one point by a shift in the wind, but then more quickly as the southwesterly breeze returned. The ships were some twelve miles beyond the coast when the British vessel around 4:00 P.M. drew within hailing distance and asked permission to send a messenger aboard. Commodore Barron, informed that it was the fifty-gun HMS *Leopard,* granted permission and hove to.[3]

The message, brought over by a British lieutenant, was an order from the commander of British squadrons on this coast for his warships to look for the *Chesapeake* in international waters and, when she appeared, to search her for English deserters. The order, bearing the names of the alleged deserters, implied that the search should be peaceable if possible, by force if necessary. Such a demand was quite unacceptable from the American viewpoint, constituting a violation of U.S. neutrality in the European war.[4]

James Barron had been aware of the British complaint since March and had conducted an inquiry. The seamen in question, as he understood it, were four—two from Maryland and one from Massachusetts (two of them black). They had been impressed into British naval service, escaped, and were enrolled among the *Chesapeake*'s crew. (Barron may not have known that the fourth man, Jenkin Ratford, carried on his roster as "James Wilson," was a Yorkshireman and a bona fide British deserter.) Clearly, the British had no claim on native American citizens pressed into their service and, in any case, must not expect to search an American naval vessel as the message indicated they should.[5]

Barron told the messenger that he knew of no deserters on board, that his recruiting officer was instructed not to enroll British deserters. He called the *Chesapeake*'s Captain Gordon to verify that the seamen named in the message were not on the ship. As the British lieutenant took his leave, Barron noted that the *Leopard*'s gunports were open and her guns were unplugged. Surely this was carrying intimidation a bit far! He ordered the frigate's decks cleared, and the men were instructed to move quietly to quarters. A game of bluff might as well have two players as one.[6]

Within moments after the messenger returned, the *Leopard* sent a warning ball over the *Chesapeake*'s bow. Shortly afterward, there was a thundering close-range broadside of cannons, swivel guns, and small-arms fire. The blast tore gaping holes in the American vessel's hull, rigging, and superstructure, and took a toll of its astonished crewmen. Barron hailed his assailant furiously to negotiate and made futile efforts to send a boat to dissuade the British from the attack. But a second broadside followed and then two more before the shocked and now injured commodore ordered the flag to be struck in surrender. The great flagship now wallowed helplessly in the current, a crippled hulk that had returned but one errant shot before its ignominious surrender.[7]

Bemused English seamen were no doubt as startled as the Americans at the frigate's failure to get off a broadside. The grim truth would emerge only slowly in months of investigation. In fact, the *Chesapeake* was in no condition to fight. It had left Norfolk with decks littered with lumber, canvas, casks, furniture, and other impediments. Its powder horns and cartridges were mostly empty; most of its guns lacked wads, rammers, or matches. Many of its crew were unable to reach their posts during the assault, and the powder magazine was reportedly in a state of confusion. Hostile action was supposed to await the ship's arrival in the Mediterranean, by which time the problems would be resolved. On her decks lay eighteen wounded and three dead.[8]

The *Chesapeake*'s surrender was the most ignoble experience to have befallen the infant United States Navy and had wide-ranging results in the months and years ahead. For now, however, it meant that the British could board the ship, take the crewmen they sought, and, at sunset, leave the *Chesapeake* to limp back to Hampton Roads.[9] Both ships carried away a perception that another result was likely to be war between Britain and the United States.

News of the *Chesapeake–Leopard* affair reached Norfolk early on June 23, producing, said the *Publick Ledger,* "a degree of agitation beyond anything we ever witnessed or can attempt to describe." Skippers of every operable vessel in the Hampton Roads area made ready to sail in case of an immediate British invasion. The arrival that afternoon of eleven wounded was "a spectacle," the newspaper thought, to "rouse the indignation of every American . . . and *never* subside until ample satisfaction has been made." "War" was the *New York Herald*'s unabashed headline.[10]

Norfolk's agitation owed much to the fact that the *Chesapeake* was perceived as the town's own. When construction of the first six frigates comprising the new American navy was ordered in 1794, the *Chesapeake* was assigned to Gosport's shipyard, started twenty-seven years earlier by Andrew Sprowle. Norfolk's William Pennock had been the navy's procurement agent in building her, and Norfolk County's Captain Richard Dale was designated its prospective first commander. In 1801 a navy yard was established at Gosport, where Sprowle had pioneered use of the site for the British navy.[11]

After a long interruption, the *Chesapeake* project was renewed by Congress in 1798 and the frigate, displacing 1,244 tons and measuring over 152 feet long, was launched that December. By now, Captain Samuel Barron (James Barron's brother) was its commander; he was also a local man, a native of Hampton. The departure of the *Chesapeake* on its maiden voyage in May 1800 was celebrated by "wharves and houses . . . lined with people, who with three cheers welcomed her as she passed the townpoint" and an exchange of thirteen guns with Fort Norfolk. So the *Leopard*'s attack in 1807 was seen in Norfolk as virtually an assault on the town itself.[12]

On Wednesday, June 24, Norfolk and Portsmouth citizens met at a "large church," Norfolk's town hall being too small, with General Thomas Mathews in the chair. Following discussion, resolutions were passed suspending contact between the shore and British warships, forbidding pilots to man them, inaugurating a fund to aid the injured and next of kin of the dead, and ordering civic funerals for any who might die later. (The body of seaman Robert MacDonald, following his death at the Marine Hospital, was given a handsome funeral on June 28, with four thousand mourners on hand.) The meeting also created a committee to plan and oversee further action and resolved to support "any measures" of the general government, "whether of vengeance or retaliation."[13]

The issue mounted rapidly to a crisis. On Friday, June 26, a British ship anchored near the fort sent an officer upriver by boat toward the Norfolk home of British consul John Hamilton. Several boats put out from the wharves to intercept the trespasser, and two reached it before the ship below Fort Norfolk hoisted a white flag. The boat was allowed to pass but the committee of oversight that evening condemned the action. It stressed that any British officer coming to Norfolk would be considered a prisoner, pending action of the general government.[14] The committee in its zeal had overreached itself by interrupting contact between British ships and their consul and was soon sorry for it.

On July 3 came the British reply, as reported in the *Publick Ledger.* Commodore John E. Douglas demanded of Mayor Richard E. Lee that the interference be "*immediately annulled*" or he would halt Norfolk's maritime traffic pending directions from his government. He had his whole squadron in Hampton Roads awaiting the mayor's answer and could "obstruct the whole trade of the Chesapeake."[15] Again it was a case of an official overstepping his authority, for proper procedure required Douglas to take no such action against neutral traffic without orders from his government.

With local authorities on both sides claiming unfounded powers and renegade intentions, the moment was ripe for an incident that would plunge both countries into a war neither wanted. Mayor Lee answered Douglas with provocative and patriotic words—it was July 4—about being ready "for the worst you may attempt." He added, however, that the act complained of was that of individuals, "not of the government" (though the Norfolk–Portsmouth committee had clearly arrogated to itself governing powers). If the act were "wrong or illegal," it should be up to courts and governments to decide the question, not force of arms.[16]

Norfolk attorney Littleton Tazewell was delegated on July 5 to deliver a reply to Douglas aboard his ship, where he found the officer to have undergone a radical change. Douglas, with his officers, read Lee's letter with a show of gravity before observing that his own letter was "misapprehended" by the mayor: it contained no menace that he could see. When Tazewell pointed out the offending words, Douglas replied that it was owing to an error of his clerk that "had escaped his observation," that "he had no orders to committ any act of hostility." He had only to inquire if arrangements could be made to communicate with the consul, and was assured by Tazewell that there was no doubt of that.[17]

Norfolk and the nation had meanwhile set in motion preparations for war. President Jefferson ordered that old Fort Nelson, below Portsmouth, be quickly refurbished; Norfolk citizens went voluntarily to work on Fort Norfolk. The *Chesapeake,* its rigging and spars shot away, was brought up under the guns of the latter fort, and the French frigate *Cybelle* was invited to help ward off British assaults on the Elizabeth River. The state hurried several companies of troops to Hampton Roads, and the local militia was augmented by enlistment. Commodore Barron, destined for a court martial, was replaced by Captain Stephen Decatur, whose wife Susan was daughter of former Norfolk mayor Luke Wheeler.[18]

War was averted by both sides backing away from the full import of their threats. Norfolk began to simmer down with Tazewell's return from his mission, though it was months before any real sense of security returned. By August it was evident that the British government was embarrassed by the bellicose tone and actions of its naval commanders.[19] The duel of ships was a humiliation for the *Chesapeake;* the duel of nations was yet to come.

The impressment of seamen from its ships was, in a sense, a tribute to the swift development of America's merchant marine during the long European war. American shipyards turned out seventy thousand tons of shipping yearly that required four thousand additional seamen each year. Experienced English sailors were in high demand on the East Coast, and recruiters for both private and U.S. naval vessels were often eager for deserters, even enticing them to desert. The British retaliated by stopping American ships on the high seas to seek out deserters, and were not above supplying their own needs with any able-bodied men they encountered.[20]

Norfolk was a principal victim of both impressment and the seizure of ships by the English and French. The *Charles Carter,* outward bound in the summer of 1803, was stopped by a British frigate and forced to yield four crewmen, all of them American citizens who enrolled at Norfolk. Conway and Fortescue Whittle's *Eliza* fell prey to Caribbean Frenchmen in 1804, and Captain Evans and his crew were set ashore on nearly deserted Isla des Palmas. They subsisted on roots as they built a raft, sailed to Cuba, found the *Eliza,* boarded, and recaptured it.[21]

The depradations continued. When the brig *Ann-Elizabeth,* en route from Norfolk to Malaga in 1805, was taken by a British ship, boarders helped themselves to the belongings of captain and crew, including cash, books, and clothing, before releasing it. The *Norfolk Herald* in early 1801 noted that Norfolk merchants had claims against the French amounting to $2 million.[22]

Insurance covered much of the loss, and death or serious injury was rare in such episodes: the risk was well worth it. Norfolk and Portsmouth by 1804 handled three-fourths of Virginia's exports and an even larger share of its imports. Some merchants minimized risk by arming their ships and sailing in fleets.[23]

Alert merchants like Moses Myers made up in a lucky venture any losses from adverse ones. Myers came to Norfolk in 1787 and opened a trade that gave him contacts all over the North Atlantic and the Virginia upcountry. Allying with William Pennock in 1794, his firm handled up to 15 percent of Norfolk's exports. In 1800 Myers joined in a ship chandlery with Richard Drummond and Richard Bowden; he then founded his own firm with his son John in 1809. He owned several ships, and speculated in banks, insurance companies, and canal and land schemes; he could weather the occasional loss of a ship, such as the *Moses Myers* to the French in 1800 or the *Argus* to the British in 1801. His home at Freemason and Catherine streets was sumptuous, though less so than Pennock's three-story house on Main, the work of renowned architect Benjamin Latrobe.[24]

Easy money bred lax business practices, and Norfolk had a reputation for exports of poor quality and short measure. An observer in 1804 took as "indisputable truth" that Norfolk articles such as flour, beef, pork, fish, and naval stores were everywhere a source of complaint. Local inspectors routinely certified damaged or deficient goods for export. The same was true of imports: the worst produce of other markets could be shipped to Norfolk; the best went elsewhere. Inspectors certified naval stores they never saw, and even provided blank certificates to be filled out as to quantity, quality, and the like by the shippers.[25]

Profit showered down continuously, for all that. Two groups of maritime insurers, the Marine and Union insurance companies, now operated in Norfolk, and two banks—a branch of the Bank of the United States, opened in 1799, and the Bank of Virginia, founded in 1803—funded much of the local enterprise. The English, French, and Spanish maintained consulates in Norfolk.[26]

Flush times benefited the public sphere as well as the private. A revolution of sorts in the city's governance took the form of the adoption in 1803

This 1830 painting by an anonymous artist is a view from Port Norfolk, looking south toward Norfolk. Despite its title (*Blue Wing Teal*), it shows a black boy holding up a dead rabbit for inspection. (Courtesy of The Chrysler Museum, Norfolk, Va.)

of a system of eight wards, each of which might elect two members to the Common Council. (The first Norfolk Chamber of Commerce was formed two years earlier.) In 1807 the state allowed Norfolk to pave its streets, and within a decade all main thoroughfares were paved. The first thirty-six street lamps were installed in 1811.[27] These steps led to rapid amelioration of some of the town's most aggravating problems.

"The streets," wrote a visitor in 1815, were "a little too crooked for beauty" and "in some places intolerably dirty. . . . The principal ones, however, are kept clean, and handsomely lighted." (Yes, this was Norfolk, Virginia!) The U.S. customs house stood at the west end of Main, the frame courthouse and jail (built in 1800) at its opposite end. Back Creek, once the northern boundary, was still navigable for small shipping but now bisected Norfolk. Many professional people, ship captains, and skilled laborers lived on Cumberland Street. The market house, burned in 1804 with much else in the lower part of town, was rebuilt on modern lines only to burn again in 1814.[28]

Methodists had a fine brick church on Catherine Street, Presbyterians boasted a frame one on Freemason. The Episcopalians had split into feuding congregations. Their borough church problem went back at least to 1789 when rival vestries had been elected, each inviting a different minister to serve the parish. The Episcopal Convention, meeting in 1792, recognized Rev. James Whitehead over Rev. William Bland. The issue pitted the Bland men against Thomas Newton, Robert Taylor, and others, the second group withdrawing to erect what was later called Christ Church in June 1800. The latter burned in 1827 and was replaced by the present one. Bland died in 1803 and his following broke up; the borough church fell into disuse until 1832, when it was reconstituted as St. Paul's.[29]

As money spawned banks and built lovely homes and churches, it also brought recreational opportunities. Early nineteenth-century Norfolk offered copious amusement, much of it by irrepressible Frenchmen. A downtown half-acre, dubbed Vauxhall Gardens, provided band music, dancing, fireworks, and other amusements. Over on Briggs Point was Wigwam Gardens, where quoits (heavy rings thrown at a peg) and skittles (bowling) were played, and fireworks and refreshments were offered. Rosainville's Bower and Riffaud's and Burt's Gardens featured concerts and balls. A version of field hockey known as bandy was popular in streets and vacant lots; there were also cricket and music clubs. On Briggs Point and elsewhere were greens for encampments and parades.[30]

From the east end of Main, a drawbridge led to Washington Point where M. Delacoste in 1805 established a botanical garden, natural history museum, and pleasure grounds. When he advertised his first big fireworks display for July 4, 1807, he had a menagerie, rare and exotic plants, a slack-wire performer, ice cream, liquor, and "French coffee a-la-Greek." Also popular for cockfights and other entertainments was Lindsay's Garden at the upper end of Church Street near Potter's Field cemetery.[31]

The town usually had one or more thespian societies besides traveling troupes that often appeared at the theater. In 1808 a race track opened on the north side of the eastern branch, east of Newton's Creek. Joseph C. Maigne ran the "Norfolk Baths," and a "mangle machine" behind house number fifty four gave clothes a better gloss than by ironing. A gaggle of "tippling houses, in obscure lanes" was a resort of some blacks and were seen by whites as "academies, wherein thievery is matured," since fencing stolen goods was thought to flourish in them.[32]

The area's premier impresario was the proprietor of Ducoing's Long-Room, offering such traveling attractions as waxworks and an enormous water-powered automaton of figures sawing wood, feeding chickens, and making shoes. In 1812 Ducoing introduced Signor Pardi's "Panharmonicon," puffed as having 250 musical instruments and doubtless as capable of torturing "Yankee Doodle" as of maiming Mozart or Haydn, all of which were on its program. But there was competition: if a six-legged cow and calf failed to beguile the multitude, a young lady from New Hampshire without hands or feet who could thread a needle and cut paper or cloth with scissors held in her teeth would. As of yore, any excuse for a celebration, including the Louisiana Purchase and the anniversary of the Jamestown Landing, was seized with alacrity.[33]

The *Herald* sometimes carried essays by amateur analysts of the passing scene, including "Rusticus," who lamented that Norfolk had no civic character but was a hodge-podge of nationalities. Lowest were the Irish, mostly "illiberal and rude" but not far below the Scotch, "a penurious, plodding race," yet "seldom indigent." Next came the French, "a whiffling, fantastical set," much inclined to meddle in others' affairs but "cheerful, even in misfortune." The few Englishmen were haughty, though some exceptions were "humane, liberal, and obliging." The local Yankees were artful at trade, "full of tricks," and hated to be outwitted. Only the native Virginian was "free, open, hospitable, and generous, . . . he appears the only happy man we have in Norfolk."[34]

Anne Ritson, who had lived in Norfolk for a while as wife of a merchant, published a volume of travel verse in London in 1809 in which Norfolk was the main topic. Referring, for example, to the tendency of lovers to elope for quick marriages in Carolina, she wrote:

Two bridges, while I staid, were rear'd
And better to the eye appear'd;
One from Town-end unto the fort,
In evening was a nice resort, . . .
The other on the verge was found,
Just at the end of Norfolk's bound;
A very handsome bridge indeed,
And well constructed for the speed
Of lovers, who delight to fly,
And matrimony's fetters tie;
For it directly leads them o'er,
And rests them on that happy shore,
Where, clear of the Virginian land,
By the first Magistrate at hand,

They are united, and may come,
At leisure, to their native home.[35]

Norfolk's busy growth and growing wealth attracted the gifted from elsewhere in Virginia and beyond. Williamsburg's Littleton W. Tazewell, later
Virginia's governor, and Marylander William Wirt, attorney general under
President Monroe and one-time candidate for president, settled in Norfolk
at the start of the new century, though Wirt soon fled from the threat of
yellow fever. A moneyed merchant might have his portrait done in 1803 by
Raphael Peale (brother of Rembrandt Peale) or Thomas Sully, two of the
nation's most gifted young artists. (Sully, also an acrobat and trick rider, gave
a display of his prowess at Briggs Point in June 1800.) A native, Thomas
Newton Jr., served from 1801 to 1833 as Norfolk-area congressman, but the
seats of the district's state senator and two representatives rotated often.[36]

Gossips were treated to a banquet of speculation on Friday afternoon,
May 24, 1811, when merchant Richard Bowden met his former business
partner, Moses Myers, at the city market and began to strike him with his
walking stick and fists. They were separated and Myers proceeded to his
counting house. Within minutes, Myers' eldest son Samuel heard of the
incident, hurried to Bowden's place of business, and shot him dead with a
pistol. It was never clear what led Bowden to pommel Myers but this was a
society affair; the son, charged with manslaughter, was found innocent even
of that. He went discretely abroad for a season, but was soon back in Norfolk
running the family's tobacco stemmery.[37]

Town characters multiplied with the population. The *Herald* reported
with regret William Moffit's death in 1812. Moffit was a barber, ringer of
the town bell, and a periodic madcap who paraded about in "the armour
and costume of a copper-coloured warrior. His soul delighted in jollity,"
though a fondness for alcohol ruined him. Northwest across Glebe Creek
lived William Colley, whose cutlass scar across his face gave a hint of credibility to his incessant retellings of how he had once freed himself from a
pirate band. It was Colley who, around 1800, built the drawbridge linking
his farm and Fort Norfolk with the town.[38]

A cloud passed over Norfolk's prospects in 1805 when the British destroyed French and Spanish naval power off Trafalgar and seized undisputed command of the seas. Britain now began enforcing an old ban on U.S.
trade with the French West Indies, a challenge the American navy was too
weak to meet. The French, though unable to deter American trade with
English ports, harassed those trying to trade with Haitian rebels and the

British West Indies, in which effort she had the aid of her Spanish allies. Collectively, these actions were a spear pressed into the lifeblood of Norfolk's trade. They soon began seriously to hamper its commerce.[39]

Petitions of protest from Norfolk were taken to Washington by William Pennock in 1806, but it was not clear what action, if any, Jefferson could take. Between 1805 and 1808 Norfolk's losses to the three predatory nations amounted to almost $250,000. Congress in 1806 adopted a Nonimportation Act banning certain British imports and placing an embargo on American trade with Santo Domingo. It was now an open question whether Norfolk was more fatally stricken by its friends or its enemies. Meanwhile, British impressment continued unabated.[40]

For a while in 1806 and 1807 Norfolk and Princess Anne counties welcomed both the French ships that came in for repairs and British vessels that anchored in Lynnhaven Bay to blockade the French. The crews bought quantities of flour and vegetables and troubled American shipping only sporadically.[41] But the *Chesapeake–Leopard* affair drastically altered local as well as national feeling and no comfort could be found thereafter in the presence of warships of the contending powers. The Jefferson administration in late 1807 enacted an embargo on all American overseas trade in the hope of putting pressure on both sides.

Ships at Norfolk scrambled to get to sea before the embargo took effect. Elijah Cobb of Cape Cod had from Friday afternoon to Sunday morning to unload a hundred tons of ballast, load three thousand barrels of flour, hire a crew, and get to sea. He did it, too, only to have the wind fail as he reached Hampton Roads. With the customs collector almost alongside and about to take him in, the wind suddenly revived and Cobb sailed for Cadiz and a high profit. The embargo had no useful effect and was lifted in 1809 with respect to all trade except that with England and France. Even this limitation was abandoned in early 1810, though the United States promised to renew it against one if the other lifted its restrictions on American trade.[42]

The embargo, however, all but ruined Norfolk. During 1808 most warehouses closed, shipyards fell silent and their laborers found themselves out of work, unemployed sailors milled about aimlessly, and ships were moved to fresh water to reduce worm damage. Some three hundred people in Norfolk subsisted on the public dole and probably as many more on private charity. "We might as well shut up shop," wrote merchant William Couper, "for there is nothing but dullness and complaining. . . . Working people's wages here is almost reduced to nothing on account of nothing to be done." Some managed to violate the embargo, but most who tried it failed.[43]

The leading merchants and shippers of Norfolk were Federalist in politics and critical of the Republican administration's policies. In the columns of John Cowper's *Ledger,* they argued that the government was soft on France but unduly provocative toward Britain. Smaller tradesmen and skilled artisans, a voting majority, supported Jefferson and Madison and used the *Herald* to vent their ill-will toward Great Britain. But the gulf between the parties was not great, each recognizing that neither France nor England meant the United States any good. Both sides tended to support initiatives that promised some rent in the curtain of European decrees inhibiting American trade.[44]

Although most of Norfolk's venom was directed at England as the stronger seapower, anger against France sometimes boiled over as well. In 1810 a French privateer, *Revanche de Cerf,* thought to have taken some American prizes, entered Norfolk for repair. By the spring of 1811 it was understood to be recruiting along the waterfront for another privateering cruise. On April 16 boatloads of local men rowed out to the ship, overpowered the watch, and set it on fire. It burned to the waterline.[45]

A break in the deadlock seemed to appear in 1810, when Napoleon announced an intention to lift France's restrictions on American trade. The Madison government responded that it would resume nonimportation against Britain in early 1811. But this small ray of hope collapsed as Britain remained unmoved and Napoleon's ships continued their depredations on American trade.[46]

In early 1811 the American frigate *President* engaged the Britisher *Little Belt* about thirty miles off the Virginia capes in an action resulting from a cannon's accidental discharge. The *Little Belt,* smaller of the two, was badly damaged, to the intense satisfaction of some Americans, who saw it as revenge for the *Chesapeake–Leopard* affair. A few months later, HMS *Tartarus* seized several American ships off the capes, including the *Orion* out of Petersburg with a Norfolk captain. The British put a prize crew on the ship, impressed three sailors, and sailed brazenly into Hampton Roads, where they landed the rest of the Americans. Such incidents helped create an American war fever and a renewed embargo against Britain in April 1812.[47]

The American declaration of war in June owed little to either ship seizures or impressment, both of which could be tolerated indefinitely. It was mainly the inspiration of frontiersmen eager to exploit Britain's preoccupation with Napoleon to seize Canada and lands of Northwestern Indians allied with Britain. New England commercial interests opposed war almost to the point of secession and Federalists during the war gained strength in

Norfolk, whose merchants also recoiled from conflict. The War of 1812 proved to be a foolish and costly adventure.

Despite the long prelude, the coming of war found Hampton Roads ill-prepared. Breastworks hurriedly went up at Lambert's Point, Tanner's Creek Bridge, and the intersection of Church Street and the Princess Anne road, the only feasible land access to Norfolk. Militia General Robert B. Taylor directed fortification of Craney Island, a small, flat outcropping near the Elizabeth River's mouth. He had redoubts placed on the island's west side and a fort on the east side, arming them with four hundred militia besides sailors, light artillerymen, and others. In the channel between Craney Island and Lambert's Point were stationed twenty small gunboats. The wisdom of these arrangements was soon handsomely demonstrated.[48]

American forces at Norfolk were gradually increased and by late 1813 reached five thousand, though some 80 percent were short-term militia with little training. In the absence of a navy of any strength, Norfolk mariners, having converted some of their merchant ships to privateers, went in search of British shipping. A few, notably the *Roger,* enjoyed success in seizing enemy ships. It was the *Dash,* under a Norfolk officer, which made the first seizure of a ship of the Royal Navy, the packet *Whiting,* in Hampton Roads in July 1812. But most of the Norfolk ships achieved little against the immense force available to the British.[49]

Not until February 1813 did the war became dangerous to Norfolk. The USS *Constellation* was putting to sea when it spied a British squadron near the capes and ran back into the Elizabeth River. The British ships were those of Admiral Warren, who promptly declared a blockade of the Chesapeake and began sending small craft against bay towns and up tributary rivers. With Lynnhaven Bay as their chief anchorage, the British found it necessary to send frequent parties ashore in Princess Anne and Norfolk counties for fresh water, which led to skirmishes with the local militia.[50]

In June the war came to the Elizabeth River. On June 21 an enemy squadron of fourteen warships, two transports, and small craft was seen approaching Craney Island. The next morning at dawn, boatloads of Redcoats and marines left the squadron and headed for the west side of the river to attack the island by land. "Hundreds of citizens," wrote a spectator, "ran to the Town Point to witness the engagement." The defenders quickly shifted some militia to the island's west side, with three cannon dragged hurriedly from their fort. When the invaders came within range on the far side of Thoroughfare Creek, a cannonade of seven guns opened and the attackers fell back. But two columns of barges bearing 1,500 men bore down on the east side of the island, led by Admiral Warren's elegant twenty-four-oared barge *Centipede*.[51]

While still some 250 yards from shore, the leading barges began to run aground; the bottom of three to four feet of mud made landing troops impossible. Moreover, grape and canister from the defenders' cannons began to fall among the barges, sinking or disabling several. The *Centipede*, turning west to rendezvous with Redcoats on the river's west bank, took a ball diagonally that cut off a man's legs and wounded others. With his barge sinking, Warren called retreat and abandoned the attack. Thanks to Taylor's thorough planning, the assault was a dismal failure. Norfolk was spared the ruin that later befell the nation's capital.[52]

The blockade continued but local businessmen found ways to beat it. Routes south around Dismal Swamp and via South Quay on the Blackwater River were used to send produce to Albemarle Sound. From there ships of modest size could slip through the blockade to the West Indies or even Europe. British warships had to keep clear of the storms that often raked Cape Lookout and Cape Fear and the treacherous shoals of Cape Romain and Frying Pan shoals. Virginia tobacco and flour came down the James and other rivers to Norfolk, were lightered to Kempsville, and were sent overland to Carolina. Much of this produce reached West Indian and European markets and kept many Norfolk traders from bankruptcy. In June 1814 the long-delayed Dismal Swamp Canal was negotiated by a twenty-ton craft, bringing Carolina produce, including bacon and brandy, to Norfolk.[53]

In the meantime, however, the Madison government in December 1813 enacted a new embargo, followed shortly by curtailment of the provisions trade from Richmond and Petersburg to Norfolk to prevent any possibility of the goods falling into British hands. This order virtually shut off the clogged valve of Norfolk commerce. "Some years ago," wrote a subscriber to the *Ledger* in early 1815,

> walking through Wide-Water street, I was much incommoded by rum puncheons, sugar hogsheads, bales of goods, flour and tobacco hogsheads. I heard the bawling of negroes as they hoisted these goods in and out of vessels, . . . I was in constant danger of breaking my shins on the skids of passing drays. Recently I again went through Water Street, Market Square, and Main Street. No rum puncheons, no . . . hogsheads, no bawling negroes, no drays passing. Instead of plodding merchants, and busy clerks, I see only some military officers, ten or twelve idle youths, a few recruits, and a group of negroes. From the nearby dram shops come the fumes of egg-nog and cigars, and the sound of fiddles and tamborines.[54]

That somber reflection was printed on January 4, 1815, four days before the great American victory at the Battle of New Orleans and eleven days after the signing of the Treaty of Ghent, ending the war. There was much celebrating in Norfolk and considerable optimism that the town's good times, interrupted for a decade by embargoes and wars, would now resume in all their turbulent glory. It was a dream that soon turned to dust in the dawning realization that Norfolk's time of trials had only just begun.

The duel of the *Chesapeake* and *Leopard* had ended in 1807 with the surrender of the former and no credit to the latter, the duel of nations with a fruitless return to the antebellum status quo. But one duel remained to be fought and it occurred at Bladensboro, Maryland, on March 22, 1820. James Barron, convicted of negligence in the mauling of his ship by the *Leopard*, had been suspended from the service for five years, his career irreparably blighted. A son and brother of ranking naval officers, he was a thorough "navy man" for whom the sentence was the evisceration of his ambitions, the ruin of his life. Stephen Decatur, though openly critical of Barron, had sat on his court martial and fought his reinstatement five years later. It was gall to Barron's tortured soul that Decatur was assigned to succeed him in 1807.

When, after reinstatement, Barron heard that Decatur was still befouling his character, he engaged his old nemesis in acrimonious correspondence that precipitated the Bladensboro duel. Decatur was a crack shot and an experienced duelist. Barron was so near-sighted that the dueling distance was reduced from ten to eight paces. Barron was severely wounded, but Decatur took a shot in his abdomen that killed him. Barron lived in Norfolk for many years, including a lengthy tenure as head of the navy yard, before he died in 1851.

The *Chesapeake*, surrendering ingloriously to HMS *Shannon* in a duel off Boston in June 1813, was taken to England where its timbers are reported to have been used to build a flour mill.[55] As in the duels of ships and nations, there was little honor to be claimed by either antagonist.

CHAPTER 11

Whistling in the Wilderness

DAY BY DAY, week after tedious week, the mind-numbing thud of pick and spade and axe labored up out of the great trench and was absorbed in the foliage of the encompassing forest. A hard hour might see the cut moved forward by a few feet, an exhausting day by a few score yards, and still the end lay grudging miles ahead, each inch no less stubborn than those already wrought. The workmen often labored waist-high or more in the muck, plagued by mosquitoes and snakes in summer, biting cold in winter, and disease in all seasons. The sun sank only to rise again and command that the drudgery resume. The white man would have his canal at whatever cost of human toil and death.

The two crews toiled through the first year, 1793, and into a second: one north from Joyce's Creek in North Carolina, the other south from Virginia's Deep Creek, twenty-odd miles away. They were expected to meet in 1799 and merge waters of the Pasquotank and the Elizabeth River's southern branch, Albemarle Sound with the Chesapeake. But the estimate was wildly optimistic and the obstacles were woefully understated. Even slaves could bear only so much, and work often ceased for fresh levies of workmen, shortages of cash, poor management, and bad weather. Thomas Newton, the Dismal Swamp Canal Company president, still felt in early 1799 that the waters would mingle by Christmas, but two years later there were miles to go and traffic only on part of the southern half.[1]

The project's first notable result was a sandy toll road in 1805 flanking the unfinished canal. Since the late seventeenth century a soggy trail had stretched along the west side of the swamp, but the new road quickly became the route of passenger and mail coaches as well as produce wagons and gave the company its first meaningful revenues. The waters of the two rivers finally commingled in that year, but the canal's two-foot draft would bear only shingle flats no more than six feet wide, poled by their crews arduously along the narrow waterway.[2]

With the war in Europe once more flaring after a pause, funds—from the states of North Carolina and Virginia and stock sales—were readily found at the start of the nineteenth century, but the sources almost gave out after the 1807 embargo. Not until 1812 and between dry spells did the canal have the water needed for sixty-foot shingle flats and only in 1814 was it negotiated by a small decked vessel of twenty tons bringing brandy and bacon from the Roanoke River. Hereafter canal traffic mounted rapidly.[3]

It was a great day for Norfolk when, in December 1815, a raft arrived from Bedford County that had been poled down the Roanoke (with portages past several rapids), up Albemarle Sound, and through the canal to the Elizabeth River—a distance of some 340 miles. Its cargo was only a barrel of mountain flour milled at Staunton, but it symbolized how far Norfolk's reach might extend once improvements were made along the route. By resolution of the Hustings Court, Colonel William J. Lewis of Campbell County was thanked for his gift of the flour to Norfolk and more especially for "this evidence of enterprize and public spirit." Within a week, Littleton Tazewell, General Taylor, George Newton, and others formed the Roanoke Commercial Company to improve Roanoke River navigation.[4]

By now the navy was showing interest in the canal. The blockade of the War of 1812 had demonstrated that an inland waterway might someday become the means of avoiding economic strangulation. In June 1818 President Monroe visited Norfolk and was taken to see the Dismal Swamp; hope rose that there might soon be federal subsidies to promote more rapid development of the project. (A dedicated fiscal conservative and strict constructionist, Monroe would have none of it.)[5]

By virtue of a lottery and other means, the canal was further widened and deepened in the next few years. Backers had the satisfaction on April 28, 1823, of witnessing the arrival via the canal of a small schooner, the thirty-five-ton *Rebecca Edwards,* from Halifax, North Carolina. This meant that at least the smallest coasting vessels could now use the canal and that an important milestone was passed in fulfilling the dream of an inland waterway to link the Southeast with New England.[6]

The canal could mean far more than that. The treaty ending the War of 1812 did not reopen the British West Indies to American ships. American goods could be traded there only on British vessels, a serious blow to Norfolk shippers and shipbuilders. For a time, the loss was partly masked by a backlog of European demands for American produce and by the fact that many British ships called at Norfolk for cargoes. But Congress in 1818 retaliated against British restrictions by forbidding the trade of British ships between American ports; the islands were closed to Americans. Other West Indian trade remained open to Americans but it was far less valuable than that of the British islands. As if to emphasize the point, the nation now plunged into the Panic of 1819, which signaled the start of a prolonged depression.[7]

Another blow to Norfolk's business was the opening of New York's Erie Canal in 1825. With this artery to the interior of the continent, New York began to take command of the American carrying trade with Europe. New York City became a magnet to the coasting trade of Norfolk and other smaller ports, drawing ships to her wharves for return cargoes and shipping Virginia produce on to Europe. New Yorkers also built huge ships whose size and speed far outstripped that of rival ports and allowed for reduced freight charges. Even those Norfolk ships that still took cotton, flour, or tobacco to Europe were likely to bring their return cargoes to New York, where prices were higher.[8]

Some had seen Norfolk's salvation in the arrival of the first steamboat, the *Washington*, from the upper Chesapeake in May 1815. Within about a year a twice-weekly steam packet, the *Powhatan*, ran between Norfolk and Richmond, and it seemed that produce from the interior would find its way ever more readily to Norfolk wharves. But soon the New York coasters were also using steam and these craft wheezed noisily past Norfolk as they headed up the James and York. As in the early days of sail, these vessels had no need of a deep harbor and could cut Norfolk out as middleman in Virginia's trade. Year by year in the 1820s and beyond, Fall Line towns prospered and Norfolk fell further behind.[9]

So Jefferson was wrong. The president had predicted in 1806 that Norfolk would soon outstrip New York, Boston, Philadelphia, and Baltimore. It would become America's major seaport, New Orleans, perhaps, excepted. Once the rivers of the Chesapeake were fully settled, the quantity of produce coming through Norfolk, he vowed, must become "immense."[10]

Given the quadruple infirmities of British restrictions, national depression, New York dominance, and the steamboat, many Norfolk merchants clung to the resuscitating vision of a flourishing Dismal Swamp Canal as their best hope for a comeback. If the canal could be improved, if the challenges of Roanoke River navigation—especially its disruptive falls—could be mastered, Norfolk's commercial "backcountry" might include much of the central and western parts of both North Carolina and Virginia. Within this region lay 25,000 square miles that included some of the most productive farmland in America. Traffic that would otherwise go to such places as

Petersburg and Richmond could be lured through the canal to Hampton Roads; Norfolk might yet recover its lost role as Virginia's premier port city.[11]

The mercantile vision assumed proportions of imminent reality in 1826, when the navy decided to build a huge stone drydock at the Gosport navy yard and Congress bought six hundred shares of stock in the Dismal Swamp Canal Company. The canal would be needed to furnish building materials for the drydock and to facilitate coastal defense. Fort Monroe at Old Point Comfort, another site of substantial federal investment, was being expanded and by 1825 held the largest garrison in the United States.[12] Could it be that this muddy dog-leg of a ditch would save Norfolk after all?

In the years while the canal inched toward completion, the public image of the Dismal Swamp, its northern edge within a dozen or so miles of Norfolk, was undergoing subtle but significant alteration. Throughout the eighteenth century, the great swamp had been viewed as a "horrible desert," an "impenetrable wilderness" of poisonous snakes and vines, great wild creatures, and desperate fugitive slaves. A luxuriant folklore had developed of mysterious swamp disappearances and strange adventures, all of it stressing the forbidding character of the dank and dangerous morass as well as its inhospitality to human encroachment.[13]

Such gloomy assessments could not withstand the romantic age of the late eighteenth and early nineteenth centuries, and Norfolk itself fell reluctant victim to the Dismal's dark allure. When poet Thomas Moore visited Norfolk and the swamp in 1803, his attitude reflected the new mood of appreciation for the wild and untamed, the fashionable appeal of the grandly remote and mysterious. British Consul John Hamilton, Moore's host, took him on a late fall visit to the Dismal's periphery and told him a tale of a young man driven insane by the death of his sweetheart and his death while searching for her in the swamp. Moore promptly rendered the story into a popular ballad, "The Lake of the Dismal Swamp," in which

> Away to Dismal Swamp he speeds;
>   His path was rugged and sore;
> Through the tangled juniper, beds of reeds,
>   Through many a fen, where the serpent feeds,
> And man never trod before. . . .
>   But oft from the Indian hunter's camp,
> This maid and her lover so true,
>   Are seen at the hour of midnight damp,
> To cross the lake by a firefly lamp,
>   And paddle their white canoe.[14]

After construction of a canal hotel just inside North Carolina in 1802, the Dismal—or its accessible margins—became increasingly a tourist attraction and lovers' tryst, the border zone a frequented dueling ground. Lumber canals furnished hunters and fishermen access to Lake Drummond in the swamp's interior, and the incorrigibly prosaic spoke often of plans to drain the swamp for farmland or further exploit its timber resources. Henry Wadsworth Longfellow and Harriet Beecher Stowe were among distinguished American writers who would in due course contribute to the literature of the great swamp.[15]

Norfolk residents, who experienced the Dismal as a source of hardwood lumber and shingles or sometimes found the air choked by smoke from swamp fires, wrote no encomiums to its grandeur. But the city was beginning, despite economic adversity, to enjoy a serious cultural life and even produce writers of minor importance. Thomas Blanchard's ode of 1800 "To the Memory of George Washington" was widely admired. William Wirt's novel, *Letters of the British Spy,* published while he resided in Norfolk in 1803, created an audience for his later and more famous essays. Hugh Blair Grigsby, born in Norfolk in 1806, began in the 1820s to win acclaim as a biographer, poet, and newspaper editor. The city's well-stocked Athenaeum was said by a visitor in 1827 to have six thousand "well chosen books."[16]

William Maxwell, lawyer and poet, was known, partly through the popular travel books of Mrs. Anne Royall, to literary people beyond the Potomac and even the Atlantic. After meeting him in Norfolk in 1827, Royall described him as "of youthful appearance, stout and well made, his face round, . . . with a soft, dark grey eye, and handsome features, with all the heavenly charities expressed in his countenance," despite being a Presbyterian.[17]

Not so for the Norfolk Theatre, which slumped after its burst of popularity at the start of the nineteenth century. Gifted performers appearing here in those peak years included Mrs. David A. (Elizabeth) Poe in 1810, whose husband's recent death had left her burdened with sole care of her children, Rosalie and two-year-old Edgar Allan. (Mrs. Poe appeared sometimes opposite Matthew Sully, brother of artist Thomas Sully.) Traveling troupes ceased to call after the 1807 embargo and never regained popularity after the war. Some felt that theater audiences were too much infiltrated by pickpockets, "Water Street Damsels," and their sailor escorts, and that actors as a class were inclined to a wanton lifestyle. The theater, by then dilapidated, was sold to the Methodists in 1833 and converted into a chapel.[18]

Thomas Moore was delighted with a harpsichord and singing performance by Miss Mathews in Hamilton's drawing room in 1803, but deemed the town a cultural wasteland and grumped that "music here is like whistling in the wilderness." Perhaps it was, but Norfolk's first singing school was opened in the same year and the wilderness would soon resound with jubilant melody.[19]

This unexpected development owed much to the acquisition of New York's James H. Swindells as organist at Christ Episcopal Church in 1817. (Christ Church's was Norfolk's first organ.) Swindells and Charles A. Dacosta, another talented newcomer, devoted themselves to composing and arranging, leading performing groups, forming musical societies, directing sacred concerts and oratorios, and generally fostering interest in both secular and sacred music. Before Swindells moved to Portsmouth in 1831 and Dacosta to Charleston six years later, they had trained a generation in the highest standards of musical performance and appreciation the city had ever known.[20]

Early in this period, Norfolk music-lovers favored instrumental music. The German influence was strong, with Mozart a runaway favorite. There was a Mozart Band in the 1820s, along with an Appollonian Society for instrumentalists and a Handel-Haydn Society. But the 1820s and 1830s saw an era of pronounced popularity for vocal music, with the ballad the preferred medium and, later, opera. From June to September, indoor music gave way to outdoor entertainment, with steamboat excursions gradually replacing some of the more refined pleasures.[21]

Public music was a feature of the various "gardens" around town and military bands had long been available to enhance the gaiety of festive occasions. But there were also families among whom private music, as in the Hamilton household, was constantly practiced and frequently performed. Moses Myers' numerous household has left America's largest family collection of antebellum music, most of it acquired by the Myers children in the first quarter of the nineteenth century. Its nine hundred compositions include pieces for voice, piano, flute, violin, string quartet, and eight-part sinfonia.[22]

The popularity of music bred a mania for dancing, and Norfolk feet tripped both the light fantastic and grosser variations. Dances were commonplace at the pleasure gardens and a "Fancy Ball" in 1829 featured four hundred dancers costumed as Turkish and Persian princesses, French and Swiss peasant girls, Margaret of Anjou, and "a Polish Lady," among others. The local military sponsored frequent balls, sometimes on board ship.[23]

All of the city's resources of literary, dramatic, and musical expression were called forth on Friday, October 22, 1824, with the arrival of the Marquis de Lafayette, guest of the nation. The man and the moment—an epoch of intense nationalism—met as the steamboat *Petersburg* glided to the public wharf bringing the old general, Secretary of War John C. Calhoun, and other Washington and Richmond panjandrums. Lafayette had been constantly in the public eye since Yorktown, owing to the French Revolution and its tumultuous aftermath. The years had transformed him from an idealistic young aristocrat into a figure of mythic proportions, and no community felt equal to giving him the honors he deserved.[24]

Two hours before the 4:00 P.M. descent, the ringing of the courthouse bell summoned citizens and military units to formations on Market Square. The general was received at the wharf by Mayor John E. Holt and the Common Council, while a band played "Hail, Columbia." He was paraded under a handsome Main Street arch of flowers and evergreens to lodgings at Mrs. Hansford's boarding house on East Main.

The parade was led by a military guard followed by Lafayette's carriage, and groups comprising the arrangements committee, clergy, corporation officials, lawyers and doctors, army and navy officers, four companies of infantry, the Marine and Mechanic societies, "the body of citizens," and schoolchildren with their teachers. A "general illumination" from 6:00 to 10:30 P.M. featured forty-two waterfront bonfires and many homes showing transparencies with mottoes and welcoming messages.[25]

Lafayette stayed three days, during which he visited Fort Monroe, was banqueted on Saturday, was accompanied by the Masons to church on Sunday, and was honored at a Monday evening ball in the unfinished and hastily decorated Water Street customs house. Businesses enjoyed a three-day respite from hard times as concessionaires peddled revolutionary cockades and badges, Lafayette belts and sashes, and Joseph T. Allyn's bookstore did a good business in biographies of the general. Many witnesses recalled it as the grandest celebration in old Norfolk's history.[26]

A long-remembered event of another kind was a sensational murder case in the spring of 1821, resulting in two of old Norfolk's rare executions. In a small house in Fox Lane, between Cumberland and Church, lived Frenchman Peter La Gaudette and Spaniards Emanuel Garcia and Santiago Castilano, all said to be members of a band of highwaymen infesting county roads. One morning a young girl on her way to school heard cries inside the house and, through a back window, saw the Spaniards bludgeoning La Gaudette. The child summoned help, and a party led by Mayor Holt found La Gaudette's headless corpse in a trunk in the house. A hunt was organized, and the Spaniards were found at Lambert's Point.

A jury convicted them, their motive evidently being a dispute over the

division of some spoils; both were hanged at the gallows near the "old magazine" on "Pudding" (or Put-in) Creek on June 1. Garcia was hanged first,
the hangman ignoring Santiago's advice to knot the rope at the neck rather
than behind the head. Before a large crowd from Norfolk and Portsmouth,
Garcia strangled in agony rather than having his neck broken instantly. Castilano, allowed to fit his own noose, dropped to instant death.[27]

Fire gutted parts of Norfolk several times a year, though no general conflagration occurred. Serious downtown fires in 1824 and 1827 prompted
the banning in the latter year of new wooden buildings south of Fenchurch
Street.[28] The fires had the useful result of permitting rebuilding on plans
superior to those of the past, and Norfolk's appearance underwent continual
improvement. All who could afford it replaced wooden houses with brick.
The town's evolution from mud-spattered Billingsgate to a city of some
charm and taste was celebrated in the travel accounts of Mrs. Royall, the
muck-raking Washington widow.

Her appraisals could be devastating. She immortalized the keeper of
Norfolk's Steam-boat Hotel as "a wild beast, unworthy of patronage, and
his clerk no better; the man ought to be fined, and his license taken from
him." (She was convicted in a circuit court the next year as "a common
scold.") But the lady could be as lavish in praise as in damnation, and she
remarked in 1828 on Norfolk houses that were "large and elegant, and many
. . . surrounded with beautiful trees. . . . The town is not only neat, it is
beautiful. The streets are well paved, lighted, and the neatest kept in any
town in the Union, except Providence. I do not except Philadelphia." Royall,
a friend of Mayor Alexander Galt, was gilding the Norfolk lily, but the city
was taking its appearance more seriously than in former times.[29]

It seemed to her, in fact, that "the whole world had conspired" to injure
Norfolk's reputation. Its people were hospitable and polite, with more taste
and refinement than any other town in Virginia, resembling, indeed, those
of Boston. When a traveler stopped with them, they "ransacked" the markets for delicacies of the season and fasted until the next arrival. Every private house had half a dozen black servants, every tavern or boarding house
from ten to thirty. Because blacks did all the work, however, white women
tended to be "pale, bloated, slothful, and always complaining," their kitchens filthy and "cooks abominable."[30]

The city market was a delight to the lady, who, arriving in April, saw
fresh strawberries, cucumbers, potatoes, green beans, peas, and so on "in
the greatest perfection and abundance"; meat was of poor quality but offset

by fresh fish, fowl, and game. The produce carts that served the city were drawn by little horses "about the size of a two-year old cow, and nothing but skin and bone," their black drivers "the most insolent of any thing that can be called human."[31]

With business at a low ebb and many jobless, Norfolk residents increasingly associated themselves with organizations devoted to recreational or charitable activities or, like the Freemasons, to both. Among the former were musical societies, the Norfolk Dancing Assembly, thespian groups, and the Norfolk Debating Society. Charitable and religious groups included the Norfolk Bible Society, Tract Society, Provident, Dorcas, Temperance, Humane, and Benevolent Mechanic societies, and the Sunday School Union. (There were four Sunday Schools, the oldest founded in 1816 by the Presbyterians, though the Episcopalians and Methodists followed in the same year and the Baptists two years later.)[32]

Municipal authorities provided relief for certain widows and orphans, as well as aid to the "outdoor poor" and inmates of the city workhouse and poorhouse. Efforts were also made in behalf of sufferers elsewhere, as when a major fire hit Savannah in 1820 and in the Greek revolution four years later. Such causes lost a strong advocate with the death of George W. Camp in 1823. Camp, in a three-year period, was secretary of the Bible Society, treasurer of the American Colonization Society, major of the Fifty-fourth Regiment of militia, and city collector and register.[33]

One glimpses in these years seedlings that became a rich harvest in later generations. The Common Council appointed Mary Booze as messenger, bellringer, and keeper of firebuckets and ladders for a period of years and hired Sarah Wells as matron and nurse at the Norfolk Infirmary. Mary Chandler was the first "directress" of the French Orphan Society. The Dorcas Society, staffed by female volunteers, aided the city's poor, especially women and children. Rachel Collins was a respected free black noted for having nursed, cooked, washed, and found lodgings for local militia in the War of 1812.[34] Through such service and activity in city churches, women began to attain official positions and exercise a measure of community leadership.

The most significant benevolent group was the Norfolk chapter of the American Colonization Society. The ACS, founded in 1816, launched a Norfolk branch five years later. The thirteen charter members included James Nimmo, president; attorney-poet William Maxwell, secretary; George W. Camp, treasurer; and six ministers. Its aim was to help free blacks and freed slaves travel to lands acquired by the ACS in Liberia. Humanitarian feelings played a part in its motives, but the removal of free blacks was also seen as a way to foster the security of the slave system.[35]

Colonizationists walked a slippery tightrope between endorsing the sanctity of slavery and the virtues of freedom. Inevitably, as in 1826, they sometimes lost their footing. In July the *Herald* carried the views of "Liber," probably William Maxwell, who assailed slavery as "the greatest of calamities and disgraces." He cited Jefferson's uncomfortable dictum that "all men are created equal," highlighting a "glaring inconsistency" in American life. The article set off a furor, capped by an angry public meeting and demands for tarring and feathering the author.[36]

The ACS survived the embarrassment, and several blacks native to Norfolk or well-known in the city became leaders of the Liberia colony. Lott Carey, a Baptist preacher with kinfolk in Norfolk, emigrated under ACS sponsorship in 1821 and became vice colonial agent of Liberia, the colony's second-highest office. Norfolk native Joseph Jenkins Roberts became a prosperous Liberian merchant, who, in partnership with a Petersburg associate, owned his own steamboat. He rose to become the first president of the Republic of Liberia, the only head of state Norfolk has produced.[37]

An interesting case of a black set free from slavery's coils was that of Old Paul, servant in the early nineteenth century to Dr. George Balfour, senior surgeon at the Marine Hospital in what is now Berkley. Sold to a Frenchman, he was taken to France and exhibited as "Old Paul the Wild Man." He was forbidden to utter a word during exhibition and denied any of the profits. Eventually, two Englishmen unmasked the charade, the Frenchman absconded, and Paul was put aboard a Virginia ship at Bordeaux. Captain Frederick Williams, a Norfolk man, brought Paul to Norfolk and set him free among "friends and acquaintances." Old Paul, converted in France to Roman Catholicism, claimed to be 104 years old.[38]

Norfolk's free blacks supported colonization and individual emigrants with funds, but showed little interest in going to Africa. They gave relief to hundreds of blacks from other areas who came looking for passage on ACS ships, but put little trust in the notion of exchanging familiar perils for unknown ones. A few, such as Rev. Abraham Cheeseman and family, were moved to help blacks in Liberia make the adjustment to freedom, but the emigration of Norfolk blacks amounted to only a trickle.[39]

Some slaves who might have gone to Liberia may have been inspired by Moses Grandy's story to stay and take their chances. Grandy was a Camden County, North Carolina slave who, allowed to hire himself out to canal boat

Joseph J. Roberts was a native of Norfolk who became the first president of the Republic of Liberia. He served from 1847 to 1855 and from 1871 to 1876. He remains the only person from Norfolk to serve as head of state. (Courtesy of the Historical Society of Pennsylvania, Philadelphia, Pa.)

operators during the War of 1812, earned the $600 his master agreed to accept for his liberty. After his final payment, his master sold him to a merchant, with whom he repeated the experience, paying $600 for his freedom only to be sold locally once more. Undeterred, he made a third arrangement to buy himself by borrowing money from a Deep Creek merchant named Minner, who was outraged by the perfidy of the former masters. After working three more years on canal boats, Grandy paid Minner off and received papers attesting his freedom.[40]

As required by Virginia law, he left the state, moving to Rhode Island. He hoped to find means to buy freedom for his wife and children. During the 1820s he worked as a seaman on ships trading in the Mediterranean and both Indies. Eventually, $300 bought his wife's freedom and, later, another $450 that of his fifteen-year-old son, from a Norfolk master. He was living in Boston in 1844 when, unable to read or write, he dictated an account of his life for publication in the hope that sales might help him find and recover four other children who had been sold away to Louisiana. Whether he succeeded is unknown, but he set a noble example of perseverance in any case.[41]

The Dismal Swamp Canal that helped save Moses Grandy was also counted on to save Norfolk. An economic problem in the Hampton Roads area, the dimensions of which were only beginning to be recognized in the early nineteenth century, was the decline of farm income. The swampy, sandy soils of the region had never been very productive. Elizabeth City and Warwick counties once had fertile tobacco lands, but they were now worn out by poor farming methods. Wheat grew in limited areas of these counties but not in Norfolk or Nansemond. Only Princess Anne produced hay and cattle in quantity, and local cattle were of poor quality owing to primitive husbandry—letting the cattle forage for themselves in thickets.[42]

Area farmers were excited over prospects for short-staple cotton in the 1820s, but found that they could not compete with Deep South cotton and began to abandon the crop. With only Indian corn to sustain them, many farmers emigrated westward and Norfolk Borough's population actually declined between 1810 and 1820; it remained virtually static for decades. A Norfolk County farmer in 1834 wrote the *Beacon* that many farmers ruined themselves by reliance on "Lumber getting" and proposed that Norfolk and Princess Anne form an agricultural society to foster scientific methods. (One was organized within two months after that.)[43]

Help seemed to be coming. By 1826 the swamp canal brought in about a million staves and six or seven million juniper shingles a year. This was pitifully short of the builders' early hopes and meant little benefit either to

Norfolk or the canal company. Yet the future remained promising, in part because the Corps of Engineers was making surveys and planning improvements that could open the canal to larger payloads. A new feeder ditch from Lake Drummond guaranteed it sufficient water even in dry spells.[44]

In addition, Virginia's legislature encouraged improvements to navigation of the Nottoway and Meherrin rivers as well as the upper Roanoke, and North Carolina sponsored work on a canal around the Roanoke falls at Weldon. Such work was slowed by the Panic of 1819, but revived as business improved in the mid-1820s.[45]

The canal benefited from a series of developments in the late 1820s. Work on the stone drydock at Gosport, large enough to handle any ship in the U.S. Navy, started in late 1827. The Corps of Engineers completed its canal survey and proposed alterations in the locks, excavation to widen the canal, raising some of its banks, dredging creeks at each end, and so on. In 1829 the federal government bought two hundred more shares of canal stock to provide funds for the work. President Jackson came to Gosport in July and was taken on a barge down Deep Creek and six miles into the canal for a picnic of Virginia ham and other delectables.[46] "Uncle Sugar" had only begun to show what he could do for Norfolk.

As the improvements proceeded, the newly organized Virginia and North Carolina Canal Company (with George Newton as president) had a fleet of eleven two-masted canal schooners built at Portsmouth and Norfolk. Three small steamboats were purchased as towboats for canal barges—one for the canal itself, the rest to ply from Pasquotank River to the Roanoke and points south. A second canal hotel, called the "Half-Way House" and straddling the state line, opened in 1829, the same year traffic began using the renovated canal. By now the upper Roanoke was largely cleared of obstructions and a canal was open around its falls.[47]

The great Roanoke artery hummed with excitement as heavy traffic began to move southeastward to Norfolk. A hogshead of tobacco formerly costing over $24.00 to send from Lynchburg to Richmond went to Norfolk via the canal for only $8.50. Canal tolls tripled between 1829 and 1833 from the ceaseless cargoes of lumber, naval stores, cotton, tobacco, flour, and corn. Traffic rose to as much as a hundred vessels a month, the canal giving Norfolk a full 90 percent of its business, though many boats passed by to Baltimore, Philadelphia, and elsewhere.[48]

Manufacturers, who had always steered a path around Norfolk, sensed better prospects. The *Beacon*, in a six-month period starting in mid-1829, announced the opening of two cotton mills, a Briggs Point iron foundry, and

Captain James R. Nimmo's tobacco stemmery on Cumberland Street. An 1835 industrial inventory showed cabinet furniture and carriage works, boot and shoe makers, hatters, saddlers, tanners, and a manufacturer of oil.[49]

The navy opened its Gosport drydock in 1833, said to be the first of its kind in the western hemisphere, with a chamber eighty-five feet wide and over 250 feet long. The era of careening ships for repair ended on June 17, when the USS *Delaware* was drawn into the drydock while throngs watched from nearby stands. Navy shipbuilding on the Elizabeth River, aided by easy access to Carolina lumber and naval stores, surged ahead, as did private construction. Government spending for docks, storehouses, workshops, and warships greatly expanded the market for rope and sails, ironware and timber, the hiring of carpenters, shipwrights, and other craftsmen. Norfolk by 1836 had ten hotels, three banks, three steam mills, three tanyards, and two ropewalks. Ten steamboats operated between its wharves and those of Richmond, Baltimore, and other ports.[50]

Even so, the swamp canal brought only limited prosperity. Despite its magnificent harbor, Norfolk did not ship produce to Europe or the West Indies but still sent it in coasting vessels to Baltimore, Philadelphia, New York, and Boston. Such bulk produce as Norfolk handled in quantity made for poor payloads. Shippers complained that the canal was still sluggish. It was so clogged with logs at some points that vessels were forced to unload and lighter around some places; vessels could not pass each other between the narrow banks.[51]

None of this caused much consternation, nor, at first, did a Petersburg announcement in August 1829 that a railroad would be built from there to the Roanoke River below the falls. The line would compete with the swamp canal for the Roanoke Valley's business, but, as a sage voice of experience observed to the *Herald*, "A railroad, I believe, has never yet beat a canal."[52] It was whistling in the wilderness.

CHAPTER 12

Last Train to Margarettsville

THE *Herald* gurgled with uncharacteristic rapture over "the chimney of the locomotive, with its stream of sparks lighting up the gloom of the swamp." Perhaps, the editor seemed to imply, the sparks could transform the dark of economic blight into a noonday of prosperity. The rails "pierced the recesses of the forest, and brought within the reach of a ready market, an inexhaustible store of the most valuable timber," opening to cultivation "large tracts of rich alluvial land, for ages abandoned to forests." Even the dreary town of Suffolk on this grand morning seemed "worthy of a poet's lay," the denture-loosening ride to Nottoway River such a passage as the traveler "cannot but be delighted with over a road that has no superior."[1]

In mid-1835 there remained over forty miles and sixteen months before the Portsmouth and Roanoke Railroad reached its terminus near Weldon, but its benefits were already being felt. Horse-drawn produce cars had hauled bacon, vinegar, and lard from as far away as Southampton and Isle of Wight counties since the summer of 1834. A year later, a determined traveler could take the stagecoach at Halifax, North Carolina, alight some hours later at Murfee's east of Nottoway, and catch early morning cars to the west end of High Street in Portsmouth. Here, carriages conveyed him to the wharf for the teamboat (established in 1821) or steam ferry *Gosport* to Norfolk and the daylong steamboat trip to Baltimore.[2] Complicated it might be, but this was long-distance travel at speeds unknown to any earlier generation of humankind.

The *Beacon* urged readers to take the rail trip for the sheer thrill of hurtling cross-country at up to twenty miles an hour. A dollar bought eighty roundtrip miles of this glorious touring "through a highly interesting country in a delightful conveyance," and Murfee's Tavern, at the far end, served cool milk and "delicious apple pies" from a "splendid orchard." The five-and-a-half-ton locomotive *John Barnet* made the trip twice a day and was soon to be joined by the powerful *General Cabell*.[3]

The rail line was not simply a wondrous means of terrestrial locomotion; it was a mailed fist aimed at the thrusting chin of malignant Petersburg, a city evidently bent on reducing Norfolk to a fishing village. The Portsmouth and Roanoke was the latest tactic in a bitter rivalry between Hampton Roads and fall line towns for the teeming Roanoke Valley business. That trade had to flow either to Petersburg and Richmond or to Portsmouth and Norfolk; it was not bountiful enough to do both. The former towns enjoyed a near-monopoly of the trade before the 1828 reopening of the Dismal Swamp Canal, endured a challenge until completion of the Petersburg and Roanoke rails in 1832, and now were threatened again by the Portsmouth tracks. The line from the Elizabeth River, trumpeted the *Herald*, would "bid defiance to competition and insure us . . . the entire produce of the upper Roanoke."[4]

The new railroad, conceived in Portsmouth and headed by Arthur Emmerson of that town, soon won the support of the Norfolk business community. Faced with the swiftly progressing Petersburg project, Norfolk in 1832 initially promoted both the Portsmouth idea and tracks between North Carolina's Tar and Roanoke rivers, which might double canal commerce. But backers of the second plan, chiefly canal director George Newton and merchant James E. Roy, found few investors and focused instead on the first. Others felt that the Roanoke track, terminating at Portsmouth, might be of little use to Norfolk or injure the trade of the canal.[5]

The Portsmouth company, already two years behind Petersburg's, got off to a painfully slow start owing to a cholera epidemic in the summer of 1832. There was more delay when Petersburg blocked state aid for the Portsmouth and Roanoke in 1833. By the time a second application to Richmond won approval the following year, the Petersburg rails were handling Roanoke River produce. Norfolk churchbells rang out and rockets fired at news of the bill's passing; the borough subscribed $100,000 of the railroad's stock, Portsmouth another $50,000, in the race to catch up.[6]

The contest moved from legislative halls to accountants' ledgers as Norfolk tried to make up lost time and revenue by laying timber foundations instead of stone, iron-plated wooden rails instead of solid metal. Costs remained high because the distance to the Roanoke was greater from Portsmouth—seventy-eight miles—than from Petersburg and meant bridging the Blackwater, Nottoway, and Meherrin rivers. But early indications, after the Portsmouth trains became fully operational in 1836, were that profits would excuse the cost-cutting expedients and justify the expense.[7]

The companies now carried their battle to the scramble for Roanoke trade, where the outcome would ultimately be decided. They had reached the Roanoke almost within sight of one another, the Petersburg tracks terminating at the Northampton County hamlet of Blakely's Depot (Garysburg), Portsmouth's opposite Weldon. An advantage seemed likely for the first to bridge the Roanoke, and it was the Portsmouth firm which, by heavy borrowing, succeeded in doing so in 1837. Petersburg investors failed to get Norfolk approval for joint ownership of the bridge and rejected prohibitively high fees demanded for its use.[8]

Even though the nation at this point tumbled into financial panic and a long depression, other developments kept hopes of victory high among supporters of both railroads. A North Carolina company with steamboat connections to Charleston in 1840 completed what was then the longest rail line in the world (161 miles), between Wilmington and Weldon. These rails connected with those from Portsmouth, but a line was completed almost simultaneously from Raleigh to join the Petersburg route at the town of Gaston, a few miles northwest of Weldon.[9]

But Petersburg worked a stunning strategic manuever in 1836 by building a spur southwest to the village of Gaston, six miles upriver from Garysburg, to intercept Roanoke traffic en route to Weldon and Halifax. It also connected its tracks to others through Richmond to the Potomac, creating a north-south corridor whose speed and convenience Norfolk could not match.[10]

Norfolk clutched frantically at Petersburg's throat by slashing rates and coordinating rail schedules with those of Chesapeake steamboats and Wilmington trains. Petersburg, with deeper coffers, withstood the rivalry better, but both lines suffered sharp cuts in profits. A rumor went abroad that Petersburg would "run for nothing and give a bottle of wine" before it would be undercut. Norfolk was also soon paying the price for its shortsighted savings in construction costs when iron strips began to come loose from the wooden rails. On December 10, 1837, an engine struck a projecting strip of iron and hurtled off the track, killing two passengers and injuring eight others; South Carolina Senator William C. Preston was one of those who escaped unharmed. An August accident had injured seventeen.[11]

Its optimism sustained by its new link south to Wilmington, the Portsmouth and Roanoke revamped its management (North Carolina's Andrew Joyner becoming president) and decided to risk further debt to refurbish its equipment. Heavy engines that split the rails were replaced by lighter ones, new rails were installed, rotten ties were replaced, modern cars were purchased. Lookouts were posted atop baggage cars with a rope attached to a bell to warn the engineer if emergency stops were necessary, and the High Street tracks were extended to the ferry wharf.[12]

Petersburg and Richmond still had the great bulk of Roanoke trade, but Norfolk and Portsmouth girded their loins for an all-out assault to take the prize. (There was talk of rails to connect Norfolk with Edenton on Albemarle Sound; Edentonians, though confident that they would benefit, were said to object that it would also help Norfolk!) In the war of words, Norfolk insisted that Petersburg was too far inland to aspire to become a port; the latter replied that Norfolk was cut off from the state's productive regions by swamps and "sterile plains."[13]

Heightening the ferocity of the contest was a realization that, apart from reordering the rhythms of existence for those who used them, railroads were shown to have results their builders had not foreseen. Trains brought cheap fertilizer to farmers along their routes, turning desolate acres into shimmering green fields. Sheriffs and militia officers took note that slave revolts, such as Southampton's in 1831, could now be quelled within hours by heavy infantry and artillery from Hampton Roads and Norfolk.[14] But north-south traffic was unlikely to sustain lines to both Petersburg and Norfolk. The fight must almost certainly end in the sacrifice of one line to the salvation of the other.

The railroad came four years too late for many residents of southeastern Virginia. If October 2, 1824—Lafayette's arrival—was old Norfolk's grandest day, Monday, August 24, 1831, was its moment of epic horror. Early afternoon brought news that slaves in Southampton County, fifty miles southwest, were in revolt and indiscriminately killing whites. Here, for the first and only time in Virginia's history, was no mere rumor of some vague plot, no roundup of blacks on the eve of an aborted rising, but the authentic embodiment of the white South's worst nightmare.

Many whites assumed at once that Norfolk's blacks—two-fifths of the borough's inhabitants—had foreknowledge of the revolt and would strike their own blow at any hour. The town council convened at once on Monday afternoon and sent the navy yard a plea for arms and ammunition; the mayor was delegated to convey the alarm to Fort Monroe. Appeals for help went to the warships *Natchez* and *Warren* in Hampton Roads; militia units were assembled. Dr. William B. Selden's daughter Susan wrote her brother that she had no "chit-chat" to share because "the alarm has suspended every thing else & nothing is heard but the firing of arms . . . nothing seen but uniforms and warlike looking men."[15]

Three companies of Fort Monroe regulars with artillery were delayed in leaving until the steamboat *Hampton* returned in the evening from its weekly trip to Smithfield. But the army was en route up the Nansemond by 3:00 A.M. Tuesday and a body of Norfolk militia followed some hours later on the steamboat *Constitution.* A day or so of reflection suggested that Norfolk's blacks must have been as astonished as whites—the night of August 23, when "all the men in the place were half drunk . . . after the election," having been the optimum moment to strike. A black brass band, organized in 1830 by Norfolk's Light Artillery Blues for parades and such, was dismissed in October, its instruments sold and the proceeds divided among its members.[16]

Wild apprehension gradually gave way to edgy relief as the Southampton affair, although the bloodiest slave revolt in southern history, proved to be a local outbreak and, for all intents and purposes, was broken up within thirty hours of its onset.[17] White and black Norfolk populations, however, were profoundly affected by the incident, albeit in far different ways.

Senator Littleton Tazewell, home from Washington between sessions, rarely left his Main Street house during the alarm, fearing for his family's safety and neglecting his business and plantations. The revolt converted Tazewell, prior to his 1834 election as governor, into an advocate of wholesale emancipation and colonization, which he had previously thought unrealistic.[18]

In two years as governor, Tazewell had to address the emerging issue of abolitionism in the wake of Nat Turner's revolt. Norfolk, still shaken, was arresting suspected abolitionists as early as the summer of 1835, and a bundle of abolitionist literature was found late in the following year at the foot of Market Street. Copies of *Human Rights* and William Lloyd Garrison's *Emancipator,* addressed to free blacks, turned up in the post office in July 1835, prompting the Hustings Court to request that the postmaster withhold delivery of such material. Tazewell asked the legislature to request northern states to suppress abolitionist groups and Congress to forbid distribution of incendiary publications through the post office. The latter request was granted.[19]

In the adjacent Norfolk countryside, Nat Turner's insurrection was taken by some whites as a license to wage war against free blacks (slaves might claim a measure of protection as someone's valuable property). The Charles A. Hodges farm in the Blackwater section was especially suspect during the alarm because its black proprietor had employed Englishman Charles Blatchford to conduct a school for black children.

Hodges' son Willis later described how "They came to our house and took Mr. Blatchford, and a young colored woman by the name of Eliza Nelson, who . . . could pass for white. They . . . took all the books, papers, bibles, dresses," and so on, carrying the prisoners to the Princess Anne jail. Many of both sexes were packed into a single room, where disease broke out. Blatchford, detained for no special reason, became mortally ill; he was released after some days, but could stagger only about two miles before "he fell dead by the roadside." Others died in jail and many free blacks abandoned their property and fled the state permanently.[20]

Hundreds of Southampton's free blacks fled to Norfolk to join those of Princess Anne and Norfolk counties seeking colonization society help to emigrate to Liberia. (More than three hundred went out on an ACS ship in December.) But Kinner Flerry, a Norfolk County free black, was among those who, unable to pay his jail fees, was sold at auction. His master, Josiah Wilson, later refused to let him visit his home even when Flerry's wife died and, when he went anyway, had him beaten so severely that he "died in a few weeks."[21]

The alarm also triggered a spasm of concern over the condition of Virginia's militia, a victim of Richmond's chronic budgetary hypothermia. Ill-armed and poorly trained, the militia could make colorful displays in their white pants and bobtail coats but were a source of alternate amusement and dismay to professional military people. After a "Regimental Review" at Norfolk in 1845, a militiaman described to the *Beacon* how his company, the "Avengers,"

> carried canes, . . . what [arms] nature gave them, a few, muskets, and the greater part umbrellas (the wise ones). . . . There was no end of nodding plumes, scarlet sashes, and gleaming bayonets. . . . The music was . . . inspiring especially that of the perservering fifer; it was impossible to witness without admiration the intense efforts he made to keep a note or two ahead of the drum, and how coolly the drummer took it. It would have animated the soul of a sluggard.[22]

Veterans of the slave alarm, by climbing atop a nearby fence, might be further agitated by viewing "the crumbling battlements of Fort Barbour," as the old works below Norfolk were now called. Fort Monroe notwithstanding, local defense left much to be desired.[23]

The city suffered a more fatal shock in the spring of 1832 when a cholera epidemic, working its way down from Canada, reached Norfolk in June, attacking especially the black population. The Tazewell family lost its laundress and then a gardener who, stricken while walking along the street on a Sunday morning, died within twenty-four hours. Servants were so terrified that they could not perform routine tasks, and rural people declined to bring produce to the market. Families like the Tazewells could pack off to Old Point Comfort or some other sanctuary, but more than four hundred were dead before the malady passed. "Of all the scourges which have ever afflicted the human race, in the shape of disease," wrote Tazewell to a friend, "nothing has equaled the cholera."[24]

Free blacks relied on close-knit families for guidance and help in crises. The choice of a marriage partner, for example, might involve many relatives and weighty issues of social distinction and family respectability. Race was a factor; mulattoes sometimes rejected those of darker hue in the hope of narrowing the divide between themselves and whites. This could mean searching abroad for a suitable match, as when Nancy Fuller, a Norfolk free black, wed Alexander Jarrett, a free man from Petersburg, and *Southern Argus* pressman Richard Cowling took a Washington, D.C. bride. Princess Anne's Willis A. Hodges returned from his New York business to scout Norfolk prospects, found all "far from . . . perfection," and wed a well-to-do New York widow.[25]

Because so many free black men worked as farm or gang laborers outside the city, women far outnumbered them in town. Norfolk's 176 free black families in 1830 were almost evenly divided between male- and female-headed households. The ratio of the former fell further in the next three decades, owing to the erosion of job opportunities in the city. Free blacks sometimes took slaves for spouses but man-wife relationships tended to be egalitarian owing to the dependable earning power of women. Scarcity of black men contributed to the willingness of some black females to become concubines of white men. British Consul George Mason, on leaving for England, provided for the maintenance of his free black concubine Mary Buchanan and the education of their two children.[26]

After the twin crises of rebellion and epidemic in the early 1830s, Norfolk enjoyed a long period of relative tranquility. In the absence of significant growth and opportunities for wealth, Norfolkians focused more fully on the enhancement of the quality of their lives. They were aided by what Common Councilman Thomas G. Broughton called a "popular revolution" in city elections in the early 1830s, a local manifestation of Jacksonian democracy. Some older and more experienced councilmen were ejected by voters and others brought in "who had never before been thought worthy of serving." Despite fears that the town "was about to be turned out to grass," the new council distinguished itself by carrying out needed improvements and laying groundwork for others. Beginning in 1843 the mayor's office was filled by popular election.[27]

Now the home of some six thousand people, Norfolk on February 13, 1845, ceased to be a "borough," its charter amended by the assembly to make it a "city." Hereafter, the thirty-seven-member Common Council, elected triennially, chose from its number an eleven-member select council, city offices (except mayor) being filled by joint vote of both bodies. The Hustings Court, long occupied, as some saw it, by "old Fogies," yielded to the council's jurisdiction over streets and properties, a measure attended with useful results.[28]

The new almshouse, opened in 1839 at the northwest edge of town, replaced the dilapidated poorhouse and embodied more enlightened principles in oversight of the poor, including some free blacks. A three-story structure of forty-two rooms, it had separate wings for males and females and extensive land for crops to feed inmates and provide surpluses for sale. As in the past, inmates spent most of their time at a dull indoor routine of picking oakum (hemp fibers to fill the seams of ships' hulls). But there were now the options of tending a "cocooning room" for silk worms and six acres of mulberry trees to feed them, as well as vegetable gardens and berry patches. Norfolk also had a "Hannah More Society" dedicated to the education of poor children.[29]

A major undertaking was the filling in of the upper part of Back Creek and creating in its place a handsome public square. Back Creek had for over a century been an ugly rent in the garment of the town, "a loathesome marsh" of foul odors and pestilence, and a nuisance to traffic. With its filling-in from east of Bank Street to the south end of Cumberland Street, the new ground was planted in shade trees, laced by paved walks and ornamental railing, and crowned by a new city hall (now the MacArthur Memorial). New clerk's and register's buildings were located to the rear of city hall and Norfolk Academy soon stood on the north side of the square. By 1836 Norfolk, we are assured, had more miles of paved streets than any other city in the South.[30]

Actor George Jones brought Norfolk a welcome amenity in 1839 by opening the Avon Theater on part of the reclaimed land. The Fenchurch Street theater had been closed and sold in 1823 to the Methodists (it burned in 1845). The Avon, a stuccoed brick edifice with six impressive Doric columns on full pediments, boasted interior ornamental paintings by Jones, a fine artist. It remained popular until it, too, burned in 1850, the year the Mechanics Hall theater opened on the south side of Main Street.[31]

Campaigns were waged in the 1830s to improve water quality and supply, lay off a new cemetery, and erect a public library and new academy (some fifty or sixty boys heretofore had been sent elsewhere each year for schooling). Some of the proposals were inspired by the celebration on September 15, 1836, of the borough/city's centennial, a time for reflection on what had been achieved but still more on what had not. With such advances finished or underway, Norfolk could give éclat to its reception of the exiled Louis Napoleon, future French emperor, who put up briefly at French's Hotel as its first guest in April 1837. A suitable send-off was also given the Wilkes Exploring Expedition, which left Hampton Roads in August 1838 to probe the Pacific in the American government's first such venture.[32]

A discerning visitor was Englishman James Silk Buckingham, whose book of travels, *The Slave States of America,* appeared in 1842. In the past, English wayfarers had been unkind to Norfolk, but Buckingham's views, perhaps reflecting a budding rapport between the two countries, were more favorable. Even he noted that there seemed "little of hope or energy" in Norfolk's mercantile houses (he arrived as the latest business slump began) and found "few public buildings of great beauty or interest."[33]

But Buckingham saw much to admire despite his strong disapproval of the institution of slavery. The new Avon theater was almost complete and tragedian Jones hoped to kindle, by a return to Shakespeare and the classics, a "reform of the drama" such as England had lately enjoyed. Buckingham had visited Norfolk in 1809 and was struck by the progress since then; the streets were straighter and broader as well as paved, and the houses were often made of brick rather than wood. The city now covered some eight hundred acres and was sprouting new neighborhoods outside its boundaries. The Gosport navy yard was the best in the country, and the Marine Hospital in Portsmouth was "the best building of its kind" in America.[34]

The Englishman, though appalled that many families had disappeared in the past three decades from epidemics and emigration, was fascinated by Norfolk society. There was, he felt,

more leisure, frankness, refinement of manners, and less of nationality, than [in] Northern cities. The number of persons in easy circumstances, living on . . . landed property rather than trade, is considerable. . . . the merchants and traders are not so entirely engrossed with the accumulation of money, as to have no time for other thoughts. The tone of conversation among the men is, therefore, more elevated, and their manner more gentlemanly, than those of the mercantile society generally of the North.[35]

In a word, Buckingham felt more at home at Norfolk than in comparable northern towns. He saw "many very beautiful women" with "the same superiority of manners" as their men, the result, he supposed, of "leisure for cultivation and polish." No "absurd competition for display" was seen, no "straining everything to the utmost in dress and parties, to outrival each other." Class distinction, at least among whites he met, was muted; they seemed "to feel themselves sufficiently on a footing of social equality, . . . fresh, cheerful, and unaffected in their behaviour."[36]

The "tone of conversation" in Norfolk owed something to the accumulation of several large private libraries by members of the commercial and professional elite. Descendants of Moses Myers, for example, owned hundreds of choice volumes gathered from European as well as American sources. Moses' son Samuel had left a collection of some four hundred books, including works of Cicero and Virgil, Hume and Voltaire. The shelves of his brother John ran to more modern writers, such as Burke, Cobbett, Sterne, and Alexander Hamilton. Louisa, Samuel's widow, owned a large Shakespeare collection, along with novels, poetry, and travel accounts.[37]

Visits by Buckingham to the neat and well-furnished Episcopal and Presbyterian churches showed that the influence of Swindells and Dacosta was still powerful; the music and singing were generally superior to that in English churches. The absence of discernibly poor whites in the congregations somehow suggested that "want of food, raiment, or comfortable dwellings, is unknown among them," a notion that a stroll along any downtown street ought soon to have dispelled. Buckingham was offended, however, that blacks were separated in "side galleries" and felt that the "unappropriated" seating of Catholics and Methodists better reflected the brotherhood that all should feel in the sight of God.[38]

Buckingham reveals a Norfolk that in some measure had surmounted its narrowly dollar–chasing repute and acquired at least a high veneer of gentility and urbane self-confidence. But the Englishman failed to depict what for many visitors in these years was a more notable feature of the town: its unanticipated emergence as a place of scenic beauty. Although they dated only to postcolonial rebuilding, the waterfront townhouses impressed the new arrival with their "time-worn and venerated aspect," their seeming claim to a hallowed antiquity.[39] Springtime travelers were often enchanted by the brilliant splashes of dogwood, yellow jasmine, azaleas, and redbuds that ornamented gardens, streets, and open spaces. A Baltimorean fell quite under the spell of Norfolk's northern prospect in the autumn of 1840:

> I stood upon the shore where the still music of the waters faintly murmured. . . . The evening sun was sinking, as it were, in a cloud of gold; a few thin clouds, tinted with a thousand variegated hues, hung in matchless beauty over the gloomy deep, reflecting the rose and violet upon its surface. . . . Far as the eye could reach [were] the snowy sails of the gallant vessels moving to the gentle breeze, and then gradually disappearing in a crimson halo.[40]

Those seeking more than city streets might take a scenic walk out to Lambert's Point Road for a fine view of Hampton Roads, Craney Island, and the estuary of the James. Or, the hiker could journey out to Indian Poll Bridge over Tanner's Creek and view the patrimonial homes of the Talbots and Ivys. Crossing the eastern branch drawbridge, another walk led east to the pleasant village of Kempsville or south to Deep Creek for a view of the canal and a drink of juniper water. The more adventurous might hike out to Magagnos (now Ocean View) on the bayshore and, if overnight lodging could be had, continue to the Atlantic's rim, which, the *Beacon* confided in 1835, "is never visited" for want of a hotel.[41]

Hikers who paid attention to crops along these buccolic pathways might discern the early stages of major changes in local farming. In 1837 Edmund Ruffin, editor of the influential *Farmer's Register*, derided farming in the area as "rude and degraded" and prophesied that "the howling of wolves will be heard from the suburbs of Norfolk" unless changes were made. At his prodding, some farmers replaced unproductive crops and methods with more rational ones. Ruffin especially championed shell marl as a fertilizer, while the *Beacon's* Hugh Grigsby kept up a drumbeat for "cottage gardening" (truck farming), dairies, and orchards. Noting the many "snug farms" in 1839, Grigsby deplored the neglect of pears, plums, and nectarines, the absence in Norfolk and Princess Anne counties of first-rate peach or apple orchards.[42]

The importance of fruits, berries, and vegetables was that the mild climate and sandy soil of lower Hampton Roads made these products available for northern markets four to six weeks ahead of those of northern farmers. Here was profit awaiting Elizabeth and Lynnhaven area farmers, so much so that Grigsby was convinced that more income might be had from fifty

well-tended acres in Hampton Roads than from a five hundred-acre plantation in the upcountry. A triweekly steamboat connection with Baltimore was
established in 1840, with the early prospect of a daily boat.[43]

Grigsby argued, however, that capitalizing on the opportunity required
farmers to adopt better ditching and draining systems. Cattle must be
housed at night to be protected from inclement weather and be fed rather
than allowed to graze on the area's ill-tasting wild plants. More must heed
the example of a Lambert's Point grower who had large flocks of turkeys,
and of Richmond's W. J. Grieves, who in 1844 bought a farm twelve miles
from Norfolk and began growing fruit, flowers, and shrubs for his Norfolk
store.[44]

Another and more important arrival in 1844 was New Jersey's Richard
Cox, a seasoned truck farmer who rented land on the Elizabeth River's western branch and began reinventing local farming. Cox and other transplanted
Jerseymen, especially partners named Bates and Hatch on the western
branch (who preceded Cox by two years), introduced the area to hothouses
("glass culture") and other innovations in market gardening. Astonished
neighbors noted that the Jerseymen got $40.00 to $50.00 a barrel for cucumbers, $15.00 to $20.00 for peas. Many turned quickly to growing these as
well as tomatoes, cabbages, strawberries, squash, lettuce, beets, and so on.[45]

By 1849 annual income from Norfolk County truck farming was more
than double that of a decade earlier. Truck farms, soon "situated in every
direction for many miles," offered "a striking contrast . . . to the old-
fashioned Virginia farms, among which they are scattered." Greater sensitivity to the tastes and needs of the northern urban market had resulted in
a large increase in growing Irish and sweet potatoes. By midcentury the long
agricultural depression of the lower Tidewater was over.[46]

The Portsmouth and Roanoke Railroad in the meantime had become a
keen disappointment to investors and the region in general. Petersburg's
astute interception of upper Roanoke trade at Gaston, a huge burden of
debt incurred by the Portsmouth line, and debilitating rate wars of the two
companies were only the more obvious problems of the P. and R. The closing of Norfolk's United States branch bank in 1836, a result of Andrew
Jackson's war against the bank's directors, led to a recall of large loans in the
Norfolk area, injuring some of the most active Elizabeth River businessmen.
The federal government suspended funding of improvements on its Hampton Roads facilities, laid off many workmen, and even closed the Dismal
Swamp Canal for a time owing to damage at its lower end in the summer
of 1834.[47]

Such problems intensified the Hampton Roads–Fall Line rivalry. What historian T. J. Wertenbaker has called the "Fall Line Blockade" was now in place, Petersburg and Richmond successfully manipulating the state legislature to help draw the bulk of western trade in their direction rather than Norfolk's. Lacking the fall line's industrial strength and access to Virginia's main crops, the Hampton Roads towns had neither the capital nor political influence to pierce the blockade. Even the appointment of a well-qualified Petersburger to the presidency of Norfolk's Exchange Bank in 1840 was seen by some as a plot to bring Norfolk more surely under the control of its upcountry rivals.[48]

Ironically, a Norfolk man was in these years making a national name for himself as a pioneer in railway technology. Edward A. G. Young, reputedly the first American to operate a steam locomotive, was the son of a Norfolk ship's captain. Among his inventions in the service of a Delaware railroad in the 1830s were a new type of locomotive and a spark catcher to prevent fires along the tracks. Isaac Clowes of Norfolk was inventor in 1834 of a device for overcoming friction in railroad cars. Perhaps even more gifted was a Norfolk slave-artisan named Jasper, said to have invented a reaper a decade before Cyrus McCormick, a machine for weaving fishnets, and a powder-making machine.[49]

The P. and R. continued to turn a modest operating profit but paid little on its debts and no stockholder dividends. Its looming collapse was signaled in 1843, when leading creditors pressed for payment. The largest of these, the firm of Clements and Rochelle, builders of the Weldon Bridge, sold its claims against the line to Captain Francis E. Rives. As a Prince George County legislator, Rives had fought the chartering of the Portsmouth route and was thought to be an agent of Petersburg interests. When the Weldon Bridge and seventeen miles of P. and R. rails in North Carolina were sold in 1843 to satisfy debts, Rives got control of the property. A diabolical, if hilarious, scheme was now hatched for the P. and R.'s ruin. Norfolk was shocked to learn in January 1844 of Rives' strategy.[50]

"In the dead hour of the night," on January 5, Rives sent forty black workmen to Margarettsville, North Carolina, near the southern termini of the two railroads. Next morning Rives' crews set to work tearing up two miles of the Portsmouth tracks. A train from Portsmouth, halted by the destruction, raced back to report what was happening to P. and R. President (since 1842) Walter Gwynn. Gwynn called on fellow citizens of Portsmouth to turn out en masse to save the railroad, and between thirty and forty answered his appeal in a headlong rush by train to Margarettsville, where Rives was remorselessly ripping up tracks.[51]

Arranging orders for timber en route, Gwynn reached his destination in late in the afternoon of January 7, posted men to prevent further destruction, and led ten to Garysburg, where Rives was reported to be at the hotel. Gwynn presented Rives a written demand to desist from his wrecking and warned that he would use force if necessary to stop it. Rives replied that he could raise as much force as Gwynn. The latter now sent for the Northampton sheriff to meet him at Weldon, and dispatched workers to repair the tracks and remove obstacles from them.[52]

Outnumbered, Rives sent an engine to Petersburg for reinforcement. The next morning he and others began throwing rails off the Troublefield Bridge and cutting its braces. The Northampton sheriff arrived with a posse and arrested Rives. When the case came before the North Carolina supreme court in 1845, the justices were asked to decide whether a railroad, as a public right-of-way, could be sold. They held that it could and that Rives, as lawful owner of P. and R. facilities in North Carolina, might destroy them. Outgunned and outwitted at almost every turn, the P. and R. was sold in 1846 to a Boston firm and reorganized as the Seaboard and Roanoke.[53] The fall line route savored the fruits of victory, and Rives was elected mayor of Petersburg.

At this low point in Norfolk's corporate fortunes one began to hear serious argument that the city should secede from Virginia and seek annexation by North Carolina, whose future seemed more closely allied than Virginia's with Norfolk trade. Norfolk investors were persuaded that the state government was an alien entity, their own town "the goose to be plucked by our more favored neighbors." Fittingly, the largest gain from all this regional and municipal conflict was that of Baltimore, which had quietly run its own rails all the way to the Ohio River, giving westerners a convenient route to the upper Chesapeake while its Virginia neighbors flayed one another toward bankruptcy.[54]

The Portsmouth and Roanoke Railroad consumed almost $1 million in construction and maintenance expenses, cost Norfolk Borough and its investors nearly as much, and never paid a dividend.[55] Its revenues had risen almost yearly up to 1842 but did little more than cover operating costs. Norfolk's one percent annual growth rate since the century's early years was not appreciably altered during the railroad's lifetime. The city's economic malaise now reached back over four full decades and had resisted all efforts at amelioration.

The newspapers sometimes lamented failings of local character and initiative, but most Norfolkians saw their city as the victim of evil outside forces. Federal and state policies as well as the ugly jealousies of rival cities were chief among these and no doubt played their part. But beyond all guilt and blame lay the workings of ineluctable Fate, concatenations of uncontrollable world events that brought unanticipated windfall as readily as unpredictable disaster. Norfolk was to experience an extraordinary measure of both in the years immediately ahead.

CHAPTER 13

The Ghosts of Julappi

It came, as hostile Armies come,
    At night upon a camping host,
With muffled tread and noiseless drum,
    When sentries sleep upon their post,
It came, as bursts the surging flood,
    Unwarned by storm or clouds of dun;
The moon's bright robes changed not to blood
    Nor darkness veiled the stars and sun.
—DR. SAMUEL SELDEN, "The City of Pestilence."

AFTER so frightening a final week of July 1855, it was good to hear from the lips of a physician that "the yellow fever was not so bad in Norfolk as people made out—that they were more scared than hurt." In fact, there was no reason why the Lamb family should not return on August 2 from "Palestine," its country place seven miles downriver, to its newly enlarged and remodeled Catharine Street house. The *Herald* had lately reported that "at no point within our memory, has Norfolk been more healthy than it is at present." Like others, the Lambs saw it as "ridiculous" that the Richmond and New York steamers would come no nearer than Old Point and that some excitable people were fleeing Norfolk altogether.[1]

July did, however, offer Norfolk a sobering scare. On the twenty-fifth, Robert W. Warren, a Norfolk clerk at the Gosport works of Page and Allen, took ill with the fever; he died four days later. On the twenty-sixth, the Norfolk board of health prudently ordered all vessels that arrived in the Elizabeth River from places south of Charleston quarantined. There must be no repetition of the fatal summer of 1852, when several hundred cases had been reported locally and between fifty and a hundred died.[2]

The latest outbreak, now evidently receding, began after the steamer *Ben Franklin* arrived from St. Thomas on June 6 with several victims on board.

The June 24 death of a Mrs. Fox, at Scott's Creek below Portsmouth, was the first local case, but it was July 8 before Portsmouth's town council sent the *Ben Franklin* from Gosport back to the quarantine grounds where it had earlier spent thirteen days. By now, a Gosport machinist named Carter was dead and several other Gosport victims were in the Marine Hospital. Despite a police barricade at the Gosport navy yard entrance and five hundred barrels of lime on Portsmouth's streets, there were eighteen cases south of the river by July 23, eight of them fatal. But it still seemed likely that the epidemic could be confined to the Gosport and Irish Row communities, the latter a slum near the navy yard "overcrowded with inhabitants, and filthy in the extreme."[3]

Norfolk's hopes were dashed on July 25, when the fever was found in squalid Barry's Row, a block of fourteen tenements south of Main Street, to which some Gosport families were allowed to move to escape the malady. The outbreak here was, perhaps, predictable; as William Lamb reflected in his diary, "The row of shanties is a perfect cess pool of pestilence. The Irish living there are almost in as degraded a state as they are in the half-starved districts of Ireland." The board of health on July 30 finally conceded that an epidemic existed and had the district vacated; a twenty-foot-high board wall was erected along Church Street from Union to Water streets in hopes of restricting the disease.[4]

By August 1 Portsmouth was in a panic. Tar fires were set in the streets to combat noxious air but seemed to have no effect. A pesthouse was opened near the Portlock Cemetery, but stores and hotels were closing, the telegraph office had shut down, and over four hundred employees took leave from their jobs at the navy yard. A new sanitary committee began inspecting streets and lots for places that might breed disease and ordered physicians to report each day's new cases by sunset. That these measures had little influence with the public was indicated by the two to three thousand who abandoned Portsmouth by August 3.[5]

William Lamb, freshly graduated from the College of William and Mary, was pleased to see many of his friends in Norfolk on August 3, including Miss Ann Lighthisse and cousin Agnes Suffern, and enjoyed an evening walk with Margaret Reardon. Norfolk seemed, indeed, "more scared than hurt," the fever being now "on the decline," though "raging terribly in Portsmouth." Mayor Hunter Woodis, Dr. George P. Upshur, Father O'Keefe, and the Catholic Sisters of Charity earned the city's gratitude, in Lamb's view, by tending the sick at the height of the crisis.[6]

Norfolk, however, was about to share not only the Portsmouth fever but that town's stricken response. On August 9 several cases were reported on Main Street and areas outside Barry's Row. When a report circulated that some poor families were returning to Barry's Row quarters, the area was again cleared on the night of August 9. With the approval of some three thousand onlookers, it was set on fire in three places and burned down, though it was unclear who was responsible.[7] Two days later the *New York Times* reported that seven thousand people had fled Norfolk and Portsmouth, with more leaving as fast as they could arrange transportation. Norfolk reported seventeen new cases and two more deaths up to 2:00 P.M. the previous day. Victims usually languished five or six days after the first symptoms appeared, though some died within forty-eight hours.[8]

Norfolk's slalom into hysteria, worsened by the closing of city newspapers, was also abetted by the response of places where its residents sought refuge. The commandant at Old Point was said to have turned back "at the point of the bayonet" those trying to land there; the town of Weldon imposed a $100 fine on anyone coming from "an infected city." A Portsmouth mail stage to Elizabeth City, North Carolina, was turned back ten miles short, only the mail being allowed to pass. Hampton, Suffolk, Smithfield, and other towns, with Baltimore, New York, and other Norfolk trading partners, took restrictive measures, some interrupting all contact, against Elizabeth River persons and produce. Mathews and Gloucester counties and the eastern shore were among the few places offering hospitality from the start, though Fredericksburg and other towns were again accepting Norfolk refugees by late August.[9]

By August 14 the fever had advanced north from Main Street; the district to the south was all but deserted. Only the hacks and carriages of scurrying doctors and nurses moved in the streets. Nearly all shipping left the harbor, warehouses were locked, Sundays saw no church services anywhere in the city. Famine gripped some districts; the city market ceased to function except for fishermen and rural blacks hawking a few vegetables. Every Bermuda Street household was said to have fever cases; on Briggs Point victims died by the dozens daily. Even the wealthy district north of Back Creek was swept from end to end. In the surrounding country, some found refuge in private homes; others commandeered cabins, schoolhouses, churches, tents, and barns.[10]

By August 24 Norfolk and Portsmouth were experiencing one of the most deadly epidemics ever to invade urban America. The former had at least five hundred cases of yellow fever, with more reported hourly. There were twenty-five burials the next day; the daily figure soon rose to eighty or more, with up to thirty additional deaths in Portsmouth. Thirty-four deaths were reported among thirty-six occupants of two adjacent Norfolk houses. Instinct associated the disease with refuse and bogs but none could guess its cause or any way to combat it.[11]

Gravediggers ceased to dig individual graves, hacking out pits and trenches for as many as forty coffins each, two or more corpses to a coffin. Coffins, now almost unobtainable, were stacked in as many levels as a grave allowed. Those for whom coffins could not be had were simply wrapped in blankets. Though burials continued, funerals ceased. "Arrived at the lot belonging to the family," wrote Dr. George Armstrong, "we find no grave dug there as yet. . . . The hearse cannot wait; all we can do is to deposit the coffin where the grave is to be dug, and, offering a short prayer, there leave it."[12]

Years afterward, Norfolk's Dr. Samuel Selden recalled these weeks in grieving verse:

> The watchman from his post retreats;
> The dogs in packs all night now prowl,
> Through empty lanes and dreary streets;
> Like famished wolves they mourn and howl;
> . . .
> Some staggering by the wayside lie;
> In solitude some wavering sink,
> No friend to close the glazing eye,
> No hand to give the cooling drink;
> Hearts that could once with pity throb,
> Are changed to stone or cold as dead,
> And find that some the dying rob,
> Ere yet the gasping breath has fled.[13]

Not only the poor and overcrowded were afflicted, but leading families as well. The disease carried off Mayor Woodis, Select Council President John G. H. Hatton, Farmer's Bank teller Alexander Feret, legislator-elect William D. Roberts, and others of prominence. City government ground almost to a halt because of the death, illness, or flight of officers. "Our city," wrote a resident, "may be aptly compared to a ship at sea without a rudder, or compass, or officers to direct, and with only a few hands at the pumps to keep her from sinking, and these nearly exhausted with fatigue."[14]

On September 6 martial law was declared so that private vehicles might be seized for use by doctors and undertakers. Although almost two-thirds of the city's residents were said to have left, four hundred bodies were buried in the first week of the month. With the city government all but closed down, its treasury locked, and revenue collections halted, the board of health served as a virtual committee of safety struggling to continue some public functions. Hospitals so overflowed with patients that the Julappi Racecourse buildings on Lambert's Point, three miles from town, were pressed into service as infirmaries while other sufferers were packed into the City Hotel.[15]

Those who remained seemed like zombies, "appalled and chilled, careless and reckless," going about "the work of boxing and removing the dead, with but little appearance of fear or agitation." Since it was deemed too late to flee, they waited for "the venom" to enter their blood and add them to the mortality lists. "Poor unfortunate Norfolk," wrote William Lamb. "The reign of Know Nothingism has been visited by a curse."[16]

Lamb's reference was to the new political alliance, officially the American Party, which won control of the city government in 1854 and retained most offices in 1855. A movement founded on opposition to American Roman Catholicism and liberal immigration laws, Know-Nothings were supported by the *Beacon* and other elements of the community, including many shipyard workers. With the Whig Party in decline in the 1850s, many Whigs affiliated with the Know-Nothings purely in the hope of defeating the Democrats. Whigs were especially attracted by KN support for the Union against secessionists, but many were quite as willing to bait Catholics and immigrants if it produced votes.[17]

Despite Norfolk's tradition of tolerance for religious and national minorities, Know-Nothingism found fertile soil as soon as it arrived in 1854. Most of those attracted to it were disconsolate Whigs, but Know-Nothings tapped a well of resentment against the city's six hundred or so Irish Catholics and the ire of native workers over competition from a few German artisans. The *Beacon* was given to calling immigrants "the scum of other countries who would rather beg than work, and rather steal than beg." The Know-Nothings lost to Democratic gubernatorial candidate Henry A. Wise in 1855, but had the year before elected as mayor former Whig City Attorney Simon Stubbs and took over the councils. Though Democrat Woodis defeated Stubbs in 1855, Know-Nothings kept nearly all other city offices.[18]

Normally a Whig bastion, Norfolk was the only area of the state to change parties from 1852 to 1855, and it remained for several years a hotbed of Virginia's KNs. The sentiments they fed gained strength in 1856 from revelations of Josephine Bunkley who, by her account, fled from a Maryland convent to Norfolk with her father to escape Catholic debauchery. A book under her name sought to expose not only the convent but an alleged plot to take over the country in the pope's name. The damage had been done by 1859 when Miss Bunkley recanted her allegations and apologized to the church. By that time Father Francis O'Keefe of Norfolk's St. Patrick's parish had barely escaped an attempt on his life, and Irish and German immigrants had been subjected to ugly campaigns of abuse.[19]

The epidemic rescued surviving Catholics from their oppressors. Father O'Keefe and the Sisters of Charity were conspicuous among those who, refusing to desert the city, stayed through the crisis to aid victims. When many gravediggers died, O'Keefe and Dr. Armstrong dug graves. Sister Mary Augustine, director of St. Mary's Asylum and Free School, was another heroine of the epidemic and Portsmouth's Father Devlin died a martyr while attending to the sick. Know-Nothing political strength continued until 1859, but attacks on Catholics and immigrants became more muted and indirect. Catholics celebrated vindication in 1856 by opening the Academy of St. Joseph and De Paul Hospital. With the burning, probably by arsonists, of St. Patrick's Church, St. Mary's (still standing) was erected two years later.[20]

Whether in the hands of Whig, Democrat, or Know-Nothing, the municipal government in the decade preceding the epidemic was emerging as a powerful instrument for change. This awakening activism owed much to southern concern over increasing northern dominance of the nation's economy. That dominance, it was clear, was rooted in the strength of the North's industries and cities. If Virginia and the South were to avoid permanent dependency on the North, they must find ways to invigorate their own cities and manufactures. State goverment must adopt a more supportive attitude toward the role and function of cities.[21]

A reflection of this view was the dawning awareness on the part of Norfolk leaders of factors that contributed to a city's economic health and attractiveness and how city government could affect these. This awareness found a Norfolk voice with the establishment in 1847 of the *Southern Argus*, a daily whose stated aim was "to stimulate to active enterprise our commercial community." Editor Hugh Grigsby became spokesman and cheerleader for a militant philosophy of urban progress. (The ardent boosterism of the *Argus* led it to suppress for six weeks news of the yellow fever epidemic!)[22]

A vibrant economy presupposed conditions far outside the narrow nexus of cash for goods. A long-standing complaint agitated in councils and newspapers was teenage gangs who on Sundays lounged about the wharves "smoking segars, chewing tobacco," quarreling, fighting, and pilfering fruit from Market Square produce carts. Many carried clubs, dirks, slingshots, and pistols, and on Sundays and evenings vandalized lumberyards and warehouses. Illegality and immorality flourished in such ghettoes as the "red-light" district around the intersection of Avon and Wolfe (later Court and Market) streets and the "Frog Town" area between Church and Fenchurch streets. Such problems made Norfolk less inviting to commercial agents and country vendors. They were arguments for a larger police force, which was increased in 1854 to twenty; Richmond, with twice Norfolk's population, had only thirty.[23]

Other nuisances included cows allowed by their owners illegally to roam the streets and packs of dogs that attacked pedestrians and one another and howled horrendously throughout the night. A new "cow law" at the start of 1852 netted eighteen street-browsing strays on the first day, but canines defeated all campaigns against them. The city might never have the wheat and tobacco processing plants it needed unless such annoyances were eradicated.[24]

The black draymen who hauled produce and imports back and forth from the river were often assailed for galloping and racing. The *Beacon*'s sardonic "Rules for Draymen" included: (1) "Excite . . . your horse by seizing the reins and jerking them" violently, (2) "Spring upon the hindmost edge of your dray, and pull upon the bit, leaning back . . . , until the shafts make an angle of 45 degrees with the ground, . . . their ends above the horses neck," (3) "Cut your horse severely, and travel the streets without regard" to anyone's safety. But draymen were a scarce and independent lot. In 1822 they went on strike against a $20.00 annual city tax and won public support to get it rescinded.[25]

Some city streets gave promise of successful resistance to improvers. "Frogtown Marsh" was a stagnant sump that bred malaria for a quarter-mile around. "Hen-house Lane" was a gloomy black enclave where fortune tellers and conjurers plied their trades. The intersection of Fayette and Broad Water, like the ends of nearly all streets in the lower part of town, was usually "in a swimming condition" for want of proper drainage. "Cow Bay" was "a miserable little alley" running out of Little Water Street. A black ghetto, it was "bordered on all sides with dirty and filthy houses—a hive" of eight-to-ten room buildings (including cellars and attics), each crammed with up to two or three hundred people.[26]

Blacks annoyed some whites by their very existence. Letters to newspapers demanded that they be forbidden to walk two abreast on the sidewalk, that black women not be allowed to wear bonnets or silks, that blacks not carry canes or umbrellas. A group of blacks was arrested at a white proprietor's "rum mill" on Broad Water on the Fourth of July 1852 and reprimanded at the Mayor's Court because six had danced noisily to a fiddle played by a seventh. Discovery of an illegal Masonic Lodge and a "colored benevolent society" led to concern over black "secret societies."[27]

Among the offending groups was an "underground railroad" of agents who spirited slaves off to freedom. A black named Henry Lewey, code-named "Bluebeard," not only helped slaves flee to Canada and the northern states, but handled the transmission of mail and belongings between those who escaped and Norfolk-area friends. When local authorities began investigating his affairs in 1856, Lewey fled to Canada. Sam Nixon, who learned dentistry under his owner Dr. C. F. Martin, was another agent of the network, eventually escaping to New Bedford, Massachusetts, where he opened a dental practice. A group of fifteen slaves escaped to Philadelphia on the ship *Keziah* during the yellow fever epidemic.[28]

The state of race relations in the aftermath of Nat Turner's revolt and the ensuing abolitionist campaign was evinced by a judge's action in lightly reprimanding two whites who stoned a black laborer to death in 1852. When the mayor let some blacks stay out past 10:00 P.M. curfew to hold a ball in 1850, there was angry public reaction. Even the use of thirty-six blacks to light the way for a torchlight parade of William Lamb's militia company in 1858 drew public criticism. Lamb's *Southern Argus* was harsh on blacks, meticulously printing any news item that cast aspersions on them and editorializing vehemently against them.[29]

A concern of many whites, partly accountable for the popularity of the Know-Nothings, was competition for available work among native whites, Europeans, and blacks. Loammi Baldwin, an engineer at the Norfolk navy yard, used black stonecutters in the 1830s at a fraction of the cost to the public of whites. The practice apparently spread, for in 1851 Norfolk's white artisans appealed to the state to ban free blacks from all trades. The hiring-out of slaves was another irritant to white workers as was the employment of white women in counting rooms and other positions, a practice favored by the *Argus* in the labor-short early 1850s.[30]

Owing in part to the absence of satisfactory urban transport, many free blacks lived in shanty towns interpersed among white residential and commercial areas, chiefly in the city's northern half. Such ghettoes were often only a short distance from places of black employment. Even within predominantly white areas it was not unusual to find integrated streets or tenements where whites could keep a vigilant eye on slaves, who might live with or frequent the homes of free blacks. Since black women were more often emancipated than men and found work more readily in white homes, most free black families were headed by females. The social results included a high incidence of concubinage of black women to white men and a high proportion of mulattoes.[31]

By 1851 Norfolk blacks were served by four evangelical churches where service as deacons, stewards, wardens, and trustees prepared many for leadership in the black community. The Cumberland Street Methodist Church in 1840 established a mission for slaves; the congregation's growth was so rapid that it acquired a second meeting place in 1848 at an old soap factory near East Main. (In 1863 it would join St. John's African Methodist Episcopal Church, said now to be the country's oldest black Christian organization.) First Baptist met between 1830 and 1859 in an old warehouse near the corner of Catharine and Freemason, moving in the latter year to Bute Street. Other blacks were members of the Cumberland Street Baptist Church, formed when First Baptist Church split in 1816.[32]

Norfolk's Catholic church also had black members from an early date, sometimes even solemnizing illegal marriages between free blacks and slaves. In 1839 the First Baptist Church minister officiated at the marriage of a Catholic priest to a free black woman, causing a critical division within his congregation. The result was the withdrawal of the remaining First Baptist whites, who then formed what became the Bank Street Baptist Church. Racial hostilities borne of such incidents may have been behind the torching of Third (or Hawk Street) Baptist Church and fire damage to the new First Baptist Church in 1855.[33]

By the 1850s, if not before, city fathers began to see inferior social conditions in terms of their negative effect on business. A way to get white boys off the streets was to put them in school, where only 40 percent of Norfolk's boys between six and sixteen were enrolled. So city leaders in 1855 created four free school districts. Voters in each chose a commissioner to administer its school; the commissioners formed a board of education that chose one of their members to serve as superintendent. All four schools opened in 1856, with any white male between six and twenty-one eligible to attend and costs paid from a $2.00 tax on white men. The new system put Norfolk at the forefront of public education in Virginia. A manual-labor school opened in 1854.[34]

Blacks, free and slave, were barred by law from such opportunities, though Christ Church had a large, illegal Sunday School where black children learned to read and write as an inducement to Bible study. Mrs. Margaret Douglass and her daughter Rosa were arrested in 1853 for running a school for twenty-five free black children. Mrs. Douglass cited the Christ Church precedent and called as witnesses court officers who taught at the Sunday School for blacks. A Charleston native, she suffered under the infirmity of having lived in Norfolk only eight years; convicted, she was sentenced to a month in jail. After her release, she moved with her daughter to Philadelphia. (Bute Street Baptist Church in the 1850s had six black Sunday School teachers.)[35]

Margaret Douglass's spirit lived on in the town of Hampton where, in the early 1850s, a black Norfolk native, Mary Smith Kelsey Peake, headed an illegal school for blacks. The daughter of a free black woman and an Englishman "of rank and culture," Mrs. Peake had been educated in Alexandria. At Hampton she conducted classes for as many as five hundred pupils at a time before losing her house to a fire that swept Hampton in the early months of the Civil War. She died of tuberculosis at age thirty-nine in 1862.[36]

A healthy business climate demanded serious efforts to aid the uninstitutionalized poor. Attorney Tazewell Taylor and banker John G. H. Hatton led a movement in 1848 to make such aid more effective by forming the Norfolk Association for the Improvement of the Condition of the Poor (AICP). The group periodically visited homes of the poor to gauge needs and ferret out "artful mendicants." Its efforts gave the city poor the first year-round aid they had ever had, supplementing the work of the all-female Dorcas Society—active only in winter and emergencies—and the Humane Society, an all-male counterpart. The Norfolk Howard Association started during the yellow fever plague.[37]

Norfolk became more livable with the establishment of the Norfolk Gas Lighting Company on Briggs Point in 1849. First Freemason Street, then others, were equipped with pipe-fed gas lamps as were many buildings and private homes. The plant burned twice before rosin replaced coal in gas production. Though the new lighting system tended to be erratic, the *Argus* revelled in "all the mantled and silvery light, . . . the friendly lamps . . . like so many faithful sentinels at their posts." A handsome granite customs house with an elevated Roman portico, the city's third since 1789, was finished in 1859 (and still stands).[38]

An important investment for the future was the purchase by a group of forty Norfolk-area men of the 360-acre Magagnos farm on the bay shoreline in 1854. The group announced its intention to erect villas along the beach as summer retreats for themselves and friends. The site, already celebrated for its pleasant beaches, breezes, and vistas, would later become known as Ocean View.[39]

Norfolk's leadership elite in these years, comprising only about three-score individuals, also sought the city's advance by promoting direct trade with Europe to reduce subservience to northern ports. Virginia's first direct-trade convention was called by Norfolk in 1850, and three years later Dr. Francis Mallory was sent abroad in the hope of initiating a direct steamship line with Belgium. The new Seaboard Agricultural Society sponsored an agricultural fair in 1854, which helped stir the issue of the lack of a first-class hotel for visiting farmers and businessmen. (There were four of small repute, and visitors often had to seek lodgings in private homes or in Portsmouth.)[40]

Among the most effective members of this leadership elite was Henry Irwin, a commission merchant who, during the 1850s, was a founder and vice president of Norfolk's board of trade, director of two banks, officer of the Seaboard Agricultural Society, and city councilman. Irwin in this decade organized and managed a hotel and a steamship company, founded an insurance firm, headed the New Orleans Relief Society after that city's 1854 yellow fever epidemic, and was a leader of Norfolk's Association for the Improvement of the Condition of the Poor.[41]

A singular element of the effort to refurbish Norfolk's trade and its image was William S. Forrest's *Historical and Descriptive Sketches of Norfolk and Vicinity*. Published in Philadelphia in 1854 with an eye to attracting northern recognition of Norfolk, it was full of the kind of special pleading that undergirded urban boosterism. "Our coloured people," readers were assured, "the slaves particularly, are generally happy and contented."[42]

As to Norfolk's reputation as an unhealthy place to live and a danger even to visit, well, that was all a notion rooted in the experience of dissipated soldiers stationed there in the War of 1812 and some unfortunate remarks in William Wirt's "Letters of the British Spy." The truth, in Forrest's estimate, was that "the climate of Norfolk is utterly unsuited to the dissemination" of yellow fever and the health of its vicinity "for miles around" had "greatly improved" in the past twenty years.[43]

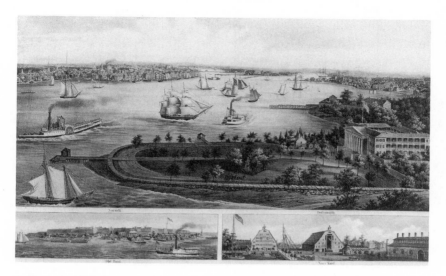

E. Sachse's 1851 drawing shows the steamboat *Herald* (left) leaving the harbor on its regular Baltimore run. (Courtesy of The Mariners Museum, Newport News, Va.)

The necessary condition for civic progress was universally held to be railroads, and the gathering intersectional crisis was eroding the old animosity among Virginia's cities. It had also become clear to wealthy farmers and other rural denizens that the countryside gained from the growth of its market centers. With intercity and rural–urban jealousies in retreat, Virginia between 1847 and 1861 built more railroads than any other state. Norfolk, its lack of rail connections retarding both industry and direct European trade, stood to benefit from the new mood.[44]

The favorable new view of internal improvement led to the rebuilding of the Seaboard and Roanoke Railroad; it opened to Weldon in 1851, joining there with the Wilmington route. Two years later, the Raleigh and Gaston laid rails from Gaston to Weldon to allow a Raleigh–Norfolk connection. Especially coveted was a line to Petersburg and Lynchburg to link up with the Virginia and Tennessee Railroad, which eventually extended to the Mississippi. Petersburg interests opposed it and the legislature dragged its feet, but the Norfolk and Petersburg road began operations in 1858.

A survey was directed by Norfolk resident William Mahone for a railroad between Norfolk and New York. Meanwhile, the James River and Kanawha Canal was extended below the falls at Richmond and the Albemarle and Chesapeake Canal was cut in 1859 between North Carolina's North River and the Elizabeth River's eastern branch as a deeper and faster alternative to the Dismal Swamp Canal.[45]

Such extensive and expensive projects seemed likely to transform Norfolk into the world-class market and industrial center it had long dreamed of becoming. But they had not produced, by early 1854, results that would necessarily impress critical visitors. Frederick Law Olmstead, future designer of New York's Central Park, came through in January 1854 and found Norfolk "a dirty, low, ill-arranged town, nearly divided by a morass." He saw but one "creditable public building"—presumably city hall—though there were some handsome private homes. Conceding the "agreeable, refined, and cultivated" society—attributable to "the families of the resident naval officers"—he felt that Norfolk had "all the immoral and disagreeable characteristics of a large seaport, with few of the advantages that we should expect."[46]

In particular, Norfolk had no public library, garden, or art gallery, "no public resort of healthful and refining amusement, no place better than a filthy, tobacco-impregnated bar-room or a licentious dance-cellar . . . to pass the hours unoccupied by business." Indeed, "if a deadly, enervating pestilence had always raged here, this Norfolk could not be a more miserable, sorry little seaport." As with nearly every other objectionable thing Olmstead saw on his lengthy southern journey, he was inclined to blame all symptoms alike on the institution of slavery.[47]

No doubt Norfolk's deficiencies impressed other observers this way, but it was an unbalanced characterization nonetheless. Evidently Olmstead could get no ticket to the New Orleans Opera Troupe at Ashland Hall on the evening of his visit—the *Beacon* called it "an unbounded success."[48] If the city's sense of the proper use of taxation did not yet encompass art galleries and libraries, it was not that Norfolk was culturally deprived.

An invitation to the Grigsby home on East Main would have allowed Olmstead to inspect Raphael's *Madonna of the Straw Chair*, other Madonnas by Murillo and Correggio, Sully's *The Maid of Athens*, a moonlight view of the harbor of Messina by Claude Lorrain, and other works of modern and classical art. Sculpture interspersed among the paintings in this home included a bust of Cleopatra from excavations at Alexandria and a collection of the work of Norfolk's own Alexander Galt (son of a former mayor), whose career Hugh Grigsby had assiduously patronized.[49]

The Grigsby library, including many volumes from that of John Randolph of Roanoke, would have introduced Olmstead to a 1630 translation of Ovid by Jamestown Colony secretary George Sandys—perhaps the rarest literary work in Virginia. Grigsby's volumes included works of Bolingbroke, Lyttleton, Burleigh, Fox, Walpole, Addison, "and a thousand others" in the fields of science, geology, zoology, art, architecture, mythology, political economy, and poetry in many languages. Grigsby himself was author of several books, including a life of Governor Tazewell (1860) and some pleasant verse. Olmstead was in town too briefly to become acquainted with the Philharmonic Association, a sponsor of musical entertainments, or the Washington Library Society, which maintained a subscription library and supported a public lecture series.[50] Forrest's history of the city in the same year as Olmstead's visit contained poetry and essays from a gallery of Norfolk writers. Notable among them was Martha Haines Butt, whose work appeared in national magazines and periodicals. Richard Halstead, R. James Keeling, Abram F. Leonard, Byron Walthall, S. S. Dawes, and attorney William Wallace Davis also warranted mention.[51] Though Norfolk claimed no special notice for the effusions of such scribblers, the city had ten newspapers—three triweeklies, a weekly, and six dailies—in which amateur talents vied for notice.[52]

Norfolk in the 1850s, with its 185 streets and lanes, was a town of fourteen churches, nine schools and seminaries, and a telegraph company. Its social life was enhanced by the Oddfellows, Masons, Sons of Temperance, Druids, Rechabites, Red Men, and United Mechanics. Regular steam packets connected the city with New York, Philadelphia, Baltimore, Washington, Richmond, and other cities, besides stagecoach and railroad routes. Its mile-long wharf district, from Town Point on the west to the eastern branch drawbridge on the east, accommodated forty warehouses. There were some seventy wholesale and retail grocers, with a great variety of dealers in other commodities and services. Industry was scattered about town: steam mills, a ropewalk, a tannery, and a cotton factory on Smith Creek and its tributaries, waterfront shipyards, carriage and harness works, iron works, block and pump makers, and so on.[53] Norfolk was no sprawling metropolis, but a town possessing the sinews of a place of potential consequence.

Wealthy merchants and professional men built homes on Main Street east of Church Street or in the northwestern part of town, notably on Bute, Freemason, Boush, and Granby streets. The lower classes crowded tenements on narrow streets off West Main, along Church, Bermuda, Hartshorn's Court on Briggs Point, Holly Place off James Street, and the labyrinth of alleys off Water Street known as "Cow Bay." Blacks huddled in the northern half of town, especially on Charlotte, Amelia (later Boush), and Church streets and the vicinity of the Almshouse and the cemetery near the Church

Street–Princess Anne Road intersection. A hotel district had risen around the intersection of Main and Church. Numerous eateries were found on lanes and streets just off Main.[54]

Know-Nothing rule, however, appears to have left a legacy of fiscal mismanagement that generated allegations, never proven, of possible embezzlement of tax revenues. By early 1860 teachers' and janitors' salaries were $2,500 in arrears and the city treasury lacked the funds to pay them. There seems to have been no investigation, and the problem was evidently soon swallowed up in the radical dislocations of the war-year 1861.[55]

It was the grotesque shift in fortune's winds that spun the city about in midcourse, as in 1776 and 1807, and cast it again on the rocks of ruin. Yellow fever shattered the city at the threshold of its Reform Age renaissance and placed in jeopardy the gains of the preceding decade. In September 1855, at the plague's height, a physician observed of the bustling suburban cemeteries: "The city and country have exchanged character. The latter now wears the busy aspect which of right belongs to the former, and almost the silence of death reigns in the deserted streets."[56]

Even the deity appeared to frown pitilessly on dying Norfolk. A day of thanksgiving had been declared by Mayor Stubbs in the previous November for the city's escape from epidemics that prevailed in other cities, and a day of fasting and prayer was observed in August of this appalling season.[57] The fever raged on with ever-heightening intensity for all that.

Yet a cause for thanksgiving amid the wails of the dying and bereaved was the outside aid Norfolk and Portsmouth received. By late August, coffins from Richmond, Baltimore, and other cities helped relieve a critical shortage. There were gifts of clothes, food, cigars, wine, and leeches (for medical bleeding). Baltimore sent bread, rice, pork, beef, butter, coffee, cheese, and milk. (The Baltimore boats were met and unloaded well out in Hampton Roads to minimize the chance of infecting Maryland.)[58]

Communities across the nation held fund drives, and numerous individuals sent cash or checks. These eventually totaled an estimated $250,000 for Portsmouth and Norfolk combined. Most was used or distributed by the Howard Association, a relief agency formed in August under the presidency of William B. Ferguson and, after his September death, A. B. Cooke. Among the many works of the organization was the creation of an asylum for hundreds of newly orphaned children. By the end of August the specter of famine, at least, appeared to subside.[59]

More gratifying still were the legions of volunteers who came to Hampton Roads communities to offer their services to the sick and dying. The first of these, Miss Annie M. Andrews of Syracuse, New York, who arrived in mid-August, was followed by many volunteer nurses and doctors, most of them from places such as New Orleans, Mobile, and Charleston, where yellow fever was a familiar phenomenon. Railroad and steamship companies offered free transportation to medical personnel bound to and from Norfolk and Portsmouth.[60]

More than sixty volunteer doctors, eight each from New Orleans and Philadelphia, were swept off by the fever, along with ten resident doctors, seven local ministers, and many nurses. A martyr-heroine was Miss Ann Plume Behan Herron who, after making her home available as an infirmary, died of the fever. She left her estate to the Sisters of Charity of St. Vincent de Paul for use as a hospital, the origin of today's De Paul Hospital. Out of some 15,000 inhabitants on the epidemic's eve, about two-thirds were stricken; over 2,000 died, besides nearly 1,300 in Portsmouth.[61]

The fever began to abate in early October owing to cooler weather, the flight of susceptible residents, and the availability of adequate medical services. Refugees were advised not to return until after the first frost, which came on October 15; Norfolk's last reported case occurred on October 29. (A considerable number of former residents elected not to return at all.) Many of the volunteers had by this time returned to their homes, and businesses had begun to reopen all over the city.[62]

Few of the city's blacks, and those probably slaves of the more prosperous families, were able to flee the epidemic. As a result, many blacks died despite a resistance to the disease perhaps owed to their ancestors' long exposure to yellow fever in Africa or the West Indies. Black hearse-drivers such as John Jones, and nurses, including nineteen from Charleston, were of great service and much more likely than whites to suffer only mild cases of fever. While mortality among whites who contracted the disease was over 40 percent, that among blacks seems to have been under 10 percent.[63]

In retrospect, it was perhaps especially perverse that the epidemic came while Know-Nothings controlled the city government. William Lamb was among those who suspected that the city's political leaders gave less attention to the fever in its critical early stages because it was "an immigrants disease" attacking mainly Roman Catholics in ghetto neighborhoods. The suspicion is probably not subject to proof, but the bigoted rhetoric of the Know-Nothings played readily into the hands of critics.[64]

Some doubted that Norfolk could recover in a generation from so unspeakable a blow to public morale, leadership, labor supply, and business relations. The numbers of orphans and of persons who lost livelihoods and living-quarters (as in Barry's Row) represented a long-term burden. Damage to Norfolk's self-confidence, its image with prospective inhabitants and visitors, is inestimable but must have been grave. Fate's final antebellum flourish was a horrendous January 1857 storm that buried the city under twenty-foot drifts. Many walked "all the way down the Hampton Roads on the ice," a hike that could be refreshed with a hot toddy from a booth midway between Norfolk and Portsmouth.[65]

But recent studies indicate that the city regained preepidemic business levels as early as 1859. Population figures by that time had already recovered and per capita income almost doubled during the decade, the epidemic notwithstanding. In addition, Norfolk boasted Virginia's only system of free public schools, the state's most exemplary program of poor relief, and "the largest and most active system of disease-control machinery between Boston and New Orleans." Its truck produce business with Baltimore and New York had earned it the sobriquet "The Atlantic Garden."[66]

Even so, the gain in commercial prospects in the 1850s was far short of what Norfolk's molders and builders hoped for. Fall Line interests bought control of the Seaboard and Roanoke Railroad and diverted much of its potential traffic northward. The Norfolk and Portsmouth, almost ruined at the start by the epidemic, had not yet built a profitable business when the Civil War began. Moreover, significant direct trade with Europe was not realized—possibly because profits of coastwise truck produce sales in Baltimore and New York proved in the 1850s to be so thoroughly satisfactory.[67]

A commission of physicians appointed by the city to ascertain whether the fever was local or foreign in origin correctly called it "an imported disease." But Norfolk's image as an unhealthy place was not likely to be improved by it. An exchange, organized in 1857 to marshall ideas for rebuilding the city, sponsored a company to build hotels and a venture to connect Norfolk with the James River Canal by steam packets.[68] Yet Norfolk in 1860, still a satellite of northern markets, was unlikely to become a major city by remaining so. For this, yellow fever was not to blame.

CHAPTER 14

The Cheesebox
and the Turtle

THE impression that would last for decades to come was a silence so grand and terrible that none in the witnessing multitude ever forgot it. One supposed that such scenes must be accompanied by thundering salutes of cannon and rockets, by martial music and lusty cheers. But the CSS *Virginia*, its engines well below the waterline, moved soundlessly downriver as if impelled by the unseen hand of the Almighty, its image that of some preternatural creature of irresistible power and resolution.[1]

The *Day-Book* reporter felt a thrill of anticipation in the "grim and ominous silence" emanating from the ship itself, whose gun-crews were instructed to remain quiet—"not even to whisper." The crowds pressing to the riverbank on both sides seemed "too deeply moved by the gravity of the moment to break into cheers." Seamen on Union warships peered incredulously across Hampton Roads as the spectral boat took discernible form, but "Not a word was spoken, and the silence that prevailed was awesome."[2]

Some sought afterward to distill these first impressions of the ship, its bow and stern both underwater, by resort to analogy. The man from the *New York Herald* made out, coming down the Elizabeth River, "a submerged house, with the roof only above the water." The menacing contours of the *Virginia* were perhaps more aptly captured in a Union sailor's impression of "a half-submerged crocodile." A bemused Frenchman could only think of "a barracks roof surmounted by a large funnel."[3] But unsatisfactory similes must suffice, for no one had ever seen such a thing before.

Notwithstanding the danger, officers and crews of the Union warships seemed eerily trance-like and immobile, as though the apparition on the river were only that—an illusion conjured up mischievously by the haze and the shimmering midday sun. "Did they see the dark hull?" wondered the *Day-Book* man. Freshly washed laundry still hung carelessly from the rigging of the federal ships; small boats swung lazily from their booms.[4] Was this any way to react to the Gosport monster? Did the Northerners have any conception of the Leviathan that bore down upon them?

A little Union tugboat ran up smartly toward Sewell's Point and lobbed several shots at the ironclad, startling the blockaders from their hypnosis before darting back to safety. But Captain Franklin Buchanan ignored the gesture so as to concentrate on his main objective, the warsloop *Cumberland* off Newport News. The *Cumberland*'s new rifled guns represented the blockading squadron's only credible threat to the ironclad, and the sloop's death must give the Confederates undisputed rule over Hampton Roads.[5]

At anchor in the *Virginia*'s path as it executed an ungainly turn northwest past Craney Island was the luckless fifty-gun sailing frigate *Congress*, ordinarily a formidable adversary. But the frigate's first sterngun shots around 2:00 P.M. caromed off the ironclad's sloping turret like the pebbles of a truant boy. Taking a withering blast of grapeshot in return, the *Congress* got off a thirty-four-gun broadside as the *Virginia* passed; dismayed gunners watched their volley beat a pathetic tattoo on the walls of the ironclad. A three-hundred-yard salvo from the *Virginia*, still plowing remorselessly toward the *Cumberland*, left the gun deck of the wooden *Congress* a wrecked "slaughter-pen." Its main hold and sick bay aflame and taking water rapidly, it limped toward shoal water to avoid submerging altogether.[6]

Veteran seamen had never witnessed so one-sided an encounter between ships of war. The ironclad had destroyed the great Union ship (on which Captain Buchanan's brother was paymaster) almost offhandedly, scarcely deigning to notice the *Congress* as it rumbled toward the primary target. A Confederate officer who boarded her could only exclaim of the bloody scenes there: "My God, this is terrible. I wish the war was over."[7]

Meanwhile the *Virginia* passed across the bow of the *Cumberland* and slowly circled for optimum position from which to plunge its two-and-a-half-foot underwater battering ram into the hull of the federal warship. The guns of both ships poured volley after volley into one another, the cascade of Union shells now and again effecting some small injury to the *Virginia* while the decks of the *Cumberland* deteriorated into "a scene of carnage unparalleled in the war."[8]

Carefully gauging his speed and distance, Buchanan took dead aim on his prey from a mile away and pushed the ironclad forward at full speed. When the *Virginia*'s momentum was deemed sufficient to split the *Cumberland* open, he stopped engines and signaled reverse; the ram gouged horrifically into the Union ship's starboard bow and broke off. Yet there was no

An artist known only as "H." painted this scene of the ironclad CSS *Virginia's* ramming of the frigate USS *Cumberland* in Hampton Roads on March 8, 1862. The following day, the *Virginia* met the USS *Monitor* in history's first battle between ironclad ships. (Courtesy of The West Point Museum, United States Military Academy, West Point, N.Y.)

pause in the hideous cannonade. The crew of the *Cumberland* dismissed shouted demands for surrender and kept firing furiously even as their ship began to break up. Buchanan had to back off and ram again before the *Cumberland*, its decks "covered with dead and wounded and awash with blood," plunged defiantly beneath the waves. Even the *Day-Book* was moved to praise the *Cumberland*'s courage, "at once a monument and an epitaph to the gallant men who fought her."[9]

By now the *Virginia* was joined by the hitherto bottled-up "James River Squadron," the twelve-gun sidewheeler *Patrick Henry*, a small gunboat, and an armed tug. The *Cumberland* was gone, but the frigate *Minnesota* and other federal ships rushed to join the fray, and Union shore batteries around Fort Monroe pounded angrily at any Rebel vessel within range. The *Virginia*, after negotiating an awkward turn in the mouth of the James, steamed again toward the stranded *Congress*, which still hurled shells at her enemies. The *Congress* at length hoisted a white flag, but her captors could remove only a few prisoners before shore batteries drove them off. Subjected now to heated cannonballs and incendiary shells from the ironclad and her escorts, the *Congress* took fire again and eventually exploded in the early hours of the next morning.[10]

Elsewhere, all was confusion and anxiety among the sixty ships of the blockading squadron and their shore batteries. The frigates *Minnesota* and *St. Lawrence,* hurrying from beyond Willoughby Spit, ran aground and seemed likely to be picked off by the lumbering ironclad. "A general panic," wrote the Frenchman, "seemed to possess everyone." Some of the federal vessels made ready to run for open sea if the *Virginia* turned their way. At Fort Monroe, drums and bugles dinned out all manner of signals and countersignals, and boats and ferries scurried about in what passed for purposeful response.[11]

The ironclad, now under Lieutenant Commander Catesby Jones—a minié ball had punctured Buchanan's thigh—bore down on the wallowing *Minnesota,* intending to ram her. But the water proved too shallow and the *Virginia* could only stand at a considerable distance and blast away. By now, however, 5:00 P.M. was approaching, night would soon fall, and ebbing tides were complicating the ironclad's movements. On the advice of his pilots, Jones broke off the firing and wheeled about toward the Elizabeth River, exchanging broadsides with the *St. Lawrence* as he retired.[12]

The ironclad sustained some injury in the four-hour action—a couple of guns damaged, a few iron plates loosened, some beams split, ram broken off, its smokestack honeycombed with holes. Its dead and wounded numbered some sixty men. But behind lay a shocked and dejected Union squadron, which that morning had conceived itself absolute master of the Chesapeake. This Saturday, March 8, 1862, had been the worst day in the history of the United States Navy, with nearly three hundred dead, a hundred wounded, two major ships lost and a third helplessly stranded, besides other damage. The ironclad had also blown up a transport at a James River wharf and sunk another while silencing some shore guns.[13]

It appeared that the whole strategy of the war must be revised, and equations reformulated to take cognizance of a ship possibly superior to the combined strength of the entire Union fleet. An immense federal assault on Richmond from the Chesapeake was jeopardized by a single ship that seemed more than a match for General McClellan's aborning armada. What, indeed, lay between the *Virginia* and Washington, D.C., save for open water and matchstick boats?

It had been the most public sea fight in history, witnessed by thousands along almost the whole periphery of Hampton Roads, and great throngs were on hand to cheer the *Virginia* as she anchored off Sewell's Point. By a miracle of modern technology, Norfolk and Portsmouth appeared to be rescued from the clutches of the mighty enemy. The strength of Lincoln's fleet, so intimidating at the assaults on Hatteras and Roanoke Island, seemed no longer a matter of much consequence. The balance, one imagined, had shifted abruptly in the Confederacy's favor, and messages of hope and deliverance pulsated along telegraph wires to the farthest reaches of the beleaguered Southland.

It was well after sundown when what appeared to be a squat barge bearing what might be a large circular water tank was first noted at the entrance of Hampton Roads.[14]

In spite of the harrowing political conflicts leading up to it, the Civil War descended upon Norfolk with breathtaking suddenness. Throughout 1860, the last full year of peace, city newspapers seemed only to go through the motions of demanding intransigent defense of "Southern rights" and warning of possible secession if those rights were violated. The city's economic life had never been so firmly shackled to that of Northern port cities and it was unthinkable that Norfolk could sever those ties without sinking quickly into commercial torpor. The August stopover of the gargantuan British steamship *Great Eastern* whetted again Norfolk's spasmodic direct-trade fantasies, but there was little real hope that the steamer might become a regular visitor.[15]

John Brown's Harper's Ferry raid in the fall of 1859 set off frenzied agitation over slavery in Norfolk as elsewhere. More closely than before, blacks were watched for signs that they regarded themselves too seriously, pondered too reflectively the rhetoric of black Republicans and abolitionists. When a free black was arrested in Petersburg in May 1860 for "smoking cigars in the streets" (and got thirty-nine lashes), the *Argus* groused that Norfolk was "the only southern city that gives this valuable privilege to the negro." Indignant "Old Dominion" advised abolitionists to attend a black funeral in Norfolk and see "a procession of . . . carriages, with handsomely dressed pall-bearers in 'fine linen' and . . . expensively dressed people, whose color is the only indication that they are not sovereigns of the soil."[16]

Such deportment implied arrogance which, in turn, signaled danger for whites. It was almost obligatory during the summer and fall that the Norfolk area exercise itself over another fancied slave plot. The latest arose from reports that Princess Anne, Currituck, and Norfolk county blacks would converge on "the Hickory Ground" in the latter county on the night of

October 7 and launch a revolt. A patrol searching for purported ringleaders startled Irish laborer Michael Flynn from sleep at his Norfolk County shanty and, when he reached reflexively for a weapon, shot him dead.[17]

Portsmouth and Currituck jails were soon filled with black suspects and twenty-one others were taken up in Princess Anne. Norfolk detained only two, letting them go as soon as it became clear that the rumors lacked substance. But Princess Anne ordered the sale out of state of David Corprew's Denson and placed other slaves under bond for their good behavior.[18]

White uneasiness over black behavior may have betokened an awareness of increased economic pressures to which local blacks were subjected. Hundreds of immigrants from Germany, Ireland, and elsewhere had settled in Norfolk from the 1830s, and many of them invaded occupations traditionally held by blacks, such as domestics, seamstresses, laundresses, draymen, and barbers. At the same time, native white artisans tried to eliminate blacks from various lucrative trades. As free blacks were relegated to the most dangerous and ill-paying occupations, their resentment grew accordingly.[19]

It was taken pretty much for granted that abolition agents often came through Norfolk to incite the slaves to flight or rebellion. The situation seemed to call for vigilance, not just when plots were detected but around the clock and calendar. Prompted by the local implications of national events, a company of dragoons was organized in Norfolk County in July, with A. M. Wilson as captain; the "Norfolk County Rifle Patriots" were formed in the fall under William H. Etheridge. There was talk of a "minute man" outfit to supplement existing units.[20]

These vigilante groups evidently had an appeal that Norfolk's five regular militia companies did not. The *Day-Book* in August found F. F. Ferguson's "Junior Volunteers" in "a delicate state of health," with no more than "a corporal's guard" at parades. The "Norfolk Blues," the city's largest unit, had increased nicely over the past six years, but the Fifty-fourth Virginia's Company F borrowed muskets for parades, having none of its own. The "Riflemen" were in sound shape though many had not appeared for its latest inspection. Virginius D. Groner's "Norfolk Greys" numbered only about a dozen and lacked the spirit that once made them "the best military organization on the Seaboard." "Were the volunteers ordered out to-morrow," warned the *Day-Book*, they could not parade 150 men nor "find muskets for but four companies."[21]

Groner's problems with the Greys doubtless owed something to his preoccupation with a more adventurous military enterprise. He was Norfolk's leading promoter of the Knights of the Golden Circle, whose aim was to invade Mexico with filibuster troops and carve slave states from it. This was the brainchild of "General" George Bickley of Cincinnati, who founded the KGC in 1859 and claimed a national enrollment of fifty thousand. Bickley spoke at Portsmouth in July 1860 and gained a following in the area, though fire-eaters such as Groner were apparently few.[22]

James R. Hathaway's *Day-Book* was especially keen on the KGC and kept readers apprised of the organization's reported progress. Groner left in August with KGC companies from Norfolk, Petersburg, and across the South for a Rio Grande rendezvous. But few reached Texas, organizational and logistical problems intervened, and Groner was back in December, the KGC's bubble having been permanently pricked.[23] Groner's niche in history was assured, however, when he carried to General Beauregard the telegram that sent the first shot into Fort Sumter on April 12, 1861.[24]

The possibility of war seemed only hypothetical in November 1860, when Norfolk cast its presidential vote for Senator John Bell and the Constitutional Union Party. Bell received more than twice the Norfolk votes cast for Democrat John C. Breckinridge (Lincoln got none). South Carolina seceded in December, but the *Herald* advised Virginia not to "dance crazily out of the Union to the fiddling of" the Palmetto State. When Virginia called for a convention for February 4, 1861, to consider secession, Norfolk joined a majority opposing the breakup of the Union.[25]

Norfolk had vocal secessionists before the end of 1860, and their numbers swelled at the start of the new year. In December, a local woman wrote the *Argus* that she would shed her "last drop of blood" for the right of secession, "and if I thought my life would be free forever from any interference from the North, I would gladly give it." When a convention was called in April, Norfolk instructed its delegate, General George Blow, to vote for secession and a group of young men raised a Confederate flag over Craney Island. So decisive was the change that boisterous rejoicing followed announcement of Virginia's secession on April 20.[26]

To accept the conversion at face value would be unwarranted. Many in Norfolk and the state interpreted events less in political terms than in how they bore on family relations, business and personal circumstances, and so on. Parades and music greeted news of Fort Sumter's fall on April 14, but some Norfolk residents shuttered their windows in token disapproval.[27] When secession came up for popular ratification on May 23, Colonel Roger Pryor released the first fifteen men of his Portsmouth infantry unit to vote. Told that all but one voted against secession, Pryor confined them until required by Governor Letcher to let them go. The next day Pryor disbanded the whole company for "disloyal conduct." (He had declined an invitation, accepted by Edmund Ruffin, to fire the first shot at Fort Sumter.)[28] It seems clear that some coercion attended voting throughout the district, if not the state.

Owing to Lincoln's quick proclamation of a blockade, Norfolk imagined itself under siege from secession's first hours. Rumors were afloat on April 20 that the navy yard was to be burned, all naval vessels were to be scuttled, and the *Cumberland* was to bombard the city. Richmond and Petersburg troops began arriving that day and General William B. Talia-ferro, commanding some 850 ill-armed militia in the Norfolk area, contem-plated seizing the navy yard although he was sure he could not hold it against warships. Besides the *Cumberland,* the only vessel fully in commis-sion, there were the huge old *Pennsylvania, Merrimac, Columbus, Delaware,* and assorted smaller ships, representing one-seventh of the navy's strength.[29]

Taliaferro's April 20 demand for the navy yard's surrender was relayed to Washington, but Commodore Charles McCauley, in charge of the base, took responsibility for destroying the yard and ships to keep them out of Confederate hands. Marines rushing south to hold the base arrived that night to find all ships but the *Cumberland* scuttled and the yard about to be torched. It was decided to finish the destruction, and crews worked far into the night pouring turpentine and powder trains. At 4:20 A.M. a rocket sig-naled the igniting of combustibles. In a conflagration "grand and terrific beyond description" and seen for thirty miles around, the ninety-acre yard was left crumbling to ruin. The *Cumberland* was towed out of the river and Union personnel were evacuated to Fort Monroe and other nearby installa-tions.[30]

Virginia troops raced to salvage what they could from the fires and were able to save many valuable buildings and prevent the total loss of several ships, notably the big *Merrimac.* A federal effort to blow up the drydock went awry, and hundreds of cannons were found spiked but in repairable condition. Experts felt that what was saved at Gosport might, within a few months, constitute a respectable Confederate Navy and provide the South with a chance to defend its self-proclaimed independence.[31]

The Elizabeth River's defense included placing gun batteries at Sewell's Point and Fort Norfolk, establishing earthworks at Hospital Point, and re-pairing Craney Island's defenses. Gangs of slaves and free blacks were set to work at Lambert's Point, the Naval Hospital, Tanner's Creek, Pig Point, and elsewhere. Over 1,500 blacks were used to sink small boats and anchor rafts across rivers. (Three who escaped from Sewell's Point on May 23 were judged by Fort Monroe's General Benjamin Butler to be "contrabands" who must not be returned to their masters. Many more soon followed.) This work became critical when Newport News fell to Union forces on May 27. Work at Craney Island was unfinished on May 19 when the *Monticello* and an armed tug shelled the island and a Sewell's Point battery. Shelling resumed the next day until Confederate guns were in place and drove off the assailants. Soon, over a hundred cannons bristled from vantage points at Boush's Bluff, Pinner's Point, Fort Nelson, and other sites.[32]

Additions were made weekly to the defending forces as units from Georgia, North Carolina, Alabama, Louisiana, and the Virginia interior encamped at sites in Norfolk and Princess Anne counties. These were routinely greeted with gala receptions, but Norfolk's relations with her defenders were soon a matter of journalistic quarreling. "Loroque," reporting for the Petersburg *Express,* complained that Norfolk had "done nothing" for the troops she sent to war. To the taunt that Lynchburg donated $50,000 to the war effort and sent a tailor to fit its artillery unit with "their second suit of clothes," the *Day-Book* responded in high indignation but with little contradictory data.[33]

As in the Revolutionary War, many Virginians suspected Norfolk of being less deeply committed to secession and war than the rest of the state. The *Day-Book,* by mid-August the only Norfolk paper still publishing, carried letters citing the daily visits of female volunteers to hospitals to offer services and gifts of mattresses, pillows, food, and other supplies for the soldiers. The paper conceded that Norfolk's "losses in an almost total cessation of business" left little to share but thought the Soldier's Aid Society, under the management of local women, was doing all it could. The letters of soldiers themselves appear to bear out the response, though none addressed "Loroque's" specific criticism.[34]

By the fall of 1861 slaves from the Norfolk area, and no doubt some from well beyond the city limits, were absconding in large numbers across Hampton Roads. Eight of them, armed with stolen Bowie knives and Colt revolvers and about to embark for Old Point, were intercepted at Todd's riverside "observatory" on the night of December 6 and ten more farther downriver. When they appeared before Mayor William Lamb, evidence suggested that they were aided by a black secret society known as the "Grand Enterprising Sons," thought to be part of an underground railroad. Fifteen more were known to have escaped from Sewell's Point on January 26, but hundreds simply vanished.[35]

The war brought a steep rise in prices and the rapid disappearance of imported goods from store shelves owing to the blockade of the Chesapeake Bay. Newspaper reports accused Norfolk shopkeepers of profiteering from the war by inexcusably high prices, which prevented soldiers and the poor from buying fresh produce. With Confederate money scarce, merchants issued "shin-plasters," small pieces of paper reading "good for ten cents," and so on. Street and sanitation problems grew because key personnel went into military service and tax revenue fell sharply.[36]

Union observation balloons above Fort Monroe and ships in Hampton Roads reconnoitering Confederate fortifications were often seen. At night, balloons were useful for surveying campfires for intelligence on the size and distribution of Rebel forces (Huger had some 16,000 men). Both sides received reports about the other from prisoner exchanges and the transfer of refugees, Norfolk being a principal conduit for these purposes. Soldiers fought innumerable fistfights at local bars; it was early 1862 before Major General Benjamin Huger of South Carolina, who succeeded Taliaferro in command of the Norfolk area, shut down the drinking houses and restored a measure of order.[37]

Norfolk may have felt well enough defended by late summer to make assault from the bay or seacoast too costly for the Union to contemplate. But the fall of Hatteras Island in August posed an avenue of attack against which the city had scant means to protect itself. The enemy's presence in eastern North Carolina threatened to choke the supply routes Norfolk depended on in the absence of seagoing commerce. At first, Union forces seemed content with Hatteras, but in January 1862 came the Burnside Expedition's seizure of Roanoke Island, the strategic key to all of North Carolina's northeastern sounds and rivers. This success rendered the canals all but useless, endangered the Seaboard and Roanoke rail line, and drew a noose almost all the way around Norfolk's neck.[38]

Norfolk might still hold out if Huger was reinforced on his southern flank and Hampton Roads could be freed from Union control. Since the Confederacy could not hope to compete in wooden warships, the only hope to recover the harbor was an ironclad, and the Confederacy had been racing since taking the navy yard to build one. As first conceived, the rebuilt *Merrimac,* now dubbed *Virginia,* would serve this purpose in an assault coordinated with a Rebel land attack on Newport News. Success would facilitate communication between Norfolk and Richmond and make both cities less vulnerable to attack from the sea. General John B. Magruder, distrusting the ironclad, opposed an attack by his forces on Newport News and rejected that much of the plan.[39]

The *Merrimac* was raised and put in the Gosport drydock in May 1861. Its hull and machinery were found to be in good condition. A design, apparently the work of naval constructor John L. Porter, was adopted, and high priority was given to the work. Details of the ironclad's construction were reported to Washington by spies; a Norfolk black woman, Mrs. Mary Louveste, went personally to Secretary of the Navy Gideon Welles. She was later praised by Welles for crossing the lines "at no small risk" to bring valuable data from a mechanic at work on the ship.[40]

Lincoln's Congress took up the question of vessels capable of opposing the Southern ironclad and funds were voted for the purpose in August. But it was November before work began on John Ericsson's design for the *Monitor*, and federal officers in Hampton Roads already feared an early descent by the *Virginia*.[41]

It took nearly all of the next winter to resolve complications inherent in the *Virginia*'s design, to manufacture and mount two coverings of two-inch iron plating over double-layered four-inch oak planks. Finished in February, the vessel had ten guns inside its turtleshell iron turret—four on each side and one each fore and aft. With a complement of 260 men and twenty-four officers, it could carry coal for up to a week's cruise. Displacing 3,500 tons and capable of a speed of only about six knots, she rode deeply in the water and was so unwieldy that a half-hour or more was needed to execute a full tactical turn. Those who envisioned her as aiming to break the blockade, maybe threaten Washington or New York, failed to appreciate that she was not a seagoing ship; her capabilities were essentially defensive and short-range.[42]

After her stunning victories in Hampton Roads on March 8, it remained for the *Virginia* to go out again the next morning and complete the destruction of the grounded *Minnesota*, the prelude to clearing the Chesapeake of federal ships. This task she set off to accomplish at 6:00 on the morning of Sunday, March 9. Only acting commander Catesby Jones knew the *Monitor* had arrived the evening before, having caught a glimpse of her in the light of the exploding *Congress*. It was a surprise to the *Virginia*'s crew, when, soon after the *Minnesota* fired an opening shot to begin the day's battle, the *Monitor* came sliding slowly out from behind her and immediately made toward the *Virginia*.[43]

Few Union observers thought the *Monitor* had a chance against the much larger Confederate ship. But the Union vessel, under Commodore John Worden, made up in maneuverability and massive armor what it lacked in size. The 990-ton *Monitor*'s low deck and sides were covered by heavy wood and iron plating; her nine-foot-tall turret had two nine-inch Dahlgren guns, protected by iron plates eight inches thick. It was as slow as the hulking *Virginia*, but its low silhouette made it a poor target for the larger ship.[44]

Jones aimed for a showdown with the *Monitor* and, after heading down the channel toward the Rip Raps—an island built at the entrance to Hampton Roads when Fort Monroe was constructed—veered toward the *Minnesota*. As the *Monitor* came in view, the *Patrick Henry* and three other escorts peeled off and headed back under the protection of the Sewell's Point guns. Worden pointed the *Monitor* at his foe's starboard bow but came parallel, his bow pointing in the opposite direction, as the distance closed to six hundred yards. The two ships opened fire, the Confederate vessel with murderous volleys, the *Monitor* with a shell every eight minutes or so as its turret was cranked slowly about to bring its guns alternately into position. Given the *Virginia*'s huge profile and tendency to overshoot targets, her advantage in firepower was offset by the *Monitor*'s ability to make almost every shot count.[45]

Marksmanship counted for little. The *Monitor*'s shells had little more effect on the *Virginia* than those fired the previous day by federal ships and shore guns. At intervals, the *Virginia*'s crew used riflefire to hit the enemy's helmsman or commander through narrow openings in her turret, but it availed nothing. Smoke soon enveloped much of the action, but witnesses now and again had glimpses of the fight, the adversaries "backing, filling and jockeying for position, then at it again, [and] again the cloud of smoke . . . settled over their struggle." Meanwhile, shore batteries from both sides and the *Minnesota*'s guns joined in with the same disappointing results.[46]

Worden sought at one point to break the *Virginia*'s propeller by running in close to its stern, but he missed by two feet. At another point, the Confederate ship was briefly grounded and Worden had a chance to come in at a safer angle and slam shells into what might be vulnerable points in the *Virginia*'s hull. Jones' boiler crew threw waste cotton and chunks of splintered wood on top of the coal, whipping up the boilers to a dangerous pitch, and had almost given it up when the ship shuddered loose from the mud.[47]

Jones, convinced now that gunfire could not win the fight, maneuvered to ram the Union vessel despite the loss of his ramming prow the day before. But he was unable to get a full mile of headway and, owing to his damaged bow, ordered stop and reverse earlier than he might have otherwise. With the *Monitor* churning "hard aport," the *Virginia* hit its target only a glancing blow which, though it spun the Union ship like a top, did no real damage. Now Jones tried to get between the *Monitor* and *Minnesota* to sink the latter, but could only engage the frigate in a brief exchange before the *Monitor* again came between them.[48]

As the *Monitor* made this move, she passed under the *Virginia*'s stern, again trying to hit the Rebel ship's propeller. Momentarily, the vessels were within twenty yards of one another. The *Virginia* got off a shell that "dislodged the iron logs sheltering the . . . [*Monitor*'s] conning tower, carrying away the steering gear and signal apparatus." Worden was temporarily blinded by the blast and had to be relieved by his executive officer. But the ship was still serviceable and the contest no nearer a decision than before. Both crews were by this time—nearly noon—covered with black powder and almost exhausted. In addition, the *Virginia*'s powder had run short and again an ebbing tide was inhibiting the larger ship's movements.[49]

Jones turned his vessel toward Sewell's Point, intending to resume the fight at higher tide and with replenished munitions. The *Monitor,* electing not to pursue, drew off toward the *Minnesota,* the defense of which was Worden's main purpose and achievement. (The crippled frigate was afterward towed to Fort Monroe.) Neither vessel had been able to injure the other enough to claim victory. The federal ship was hit at least twenty-one times, the *Virginia* more than a hundred in the two days of conflict, but both remained operational. They had not proved in their four-hour fight which was superior—only that the day of the wooden ship was over.[50]

Norfolk, badly in need of some kind of reassurance, could be forgiven if it treated the indecisive action as another victory for the *Virginia.* "You cannot imagine the triumphant thrill of exultation," wrote "Rifleman" to the Petersburg *Express,*

> with which the return of our little flotilla galvanized the torpidity of this undemonstrative town. . . . As they passed up the channel . . . the paeans of welcoming triumph leaped from point to point and headland to headland, until ten miles of this beautiful harbor was vocal with the plaudits of a grateful and admiring people.
>
> "Gratulatory words are passing from one to another as people meet in the streets. . .," wrote Stella, "thanksgiving is made in the churches and the harvest of 'Amens' . . . fills the aisles and corridors and floats up like incense on the Sabbath air."[51]

In the few weeks the Fates granted Norfolk to savor a sense of deliverance, the city experienced a burst of vital energy. A fund was started to build another of the wonderful ironclads. Freemason Street Baptist Church donated its 1,785-pound bell to be cast into weaponry. Local women formed an organization of nurses. "Blind Tom," a black lad with prodigal musical gifts who was a favorite on the Norfolk stage, made appearances in both Norfolk and Portsmouth as if the war were already over and the South had won.[52]

The *Virginia* was drydocked for repairs; her plating was broken in many places, timbers were cracked, she needed a new ram and funnel, her old engines were in poor condition. She was soon ready for action, but her new commander, Josiah Tatnall, had orders not to risk the vessel since Norfolk would be lost without her. She made several short runs into Hampton Roads in succeeding weeks but without significant contact with enemy vessels. The *Monitor* was anchored under Fort Monroe's guns and others kept a respectful distance.[53]

Reality returned in late March when residents realized that General George B. McClellan was landing his Army of the Potomac on the Yorktown peninsula to drive on to Richmond from the east. McClellan, irked that the navy could not assist his invasion because the blockaders were concentrating exclusively on watching the *Virginia,* brought one hundred thousand men ashore and made ready for a quick capture of the Confederate capital and an end to the war.[54]

The Confederate high command concluded that Norfolk, endangered from the south by Burnside and from the north by McClellan, could not be held. It appeared to be within Union capacities to seize the river and railway routes connecting Norfolk and Portsmouth with the interior and so entrap any Confederate forces south of Hampton Roads. By May 2 steps were being taken to remove troops, rolling stock, munitions, and other items of military value from the two cities. A massive military and civilian evacuation took place in the next few days. Various schemes for saving the ironclad were explored, including a late, unsuccessful effort to lighten her sufficiently for a run up the James River. What must be avoided at all costs was her capture by Union forces.[55]

Assured that Norfolk was all but abandoned, President Lincoln, with a party including Secretaries Chase and Stanton, left Washington on May 5 for Fort Monroe, arriving the next day. Informed that Norfolk was clear of Confederate troops, Lincoln and his party came over to Ocean View on a tug for a look around on May 9. (The Ocean View vicinity was abandoned early by the Confederates because it was exposed to fire from the largest cannons at Fort Monroe and the Rip Raps.) Lincoln himself called for a

Union landing, and that evening a force of some six thousand men arrived to accept Norfolk's surrender and to occupy it.[56]

On Saturday morning, May 10, Fort Monroe's commander, old General John E. Wool, in company with Lincoln, Stanton, Chase, and others, came around the head of Tanner's Creek (its bridge being in flames) and approached Norfolk along the Princess Anne road. Around 4:00 P.M. they passed some deserted Confederate earthworks and were in sight of Norfolk when they were met by Mayor William W. Lamb and some of his councilmen carrying a flag of truce. Assured by Lamb that there would be no resistance, the Union forces bivouacked outside of town while Wool, with General Egbert Viele, designated as Norfolk's military governor, and others, went on to city hall. Lamb addressed a crowd of citizens, counseling that they accept the unhappy situation and joining them in three cheers for Jefferson Davis before they formally surrendered the city.[57]

That evening, Norfolk blacks celebrated the new era by crowding the streets, the women shouting "O Lord! Too good to be true! Bless the Lord!" and similar ejaculations of joy. Police sought to enforce a slave curfew, but Union officers indulged the demonstrations, which continued all night. Shortly afterward, Wool allowed blacks to observe a day of public thanksgiving and prayer, including sunrise services at black churches. These were followed by a parade of some five thousand led by "Father Dick Parker," who had served Norfolk's black community as a minister for over thirty years. Parker and Wool addressed the crowd, bonfires were lit, guns boomed, and bells and horns sounded the death knell, somewhat prematurely as it proved, of the old system of oppression.[58]

As federal forces occupied Norfolk, Confederate wrecking crews busily destroyed the Gosport navy yard, making a better job of it than the previous tenants. The drydock was mined and heavily damaged, buildings were torched, machinery was destroyed, stores of tobacco were thrown into the river, and the remaining Confederate vessels were burned. Onlookers were reminded of a panorama of the burning of Moscow that had lately been on display in Norfolk, "the scene one of terrible grandeur."[59]

The doomed CSS *Virginia* was that night destroyed off Sewell's Point. After being run ashore half a mile below Craney Island, the ironclad was coated with tar, oil, fat, and grease, and her crew sent ashore. Tatnall and a few others remained to ignite the vessel just before 5:00 A.M. After burning for an hour and a half, the ironclad exploded, huge sections of hot iron plates and pieces of timber erupting over the surrounding waters and shoreline. "The noise made by the explosion," said a newspaper account, "was perfectly terrible, shaking everything, even the very ground, apparently, to its centre"; within moments, "not a vestige of her remain[ed] above water."[60]

Lincoln stayed long enough to ride through the streets of Norfolk on May 11 and view with satisfaction the wreckage of the *Virginia*. Steaming back to Washington, Secretary Chase wrote his daughter that, if Lincoln had not come down personally, "Norfolk would still have been in the possession of the enemy."[61] The old borough, which had so often in the past seen its livelihood destroyed, which had endured the heel of the conqueror, the worst ravages of storm, depression, pestilence, and fire, shrugged its careworn shoulders and resolved to make what it could of the new adversity. If for a city, as for an individual, such circumstances build character, Norfolk might stand comparison in civic rectitude with any place in America.

CHAPTER 15

A Question of Insanity

IT WAS one of those close, sultry "dog-day" afternoons in downtown Norfolk, and Dr. David M. Wright was anxious to fetch his horse from the Hill Street stable. It was already about 4:00, he still had patients to see, and he had left home in sufficiently irritable spirits for his wife to have extracted from him a promise to "keep out of any fuss" while completing his rounds. The doctor stopped briefly at the big Foster and Moore dry goods store at seventeen Hill Street opposite the stable and was just leaving when "the incident" occurred.[1]

Before he could cross the street, Dr. Wright had to duck back into the store entrance to avoid colliding with a column of federal soldiers marching to a drumbeat along the sidewalk, forcing pedestrians to scurry left and right from its path. The column was Company B of the newly organized First Regiment, U.S. Colored Troops, and it was led by Second Lieutenant Alanson L. Sanborn, lately a schoolteacher in Whitford Centre, Vermont.[2]

Black solders were a novelty in Norfolk in the summer of 1863; many whites felt keenly the humiliating irony of kowtowing to men who had for centuries formed the "mudsill" of Southern society. Dr. Wright, a secessionist and slaveowner, was known as a kindly master, but this was really too much! What was one to make of this smartly dressed Yankee and his sable entourage, a strutting phalanx whose very existence mocked the South's history? Wright shot an almost involuntary "exclamation of disgust" at the white officer; bystanders caught at least the word "cowardly" in what he said.[3]

Lieutenant Sanborn heard the doctor and immediately ordered his company to halt, a file of eight men to turn and face the assailant, all to order arms. He directed one of his men to the customs house on Main Street to summon the provost's guard and approached Wright with an announcement that he was under arrest, to which the doctor made a reply inaudible to others nearby.[4]

By now Wright, apparently through the agency of someone behind him in the store, held a pistol behind his back. He now pointed it at Sanborn, who turned partially away, but a shot struck his right arm. Almost simultaneously, a second shot penetrated the officer's upraised left arm, lodging in his shoulder near the collarbone. Sanborn shoved Wright back through the doorway, grasping the pistol barrel as his excited soldiers pushed through the door behind him. Another federal officer, Lieutenant Colonel Hugh C. Floyd, also burst in, seizing Wright and ordering the soldiers not to molest the doctor. Sanborn, sliding semiconsciously along the counter, crumpled to the floor and was dead within fifteen minutes. Wright was hurried off under arrest to the customs house, which served as headquarters for the provost's guard.[5]

Many of Norfolk's prewar residents had fled by mid-1863, but many who remained were admirers of Dr. Wright and the episode was a local sensation. A Nansemond County native, he had practiced medicine in Edenton for over twenty years before moving to Norfolk in 1854. He was a beacon of service in the next year's yellow fever epidemic, contracting the disease himself but recovering. Tall and dignified, with long gray hair, full beard, and mustache, he was said to be "an upright, amiable and peaceful citizen, in his domestic affairs, an affectionate husband and father." His household at twenty West Main included his wife Penelope Creecy Wright, eight children, and (in 1860) six slaves.[6]

As Wright's arraignment proceeded, military authorities named a commission of officers to conduct his trial, and it formally charged him with murder. The doctor chose as his attorneys Unionist lawyers Lucius H. Chandler and Lemuel J. Bowden, who entered his plea of not guilty. Meanwhile the city on July 14 gave Lieutenant Sanborn a civic funeral, with all places of business closed, all church bells tolling, and the city council in attendance.[7]

Dr. Wright's trial opened on July 20 in the customs house. His lawyers contended that the military commission could not legally hear the case because Norfolk was under a properly constituted civilian government. Murder was a crime under state, not federal, law and fell under the jurisdiction of the city's circuit court, which would meet next in November.[8]

The military establishment was convinced that a civilian jury would find Wright innocent owing to community support for him. Judge Advocate Major John A. Bolles, therefore, answered the jurisdictional challenge by citing War Department Order Number 100, placing under martial law territories formerly occupied by the Confederates and an Act of Congress recognizing

the right of military commissions to try capital cases. "May malignant secessionist traitors," Bolles queried, "shootdown . . . every soldier and civilian?
Thank God . . . there is . . . a tribunal like this, competent to try [and] swift
to punish."[9]

The commission dismissed defense objections to its jurisdiction and the
prosecution presented its case, with several witnesses offering roughly similar versions of the shooting. But when the moment came to open Wright's
defense on July 27, Chandler and Bowden announced their withdrawal from
the case. They and their client had evidently decided that he could not have
justice in this setting and that a remedy must be sought elsewhere. They
may also have expected a postponement to ensue. It didn't.[10]

On July 29, nevertheless, Wright gave the commission a statement challenging once again the court's jurisdiction and recounting what he perceived
to be errors in the witnesses' testimony. He was of the opinion that black
troops were brought to Norfolk chiefly to provoke and harass white citizens,
and thought the court should have considered Lieutenant Sanborn's likely
motives for approaching him with offensive remarks. Blacks, moreover, became ungovernable when excited. Could it be expected that "a citizen of
Norfolk, himself an owner of slaves, not knowing but what one of my slaves
was in the company, would be arrested by Negroes [and] marched off to the
guardhouse? No sir, I would not submit to that."[11]

The commission decided unanimously that Wright was guilty as charged
and ordered that he be hanged at such time and place as the district commander, General John G. Foster, directed. Dr. Wright's fate now rested with
Abraham Lincoln, who was asked by attorney Bowden for an interview, that
he might "present the mass of testimony" to prove Dr. Wright's insanity.[12]

But Lincoln may not have appreciated the underlying issue. For fourteen
months Norfolk's civil and military officials had been locked in conflict over
who should rule the city, and inhabitants were caught brutally in the middle.
Dr. Wright was a pawn in the struggle, but the wider ramifications included
the continuing Union blockade of Norfolk—almost as if it were still a bastion of the Confederacy. Provisions were scarce and expensive for a teeming
and mostly destitute population, streets were unlighted at night, filth
abounded, pavement was broken, and Norfolk's "lamentation visible at every turn and corner was [that] nobody cares for me now."[13]

The sorry state of affairs owed something to military incompetence and
corruption, but more to civilian leaders whose misplaced loyalties consigned
Norfolk to at least three years of needless misery. Promptly after arriving in
Norfolk in May 1862, General Viele requested Mayor Lamb and his council

Crowds watched from Norfolk in May 1862 as fleeing Confederates torched the navy yard on the eve of Union occupation of Norfolk. (From *Harper's* magazine)

to signify whether they would cooperate with the occupying forces. The civil officials replied that they preferred that Norfolk's citizenry be regarded as a "conquered people," an indication that at least passive civil resistance could be expected. General Wool, Viele's superior, now called on the magistrates to take the oath of allegiance to the Union but was refused. The elected government was thereupon dismissed and replaced by martial law.[14]

General John Dix replaced Wool on June 1, 1862, and Viele informed Dix that he had difficulty procuring supplies both for relief of the poor and for those with means to buy. Norfolk by now was transformed into a city mainly of paupers as whites lost their means of livelihood and slaves sought refuge from nearby North Carolina and Virginia counties. Many black refugees were reduced to begging for food; as many as two or three women and children died each day from starvation. The problem might be alleviated if the blockade were lifted, as in the case of some conquered Southern cities. But the decision lay with Lincoln's cabinet, which continued blockading because Secretary of War Stanton had heard that Norfolk was "hot with rebellion." (Dix thought that at least half Norfolk's inhabitants were Unionists and that the blockade should be lifted.)[15]

With the federal policy toward slaves as yet ambiguous, Viele at first announced that all ten thousand slaves in his Norfolk command were free. The policy was soon revoked since the government, although recognizing the city's fugitive slaves as free, was not disposed to confiscate slaves of Norfolk residents. This led to the flight of some three hundred Norfolk slaves to Fort Monroe where, white slaveowners having all but deserted the vicinity, all fugitive slaves were viewed as free people.[16]

Thousands of fugitive slaves were initially lodged at several Norfolk-area camps, including Fort Norfolk, the largest being on Craney Island. The fugitives had little shelter and only the clothes on their backs. Every available parcel of Craney Island land was pressed into cultivation, but blacks complained that the camps were little better than slave pens. Meanwhile, 175 blacks were organized to assist the city fire department. Sisters Sarah and Lucy Chase, sent to Norfolk by the philanthropic Friends of Worcester, Massachusetts, reached Craney Island in early 1863 to find two thousand hungry and homeless blacks, so poorly was the army serving them.[17]

The military began moving many blacks to forty-six abandoned Norfolk and Princess Anne County farms; others worked for the remaining white farmers or found jobs in the city. Black farmhands were at first made to work in gangs under Northern white overseers but, this proving to be too much like slavery, were provided individual ten-acre plots on which they could erect their own houses. The program was undermined by the rising availability in Norfolk of missionary and army supplies and the desire of refugees to remain there in the hope of reuniting with still-awaited loved ones.[18]

Supervised by Colonel Orlando Brown, freedmen's schools were opened in former public schools by Northern missionaries. The Chase sisters in 1863 started one at former Governor Henry Wise's Norfolk County farm. Life remained hard for most blacks, but those in Norfolk gradually gained the self-confidence to leave white churches and form their own. (Craney Island blacks held their own services, appalling straitlaced New Englanders by their tendency to "begin with a meeting and end with a party.") Blacks began weekly meetings in 1863 to promote relief programs and made deposits in a freedmen's bank, later the Norfolk branch of the Freedmen's Savings and Trust Company, on Main Street. Cashier H. C. Perry reported over $12,000 in deposits in early 1866.[19]

Viele struggled to feed Norfolk though no military funds were appropriated for it and the city's only revenue was a trickle from fines and licenses. The blockade was modified in late 1862 to allow trade in goods essential to the military, but material privation made even Unionists hostile to army rule. Growing fear and frustration boiled over in a series of ugly episodes. A white woman who snatched an American flag from a black boy on July 4, 1862, was arrested. Unionists adopted a game of torment in which flags were hung across sidewalks so they might be lowered in front of passing females. The Chase sisters cited as a common view that of a white Norfolkian who reportedly said: "I'd poison a Yankee, in a moment, if I could get a chance."[20]

On the evening of March 26, 1863, Fort Norfolk's garrison was fired on by unknown assailants and attempts were made to burn the contents of some warehouses. Rebel spies were known to work throughout the city and aid was given to Rebel soldiers secretly visiting their relatives through the lines. The gas company's directors engaged in passive sabotage, neglecting repairs, refusing to take the oath of allegiance that would allow them to import fuel, and finally letting the lights go out altogether. A more capable commander might have found ways to combat such tactics, but Viele had neither the wit nor the resolution to do so.[21]

Want of discipline in military ranks underlay many incidents of abuse to civilians, white and black. "They steal everything they want," wrote George Neville from the vicinity of Norfolk. "The Yankees have stolen all the cut wood in this neighborhood, robbed smoke houses, hen roosts, stolen horses and everything else which suited their fancy." Blacks were impressed into labor gangs, and black schoolchildren were harassed by "copperhead" soldiers. A race riot between Portsmouth blacks and New York soldiers in 1862 ended with between six and ten blacks dead and a hundred wounded.[22]

Two years of occupation under these circumstances left Norfolk "gloomy," as a Northern observer found,

> the people for the most part sullen. . . . Of the houses, one-fourth appear to be unoccupied, having been deserted by their inhabitants. . . . some have been seized by the government for storage . . . , of some, the newly arrived mechanics from the north have taken possession; in others the freedmen and their families have squatted. No repairs are perceptible. . . . Broken glass, crumbling walls, opening roofs, creaking doors, and general dilapidation follow disappointed hopes. . . . I left Norfolk as sad as the large company of women, both white and black, standing in front of the commissary's office to receive rations for their families, as sad as the . . . ladies I had met draped in weeds of mourning, as sad as the winds which howl through the deserted habitations of . . . secessionists.[23]

A partial answer to the plight possibly lay in a return to civil government, and the chance came in June 1863. Elections were allowed for Select and Common Councils; judges were appointed to the civil courts, though only candidates and voters taking the oath of allegiance could participate. William H. Brooks became mayor, but his administration got off to a shaky start when the Sanborn shooting occurred in its first weeks and civil and military authorities squabbled over who should try Dr. Wright. Brooks levied taxes on liquor dealers and houses of entertainment to meet some of the city's needs, but results were disappointing. The Brooks government, then, was already in trouble when General Benjamin F. Butler became commander of the Department of Virginia and North Carolina in October 1863.[24]

In Butler, Brooks encountered an elemental force of nature, a general with little battlefield acumen but an administrator of considerable energy, resourcefulness, and determination. The new district commander was by now universally known as "Beast Butler" for an order he had issued in occupied New Orleans that any woman who insulted Union soldiers be treated as "a woman of the town plying her avocation."[25] Civilian Norfolk prepared for the worst.

For his own part, Butler adjudged Norfolk to be in wretched condition and blamed the Brooks regime. Seizing the initiative almost at once, he levied a tax on all his department's imports and exports and demanded fees to issue passports and ships' licenses. He had his provost marshal take over many responsibilities of the police and the military courts handle matters ordinarily resolved in municipal tribunals. Brooks complained loudly, but Butler managed to humiliate him by jailing him on a wife-beating charge; Brooks' authority all but evaporated.[26]

Butler's police guards, many of them black, had their hands full patrolling streets, especially with the hundreds of sailors whose ships were being repaired at Gosport. Drunkenness was often the culprit, though racial feelings were sometimes at the root of the trouble, as when a riot erupted at Commerce and Main streets between guards and sailors in September 1864.[27]

The blockade of Norfolk had become leaky during the regime of General Dix, who tried to open trade on grounds of military necessity. By straining the regulations, Dix found ways to allow a growing import and export of goods and this persisted under Butler. In mid-1863 a Treasury official found business flourishing in a hundred or more stores and "a considerable immigration from the North." Butler had his own licensing system, and the canals from Albemarle Sound in the final months of war brought huge amounts of Confederate cotton in exchange for bacon, sugar, and other produce that went straight to Lee's army. It has been argued that this trade prolonged the war by supplying Confederate needs that could not otherwise have been met. But it benefited Northern traders far more than Norfolk's established merchants.[28]

Butler tried to keep the trade within his own guidelines, and could come down hard on merchants who tried to go farther. After merchants Francis Zantzinger and J. T. Daniels complained to Lincoln of Butler's "persecution," the general's agents caught them importing whiskey as "cider vine-gar." The discovery was reported in Butler's army-controlled newspaper, *The New Regime,* on June 24, 1864, the day designated for Norfolk citizens to vote on whether they wished the civilian government to continue operating. By 330 to sixteen, the Brooks administration was suspended. Norfolk remained under military rule for the rest of the war.[29]

Free of the nuisance of civil government, Butler, unchecked by laissez-faire municipal tradition or posturing by Francis Pierpont's Unionist state government at Alexandria, began dealing with issues according to his own lights. A problem in dire need of remedy was the many poor white and black families in his district. He opened an Office of Commissioners for the Poor with revenue from his new taxes and fees to provide necessities for over three thousand poor in Norfolk and Portsmouth. Jobs for those able to work were sought by a new Humane and Employment Society. Some 16,000 now worked on farms abandoned by owners; hundreds more occupied abandoned Norfolk houses. New revenue also renovated the decrepit fire department, repaved broken Main and Bank streets, reopened the gas company in early 1864, and addressed other needs.[30]

Butler hoped that cleaning up Norfolk's streets might head off yellow fever and smallpox epidemics. Toward that end he undertook an ambitious assault on filth. Owners or occupants of city property were required to clean up their premises and deposit all trash and sweepings in "a proper vessel" for removal by the city. Street cleanup was performed regularly by a force of some 250 convicted criminals, vagabonds, and deserters who could work off parts of their sentences in this way.[31]

The age-old problem of animals roaming the streets was addressed in a regulation requiring that cattle, horses, and swine found unattended in the streets be impounded, and that their owners be charged a fee and fined before the animals were returned. An order to destroy "every fourth dog" brought much amusement as to how such a determination was to be made, but owners had to register and license their dogs to preserve them. To reduce the threat of rabies, dogs had to be muzzled from May to October.[32]

To insure early discovery of outbreaks of certain diseases, physicians submitted weekly bills of mortality citing causes of death. (Some victims tried to conceal their illnesses to avoid being sent to the racially integrated pesthouse.) Smallpox, in particular, remained a significant threat, but Butler's policies probably reduced the incidence of disease as well as death rates. Living conditions after mid-1863 seem to have improved considerably because of the alterations made by the military command.[33]

A Question of Insanity

Owing mainly to efforts of the American Missionary Association (AMA) and its agent, Rev. Lewis Lockwood, Norfolk blacks had a black-taught school by October 1862. Butler saw the need for a "reconstruction" of Southern society that included educational opportunities for blacks. To this end, he closed the public schools, announcing that they would reopen for free, integrated classes. He used Northern volunteer teachers, with night sessions for black adults. Attendance was compulsory for black children from five to sixteen years old; school-age children found in the streets during school hours were sent to a government farm. Some 1,500 black children were enrolled in schools under thirty teachers; the costs were borne from proceeds of a direct tax. (Norfolk Academy was used during the occupation as a military hospital.)[34]

Most of the responsibility for the black schools fell to AMA missionaries. Two schools that opened in the Bute Street Baptist and Methodist churches in the spring of 1863 enrolled over 1,200 daytime children and nighttime adults. The missionaries engaged fifteen black teachers' aides, began a Sabbath school, and, just beyond city limits at Ferry Point, established a black orphanage. At a Sabbath school at the ropewalk, teachers reported enrolling a 108-year-old man who was determined to learn to read and write. In October 1863 the AMA began taking over formerly white public schools. Soldiers and army wives volunteered as teachers; many children were sent by wealthy patrons north for education.[35]

Having authorized formation of the war's first black regiment at New Orleans in 1862, Butler began early to recruit, sometimes dragoon, Norfolk-area blacks for Union service. Many left government farms to volunteer, most farmwork hereafter being done by women and children. The lure of army pay, warm clothes, and food drew new waves of fugitive slaves to the city. By 1864 two black cavalry regiments, three of infantry, and a light artillery unit were formed at Fort Monroe. All saw combat on the Petersburg–Richmond front in 1864; two of the infantry regiments were involved in the capture of Richmond and the 1865 Appomattox Campaign. Other Norfolk blacks served in the Second U.S. Colored Light Artillery, and the Thirty-sixth, Thirty-seventh, and Thirty-eighth U.S. Colored Infantry regiments.[36]

Eight hundred blacks comprising the Tenth U.S. Colored Volunteers were put under the command of abolitionist Edward A. Wild and designated to seek out slaves and bring them into Union lines as well as engage in combat. On a raid into North Carolina in 1863, Wild's regiment returned with 1,800 new recruits. The First and Second U.S. Colored Cavalry served briefly on the Mexican border at the war's end before being mustered out in 1866. Inured by years of servitude to taking orders, these recruits proved to be exemplary soldiers.[37]

Norfolk blacks on January 1, 1863, greeted the effective date of the Emancipation Proclamation with a joyous and colorful parade led by a line of hacks filled with women. It moved down Main Street, converging with another procession and continuing to the residence of Military Governor General Viele, who addressed them before they proceeded to the fair grounds (at Eighteenth and Church streets) and cemetery. At the latter, four thousand strong and accompanied by five hundred black soldiers, they buried an effigy of Jefferson Davis. At the 1865 anniversary, there was another parade "crammed with colored folks of all ages and sexes," a battery of the Second U.S. Colored Artillery in the van, followed by black cavalry, Freemasons, and "the Colored Charitable Society."[38]

The epic moment of emancipation was rendered in graceful verse in 1884 by Miss M. E. Chapman, a Norfolk black. "Shout forth all ye people," proclaimed the poet in her opening lines,

> from mountain to sea,
>   The fetters are burst, the captive is free,
> The taskmaster's whip is forever laid by,
>   No agonized voices to Heaven now cry,
> For freedom is come.[39]

In the eighteen months of occupation before Butler's advent, secessionists would often express open hostility toward the occupiers. A woman on the Portsmouth ferry in 1862 was overheard to say that she wished "all the Unionists had one neck, that one blow might sever the neck from the body." But Butler's regime tolerated no such public expressions. When Rev. Dr. George D. Armstrong (of yellow fever celebrity) praised a kinsman before parishioners for saying that he "would like to spit upon" a Yankee, Butler sent for the minister and upbraided him. After ascertaining that Armstrong had taken the oath of loyalty, Butler sentenced him to solitary confinement at Fort Hatteras, later amended to work with street-repair gangs. Armstrong's church was put under a chaplain from Massachusetts.[40]

Butler required Norfolk and Portsmouth inhabitants to swear allegiance to the United States before they could engage in trade, practice their professions, or enjoy other advantages of loyal citizens. Many at first refused but ultimately took the oath as an acknowledgment of passive obedience to the federal government. In some cases, however, oath-taking signified that the animosities of 1861 had grown less virulent. Well before the end of the war almost every adult in both cities subscribed to the oath.[41]

Butler's success can be measured by Norfolk's recovery before the war's end. A Baltimore journalist found most houses still dilapidated in early 1865, but "streets thronged with people." The stores "presented a more stirring aspect; the wharves were crowded with steamers and sailing vessels— and altogether there is evidence abundant that Norfolk is commencing to revive" from stagnation. The new Kimberly Brothers store covered two acres and offered a wide variety of merchandise, while other stores and warehouses were "all in full blast." There was even evidence that "old families" were "beginning to open their doors to the loyal, and old friendships are being renewed."[42]

Impresarios like S. W. Glenn arranged for many road shows in the final year or so of the war, mostly staged at the Norfolk Opera House, Church Street Theater, and Mechanics Hall. Presentations of popular plays, such as *School for Scandal* and *Our American Cousin* were interspersed with Shakespeare's *Romeo and Juliet, King Lear,* and others. Violinist Niccolo Paganini appeared in January 1865; the "greatest living pianist," Louis M. Gottschalk, performed in April. Lower-brow fare included Professor Hamilton's violin imitations of bagpipes, pantomime dances of the "Metropolitan Minstrels," and more.[43]

A gala St. Patrick's Day parade in 1864 featured Freemasons, Oddfellows, and other groups marching to a military band playing Irish and American tunes. The parade came down Church to Main and on to Granby Street between crowds of onlookers, while others watched from windows, balconies, and even lamp posts. Officials crowned the day with an eight-course meal at the Atlantic Hotel, with toasts, patriotic songs, and other tokens of respect to a people barely tolerated by white Norfolkians on other days.[44]

Perhaps as important to blacks as a measure of civil liberty was the right to racially separate churches with black ministers. As early as 1857 the white pastor at First Baptist assigned Lewis Tucker, the black church clerk, to lead services. When the minister left after Union occupation in 1862, Tucker took over the Bute Street Baptist Church, becoming the first black ordained minister in Norfolk. Another milestone came in June 1863, when St. John's Methodist Church allied itself with the African Methodist Episcopal (AME) Church's Baltimore Conference.[45]

Butler's early and decisive assault on Norfolk's civil government was a setback to those who hoped to save the life of Dr. David Wright after his murder conviction in July 1863. But some on both sides of the war and Norfolk's administrative divide argued that little was to be gained by making him a martyr. Others warned President Lincoln, who must approve or halt Wright's execution, that the enrollment, discipline, and morale of black troops would suffer if Wright did not hang for his crime.[46]

The president, after talking with Wright's lawyers and others, had no doubt of the doctor's guilt, but was troubled by the question of the condemned man's sanity. In August 1863 Lincoln sought professional advice by appointing Dr. John P. Gray, superintendent of the New York State Asylum at Utica, to determine whether Wright was insane. It was not especially promising news for Wright's supporters; Gray was known to oppose what he felt was overuse of the insanity plea in capital crimes.[47]

Gray came to Norfolk in September and interviewed Wright. The two discussed their professional interests and personal lives, Gray drawing his interviewee out on his family circumstances, views on slavery, and other matters that might bear on the case. The doctor described himself as essentially apolitical but opposed to the arming of former slaves. He suffered "the most awful agony of mind" after Sanborn's death, wept often at interviews, and joined Christ Episcopal Church during confinement.[48]

Gray took testimony from twenty-six Norfolk witnesses, who split evenly as to Wright's sanity. The more impressive statements came, however, from those who, like druggist Charles A. Santos, felt that Wright's occasional eccentricities did not suggest insanity. In his report to Lincoln, Gray noted that the doctor, up to the time of the murder, had the confidence of his fellow citizens and seemed fully in charge of the responsibilities associated with a large medical practice. The report concluded that Dr. Wright was not insane on or prior to July 11, 1863, "and is not insane now."[49]

The president on October 7 gave his decision that Wright was both guilty and sane, wherefore he should be hanged at 10:00 A.M. on Friday, October 16, a date afterward postponed a week to allow the doctor time to settle his affairs.[50]

Attorneys Chandler and Bowden continued to communicate to Lincoln their belief that Wright was of unsound mind and would be more appropriately confined for life or, perhaps, exchanged for a prisoner in Confederate hands. A rumor circulated that Wright would be rescued by Rebel guerrillas, many of whom lurked in the countryside near Norfolk. But there was a better prospect of freeing him, one not anticipated by Union authorities.[51]

On Wednesday night, October 21, about thirty-six hours before the scheduled execution, Wright's daughter Penelope, "Miss Pencie" as she was known, visited his cell. By prearrangement, he had shaved off his beard and mustache; he now exchanged clothes with his daughter and extinguished the light he used when entertaining visitors. (There were reports of "numerous fires" breaking out in these hours in different quarters of the city, evidently set as diversions.) His face covered by a veil and trying to hide his leg irons, Wright started to leave. He was discovered, however, by his guard and returned to his cell.[52]

On the afternoon before his execution, the doctor wrote his wife a farewell letter, admonishing her that "all things must have an end, so too our happiness." On the bleak morning of October 23, he was taken in a carriage to the fair grounds about a mile north of the city under armed escort. A gallows had been erected at the center of the race track; it was surrounded by a hollow square of Union troops (including elements of the Second North Carolina Colored Infantry). A large number of townspeople looked on, though most of Wright's friends remained at home.[53]

Before the black hood was placed over his head, the doctor offered the single public comment that "[t]he deed I committed was done without malice." He was buried the next day at Elmwood Cemetery north of Christ Church. The Richmond general assembly in March 1864 declared him a martyr for the Confederate cause. Long years afterward his execution was still referred to by his friends as a "legal murder." As much as any event of the war, the execution of Dr. Wright represented, for Norfolk, the end of the old and the advent of a new era in its history.[54]

That some took seriously Wright's chances of escape may perhaps be credited to the *Maple Leaf* saga, one of the few really heartening episodes of the war for Hampton Roads Confederates. The story began in New Orleans on June 2, 1863, when a group of forty-seven Confederate prisoners was put aboard a Union steamer for transfer to Northern prisons. Guarded by six hundred homeward-bound troops, the prisoners were delivered to Fort Monroe on June 9 and, within a day or so, to the steamer *Maple Leaf* in Hampton Roads.[55]

On the following morning, forty-five more captives, mostly from Bragg's Army of the Tennessee, were placed on the *Maple Leaf*, which left that afternoon for Fort Delaware. The guard, however, comprised only twelve men, and an escape plot was devised by the prisoners before they lost sight of Cape Henry. A tap of the ship's bell was to be the signal for groups of prisoners lounging strategically on deck to seize each guard. Others were to break into the captain's cabin and take control of the helm. The effort was performed with surprising ease, and the *Maple Leaf* was taken after a struggle of no more than three minutes.[56]

It was only about 5:30 P.M. and still time to direct the ship southward in daylight, perhaps to neutral Nassau in the Bahamas. Warned by the captain that there was too little coal for such a voyage, they elected to steer to the Virginia shore, destroy the ship, and make their way on foot to Rebel lines. Arriving at the Princess Anne coast, the captors were prevailed upon to spare the ship, a chartered vessel owned by its captain. Leaving sick or injured compatriots on board, the rest clambered ashore in the gathering darkness and headed down the beach for Carolina.[57]

The *Maple Leaf*'s captain promptly reported the escape to Fort Monroe authorities, and patrols as well as vessels were dispatched to round them up. Meanwhile the Confederates made their way into Currituck County, procured the assistance of Rebel guerrillas, and managed to evade the searchers. After a hazardous and difficult trek across the Pasquotank, Chowan, and other rivers and swamps, the first of the fugitives reached Richmond by rail from Weldon on June 22. Seventy-one prisoners had escaped, one of their leaders being Captain O. J. Semmes, son of the legendary Raphael Semmes of the CSS *Alabama*. The "Capture of the *Maple Leaf*" became one of the most oft-recited adventures of the war in Virginia.[58]

Benjamin Butler was unable to control graft and corruption among the horde of opportunists who descended on Norfolk in the year and a half of his regime; his department remained in a ferment of greedy conniving. Nor is it proven that many of his remedies for poor relief, schools, and so on were fully or even substantially effective in solving the problems they were intended to address. Much suffering and many aggravating deficiencies in Norfolk's management remained.[59]

But conditions in Norfolk never descended to the deprivation in comparable places under Confederate control. Butler's tenure offered a lesson in what might be achieved in a short time by a strong administration. His policies were in important ways a challenge to the tradition of laissez-faire municipal government which, though it weakened in Norfolk in the prewar decades, remained strong in 1861. His work made it possible for Norfolk to anticipate a smoother transition to Reconstruction in the postwar era than could many Southern cities.[60]

In the turbulent year before the occupation, Norfolk gave the Confederacy a full measure of support. Its five militia companies of infantry, incorporated into the Sixth and Twelfth Virginia regiments, fought in most of the great actions in the war's eastern theater. Four of these belonged to the Sixth, which saw action at Malvern Hill, Second Manassas, and conspicuously in September 1862, at Crampton Gap, Maryland, when Lee's army, having crossed the Potomac, threatened Washington. With McClellan privy to Lee's secret plans and moving to crush his army, the Sixth held the mountain gap against repeated assaults and helped make possible a juncture of Lee's and Jackson's forces that prevented a crippling Union victory.[61]

Both the Sixth and the Twelfth belonged to what was known as "Mahone's Brigade," under prewar Norfolk resident William Mahone, a gifted engineer and railroad builder. They were with the brigade at the Battle of the Crater at Petersburg in July 1864 and most of the other celebrated Virginia engagements. Other Norfolk soldiers were scattered among scores of organizations all over the South. The city also furnished the Confederacy four artillery companies besides personnel for the Rebel navy.[62]

Many of these brave men died or were permanently injured. Nothing was gained, not even, arguably, the vaunted honor that later generations would claim in their behalf. Dr. Wright, at least, was cleared of the suspicion of insanity. History's verdict was less certain for those he left behind.

CHAPTER 16

The Unbuttoning

DESPITE the April 1866 drizzle and catcalls from sidewalks and upper-story windows, the marchers were in a festive mood. A few whites accompanied them out of Market Square but the majority, some three hundred, were black men and women for whom the recent civil rights laws enacted by Congress finally brought the heralded "Day of Jubilee."[1] Not simply the freedom promised by the Emancipation Proclamation three years before was the new attainment, but equality under the law, without which freedom must be a mockery.

"The Ballot Box for All" proclaimed a marcher's banner; "The Rising Sons of Freedom" were identified by another, "The Monitor Union Society" by a third, "Sons of Honor" by a fourth. Not even a pathetic volley of missiles hurled by "some evil-disposed persons" from behind Hall Carpenter's fence at the corner of Dock and Bute streets could deflect the celebrants' good cheer on this epochal Monday morning. In any event, parade marshals and armed black war veterans on the marchers' flanks would deter anything more serious as the parade headed toward the speaker's platform in the field off Nicholson and Upper Union (now Smith) streets.[2]

Speakers were mounting the platform when the commotion broke out. From a house across Nicholson Street, a besotted, cursing, off-duty policeman, William Moseley, lurched into the crowd, reportedly to prevent a reading of the new civil rights bill. As he moved forward, two revelers engaging in a mock pistol duel fired a blank cartridge. Moseley tried to arrest the supposed assailant, cutting him with a dirk as he did so. Some of the crowd began to pommel Moseley who, now recognizing his rashness, retreated at a run across the street. By now there were several alarmed white onlookers at Moseley's house and that of a neighbor, Mrs. Charlotte Whitehurst. John Moseley, the policeman's son, apparently came to his father's aid, as did Mrs. Whitehurst's stepson Robert, a Confederate veteran armed with a pistol.[3]

The gist of later accounts was that Robert Whitehurst fired several shots at some blacks with whom he had had an altercation a few days before. One shot may have struck a black man. As members of the crowd now rushed at Whitehurst, he fired a panicked shot, striking his stepmother fatally in the throat. Pursued by several people, he ran through his house and out onto Church Street, where he was apprehended. His captors were hustling him back toward the speaker's platform when shots rang out behind him; Whitehurst fell dead in the street.[4]

Federal troops hurrying to the scene soon restored order, but Norfolk was in for a night of terror. As word spread that two whites were dead and others (including the two Moseleys) injured by a black mob, armed whites took to the streets. A black man and a boy named Mark Bennett were killed during the evening and others injured by whites, many dressed in Confederate uniforms. Even Major F. W. Stanhope, commanding the Twelfth U.S. Infantry Regiment, and his aide were fired on by a body of about a hundred men in Confederate gray later identified as members of the United Service Fire Company, who had served together under General Lee.[5]

At 11:30 P.M., Stanhope sent to Richmond a request that Norfolk and Portsmouth be put under martial law. It was promptly granted, and by the next evening reinforcements had arrived or were en route from as far away as Washington, D.C. But roving white bands continued to attack blacks for several days.[6]

On April 19, three days after the riots, seven blacks were arraigned in Robert Whitehurst's death, though no one was charged in the deaths and beatings of blacks or the attack on Stanhope. A board of inquiry at the customs house on May 2 heard sixty-eight witnesses, many of whom stressed the dangerous environment for Unionists and blacks. Edward W. Williams, sexton at St. Paul's Church, stated that blacks must "be very careful how we walk, and I never go out at night." An army surgeon felt that, but for the troops, "loyal men could not live here an hour." George Sangster, vice president of Norfolk's board of trade, accused the *Day-Book* of helping create tensions that spawned riots and ill-will. Six of the seven blacks arraigned were freed, but Edward Long was sentenced to eighteen years in prison for Robert Whitehurst's murder.[7]

Revived after the war under prewar editor James R. Hathaway, the *Day-Book* was as rabble-rousing a sheet as existed in occupied Virginia. Incidents like the riot were for Hathaway evidence that blacks must never take part in governing either city or state. On April 17, a day after the riots, he posed the question: "Does the negro suppose that freedom means to butcher indiscriminately white men, women and children whenever they [*sic*] may choose to have a procession"? Must each step toward black "superiority" mean "drunken carnivals of the blood of white people"? An accompanying article portrayed blacks as "semi-barbarous," inflamed by "wild teachings of fanatical instructors." The Norfolk *Post*, in general, shared this view.[8]

Hathaway also printed a statement by Robert Whitehurst's father that there had been no pistol in his home for over two years, and that federal troops refused to aid his dying wife while robbing the house. It was later revealed that the elder Whitehurst, at work in the navy yard when the riot occurred, concocted his testimony at the urging of a *Day-Book* reporter; it was all false.[9]

The April riots were potentially ruinous to Norfolk blacks. In the first postwar year, their leaders worked hard to show whites in both the South and North that blacks could function effectively as citizens. They felt betrayed in early 1865 when the city government was returned to former slaveowners, and when Union officials soon began restoring confiscated property to former Rebels. Slavery's end left them with a status not much above that of prewar free blacks, who had always been viewed by whites as unworthy and unwanted. Union soldiers, whose presence protected blacks, proved, on the whole, to be as bigoted as southern whites. Change was unlikely unless blacks attained full citizenship, including the vote. Yet even this might not suffice if President Johnson went on pardoning traitors for the price of an oath of allegiance.[10]

Black leaders began in February 1865 to organize against Mayor Thomas C. Tabb's administration and petitioned Lincoln for a government formed on "a loyal and equal basis." Led by dentist Thomas Bayne (formerly Sam Nixon, a Norfolk slave who fled to Boston in 1856 via the underground railroad), they created the "Colored Monitor Union Club" to foster black goals, notably the right to vote in state elections. The black population had risen from under 30 percent of Norfolk's 1860 total to over 45 percent after the war. The argument advanced was that Virginia's 1864 constitution, enfranchising only loyal white men, was "provisional," without popular ratification, and could not deny blacks the vote or other citizenship rights.[11]

Trial was made of this view on May 25 election day when over a thousand blacks assembled at the Bute Street Methodist Church and proceeded to divide themselves by the four city wards in which they lived. Residents of each ward chose three or four to go to the polls and try to vote. Only in the second ward were they allowed to vote, and then on a list of "voters whose qualifications are a matter of dispute." While additional second ward blacks hurried off to add their names to the list, those from other wards recorded their own names at the church as having been denied the right to vote. A slate of Unionist white state legislative candidates to whom black voters were pledged ran second in the city elections, no black votes being tallied.[12]

With a state constitutional convention soon to meet, black leaders began a campaign for equal suffrage. Some two thousand blacks and about 150 white allies met at the Catharine Street Baptist Church on June 5. Issues raised by the speakers were soon addressed in a publication of five thousand copies entitled "Address from the Colored Citizens of Norfolk, Va. to the People of the United States." It bore signatures of Bayne, Joseph T. Wilson, a Norfolk native who was a former Union secret service agent, and six others. It called on "Christian and enlightened people" to concede full citizenship, "indispensable to that elevation and prosperity of [black] people, which must be the desire of every patriot." It called on blacks to form labor and land associations to protect workers and buy land for blacks. William Keeling became secretary of the Norfolk Labor Association, George W. Cooke of the Norfolk Land Association.[13]

The authors of the address were proud that their campaign had been "conducted in a . . . constitutional and peaceful manner, unmarked by disorder." When Joseph T. Wilson moved Virginia's first black newspaper, *The True Southerner,* from Hampton to Norfolk in early 1866 and became its editor, black leaders felt they had an instrument for molding the views and conduct of the masses in positive ways. The voice of the city's Union League, it was Norfolk's first black-oriented newspaper.[14]

The latter half of 1865 and early 1866 were marred by ugly racial incidents, but black leaders appealed to the public to recognize that the culprits were mainly "Negro vagabonds" from Baltimore, Washington, and elsewhere—in short, "the class who followed the army."[15] But the April riots seemed to undo all that had been accomplished in shaping an image of blacks as responsible citizens. The white press gravely distorted events, and the blacks and their few white allies had no effective means of rebuttal.

Congress, however, had recently passed, over Johnson's veto, an act to strike down the "Black Codes" of Virginia and other southern states. Federal policy was still far short of granting the vote to black men, but powerful voices in Congress favored it. Suffrage for blacks could yet be gained, but urban race riots played into the hands of those who opposed it, especially where the public was led to believe that blacks were to blame.

It might easily be lost in the clamor of racial politics, but Norfolk's civic tumult was not primarily racial. The city still had many Union soldiers wandering the streets during off-duty hours, hosts of sailors and merchant seamen, prostitutes and other parasites on the military, rootless ex-slaves, and bands of Confederate veterans, many without honest means of livelihood. But the civil administration's approach to this incendiary situation called for six unarmed policemen, whose appearance on their beats was sporadic at best.[16]

The April 1866 Norfolk riots were the first major racial disturbances in the postwar South, but formed only part of a pattern of local eruptions. Union troops rioted as early as June 22, 1865, roaming through black districts carrying bricks, rocks, and pistols and raiding dance halls. That night, blacks armed with bludgeons assaulted a soldier on Main Street and were attacked in turn by a body of troops. There was firing by blacks on soldiers at the circus grounds and a march by soldiers from there to Roanoke Square with assaults on every black they encountered. Subsequent months brought frequent incidents of the same kind.[17]

Norfolk in the months after General Butler's departure had become a roistering, carousing, gun-slinging, mining camp of a town. When it was not blacks against their liberators or old oppressors, it was sailor against soldier, civilian against military, Union versus former Confederate, women battling women, and town watchmen in combat with all and sundry. The defendants in the Whitehurst case eventually won release for want of evidence against them, but city jails and stockades remained packed with miscreants of both races and all persuasions. Even newspapers not given to exploiting racial and political conflict carried frequent accounts of urban mayhem from mid-1865 through most of 1866.[18]

Street violence was only an example of the city's postwar ambience. "Norfolk," wrote a Petersburg journalist in March 1866, "is a strange place." By day, downtown was a glittering bazaar of eating and drinking saloons, billiard rooms, and "ladies restaurants," the latter adorned by "beauty and fashion." "For oysters, for beautiful girls, and for French brandy, we stake Norfolk against the Union." But the staid prewar image was gone. Instead, indulgence among the upper and wealthier classes had "engendered a recklessness of dissipation and an openness of vice" among poorer classes, "which is not common in Virginia."[19]

The latter trait was most visible at night. As soon as the moon arose "over the oyster shell roads of Church and Little Water and other streets then the sound of fiddling and dancing begins." By early morning, "the *purlieus* of vice are thronged with the falling and fallen, indulging in open revelry." Unblushing "servants of shame attempt not to conceal their profession, but every branch and calling of vice keeps open house with shingles out and hospitable latch."[20]

Hard by the Opera House stood "The New Idea," a beer hall with "pretty waiter girls"—an innovation in customer service—"in peasant costumes—balmoral boots and red strings, plaid stockings, . . . short, red skirts, which need no looping, black bodices laced with ribbon, and jaunty headdresses." Nearby dance halls featured a "free and easy style of dancing" and urgings at the end of each number for men to "promenade to the bar and treat your partners." The eight tables at Beardsley's billiard saloon were constantly employed, the proprietor having put $12,000 in it in 1865 only to make a fortune in the first six months.[21]

Many Norfolk white women had enjoyed at least a brief liberation of their own since the outbreak of the war in taking occupations heretofore denied them. The *Day-Book*, before its stoppage by Union authorities in 1862, had a staff of female compositors in place of employees in the Confederate Army. After the war, men returned to their old occupations and, in some cases, those traditionally held by women. The *Virginian* in January 1866 heard from a female reader, "a first class milliner" before the war, who could find no work because all the milliners were now men. "Pretty waiter girls," on the other hand, were in demand.[22]

Permanent residents, black as well as white, were dismayed by the brawling, wide-open lifestyle that enveloped the town. In January 1866 Mayor Tabb called a public meeting at the courthouse to consider ways to upgrade police protection. A committee was formed to recruit a volunteer force of a hundred men to join police on their beats until order returned and as needed thereafter. But few answered the call and disorder persisted.[23]

What Norfolk experienced was the breakdown of traditional modes of behavior and their replacement by alien ways and ideas. Apart from the inundating swarms of outsiders, it was the result of a release from customary cultural and social restraints for all races and classes. Norfolk had become quite unbuttoned and needed time to find modes better adapted than the old ones to the new order.

The change was conspicuous in recreational pastimes. As early as October 1865 some young men organized a baseball club, the Junipers, and played against an army team, the Unions. Many spectators had never seen the game and were impressed by "the feats of dexterity displayed by the fielders." Soon the Junipers challenged a second civilian team, the Creightons (named for baseball's supposed founder), and, by mid-1867, according to the *Landmark*, Norfolk had "baseball on the brain." Clubs at Suffolk, Petersburg, Fort Monroe, and elsewhere were eager for intercity matches, with businesses and schools close behind in forming teams. Black teams such as the Quickstep Club and the Red Stockings came in the early 1880s.[24]

In the black community, popular recreational activities were lectures, picnics, and weekend excursions, but nothing matched the lure of a parade. Parades meant military units and benevolent and social societies in full regalia, with bands and clamorous fanfare. Fairs and dances, outings to Portsmouth, Hampton, and Petersburg, and similar events were also welcome.[25]

Partly owing to Yankee soldiers and carpetbaggers, Norfolk was exposed to a breathless new world of recreational opportunity. Horseracing, cockfighting, and other traditional events endured. Billiard halls sponsored individual and intercity matches with the alacrity of baseball promoters; W. F. Brough emerged as the city's premier cue-stick artist. Norfolk had three velocipede schools by 1869, though the clumsy device soon yielded to its chain-driven stepchild, the bicycle. Breezy journalists dashed over to Burke's Hotel in Hampton for hogfish, crabs, and mint juleps and evenings of "music and moonlight" at Ocean View or Broad Creek. Blacks picnicking at a grove below Fort Norfolk in July 1869 enjoyed dancing and singing, though five drowned before the outing ended.[26]

A town with so many boatmen and fishermen took eagerly to any new water sport; yacht racing had been popular with those of means even before the war. Postwar years saw the beginning of the Phoebus Cup races at Old Point Comfort, a typical race being from the Craney Island lighthouse to Willoughby Spit. Catboat regattas were favored by the middling sort, as were sculling, skiff, and other oarboat races, with the Undines rowing in the Elizabeth River against the Chesapeakes (outfitted in white pants and blue shirts) and out-of-town guest crews. Spectators watched from sailboats and steamers in the harbor; crews returning from matches elsewhere could expect elaborate public receptions, with banquets of green turtle soup and ice cream.[27]

Steamboat and sailing excursions remained popular, though the idea of a few days or weeks in a seaside cottage or hotel grew more attractive as the bustle of the city began to pall on some urbanites. A fortunate few had enjoyed such facilities for many years past at Old Point's Hygeia Hotel and at Nag's Head, but the postwar era brought it within reach of larger segments of the population. Ocean View, started as a private summer resort in 1854, was beginning by the 1870s to attract numbers of Norfolk sea bathers and wealthy northern invalids. Hopes for its further development rose in 1871 when a group of northern investors visited to consider building a hotel and cottages.[28]

A pioneer in fostering Norfolk's resort prospects was Colonel William E. Lamb (the yellow fever diarist), who in 1869 helped organize the "Vue de

The Unbuttoning

A German artist captured this busy Commercial Place scene in 1865. (Courtesy of Norfolk Public Library)

l'Eau" Company to build a Sewell's Point resort hotel. It opened with a grand ball in June 1872. Lamb was one of a new breed of capitalist city-improvers whose activities were propelling Norfolk toward that leadership in state affairs her citizens had long desired but had yet to attain.[29]

As commander of Confederate forces at Fort Fisher, guarding the mouth of Cape Fear River, Lamb had made contacts among British firms involved in blockade-running and had seen the advantages of "direct trade" with Europe. A son and grandson of former mayors, he was well connected in Norfolk and had been a partner in publishing the *Southern Argus* in the last years before the war. Not yet thirty in 1865, he came home a war hero still on crutches but full of ambition for himself and his community.[30]

Lamb used his British connections almost at once to initiate Norfolk's first direct steamship trade with England. He arranged for a London firm to send the steamer *Ephesus* from Liverpool in early 1866, and secured the cooperation of dynamic General William Mahone in his direct-trade plans. Before the *Ephesus* arrived, Lamb had opened a cotton press and persuaded the city to deepen the river opposite his warehouse. The steamer arrived in early June via Boston and cleared at the month's end with 800 bales of cotton, 3,000 barrels of naval stores, 43,000 staves, and some tobacco. Direct trade got off to a bad start when the *Ephesus,* with Lamb aboard, was wrecked on Sable Island, a treeless ship graveyard off Nova Scotia. But much of the cargo was saved and Lamb returned home to arrange more shipments.[31]

Lamb's name popped up everywhere in city business and public affairs. Soon after his shipwreck he became a director of the Merchants and Mechanics Exchange, began supplying coal to Atlantic steamers, and was elected vice president of Norfolk's First National Bank and a director of the South Mills Company across the line in North Carolina. In early 1867 he became president of First National, in March secretary-treasurer of the Norfolk Printing Company (a job printing and newspaper firm), in May president of the Seaboard Insurance Company, in November president of the exchange. He scrupulously avoided business on Sundays (he was also active in St. Paul's Church), but his list of executive duties continued to lengthen throughout the 1870s.[32]

Direct trade could work only if Norfolk had the communications network needed for loading big steamers. Truck farming would never supply such cargoes, but what if rail connections were extended to the most productive cotton and coal country—the Mississippi River and West Virginia? Mahone agreed in early 1866 to extend his recently reopened Norfolk and Petersburg line to Lamb's warehouse. Wartime "Hero of the Crater," Mahone also worked to consolidate three small lines to connect Norfolk with Bristol, Tennessee, and from there to both Memphis and the West Virginia coalfields. This became the Norfolk and Western and helped make Norfolk, one of the nation's great cotton ports, into the world's biggest coal port.[33]

Norfolk's trade with Carolina and the South began to flourish again. The Seaboard and Roanoke, closed and badly damaged by the war, reopened in late 1865, and in 1870 the Elizabeth City and Norfolk (later Norfolk and Southern) was chartered. The canals continued to handle a busy traffic, but were soon overshadowed by rail competition. Much of the nation was injured economically by a depression that began in 1873, but Norfolk's momentum saw it rather nicely through the crisis.[34]

Meanwhile, Lamb pushed Norfolk voters to support bonds to facilitate laying rails to Danville—the Norfolk and Great Western—but had to wait until the early 1880s to see construction begin. In February 1872 he called on New York railroad tycoon Collis P. Huntington about making Norfolk the eastern terminus for Huntington's Chesapeake and Ohio. Lamb was told that "a good piece of real estate" might be an inducement. Huntington finally chose Newport News instead, but Norfolk could not be hurt by the added business for Hampton Roads.[35]

The new western rail routes bypassed Richmond, enabling Norfolk in the 1870s to outstrip its old fall line rivals. The largest transatlantic steamers, much to Norfolk's benefit, could no longer negotiate the James River. In late 1866 the Norfolk *Post* chortled that "Everywhere there is bustle and noise, and the pleasing sound of labor." "Turn where we might," added the *Journal,* "we saw huge piles of cotton." Wharves groaned under Carolina products—tar, turpentine, rosin, staves, shingles, and lumber. "Hundreds of merry-faced laborers were busy discharging or loading the many vessels that lined the wharves." Only one born before the century began could recall such irrefutable proof of local prosperity.[36]

The coasting trade regained prewar intensity and found a profitable new crop—peanuts. A humble slave-food in antebellum times, the peanut became a favorite snack of federal troops and other newcomers during the war. Norfolk by 1876 had a peanut polishing and sorting factory; it soon served one of the nation's most productive peanut-growing regions. Fleets of steamers were being developed by the Old Dominion Line to New York, by the Merchants and Mariners Company to Baltimore and elsewhere, and by other firms.[37] In gleaning a livelihood as in recreation activities, Norfolk was undergoing a liberation from old constraints.

Postwar prosperity caught Norfolk unprepared. The city proper was still confined between Smith's Creek to the north and Newton's Creek on the east; its area in 1865 (one and a third square miles) was the same as it had been in 1809. But pressures of growth toward Tanner's Creek and along the riverfront spawned new settlements—Brambleton, Atlantic City, Huntersville, Eureka (a black community beyond "Mrs. Colley's"), Fairfield, and others. Growth patterns were influenced by the Norfolk City Railroad, a horsecar system that put five cars in operation in August 1870. The first tracks led only along the length of Main Street to wharves of the Providence, Baltimore, and Washington steamship lines but soon extended down Church, Granby, and other streets and to residential areas.[38]

After the police force (gradually being enlarged), water was the most urgent postwar need, and voters in October 1865 endorsed a plan to borrow $500,000 for a waterworks. Given Norfolk's poor credit, this proved to be a daunting problem requiring a serious drought in 1869—when pump water was too brackish to drink and supplies had to be shipped from Washington—to force action. Four years later water began flowing through pipes from the new waterworks at Moore's Bridges. It was still many years, however, before most citizens ceased to rely on their accustomed pumps and dust-collecting cisterns.[39]

Piped water from hundreds of faucets exacerbated the old problem of rainwater collecting in streets and vacant lots. This gave rise to a demand for a drainage and sewage system, but nothing was done until a Memphis yellow fever epidemic in 1878 reminded Norfolk of the risk it ran. The new cesspool system, from which sewage was pumped directly into the harbor, was still incomplete, however, a decade later. A benefit of the waterworks was seen in February 1874, when fire swept Main Street between Market Square and Union and was doused by one of three fire companies using a new water main. Norfolk moved in 1871 from volunteer to paid firemen after two of the companies had a brawl and a man was killed.[40]

A by-product of the new facilities was the filling in of the rest of the "pestiferous, noisome, odorous, odious, and unsightly" Back Creek marsh, between Granby and Bank streets, adding sixty acres to the downtown business district. By 1884 the creek, reduced to a ditch, was enclosed in an iron culvert and city hall Avenue was built over it between Granby Street and City Hall. Newton's Creek was meanwhile closed by a railroad causeway and gradually filled in by other development. In 1874 a telegraph line was established between Norfolk and Cape Hatteras, providing early warning against tropical hurricanes.[41]

Those who knew Norfolk in 1860 could be forgiven for finding it unrecognizable by 1875. There were surface similarities between the prewar town and its postwar offspring, but it was a different city all the same. Not only did a great many people from other parts of the nation and world take root in Norfolk in the intervening years but the spirit and outlook of many natives were altered. William Lamb, director of the projected Norfolk and Great Western Railroad, treasurer of the International Commercial Company, vice president of the Seaman's Friend Society, and member of the board of visitors of the College of William and Mary, typified a new breed of homegrown citizen.[42] These were only roles he added in 1868–69 to former ones; ahead lay greater challenges.

Equally representative of the new type of municipal leader was Walter H. Taylor, three years Lamb's junior and, like him, a son and grandson of prominent Norfolk citizens. Taylor, confidante and aide-de-camp to General Lee during most of the Civil War, returned home to enter the hardware business. He became president of the Seaboard Fire Insurance Company and the Marine Bank, as well as controlling or sharing management in numerous other companies. He was active, on and off the city council, in promoting waterworks, railroad consolidation, development at Ocean View, the Norfolk and Portsmouth Cotton Exchange (founded in 1874), and other enterprises. He was a founder and president of the prestigious Virginia Club and briefly a state senator.[43]

Some blacks shared in the new prosperity, brickmason J. B. Capps accumulating $9,000 in real estate by 1870. Leading black entrepreneurs, such as butcher Robert Francis and barber William Lee, lived south of Cedar Grove Cemetery in an area bounded by James, Nicholson, Lodge, Smith, and Queen streets and deemed by most whites wasteland remote from city markets. By 1872 Norfolk had seventy-four black businesses (including all six oyster dealers), many on Church Street or in rented city market stalls. The Freedman's Bank had four blacks—Chairman Rev. W. D. Schureman, James E. Fuller, Rev. E. G. Corprew, and Randall Harper—on its advisory board, but misdirection from Washington and the 1873 depression were fatal to it. Not only individuals and businesses suffered, but social and benevolent groups—the Oyster Association, Wandering Pilgrims, Humble Sons of God, and some three hundred other black institutions and societies.[44]

A signal example of enterprise was the career of Richard G. L. Paige. Son of a Norfolk slave and a prominent white woman, he was sent to Boston to train as a machinist, returning home after the war. Graduating in 1879 from Howard University Law School, he opened a successful Norfolk practice, won election to the House of Delegates, and owned real estate scattered across the city.[45]

Blacks saw education as the key to economic and cultural progress, a faith nourished perhaps naively in the grim postwar atmosphere. They lost all but two of their wartime schools, AMA facilities on Queen and Holt streets, when whites recovered the buildings in 1864. In early 1867, however, aided by such groups as the New England Freedmen's Aid Society and AMA, ten black schools were in operation, several with adult night schools as well as daytime classes. Under the superintendency of AMA missionary H. C. Percy, they were well conducted and their students proficient in math and reading.[46]

In 1867, with AMA and Freedmen's Bureau help, four black schools with over five hundred students were united in a public system under Superintendent Percy, though without public funding. They were at Bute Street AME Church, the U.S. Dispensary on Fenchurch Street, Calvert Street, and a ropewalk near the gas works. Several missionary schools closed for want of funds and the failure of their teachers to return south after the 1867 summer holiday.[47]

Virginia's 1868 constitution authorized creation of the state's first public school system; the new program was initiated two years later, though again without funding. Pressed by the Freedmen's Bureau and such black leaders as Joseph T. Wilson, the city council agreed in 1870 to underwrite black public schools. The two public schools still open united with the white system, though all their teachers were to be black. To no one's surprise, funds for black schools fell well below those for white ones.[48]

After the Civil War it seemed that blacks would gain little by the Union victory. Many refugees appealed in 1865 to the Freedmen's Bureau for work, but jobs were found for barely half who applied. To care for the destitute, the bureau opened a "soup house" at its hospital (established in 1855 for yellow fever victims) in the ropewalk section. Marcia Colton was matron of the hospital's "Home for Old Ladies." But the number of destitute fell slowly for several years.[49]

As hope of large-scale redistribution of confiscated farmlands faded, freedom seemed a tainted gain. Thousands of Norfolk-area blacks acquired rudiments of literacy, but such minimal attainments opened few doors of opportunity. By 1870 black churches included Bute (the city's oldest black congregation) and Catharine Street Baptists, St. James Methodist, and St. John's AME. But white leaders seemed determined to keep blacks servile, whatever Washington might desire. A white mob in late 1866 wrecked Joseph T. Wilson's paper, *The True Southerner*.[50]

Blacks could hope for a voice in the city and state only if they gained the vote. The black population doubled in the war years, in 1870 comprising almost half the city's 19,000 people. With the spectacle of race riots and the "Black Codes" before it, and a growing unrest with Andrew Johnson's policies and personality, Congress in 1867 turned to radical solutions to Reconstruction's challenges. The war-spawned Pierpont regime was abolished and Virginia became a military district under a Union general. Norfolk officials refusing to take an oath of allegiance to the federal goverment were replaced by those who would.[51]

The congressional plan required Virginia to adopt a new state constitution, with blacks eligible to vote and serve in the constitutional convention. Whites who held prewar federal office but aided secession were disenfranchised. For the moment, this gave Virginia a black majority of eligible voters, including a small preponderance in Norfolk. It was a chance for blacks to join in shaping a future in which they might have full citizenship and representation at all levels of government.[52]

Norfolk blacks eligible to vote exceeded whites by 2,049 to 1,910.

Voting for the first time in October 1867, they chose a white, Henry M. Bowden, and black leader Thomas Bayne as delegates to the constitutional convention. A Norfolk County black, George Teamoh, was also a delegate. All were Republicans (usually called Radicals for endorsing a constitutional black voting franchise); their opponents, mostly white, were known as Conservatives. Radicals dominated the convention (twenty-five of 105 delegates were black), which endorsed the black franchise, though Bayne, its leading black, lost a fight to integrate public schools.[53]

Conservatives resisted provisions in the draft constitution barring former Confederates from voting and holding office. They successfully lobbied Grant's administration to let Virginians vote in referendum separately on the disqualifications and, possibly, endorse the constitution's main features while rejecting what they saw as its most offensive parts. The referendum was held on July 6, 1869; voters also chose state officers and congressmen.[54]

In an exciting campaign, Radicals carried Norfolk for gubernatorial candidate Henry H. Wells, though a split between Bayne and Vermonter James H. Platt gave a Conservative the second district congressional seat. Conservative Gilbert Walker of Norfolk became governor, his party gaining control of the assembly. Twenty-one blacks won assembly seats. Norfolk Conservatives celebrated on July 7, with Walker on a Granby Street balcony cheering his triumph over "vampires and harpies."[55]

It remained for Conservatives to capture the city government. Their hopes rose as former Confederates regained the vote, many carpetbaggers returned north, and the black voting majority dissolved. In the May 1870 city elections Conservatives won most offices, John B. Whitehead defeating Radical Peter Dilworth for mayor. Conservatives took over the city councils, although four blacks, including Thomas Paige and Joseph T. Wilson, won seats as did several white Radicals. The councils soon gerrymandered most blacks into the fourth ward and reduced that ward's representation from eleven to five.[56]

In essence, Virginia's Reconstruction was over. Norfolk blacks had a small role in city affairs and might perhaps exploit splits among Conservatives. But the withdrawal of federal troops in early 1870 left them without their main defense against exploitation. Economic and educational gains were meaningful but neither widely dispersed nor deeply rooted. Efforts by the Colored National Labor Union in 1869 to organize black dockworkers achieved little, owing in part to uncertainty over whether blacks should organize with or without white co-workers.[57]

White Conservatives saw the 1870 result as rescuing city and state from immoral men. H. W. Burton's 1877 *History of Norfolk* hailed a triumph of "white men with white men's principles," a government "'redeemed, regenerated and disenthralled.'" The state legislature reduced black voting by means of a poll tax, loss of voting rights for those convicted of petty larceny, and a return to voice voting.[58]

Although politics was now thoroughly polarized by race, the Conservative measures did not achieve their goals. Blacks still voted in proportions almost equal to whites, even controlling some counties. They sent Norfolk's Henry Platt to Congress in 1872 as Grant carried Virginia. Platt was re-elected in 1874 and 1876, but the result in the latter year was overturned by charges, probably true, that he bribed his way to victory. The conservative *Virginian*, historian Burton's employer, paid poll taxes for some six hundred blacks to buy their votes in the contest.[59]

Norfolk blacks holding office in this era included, besides Bayne, Rev. Miles Connor, elected to the House of Delegates in 1875. Also in the House were Norfolk County's Charles E. Hodges (1869–71) and Richard G. L. Paige, who served three terms in the 1870s and 1880s. Fourth ward delegates to the city council included H. H. Portlock, J. D. Eps, and barber Jacob Riddick. The county sent George Teamoh to the state senate in 1869.[60]

Black voting strength translated into some social gains, including unsegregated trains and the right to dine at most restaurants and hotels and attend theaters and other places of amusement. It killed a proposed railroad bond in 1870 and carried one for a trolley to Ocean View soon afterward. The black community maintained cohesion through its numerous organizations—the Monitor Union Society, Sons of Houn, Humble Sons of God, Zion's Sons, the Independent Society, and others. The Eureka Lodge of Elks was said to be the nation's oldest black fraternal organization. Black pastors played key roles in politics as in other endeavors.[61]

For all its racial tensions and inequities, Virginia had no Ku Klux Klan to intimidate black and white Republicans. Despite friction, the races in Norfolk and the state handled the transition to a new society with a measure of forebearance. For blacks as well as whites, the postwar era was one of liberation from old constraints, but the unbuttoning did not dissolve into chaos. On the other hand, it did not provide blacks that share in the national wealth that was their just reward for generations of productive toil. For this reason, they would be unable to resist the concerted assault on their civil liberties that closed out the nineteenth century.

CHAPTER 17

Ruffles, Truffles,
and Scuffles

THE *Svetlana* had scarcely dropped anchor below Fort Norfolk on the morning of January 13, 1877, when a report was out that navy yard officers were planning a "grand ball" to honor their Russian counterparts. It was news to gladden the hearts of Norfolk's social elite, especially the young people. The pre-Lenten social season was already in a glossy blur of crinolines and Prince Alberts, and a smart military dance would be a fine way to top off the winter's agenda of parties, hops, and Germans. Only gradually in the next few weeks would Norfolk realize that the Russians meant to spend the winter, and that the navy men were plotting an extravaganza beyond anything the city had ever seen.[1]

It got off to an awkward start. Navy men gave a German for the Russians at the Masonic Temple on the night of January 13, but the visitors had dismally unpronounceable names and few spoke English. They were unfamiliar with local dance styles, seemed perhaps rather stiff, and tended to leave early. Managers of the Opera House, however, invited the principal Russians to Miss Neilson's *Juliet* on January 22, and here Norfolk began to gain some awareness of the social whirlwind gathering strength around it.[2]

The Russians made their appearance just after the curtain rose at 8:00 P.M., passing in full dress down both aisles to reserved boxes decorated with "flags of all nations." In the lead was Grand Duke Alexis, son of Czar Alexander II, and his cousin, Grand Duke Constantine. Frenzied whisperings carried about the hall the identities of Barons Sternberg, Schilling, and Englehardt, Ensign Prince Bariatinsky, Prince Gargarin, Sub-Lieutenant Princes Obolinsky and Scherlatoff, Flag-Lieutenant Prince Alexieff, Count Conovnitzin, and others. Only now was it clear that the imperial Romanovs, among the world's most extravagant and incorrigible party animals, had descended in force on Norfolk and no doubt meant to wring from the town as

Grand Dukes Alexis and Constantine take their morning exercise aboard the *Svetlana* during the memorable visit of Russian ships to Norfolk in the winter of 1877–78. (From *Frank Leslie's Illustrated Newspaper*)

much winter amusement as it could be made to yield. Miss Neilson did her best, but no mere Montague or Capulet could rival the glamorous occupants of the lower boxes.[3]

The Russians turned up everywhere. Grand Duke Alexis returned to the Opera House on the twenty-third to see Neilson as Viola in *Twelth Night.* (Four policemen guarded against a reappearance in the cheap seats of raucous boys who repeatedly interrupted the *Juliet* with derisive howls.) A party at a restaurant on the twentieth tried in vigorous Russian to order a bottle of claret but got a leg of mutton instead. *Svetlana*'s thirty-eight-piece band played on the twenty-fifth at the Norfolk German Club dance. Alexis joined the Norfolk Fox Hunting Society at Thomas Morrisett's "Witch Duck" farm on the January 26; he hunted ducks a few days later in Currituck and got four with one shot. He was at the Opera House again on February 5 for the Boucicault Dramatic Company's *Forbidden Fruit,* and was seen often at the Atlantic Hotel.[4]

Out on the river, navy brass exchanged visits and honors daily; the *Hartford* dined the royals on February 7. The menu featured oysters with Chablis, gumbo soup with Amontillado, baked black bass with Sauterne, cotel-lottes a la Milanese with Nefersteiner, roast turkey with Chateau Leonville, canvasback ducks and quail on toast, ice cream, wine jelly, chocolate custard with Madeira, Bordeaux, and Champagne, and other improbable staples of the galley. The *Hartford* band rendered Verdi's overture, Shubert's serenade, and other tasteful selections.[5]

All this and more was but preliminary to the ball on February 8 in two "elegantly dressed" three hundred-foot-long rooms of the Navy Yard Pro-visions and Clothing Department in Portsmouth. The 1,400 guests in-cluded many from Norfolk's leading families who came over at 9:00 P.M. on the *N. P. Banks*, lent by Old Dominion steamship line, or on navy launches. There were guests from Brooklyn and Grammercy Park, New York, Wash-ington, Baltimore, Charlottesville, Richmond, and elsewhere, many of them state and federal dignitaries and their ladies. Among nineteen numbers danced were quadrilles, waltzes, galops, polkas, lancers, and a Virginia reel, the ladies' gilt-edged dance cards furnished by Tiffany of New York. At midnight intermission, guests moved to other rooms with festive boards set for dinner before once again taking the dance floor.[6]

Landmark editor James Barron Hope was atwitter over "gilded creatures more fair than ever peopled the raptest dream of love from poet's brain. Laughing, chattering, flirting, winding through unnumbered labyrinthine mazes were beings more . . . beauteous than the Houri of Mahometan Para-dise." There were "fair Blondinas in blue, laughing divinities in satin and lace . . . , Rowenas in pure white, with locks of sheeny flaxen, Evangelines with tresses 'like imprison'd sunbeams,' dark-eyed, languishing Virginias, whose every motion made the air seem fragrant as the tropics." Ports-mouth's Eugenia Murtaugh was a vision in blue silk "the hue of the cloud-less sky," priceless old lace at her throat and wrists; Norfolk's Sally Newton was dazzling in white brocaded satin, blue silk overskirt trimmed in white lace, with pearls and diamonds.[7]

Not since antebellum years had Virginia seen such a spectacle. (Mark Twain, who coined the term "Gilded Age," was all but overlooked in the champagne mist of elegant folderol when he spoke at the Masonic Temple February 1 on "How to Edit an Agricultural Newspaper.") The event came off with "a brilliancy and éclat," wrote Hope, "that will mark it an era in the memory of all the fortunate participants." The *Landmark*, with its flattering commentary on the dress of female guests, sold out three navy ball editions, the largest newspaper sale so far in Norfolk's history. Nor was the season over. Alexis hosted a *matinee dansante* on *Svetlana* on February 14 with a repast of Ros Bif a l'Anglaise, truffles, patés de foie gras, and cotelottes Po-jarske, alongside Jambon de Norfolk and Terinne de Sarcelles de Norfolk.[8]

So far, at least, the visit of the Imperial Russian Navy had been a re-sounding success, but there remained weeks in which many things might go awry. Little notice, for example, had been given to the scores of Russian sailors who roamed the downtown streets by night. These, too, soon found means of introduction to the public.

Lavish entertainment was only a lighter side of the dynamics of the Gilded Age, which could express itself in more volatile ways. In particular, politics in the era was corrupted by forms of vice and fraud more vicious than any hitherto seen in a democracy. Norfolk was spared the excesses of graft that despoiled some governments, but William Lamb and Michael Glennan provided the kind of barefisted vendetta that in 1881 cost the na-tion one president and ere long deprived it of another.

Surely Glennan, the *Virginian's* editor, prodded Mayor Lamb with a sharp stick in printing a letter of August 23, 1882, from "H." in Surry County. In "H.'s" view, Lamb had lately been bested on the stump in Surry by a black opponent when the mayor tried "in the most ranting manner" to show that Bourbon politicians had for sixteen years oppressed Virginia's poor, both black and white. Lamb appealed to the "lowest passions and prej-udices," urging the poor of both races to "stand shoulder to shoulder against the better classes, . . . their natural enemies and oppressors."[9]

The letter no doubt misrepresented Lamb, but he did his cause no good by publishing an ill-considered "card" on September 9 against the "infa-mous liar" who wrote the letter and Glennan for printing it. Lamb called Glennan "a base ingrate and contemptible scoundrel" who would be hereaf-ter "treated by me, if he goes too far, precisely as I would treat a mad dog that attacks me."[10]

Stung by this harshness, Glennan used his September 10 front page to review his twenty-five-year relationship with Lamb. It was the tale of a poor, crippled Irish boy who sought work at Lamb's office in 1857. Hired at $4.00 a week, he had regarded Lamb "with all the love and confidence that ever youth paid to character." Lamb seemed "the ideal of true worth and man-hood . . . no other man like him." Barred by lameness from the army, Glen-nan followed Lamb to Fort Fisher anyhow, served him there as devotedly as in Norfolk, and fought by him in many battles. When the fort fell in 1865, Glennan found Lamb severely wounded, sent for help, "watched by his side, attending every want," and saved his life.[11]

Returning home, Glennan continued, Lamb promised him work in token of his loyalty, even reiterating "his *written* promise." But Glennan, now a young man of nineteen, arriving at Lamb's office, was told that his idol's affairs "would not admit of him giving employment" at that time. It was Glennan's "first experience of how little there is in the word friendship." He resolved never again to ask a favor of Lamb, found other work, and rose through bitter struggle to acclaim as a journalist.[12]

All loyalty forfeited, Glennan could now reveal Lamb's record of infamy: his rumored breech of honor on a William and Mary examination, his contempt for Norfolk war veterans in giving work needed by whites to former slaves. There was Lamb's enticing of investors' funds into a failing bank (First National) while he was president, those who lost all by endorsing his notes and, since his 1880 election as mayor ("under false colors"), his "cunning and despicable" bullying of the police. Lately had come the new Norfolk charter "that could only have emanated from a mind that combined . . . the qualities of Caligula and Nero." As for Lamb's "cowardly threat," Glennan stood ready to "meet him, defending myself by the rights that God and the law gave me."[13]

It was an editorial assault as furious as any public figure in Norfolk had been compelled to endure. On a personal level, Glennan's rage was that of mingled envy and unrequited love, an affirmation of the claims of virtuous self-reliance against the arrogance of inherited status. But it was something more, for 1882 was seething with battles of Funder and Readjuster to control state government, ruled for three years past by the latter. Glennan stressed Lamb's recent about-face that swung him from the Funders to the camp of the Republican-Readjuster coalition. The mayor, in short, was no less unfaithful to political than personal friends.[14]

For Glennan and the Funders, who controlled Norfolk's three major newspapers, Readjuster success in scaling down the payment of Virginia's prewar debt to bondholders was an assault on property rights and integrity in government. That Readjusters crusaded for black political equality, aid for farmers and small businessmen, more funds for public schools, strict regulation of middlemen, and so on, smacked of communism—a revolution in the relationship between government and governed.[15] Only by the defeat of bosses Lamb, Mahone, and their cohorts could the stench of indecency and malign policy be purged from the Old Dominion.

In this fetid atmosphere, it mattered little that Glennan stooped to purveying gossip and unfounded charges. Lamb, as the editor soon conceded, was not president of First National when it failed. If he rejected Lamb in 1865, they were evidently friends as recently as 1881, when Glennan wrote what Lamb called a "splendid article" on Lamb's role at Fort Fisher and Lamb visited Glennan's home, met his wife, and was shown his baby.[16]

In spite of their personalizing of the issue, the origin of the hatred between the men was narrowly political. Lamb was elected in 1880 and 1882 by a coalition not unlike that of the progressives, Republicans, and blacks who defeated the Funders at the state level in 1879. He incurred the wrath of local Conservatives as mayor by a campaign to clean up the police department. Owing in part to rapid growth, Norfolk, its population 22,000 by 1880, was reputed to be a den of gamblers, drunks, and prostitutes. Lamb, before taking office, promised his diary to "get rid of as much of the Police court as possible." His election, with both white and black majorities, seemed to him a mandate for reform.[17]

Soon after taking office, Lamb had Assistant Chief Jacob R. Mowle and Sergeant J. R. Pettis dismissed for violating police board regulations. He was soon after Sheriff Andrew J. Dalton for instances of drunk and disorderly conduct, and in early 1882 got Dalton and several other policemen dismissed. These actions were assailed by the newspapers as a vendetta against political foes. Lamb also had increasing trouble with the police commission—a creature of the city council—which obstructed him in various ways, hiring and firing personnel over his objections.[18]

Lamb fought back by amending Norfolk's charter to give him further powers. He drew up the proposals himself and sent them to Richmond, where a Readjuster legislature in April 1882 passed all but one, giving him more control over the police. They gave the mayor, reelected in May, a veto over the council and called for filling select council seats in at-large elections to reduce the power of Conservative ward organizations. Conservatives blasted the changes as a power-grab without popular endorsement and detected enough in-fighting among Readjusters to sense a possible victory in 1882. Giving up the debt-funding issue in favor of a cry of "Negro domination," they resolved to destroy Mahone's insurgents once and for all.[19]

The city press focus on Lamb's ties with Readjusters and Mahone aided Norfolk's budding ring of vice-den proprietors and ward bosses. Lamb recognized that the city government's power was so dispersed among boards and commissions that he must try to gather the loose strands of administration into his own hands. But he did not persuade the editors, who discerned in his efforts little more than self-promotion. Attempts to establish a Readjuster or Liberal paper failed, and Lamb had to vie with the vice lords on an uneven field. By the time he left office, a ring existed that even reforming Democrats would find almost unassailably powerful.[20]

Lamb's reforming zeal, expressed in orders to arrest anyone found publicly drunk on Sunday (twenty-four were taken the first Sabbath) and occasional jihads against disreputable neighborhoods, was not universally popular. Profits from such places had bought some leading families their claims to respectability. A sound police force was deemed to be one that understood which vice-dens to harass and which to ignore. Lamb, some felt, lacked a keen sense of the proper nuances of municipal leadership.[21]

Lamb responded to Glennan's attack on October 9 in a pamphlet giving his own view of their relationship. Mailed to hundreds of Lamb's allies, it cited his long solicitude for Glennan's welfare as well as his struggles in behalf of the rights of Irish and Catholic immigrants. He denied that his wartime association with Glennan had been very close, that the editor saved his life.[22]

The stakes in this squalid dispute were high. Lamb, a close associate of Mahone, was honored in 1880 as Norfolk's "most popular citizen"; his personal standing was a key to Readjuster and reformist strength in the Hampton Roads area. If public perception of him could be altered, Virginia Readjusters might suffer a heavy blow and, if so, what a Danville paper called "the viper of negroism" might be eradicated.[23] One more election campaign might topple the popular mayor and his Readjuster allies.

An obvious point of attack for Funders was Lamb's debt to fourth ward blacks who, after splitting into Republican factions in 1881, reunited under the leadership of Readjusters Thomas F. and R. G. L. Paige, the latter a member of the House of Delegates. (R. G. L. Paige petitioned the lawmakers successfully for a black college, now Virginia State University; Thomas F. in 1885 published *Twenty Two Years of Freedom,* recounting black gains since slavery.) Eight blacks served on the councils in the 1880s, James E. Fuller for eight years. Such examples might be treated as threatening black domination, with Lamb partially to blame.[24] The lines were drawn for a vicious showdown.

Gilded Age moral standards conflicted sharply with the tenets of Victorianism. When not in the ballroom, Norfolk women were likely, wrote a male observer, to abandon "loose draperies, floating gauziness or ethereal accessories of any kind." The new style, called "Henry II," was worn "tight as human nature can endure" and "Everything in sight is real and solid." Some males professed to be scandalized by women wearing "semi-nude or transparent garb" to church, especially "tight fitting . . . white muslin . . . without an outer garment." When an anonymous placard appeared near some churches on a Sunday in 1879 denouncing the style, the police chief sent officers to search out the culprit for insulting women, an initiative warmly endorsed by the newspapers.[25]

Leisure activities continued to expand, by the 1880s embracing the sports of "pedestrianism" (walking races), pigeon shooting, roller skating, trotting races, football (between police and fire departments), "gymnasium clubs," and so on. Fishing had always been popular but never so frenetically as when three Norfolk men caught one thousand fish in a half-day's outing in August 1882. A railroad through "a seemingly almost interminable forest" to Ocean View was finished in 1879. Virginia Beach was predicted to become one of the South's great summer resorts when the Seaside Hotel and Land Company bought five miles of its waterfront in 1882. In the next year, the Princess Anne Hotel opened, as did a railroad between Virginia Beach and Norfolk.[26] (*Light* rail, at that!)

Still popular, though reviled by many, was cockfighting. One of the memorable sporting events in late nineteenth-century Norfolk County was a two-day "main of cocks" matched at the "Monkey House," a Lambert's Point warehouse favored for such events, in April 1888. It set twenty-five North Carolina cocks individually against twenty-five from Virginia. In a final and deciding match, "D. D.," the Tar Heel entry, plunged its gaff "so deeply the cocks were stuck and the gaff had to be pulled out." But the dying Virginia bird delivered a *sic-semper-roosteris* cut that caught its adversary in the throat and ripped it open, the Carolinian expiring before its rival and giving Virginia victory.[27]

The *Virginian* described it as "marked by the most orderly conduct, and remarkable from the fact that those present [were] of the highest order of sporting men." A fan long afterward recalled it as the last cockfight "in which people of any prominence socially in North Carolina had a part."[28]

Despite rapid growth following the war, Norfolk in the mid-1880s retained its boundaries of a half-century earlier. Main Street had evolved into rows of three-story brick stores, many with wooden Indians and other figures attached to front walls and jutting onto the sidewalks under canvas awnings. The new Atlantic Hotel was a prominent edifice (an older one had burned), stretching from Granby Street to Randolph in French chateau style under a mansard roof. To the east were the new Academy of Music, several banks, and the Purcell House, where Frank James, Jesse's brother, stayed briefly with his wife around 1882. (On the run from lawmen and looking for a place to settle, he registered as "Warren." He later told a Missouri judge he "didn't like" Norfolk and went on to Lynchburg, where he rented a house.)[29]

As of old, the busiest part of town was Market Square, served by two ferries and a streetcar line. Here gathered before dawn each market day hundreds of fish and oyster carts, seasonal wagonloads of fresh fruits and vegetables from nearby truck farms, and Currituck Sound and Dismal Swamp vendors of game. On Saturday nights, hawkers of every kind of portable commodity crowded the square under torchlights to magnify the merits of their patent medicines, soaps, and other goods.[30]

The Academy of Music was packed almost nightly with audiences relishing performances of New York dramatic companies, some of which opened their touring seasons there. Al Field's minstrels, giant burlesque comedian DeWolf Hopper, operettas such as *HMS Pinafore* and *Pirates of Penzance,* and tragedians Fredericke Warde and Louis James, among others, performed there. Minstrel parades were second only to circus parades in outdoor crowd appeal. From 1870 a free public library had been maintained at the Norfolk Academy (now the Chamber of Commerce) on Bank Street; earlier libraries had been open only to subscribers.[31]

Church Street teemed with stores and bars, but also synagogues, churches, and hospitals, along with Odd Fellows Hall, and, just over the city limits (in Huntersville), Lesner's Maplewood Gardens, the area's nearest approximation of a public park. On the east side of Church Street extension, Sheriff John Lesner had excavated an oval lake fed with well-water by a windmill-operated fountain. The surrounding park was dotted with magnolias, maples, and other shade trees. Its fenced paddock held deer, swans, geese, ducks, cages for black bear, raccoons, wild cats, and other animals. Entry was gained through a brick building with a multistoried tower and other architectural flourishes.[32]

Urban living gained added attraction with the introduction of telephone service (the exchange was over L. W. Jordan's Roanoke Square store) in 1879 and, two years later, electric lights. The first building illuminated was the Atlantic Hotel. Richmond installed the nation's first electric (or trolley) cars in 1887; Norfolk replaced her horsecars with them seven years later.[33]

Gilded Age Norfolkians could choose among nearly five hundred places of business within city limits, including twenty-six restaurants and saloons and eleven banks. By 1877 there were four Masonic lodges and two of Oddfellows, besides Knights of Pithias, Heptasophs, Rechabites, and other fraternal orders. Jews were welcomed in all of these; they also had their own Orders of B'nai B'rith and Kesher Shel Barzel, with Moses E. Myers, Jacob Hecht, Zachariah Hofheimer, and Samuel Weil among their leaders. Women as well as men were being drawn into an increasingly potent temperance movement, led by the Women's Christian Temperance Union (Mrs. Eliza O. Scott was first president of the Norfolk chapter) and the still more ambitious Roman Catholic Total Abstinence Society.[34]

Public education for whites was still limited in 1876 to the original, un-derbudgeted elementary schools on Fenchurch, Charlotte, Queen, and Boush streets. The seven hundred students in Superintendent H. C. Percy's black system merged administratively in 1871 with the whites. Overcrowd-ing forced split school days at the two remaining black schools, on Bute and North streets, each accommodating sixty pupils in the morning and as many more in the afternoon. Many of the black teachers were products of Hamp-ton Normal Institute. Of a school-age population of 3,500 in 1886, only two thousand were enrolled. Public school overcrowding was a boon to private schools, but Superintendent George W. Taylor noted in 1887 that "not one step of advancement in the curriculum" had occurred in fourteen years.[35]

A notable private school was started for girls in 1873 by Irene Leache and Anna Cogswell Wood. Leache–Wood Seminary on Freemason Street (after 1882) offered not only traditional women's studies in art, music, and literature, but English, Latin, and math. The ladies held soirees for "fine conversation" and dancing, these evolving into a Fireside Club for discus-sions of literature, art, religion, and philosophy. After Miss Leache's death in 1900 (the seminary was sold two years earlier), Miss Wood established a memorial art collection in the public library. These seedlings were the source of much of Norfolk's twentieth-century high culture.[36]

Because the seminary accommodated only small numbers, lumberman John L. Roper and other prominent citizens in 1880 organized the Norfolk School for Young Ladies. Located at the corner of Granby and Washington, it offered gas lights, steam radiators, and hot water, besides elocution, calis-thenics, music, art, literature, math, French, German, and a "domestic de-partment." Bookkeeping and secretarial skills were added by the 1890s as opportunities for women increased. It closed in 1899 but another, Mary Washington College, under Misses Virginia Reynolds and Mary Buchanan Randolph, operated in the same buildings for several years. Alumnae of the Norfolk College by 1948 had helped over fifty young women further their educations through loans and scholarships.[37]

Norfolk native Mary Jeffry Galt in 1888 founded the Association for the Preservation of Virginia Antiquities (APVA). The loss of such historic structures as Powhatan's house in Gloucester County and the vandalized and neglected rubble at Jamestown ignited in Miss Galt a fire for preserva-tion that led APVA to acquire Jamestown Island in 1893. The site was made presentable for tourists by the time of the 1907 Jamestown Exposition. With the aid of Barton Myers and its Norfolk chapter, APVA was instrumental in saving many old buildings, including Bacon's Castle in Surry County and the Cape Henry Lighthouse at Virginia Beach.[38]

In 1905 Leache–Wood graduates formed an alumnae association aimed at collecting art objects as a memorial to Miss Leache. The group evolved in 1917 into the Norfolk Society of Arts, which won city council support for an art museum "in the vicinity of Lee Park and west of Duke Street," site of the present art museum. When Miss Wood died in 1940, she left an endowment that was used to purchase art, sponsor exhibits and programs, and offer prizes in poetry and essays. Meanwhile, another pair of maiden ladies, Evelyn Southall and Ethel Neely, started St. George's, a school of high quality where began the career of Miss Caperton Preston, founder of the celebrated Preston School of Dancing.[39]

In 1881 George M. Bain (later Norfolk's first high school principal) proposed to Mayor Lamb the consolidation of Norfolk, Portsmouth, and surrounding villages. Not until 1887, however, was the first step taken toward old Norfolk's enlargement with the annexation of Brambleton. This was an eastern suburb on the old George Bramble farm where nearly nine hundred families had settled from the early 1870s. Three years later Norfolk added Atlantic City on the west, home of the Norfolk Knitting and Cotton Manufacturing Company (employing two hundred girls and women) and lumber enterprises. Both additions were soon served by the Norfolk Railroad Company. The annexations were one reason for Norfolk's population leap from 22,000 in 1880 to 35,000 a decade later.[40]

The economic rationale for Norfolk's expansion was the growth of the cotton and coal business and continuing success of its truck farming and older enterprises. (Some three million quarts of strawberries were harvested locally in 1878, and J. R. Young's 150–acre Norfolk County strawberry farm was said to be the world's largest.) Oystering alone employed over five hundred local boats apart from thousands involved in "catching" them with tongs and dredges. Almost half a million bushels were packed annually by the 1880s for shipment coast-to-coast and to Europe. Lynnhaven River oysters had a reputation as being among the world's most flavorful.[41]

Cotton, the core of the city's foreign trade, gained importance with each new mile of track to Norfolk. The Atlantic Coast Line, through Suffolk and Tarboro, North Carolina, opened in the late 1880s, the Atlantic and Danville in 1890. These and older lines to the coalfields gave Norfolk abundant cheap coal, making it a favored stopover for refueling steamships. Norfolk and Western put a huge coal pier at Lambert's Point and shipped to buyers from

Most of Norfolk's 1,200 or so oyster shuckers were black. By the 1800s, however, they had been driven out of the dredging and sale of oysters by well-financed outsiders. (From *Frank Leslie's Weekly Illustrated Newspaper,* 1885)

Maine to Cuba. Hampton Roads, supplied mainly by Norfolk and Western, Virginian, and Chesapeake and Ohio rails, was the world's leading coal port.[42]

Black property owners more than doubled (to 167) during the 1870s, but black businessmen were driven out of the lucrative oyster business by commercial developments. As the fame of Norfolk-area bivalves spread, investors from the North and elsewhere took over the business. By 1884 northerner J. S. Darling, a post–Civil War settler at Hampton, packed up to two hundred thousand bushels yearly, the world's largest oyster concern. Black oystermen quit or, like John Billups, who opened a Church Street store, switched to related work. Many black laborers remained, the city's fifteen packing plants in 1880 employing 1,200 shuckers, mostly black.[43]

Possibly one-third of the black laborers worked seasonally on truck farms; wages earned this way were the only income available to many. Most probably had no regular employment and could be hurt, even at the height of farming season, by bad weather. Because many women and children were required to take farm work, the latter often missed school; this meant a long-term deficit for the black community. On the other hand, many of the small boats in the "mosquito fleet" that carried farm produce to market were black-owned and sometimes swarmed up to 150 at a time along the wharves.[44]

Leading black organizations included the Grand United Order of Tents, Virginia's oldest female lodge and originally part of the underground railroad. The Tents, destined to become one of the nation's largest black female organizations, was founded in Norfolk. Along with the Colored Female Providence Society and others, Tents provided members with burial and accident insurance, housing for indigent women, and relief for the poor and widows—services often not otherwise available to members.[45]

The "Farmer's Revolt" of the 1880s produced black as well as white Farmers' Alliances seeking aid for southern and western agriculturalists. In Norfolk, a Colored Farmers' Alliance appeared in 1888. It was organized and led by Joseph J. Rogers, a white who sought help from the national white Alliance by talking of white "superiority and intelligence" and the benefits of segregation. Blacks tolerated his strategy until an 1891 investigation revealed mishandling of Alliance money. Rogers absconded during the inquiry with most of the funds, and the organization soon folded.[46]

The winter's visit of the Russian Imperial Navy in 1877–78, despite its social glitter, was not an unqualified success. There was dash and color to spare but, while Brahmans filled ball and banquet rooms, Russian sailors prowled the city's nether regions in search of earthier recreation and had little trouble finding it. The *Svetlana*'s crew of five hundred was soon augumented by the corvette *Bogatir*'s 380 and the *Askold*'s 325, an aggregate large enough to tax even Norfolk's considerable resources for vice and mayhem. Newspapers initially treated the sailors indulgently, citing, for example, the "amusement" offered by Russians who, "after taking a drop too much," were apt to "make things lively."[47]

They were apt, in fact, to make things downright anarchic. In late January a drunken Russian tried to strike a patrolman; he was required by a witnessing officer to kneel and kiss the back of the patrolman's hand three times. Offenders at first may have been escorted to their ships but, by February, Mayor Tucker's court was fining them for drunk and disorderly conduct. On February 14 some Russians engaged in a half-hour fight at Taylor and Loyall's store on Main Street before police broke it up. When a policeman tried to halt a fight in a house at Church and Union, some Russians threw him down a flight of stairs.[48]

By now Norfolk, inured as it was to off-duty Saturnalia, began to complain. The *Virginian* pouted that the visitors' behavior "is disorderly in the extreme," and should not be tolerated. They had several times trespassed, added the *Public Ledger,* on the premises of citizens in the upper part of the city, "and yesterday one . . . entered a residence on Main street and frightened the Lady of the house so badly as to cause her to jump out the back window." Notwithstanding colorful parties, the city sighed in relief when the Russians sailed on March 20.[49]

Time and legend embellished the Russian visit into a symbol of Norfolk's Gilded Age. Folklore immortalized a young lady who, swooning in Grand Duke Alexis's arms at the navy ball, was adroitly passed off by him with the terse remark: "Toodamthinovitch."[50] Norfolk was no gilded city, but the episode gave it cause to imagine itself not unequal in social tone to Richmond and Washington—given the proper circumstances. For Norfolkians, this was a heady recognition, the advent of an epoch in their history.

The Lamb–Glennan feud ground to a standoff in the winter of 1882–83 after Glennan issued another windy pamphlet: "A Review of a Reply to a Paper which Included the Sketch of Two Lives." Lamb's Readjusters lost assembly seats in the 1883 state elections. But the assembly had lately awarded Norfolk's fourth precinct a sixth council member and two Select Council seats, doubling the four wards to eight. Councilman Peter Wilson evinced a new mood on the part of blacks, announcing that he would not vote for city electric lights unless the fourth ward got its share.[51]

Conservative Democrats, buoyed by success elsewhere, resolved to finish Mahone, Lamb, and the other Readjusters. The *Landmark*'s James Barron Hope took up the attack, again focusing on Lamb's handling of the police. On Sunday morning, March 23, 1884, police Sergeant Phil Mordecai led a raid on J. E. Brown's black Queen Street "gambling house," seizing twenty-five men, four women, and gambling "paraphernalia." Lamb was out of town but, returning on the twenty-fifth, suspended Mordecai and eleven others, a third of the force. Police Commissioners R. Y. Zachary and Washington Taylor contested Lamb's action and were told that the raiders had no warrant, that "the Commissioners had put thieves and cut-throats on the force."[52]

On the twenty-seventh Zachary and Taylor exchanged hot words with Lamb in his office: "Do you mean, Colonel Lamb," Zachary demanded, "that I have lied?" "Yes," Lamb replied, "you are a liar and a puppy." Zachary slapped Lamb's face and others seized both to prevent a fight. The *Landmark* huffed that other cities tried to strengthen the police "in dealing with the criminal classes. With us this department has been made a political machine."[53] This was true enough, though the machine was demonstrably not of Lamb's making.

Norfolk's microcosm reflected tactics used elsewhere to shatter Mahone's legions. In 1883 the Conservatives changed their name back to Democrats, came out strongly against "Mahoneism," and set off a wave of hysteria, including five deaths in a Danville riot, over the threat of black social equality. They won decisively, and began molding Virginia into a one-party state. Readjusters won Norfolk's House of Delegates seats, but the result was challenged, the Democratic House declaring the seats vacant. Readjusters won a second election in early 1884, but Mahone was ousted from the senate a year later and Democrat Barton Myers became mayor in 1886. Lamb's charter revision was soon repealed.[54]

Democrats could now afford to be generous. Myers, reviewing Lamb's three terms, cited what he saw as its main achievements, "probably more than any equal period before." They included: departmental improvements, opening City Hall Avenue and Plume Street to give businesses more frontage, Main Street's granite paving, paving or repair of other streets, extension of Queen and Bush, a fireproof clerk's office, additions made to the jail and police station, sheds built at white schools to shield pupils from the sun, and the adoption of the Waring system of sewerage. The new waterworks had four times the capacity of the old, the fire department was one of the state's best equipped, and so on.[55]

Lamb would no doubt have added his closing of illegal raffles and vice-dens in Cove, Cumberland, Wolfe, and Church streets. But vice-dens arose as quickly as they closed, and liquor dealers almost doubled (to 107) during his tenure. Two years later he noted bitterly that, though he was elected as a reformer, leading citizens "resisted my interference with their pastimes." The "moral portion of the community" allowed him "to be maligned . . . by the pimps" and others. To expect new mayor R. G. Banks to cure such evils, he added with characteristic overkill, was "a roaring farce," the grand jurors including men who played keno "and drink on Sundays at the nearest bar."[56]

Despite depending on black votes, white Readjusters did not seek social equality for blacks and were ambivalent about fostering black aspirations. In 1881 Lamb shunned a march commemorating Yorktown's centennial because white groups refused to parade if blacks did (and maybe because the commemoration was Glennan's idea). He sent police to prevent white stevedores from excluding blacks from jobs at the wharves, but also ordered separate chain gangs (formed in 1872) for white and black convict street workers. In 1880 he opposed "any colored man . . . being put on the [Readjuster] city ticket," though he allowed some in the nominating convention, and he tried to remove black leader James E. Fuller from his superintendent's post at the navy yard.[57]

Even so, blacks enjoyed tangible gains. Readjusters in 1879 turned out a one-legged Confederate-veteran doorkeeper in the House of Delegates in favor of G. W. Cook, a Norfolk black. Councilman James E. Fuller in 1881 ran on a promise to push the city's first public school built for blacks and, with two new black school commissioners, Jacob Riddick and John Gibson, fulfilled his promise with the construction of the Samuel C. Armstrong School. (Fuller was later secretary of Norfolk's Republican executive committee.) But Readjuster defeat would mean reversal of most black gains from the late 1860s.[58]

A token of continuing black political influence was the quiet struggle for a black cemetery. Historically, blacks had no formal cemetery, but utilized the Potter's Field just beyond the city's limits, vacant lots, back yards, and so on. In 1873, evidently responding to black appeals, the councils authorized another Potter's Field on Smith's Creek, west of Elmwood Cemetery. A decade later, Councilman Fuller petitioned that it be renamed West Point Cemetery, with a section for a memorial to black Civil War dead, a proposal ratified in 1885. Meanwhile, the councils in 1874 acquired fifty-three acres on Princess Anne Road for a black burying ground. The Civil War monument, a shaft topped by a black soldier standing amid the graves of nearly a hundred black veterans, was at last completed at West Point Cemetery in 1920.[59]

As the noose of Jim Crow segregation tightened, blacks created more social organizations for self-protection and self-fulfillment. Good Samaritans, Knights of Pythias, Odd Fellows, Knights of Gideon, Rose of Sharon Household of Ruth 100, Seven Wise Men, and others offered burial and insurance plans, fellowship, and help with urban adjustment. Norfolk blacks, led by William A. Hunton, in 1888 opened the nation's first black YMCA and, in 1886, their first high school, called Norfolk Mission College, on Princess Anne Avenue. Opening with ninety-six daytime and sixty-four evening students under an integrated faculty, the school soon produced well-trained graduates, many of whom became teachers in Norfolk's public schools. Booker T. Washington High opened in 1916.[60]

Excluded from white-owned restaurants and hotels, blacks compensated as well as their resources allowed. Thomas F. Paige's hotel, opened in the late 1870s on Market Square, was Norfolk's first for blacks; Fitchett and Porter's and George Richardson's boarding houses were established about the same time on Church Street. Among the more popular black eateries were those of James Carter, William Emmerson, and King, Moseley and Company downtown. Black-owned fish shops, groceries, and tobacco stores sprang up, along with Warren and Carle's Church Street furniture store, several butcher shops, doctors' offices, and others.[61]

Joseph T. Wilson, exiled to Petersburg when his newspaper was burned in 1866, returned in 1880 to open the *American Sentinel* to boost James A. Garfield's candidacy for president. Switching his political allegiance in 1885, he founded *The Right Way*, a Democratic paper. In 1890 he published *The Black Phalanx*, a volume on black soldiers from the Revolution to the Civil War. He established another paper after moving to Richmond in 1888.[62]

The fragile Readjuster coalition, truly united only in opposing Funders, collapsed when Conservatives concluded that Richmond was "worth a Mass"—or abandoning the albatross of debt-funding. But aftershocks of Readjuster defeat were felt in Norfolk and across Virginia for over a century. The absence from public life of such men as William Lamb, perhaps the most effective mayor Norfolk had ever had, and William Mahone, a genius at harmonizing factions, left Virginia in the hands of men with narrower vision.

Little affected by these events, Norfolk and Hampton Roads continued to grow in the 1880s under both Readjusters and Democrats. Both pursued progressive economic goals and fostered Norfolk's bounding prosperity. The *Public Ledger* mourned that Virginia's "high moral and political character . . . departed when we ceased to be a purely agricultural community," citing Jefferson's dictum that "cities are sores upon the body politic."[63] But there was little virtue in opposing what could not, in any case, be prevented.

If, on the other hand, cities were an inexpungible fact of life, it did not necessarily follow that urban vice must be an eternal given. Traditional politics had failed to rid Norfolk of its reputation for sin, but maybe nontraditional means deserved a trial. They soon got it, though the new wave of reformers had no idea how tenacious the Hydra they were setting out to slay was.

CHAPTER 18

The Brambleton Insurrection

THE TROUBLE was that those best qualified to answer the question were never asked. "Lottie Freeman," the Portuguese girl who hustled drinks at the Mascot Saloon, could probably have settled the issue at once. Cora Ray and Clara Ford at "The Slide" knew well enough, as did Belle Scheurman at Fentress's Bar. If none of these was available—they usually were—the question might be posed to Mollie Hogwood over at the Washington House or Flossie Freeman at the Novelty Theatre.[1]

Was Norfolk, as the New York *Town Topics* concluded, "the wickedest city in the United States"? Had the fair claims of Lexington, Kentucky, been adequately considered? Were Savannah and Omaha no longer in contention?[2]

The *New York Voice* tried to settle the matter on the front page of its June 7, 1894 edition with a diagram of a portion of downtown Norfolk. It was bounded north by Washington, east by Church, south by Water, and west by Bank. Within the zone lay Norfolk's "Hell's Half-Acre"—actually more like two hundred acres—seat of most of the city's 240-odd retail liquor establishments, including bars, saloons, gambling parlors, "policy shops," brothels, and "variety theaters." Those owned by ring politicians were helpfully noted on the map; conspicuously at dead geographical center of the zone lay the Norfolk police department.[3]

The Miller girls would have voted for Norfolk in the sin sweepstakes. When they signed with a booking agency in 1892 to take their song-and-dance act to the Novelty Theatre, they did not know its character and objected when manager Sam Wasserman made them hustle drinks between performances. When the elder sister took sick and wanted to return to New York, Wasserman held back part of their $15-a-week salary so she could not go. Judgment for the plaintiffs.[4]

Young Felton from over near Petersburg would also have voted for Norfolk. On the evening of February 22, 1893, he entertained some Novelty ladies over six quart-bottles of $5.00 wine in a private balcony box and was disencumbered of $970. . . . Misses Dora Lennon and Flossie Freeman gave the court little help, though perhaps it might have called on Florence Edwards, accused some weeks before of lifting $15.00 from a Novelty patron. In the meantime Nora Wells and Mollie Bassett brought up R. L. Dawes, who had "bruised and battered [them] in the most shocking manner" at his Water Street saloon.[5] Almost every night the police docket contained similar incidents.

The vice district could also be deadly, as when a Spanish sailor died in March 1893 from a beating at the Slide by proprietor Al Gillingham. George F. Taylor's Dismal Swamp Lottery Company, operating from rooms over the Novelty Theatre, was called by a state senator the "worst fraud east of the Mississippi," daily spinning illegal numbers on a glass wheel and telegraphing results to New York, Philadelphia, Washington, and elsewhere.[6]

Norfolk's sordid underworld, often explored in the city's newspapers, was the focus of a grand jury investigation in 1893. But it all sounded somehow more thrillingly sinister when itinerant Prohibition evangelist Sam Small arrived in April 1894 to diagnose the municipal ailment and prescribe a cure. A guest of the local Prohibition Party, Small drove Academy of Music audiences to righteous frenzy by delving in exquisite detail into Norfolk sin in what the *Landmark* called "the most severe arraignment of Norfolk's municipal government ever heard."[7]

For ten days the spellbinding Small hammered at the police commission for retaining men found drunk on duty, letting patrol wagons take home policemen too drunk to walk. What could be expected where six councilmen were whiskey dealers, where young men of Third Baptist Church were "brutally assaulted" for reporting a saloon that sold whiskey on Sunday, where most of the Norfolk Bicycle Club were underage yet their clubhouse sold illegal hooch? There must be an end to Peggy Temple, black "Queen of the Dance," performing shameful exhibitions in the bar at Talbot and Hill, to scarlet women working main thoroughfares "in extravagant finery, riding in open carriages with coachmen in livery."[8]

To audiences up to six thousand-strong and roaring with cheers and applause, Small raged at the council for running Norfolk $3 million into debt, wasting $114,000 on a malarial bog to be used as a public park. Worse was the decrepit public school system, still using its forty-year-old original buildings, all of them dark and poorly ventilated, packed fifty and sixty to a room. Norfolk had "the poorest school accommodations . . . of any city in the country"; it was the nation's only city of over five thousand with no high school. There was fraud in granting the horsecar franchise, skulduggery in issuing liquor licenses, chicanery in elections, bribery in tolerating thirty-five policy (lottery) shops, scandal in allowing eighty-one brothels "within the circle of the shadow of one church spire."[9]

There was much more of the sort, and any muck Small omitted was supplied by fellow crusaders—Lou J. Beauchamp, "the Prince of Southern Prohibition Orators," Colonel J. R. Miller, "Prohibition's War Eagle," John H. Hector, the "Black Hawk of Prohibition" (for black audiences), and others. Prohibitionists packed thrice-daily sessions at the Academy of Music, always with the imported Silver Lake Quartette, "one of the greatest musical attractions in the country." Norfolk was saturated with Prohibition talent from Alabama, Tennessee, Maryland, western Virginia, and elsewhere, who took over, as needed, Festival Hall, a hastily erected outdoor stand in Brambleton, the Norfolk and Atlantic City YMCAs, Armory and Oddfellows halls, and sundry churches.[10]

The ten-day crusade in April 1894, preceding another in mid-May by the same team, was not simply one of those periodic scoldings administered by scowling puritans—though Mr. Ernest Christian was, indeed, a fervent leader of the Atlantic City Drys. It challenged the Democratic machine in the May 24 election. Drys had a full slate of municipal candidates and were supported by many defecting Democrats and some Republicans sick of the arrogant corruption of the Democratic bosses.[11] When Norfolk's depravity and misrule were ridiculed in the New York papers and compared unfavorably with the most unsavory cities in America, it was past time for decent citizens to rebel.

The Prohibitionists blew the Democrats wide open. Academy of Music rallies were nothing more than old-fashioned religious revivals heavily spiced with politics. They opened with invocations by ministers, and featured prayers, hymns, collections, and frequent affirmations of the will of God Almighty. Small declared on April 26 that "the issues of right and wrong are now before us. Which side will you take? The Prohibitionists have placed before you a ticket . . . composed of men of pure and upright character, . . . who, if elected, will advocate the laws in the fear of God and for the welfare of the whole people." "'I want everybody here to stand up,'" he called on April 30, "'who will help purify Norfolk.'" The huge audience stood in a body.[12]

Against this onslaught, demoralized rump Democrats made feeble and ineffectual response. The most cynical of ward-heelers grew uneasy instructing clients to vote even once against God, let alone the several times each it might require for success. On May 24 the Prohibitionists and their allies had agents everywhere, guarding against the purchase of votes with free booze, ballot-box stuffing, and other time-tested methods of determining the people's will. The Drys swept triumphantly into power and Norfolk appeared to be delivered at one mighty stroke from the twenty-year reign of the Devil.[13] If Sam Small had not gained the Kingdom, he at least gained himself a medium-sized city.

Norfolk's fledgling Prohibition Party had existed for scarcely two years when it stormed to power in 1894. Its national party in 1892 fielded a presidential candidate who got only 110 Norfolk votes. But in 1893 the local Dry vote rose to 15 percent despite the party's negligible showing in Virginia as a whole. They were helped in Norfolk by a split that began among local Democrats in 1888 between reform- and ring-controlled factions. Reform Democrats were not, for the most part, Prohibition-minded but an alliance with raging Drys seemed the only way to defeat the ring and effect change in municipal government.[14]

The normally reliable Democratic ring was led by a trio of ward bosses just rising to power in the 1890s. In the first ward, it was James V. Trehy, native Norfolkian and son of a deliveryman. Educated at Father Matthew O'Keefe's Christian Brothers School, he was a bookkeeper in his teens; by age twenty he owned the Norfolk Carriage and Cab Company. Only twenty-four in 1894, he was already a member of the city's Democratic Executive Committee. The second ward's James E. Prince came to Norfolk in 1886, climbing from stevedore to ownership of several saloons. In the predominantly black fourth ward, Napoleon Bonaparte "Bonney" Joynes held sway, rising from bartender to saloon owner after coming to Norfolk in the 1880s. The strength of each was the ability to deliver his ward to the Democratic Party.[15]

An old-timer half a century later recalled Trehy as "King of Norfolk"; he was said to control the cabs and nearly all else that defined the free-and-easy "wide open" policy of the hell-roaring seaport town. James Prince was "a sort of first lieutenant in the small town 'Tammany' organization. . . . he was a master politician probably smarter than his older superior, and made most of the personal contacts necessary to keep the 'king' on his throne." Trehy had a popular Market Square saloon where customers gorged on white beans, bologna, potato salad, sliced onions, and slaw for the price of a beer—a nickel.[16]

Hindsight showed the bosses what went wrong. Both moral and political reformers had chiefly the new Brambleton (fifth) ward to thank for their 1894 victory. An enclave of mostly rural-born Virginians and Carolinians committed to traditional values and fearing the moral erosion of city life, Brambletonians cast a large share of the reform votes. They made the difference against lower and lower-middle-class downtown wards, the ring-dominated first, second, and fourth wards. (The third ward was a middle-class district east of and similar to Atlantic City's sixth ward.)[17]

Behind the reformers' victory lay seven years of remarkable work by the Women's Christian Temperance Union. Formed locally in 1887, the WCTU within a year got voters to petition successfully to close all saloons on Sunday. By 1894 it persuaded city schools to add physiology and hygiene classes, started an Atlantic City night school for working children, got city churches to adopt four annual Prohibition Sunday School lessons, and launched a newspaper that soon became the official WCTU state organ. Union women opened lending libraries, held street prayer sessions, picketed bars, distributed literature at almshouses and jails, and even joined the state body to attack an alcohol-laced soft drink, Hines Root Beer. By 1894 Norfolk also had a two hundred-member black WCTU.[18]

There had never been a public issue that touched the lives of women so dramatically as the politicization of alcoholic drink in the late nineteenth century. The Prohibitionist–reformer victory evinced a startling new activism by women in general, but especially those in Norfolk. The city's WCTU in the 1890s was the state's largest; its own Mrs. Richard H. Jones was state president from the first WCTU state convention in 1888 until she retired a decade later. Mrs. William D. Southall, Mrs. Lillian A. Shepherd, and Mrs. Mary E. Webb were other Norfolkians holding state offices in those years.[19] This generation of women would not enjoy access to the ballotbox, but their success in the 1890s was ample proof of their ability to organize effectively and mold public opinion. Norfolk women were a beacon to those throughout the state.

Sam Small made a great point of appealing to women to sway the votes of their husbands; many of his audiences were about equally divided between the sexes. This was, in fact, the first time women had formed a significant element at political meetings. A foretaste of this came in 1892 when General James Weaver of Iowa, Populist presidential candidate, appeared at Lesner's Garden with Kansas's Mary Ellen Lease, of "raise-less-corn-and-more-Hell" fame. The newspapers seemed mildly surprised that she was "a good speaker and certainly entertained her hearers." The Granby Theater manager, on the other hand, perhaps recalling Mrs. Lease, rejected a proposed visit by Carrie Nation in 1902, as much a tribute, in its way, as editorial gallantry toward the lady from Kansas.[20]

Every week came news of women in one or another unfamiliar pursuit. Mrs. A. L. Seabury of Granby Street in October 1892 became the first Norfolk woman admitted to the new Daughters of the American Revolution. Portsmouth's Katie McHugh was appointed a few weeks later to a clerkship in the Norfolk office of the Internal Revenue Service. In 1899 an unidentified Church Street girl of sixteen shipped out as seaman "David McKinley" on a steamer to visit a lover in London; her imposture was detected only after twenty days at sea. The *Virginian-Pilot* in 1902 hired Miss Annie K. Henry as Norfolk's first female correspondent.[21]

There remained innumerable women, mostly single and homeless, who could find employment only along honky-tonk rows, though Mollie Hogwood of Washington House was said to own more diamonds than any other woman "of her class" in Norfolk. Some unfortunates found furtive shelter at two or three "homes for fallen women." "Dutch Lou's," for example, a Church Street saloon, was converted to the nurturing "White Ribbon Anchorage" (later the Florence Crittenden Home). But many women roamed darkened streets at the service and mercy of a huge transient population. A Williamson's Lane ("Henhouse Alley") black woman who tried to commit suicide one night in 1899 by drinking laudanum was only a pathetic statistic from an area where suicides or attempts at it were reported at a rate of one a week.[22]

Yet when the fog of 1894 campaign rhetoric lifted, some noted that Sam Small, for all his flamboyant indignation, had stooped frequently to demagoguery in fulminating before Norfolk audiences. The *Public Ledger*, in particular, kept an eye on his off-duty hours during the crusade and documented a succession of visitors to his rooms who wrung from him admissions of having misstated facts and, sometimes, promises of retractions. It was true, for example, that Norfolk had no high school, but negotiations were underway to buy the old Hemenway School and it was reopened in September 1894 as Norfolk's first public high school. The original 1850s schools were, as Small charged, still in use, along with five new ones.[23] Moreover, the most notorious of the saloons and hangouts, including The Slide and the Novelty Theatre, lost their liquor licenses before Small's advent. His most damaging statistical indictments—the 240 liquor dealers, eighty-one brothels, thirty-five policy shops—were hypothetical, for no one knew whether the city had more or less, though such figures left an impression of dogged research into the issue. The liquor sellers included the city's best hotels and restaurants along with various gentlemen's clubs and social organizations, to which some of Small's strongest allies belonged. Norfolk was naughty enough, but Small's efforts were directed at making it seem even worse.[24]

The new public park was a case in point. The Chamber of Commerce's committee of local improvements recommended a park in 1890. The chamber sent the idea to the councils, which set out to see if tracts at the mouth of Newton's Creek and on the river west of Freemason Street (twenty-five and nine acres, respectively) could be had. These apparently proved to be too expensive, but the council soon bought the ninety-seven-acre Spratley farm at the head of Tanner's Creek. It was a disappointing two miles from downtown and ridden with swampy mudflats, but it was successfully developed (and is now the site of the Norfolk zoo).[25] The site may not have been the wisest but was clearly eligible and involved no discernible malfeasance.

The challenges of governing a rapidly enlarging city constantly outran the institutional machinery available for the purpose. Adverse farming conditions in the late nineteenth century drove many rural people to Brambleton, Atlantic City, and other peripheral areas, and numerous immigrants, especially from the eastern Mediterranean, settled in Norfolk. Naturalization records showed many Italians, Greeks, Russian Jews, Austrians, and others, with small synagogues and congregations of the Eastern Orthodox springing up around the city. (Older Jewish families associated chiefly with Ohef Sholom Temple on Church Street.)[26]

Norfolk had a Chinese community sufficient for a celebration of Chinese New Year in February 1898 with fireworks at George Hop's Main Street laundry and elsewhere. (Hop Sing's gambling joint was just down the street.) The local Chinese experienced a trying era during the Boxer Rebellion in 1899 when street urchins assailed their businesses with stones, breaking windows and, at a Church Street laundry, throwing horse manure into newly cleaned linen. "Jimmy Jones" was an Americanized Greek who ran a first-class bar and restaurant near Irishman Mike McKevitt's saloon. It was to McKevitt's that patrons of the Academy of Music, across the street, rushed between acts to down a schooner of frosty brew.[27]

An increasingly diverse population made Norfolk a mecca for social outcasts and eccentrics who could not be assimilated by smaller communities. An Arab with four ears and five tongues was too bizarre even for Norfolk and was jailed for thirty days in 1892 for frightening ladies on Main Street. Albert Brooks, a black "horse doctor," won a following by predicting in the fall of 1898 that Norfolk would be destroyed by an earthquake at 2:00 P.M.

This aerial map, drawn from a balloon, depicts Norfolk during a period of rapid growth. Note the large area at the north end of the Norfolk and Western bridge entirely given over to industry and commerce, as well as the thick clusters of houses and other buildings beyond. (Courtesy of Norfolk Public Library)

on November 11. At a Queen Street rally on the tenth, Brooks offered to postpone the event six months if he could raise $35.00 from his audience. The sum collected was not known because he left town within hours, but the entire cancellation of the tremor argued for the generosity of his contributors.[28]

A Norfolk resident in these years was E. K. Alexander, a black from Australia with some claim to the title of "world's fastest human." A longshoreman at the Old Dominion wharves, Alexander won a ten-mile footrace in 1888 at Manchester, England, before Queen Victoria and claimed in 1893 at age twenty-four to hold 117 medals for running. He ran short distances as well as long ones, outsprinting a Petersburg horse over a quarter-mile path in forty-seven seconds.[29]

A compelling figure was George I. Nowitzky, who migrated to the American West in 1857 as a boy from Prussia. Joining the army, he fought Indians in the Wyoming Territory before joining "Buffalo Bill" Cody's Wild West Show as a fancy rider and trick-shot artist. He arrived in Norfolk around 1880, as a patent-medicine peddler with a wagon rigged as a stage for a Punch and Judy show. Nowitzky was "a most commanding personality, resembling Buffalo Bill strikingly"; his sleight-of-hand and card tricks made him popular despite the worthless goods he sold. In 1884 he began publishing *Nowitzky's Monthly,* a magazine miscellany of stories, poetry, and tips for travelers. "Buffalo Bill's" show played intermittently in Norfolk, giving Nowitzky opportunity for reunions with his former employer.[30]

At Hume Minor Music Company on Main Street opposite Commerce Street was salesman James Casey, who, one night in the 1880s, composed a hit tune, "Sing Me a Song of the South," which propelled him to a career with a New York music publisher. At Joe Seelinger's "Onyx" saloon on East Main was an elaborately decorated second-floor dining room where President Cleveland regularly gorged on game and seafood during his frequent duck-hunting trips to the area. Seelinger was one of four brothers, each of whom operated a Norfolk saloon. At the corner of Main and Commerce was the first of R. W. McDonald's snug five-cents sandwich shops, later found all over the city, which inaugurated the tradition of "eating downtown" rather than going home for meals.[31]

Norfolk by the 1890s counted on a succession of road shows, circuses, and traveling acts for its entertainment. But the city came most alive on special days, such as Columbus Day 1892 and the Naval Rendezvous, related to the Chicago World's Fair, in 1893. The first was the occasion of the biggest parade Norfolk had ever seen. Fifty thousand spectators viewed the marching societies and groups, notably a body of forty-two Italians from

Norfolk and Catholic organizations from around Hampton Roads. The Naval Rendezvous drew men-of-war from Great Britain, France, Germany, Argentina, Holland, Italy, Russia, and Brazil, besides America's own "white squadron." There were boat, bicycle, and other competitions, a ball, bands, fireworks, a military fair, and varied accompaniments.[32]

No further annexations were made to the city for a dozen years after 1890, but the outlying metropolitan area grew as impressively as Norfolk itself. A development company bought the old Taylor country-place on Willoughby Spit in 1891 and laid off 150 lots where residents might enjoy "a panoramic view of the great ocean gateway of Virginia." West Ghent sprouted apartment buildings, and Ocean View and Virginia Beach added more hotels and recreational facilities as they became yearly better known to excursionists and vacationers. The globe shrank noticeably when long-distance telephone service was introduced in 1897.[33]

Norfolk gained a landmark in 1898 with the big Monticello Hotel on land where Back Creek formerly ran. (The creek's last remains were filled in by 1905, when City Hall Avenue was extended west to Granby.) A new stone post office opened in 1900 on Plume at Atlantic and the Bank of Commerce was planning its thirteen-story "skyscraper," Norfolk's first, which opened in 1904 on Main at Atlantic. Culturally, however, many lived less in the vibrant present than in exculpatory recountings of the Civil War, as seen in two Norfolk books of 1893: John W. H. Porter's history of Norfolk County in the war years and Judge Robert M. Hughes' biography of General Joseph E. Johnston. William Lamb was constantly on call to rehearse the defense of Fort Fisher, and there was much public discussion of memorials to the Confederate dead.[34]

Norfolk's first automobiles appeared at the century's end but seemed unlikely to play any more vital role in the city's future than hot-air balloons or unicycles. Someone (Arthur O'Neil?) was running a Locomobile steamer, reputedly the state's first automobile, around town in mid-1899. Peter Wright, manager of the Norfolk Railway and Light Company, was the first resident to own one when he returned from New York with a Mobile and ran it down Main on June 27, 1900. The *Dispatch* called it "a handsome affair" that "ran noiselessly and with the speed of greased lightning." But its engine "registered a protest" in a lane between the Columbia Building and the Atlantic Hotel; it "bucked and ran backward into the street, narrowly missing a trolley car." It had to be "towed to its stable" for repair.[35]

The signal world event affecting Norfolk toward the century's end was the Spanish-American War of 1898. The conflict, except for a prolonged struggle in the Philippines, was of short duration, but the navy yard and the

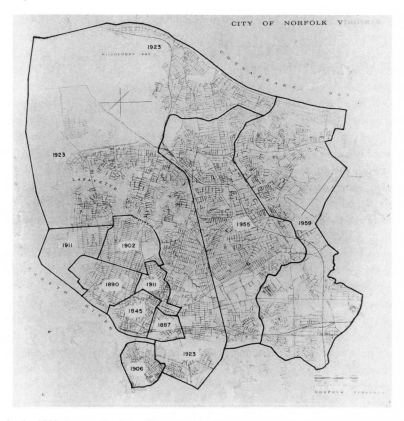

As the 1880s began, Norfolk still retained its boundaries of over a half-century earlier. But the city stood at the threshold of a wave of annexations that greatly enlarged its area, as shown by the dates on the map, in a short time. (Courtesy of Bureau of Surveys, Norfolk, Va.)

Newport News Shipbuilding and Drydock Company got major orders for construction and repair, a boost for the local economy. The sailing of the Spanish fleet from Cadiz led to the placing of mines and torpedoes between Fort Monroe and the Rip Raps and guard boats at Fort Monroe to conduct ships through the narrow opening in the defenses. The first steel ships built in the South, the cruiser *Raleigh* and battleship *Texas,* had been launched at Gosport in 1892, though structural defects gave the *Texas* a reputation for being "more trouble to the Government than any other vessel in the service."[36]

Several military units, both black and white, from in and around Norfolk served in the war's far-flung campaigns. News that Spanish Admiral Cervera's flagship *Maria Teresa* had been raised from Santiago harbor and would be repaired and commissioned for the navy at Gosport was treated by the newspapers as a godsend that would employ hundreds for up to eighteen months. Most of the tugs in the harbor were contracted to tow the big ship upriver, and excursions were planned for the influx of tourists it was expected to draw. Loss of the vessel while it was being towed to Norfolk was seen by local editors as an economic disaster. In May 1899 the mangled cruiser *Reina Mercedes*, the only other consequential Spanish ship raised at Santiago, was brought to Simpson's Drydock for refurbishing over a period of eighteen months.[37]

Almost inevitably, Prohibitionists and reform Democrats did not work in harmony, a study in the danger of assignations by strange bedfellows. Having won twelve of fifteen paid city offices in 1894, they named a joint committee to choose for nonelective offices candidates the councils must accept. This was properly scorned by the press for transferring initiative from the councils to a body reeking of ring "bossism." But the appointments were also heavily weighted on the Prohibitionists' side, leaving their Democratic allies ill-rewarded for supporting Dry planks.[38]

Enemies (and some friends) of the reformers were galled by the dismissal of twenty-one white street maintenance workers (half the force) in the summer of 1894 and their replacement by blacks. Black leader William Thorogood demanded it as the "spoils" owed to blacks for aiding the reformer ticket in May; they wanted better treatment from the police and more jobs. Thorogood also had candidates for city hall janitor and keeper of Calvary Cemetery and wanted the office of high constable for himself, but evidently got neither. The *Public Ledger* somehow saw in this the basis of a new party, "with the negro as its cornerstone."[39]

Blacks could hope for only the humblest city jobs and looked to Washington Republicans for additional work. The customs house had numerous black employees, including Thorogood as watchman, boatmen Isaiah Connor and J. W. Watts, laborer Abram Beckett, and others. Democrat Grover Cleveland's victory in 1892 cost blacks federal jobs but they looked for more with McKinley's election in 1896. Black longshoremen and female domestics, dominant in their occupations but barred from white unions, formed their own; hundreds of black longshoremen walked off their jobs in 1899 rather than work beside nonunion men. That year some 1,500 oyster shuckers, mostly unionized blacks, struck against their employers, charging illegal tactics. Black Catholics, meanwhile, opened St. Joseph's chapel and school on Queen Street in 1893.[40]

Liquor drove another wedge between political and moral reformers. Drys in early 1895 got the council to set 5:00 A.M. to midnight hours for liquor sales and other limits on the trade. This presupposed police sympathetic to the cause but factions bickered over the office of police chief, police force personnel, and the snubbing of Mayor Pettit by fellow police commissioners John T. Bolton and C. E. Verdier. Pettit lamented that the force was "disorganized and undisciplined," that fellow commissioners blocked efforts to change it.[41]

Restrictions on bars and saloons spawned over a hundred "social clubs" to circumvent new laws, including a ban on Sunday liquor sales, by serving "members" who paid "dues"; membership was gained by signing a register. Rather than slipping into some "dive," thirsty patrons now walked through a club's front door any day of the week. Drys hailed an ally when Sam Small in mid-1894 settled in Norfolk and opened a newspaper; the first edition of his *Daily Pilot* appeared on October 6, 1894. His first editorials championed moral reform but Small, never so happy on defense as offense, was soon assailing reformers for their failures. Mayor Pettit seemed to him a "do-nothing" who reneged on campaign promises and went "to ring lawyers for advice."[42]

The rhetoric of moral zealotry was more safely delivered from an orator's rostrum than in newsprint. In early 1895 Small was hit by two libel suits. The first, by State School Superintendent John E. Massey, involved *Daily Pilot* allegations that the American Book Company bribed Massey to buy its books for state schools. The second came after Small printed an eastern shore rumor that a prominent Onancock man was having an affair with a Baptist preacher's wife. The latter was quickly exposed as a hoax; Small retracted it too late to avoid a suit. He lost both actions, and, financially crippled, sold out in August 1895 and left town.[43] Few mourned his departure.

The main failure of the Drys and their allies was in political reform, where they found little common ground. Neither had strong leaders and reform Democrats never articulated a coherent program. Even reformers were not expected to be perfect, but Commissioner Verdier pushed his luck by entering a horse in a Suffolk race (and winning) while he was supposed to be attending commission meetings. Calls for his resignation were unsuccessful.[44]

Even so, reformers purged the police of ring allies and cracked down on saloons and bawdy houses. Arrests for drunkenness jumped 90 percent by 1896 (to 7,115 for the year), for the illegal sale of liquor from four in the year ending June 30, 1894, to 209 two years later, and proportionately in gambling and offenses against decency. Norfolk was probably better behaved in these years than it was before or afterward. If prostitutes only relocated to unaccustomed parts of town, they were at least put to the trouble of re-structuring their business arrangements.[45] But a continuation of such prog-ress depended on perpetuating a revival atmosphere that by its nature must be short-lived.

City papers turned from tentative support of Pettit's regime to sneering rejection. Reform Democrats by 1896 were abandoning the leaky Prohibi-tion ship to rejoin their old ring cohorts. The *Virginian* in March reprinted Sam Small's parting shot, that the reformers were "sycophantic, spaniel-eyed, but snake-fanged frauds whom I helped to foist upon . . . Norfolk, and whom I will delight to force back into the dirty bogs that bred them." Prohibitionists renamed themselves the Citizens Reform Party and carefully included Republicans and Democrats on their ticket. But even "old sober Brambleton" voted in May against them. Democrat Wyndham R. Mayo be-came mayor, his party taking all other offices by wide margins.[46]

The triumphant ring was soon back to its old tricks. In the fall congres-sional campaign, its delaying tactics in the fourth ward held up lines as much as seven hours so that only small numbers voted; similar means in-sured victory in 1898 and 1900. Soon after a police pay raise was rejected in 1899 as too costly, Boss Trehy and associates got the council to reduce saloon licenses from $350.00 to $250.00; by 1903 the number of saloons had in-creased from eighty-one to 129. Up to a dozen poker games a night were reportedly played in an upscale hotel and some forty Main Street gambling houses (among the city's one hundred or more) offered all-night roulette and other illegal games. So pervasive was corruption that a new reform movement, the Good Government Association, was launched in 1900.[47]

The new century began on an ominous note, the reverberations of which have not yet ceased. A plan pondered in legislative circles from the 1880s was adopted in July 1902 when Virginia's blacks were largely disfranchised. Democratic and Republican whites agreed that the black vote was a source of glaring political abuses; it could be bought or coerced in many, especially urban, areas, and gave rise to cynical manipulation at elections. When the federal Supreme Court in 1898 held constitutional Mississippi's disfran-chisement plan, Virginia's gained momentum.[48]

There was little to be said of some black voters that could not be said about large segments of whites as well, but party leaders favored sacrificing some white votes in order to disqualify most blacks. Underlying the issue of black votes was the success of the Populists, a grassroots third-party reform movement with strong black support in state elections during the 1890s.[49]

By the new state constitution, a literacy test and poll tax were required of all voters except property owners, Civil War veterans and their descendants, and those paying annual taxes of at least a dollar. Some blacks still qualified, but white registrars could reject any by means of the literacy clause. Norfolk's ring delegates to the constitutional convention, attorney A. P. Thom and Judge D. Tucker Brooke, voted for disfranchisement. In the largely black fourth ward, the vote of 1,240 in 1901 fell to eighty-six (mostly white) in 1903, a crucial blow to black ward-boss Bonney Joynes, though perhaps aiding his white colleagues, James Trehy and other ring leaders. In 1904 Norfolk's black vote fell to 504; in 1910 only forty-four paid the poll tax, a voting prerequisite.[50]

Norfolk emerged sadder but maybe wiser from the nineteenth century, which opened and closed on waves of prosperity despite seven decades of tribulation in between. Prosperity itself seemed a snare to those most sensitive to the city's social ambience. But the century purged some of Norfolk's worst faults: its reliance on chattel slavery (and guilt-ridden paranoia over the potential for slave revolt), its awful vulnerability to epidemic disease, and its parochial jealousy toward sister cities. It liberated the city from the isolation imposed by nature, brought belated recognition of its strategic ascendancy, and integrated it securely into the mainstream of American commerce.

An inability to accept the full implications of democracy, a self-devouring racism, were attitudes that a more sophisticated century would find as worrisome. But the failings of crusades by William Lamb and Barton Myers, the collapse of the 1890s reform campaign, did not sap the optimism of those still cherishing the idea of progress. As the twentieth century began, new reformers were in full cry and leading Norfolkians had the impertinent vision to see their often maligned city as a proper setting to celebrate the totality of the American experiment in its first three hundred years. It was an odd conceit, but if Chicago claimed the right to host for the western hemisphere its "Columbian Exposition" for four centuries, who could begrudge Norfolk its own grandiose notion?

CHAPTER 19

The Jimstowne Follies

THE DREADFUL word was out before the end of April: Norfolk's heralded tercentennial exposition was a colossal failure—"the Jamestown Imposition," as it was soon widely known. Opening day, April 26, 1907, found the Sewell's Point grounds in disarray—littered with building materials and debris, some structures surrounded with scaffolding and without roofs or windows, others not yet started. Two large exhibit halls were empty; several were only partially filled. Faulty electric lines made the trolley ride from Norfolk an irritating adventure of fits and starts; soggy foundations caused derailments on the miniature interior railway; piers clogged with steamboats made for long delays. The burning of two new hotels just off the grounds seemed eerily appropriate to a day abounding in disappointments.[1]

The national press, annoyed over inadequate accommodations for journalists, poured scorn on the venture. The exposition, carped a New Jersey paper, "is situated in the swamp and ooze contiguous to Norfolk"; military authorities warned fair-going servicemen to take precautions against malaria, sunstroke, typhoid, ptomaine poisoning, and other dangers. Japanese sailors came ashore with their own canteens rather than risk drinking local water. "When the buildings are completed," offered Chicago's *Tribune*, "the exhibits are in place, . . . walks laid, the mess . . . cleaned up, the landscape gardeners complete their work, and the railroads and steamship companies solve the problem of moving crowds back and forth the same day, the . . . Exposition will be all right."[2]

Even the purpose of the event, commemorating the three-hundredth anniversary of Jamestown's founding, seemed a poor excuse for a celebration. History books routinely treated the Jamestown saga as a woodsy soap opera, starring John Smith and Pocahontas, which unfolded as the seeds of liberty and democracy were being sown at Boston and Plymouth. Exposition publicity countered New England doctrine with shrill embellishments of local history and folklore. Norfolk's defiance of the Tea Act was recounted under the title "Where Independence Was Born"; it was "certain" that Powhatan had "often quenched his thirst" at a spring on the exposition grounds and "more than probable" that Pocahontas did too.[3] A better appreciation of the nation's heritage seemed unlikely to emerge from the exposition.

More distressing to those who had spent up to six years planning the exposition was the sparse attendance. Over 44,000 showed up the first day to see President Theodore Roosevelt officially open the event, but the second day brought less than 7,500, most of whom had free passes. Predictions of a total attendance of fifteen million during the exposition's seven months were progressively scaled down, as was initial optimism that the cost, over $5 million, might somehow be met from its revenue.[4]

Surely Norfolk deserved better. The commemoration was proposed in early 1900 by state historian Lyon G. Tyler, and the *Norfolk Dispatch* shortly began to press the city's claim as an appropriate site. The state legislature in 1902, rejecting the case for Richmond, awarded the charter to Norfolk and sister Hampton Roads communities contingent on $1 million being raised by January 1, 1904. Fitzhugh Lee, former Civil War and Spanish-American War general and nephew of "Marse Robert," agreed to head the Exposition Company and Norfolk's leaders pledged support. Subscriptions of company stock were slow, however, and it was New Year's Eve 1903 before the million-dollar goal was reached. The exposition was expected to require $2.5 million, so federal help was essential.[5]

Lee and his lieutenants—Norfolk's T. S. Southgate, Walter H. Taylor, hotelier David Lowenberg, and others—made frequent trips to lobby a resistant Congress, and in early 1905 took a whirlwind tour of nine state capitals. (Exhausted, Lee died of apoplexy two days after addressing the Massachusetts assembly and was succeeded by former Congressman Harry St. George Tucker.) Congress in 1906 awarded the exhibition a paltry $250,000, but provided funds for government involvement as an exhibitor and in other ways. The state came up with $200,000 to acquire a 340-acre site at Sewell's Point with a mile of Hampton Roads frontage. With cost estimates rising, it was still necessary to seek a million-dollar congressional loan to keep the project afloat.[6]

Legislative wrangling over funds, bad weather in the fall of 1906, and bickering among exposition officials helped insure that everything would be behind schedule. The exposition site was a picturesque wasteland that required draining marshes and small lakes, removing or replanting hundreds of thousands of trees and shrubs, and so on. A boulevard had to be built across the seven miles between Norfolk and the site, steamboat piers constructed, sewage, water, electric, telephone, and gas lines installed, rails laid for trolleys and trains. Dozens of large buildings, several of them permanent, had to be erected, besides boardwalks, entrances, concession stands, and other facilities.[7]

Exposition directors rejected anxious calls for postponement and instructed their "Exploitation Department" to announce on opening day that preparations were "practically complete." Local newspapers winked loyally at the verbal hanky-panky, but journalists from a distance were outraged. That the exposition chose mainly billboards and other forms of promotion over newspaper advertising incited many editors to flay the commemoration long after its worst problems were resolved. Yet exposition supporters persuaded themselves that all was not lost, that a few finishing touches and better weather—April and May were perfectly miserable, June the coldest in thirty-seven years—would yet bring spendthrift millions trooping out to Sewell's Point and all would be well.[8]

Mr. R. C. Parks, at least, would not be among them. A North Carolina farmer, Parks arrived in Norfolk on the exposition's opening day. He met a cordial gentleman who took him on a tour of the Citizen's Bank building on Main Street. He admired the view of the harbor from the seventh floor, enjoyed riding in the elevator, and was impressed when his guide offered to sell him the building for $2,000. Parks had only $800 with him but the gentleman graciously agreed to accept that much as a downpayment. It was later in the day when Parks learned that cities could be wicked places—and no less so when hosting great celebrations.[9]

Norfolk was a bride left at the altar; even opening-day crowds were judged to be "woefully small." Five downtown public buildings, including the sewer-pump house and fire headquarters, besides some private structures, were handsomely decorated. City hall, its dome freshly painted white and festooned in flags and red, white, and blue bunting, had huge portraits of Walter Raleigh, Pocahontas, Lord Delaware, and Captain John Smith mounted on its four columns. The Granby Theatre booked *It's Up to You, John Henry;* the Majestic, *Sheridan Kean, Detective.* The Academy of Music put on *The Clansman* (its third appearance) plus Walter Damrosch and his orchestra for the throngs that did not show up.[10]

Whatever might come of it, the exposition ignited a surge of building and improvements in and around Norfolk. City leaders en route to Richmond to lobby for it in 1902 conceived the conversion of a disheveled area around lower Newton's Creek (Mahone's Lake) into a park. Led by Councilman

Jesse O. Reid and City Attorney Walter H. Taylor, the city acquired the site; Jackson Park, more accessible for most residents than the Tanner's Creek facility, opened in 1905. The Woman's Club, troubled by Norfolk's unsightliness as the exposition neared, asked householders to help get rid of trash and refuse; Mayor Riddick declared April 11, 1906, housecleaning day to target ugly alleys and streets, plant bushes and shrubs, and undertake other projects.[11]

Anticipations of a tourist tidal wave in 1907 sparked the greatest building boom so far in the city's history. When the exposition opened, Norfolk and its environs, long reviled for few and uninviting hotels, had forty within easy reach of the grounds. Some were jerry-built firetraps, but others, like the new Lorraine at Tazewell and Granby, the Victoria on Main Street, and the Union Square at Granby and Freemason, were tasteful and pleasant. New theaters—the Majestic on Main, the Colonial on Tazewell Street, and others—provided hotel guests with evening entertainment. The Princess Anne at Virginia Beach added eighty rooms in the fall of 1906, while Ocean View expanded its amusement offerings.[12]

Economically, exposition year was the best so far in Norfolk's history despite a Wall Street panic. On a day in March 1907 the new *Ledger-Dispatch* afternoon paper (merging namesake predecessors) carried 323 classified ads, the largest number ever in a Virginia newspaper. A million-dollar Union Station was planned by the Virginian and Norfolk and Western railroads on East Main Street to open in 1909. More gratifying to the *Virginian-Pilot* editors was the civic awakening, inspiring all classes to work together for the city's well-being.[13]

Much of the building boom was unrelated to the exposition and continued well beyond it. F. S. Royster's skyscraper office building, the city's tallest, arose at Granby and City Hall Avenue. The thirteen-story Bank of Commerce was begun in 1905 on Main at Atlantic. Granby, in 1890 a residential street lined with huge elms, maples, and sycamores shading stately antebellum homes, had been transmuted into a bazaar of busy stores and eight-story office buildings. The business center was shifting from Main Street and old Market Square, site of the Commercial Bank, north and west to streets such as Tazewell, City Hall Avenue, and Brooke Avenue, which had not existed fifteen years earlier.[14]

Conscious of its expanding role in the life of the region and nation, Norfolk scurried to assume those attributes of urban dignity so far left unattended. A new Chamber of Commerce was formed in 1902 to help capture the exposition and, in the words of an enthusiast, ensure Norfolk's "proper position as the greatest city in the South." In June of that year the Norfolk Conservatory Symphony, brainchild of Professor Charles Borjes, gave an inaugural concert that made doubtful, in the *Landmark*'s view, that "any other Southern community of the size of ours possesses such an orchestra." Newspaper editors urged Norfolk and Portsmouth to merge into "the largest city in Virginia," though the *Public Ledger* conceded, in a let-them-keep-their-horses gesture, that Richmond might remain Virginia's capital.[15]

Norfolk's public library dated from 1872, when Dr. Samuel Selden and the new Norfolk Library Association stocked a reading room in the Norfolk Academy. The library was shunted from one place to another for three decades, but in 1901 steel tycoon Andrew Carnegie offered $50,000 for a building if Norfolk would guarantee to maintain it and provide a site. An agreement was struck and the cornerstone was laid in 1903 on Freemason Street, the land donated by Dr. William Selden's heirs. Reporting on books most called for in 1911, the staff noted that over four-fifths were what a critic called "that love stuff."[16]

New residential developments sprouted like dandelions within and near the city limits: Larchmont, Chesterfield Heights, Virginia Place, Lafayette Park, Old Dominion Place, Riverview, Colonial Place, and others. Most were along the trolley lines that stretched toward Ocean View, up Colley Avenue, and out to the exposition grounds. The annexation of Park Place (between Norfolk and Lafayette River) in 1902 and Berkley in 1906, followed by Huntersville (predominantly black but highly cosmopolitan), Lambert's Point, and part of Villa Heights five years later, brought the city's population to more than eighty thousand.[17]

Blacks lived in all wards but clustered mainly in communities such as Titustown (annexed in 1923), distinguished by the fact that it was all-black and every family owned its own home. Dr. Samuel D. Proctor, growing up there during these years, remembered that whites "did not touch our lives." The blacksmith and ice man were black: "The fish man was black. The dentists, the physicians and the morticians. . . . We had self-sufficient communities. . . . These people stood for something. They amounted to something. . . . They didn't have any money. I had to work my way through college. . . . All six of us got a college education."[18]

The church played a central role in the lives of many blacks. Dr. Marian Palmer Capps, a child in the century's early years, long cherished the memory of St. John's Methodist Church on Bute Street. Sunday congregations regularly had up to nine hundred people. "My first memory of going to the library," she recalled, "was in that church. They had a library for Sunday

School people. . . . I remember *Little Women* was probably the first one that I read." There was a choir, a Sunday School orchestra, a men's Bible class of about seventy-five, another of about sixty, and a women's class.[19]

Barbersville, the Palmers' neighborhood, was made up of "people who were interested in everybody else's children plus their own. And they didn't hesitate to report to your parents if you did anything . . . out of line." Next to church, school was the main influence in children's lives. "I can remember that . . . [college] students were ashamed" if they did poorly. "And . . . if you did not do well, at the end of your first semester you packed your bags and came home." Most attended Hampton Institute or Virginia State, the normal schools, or Howard, Lincoln, and Union universities. "They expected you to come back having achieved promotion if nothing more. And . . . students would rather do anything than . . . let them know they had failed."[20]

Jim Crow laws and city ordinances multiplied after black disenfranchisement; restrictive codes developed in transportation, housing, and other public facilities. Norfolk and Western Railroad was convicted in 1904 of letting blacks share cars with whites on an excursion to Princess Anne. Separation of races on streetcars began in 1906. By this time, a migration of blacks to the North and West was underway as life grew intolerable to many in the South. Lynching, at least, though performed as nearby as Princess Anne and Nansemond counties, was a terror that was spared Norfolk blacks. (A sizable police force was perhaps more accountable than a liberal humanity, though the city's cosmopolitanism made for at least minimal acceptance of ethnic differences.)[21]

Several efforts had been made to give Norfolk a black newspaper, most recently in 1897 with the *Daily Record,* but it moved two years later to Newport News. (White-owned papers carried little news of blacks besides criminal activity.) In 1910 Plummer B. Young bought the *Journal and Guide,* for which he was a reporter, from the Knights of Gideon's Lodge. From a circulation of only five hundred, Young, a voice for self-help and racial cooperation, built a readership of 75,000, one of black journalism's largest. Other reputable black newsmen were George R. Moore of *The New Century* and William H. Tabb, who once cleaned *American Beacon* offices as a slave boy but was later a pressman with the *Landmark* and other papers, retiring in 1911 after sixty-six years in the business.[22]

Berkley's annexation drew into Norfolk the strongly Orthodox Jewish community that had grown up there. The first Jewish cemetery in the area had been opened there (then called Washington Point) in 1820, but it was not until 1884, when Abe Legum arrived, that Jewish settlement of Berkley began. Legum and his brother Isaac opened a Liberty Road drygoods store (on the old route to Great Bridge) and many subsequent Jewish arrivals, mostly Lithuanian refugees often closely related to one another, opened stores on the same street. Their congregation, formed in 1889 and called Mikro Kodesh, was one of the most conservative and closely knit in the southern United States.[23]

Norfolk Judaism went back to Moses Myers, the first permanent Jewish resident in the late eighteenth century. By the early twentieth century, the town had at least three synagogues: Ohef Sholom, a Reformed body of German Jews and their offspring at Freemason and Tripoli (now Monticello); Beth El, a conservative German group on Cumberland; and Beth Israel, also on Cumberland, seat of recent Lithuanian and Russian immigrants. The Jewish community had numerous charitable and social organizations and was active in civic affairs: Michael Umstadter as founder in 1903 of the Norfolk Retail Merchants Association, David Lowenberg as director-general of the exposition until 1905, Benjamin A. Banks as the first Jewish member of the House of Delegates (1911), and others.[24]

In 1905 a right-of-way around the city allowed the Virginian rail line to connect its Deepwater, West Virginia coal terminal to a 1,040-foot steel pier at Sewell's Point. Four vessels at once could take on coal there, and by 1913 the line was delivering four and a half million tons annually, while Lambert's Point continued to flourish as a coaling station. Five steamship lines regularly serving Norfolk brought visitors to the exposition: the Old Dominion from New York, the Old Bay Line and Chesapeake Line from Baltimore, the Norfolk and Washington, and the Merchants and Miners from Baltimore, Savannah, Boston, and Providence.[25]

The new residential developments and annexations were made possible by automobiles and trolleys. The temperamental toy of 1900 became the favored mode of transportation by 1906—when the Tidewater Automobile Association was formed—by those who could afford one. By 1910 there were automobile and motorcycle races at Fairmont Park fairgrounds. The city in 1911 bought its first "automobile firewagon," Protestant Hospital an "auto ambulance." The *Landmark*, noting sagely in 1904 that "the automobile will never take the place of the horse," predicted that horseless carriages would be available before long for $100.00 or $150.00, a boon to "families which could not think of owning a horse."[26]

Editors were still less sanguine about flying machines. The *Virginian-Pilot* in May 1903 made clear that aerial navigation would never be of com-

Aviator Eugene B. Ely on November 14, 1910, flew a Curtiss Hudson Flier from a plat-form on the USS *Birmingham's* deck to demonstrate that planes could be launched from ships. (Official U.S. Navy photograph)

mercial value owing to its inability to compete with methods of land and water travel and the likelihood that accidents in operation would be fatal to passengers. But the same paper scored the journalistic coup of the young century just seven months later when it publicized a successful flight on the Outer Banks by a pair of bicycle mechanics. No other paper, not even in the aeronauts' hometown of Dayton, Ohio, would print the story when it first appeared.[27]

Norfolkians had more reason than most to be skeptical of the claims of those who professed to skim the clouds and ride the wind. "Professor" Harry Hucheson in 1893 brought his passenger balloon to Ocean View where his nineteen-year-old daughter and pug dog performed three ascensions, the first two ending in near-tragedy in treetops, the third with a fire in the operator's basket. A fourth by another associate produced a levitation of some two thousand feet before descending suggestively into Elmwood Cemetery. Heavier-than-air experments seemed unlikely to be any better.[28]

The Jamestown Exposition had an aeronautics building and attempts to fly in motorized balloons, one of which performed an involuntary kamikaze crash into the battleship *Alabama*. No airplanes came to the exposition (the Wright brothers decided against it), but in 1910 the *Ledger-Dispatch* arranged for Glenn Curtis and his team to appear on the exposition grounds for biplane flights, one of them a breathtaking ten-minute jaunt over Norfolk. Meanwhile, the brothers Wright conducted more experiments at Kitty Hawk, passing frequently back and forth through Norfolk and utilizing it as a source of supplies. Also in 1910 pilot Eugene Ely performed the trick of flying a biplane off the deck of the cruiser *Birmingham* in Hampton Roads, the first such flight from a ship.[29]

Another technological advance was that of *Virginian-Pilot* photographer John Ernest Williamson who, in June 1913, took the first undersea photos. Williamson's English-born father had invented a "submarine tube," allowing descents of considerable depth into a cast-iron, portholed observation chamber. Going out into Chesapeake Bay in a launch, Williamson lowered four tungsten electric lights into the chamber and climbed down the tube with a camera. His pictures were published in the next Sunday edition of the *Virginian-Pilot*. Within a year, he launched a lifelong career by making undersea motion pictures in the Bahamas. In 1915 he filmed *Twenty Thousand Leagues under the Sea* for MGM.[30]

Norfolk's saloon-and-gambling-supported ring remained in power from 1896 to 1904, reopening the city to all the sleazy influences of the 1880s and early 1890s. Reformers regrouped in 1900 as the Good Government League but made little headway until the ring began to experience internal conflict over issues of patronage and the like; Trehy (now clerk of court) and Prince factions weakened each other in municipal turf battles. As the new century began, reformers were goaded to renewed effort by rising civic violence, city partiality in granting streetcar and telephone franchises, and recurring election frauds.[31]

Reform mayoral candidate Dr. James G. Riddick, a popular figure mistakenly seen by the ring as amenable to its influence, was elected in 1902 with a majority of reform candidates for the city council. The reformers set out to curb Sunday liquor sales, close gambling and policy shops, and revamp the police. Saloon owner James Prince and other ring men could abide some polishing of the city's tainted image, but soon soured on reform moralism and unexpected difficulty in manipulating Riddick. He was all the more dangerous because the city charter was amended in 1902 to give the mayor a veto over the council. With added help from the fledgling Working-man's Political Club, an arm of union labor, Riddick and the reformers won again in 1904, this time for a four-year term provided in the new state constitution.[32]

But Riddick, uncomfortable amid zealots, became alienated from some of his allies. As a result, his administration had as little success effecting meaningful change as the Drys of the 1890s. His effort to amend the city charter toward more centralized government only allowed the ring to proclaim itself champion of "the people" against "the politicians." Reformers also generated unfavorable publicity with closed meetings and a partisanship as notorious as that of the ring: a bricklayer was a suitable appointee to the detective bureau because he voted reform. They also did little to merit continued support from labor unions. When the council sought to gerrymander the city to eliminate the ring-dominated fourth ward, they handed their foes a big club.[33]

Riddick, ever the individualist, bickered with the reformers. When they campaigned in 1908 on another wave of saloon-busting, the mayor and other political moderates broke with the Good Government League and sided with the ring. (Only true believers had the stomach for another Sam Small-type revival to save Norfolk from demon rum.) Riddick had strong personal support whatever side he was on and, with ring approval, was reelected in 1908. Once again the ever resourceful ring was in power.[34]

Norfolk, however, was no longer the tight little riverside town that could be held captive to two or three downtown wards. The newer wards were heavily middle-class, and business interests were becoming too diversified to be dragooned by saloon and gambling lords. The Brambleton insurrection was but a foretaste of major changes in Norfolk's urban character. The ring was doomed: the Progressive Era still gathered momentum across the land and local reformers, painfully gaining political savvy and sophistication, had yet to deliver the ring their Sunday-punch.[35]

The tercentennial, little touched by city hall tempests, struggled bravely through 1907 to recover from its dismal opening. To visitors not put off by lingering incompletion (endemic to such affairs), Sewell's Point had much to offer. Even had the fair been uninviting, Hampton Roads hosted the largest gathering of warships in history. Displayed on opening day was most of the Atlantic fleet—sixteen battleships (including the *Virginia*), three cruisers, six destroyers, and sundry torpedo boats, monitors, and auxiliaries. Four British ships, three Brazilian, two German, two Austro-Hungarian, an Argentinian, and a Chilean rounded out the armada. Some departed almost daily as others arrived from Italy, France, Holland, Portugal, Norway, Japan, and Sweden.[36] (The czar's navy had lately been Pearl-Harbored by Japan.)

The warships not only provided a spectacle, enhanced by decorations, evening illuminations, cannon salutes, and colorful pomp and protocol, but furnished bands and escorts for occasions ashore. Naval personnel held rowing contests and sailing regattas, carnivals involving tugs of war, wrestling on horseback, and other competitions. There were also athletic events by such groups as the Amateur Athletic Union and the annual Intercollegiate Championship Meet, when Guy Haskins of the University of Pennsylvania won the mile in 4:28 and teammate McSwain tied Princeton's Vozin at eleven feet four in the polevault.[37]

The exposition grounds were set off by two 2,400-foot-long federal government piers (finished only in September) joined at the sea-end by an ornamental arch to form an attractive forty-acre basin. On shore, the piers fronted Roanoke Square, which led south to the Court of Honor, with its Tyrolean fountain flanked by twin lagoons. Beyond lay the administration building, south of which stretched the Lee Parade and an encampment for the seventy-five military units that visited at one time or another.[38]

West and east were the exhibition halls and buildings. Two government halls housed displays from every Washington department; twenty-two states erected their own buildings, many of them historic replicas, such as Kentucky's "Fort Boonesboro." Some special exhibitors also had their own buildings, including Richmond and Baltimore, Baptists, Presbyterians, and others. There was a single hotel on the grounds, but restaurants, amusement concessions, and other facilities dotted the premises. Each day had its special events: balloon ascensions, carrier-pigeon races, military parades and drills, and reunions of notable families.[39]

Besides federal and state exhibits, exposition buildings held displays in history, education, social economy, manufactures and industrial arts, machinery and transportation, marine appliances, mines and metallurgy, and agriculture. A federally sponsored "Negro Building" held exhibits from scores of black universities, colleges, and schools. Norfolk Mission College and Princess Anne Academy took silver medals in the education division. There were glistening automobiles from the Rapid factory in Pontiac, Michigan, public and private collections of portraits, firearms, silverware, historic documents, exhibits by foreign countries (including a complete Japanese village), and whatever else might spark a moment's attention from footsore spectators.[40]

Organizations took advantage of the occasion to hold annual meetings there: the National Council of Mothers, the Association of Seaboard Airline Railway Surgeons, the Women's National Press Association, the National Council of Jewish Women, and many more. Every day had its special recognition; hence Osteopathy Day came between North Carolina Negro Day and Negro Physician Day, and Nova Scotia Day was held just before Greater Norfolk Day. A Seattle high school baseball team played games across the country to finance its trip; a group of twenty-one heiresses from Oregon came in their private Pullman cars; Floyd Pegg rode a horse from Chicago to Washington in twenty-one days, doing the final lap to Norfolk by rail. He lost a $1,500 bet that he could make Washington in twenty days.[41]

Visitors interested in just having fun had an array of possibilities. Emmet McConnell's "spectatorium," featuring electric-powered moving scenery that depicted the *Monitor–Merrimac* battle and cycloramas of the battles of Gettysburg and First Manassas were crowd-pleasers, as were his Shoot-the-Chutes and Scenic Railway. Many such attractions lined a midway section called "The Warpath": Beautiful Orient, Streets of Cairo, Temple of Mirth, Destruction of San Francisco, Ferrari's Wild Animal Show, and more. To the west of the exposition lay the new town of Pine Beach, an "outside amusement park" with rides and games of chance, animal shows, pickpockets, and women of inconstant virtue. The completed exposition stretched two miles along Hampton Roads and another half-mile beside Boush's Creek.[42]

Singular in drawing power was the "101 Ranch Wild West Show," which arrived in sixty-five railroad cars and boasted a cast of five-hundred cowboys, cowgirls, Mexican *rancheros,* and Ponca and Otce Indians. A special treat was Bill Pickett, a black cowboy from Texas who could throw a steer "by the sheer strength of his teeth." Bostick's Wild Animal Show was another of immense size and variety with its eighty lions, sixteen polar bears, twelve hyenas, and other four-footed attractions. There were "ostrich farms" both inside the grounds and at Pine Beach.[43]

Politicians and persons claiming expertise on any subject at all were in high demand. There seemed to be no end (literally) to discourses such as "Compression Ice Plants Using Ammonia as a Refrigerant," "Claiborne Genealogy," and "The Uses of the Peanut." Mark Twain gave an amusing talk, Dr. Woodrow Wilson of Princeton University a high-minded one, President Roosevelt one that scorched monopolies, Booker T. Washington one on "the peculiar advantages presented by the South" to black people. There were also William Jennings Bryan, Samuel Gompers, and assorted governors, department heads, men of the cloth, diplomats, and ladies in large hats.[44]

Indian artifacts were prominent in the history building, where an exhibit featured "the Mound Builders." But the arrowheads and clay pipes could not compensate for an act of criminal desecration that occurred two years before the exposition opened. In April 1905 workmen digging the foundation for a Pine Beach hotel excavated "a sand hill" or "mound" containing fifty or more Indian skeletons (the *Virginian-Pilot* said it was hundreds) "buried in a circle," with "an Indian arsenal" nearby and other evidences of thick native American habitation on Sewell's Point. Some of the bones and artifacts were salvaged for display with the history exhibits, but the likely site of the Chesapeian town of Skicoak, known to Ralph Lane in 1585, was thus destroyed.[45]

The exposition gave encouragement to every kind of creative talent, or at least the aspiration to it. "Virginia Day" featured Thomas Nelson Page reciting his epic poem, "The Vision of Raleigh." Signor Patricolo, "one of the world's great pianists," incongruously chosen to compose an official musical score, responded with an impermanent piece entitled "Jamestown Dixie," with snatches from the Rebel rallying song interwoven with classical strains. There was also an "Official Hymn" by two Baltimoreans—forty lines on how the pioneers "struggle on, impelled by conscious right," and so on. Norfolk native William Couper, "perhaps the most eminent contemporary American sculptor," did a heroic John Smith for the history building besides a bronze Confederate soldier for a Commercial Square memorial downtown.[46]

Hundreds of prizes were awarded to exhibitors of many states and countries, from the Yuji Onuma Fish Culture Company of Tsuchiura, Japan, to D. Carpenter's furniture and furnishings in Norfolk. Head-to-head with some of the world's best, Norfolk individuals and businesses took numerous medals, including John G. Helvin for handmade copper horseshoes, the Pocomoke Guano Company for fertilizer, the Chesapeake Launch and Motor Company, and A. Wrenn Carriages and Buggies. Norfolk's J. R. Cromwell got one for cantaloupes, Wallace Hawkins and L. M. Sylvester for vegetables. Anyone able to carry a tune, play an instrument, or plausibly fake it could find fulfillment with an exposition band or chorus.[47]

Of more enduring value was the national airing of facets of Virginia's history of which even the local public was largely unaware. The *Jamestown Magazine*, published monthly after June 1906 and mailed to destinations throughout the country, carried a lot of sheer puffery but also such articles as "Historic Yorktown," "An Early Virginia Witch" (Grace Sherwood), "Historic Williamsburg," and "The First University in America" (Henrico). Dozens of orators held forth on Bacon's Rebellion, Patrick Henry, John Randolph, and so on, besides innumerable eulogies to the settlers of 1607. Frequent tours to Jamestown and other historic sites deepened the impression that the history of the Old Dominion had not received the notice it deserved.[48]

The most obvious impact, of course, was on Norfolk and nearby towns. The *Jamestown Magazine* and other exposition literature trumpeted Norfolk's prospects as a commercial emporium and the recreational assets of Ocean View, Virginia Beach, Old Point Comfort, and other local spas and pleasure grounds. Attendance at the exposition was almost three million, and many who would not otherwise have set foot in Norfolk no doubt became regular visitors and even residents. The exposition gave temporary work to thousands of Norfolk's black and white laborers and, though not living up to its promise, was still of considerable moment to area businesses.[49] The coming years must inevitably witness a thrusting growth of Norfolk toward the exposition grounds and beyond.

A summing-up in the *Jamestown Magazine* credited the exposition with the "grandest naval rendezvous in history," "the greatest motor boat regatta ever held," and "the greatest military and naval parades ever witnessed" on "the largest military parade ground in the world." It had "more naval and military bands than were ever assembled" in peacetime and "the only privately owned collection of Egyptian mummies in the world." Officially in receivership, it was also the most fiscally catastrophic in an era that included the Louisiana Purchase Exposition in St. Louis and others in Chicago, Omaho, Charleston, Buffalo, Philadelphia, and Atlanta. But the Exposition Company owned some four hundred acres of waterfront property and might yet sell it a price that could recoup most losses.[50]

Given the small local interest in the site, the *Ledger-Dispatch* proposed that the navy take it over as a training center or storage facility for coal. The navy showed interest, but new military facilities were always the subject of congressional donnybrooks and it would be years before action was taken. In the meantime, navy commitment to Hampton Roads increased month by month. War clouds in Europe and Roosevelt's initiative in naval shipbuilding led to expansion of Norfolk navy yard's drydock into the world's largest to accommodate the latest battlewagons and the deepening of the channel— to thirty-five feet in 1911. Norfolk was homeport for twenty-one warships, the Atlantic fleet's second division. It was also in 1911 that the government resolved to give Cape Henry the strongest fortifications on the Atlantic coast.[51]

A final emanation of the exposition was a handsome *Official Blue Book* of over eight hundred pages, which appeared in 1909 and was called the most elaborate book ever published in Norfolk. Bound in Persian Morocco with the exposition seal embossed in gold on its cover, the volume contained 1,400 illustrations and texts by many leading players in the exposition experience. It was edited by Charles R. Keiley, who had served as "chief of exploitation," and contained a surprisingly candid review of the fair in all its calamitous grandeur.[52] It was a welcome return to sober evaluation after an era of stentorian exposition bombast.

A similarly useful reflection was the clear-eyed review of Norfolk's most pressing needs carried by the *Ledger-Dispatch* at the start of 1913. In five columns under large black letters, the editors listed an unlimited supply of good water, a new hospital on the grounds of the naval hospital across the river, and consolidation of Norfolk and Portsmouth. There must be an immigration station for Hampton Roads, "a united business body . . . to make local efforts more effective" (earlier chambers of commerce having proved unsuccessful), "a hundred factory whistles," and other goals. The list might have been extended indefinitely: automobile owners, for example, pointed to macadamized roads as one of the major needs of the twentieth century in Norfolk as elsewhere.[53]

A principal legacy of the Progressive Era was a consensus that cities of the twentieth century would live or die by careful and elaborate planning, and the Jamestown Exposition drove home this lesson with impressive urgency. The casual, rollicking days of rings and robber barons must yield somehow, for better and worse, to the age of managers. The epoch of unbuttoned deliverance was over, that of the bureaucrat was at hand.

CHAPTER 20

Kaiser Willi's Boomtown

NORFOLK in a rare transport of patriotism was not an altogether attractive sight. The five thousand people who jammed Armory Hall on the night of March 31, 1917, craved raw meat and a battery of speakers was assembled to throw it to them. The invocation by Dr. L. D. Mendoza of Ohef Sholom was followed immediately by Governor Henry C. Stuart's tirade against pacifists who would meet invading armies with the Ten Commandments and the Golden Rule. Rev. Francis C. Steinmetz of Christ Church skewered the kaiser with harsh invective and Captain J. W. Happer of Portsmouth invoked Patrick Henry's memory as somehow pertinent to the wars among Europe's emperors.[1]

Solos by contralto Blanche Consolvo and others and stirring music by the Naval Port Band stiffened the crowd's resolve to send young men to defend whatever it was someone threatened. Jacob Leicht, a native of Bavaria, declared unswerving loyalty to America (applause). North Carolina Judge Francis D. Winston was of years sufficiently advanced to assert that he would rather die in France than that the humblest American "lose his life to the barbarian submarines of the war-crazed kaiser." (Loud applause.) But it was left to D. Lawrence Groner, bred to a still more unabashed jingoism, to pledge that "whatever the sacrifice, whatever the treasure, whatever the life, it is none too dear to be placed upon the altar of freedom and honor."[2] (Prolonged applause.)

Fired by recent news of the sinking of American ships by German submarines, Norfolk knew that President Wilson would ask for a declaration of war in a day or so and that Congress would grant it. The April 6 headline— "U.S. DECLARES WAR"—was accompanied by a *Virginian-Pilot* "Honor Roll" of fifteen local people who enlisted in the services the day before, including Misses Alice B. Hines and Ruth M. Baldwin as navy yeomen. The editors wondered if Norfolk's women were not in fact more patriotic than its men; Mrs. Pauline Adams called for a "Women's Home Guard" to displace men at guard duty. (Such a unit, with a full complement of sixty women, was soon drilling twice a week at the Fergus Reid Building.)[3]

The nation's entry into the war provided outlets for the patriotic impulses of virtually every citizen. The Norfolk branch of the surgical dressing committee sent an average of 1,800 dressings a week to France even before war was declared, and the Fund for the French Wounded had been at work for a year collecting donated pajamas, shirts, underclothes, socks, and so on. Nineteen doctors and surgeons at Protestant Hospital offered their services to the government at once. The Belgian Orphan Fund was being conducted by Belgian Consul J. P. Andre Mottu, and the Women's Auxiliary of the Navy League was actively recruiting.[4]

To recruit for the battleship *New Hampshire*, at anchor in the Elizabeth River, some teenage girls—Anne Byrd, Margaret Grandy, Virginia Hughes, Anne Groner, and others—agreed to occupy a tent at Granby Street and City Hall Avenue to buttonhole young men about volunteering. When twenty men applied the first day, the *Nevada* and other ships procured their own tents and girls. The daily Honor Roll swelled to fifty and more, though young women could only enlist as clerks and the like with the navy and black men only for the army. Peppery George F. Viett was denied enrollment in the army on the technicalities that he was an old man and a cripple.[5]

It was rumored that blacks might be unwilling to fight, that "German influence" would undermine their patriotism. Black leaders such as P. B. Young, Boy Scout official Benjamin Braxton, Professor D. G. Jacox (Tidewater Teachers' Association president), and others called a black mass meeting at Booker T. Washington School on April 10 to display solidarity with the nation. The papers reporting the meeting noted city council steps—unconstitutional as it turned out—to force black residents and businesses out of predominantly white blocks and vice versa. All black military units, however, were enrolled to maximum strength by the end of April.[6]

The hysteria of the war's early weeks sowed new suspicions over the cause of every downtown fire, every breakdown of a public utility. The kaiser was thought by many to have sent agents from Berlin expressly to burn a shoe shop on Colley Avenue or to spook the horses at Plume Street stables. On April 17 a young man was arrested for asking a YMCA clerk the cost of sending a letter to Germany. Found on his person was a letter with queer markings, possibly a code, to a Rhode Island woman. There could not be too much vigilance against so devious a foe: on April 12 Mayor Wyndham Mayo ordered all alien enemies in the city to surrender their firearms.[7]

If anyone had a right to rejoice over the war, it was Theodore J. Wool, nephew of Civil War General John E. Wool. A Norfolk lawyer, Wool had tried for a decade to sell the government the Jamestown Exposition site for a naval facility. Several bills came close to passage in Congress only to fail. He and other investors in 1908 bought the site in hopes of a windfall when they sold it. In late 1916 Secretary of the Navy Josephus Daniels came down with the House Naval Affairs Committee to examine the site, but decided it would be too costly to develop. But Norfolk in early 1917 became head-quarters of the Fifth Naval District (offices in Citizens Bank), and Wool's hopes soared.[8]

American entry into the war pushed Daniels to propose leasing the Sew-ell's Point land (including Pine Beach), but the navy now decided to buy it for long-term development. Funds for the site were voted by Congress on June 15, 1917; Wool and his associates received $494,000, substantially less than they hoped but nearly twice what they had paid for it. In the words of the late Lenoir Chambers, "Nothing of greater importance had come into the life of Norfolk since it was established as a town."[9]

Apart from long-unused Fort Norfolk, the only military facility in Nor-folk was Berkley's St. Helena Training Station. But Sewell's Point was envi-sioned as a full-blown naval base, not a training camp or coaling station. A training center was ready by mid–October, followed by a supply depot, naval aviation lagoon for seaplanes, airfield for planes and dirigibles, thirty-one-vessel submarine base, storage for medical supplies, oil, mines, nets, torpe-does, and a fleeting grounds. In short, Norfolk, its ship channels deepened to forty feet, would be one of the navy's major operating bases and as rapidly as the nation could create it. In addition, the army began building its largest base at Boush's Bluff just south of the exposition grounds.[10]

The navy adapted the old exposition entrance as the main gate to its new base and occupied the administration building and other structures still in good repair. Land was soon acquired for the great concrete hangars, six-story warehouses, barracks, mess halls, garages, bakeries, laundries, an ice plant, machine shops, and hundreds of other buildings that had to be con-structed at Sewell's Point. The navy wanted two 1,400-foot piers built into the river with thirty-five-foot access channels, a mammoth bulkhead over 22,000 feet long, and miles of streets and railroads.[11]

Besides the new navy and army bases, older military facilities had to be altered and enlarged. Gosport would have new piers equipped with cranes, tracks, trolley, capstan, and conduits. It would have a forty-foot-deep dry-dock over a thousand feet long to accommodate the greatest battlewagons. The naval hospital at Portsmouth would be enlarged with emergency buildings and eight temporary wards to make it the largest on the Atlantic Coast.[12] The government was building what amounted to a whole new city on the south shore of Hampton Roads.

Norfolk relished the idea of the trade to be generated by so much activity, but did not yet imagine how thoroughly it would be transformed. The military plans meant tens of thousands of laborers, and scores of thousands of military personnel added to the local population. The human tidal wave implied vast demands on Norfolk to help house, feed, entertain, and otherwise accommodate them, and more immigration to supply multitudes of human services. With its creaky nineteenth-century administrative system, fossilized Victorian institutions, lingering river-town perspective, and scanty and outmoded service economy, Norfolk might not be equal to the task. There must be limits on how far a small city could be stretched without breaking altogether.

Old World rivalries seemed of slight consequence when an heir to the Austro-Hungarian throne and his wife were shot to death in a European town in June 1914. Of more concern were Pancho Villa and the Mexican rebels, whose resistance to their government sometimes took forms inconvenient to American interests and in 1916 summoned Norfolk's Light Artillery Blues to brief duty in Texas. But most Norfolkians were still more preoccupied with the opportunities the twentieth century offered for richer and, sometimes, more enjoyable lives. (An exception was the seventy-one-member Amish Colony located six miles out toward Kempsville.)[13]

In March 1915 a German commerce raider, the *Prinz Eitel Friedrich*, entered Hampton Roads after a long Pacific and South Atlantic cruise to apply for coal and repairs at Newport News. British cruisers took position off the coast to sink her when she left, so the German commander decided to let her be interned for the war's duration. She was brought to Norfolk navy yard in April as thousands of spectators lined the river. The crew lived aboard ship until the United States joined the conflict; they then became prisoners of war. (A second raider, the *Kronprinz Wilhelm*, was interned soon afterward.) The *Prinz Eitel* later became an American transport and, after the war, a passenger liner.[14]

By the start of the European war several "photo-play houses," such as the Strand on Granby, offered silent movies at five cents a showing. The year 1915 brought *The Birth of a Nation*, D. W. Griffith's adaptation of the racially inflamatory novel and play, *The Clansman*, though the film stirred less prejudice and was hailed chiefly for its technical virtuosity. Norfolk's Alva Lee Turrentine, Annie Russell, and Winnie Davis were finalists in a

Photoplay magazine contest to find Hollywood talent, and won a course of dramatic arts lessons in New York. The war was brought home to Norfolk in such films as *Fighting for France,* a documentary with frontline footage, though a Keystone comedy appeared on the same bill to lessen the harsh impact.[15]

The hustling Norfolk Moving Pictures Company in 1914 offered "Norfolk–Portsmouth Animated Weekly Views" at the American Theater. Subjects included Park Place School's teachers and pupils passing in drill-formation review, the Elks Home and members of the order, "beautiful Larchmont" homes and children at play, crowds leaving the ferry, scenes on Main and Granby, part of a Newport News–Portsmouth baseball game, and other local footage.[16] But the novelty of familiar scenes in living motion seems not to have held its own long with the Silver Screen witchery of Mable Normand, Fatty Arbuckle, Billie Burke, and Douglas Fairbanks.

In the summer of 1914 an anonymous young man, lately home from a world tour, introduced at Virginia Beach a sport identified as "shooting the waves on an Hawaiian surfboard." Sportsmen who had used canoes for this purpose for several seasons past soon mastered the art and ordered boards from local lumber dealers. Newspapers acclaimed the exploits of airman Theodore Macauley, who flew a big seaplane from Newport News to Baltimore in 1916 with five passengers, setting several records, though two died when the craft plunged into the Potomac on an attempted return flight.[17]

By now Norfolk's heart was captivated by the automobile, though many horses and horsedrawn vehicles still used the streets. In 1912 the *Landmark* dubbed Norfolk Virginia's leading auto seller and shipper. Norfolk dealers handled thirty-six makes of "pleasure cars," ten kinds of trucks, and several motorcycles. The first "jitney bus" (any vehicle carrying two or more paying passengers) was introduced in early 1915 between the Commercial Place ferry and points uptown.[18]

In 1916 Main and Granby were clogged with up to 2,500 autos a day besides jitneys, trolleys, trucks, and horses; Norfolk now had its first one-way streets. Carnival proprietor K. H. Barkoot in 1917 sought investors for a plant to make an electric gimcrack which, worked by a button at the steering wheel, caused tail lights to signal when cars turned left or right, stopped, or backed up.[19]

If downtown traffic was at a critical stage, beyond city limits it was excruciating. Norfolk and Princess Anne counties were confidently said to have the state's worst roads. Norfolk County's only highways connected Pine Beach with Ocean View, Deep Creek with Great Bridge. Princess Anne had no properly graded roads whatever and insufficient means to convert existing dirt and shell roads into highways. Many formerly straight segments were turned into corkscrews by users twisting right or left around deep holes and ruts. A Princess Anne mass meeting was called in 1915 to discuss the roads, but only fifty of two hundred invitees showed up owing to recent rains that left many routes impassable.[20]

Norfolk's business, good before the war, got better after it began; 1915 exports doubled over the previous year and almost doubled again in 1916. (The Panama Canal's opening helped.) Even without a war the city was the world's biggest peanut market, the Atlantic Coast's second largest lumber market, one of the world's great truck-farming centers, the fourth-ranking cotton port. The war's effects were seen in such phenomena as passage through town in 1915 of 132,000 horses en route to France. City businesses in 1913 included some 360 manufacturers, mostly tiny shops and mills specializing in a some handcrafted item or line, and war would add 20 percent to the industrial workforce. The British-American Tobacco Company soon opened four cigarette-making plants and the shipbuilding firms enlarged their facilities.[21]

Representative of the more successful enterprises was Pender's Grocery. David Pender came to Norfolk in the late 1800s as an unemployed clerk with $10.00. After buying his employer's small grocery in the early 1900s, he divided the business by departments, each of which had to show a profit or a good reason why it could not. He cut out many middlemen, and learned to package his own goods, run his own lunch counters, and produce baked goods. By 1915 he had three stores, two of them at the corner of Wolfe (later Market) Street and Monticello Avenue. Nicely positioned to meet wartime challenges, Pender created a chain of stores across Virginia and North Carolina. In 1921 he had sixty-two stores, a figure that quadrupled before he sold out five years later to what became Colonial Stores.[22]

More common were such operations as the Gin-Gera Company on Commerce Street. Formed in 1912 with Frank B. Howard as president and treasurer, Gin-Gera made a ginger-flavored sweetwater deemed by some "the best soft drink ever produced." But the company had early financial problems that continued after introducing a cola—Ginco—in 1915. What probably led to the company's demise in 1918 was its inability to find capital for effective advertising and the purchase of barrels, boxes, and trucks, despite unsolicited help from the state, which in November 1916 adopted Prohibition, a boon to soft-drink sales.[23]

Some of the more successful enterprises were operated by immigrants such as John P. Bombalis, a Greek who owned the Bombalis Hotel and Cafe and was part-owner, with other Greeks, of the Virginia Beach Casino. The sale of two small battleships, the *Mississippi* and the *Idaho*, to the Greek government in 1914 was celebrated by the Greek community as a patriotic event. Bombalis obtained from New York a Greek flag for the *Mississippi*, newly christened *Kilkis* and at anchor in Hampton Roads, and entertained its new officers and others with a banquet at his casino in July. The ship steamed off almost at once, war having broken out in Europe in the same month.[24]

Among successful black businesses was Little Bay Beach, near Ocean View, operated by the L. W. Brights. During the warm months of 1915, they hosted outings of such groups as the Priscilla Art Club, Philharmonic Club, Ladies' Art Circle, Hawthorne Club, Premier Band, and St. Joseph Catholic Sunday School, all of Norfolk, as well as groups from Portsmouth, Smithfield, Hampton, and elsewhere. C. C. Dogan's Home Building and Loan Association, founded in 1905, had over $80,000 in assets by 1920. In 1916 Brown's Savings and Banking Company (BSBC) of Norfolk, the first black institution to open a Christmas Savings Club, led all black banks in the country in savings accumulated that way. In 1919 founder E. C. Brown converted BSBC into the Metropolitan Bank and Trust Company, with stock capitalized at $2 million.[25]

P. B. Young's *Journal and Guide*, struggling to establish itself and modernize its equipment, suffered a staggering setback in December 1913 when its Church Street plant burned. Despite losing his machinery, stocks, records, and files, Young never missed an issue. He moved to new Queen Street quarters, and by 1919 had four thousand readers in Tidewater Virginia and northeastern North Carolina. By now Young had adopted the roll of spokesmen for Norfolk blacks in lieu of Church Street's influential black merchants, too inclined toward reticence, and the community's preachers, who seemed to him out of touch with practical affairs.[26]

The war found Norfolk more attuned to national and world affairs than ever before, virtually every national cause resonating in the form of some group or campaign. For Jews, the war gave opportunity for Zionists, especially popular at Beth El, to seek fulfillment of their dream of a Palestinian Jewish homeland. In 1913 Mrs. Miriam Blaustein founded Norfolk's chapter of Hadassah, a women's organization initially devoted to providing health care for Jews in Palestine. Norfolk Zionists gave liberally to the Jewish National Fund and its aim of buying land for Jews wishing to settle in Palestine. In 1916 Virginia Zionists held their first state convention in Norfolk, with Bel El Rabbi Louis I. Goldberg as president and Mrs. Blaustein as executive secretary. B'nai B'rith formed its first Norfolk chapter in 1921.[27]

Norfolk women were intrigued by the Equal Suffrage League, aiming to cap off the Progressive Era with a constitutional amendment giving women the vote. Weekly meetings at the Lynnhaven Hotel explored such issues as raising the female age of consent from fourteen to eighteeen and the need for a public Declaration of Principles. Mrs. Pauline Adams, Mrs. C. E. Townsend, and Helen Hewitt Greene were among suffragists trying to educate the public on the issue despite the fact that President Wilson, eminently progressive in other ways, saw it as a state matter rather than a constitutional one. The war put the question on hold and the Lynnhaven Hotel meetings declined to once a month.[28]

Prohibition remained a leading issue until 1914, when voters adopted a statewide ban on making and selling alcohol, effective November 1, 1916. Norfolk voted wet by a thin margin but the result denied ring politicians the saloon vote, long one of their essential constituencies. Sensing the ring's evaporation, reformers in 1914 put together the Citizen's Party to oppose it. The new party represented mainly the business community, now more concerned with economical and efficient government than liquor, the merit system of officeholding than prostitution, better streets and schools than gambling. In the 1914 city elections, the new party took fourteen of twenty council seats and was soon in firm control of municipal administration.[29]

The war made acute the problems of water supply, a needed gas works, street maintenance, and other practical matters that seemed to many to dwarf in importance the old moral questions. The city acquired two more lakes in 1917, for the moment deemed adequate to Norfolk's long-term water needs, but even at the war's end less than half its 172 miles of streets were paved. To these needs were also added public docks, a new city market, armory, convention center, schools, and playgrounds.[30]

The key obstacle to ready answers appeared to be the unwieldy structure of local government, in which the buck might pass indefinitely through rival centers of authority and questions were often discussed into oblivion. The city council, always large and unwieldy, had grown in 1911 into a sixty-four-headed monster that devoured civic initiatives like small children. Pared down to twenty-five by 1916, it was still a shaggy beast, immovable except by sharp blows to its hind quarters.[31]

Reformers—I. Walke Truxton, Tazewell Taylor, members of the Citizen's Party, the Chamber of Commerce, and other business leaders—favored a new city charter modeled on Galveston's commission system or

Staunton's city-manager plan. A referendum on charter changes failed in 1915, as many voters were on vacation, but Portsmouth adopted a council-manager system in 1916. A second try in November 1917 gave Norfolk a charter providing a council of five at-large members who chose one of their own as mayor *ex officio* (eliminating the ward system) and hired a city manager. The councilmen were mostly top bankers and businessmen living in suburban Brambleton, Colonial Place, and West Ghent. As city manager, they chose engineer Charles E. Ashburner, who had been the nation's first city manager at Staunton.[32]

The new administration was put to a swift and severe test of its capabilities. To the dizzying rush of growth and the complexity inherent in implementing the new charter was added the strain of a war abruptly concluded and a skidding swerve back to peacetime status. If the new system could survive such a succession of crises, its merit would be proved beyond cavil.

As the war wore on, downtown could be seen to have changed only marginally in the latest decade. Between Water Street (now Waterside Drive) and the river lay a long row of warehouses and rail and steamship terminals. Behind it was East Main, a dozen or so blocks between Union Station and Granby, with its fruit stores, garment and tailor shops, groceries, restaurants, lunch counters, and cathouses. The Boston Cafe, under the unlikely dominion of Hop Sing and Joe Eng, shared a block with Demeteirous Feleron's New York Lunch Room and not far from Antonio and Philip Tagliavaria's fruit store. Hofheimer's Shoe Store was farther down Main, with Near Eastern and Latin tenants interspersed among Greeks, Chinese, Italians, and Jews in pre–Babel amiability.[33]

Most produce dealers congregated in the vicinity of Roanoke Square, to the west of Commercial Place and the big Miller, Rhoads, and Schwartz store. The Piggly-Wiggly at Twenty-Seventh and Granby was the city's only rival to the Pender chain; the new Flatiron Building on Upper Granby now housed offices of the fifth naval district. On the same street were most of Norfolk's automobile showrooms, repair shops, and automotive supply stores—"Automobile Row," as it was termed. The city market off City Hall Avenue held dozens of stalls for meat and fish vendors.[34]

From Sewell's Point, the war was a maritime galaxy of "French Barks and British merchantmen, ships from China," Scandinavia, the West Indies, Russia, Argentina, and elsewhere, "beaten by the seas until they are the sea's own gray." "The whole beautiful expanse of Hampton Roads," sang the *Virginian-Pilot*, was dotted with ships loading cargo and coal or awaiting turns, "while all about them ply the small, busy harbor craft, and an occasional big government dredge. . . . In the distance, tramps and sailing vessels, barges and schooners, show dim against the horizon." Ashore, immense coal trains lurched and moaned against burdens amounting to 95 percent of all the Elizabeth River's export tonnage in 1917. There were also huge amounts of fertilizer, fruit, vegetables, seafood, lumber, and so on daily passing through the terminals.[35]

The most pressing need by the winter of 1917–18 was housing; Norfolk's 67,000 residents of 1910 had doubled to 130,000 in 1917, with more train loads arriving almost daily. They came from as far away as Minnesota and Texas and needed rooms at once. Norfolk, growing rapidly for the past four decades, had little land to spare and much of that was uninhabitable. Older residents found a welcome source of income in renting spare rooms and did not hesitate to raise rents and leases as fast as the traffic would bear. The federal government finally put up $9 million in early 1918 to build housing for its Norfolk employees. But the new communities in Glenwood Park (near the naval base) and Cradock on Paradise Creek were still in early phases of development when the war—and the need—ended.[36]

Even with people practically standing on each other's heads, the labor shortage was extreme. The government, one way or another, met its needs but often at the expense of civilian employers. Blacks and women found themselves in unaccustomed high demand, 250 females, for example, replacing an equal number of male clerks at the new army supply base in October 1918. But farmers grew accustomed to crops that went unharvested for want of labor (or lack of transportation for what *was* harvested), while hotels and restaurants jostled one another viciously for the available cooks, waiters, waitresses, maids, bellhops, and so on.[37]

The flourishing war years enabled much of the black labor force to organize effectively for the first time. Black longshoremen had two unions, the Coal Trimmers Local 15277, formed in 1914, and the Transportation Workers Association (TWA), started before the war as a fraternal group. The former won an early victory when it struck and won a pay raise. In 1917 TWA, threatening three Norfolk shipping companies with a walkout, won a pay increase, guaranteed minimum wages, and better working conditions.[38]

TWA had less success in other respects. It was behind a decision of the American Cigar Company's female stemmers earning less than $5.00 a week to unionize and demand higher pay and shorter hours. The firm granted a small pay increase but endured a strike of several months in order to break the union. When TWA approached black oyster-shuckers in Norfolk's ten plants, the ensuing strike was broken, in part, by police, who dispersed picketers and escorted strike-breakers to work. Black female domestics, incited by TWA to threaten a strike in 1917, were defeated by a police sweep of "loafers" and "slackers" in the black laboring class, including domestics. But wartime union activity was sufficiently successful to persuade many blacks of the value of organization for the common economic good.[39]

Police made periodic sweeps to round up loafers; two-hundred blacks and whites were taken in a descent on pool rooms in August 1918. Black women took the initiative in hunting down shirkers and reporting them to authorities, who offered a choice among workplace, battlefield, or jail. Workers, conscious of improved bargaining positions, struck often for higher wages and other benefits; eight thousand building tradesmen struck in November 1918 for a dollar-an-hour raise. Little violence accompanied the walkouts.[40]

Norfolk's chief disaster of the war years came not from U-boats or saboteurs but from a fire that broke out about 4:00 A.M. on New Year's Day 1918 in a building next to the Monticello Hotel. With the temperature as low as twelve degrees and Hampton Roads nearly frozen over, firemen from Portsmouth and Suffolk as well as Norfolk fought through the day and into the next, three dying in the effort to halt the flames. Citizens and off-duty sailors and soldiers manned the hoses of trucks and tugboats, the sailors using semaphore from rooftops to coordinate efforts over the bedlam below. But $2 million worth of shops and stores, the Monticello, and other buildings were lost in Norfolk's worst blaze since 1776, 142 years earlier to the day. Editors blamed incendiaries, quite possibly German agents.[41]

Other perils of 1918 included a wave of influenza, not so fatal in Norfolk as elsewhere, and a national coal shortage that closed local businesses for part of the winter. Not low coal supplies but scant means of shipping it turned out to be the problem. Nature offered a clumsy compensation in the following summer with a searing heat wave that felled farm horses in the fields and curtailed productivity. The influenza epidemic, beginning in September, ended in November with almost nine thousand reported cases but only 273 deaths. Schools and theaters closed for much of that period.[42]

Also temporarily closed by the flu were dance halls, which had become a source of friction between the military and some of the townsfolk. In May 1918 Rev. Steinmetz delivered a philippic against "immoral indulgences" by military men that handicapped Norfolk's ability to confront the war; especially heinous were dance halls and triweekly dances at Armory Hall. Dancing, Steinmetz maintained, enabled servicemen to meet prostitutes, over five hundred of whom, many under eighteen and diseased, had lately been arrested in a ten-week period. But voices from both military and civilian ranks protested that the Armory Hall dances, at least, were well chaperoned, dancers carefully screened, and service immorality the exception more than the rule.[43]

Dancing continued, but the controversy brought to a head a festering issue of military-civilian relations. By 1918 Norfolk had a reputation throughout the navy as a poor liberty-town where residents allegedly put up signs such as "Sailors and Dogs —Keep Off the Grass." Many townspeople, their streets and facilities inundated by uniformed strangers, were sick to exhaustion with the intruders and wished them all in Hell or Heidelberg, whichever was farther from Town Point. The main problem, the fault of no one in particular, was that Norfolk's recreational facilities, wholesome and otherwise, were swamped by ceaseless hordes of blue and khaki. The bad reputation, fair or not, was destined to endure.[44]

New Year's Eve revelry at the end of 1917 had led to a serious riot, broken store windows, a sailor's death, and injury to others before marines cleared the streets with rifle butts. Another came on September 22, 1918, when the arrest of a black soldier on a dubious robbery charge brought nearly one thousand blacks to the police station at Queen and Church and fighting that caused injuries on both sides. A few weeks later, Halloween hijinx erupted into a downtown melee in which a policeman was killed. Navy authorities in early 1918 put the South Church Street black area off-limits to sailors and set up a naval guard (forerunner of the shore patrol) for streets and public conveyances.[45] Civilian-military and racial friction continued but within controllable limits.

Norfolk was several times faced with navy threats to pull out and go to Yorktown if the city could not address its needs promptly and effectively. Water was a principal irritant until Norfolk agreed in March 1918 to connect its two reserve-supply lakes to the base. Arrangements were made to upgrade Jamestown Boulevard to the base and acquire more land as navy needs expanded. The newly reorganized Chamber of Commerce canvassed the city for housing pending the start of the government's own building programs. Meanwhile, the navy built its own railroad so that it need not hire trucks from private firms.[46] Everything was strained to the point of breakdown, but chaos was averted by forebearance on all sides.

Norfolk's own soldiers comprised four infantry companies, one each of infantry headquarters, support, machine gun, and ambulance personnel, an artillery battery, and a sanitation unit; many of the soldiers were draftees. Few local men became marines, but many joined the navy, which finally accepted blacks as mess attendants, cooks, and stewards. The National Guard units, the Fourth Virginia Infantry and Light Artillery Blues, were mustered into service, the latter seeing action notably in the Meuse-Argonne offensive of September 1918. A home guard, without age-limits, replaced the militia and also aided bond drives and other patriotic activities. The troops were welcomed back in May and June 1919; the third week of June was "Home-Coming Week," with parades, festivities, and services.[47]

In John Dos Passos' novel *1919*, a returning merchant mariner thrills at entering the "smooth brown water of Hampton Roads" and finding it "crowded with shipping; four great battlewagons at anchor, subchasers speeding in and out and a white revenue cutter, camouflaged freighters and colliers, a bunch of red munitions barges anchored off by themselves." He "hardly knew the town walking up from the ferry," the store windows full of liberty-loan posters, bands playing, streets thronged with uniforms, and "two minute speakers" holding forth at Main and Granby. The war workers would leave only gradually; the military presence diminished by imperceptible degrees in the coming months.[48]

The euphoria of peace gave Congress an opportunity to pass the Prohibition and Equal Suffrage amendments in 1919, the first over Norfolk's objections, the second with its grudging consent. Women must have the vote, some said, to help keep alcohol under control. Previously, possession of booze was legal in Virginia and many Norfolkians were accustomed to receiving it by mail and consuming it without interference.[49] New strategies were required to keep alive the sacred traditions of Old Virginia.

Newspaper sales soared during the war and remained high as Norfolk followed President Wilson's triumphant voyage to Europe and the Peace Conference. America had been at war less than two weeks when Norfolk's C. Whittle Sams warned *Virginian-Pilot* readers not to interpret the conflict as one of democracy against aristocracy. England, he noted, was a monarchy, ally Japan an empire, Russia in transition from an empire to God-knows-what. We fought Germany for sinking our ships, not because the kaiser was an emperor.[50] But his reminder echoed too faintly in 1919 and the president seemed to claim victory in a war that had not been fought.

An unhappy residue of war was the persistence of the ferocity it had been the particular design of the nation to foment. Popular hatreds that proved serviceable against "Huns" and other malefactors were not abruptly buried and forgotten with the war's end but directed toward other objects. From Washington and Stone Mountain, Georgia, came warnings that alien immigrants, feminists, Jews, blacks, Reds, and maybe Sears, Roebuck and Company were as little to be trusted as the former enemy. Strikes, naughty movies, high prices, and cosmetic creams were said to be linked by subterranean threads worked by networks of conspirators.[51]

The *Ledger-Dispatch* applauded a Park Place rally against the Red Menace in 1919 and proposed police reserves to "defend Americanism." When the American Citizens League undertook to save Norfolk from foreign agitators, the paper cited agents "whose purpose is the overthrow of American institutions" in favor of "Red Anarchy and a Bolshevist form of government." A raid on IWW union headquarters in Portsmouth turned up radical propaganda testifying that V. I. Lenin had taken up where the kaiser left off. But the *Virginian-Pilot,* coming in 1919 under editor Louis Jaffe, whose parents were Jewish, took a less paranoid tone in the first of his thirty years with the paper.[52]

Late in 1919 a huge tabernacle arose at the corner of Twentieth Street and Monticello Avenue, where evangelist Billy Sunday was to appear in January. Worried about the prolonged drought, local supporters asked Sunday to pray at his initial program for rain and he did so. The rains soon came in the form of a terrible storm that rammed a channel across Willoughby Spit, destroying several cottages. Some hours into the tempest it was proposed that the faithful invite Sunday to consider whether this was not enough already and that he use his influence to stop the storm. Sunday prayed and the storm ended. Norfolk's hurricanes, like its earthquakes, it seems, were equally susceptible to benevolent intervention.[53]

Even Billy Sunday was powerless against postwar unemployment. As troops and crews returned to civilian life, ships were decommissioned, and plowshares beaten into four-speed transmissions and three-bearing crankshafts, the hyperactivity that showered blessings on Norfolk during the war ended. Returning servicemen found few jobs available and those mostly low-paying. The government laid off the first of 13,000 Norfolk civilian workers it would dismiss over the next five years. The jobless from elsewhere flocked to Norfolk in the belief that there was work for them, and the city was compelled to try to care for them. Rising prices brought a new round of strikes in early 1919 by ironmasters, telephone and electrical workers, and others. A shipping strike on the Roanoke docks in 1921 resulted in a pitched battle.[54]

But the navy's commitment to the city was permanent, and postwar Norfolk retained major assets over prewar Norfolk. Appropriations in 1919 were voted to make Norfolk the nation's largest navy yard. A new $6 million plant was begun by the Norfolk and Hampton Roads Dry Dock and Ship Repair Corporation. In April 1919, when the city issued 185 building permits, Norfolk seemed likely to settle back into the less dramatic but highly satisfactory growth rate it had known prior to 1915.[55] Even the tense animosities nourished in wartime yielded in due course to a more humane outlook. Satisfied that she had played her role well despite unprecedented challenges, Norfolk, more than many cities, could view the transition with confidence and equanimity.

CHAPTER 21

"Cap'n Whiskers" on Rat Patrol

IT WAS commonly thought that there was never an ordinary epoch in the career of "Cap'n Whiskers," and the first weeks of 1923 were no different. January began with his inquiry into Teresa Lacava De Bona's melancholy death. This elderly Italian peanut vendor who begged near Smith and Welton's on Granby Street was unable to accumulate the $11.00 monthly rent due on her tiny quarters. On New Year's Eve she turned on the gas in her peanut roaster and ended her life. Detective Leon Nowitzky—"Cap'n Whiskers" to those daunted by his surname—made the police department investigation and, as usual, ascertained the facts.[1]

January 2 was little better. Nowitzky was obliged to bring in seventy-year-old Fred Buckner for operating a thirty-gallon whiskey still on the second floor of his Castner Avenue home. The detective apologized to Police Court Justice Richard B. Spindle that he had not the heart to arrest Buckner's seventy-year-old wife, and the justice concurred in the decision.[2]

The pace quickened in the early hours of January 3. Harry G. Williams Jr., a wealthy Oldsmobile dealer, was found dying in his West Ghent home and Percy A. Page, a prominent Larchmont resident who spent the night there, was booked for murder. They had been to a party and a fight at Williams' Hampton Boulevard office. Nowitzky found that Williams came home drunk and called the Union Taxi Stand for two pints of whiskey. Williams insisted the driver give him a ride and was refused; he jumped on the runningboard, was pushed off, and broke his skull in the fall. This solved the case, though the papers kept it alive for a while with juicy tidbits about Williams' stormy relationship with his wife.[3]

Now Nowitzky was preoccupied with the "Boy Bandit." A teenager robbed several businesses and homes in December, including two A and P stores and Charles Chinn's Thirty-third Street laundry. On the night of January 8, he stuck a pistol in the ribs of Jake Feinstein, who owned a West Main naval supply store, and forced him to open his safe. The boy coolly

"Cap'n Whiskers" (right) poses with a partner after breaking up the "Tri-state Gang," notorious bootleg whiskey dealers, and seizing its arsenal (ca. 1927). (Courtesy of Richard B. Nowitzsky Personal Collection)

took over $200.00 from the safe and cash register. Three days later he hit S. P. Everette's store on Wood Street and then O. P. Joseph's place on Bute.[4]

A brown cap dropped at Everette's on January 11 helped Nowitzky identify him as Benjamin Liverman, or Moore, and learn that he might be in Petersburg. A call to Petersburg led to his arrest. Nowitzky went there and brought him back to face eight counts of robbery and housebreaking. The lad confessed all to Nowitzky, including a burglary at Mrs. S. Greenblatt's on Westover Avenue. She had come home, caught him at work, and vowed to spank him unless he returned her valuables, which he did. He was seventeen, five-feet-four, 120 pounds, had gained $279.00 from his spree, and admitted having once before been arrested—for fighting.[5]

Through fingerprints, Nowitzky found that his real name was Donatto Siravo. He had been arrested in New Bedford in 1920, put in a Massachusetts reformatory, escaped, and was wanted on nineteen counts of housebreaking and larceny. He was picked up in 1922 for crimes in Columbia, South Carolina, sent up for ten years in the state penitentiary, and escaped again. Facing up to eighty-seven years in Virginia, he was given fifty-three of those in the state prison at Richmond. He escaped in July but was taken six days later at the Petersburg room of a blonde girlfriend.[6]

The capture of the Boy Bandit, two-year scourge of the East Coast, was vintage Nowitzky. He broke the case by showing the brown cap to a young woman who turned out to know Siravo and the Petersburg address where he might be found. It took no undercover work, no scientific data, but only Nowitzky's personal network of contacts, his uncanny knowledge of Norfolk's underworld, and persistence. "Your best friends are people," he told a reporter. "The more you let them know the more they help you."[7]

Nowitzky, son of medicine-man George I. Nowitzky, joined the police force in 1918 and was still a twenty-four-year-old rookie when he made detective soon afterward. He was soon universally recognized, clattering about in a superannuated Model-T, emanations from his squat corpulence scanning every doorsill. Stories of his good humor and acumen captivated city editors, who vied with each other in Nowitzkyisms: "The thrill that comes once in a lifetime," mused the *Post*, "is a wild ride . . . in Leon Nowitzky's leaping Lizzie. . . . Telegraph poles look like fences." "Nowitzky's Head Deflects Inkwell Hurled at Woman," chortled a paper; "Hurtling Milk Bottle Barely Misses Nowitzky," hailed another.[8]

By 1923 Nowitzky was reputed to be a "super-sleuth," a term often used of him in print. Questioning a man "too clean looking to be wearing overalls," he caught a deserting sailor; a "soiled hat" revealed another. Intrigued by a former peg-leg riding a bicycle, Nowitzky found that the man had a new artificial foot—and a sack of stolen lead pipe on the handlebars. Sipping coffee at a restaurant, he caught sight in the mirror of a large man riding by on a girl's bicycle; he ran down the cyclist and recovered a stolen bike. Stepping from the United Bakery, his knee collided with a bag carried by a passer-by; alerted by a tinkling sound, he had the bag opened and caught a bootlegger with several bottles of unbaptized firewater.[9]

Nowitzky saw public attention as vital to his work. He joined the Knights of Pythias, Woodmen of the World, SPCA, Masons, Eagles, Elks, and Moose, among others, and was a leader in many. He let the papers invade the birthday parties of his eight children, dog his tracks to his Ocean View cottage, solicit his views on everything. He rushed onto the field at a Norfolk Tars baseball game to berate a visiting coach for arguing with the umpire.[10] Attention was his glory and a key to his success.

While hunting the Boy Bandit, Nowitzky worked on numerous other cases. Observing too large a procession entering a Roanoke Avenue brokerage on February 21, he arrested over a hundred men for cockfighting. Finding a gypsy couple sharing an East Freemason room, he was told that they were united by "Romany hymeneal vows." Unsatisfied with that state of matrimony, he took them to Corporation Court for a license and Father Brennan of St. Mary's for proper nuptials. Other cases involved poisoned whiskey at the Crystal Restaurant, a barber's fake suicide note, the arrest of "Hot Tamale" Slater on an assault charge, and more.[11]

Norfolk in the age of motorized crime and with the incentive of Prohibition was an uncommonly violent place; law-enforcers might make it less so, but it was brutal work that often cost the lives of the best and brightest. Nowitzky took needless risks: off-duty and unarmed, he chased a knife-wielding purse-snatcher down Botetourt Street, hurled his 250 pounds after the man, and caught him with a flying tackle.[12] Unless some forgiving star shone on him, there was little hope that Nowitzky, force of nature though he was, would live to tell his grandchildren about it.

Besides normal wrongdoing, Norfolk conceived itself to be menaced by Red and Yellow perils. Nowitzky lectured American Legionnaires about schools where children were taught disrespect to the flag, about local Reds who started by talking of unions but ended "by tearing the flag in two." It had a ring of paranoid nonsense, but in March 1919 he busted a gang of fifteen live Bolsheviki at Pete Boyko's house at 408 Fenchurch Street. Its leaders meant to use a nationwide May Day strike to bring down the government.[13]

In early 1925 Chinese businessmen warned police of a threatened "tong war." Rival tongs or secret societies (some said fraternal orders), the On Leong and Hip Sing, had members among Norfolk's three hundred or so Chinese. On March 12 Church Street laundryman Wong Lee told Nowitzky a tong had ordered him to shut down. Police in his "Chinatown" neighborhood had lately quelled a disturbance there when a spy of one tong allegedly gathered data on the other.[14] The danger was probably even smaller than the Red menace, but it fed a civic queasiness that beckoned alluringly to the Ku Klux Klan.

The reborn Klan put in an initial Norfolk appearance in June 1921 with signs on Ocean View and Willoughby telephone poles warning that "All Undesirables must leave town," especially gamblers, bootleggers, high spenders, thieves, crooks, grafters, and bawdy-house operators. Another recruited "native-born, white, American citizens" believing in "the Christian religion, free schools, free speech, free press, law enforcement, and white supremacy." Colonel J. Q. Nolan of Atlanta appeared before a large Armory audience on July 19 to expound KKK principles and demand stronger immigration laws "to preserve racial integrity and white supremacy . . . in pristine purity." But an Ocean View Klan parade on the thirtieth drew only about one hundred marchers.[15]

There was a flurry of bedsheet bedlam in September when Police Chief Charles Borland was forced to deny that he was a Klansman, but little was heard from the Norfolk Klan for several years. In July 1924 it hosted a big rally at Fairmount Park fairgrounds and inducted several hundred members. A Klan spectacular there the next July brought out 35,000 people for a program of fireworks, singing, sports contests, band concerts, and a picnic lunch; another one thousand joined KKK ranks. There were local Klan gatherings in the following months, but it was 1926 before the order appeared to make important headway in Norfolk.[16]

The Klan in May sponsored *The Awakening* (a musical based on *The Birth of a Nation*), which ran two weeks at the Academy of Music. Heralded by a Klan parade with motorcycle-police escort, it featured a "galaxy of graceful girls," and Charleston, toe, tap, ballet, and "old fashioned cake walk" dancing. It was said to have set city attendance records, but proceeds intended for a Norfolk Klan temple went elsewhere. City papers set up a drumbeat of criticism of the Klan, the *Pilot's* Jaffe (awarded Virginia's first Pulitzer Prize in journalism in 1929) leading the pack. Albert Pike Klan No. 32 for a time had a Boush Street clubroom but evidently fell victim to internecine strife.[17]

The Klan overreached itself on the night of September 1, 1926, when twenty-eight KKK in seven automobiles arrived at a Princess Anne farm. The occasion was a concert by the Negro Boys Band from a school conducted by Father Vincent D. Warren and St. Joseph's Catholic Church. Klansmen dragged Warren off at gunpoint and drove him about two miles for an interrogation. Assured that his school was not racially integrated, the abductors released him. Princess Anne's sheriff and commonwealth attorney refused to investigate, but Norfolk's city council adopted an antimask ordinance.[18]

That fall saw a last hurrah of Klan incidents. *The Journal and Guide* cited a reign of terror against rural blacks. Four service station attendants near Ward's Corner were flogged by hooded men who accused them of selling liquor and insulting women. A Norview grocer reported a Catholic customer flogged by masked men. One or more city policemen, many of whom were thought to be Klansmen, were reportedly among the floggers. Public, especially newspaper, reaction was strong and the local Klan, like the national, went into steep decline in the late 1920s. On the whole, it had made little impression on Norfolk.[19]

Most of the black community went about its business with little concern for the Klan. One of the fifty-three schoolteachers charged with the education of 2,500 black students filled her week with a Monday hospital auxiliary club, Tuesday after-school art class, Wednesday music club (as its president), Thursday choir practice, Friday extension classes for Virginia State College, Saturday afternoon theater, and church at least twice every Sunday. She also found time for such events as the big Hampton versus Greensboro A. T. and T. football game in Norfolk—"our classic of the season." Bed-sheet bullies needed an appointment.[20]

More troubling than Red, Yellow, or black perils was "white lightning." The city showed little enthusiasm for the Eighteenth Amendment and did not give itself heartily to enforcement. A great deal of illegal alcohol was made and consumed during the 1920s within the city and brought in from elsewhere. (The Old Dominion Distilling Company, however, only made molasses.)[21] The foremost avenues of entry were the Dismal Swamp and Albemarle and Chesapeake canals, reaching into untamed portions of eastern North Carolina.

One heard tales of a "hidden city" in the bowels of Alligator Swamp in Tyrrell County, North Carolina, from which motorboats sped corn liquor eighty-nine miles north to thirsty Norfolk, loaded with sugar and corn mash, and sped back. The rot-gut metropolis, with its own electric light and water systems, lay "buried in swampy jungle." Heavy undergrowth masked more than twenty stills from which whiskey barrels and jugs were sluiced down flumes five miles long to waiting boats. Agents now and again caught a boat but the traffic continued. Some rum-runners complained that Norfolk had too few access routes for profitable bootlegging, but others dealt efficiently with the geographical hazard.[22]

Retail outlets included half a dozen in the vicinity of the second precinct police station. Four *Virginian-Pilot* men inspected one of these, Jennie Williams' in the Lincoln Street red light district, in November 1920. They found several bemused policemen observing a bacchanalia of illegal hooch and jazz dancing by white and black patrons. Shamed into raiding a Queen Street cabaret just opposite the police station a few nights later, the police chief could find "nothing irregular."[23]

More modest entrepreneurs ran off small amounts of liquor at locations throughout Norfolk, mostly for personal use. Readers of the *Ledger-Dispatch* were edified in 1924 by serialized revelations of Mrs. Texanna Chappell, ex-moonshiner. Despite her upbringing "in a good family down in Carolina," she turned to corn-squeezings in Norfolk to feed her three children. With a recipe from a relative, two copper kettles from different stores, a worm and copper piping, a dozen pint jars, and a small gas range, she set up shop "in a little room on the second floor." She operated wholesale since she "wouldn't have any chance of being successful if a lot of people knew about it." A $50.00 fine and thirty days, she felt, saved her from a life of crime.[24]

Women in the 1920s figured more largely than ever in the city's public life, legitimate as well as criminal. A column of advice to the lovelorn by "Beatrice Fairfax" (Stella Upshur) roused more female interest in the *Ledger-Dispatch* than any prior feature. Mrs. Upshur began with the paper at age fifty-one in 1918, writing society and women's news. One day she volunteered to reply to a letter seeking personal advice; she ran her column for the next twenty years, receiving an average of some twenty letters a day. She also wrote food columns advising housewives on good buys.[25]

Female role models emerged all over town. Anne M. Brown in 1920 became the first Norfolk woman to earn a law license, followed in 1921 by Mrs. Pauline Adams, who had once picketed the White House as a suffragist and served a sixty-day sentence for it. Bertha L. Douglass in 1926 became Norfolk's first black female lawyer; in August 1920 Mrs. Aileen Robertson was the first Norfolk woman to qualify to vote under the Nineteenth Amendment, just ahead of Bertha E. and Kate L. Cannon, Kathryn Peebles Cooper, and the irrepressible Pauline Adams. The Housewives' League, headed by Mrs. John H. Inglesby, in 1920 began issuing a journal, *The Norfolk Housewife*, to advocate a new city market, lower gas rates, and other goals. But women were slow to register, the young and businesswomen moreso than the middle-aged and married.[26]

In 1923 a schoolteacher and Brambleton native, Mrs. Sarah Fain, surprised many in Norfolk by making a bid for the district's seat in the House of Delegates. Owing to what the newspapers called her "charming personality" and progressive platform, she won the seat. She was reelected in 1925 and 1927. She lost a bid as Democratic nominee for Congress in 1930.[27]

Mrs. Emilie N. Plack gained national attention in 1925 when she became a director of Norfolk's Morris Plan Bank, reportedly the first woman to hold such a bank position. She had joined the bank in 1919 and was to become its executive vice president and cashier; when it was absorbed by the Bank of Virginia, she served the latter as vice president in charge of operations.[28]

A role model of sorts was Peggy Hopkins Joyce of Berkley. News that she was to divorce her fourth millionaire husband in 1921 created a stir. Born in 1893 to the wife of barber Sam Rudd, Peggy—or Marguerite as she was baptized—early showed a flair for schoolwork and drama. A striking blonde at fifteen, she ran away, meeting her first millionaire husband on a train to Denver. A quick annulment gave her funds to attend school in Washington, D.C., where she married Sherburne P. Hopkins, son of a prominent lawyer. In 1917 she left him and went to New York, where Flo Ziegfeld starred her in a revue, *Miss 1918*. On a traveling Ziegfeld show in 1920, she met and wed Chicago lumberman J. Stanley Joyce.[29]

Peggy locked herself in a bathroom on her wedding night with Joyce and refused to come out until he slid a check for $500,000 under the door. She was soon off to Paris and later took Joyce for $2 million in a divorce settlement. She returned to New York and a new stage vehicle, *Vanities of 1923*, at $5,000 a week. By now a leading socialite, she was showered with diamond necklaces and other trophies by Averell Harriman, Hiram Bloomingdale, Prince Christopher of Greece, the Maharaja of Baroda, and others. A smitten Walter Chrysler was reported to have given her $2 million in gems as she waltzed through several more marriages. Curiously, *Life* magazine named her one of the most important women of the first half of the century prior to her death in 1957.[30]

Lovely ladies of more sedentary habits might seek to emulate Dorothea Prince who, crowned first "Miss Norfolk" at the Virginia Beach Casino in July 1925, was soon off to Atlantic City and a shot at "Miss America." Unfortunately, she missed. But women also had access to local chapters of the

Peggy Hopkins Joyce kept her native Norfolk and much of the world agog in the era of World War I and afterward by her romances with, and marriages to, a succession of millionaires. She also starred in shows produced by Florenz Ziegfeld. (Courtesy of Culver Pictures, Inc.)

League of Women Voters, the American Association of University Women, and other groups catering to the intellectual rather than the purely sexual.[31]

Automobiles and airplanes continued to fascinate Norfolk, and the Tidewater Automobile Association in 1926 found it necessary to urge motorists "not to make such free use of their horns." Association President Robert W. Pollock rebuked motorists who tried "to raise the Norfolk and Western crossing gates with their horns." Pedestrians not attending to the horns were at high risk. Norfolkians killed each other with their cars at a rate greater than those of New York and Chicago.[32]

Airplane enthusiasts got a treat in November 1926, when Norfolk was the site of the annual Schneider Cup seaplane races. The United States was defending champion and Italy had earned the right to challenge. Each team flew three planes in a closed course from the naval air station, over Willoughby, around a pylon northeast of Thimble Shoals, to Old Point Comfort, and back to the start. The cup was taken by Major Mario de Bernardi, "the Flying Fascist," in a Macchi averaging 248 miles per hour. De Bernardi already owned most of the world's speed records and soon broke another off Ocean View by flying a closed course at 258 mph. Airplanes now delivered Norfolk mail to LA and San Francisco in forty-eight hours, and to Washington, D.C., in just over three hours.[33]

The local Italian colony named a committee, headed by Hugo Bernagozzi and A. Lagiglia, to arrange a celebration of their country's victory. On November 21 some three hundred guests at the Roma Club attended a farewell dinner party for Italian flyers still in town. American aeronauts got more bad news three days later when navy seaplanes attempting a nonstop flight from Norfolk to Panama were forced down well short of their destination.[34]

A new love for many was radio. Four young Portsmouth and Norfolk men, including Norfolk's Roger Wolcott, improvised radio sets in 1912 and tried unsuccessfully to communicate across the river. By 1920 the Hampton Roads Radio Association had forty members. They were in regular radio contact with others as far away as Canada and Key West, on occasion picking up signals from Germany and the Eiffel Tower. WTAR, Norfolk's first broadcasting station, began operation in 1923.[35]

Norfolk's pulsating wartime growth survived the war's end. A Norfolk Booster Club, formed in 1920 with four hundred members, hoped to capitalize on the fact that the city had more railroads than Baltimore, only one less than New York. Norfolk's steamship and rail lines and individual businesspeople owned 165 wharves with two and a half million square feet of warehouses. A priority, soon realized, was a collective port council to mobilize the interests of Norfolk, Portsmouth, and Newport News. A problem less amenable to quick solution was that Norfolk's imports, only 15 percent of her foreign trade, compared very unfavorably to, say, Boston, where imports exceeded exports by 600 percent.[36]

The year 1923 opened with the annexation of twenty-seven square miles and thirty thousand residents across the Lafayette River and the eastern branch. These areas included the army and navy bases, Ocean View, and suburbs across the eastern branch opposite Ohio Creek. Meadowbrook, Titustown, Lochaven, Willoughby, Fairmount, Larchmont, Newton Park, Campostella, Lenox, and other neighborhoods were thus drawn into the city. Also incorporated were the army piers, which were leased by the city in 1922 to give it a facility properly equipped for foreign trade. That year voters approved $5 million for a grain elevator and terminal between the military bases to provide "ballast freight" on ships with light cargo such as cotton and tobacco.[37]

The new additions reflected the benefits of city-manager government. City Manager Ashburner, abetted by Mayor Albert L. Roper and his successors, provided more and better schools, white playgrounds and parks, a new armory, better streets, food inspection, fire protection, a juvenile and domestic relations court, and other attributes of a thoroughly modern city. Ashburner resigned in 1923, but the system he developed continued to function smoothly under I. Walke Truxton, who converted a city deficit into a surplus, sought to dismiss policemen who coddled bootleggers and speakeasies, and waged war on flies, mosquitoes, and other menaces to public health and safety.[38]

Its population approaching 150,000 by the decade's end, Norfolk let itself dream grandly of becoming a great city, a goal requiring its consolidation with Portsmouth and, perhaps, Newport News and Hampton as well. As early as 1919 the *Ledger-Dispatch* pushed the idea of a tunnel to Portsmouth, which found itself the blushing recipient of ardent proposals from across the river. A modishly modern miss, she seemed reluctant to lose her identity (not to say virginity) in the "Greater Norfolk" that was held out as her best hope for security and happiness.[39] Norfolk, an inept swain, was spurned as perhaps desiring a servant more than a partner.

Norfolk in 1919 became the first Southeastern city with dial telephones, and Coca-Cola announced a big bottling plant for College Place. A new city market, bounded by Monticello Avenue, Market, Brewer, and Tazewell and hailed as the country's finest, opened in 1923. South Norfolk's Virginia Portland Cement Company, called the world's most modern facility of its kind, expanded to produce a million barrels a year. Ford Motor Company in 1925 opened an auto assembly plant with six hundred workers and prospects of hiring many more. Marcus Loew and Otto Wells vied with each other in building movie theaters downtown—the Strand, Norva, Granby, Loew's State, and others at Ocean View and elsewhere in the area.[40]

The Crispus Attucks on Church Street was the leading black movie house. Besides top motion pictures they could not see in white theaters, black audiences were treated to vaudeville shows and such artists as Ethel Waters, Dinah Washington, Bessie Smith, and Cab Calloway. The Attucks had opened just prior to World War I, its design by Harvey N. Johnson, a black architect from Richmond who settled in Norfolk as a young man. (Closed in 1955, the Attucks was listed in 1982 in the National Register of Historic Places and a movement, still uncertain of success at this writing, was later launched to renovate it.)[41]

Postwar conditions undercut black unions. By 1921 the Coal Trimmers Union and much of the Transport Workers Union were drawn into the International Longshoremen's Association (ILA), with George Milner as local head. But the added clout of the ILA was offset by members feeling that the focus on local issues was gone. An economic slump, starting in 1921, forced dockworkers to take pay cuts, some losing their jobs. The new Ford plant banned blacks, though the American Chain Company hired them at all levels, including Dr. G. Jarvis Bowen as director of hygiene and welfare. Pressed by some whites to alter its policy, the company left town. Many blacks took extra work on area truck farms, where the nature of the work discouraged unionization.[42]

From 1914 an ordinance had barred blacks from living in white neighborhoods (and vice versa). Black residents, driven increasingly to rely upon their own resources, gave themselves more fully to their churches and social organizations. St. John's, still the leading African Methodist church, vied with Presbyterian, Baptist, Methodist, Episcopal, a Catholic, and various Holiness churches. Many blacks belonged to one or more social groups, such as the Ladies Aid No. 1, Grand United Daughters of Tents, White Lily Social and Benevolent Association, and other orders.[43]

Blacks by the 1920s also had a variety of social protest groups and movements. Chief among these were the interracial NAACP and Marcus Garvey's Universal Negro Improvement Association (UNIA). The NAACP was distinctly middle-class, led by businesspeople, physicians, and teachers (P. B. Young was president), but the UNIA catered to the working class. Garvey himself addressed a packed Attucks Theater in July 1922, sketching plans for a black nursing corps, an Afro-centered version of Christianity, and a Black Star Shipping Line to take American blacks to Africa.[44]

There was plenty to protest. In 1925 the city rewrote its residential segregation ordinance to circumvent U.S. Supreme Court displeasure over such laws. Two years earlier, a black family that moved across the informal Corprew Avenue racial divide into white Brambleton had been forced out by eighty to one hundred armed whites. Urged on by the national NAACP, the local branch under attorney David H. Edwards brought suit against a Jewish shopkeeper in a black community to test the ordinance. When Police Court Justice Spindle ruled the ordinance unconstitutional, residential segregation in Norfolk became de facto (by practice), rather than de jure (by law), though no less effective. Blacks felt it patently unfair that white Jewish merchants operated in black neighborhoods, though blacks could not do so in white areas.[45]

Most blacks lived in rental housing, much of it in abominable condition. City Health Commissioner Powhatan S. Schenck in 1920 reported a black death rate of twenty per thousand, more than double that of whites. The city's twenty-one parks included none for blacks until 1928 when, at the urging of Mrs. Frank Anthony Walke, a prominent white, the city council authorized a park for blacks on the Barraud farm east of Huntersville. Blacks formed community leagues in Lindenwood and elsewhere to contend with the city for improvements, but a better hope lay in bringing voters out in larger numbers at election time. Drives toward that end were hampered, however, by the onset of the Depression; in 1931 only fifty-seven more blacks paid poll taxes than in 1921.[46]

Union and business restrictions still kept blacks from skilled trades. By 1926 the black population was shifting from downtown to areas east of Chapel Street and north of East Brambleton Avenue, many building homes in Douglas and Bruce parks and Wesleyan Heights. Succcessful realtors guiding the transition included J. C. Brooks, J. T. Tanner, and, in 1925, Norfolk-born Miss Virginia R. Collette, the first of her gender to invade this male realm. Among the prosperous black firms were the Metropolitan Bank and Trust Company, advertised as the world's largest black bank, the Norfolk Home Building and Loan Association, and the *Guide* Publishing Company. A leading employer of blacks was the American Cigar Company, with some five hundred black women working as stemmers.[47]

P. B. Young's *Journal and Guide* emerged from World War I as the South's largest black newspaper. Young, an ardent but unrequited Republican, trod the line between accommodation to maximize white support for black aims and militance toward the KKK, lynching, and other racist evils. His success in fostering racial cooperation was, for some, offset by his weakening support for the local NAACP, which was divided and ineffective during the 1920s. His own Negro Forward Movement stressed "self-respect, self-trust, and mutual confidence" but was no forum for grievances. Though prodded by the national NAACP and others, he avoided attacking Norfolk's pattern of residential segregation. His paper helped many families keep track of distant kin, encouraged local business ventures, and kept black hope alive in a trying time.[48]

A promising venture was that of the Truxton Home Corporation. In 1923 this black syndicate persuaded the United States Housing Corporation to sell Truxton community, built by the wartime government on Deep Creek Boulevard a mile south of Portsmouth. Investors included banker W. H. C. Brown, Rev. J. Albert Handy, and Dr. A. J. Strong, all of Norfolk, and others. It had 253 houses, mostly five-room bungalows with electric lights, indoor plumbing, and hot water. The government had sold only about half. There was also a modern school building and streetcar service. The corporation aimed to revise prices and payment schedules to put the homes in reach of large numbers of black families.[49]

Norfolk's six synagogues by 1926 had 7,800 members, many with an active interest in Zionism as supporters of the United Palestine Appeal (launched in the city that year). A native Norfolk Jew who gained national acclaim was Polan Banks who, as a sixteen-year-old Maury High student in 1922, published fiction in the *Ledger-Dispatch* in preparation for greater things. Before graduation, he wrote his first novel, *Black Ivory*, which went through six editions, earned him a decoration from the French Academy, and became a Warner Brothers movie. All this was before he turned twenty-one. He later wrote some ten novels, formed his own movie company, married a niece of Bernard Baruch, and got his name on one of Admiral Byrd's Antarctic peaks.[50]

Norfolk's age of prosperity, a recompense for so many ages of adversity, flowed on toward the 1930s, each year in important ways better than the one before. Super-sleuth Leon Nowitzky remained a pillar of strength amid the fraud and violence that screamed from the daily headlines. It was calculated near the end of his thirty years as detective that he had handled some 1,250 homicide cases, 95 percent of which were solved. He was a law-enforcement legend, and the hero of numerous stories in detective magazines.[51]

His most dramatic case began on Wednesday, May 11, 1938. The body of Mrs. Audrey Abdell of 1318 Lafayette Boulevard was found by her teenage sons on returning from school. She had died of gas from a kitchen range, her body crouched nearby in a blanket. James C. Abdell, her husband, was in Washington, D.C., on vending-machine business but rushed home the next day.[52]

Nowitzky arrived in the late afternoon to investigate an apparent suicide. As usual, untidy details must be reconciled with initial presumptions. Scratches and bruises covered most of the body; suicides did not often flagellate themselves before taking gas. As Nowitzky pondered this, Bobbie Abdell, thirteen-year-old son of the deceased, handed him a note. It was from his father and counseled the son to contact him at Hotel Harrington in Washington "if you need me before I get back. . . . You be a good boy and always remember your Daddy loves you no matter what anybody says."[53]

Shortly, Jimmie Abdell, fifteen, blurted out that, if his mother killed herself, his "father had something to do with it." He told of Abdell's threats against her; the night before, Jimmie had put a bolt inside her bedroom door. It appeared that Abdell lived with another woman, though maintaining an office in his Lafayette Boulevard house and visiting it often, and that Mrs. Abdell had lately sued for nonsupport. It was Jimmie's understanding that his mother and a neighbor, Lola Dorman, had gone to Domestic Relations Court the day before with two handwritten notes.[54]

Nowitzky visited Mrs. Dorman and learned that Mrs. Abdell had said the notes were written by her husband; she found them among his things while cleaning. A call to the coroner fixed her death before 10:00 A.M., after the boys left for school about 8:25. The detective called the District of Columbia Detective Bureau to have Abdell told of his wife's death and a tail put on him. The next morning he drove to Domestic Relations Court to see the notes turned in by Mrs. Abdell.[55]

The notes, in Abdell's hand, were written ostensibly by his wife. One said she was leaving and confessed that she had "not been the kind of wife" she should have been. The second prayed Abdell's forgiveness for her "jealousy and madness," the trouble she caused "by talking about you to everyone, . . . and by making the children work against you." While still at court, Nowitzky was approached by attorney Ivor A. Page Jr., accompanied by Abdell, just back from Washington, his alibi in good order. The detective asked Abdell about the scratches on his throat. Bit of a scrape with his girlfriend. What did Abdell make of the two notes? Well, he wrote them "as samples for her to consider."[56]

Nowitzky wished to pursue this, but Page cut his client off. So "Cap'n Whiskers" drove to the home of Mrs. Anne Dunn Williams, Abdell's mistress. She revealed that Abdell had left there for Washington on the tenth, the day before Mrs. Abdell's death. "Have you seen him since?" Well, yes, he came in about 1:00 A.M. on Wednesday and left two hours later. Was his throat scratched? No, not until he came in from Washington this morning; he said it was from shaving.[57]

Abdell's absence in Washington at the time of his wife's death now seemed more problematic. Nowitzky must show that Abdell was in Norfolk between 8:30 and 10:00 A.M. on the eleventh. It was now that Marie Facchini, who lived down the street from the Abdells, came forward. She told Nowitzky of leaving Norfolk by car early on May 11, stopping at a restaurant near Fredericksburg about 1:30 P.M., and noticing Abdell's car parked by the highway with the owner, his neck scratched, at work on it. She asked if she could help, was thanked, and departed on her trip; Abdell later passed her, "speeding toward Washington."[58]

The case was rounded off three days later when Mrs. J. M. Palmer, a neighbor of Abdell, reported passing his house about 9:30 A.M. on the fifteenth and seeing an excited man come out. Taken by Nowitzky to jail, she fingered Abdell as the man. At the trial, a paperhanger insisted that he had worked at Abdell's on the eleventh, arriving about 10:00 A.M. Mrs. Abdell said her husband was not in and the workman left. But Abdell's diary showed that the work was done the week before the victim died.[59]

A final hurdle was Janyce Mattox of Lafayette Boulevard, who said she could see Abdell's house from her front porch, saw him leave that morning, and saw the paperhanger arrive and leave. Nowitzky and a photographer went to her house and found that Abdell's front porch was not visible from there. Miss Mattox was later shown to have been a patient in a mental institution. Abdell was electrocuted on January 5, 1940, the first person sent to death by a Norfolk jury in thirty years.[60]

Retiring in 1950, Nowitzky guessed he had shot forty-five people in the line of duty, killing seven, since his days on "rat patrol" down by the wharves. He most regretted that of a shotgun-carrying black preacher at the corner of Olney Road and Monticello Avenue who "was shooting at people and shouting that the Lord had sent him to kill all sinners." A memorable wild-goose chase was a night he was called about a body with its throat cut in a Water Street boxcar; it was a dressed hog. "People in every line of life," he reminisced, "have helped me, and I am indebted to all of them."[61]

CHAPTER 22

The Misunderstanding

THE NORFOLK school board was surprised, perhaps a bit annoyed, but it knew perfectly well how to handle the matter. Chemistry teacher Aline Black's request in October 1938 for a pay raise was duly considered and, in December, denied. Curiously, Black, a twelve-year veteran at black Booker T. Washington High, based her request on the difference between her pay and that of comparably qualified white teachers at Maury High. No matter, she had already signed this year's contract. She was reminded that salaries were fixed between the board and individuals, and were not subject to "any law, rule, or regulation affecting civil rights."[1]

Christmas vacation passed and the matter seemed ended; but in January, Black again petitioned for pay equal to that of white teachers. As this impertinence was being digested, Richmond attorney J. Thomas Hewin, representing Black, received permission to examine the school board's minutes for the past ten years. (School board figures would reveal that black teachers received only about two-thirds of what comparably trained white counterparts earned.)[2] Clearly, something out of the ordinary was afloat in the normally staid Norfolk school system, and it behooved officials to get to the bottom of it.

Norfolk, after all, as the 1937 *City Directory* proclaimed, was a city where the races "understand each other and it is to the credit of Norfolk's people—both white and colored—that in all Norfolk's history there has never been a serious racial misunderstanding." There was no misunderstanding as to the white-only restrooms and fountains, "blacks-to-the-rear" seating on street cars and buses, the exclusion of blacks from public facilities. That janitors at black schools earned $140 a month while the top pay of black teachers was $115 was well understood by both races. If, therefore, a misunderstanding arose over Aline Black's salary, it could not be a "serious" one.[3]

Inquiry disclosed that Aline Elizabeth Black held a bachelor's degree from Virginia State, a master's from the University of Pennsylvania, and was working toward an NYU doctorate; her teaching was commendable. Her petition was supported by the national and local NAACP and the black Norfolk and Virginia teachers associations. She could probably be expected, therefore, to take the issue to court as a test of the pattern by which black teachers throughout the South for seven decades had been compensated at rates far inferior to those of white colleagues. Doubts vanished in March when her lawyers filed for a writ of mandamus against the board and for an end to racial discrimination in school salaries.[4]

A Norfolk circuit court hearing was set for May 31. Black's attorneys, led by young Thurgood Marshall of Baltimore, contended that salary differences based solely on race violated her rights under the due process and equal protection clauses of the Fourteenth Amendment. School board lawyers Alfred N. Anderson and Jonathan W. Old held that Black, in signing her contract, waived any right to redress. Judge Allen R. Hanckel, sidestepping both arguments, dismissed the suit on the technicality that a mandamus was not the proper action in such a case.[5]

The decision settled nothing but Aline Black's hash. The school board had decided two weeks before that her contract would not be renewed for the 1939–40 school year, and she was so informed a few days after Hanckel's decision came down in June. In a gratuitous flourish, the board deducted $4.01 from her final paycheck for a teaching day she spent at court. It would reconsider only when "the suit has been finally decided and Miss Black ceases to occupy the position of plaintiff."[6]

This action was less popular than the school board had anticipated. On Sunday, June 24, 1,200 blacks, normally disinclined to public protest, gathered with a few whites at St. John's AME Church. On hand was the Negro Boy Scout Drum and Bugle Corps, which had marched from Dunbar School accompanied by many children carrying banners with such slogans as "School Board Must Go," "Dictators: Hitler, Mussolini, Norfolk School Board," "Our School Board Has Vetoed the Bill of Rights," and similar expressions.[7]

The crowd heard remarks by publisher P. B. Young, local and national NAACP leaders Jerry O. Gilliam and Walter E. White, respectively, and Thurgood Marshall, among others. Marshall assured his listeners that the NAACP had a "war-chest" sufficient to see Black's case through the courts. Most signed a petition calling the school board's action "utterly shameless, a blot on the city of Norfolk," and demanding Black's reinstatement.[8]

On Monday, the *Virginian-Pilot*, though impressed that "never in the city's modern history have Norfolk's Negroes staged so formidable a demonstration," was sure no school board member would stoop to "petty reprisal." Still, some clearly felt that Black was fired "for seeking a peaceful, judicial determination of a disputed legal right." The editor noted that her position paralleled that of city firemen who sought in 1934 to establish a chapter of the American Federation of Labor: they lost in court but none were dismissed. The board must honor "the historic American right of peaceful petition"; Black's contract should be renewed.[9]

The school board had defenders. J. L. Smith's letter to the *Virginian-Pilot* observed with somewhat imprecise relevancy that a drive along Broad Creek Road revealed many above-average black residences in Atlantic City, Brambleton, Lambert's Point, Fairmount Park, and Park Place. He knew of a black attorney and two doctors who were affluent and influential citizens. Such facts testified emphatically that teacher-pay differentials were "not a matter of race." Anyway, they testified something.[10]

More cogent was the view of white attorney W. H. Venable that whites paid more taxes than blacks and bore much of the burden of black education. Blacks, he wrote, "have a good deal more climbing to do before there can be any serious thought given by sensible people of either race, to your far-off dream—social equality in Virginia." Again, however, the pertinence of the observation seemed uncertain. Miss Black's Pennsylvania master's degree presumably carried no label warning that the recipient had black skin and should therefore not be taken seriously.[11]

Hanckel's decision and the school board's punitive action threw Black's supporters into a dither. Her lawyers filed for a writ of error in the state court of appeals, but the Norfolk Teacher's Association (NTA) seemed ready to chuck the whole thing. Attorney Marshall decided that Black's "legal interest" in the case was not enough for her to remain a litigant; someone else must be found to serve in the role. After some hesitation, NTA president Melvin O. Alston agreed to be the guinea pig. On September 29 he petitioned the school board that all black teachers' salaries be equalized with whites, effective on October payday.[12]

But the paycheck issue was secondary to a more urgent question: What demon was loose in the black community to bring it flooding into the streets like that? What was become of the traditional deference owed by blacks to white authority, the superb harmony that had always spared Norfolk from any "serious racial misunderstanding"? What, in short, was the world coming to?

For much of Norfolk's population, the Great Depression was little more than a temporary inconvenience. With the news media full of stories of soup kitchens, mass unemployment, and suffering elsewhere, Norfolk in the crisis years of the early 1930s fared relatively well. Partially insulated from national economic woes by its military and other federal facilities and the government's $24 million payroll, its seaborne trade still fairly strong, Norfolk was weathering the tempest better than most.[13]

Trouble there was and sometimes critical. The Seaboard Air Line Railroad went into receivership in late 1930, the Norfolk and Western and Monticello Hotel in 1932. Ford's Norfolk assembly plant closed for several months in 1932 and early 1933. Lagging tax collections brought a 20 percent pay cut for city employees (higher for top officials), suspension of public summer and night schools, and cancellation of a new harbor fireboat. But no city banks closed and no soup kitchens were established.[14]

That Norfolk was meeting the challenge of Depression rather nicely gave little comfort to thousands out of work or otherwise miserable. Relief agencies associated with the Community Fund found it hard even in 1929 to meet the needs they addressed and complained that fund-raising goals for 1930 were inadequate. They were right: the city by June 1930 had over 3,800 (and perhaps many more) jobless; a "Hooverville," or "tent city," for the homeless was emerging on the grounds of the municipal hospital. The fund managed slightly to exceed its 1930 goal, but fell 9 percent short in 1931 and raised only two-thirds of its goal for 1932, the city's worst year of the Depression decade.[15]

Frank and Myrtle Vann's story could be multiplied many times over. Moving from rural eastern North Carolina in 1929, Frank found work with the city bus company, lost it to the Depression, was hired at the Ford plant, and lost that too when it closed in 1932. The Vanns and their three children moved from one run-down Lambert's Point or Atlantic City house—the main white working-class neighborhoods—to another because they could not pay the rent. Lambert's Point in 1936 had paved streets, sewers, and electric lights, but no sidewalks except dirt paths; most houses had only a weed patch for a lawn. The railing on the Vanns' porch collapsed from disrepair, the wood floors lacked carpet or linoleum, and the house was unpainted.[16]

Frank picked up work driving taxis or sometimes got back on at the Ford plant to keep his family in fried potatoes and biscuits, with "tomato gravy" or fried pork brains now and then. He did most of the cooking while Myrtle, intent on having things her husband could not afford, sold her body to a carefully selected clientele of middle-class men she met at assignations or

even brought home. She could attract business just by sitting on the dilapidated front porch or yard clad in her finery. Meanwhile, her son Gene came
down with rickets; his legs became so hideously bowed that doctors had to
break and reset them.[17]

Myrtle, who spent the proceeds of prostitution on herself, was unlike
most working-class women, who might go on a bender now and then but
mostly took seriously their roles as housewives and mothers. The Vann children never had a Christmas tree or a Thanksgiving turkey. John Paul, the
older son, lived in humiliation over his mother's immoral lifestyle. In later
years, however, he became a legendary hero of the Vietnam War and the
subject of a Pulitzer Prize-winning 1988 biography, Neil Sheehan's *A Bright
and Shining Lie.*[18]

Laid-off workers, drifters, and others tried to cope with the situation by
makeshift. Blacks took up stands or pushcarts as vendors of fruit, vegetables, fish, ice, coal—whatever might garner a few pennies against the spur
of hunger. A *Virginian-Pilot* reporter in August 1935 found hundreds of
blacks and some whites fishing and taking crabs along the waterfront. Some
had lately taken to it to hold back starvation, but black "Old Aunt Mary"
had been at it thirty years. "Sometimes," she said, "I don't have anything
else to eat but maybe some bread." She never sold the crabs she caught but
gave away any excess to those more needy than herself. "This is God's water," she declared, "and what He has given He gives to everybody, white
or black."[19]

Andrew Dickson, an elderly black ensconced in a shack at 2528 Reservoir
Lane, lightened the Depression's burden by minting coins from 125 brass
plates containing every denomination. He told incredulous police that the
coins were only for his living expenses. He thought it legal since he used
only a twenty-pound pig of silver made from teaspoons, cups, and other
sources he was "given by friends." A conscientious craftsman, Dickson
made even his nickels from pure silver, using a higher ratio in his coins than
did the federal government. He had, by his estimate, been at the business
ten or fifteen years.[20]

Mary Perry, a black school teacher, often bought shoes out of her meagre
$45-a-month salary for her students who wore theirs out. At home, her fam-
ily kept "one light on at a time. We only heated one room at a time." Fuel
was mostly reburned cinders of coal picked up beside railroad tracks. There
were many in still more wretched circumstances.[21]

City fathers were closely in tune with President Hoover, who saw poverty
and joblessness as local and state problems; private and local public charity

would relieve those in want until the crisis, surely temporary, passed. If the city made it through winter, warm weather—bringing low fuel bills and work at truck farms and resort facilities—would ease problems. But the growing desperation of agencies such as Travellers' Aid, the Seamen's Fund, the Council of Jewish Women, the black Philiss Wheatley Association, and the Union Mission slowly eroded confidence. When Hoover seemed to concede his policy's failure by authorizing the Reconstruction Finance Corporation in 1932, many in Norfolk began to see federal intervention as the only hope.[22]

Still, the city council came under fire in 1932 for running up a sizable deficit, and Mayor P. H. Mason resigned in January 1933. To replace him, the council named Samuel L. Slover, publisher of the recently merged *Virginian-Pilot* and *Ledger-Dispatch*. Slover faced an immediate crisis, that of imposing salary cuts approved before he took office. At his first council meeting, held at City Auditorium to accommodate a crowd of a thousand worried city workers and others, the council not only endorsed but increased the reductions. This was hailed by many as a personal triumph for Slover; the Suffolk *News-Herald* nominated him for governor. Half a million in budget cuts in his first two weeks ended the deficit. He resigned at year's end, the city's debt much reduced and his mission fulfilled.[23]

Many blacks thought Slover's mission was far too narrowly conceived. Domestic and personal servants were often the first fired; experienced blacks everywhere were laid off, their jobs taken by inexperienced whites. Its funds drying up, the Metropolitan Bank and Trust Company, Norfolk's leading black financial institution, shuddered and, in 1933, died, sending ripples of disaster through the black business community. No city government jobs were open to blacks; white Church Street stores, their clientele mostly black, employed no black clerks. (The *Journal and Guide* rejoiced in 1936 when the white-owned Miller Drug Store at Church Street and Olney Road hired Almeda Faulkner, a black clerk.) By 1935 black unemployment stood at 8 percent, white unemployment at 2.5 percent; in 1930 blacks were only a third of those on relief rolls, in 1936 over three-quarters.[24]

The Communist Party sent organizers in the early months of the Depression and found eager listeners. Red speakers lured blacks for the Trade Union Unity League, which aimed to destroy capitalism and the prevailing form of government. They set up Unemployed Councils to demand free or low rents, building repairs, and tenants' rights to negotiate directly with landlords. Rallies along Olney and Princess Anne roads and Church Street drew up to five hundred people to hear Rufus Beaverbrook, head of South

Norfolk's Unemployed Council, Rev. Haywood Parker, and other radicals. Sometimes even mainline churches such as St. John's AME or Second Cavalry Baptist provided the setting for communist harangues.[25]

The listeners were mostly black workers who saw a friend in any group willing to intercede in such cases as that of Julia Jones. She and her twelve-year-old daughter occupied a ramshackle one-room tenement on St. Paul Street. She lost her job after back injuries suffered when her porch railing collapsed. Evicted by landlord H. M. Hardee when she could not pay her rent, she refused to leave, and Hardee in January 1933 sent a crew to remove the windows and doors. The Unemployed Council put cardboard in the openings and sued Hardee for compensation for Julia and repairs on this and his other tenements, but the suit does not appear to have been successful.[26]

Yet the problems faced by Norfolk's blacks were clearly more associated with race than class, and communist doctrine had little appeal for black leaders. Ministers and NAACP officials sought to lure blacks away from communist groups. Some victims of the Depression found a more persuasive panacea in the doctrine of "Sweet Daddy" Grace's House of Prayer on Church and Seventeenth streets. Spurred by the New Deal, the new Congress of Industrial Organizations (CIO) recruited black members nationally, in 1938 affiliating with Norfolk's ILA Local 978, while federal relief and reform took some of the sting from the economic malaise.[27]

Communism's allure faded in the late 1930s, blacks meanwhile finding less radical ways to solve some of their problems. An old grievance, for example, was that Norfolk, all but surrounded by golden beaches, had none for blacks. In 1930 the Interracial Commission proposed that the city buy from the Pennsylvania Railroad a Little Creek site. Whites with property nearby opposed it as a threat to land values; a trio of council candidates campaigned against the proposed beach and lawsuits further delayed action. Aided by the New Deal's Civil Works Administration, however, the council bought the tract and by June 1935 Norfolk blacks finally had their own beach.[28]

Longer-range recovery owed much to New Deal spending and the aggressive way city officials pursued a share in it. Some councilmen initially opposed what seemed to be federal extravagance. But the Depression lengthened and philosophic objections proved malleable. Reasons related to national defense could be argued on behalf of innumerable improvements in highways, bridges, piers, pollution-control, waterworks, and airfields, as well as military facilities. But equal energy was shown by new (1933) City

Manager Thomas P. Thompson and others in quest of government help for schools, colleges, museums, and so on.[29]

The Civil Works Administration (CWA) provided jobs in a mosquito-control program, repairing hurricane damage, building jetties, bulkheads, playgrounds, and athletic fields, repainting and repairing schools, beautifying cemeteries, putting in a pool at Lafayette Park and a canning project at the City Home, and so on. The CWA was temporary, but the Public Works Administration (PWA) took up where it left off, adding many new projects.[30]

With the Elizabeth River's wooden Campostella Bridge rotting away, Norfolk sought federal aid to rebuild it four lanes wide with a steel and concrete draw span; in July 1933 the city got $400,000 toward the purpose. The new span was toll-free; the first access to the city in a century with no fee on entering vehicles was a spur to business. Other wooden bridges, including Granby Street's over the Lafayette River, were also replaced. The Jordan Bridge between Norfolk and Portsmouth had opened in 1929.[31]

Norfolk had been embarrassed for years for want of a municipal airport. The city's first passenger and mail service, to Pittsburgh via the Philadelphia Rapid Transit Air Service at East Camp landing field in 1926, folded within months. In 1929 airman Ben Epstein used his Grand Central Air Terminal, a strip on Granby Street opposite Forest Lawn Cemetery, for an air-taxi service to Richmond. This failing early, the Ludington Line in 1929 began flights to Washington from the same strip, renamed Norfolk Airport. When Eastern Air Transit (EAT) soon began a twice-daily hop to Richmond, air service seemed here to stay. But the navy objected to EAT's field as too near the naval air station and East Camp field, which was earmarked for navy purchase. Ludington and EAT pulled out in 1933.[32]

Federal aid enabled Norfolk in 1937 to acquire Truxton Manor Golf Course, where the operations of three small airstrips could be merged (into what is now Norfolk International). Even before the terminal was finished, Pennsylvania Central Airlines in April 1938 inaugurated service from there to Washington in two big Boeing airliners. Private flying was also increasingly popular; pilot Dave Driskill opened a flying school at Grand Central Terminal in 1930. He had a class of forty in that year, among whom Miss Britta Aspegren of North Shore Point was the star, soloing after only ten hours of flying time. Three years later, Driskill launched Witch Duck Airplane Lines with two flights daily to Cape Charles with Norfolk newspapers.[33]

The New Deal also invigorated Norfolk's cultural life. The Norfolk division of the College of William and Mary opened in 1930 after the faculty had commuted from Williamsburg for eleven years to extension classes at Larchmont School. It gained federal funds for the 18,000-seat Foreman Field stadium (opened in 1936 on Hampton Boulevard), a gymnasium, and a classroom building. A junior college (now Old Dominion University), it had an initial faculty of ten—soon joined by engineering instructors from VPI—some two hundred students, and a winning football team. In October 1935 Richmond's Virginia Union University opened a branch junior college at the Negro YMCA on Brambleton Avenue, with a faculty of four and seventy students. It became Norfolk Polytechnic Institute in 1942, was taken over by the state two years later as a branch of Virginia State University, and is now Norfolk State University.[34]

The Museum of Arts and Sciences was finished in 1939 with New Deal money by adding an assembly hall, new galleries, a library, and a hall of statuary. The museum had opened in 1933 under sponsorship of the Norfolk Society of Arts (the former Leache–Wood Alumnae Association) on land provided by the city and with a tasteful garden of yaupon hollies, cherry laurels, dogwood, and other trees and shrubs. Granby High (opened in 1938), Ocean View and Berkley schools, and improvements to Booker T. Washington High were among other projects with federal support.[35]

The Azalea Garden near the new city airport was conceived in 1938 as a WPA project employing black women, who had gained little from federal largesse. They set out thousands of rhododendrons, azaleas, camellias, and other plants, and did much of the heavy work of clearing land, laying off five miles of trails, and erecting levies around a lake. A stir of disapproval spread through the black community when it was learned that the women, displaced from a WPA sewing project by white women, used shovels and axes, pushed loaded wheelbarrows, and performed other heavy labor. In 1958 the city would add to the 125-acre grounds a 75-acre botanical garden, an educational workshop with many plants from the Dismal Swamp as well as exotic varieties from across the continent and abroad.[36]

Music lovers, yielding little to economic pessimism, were often beguiled by Norfolk's Feldman String Quartet, Society of Arts concerts, the Community Concert Series, the Lyric Trio, the Norfolk Orchestral Association, the Norfolk Choral Society, and others. Such international artists as pianist Jose Iturbi, Jascha Heifetz, Lily Pons, Lawrence Tibbett, and Jussi Bjoerling performed to large and appreciative Norfolk audiences through the darkest days of the Depression. Sculptor William Marks Simpson Jr., a Norfolk native, was in 1930 awarded the Prix de Rome, one of the most coveted prizes in the plastic arts.[37]

A cultural watershed of sorts was marked by the publication in 1931 of Thomas Jefferson Wertenbaker's *Norfolk: Historic Southern Port.* It was the first time the city's story had been told by a professional historian. The author, a grandson of Jefferson's own choice for the first University of Virginia librarian, was a Princeton professor of sound scholarly credentials. He was especially adept at explaining the economic bases of Norfolk's development, but his book, in keeping with the tenor of the times, was shamefully abusive and dismissive of the city's black people, early and late.[38]

Economic necessity might mean doing without but it was also the mother of a numerous progeny of better ideas. The municipal grain elevator and terminal, which proved too costly for the city to operate, was leased under Mayor Slover to Norfolk and Western, releasing over $250,000 a year in city funds for other purposes. Traffic lights were installed at major downtown intersections; Norfolk as late as 1933 had only one such light (at Monticello Avenue and Princess Anne Road) and was reportedly the last American city still using policemen to direct traffic. Three intercity bus companies joined in 1935 to build the Union Bus Terminal at the city market's south end.[39]

The Depression grew more tolerable for many with repeal of the Eighteenth Amendment in 1933, Norfolk joyfully joining the majority by 6,823 to 1,142. If drunk driving arrests doubled in the first four months after repeal, well, some still wondered, with Omar Khayyam, "what the vintners buy one half so precious as the stuff they sell." Interest in professional baseball had declined in the late 1920s with the death of the old Virginia League but in 1934 surged anew, perhaps as a diversion from hard times. The New York Yankees established the Norfolk Tars as a farm-team; the club won the Piedmont League title in its first year, Ray White pitching eighteen straight shut-out innings in the playoffs.[40]

And still the life-giving cloudbursts from beyond the Potomac poured down: the federal building at Granby and Bute opened in 1934; next year came news of five destroyers to be built at the navy yard. There was a battleship each for Norfolk and Newport News shipbuilders in 1938, Norfolk's *North Carolina* having been scuttled, when over a third finished, by 1920s naval limitation treaties. The naval air station was enlarged, funds provided for a sewage disposal plant, a main building for the new naval hospital started in 1937, the old post office building converted in 1939 into a new city hall.[41]

Sometimes nature and circumstance seemed determined to inflict upon Norfolk what the Depression could not. The economy took a gratuitous Sunday-punch in 1932 when many naval vessels stationed in Norfolk waters were summoned to Pacific war-games; as it turned out, they would be gone for years. In June 1933 the piers of the Buxton and Clyde Line steamship companies were destroyed in a $3 million fire that consumed sixty buildings in the wholesale area east of Commercial Place and south of Main. In August the city experienced the worst hurricane in its history; tides lapped onto Granby and Freemason streets for the first time in memory, and many homes and cottages were swept away at Ocean View and Willoughby.[42]

The slums where most blacks lived comprised only one percent of the city area but housed an eighth of its population. Overcrowding meant poor sanitation and high susceptibility to diseases, notably typhoid fever, influenza, and tuberculosis. An outbreak of typhoid in 1933 was attributed by doctors to the cutting off of water to blacks unable to pay their water bills. Black illiteracy was over 11 percent, that among whites under one percent. Crime festered in these conditions; blacks accounted for just over a third of the city's population but over half of its jail inmates. The *Journal and Guide* returned continually to the cry that city authorities apply to federal agencies for housing programs for the poor, but its pleas went unheeded.[43]

The small black upper class included publisher Young, attorney J. Eugene Diggs, mortician J. H. Hale, Dr. Edward Murray, and Rev. Walter L. Hamilton of Shiloh Baptist Church. In 1930 Norfolk had twenty-five black doctors, eighteen attorneys, eight dentists, and four pharmacists. Norfolk Community Hospital, founded in 1931, rejoiced when its PWA-funded facilities opened at Memorial Park in 1939 and when Norfolk-born soprano Dorothy Maynor, fresh from Carnegie Hall and New York rave reviews, in 1940 performed a benefit concert for the hospital at City Auditorium. Leading black organizations included the Masons, the Elks, the back-to-Africa Universal Negro Improvement Association, and various sororities and fraternities. The sixty-nine black churches played a major role in all sorts of social, spiritual, political, and community concerns.[44]

Red-letter days in the black calendar were Emancipation Day, declining in appeal but still recognized with parades, music, and festivities, and History Week, with its lectures, informational and instructional programs, exhibitions, and concerts. Conspicuous at most celebrations was the Eureka Lodge's famed Excelsior Brass and Reed Band, and sometimes the Norfolk Players' Guild, a drama group made up mostly of school teachers.[45]

Even the black elite found it hard to register and vote; registrars often used technicalities to bar black graduates of professional schools as well as common laborers. Of nearly fifty thousand Norfolk blacks in the mid-1930s, only about seven hundred were registered and few of them could count on voting. For most blacks, huddled in Huntersville, Lindenwood, Young Park, and near Washington School, Virginia's poll tax, which had to be paid three consecutive years and six or more months before voting, was, in the Depression's depths, an insuperable obstacle. Through 1932 most black voters remained loyal to the Republican Party, which paid them little heed but still seemed less repugnant than the Democrats. The New Deal provided blacks only marginal benefits.[46]

Even so, the influences confronting the school board with Aline Black and her lawyers in 1939 probably included the glimmer of hope offered to blacks by the New Deal. Roosevelt's advisory "black cabinet" and the extent to which Mrs. Roosevelt, Interior Secretary Harold Ickes, and others around the president seemed committed to racial justice, were elements behind a massive black shift to the Democrats in 1936. Blacks also drew encouragement from occasional court victories around the country over issues involving racial segregation and discrimination. After Massachusetts in 1935 refused to extradite a black man to Virginia because blacks were not allowed on Old Dominion juries, Norfolk and several other cities began adding black names to jury panels.[47]

Signs of an alteration of the tradition of black deference, caused in part by economic fears, were the protests when the city council in 1933 closed Blyden Branch Library as an economy measure. Grumbling in the black community grew so intense that the decision was reversed. Blacks grimaced again in 1934 over rear-seating in city buses, but Young's newspaper complained to no avail. A fourth of the eight thousand black school students (but no whites) were put on a part-time basis in 1934, and black teachers, like whites, incurred a 10 percent cut in their paltry salaries.[48]

Many black Norfolkians could tolerate bias if they had some assurance that their children would fare better. For this reason, blacks took their schools very seriously, regarded their teachers highly, and resented white-imposed shortcomings in education more than elsewhere. The black school term of 151 days was a month less than that for whites. Norfolk's expenditure for black students was just over half the annual $50.00 average for white students. Overcrowding in black schools was moderately relieved when the Henry Clay School on Chapel Street was assigned to blacks in 1935 and renamed Laura A. Titus Elementary, but their school conditions remained far inferior to those of whites.[49]

Norfolk seemed to enter a historic new phase of race relations in 1937 when Rev. Hamilton, president of the local black ministers conference, set off one morning to represent blacks at the Community Fund directors' annual meeting. Refusing to ride a freight elevator to the hotel room that whites reached on the main elevators, Hamilton missed the meeting. This small but symbolic event generated formation by blacks of the Committee on Interracial Welfare to assist blacks encountering local humiliation or injustice. Sensitive observers of the incident may have been less surprised than most by Aline Black's crusade in the fall of 1938 and the months following.[50]

There were black appeals to the city in years prior to the teacher-pay equalization matter for equal but separate parks, beaches, and playgrounds. But that of Aline Black, and then Melvin Alston, was a class action aiming for precisely the same salary schedules guaranteed to whites, an absolute end to racial distinctions. Segregation was not at issue, but a victory by the plaintiffs must raise questions as to whether legal and public views on the federal Constitution had not undergone a sea-change since *Plessy v. Ferguson.*[51]

The Alston case was heard in early 1940 by the circuit court, which again ruled against the plaintiff. On appeal in late 1940 to the United States Circuit Court of Appeals, it was heard by a three-judge panel including John J. Parker, lately rejected for the U.S. Supreme Court on accusations of racism, and Judge Armistead M. Dobie, a Norfolk native thought by the NAACP to be hostile to its cause. But the court ruled that the state's fixing of salaries was covered by the Fourteenth Amendment, in short, that Norfolk's discriminatory policy violated the Constitution. The city appealed to the Supreme Court, which declined review and remanded it to the lower court for settlement.[52]

City Attorney Alfred Anderson called a meeting of city officials, school board, NTA, and black leaders in the hope of a compromise. The city offered to phase in salary adjustments over three years. NAACP leaders refused but P. B. Young, ever the pragmatist, saw merit in compromise. (Fearing a negative effect on race relations, he had tried to halt the suit by negotiating an end to the salary dispute.) If blacks did not insist on immediate equalization, it would be easier in months ahead to negotiate for a new black elementary school. His view prevailed and the teachers accepted the offer.[53]

A disgusted Thurgood Marshall called it "the most disgraceful termination of any case involving Negroes in recent years," a failure of nerve that would set back the black cause by seventy-five years. He and Young drifted farther apart with the passage of time.[54] But nothing now could hold back the equalization of black and white teacher pay across the South. With the principle conceded, it was harder to defend the equal-but-separate doctrine. Either billions must be employed to try and make conditions and facilities truly equal for blacks and whites, or whites must bend at last to the logic and humanity of racial integration.

Another new factor in the complex racial equation was that Hitler and the Nazis were achieving by the late 1930s what slavery and Jim Crow laws had been unable to do, namely, give racism a bad name among whites. Aline Black won reappointment for the 1941–42 school year and continued to teach until she retired in 1969. Like Melvin Alston, her courage had been tested and she survived to witness the coming of a new world.

CHAPTER 23

Red Lights, Blackouts, and "Norfolk County Insurance"

"CHINA Solly," in important respects, was in 1942 a local embodiment of the respectable wartime businessman. An ex-sailor who had served his country in the Far East and other theaters, Solly was an unswerving patriot. His club just outside Norfolk was called "The Stars and Stripes Forever," its interior walls painted with "fire-belching battleships" and other emblems attesting his love of country as well as his loyalty to the navy and the men who staffed it. The high wooden walls of the stockade (much like a frontier fort of old) surrounding his trailer camp out back were painted in inspirational tones of red, white, and blue.[1]

Solly had exacting standards. The trailers stood in neat rows and had curtains at the windows and understated lighting. If the trailer occupants or their clientele became rowdy, Solly was quick to banish them from the premises. He got around Virginia's law banning the sale of liquor by the drink because his was a "club" serving "members," but he allowed no drinking in the trailers. No one got a membership card until he showed Solly that he had the price in negotiable currency or its equivalent.[2]

Some of Solly's competitors, regrettably, were less high-toned. Places like "Arab's Tent," "Krazy Kat," and "Mickey Mouse" let the girls put signs on their rooms or trailers, many of them the titles of popular films: "It Happened One Night," "Boys' Town," "The Lone Ranger," "All That Money Can Buy," and so on. Many of the clubs on Cottage Toll and Sewell's Point roads and elsewhere were inside stockades, with fifty or more upstairs bedrooms around the square and parking underneath. Clients drove through narrow entrances manned by bouncers, parked, bought drinks and gambled (illegally), danced and played slot machines before assignations with a waitress or other female regular.[3]

There were hundreds of such places scattered about Norfolk and Prin-

cess Anne counties—the "Fairmount Social Club," "Norfolk County Athletic Club" (off Sewell's Point Road), "Cabin in the Pines" (Suffolk Boulevard), "Stinnett's Pool Room" (in Portlock), and others. It was not unusual
for a drink to be a "Mickey Finn," rendering the patron oblivious to the
purloining of his valuables. Booze bred frequent fights, and few bars kept
bottles where they might be struck by flying missiles or bodies.[4]

Apart from unprincipled rivals, Solly faced other hazards. Servicemen,
usually some 12,000 a night (several times that on weekends), tended to stay
downtown until the bars and dives closed at midnight and only then make
their way to clubs and other places of recreation in the county. Military
personnel in commercially significant numbers arrived, therefore, only in
the early morning hours. Sailors were generally very young, their paychecks
quickly exhausted in brief hours of carouse, their liberty-time limited. So
Solly, like many entrepreneurs, learned to cultivate mainly shipbuilders and
other working men, who were better paid and less restricted. Black servicemen were confined to the scant recreational opportunities in the black
community.[5]

Solly would probably not have had a downtown bar if his life depended
on it. Sailors were routinely victimized there as fast as they piled off the
buses from 5:00 P.M. onward. Minutes after the first naval base bus pulled
in, liquor store lines could be two blocks long. From these outlets, the sentinels of the Atlantic defense-line moved on to East Main Street and "the
most solid block of beer joints in the world." The dives were carbon-copies,
each with a large bar in the middle, hamburger grills along both walls, a
juke-box behind the bar booming out "Pass the Ammunition," "Der Fuh-
rer's Face," "The Boogie-Woogie Bugle Boy of Company B," or other pop
favorites. Tables and chairs, stalls and slot machines receded into dimly lit
rear areas.[6]

Downtown nightlife had undergone major alterations in the past two
years. At the end of 1940 there were some four hundred prostitutes in East
Main's "red-light" district. They occupied well-known bordellos, paid their
property taxes, received weekly health-checks and certificates, and were
forbidden to work outside the district at night. Then came the crackdown.
In January 1941 the city, at the navy's urging, shut down the district's
whorehouses, gambling dens, and speakeasies. Beer halls remained but
could sell no hard liquor and must close at midnight. Now, in 1943, one saw
"block after block of decaying two-story houses."[7]

There were no more bawdy houses or dance halls on East Main but
plenty of bars, penny arcades, peep shows, shooting galleries, and flop-

houses. Because the police left it to the navy shore patrol, law enforcement tended to amount to comradely rebukes or escorts home. Many of the city's three hundred–odd taxicabs cruised the street and its tributaries with prostitutes in quest of fellow riders. Once two suitably matched fares were aboard, some taxi drivers parked briefly in an alley and took a stroll, others not bothering to park at all; they got their 50 percent cut in any case.[8]

Now, instead of smutty but carefully regulated nightlife, danger haunted every corner. Tavern waitresses offered after-hours "dates" to customers ordering a bottle of $7.00 champagne. Closing time might find half a dozen men awaiting the same girl, often leading to a brawl that allowed her to escape unescorted. Those yielding to siren calls from dark alleys might find fifty cents worth of tawdry exhilaration but hazarded assault, robbery, or venereal disease. Conveniently at the center of the pub district stood the Gaiety Theater, Norfolk's only burlesque house and purveyor of such attractions as Rose La Rose, Anne Corio, or even Gypsy Rose Lee. Appreciative audiences enlivened performances by shouts of "Taxi! Taxi!"[9]

City Manager Charles B. Borland put a stop to the practice of simply fining prostitutes and sending them back on the streets. So the city jail, with facilities for forty-five females, now had 110 or more doubled up on beds or mattresses on stairway landings and floors. Norfolk also had a prison farm but it was filled to overflowing and could not help. Many downtown prostitutes, meanwhile, moved out beyond the municipal boundary, transferring the problem from city to county. Others made their way to new quarters in Ghent and other areas of the city where police and health authorities could no longer keep them under surveillance.[10]

Norfolk thrashed about for solutions, finding few that the sinmongers could not circumvent. It was bad enough to struggle on unnoticed, but suddenly the whole country in 1942 peered over the back fence and smirked at the garbage. *Collier's* magazine sent a reporter down for a piece on housing problems but his story in March dealt mostly with the title topic, "Norfolk Night," with a full-color sketch of a beer-joint packed with raucous sailors and "waitresses." The writer toured East Main and county night-spots— the "Shamrock," "Royal Palm," Professor LaPaz's tattoo emporium, and others—and drew a portrait of a city out of control. *PM* (a New York tabloid), the *Baltimore Sun, Domestic Commerce,* even the *Architectural Forum,* sensationalized Norfolk's plight.[11]

American Mercury came out in early 1943 with "Norfolk—Our Worst War Town." J. Blan van Urk studied a series of cities but came away satisfied that Hampton Roads was far the worst. At the Norfolk jail, he found five or six women to a cell, most of them confident of quick release to make room for a new batch. The main reason for holding prostitutes was to treat their infections, but the need overwhelmed every approach to a solution.[12]

Such exposés were too absorbed in the civic malady to give thought to remedies. Like the *Collier's* man, van Urk found no one especially to blame. Norfolk, he insisted, had "a progressive, honest city government, functioning as efficiently as it can . . . where it cannot hire men for its police force nor doctors and nurses for its health department." Nor could it arrest women for riding in taxis or put people in unbuilt jails.[13] Like Willoughby Spit or the Great Dismal, Norfolk's ills, readers should conclude, were caused by elemental forces beyond human control.

If city authorities lurched from one unpromising tactic to another, the county was a different matter. Investigations by a congressional committee and a grand jury heard testimony that some of the most lurid dives, including "Cabin in the Pines" and "Big Apple," were owned by police officers. County authorities, it was said, had never raided a whiskey establishment; they protected whiskey traffic at a fee of a dollar a gallon. Mrs. Elizabeth Jordan, president of the Highland Park Garden Club, complained of living across the street from a vice lord who received frequent station-wagon loads of liquor; her calls to county police brought no action. The best people agreed, she said, that "Norfolk County is the rottenest place they know of."[14]

Norfolk had heard it all before. In the 1890s it was labeled America's "wickedest city"; now it might be enclosed within the nation's wickedest county. In preceding decades, city-manager government, successive purges of the police, and other initiatives had eradicated many old evils. But in 1943 it seemed that the city could not, the county would not, address the major social burdens imposed by the war. Worse still, many Norfolkians shrugged it off as the inevitable accompaniment of a wartime boom.[15] In this climate of moral apathy, it did not seem to be appreciated that the city had a reputation that many postwar years would not live down. Allied victory over the fascists would not guarantee Norfolk's victory in the war it waged with itself.

The war in Europe seemed of small concern in 1939 when it was a Nazi invasion of Poland, another emanation of ancient Old World grudges. It grew unsettling with German attacks on Scandinavia and Western Europe in 1940. The city council thought Congress should require that aliens be registered, fingerprinted, and photographed. The navy yard was adding about a thousand people a month, making new demands on housing, while the naval operating base on Hampton Boulevard spoke of doubling its eight thousand civilian and military personnel. The navy bought a big tract near Oceana for an auxiliary airfield. Business and real estate values picked up, and the cost of living jumped by 18 percent between September 1939 and December 1941, but the full effect of international events was not yet felt.[16]

In July 1941 Norfolk began to feel the pulse of a nation preparing in earnest for war with the snatching up of over one thousand acres between the naval base and Granby Street to expand the naval air station. Barracks and mess halls sprang up overnight; the bottom of Willoughby Bay was dredged to fill Boush Creek. President Franklin Roosevelt came down in his yacht to tour the naval facilities and remind voters that he, not Wendell Willkie, was responsible for the city's newest bridges and roads. The army leased a state military reservation at the south end of Virginia Beach, naming it Camp Pendleton, and seven hundred acres of Seashore State Park to enlarge Cape Henry's Fort Story. Camp Allen, a Seabee training center south of the naval base, came later, as did Camp Ashby, for German prisoners of war, on Virginia Beach Boulevard.[17]

Meanwhile, it was found that Norfolk, which in 1936 had some five thousand vacant houses, had few left and rising rents outran most pay raises. The city council named a citizens' committee to study the situation, and in July created the Norfolk Housing Authority to help navy families find rooms. Federal funds begat the low-cost eighty-seven-acre Merrimack Park on an Ocean View peninsula next to the naval base. Admiral Joseph K. Taussig, head of the fifth naval district, had fifty more units built on the base and, because his officers faced higher rents on leases many would sign on October 1, applied for federal money for officers' quarters. Blacks had to settle for a few new houses in Titustown without recreational facilities and, in 1943, temporary housing in Liberty Park.[18]

Realtors reacted indignantly to Taussig's moves. Otto Hollowell, secretary of the Norfolk Real Estate Board, sniffed that naval officers, subject to sudden transfer, were not very desirable tenants anyhow. Not yet in the open was the realtors' view that the post–World War I experience, when Norfolk was left with a large housing surplus and a sharp decline in rents and property values, must not be repeated. Throughout the rest of 1940 and long after, Hollowell and John R. Sears, representing building and loan associations, voiced concern over new projects. If more houses were needed, let them be temporary ones that could be torn down when Europe's war ended.[19]

In W. Bruce Shafer Jr., a produce dealer by trade and ardent civic booster by inclination, realtors saw an enemy incarnate. He was close to Admiral Manley H. Simons, who succeeded Taussig in mid-1941, and foresaw a Norfolk of half a million people before the boom spent itself in maybe twenty years. The city needed ten thousand new homes now, and would get twenty thousand more defense workers within months if houses were built for them. When Sears' group sent Washington a plea that the government approve no more large housing projects for Norfolk, Shafer sent a telegram advising that Sears spoke for "home and apartment builders who seek high rents." He infuriated realtors by naming himself the "Emergency Housing Committee" and inviting out-of-town builders to help end Norfolk's shortage.[20]

Washington, as heedless of Shafer's megalopolis as of the Sears–Hollowell apocalypse, threw money in all directions. With the naval air station expanding to Granby Street and swallowing old Norfolk airport, a patrol-boat base going up at Little Creek, and Berkley's St. Helena Reservation reopening for small vessel repair, Washington anticipated needs that Norfolk did not. A three hundred–unit public project began on Campostella Road for black defense workers, a federally insured one for 175 homes at a rural crossroads called Ward's Corner, and others at Lafayette Shores, Benmoreell (on the old army base east of Hampton Boulevard), Glenwood Park, Willard Park (north of Benmoreell), and others. Long Island mogul William J. Levitt began a giant Riverdale project. All were too few.[21]

Norfolk's official 1940 population figure of 144,000 was obsolete before it was published. By mid-1941 there were 30,000 officers and sailors at the naval base or on ships stationed there. The peak of military personnel in the area would come in December 1943 when there were over 168,000, besides almost 200,000 civilians. By early 1944 the worst was over and both the military and civilian populations began to decline.[22]

Every solution to problems caused by the mass influx seemed to generate three headaches. Abruptly, water and sewage systems built for remote posterity were intolerably strained. Streets and roads dedicated to the needs of Norfolkians yet unborn were strangled with traffic. Gleaming new schools and hospitals ran out of space.[23] Like the difficulty of maintaining order amid East Main's debauchery, the physical problems appeared likely to baffle human ingenuity. The city was breaking down because some European countries were having one of their perennial tiffs. On the afternoon of Sunday, December 7, 1941, came word that the Japanese were attacking Pearl

Harbor naval base. Every problem graduated at once to a new order of magnitude.

Blacks found the federal government still discriminating against them in many ways. New occupational training facilities included few for blacks, and these operated at awkward places and times. Black women answering an urgent call for two thousand female bench and lathe operators in 1942 found that only white women had access to training shops. Rebecca Watson, applying for an opening for a registered nurse at the Portsmouth naval hospital, was told the position was filled, only to learn that a white nurse was hired for it soon afterward. Blacks lucky enough to get skilled work at the metal works division of the naval air station found that promotions went almost exclusively to whites. Complaints forced the navy to add a black to the shop committee.[24]

Change came in small and toilsome increments. Tom Tunstall, a Norfolk County black, in 1944 lost his fireman's job with Norfolk and Southern Railway and sued the white Brotherhood of Locomotive Firemen and Enginemen for protecting only the jobs of whites. The suit, on behalf of the Association of Colored Railway Trainmen and Locomotive Firemen, was decided by the U.S. Supreme Court as a class-action in favor of the plaintiffs. A decade before Rosa Parks ignited the Montgomery bus boycott, schoolteacher Sara Morris Davis took a city bus seat, the only one available, near the front between two whites. Ordered by the driver to move, she refused and was arrested. She sued the bus company, the Virginia supreme court ruling against the driver—because he ignored a white passenger seated in the black section.[25]

Yet Premier Hideki Tojo had done Norfolk a great service. For the city to be actually at war had the tonic effect on many of a liberation from petty concerns, the diminution of all obstacles to temporary inconveniences. City Manager Charles Borland, within minutes of the Pearl Harbor news and a full day before the declaration of war, had all forty of Norfolk's alien Japanese arrested on suspicion of being Japanese aliens. Local navy units went at once on wartime alert; all military personnel were ordered to their stations. By Monday morning a civil air-warning system was operational in the federal building and preparation was under way to keep it open on a twenty-four-hour basis.[26]

The air-raid business became a cottage industry. Never mind that the enemy had about the same capacity to bomb Norfolk as to simonize San Antonio, scanning the skies over the Royster Building for Messerschmidts had about it an air of total immersion in the common cause, almost like arm-wrestling with Mussolini himself. By Tuesday evening the army had ringed Norfolk with antiaircraft batteries. And just in time, new Chief Air Raid Warden Richard M. Marshall warning on the same day that "this city may be attacked by German airplanes any night now." People should not throw water on a bomb that fell into their homes—"it will explode and probably kill you." (Not to mention the need to conserve water.) On Thursday, two hundred people signed up as air-raid wardens.[27]

The experience of war galvanized Norfolk's energies as no amount of importuning "Uncle Sugar" for this and that had so far done. Uncle was much in evidence, but no guilty sense of selfish whining need restrain Norfolk's calls for federal funds or delay its own initiatives. An unused pumping station at North Landing River was refurbished and pressed into use to increase the city's water supply, and Borland got Washington to fund half the cost of a second line from Lake Prince. The Dismal Swamp Canal was tapped, as were the Nottoway and Blackwater rivers. The state geologist showed that a pipe drilled fifteen or twenty feet into the ground almost anywhere in Norfolk would start a well. Summer droughts still brought shortages and calls for conservation, but supplies kept approximate pace with demands.[28]

Traffic snarls eased when the navy improved Kersloe Road from Hampton Boulevard to Granby Street alongside the naval air base expansion, renaming it Admiral Taussig Boulevard. Federal money widened Sewell's Point Road and Hampton Boulevard north of the Lafayette River, and built a bypass between Sewell's Point Road and the toll-free route over Campostella Bridge. VEPCO scoured the country for old trolleys, ordered a fleet of buses, and eliminated half its stops and some routes to speed service. Bus and trolley operators were hard to find, especially since no blacks or women were hired, but the policy was blamed on a lack of restrooms and later abandoned. Seven steam and diesel ferries carried traffic between Norfolk and Portsmouth.[29] One way or another, despite everything, Norfolk managed to get people back and forth and in and out.

A month before Pearl Harbor, city leaders created the Council of Social Agencies (now the Planning Council) to centralize planning in social and health services. Blending business and citizen support, it raised funds to put up buildings for United Way services. Later, it helped develop such projects as the Foodbank of Southeastern Virginia, a Youth Commission, Comprehensive Health Survey, Legal Reference Bureau, an area-wide anti-poverty program, 911 emergency service, and a Teen Health Education

Center. Many of its programs later became the responsibility of government agencies, but the Planning Council by the 1990s had a permanent staff of over one hundred besides many volunteers. Its funds now came mainly from private foundations and contracts with government agencies.[30]

By early 1942 the war was at Norfolk's doorstep and slithering over the transom. Norfolk lives were lost to U-boat sinkings as early as October 1941, and January 19 saw the loss of a Latvian ship a day out of Norfolk. In March a Nazi sub surfaced almost within sight of Cape Henry to shell a tugboat towing coal barges. A steady stream of bodies and survivors came into Norfolk from sinkings off the Virginia and Carolina coasts. Thousands at Virginia Beach in June saw a tanker hit a mine five miles offshore and sink. Patrol planes depth-charged a phantom U-boat, which, as rumors spread, surfaced to fire a spectral shell at the Cavalier Hotel for God-only-knew what delinquency of service. Almost one hundred naval vessels were stationed at Norfolk; the navy yard would build forty-two warships, including the battleship *Alabama*.[31]

Still the hairy hordes, military and civilian, streamed through Norfolk's portals, sleeping in cars, using rooms in shifts, living in converted henhouses and garages. A prefabricated village rose on Broad Creek Road, and new housing went up at Roberts and Oak Leaf parks. Lewis Park, across Hampton Boulevard from Benmoreell, sprouted two hundred trailers with rows of sleeping quarters like the Tucker dormitories for blacks at Lambert's Point. Commodore Apartments, Admiral's Road Apartments, Talbot Park—all filled as fast as glass was puttied into window frames.[32]

Civil defense meant blackouts and dimouts, air-raid drills, and the like. In mid-1942 rumors circulated in the white community that blacks would stage a riot during a upcoming blackout. Gossips had blacks buying ice picks to attack whites. Newspapers and the FBI tried to trace the rumor's source, but got no closer than an informant who said he first heard it from four women at a bridge table. City Manager Borland laid it to enemy propaganda but swore in a large group of black auxiliary police on the eve of the threatened attack. There was also talk of an "Eleanor Club" (said to be directed by Mrs. Roosevelt) of black maids who would insist on using the front door on pain of refusing to cook or otherwise sabotaging what remained of white domestic tranquility.[33]

P. B. Young's *Journal and Guide* was one of four southern newspapers honored by the Office of War Information for exposing such rumors as false. Young was an ardent supporter of the war effort; he also pushed hard in his columns for an end to racial discrimination in defense industries, an aim

Roosevelt signed into law in June 1941. Young publicized weekly incidents of reprisal and subterfuge against black workers by area employers, but tried to reduce tensions caused by black workers having to push through crowds of whites to rear seats on public conveyances.[34]

The *Guide*, enraged by the scant notice given to black housing conditions, cited an eleven-room house with twenty-one occupants who, for $7.00 a week each, shared a bath and toilet that emptied through pipes to buckets on a lower floor. A federal housing administrator agreed that Norfolk's slums, mostly black, were "the worst in the nation." The city council in 1940 launched, over real estate board opposition, a program of slum-clearance and rebuilding—one of the nation's first. Exposure of such abuses led to the creation of the Norfolk Housing Authority. In failing health, Young turned over his paper in late 1943 to his sons, Thomas W. and P. B. Jr., the latter an ex-war correspondent.[35]

In the long run, only vigorous black voting could achieve real racial progress. A 1941 survey by Professor Luther P. Jackson of Virginia State College showed barely 4.5 percent of Norfolk's eligible black voters paying poll taxes and few of these voting. Jackson led a campaign that depended heavily on black labor leaders such as Rev. W. H. Bowe of the local Pile Drivers Union. Only 250 blacks registered in the first year, but blacks showed interest in politics by joining such groups as the Adams Ward Voters League. In 1944 a black representative regularly attended the City Democratic Committee, evidently as a full member.[36]

Norfolk's hospitals seemed adequate to the needs of wartime in 1939 when the Norfolk Community Hospital for Negroes opened. Within months, however, the city sought federal help to expand it as well as Norfolk General, De Paul, and Leigh Memorial. By 1941 doctors doubted that Norfolk could handle an epidemic, and sought emergency space in schools, churches, and clubhouses. Finally, it was agreed that, besides expanding the existing hospitals, De Paul must have an entirely new facility on Granby Street to replace its old one, which dated from the 1855 yellow fever epidemic. The latter opened in May 1944. Luckily, the war brought Norfolk no severe epidemics.[37]

Signs of burgeoning school needs led to plans for elementary schools on Granby Street for whites and in Campostella for Oak Leaf Park blacks (Richard A. Tucker School), with federal help. The Granby project was dropped but a combined elementary and high school opened at Broad Creek Village and an elementary school at Liberty Park, while other schools were enlarged. Some had to run on shifts and all found it hard to hire suitable teachers. Meanwhile, a city auditorium was begun in early 1942 at Ninth and Granby; it had a two thousand-seat theater and five thousand-seat arena.[38]

As the city's war historian, Marvin Schlegel, put it, Norfolk was a "conscripted city," its skies filled with the drone of cargo, training, and patrol planes, blimps, and other traffic. Its waters churned with tugs, great gray battlewagons, merchantmen, patrol boats, and smaller craft. Military vehicles sped through the streets, though never so impressively as on an October Sunday in 1942 when "an unending stream" of camouflage-painted rolling-stock rumbled out Hampton Boulevard to the piers for the invasion, a few weeks later, of Axis North Africa. The Pacific Theater had special significance for Norfolk owing to the role of Douglas MacArthur, the curiously flawed genius commanding America's Pacific forces and whose mother was a Berkley native.[39]

With its enormous truck farming, Norfolk suffered no want of food, though one might face starvation waiting for a stool or booth at one of the eternally packed eateries. Sugar was rationed, however, as were butter, bacon, coffee, cars, tires, shoes, liquor, gasoline, and other items. Pleasure driving was outlawed in 1943, gas stations having been asked to close twelve hours a day. Newton Park's Ford assembly plant was taken over by the navy. A woman seeking a ruling on whether she might drive to her wedding insisted it was no pleasure trip. (For those with the cash, a black market flourished in most hard-to-find items.) People were asked to save old iron, tin, nylon stockings, and fat drippings, and drives were held to collect scrap metal and other materials.[40]

With the military, shipbuilding, and so on draining the male labor pool, women found unprecedented opportunities. Reporter Mary Hopkins took over the *Ledger-Dispatch* sports desk. Others became air-raid wardens, drove streetcars, and volunteered at USOs and similar facilities. At the navy yard, they welded, operated cranes, drove cement-mixers, and became airplane mechanics; the federal government financed day nurseries for the children of female workers. Many ran businesses formerly operated by their husbands. Mrs. Lynette Hamlet, a Maury High teacher, was everywhere recruiting and training volunteers for air-warning and civil defense. Mrs. W. MacKenzie Jenkins, Mrs. Fred Stewart, Carol Tidball, Harriet Tynes, and others lent their energies to war-related work.[41]

High-paying government work enticed Norfolkians away from other employment and caused headaches for the operators of restaurants, hotels, and shops. Housewives unaccustomed to housework found domestic help all but extinct. Stenographers, no longer willing to struggle along on $100.00 a month, quit for better jobs. The police force and fire department were strapped; by 1944 the former had lost sixty men and found only ten to fill vacancies, but still turned down proposals to use women and blacks for certain duties.[42]

The want of police had been a factor in the sprawling growth of vice and immorality in wartime Norfolk (especially in county districts), though major crimes, fortunately, were few. Matters came to a head on Saturday night, July 24, 1943, when a sailor, W. J. Evans, was stabbed to death at the "Casablanca," a dance hall near Edmund's Corner, by civilian Charlie Van Horn. Admiral Herbert F. Leary, who had recently replaced Simons as fifth naval district commandant, was dissatisfied with testimony that Van Horn acted in self-defense. Thinking county police guilty of a coverup, Leary on July 30 put large parts of Norfolk County off-limits, including all highways into Norfolk and Portsmouth from the west. The order covered even navy personnel living in these areas, though they were not required to move.[43]

The draconian nature of Leary's order reflected frustrations of navy, city, and state officials in dealing with the county police and their head, Deputy Sheriff Frank Wilson. Shore patrol raids on county vice-dens, when conducted with the knowledge of county officers, found evidence of illegal activity wiped clean. The navy resolved as early as February 1944 to give the county no more forewarning of raids. In May a state policeman stumbled into a gambling den, the "Pelican Club," and called county officers to help shut it down. He was told that he had started the bust and could finish it. Such places were said to pay police "Norfolk County insurance" to be spared interference.[44]

Businesspeople howled in protest at Leary's order and Governor Colgate Darden, an adopted son of Norfolk, asked Judge A. B. Carney to look into it. Carney replied that county law enforcement was fine, servicemen well treated. Darden, informed by private inquiry that Carney misstated the case, called for a special grand jury. Then came raids by ABC agents and shore patrolmen on the "Fairmount Social Club," "Fairmount Billiard Parlor," "Norfolk County Athletic and Social Club," and "Sportsman's Club," which uncovered illegal liquor, gambling, and so on. When the grand jury began work in September, Leary lifted his off-limits order.[45]

Leary was soon transferred to New York but, a day before leaving, closed much of the Norfolk black business area—between Princess Anne Road and Main Street—to white sailors. The public never learned why, though Police Chief John F. Woods offered assurance that, if they knew, they would appreciate the need. This was not an answer that went down well with the *Journal and Guide,* and P. B. Young rode herd on the navy for having "damned the good Negroes with the bad" and putting "all of Negro Norfolk outside the pale of decency." Leary's action had no great economic consequence to black businesspeople, since few white sailors dealt with them, but the implications were beyond endurance.[46]

The grand jury produced evidence to support what everyone knew, that vice was rampant in parts of the county and could not go on without police knowledge of it. The grand jurors wanted nineteen county officers dismissed, four more reprimanded, and one indicted for operating "The Pines," a house of ill-fame. The county police were now reorganized, with Frank Wilson as chief of police, though he stood accused by the state corrections commissioner of having been responsible for running the state's second worst jail. All this brought on an investigation by the House of Delegates.[47]

A House committee heard testimony about open gambling and prostitution and officers who profitted from it. When ABC agents complained that more than seven hundred pints of whiskey taken in a raid on "Shack's Place" had disappeared, Frank Wilson revealed that it was stored at the jail. A check found 253 pints missing, but Wilson had by now resigned as police chief and jailer, so the jail could at least be cleaned up. Even so, the county police were woefully undermanned, the force remaining the same size as in 1940 though the county population had doubled since then and problems multiplied out of all proportion to physical growth.[48]

City vice might seem equally unyielding but municipal officers genuinely tried to improve matters. Besides the rolling-whorehouse taxi problem, city challenges included hotels not employing house detectives or alerting managers to foil bellboys smuggling women to rooms or clerks renting rooms by the hour. Police were reluctant to raid even the worst offenders lest the inadvertent arrest of married couples might lead to suits for false arrest. Then there was the aggravated liquor problem: sailors now had not only to get to town before state stores closed and stand in long lines but also present ration cards. This gave an edge to bootleggers and black marketeers, who resurrected the sordid gimmicks of the 1920s to purvey liquor at up to six times its legal price.[49]

None of this was beyond redemption, and renewed military and city vigor in attacking it began to pay off. The city began clearing with the FBI all applications for taxi licenses in order to block those with prior criminal records and clamped down on overcharging, speeding, and carrying "cab-girls." Drivers had to have their photos posted on the backs of front seats for identification, use meters to prevent overcharging, and record all trips. The cops got three cab-girls to incriminate fifty drivers, nearly all of them licensed by the county, where screening was less rigorous. City drivers added a measure of self-protection by organizing into a chapter of the Teamsters Union.[50]

Much Norfolk vice involved juveniles lured to the city from all over the country, boys usually finding work though they might fall within child-labor restrictions, girls often resorting to serial marriages with sailors or to prostitution. (J. G. Etheridge, a South Mills, North Carolina justice of the peace, performed up to fifty weddings a week and rarely asked questions.) Police began shipping delinquent girls home; Travelers Aid furnished one-way tickets. Some had no home to return to or soon reappeared; space intended for black women at the city farm was commandeered for girls under eighteen. Conditions were so abysmal that inmates rioted several times. This led the city to bring them back to the jail and apply for federal funds for new detention quarters.[51]

The police invoked a 1920 ordinance requiring hotel and rooming house operators to report within twelve hours anyone under twenty registering without parent or guardian. Parents were brought up for letting children roam the streets, judges offering alternatives of moving away or serving time in Norfolk's sardine-tin jail. The navy in October 1943 ordered sailors off the streets from 1:00 to 5:00 A.M. It now had a permanent shore patrol, staffed mostly by former policemen, who took a no-nonsense view of misbehavior. Much indignation followed, including complaints that officers were exempt, but the order got the least responsible servicemen off the streets during the most dangerous hours and broke up numerous parasitical business enterprises.[52]

Important in containing vice was Norfolk's effort, after some initial coolness and hesitation, to provide servicemen with wholesome recreation. By tradition, young ladies did not go out with sailors and it took wheedling to get them even to attend chaperoned dances and parties for servicemen. (The war, however, did tend to boost the social status of sailors as defenders of freedom.) Meanwhile, sailors had to be content with an enlarged navy YMCA at Ocean View and hostess houses and lounges run by Catholic, Methodist, and Lutheran churches. The Salvation Army renovated its building at Granby and Plume as a recreation center but it did not open until 1943; Tuesday and Saturday night dances were held in the old city hall

The Smith Street USO provided black servicemen with one of their few places of wholesome recreation and entertainment during World War II. (Courtesy of Norfolk Public Library)

auditorium. Only at baseball games did servicemen get reduced prices for their entertainment.[53]

The USO, from modest beginnings, built a formidable Norfolk organization and by late 1942 had eight centers, including one on Smith Street (one of the city's worst slums) for black servicemen. Catholic and Jewish groups set up USOs at Ocean View and on the beach at Lynnhaven, respectively. The USO sponsored outdoor dances at Lafayette Park, and in July 1943 took over the new Municipal Auditorium for dances. Free tickets were provided to service personnel for concerts, stage shows, boxing matches, and other events. The Taussig Gymnasium opened at the Navy Y and Admiral Simons launched a Fleet Recreation Park on Hampton Boulevard, with playing fields and an indoor recreation center.[54]

To the Smith Street USO were gradually added a few more recreational opportunities for black servicemen. The Hunton branch of the YMCA opened a dormitory and sponsored weekly dances at Booker T. Washington High School. Middle-class black parents often refused to allow their daughters to attend activities at the black USO because of Smith Street's mud and filth, but it served almost two million people during the war in its dormitory, recreational, educational, and personal service facilities.[55]

The worst of the overcrowding was relieved by early 1944, when both the civilian and military populations began to decline. Vice gradually receded during 1944 and the war months of 1945. Norfolkians could find encouragement in the fact that a resolute determination not to be crushed under the weight of wartime burdens had borne a large measure of success.

At 7:00 P.M. on August 14, 1945, the first horns sounded along Granby Street and, in residential areas, housewives appeared in the streets with improvised dishpan-and-spoon noisemakers to herald Japan's surrender. As the downtown air filled with soap flakes and bits of paper, suburban children formed parades of bicycles trailed by strings of tin cans. Old Jay Engle, night clerk at the Union Mission on 907 Main Street, commented that "It's all over" and fell dead in front of the building.[56] For nearly everyone else, the end was a new beginning.

There was no pause for Norfolk to accept the thanks of a grateful nation for its efforts in behalf of the 1.7 million servicemen and women who passed through the Hampton Roads Port of Embarkation, for many other contributions and sacrifices the city made to Allied victory.[57] What lingered was the aftertaste of the muckrakers of 1942 and 1943, the recollections of tens of thousands who left despising Norfolk as a snarling, booze-drenched, syphilitic flophouse. It was unfair, but love and war have their own rules in such matters. On the whole, Norfolk and "China Solly" felt that they had done about as well as they could.

CHAPTER 24

The Dixie All-American

THERE had been no previous black candidate for the city council in the twentieth century, and no one was quite sure how seriously to take Victor J. Ashe. A Villanova-educated attorney, World War II veteran, and Norfolk native, Ashe had articulated a thoughtful platform and would probably get the votes of all five thousand eligible blacks who might cast ballots in June 1946. Since there were eight whites in the field and Norfolk had never had a councilmanic contest in which over ten thousand people voted, Ashe was likely to win one of the three available seats and give blacks their first voice in the city's government in over half a century.[1]

A further guarantee of Ashe's success was the "single-shot" ploy pushed by P. B. Young, NAACP chief counsel Thurgood Marshall, and other black leaders. Blacks were urged to vote only for Ashe, passing up a chance also to select two whites and thus considerably increasing his chances. White candidates predictably deplored this strategy, the race being close enough that black support might well mean the difference for successful whites.[2]

The candidates appeared before the Norfolk Council of Clubs and Organizations at Bank Street Baptist Church on May 20, candidate George G. Martin explaining to a largely black audience why they should not use the single-shot option. "In the old days," he reminded them, "when cold, juicy watermelons sold three for $1, you never paid $1 and then took only one watermelon. Vote for Ashe, but get your money's worth. Vote for two others." Martin, who ran dead last, may never have understood quite why.[3]

If sensitivity to blacks was a problem for whites unaccustomed to courting their votes, the appeal to black self-interest also tended to go awry. Councilman Richard W. Ruffin told a black Frances E. Willard audience that "the time has not come for Norfolk to elect a Negro to the council." Ashe, Ruffin conceded, was "a credit to his race and the city, but . . . his election would be injurious to his race as well as to the white population." Why this was so did not come out but presumably was understood, Ruffin implied, by right-thinking people.[4]

The chief interest in the 1946 contest, however, was not Victor Ashe's candidacy but the fight between groups of white hopefuls. Up for reelection were incumbent councilmen Dr. James W. Reed (the mayor), Richard W. Ruffin, and C. E. "Eddie" Wright. The trio campaigned to make the Berkley Bridge toll-free, spend $2.5 million on public improvements for 1946–47, and, in general, continue council policies of the war years.[5]

The campaign's excitement came mainly from three political outsiders calling themselves the "People's Ticket." Corporate attorney Richard D. Cooke, auto-dealer Pretlow Darden (brother of retiring Governor Colgate Darden), and sand, gravel, and concrete contractor John W. Twohy II emerged as joint candidates after a secret January meeting at the Monticello Hotel. It was said to have included "bankers, shipbuilders and fertilizer millionaires," called in response to "the apparent unrest among the electorate over conditions at City Hall." If fertilizer and gravel millions was an unlikely basis for what opponents called a "silk-stocking ticket," neither was it an obvious basis for a "People's Ticket." The race cried out for clarification.[6]

Real issues emerged grudgingly if at all. When the "People's Ticket" proclaimed a ten-point platform in March, it was hailed by Mayor Reed's trio as an "almost one hundred per cent endorsement" of his own administration's policies. Struggling to define contrasts, Darden's group charged that Norfolk was "not a clean city," not "well policed," an echo of the ill-repute the city had endured in recent years. Connoisseurs of political rhetoric noted the statement that combatting these evils might require "additional municipal income, . . . an increase in certain levies." With the mayor's group pledged to "a balanced budget," the "t-word" offered as much of an issue as voters could expect.[7]

The "People's Party" assailed with unabashed alacrity the most obvious weakness of the incumbents, who claimed rather defensively to have led wartime Norfolk "safely and sanely" despite shortages of manpower, material, and equipment. The war, shot back the "People's Ticket," was "too often used as . . . a cloak for apathy and gross ineptitude." The council must not lay "the collapse of certain government functions" at other doorsteps than its own.[8]

The bland sloganeering masked a bitter power struggle. The council was understood to be dominated by the political "machine" of Clerk of Courts William "Billy" Prieur, who had controlled the city's government throughout the Depression and war years. Seen by many as overly tolerant of prostitution, gambling, and bootlegging, the council also exhibited a fiscal conservatism likely to prolong social and other problems left by the war years.

Proposed cuts in city services and improvements might even drive away the navy and deprive Norfolk of its only real "industry."[9]

The "People's Ticket" spoke for business and financial leaders who had long confined their civic energies to charities such as the Community Chest and volunteer groups like the Citizens Crime Committee; for support they looked mainly to the legion of volunteers with whom they worked. Besides thwarting the threat to business posed by council policies, they hoped to cleanse Norfolk of its seedy image and reawaken the city's sense of pride and latent energies. But both sides were beholden to Virginia's "Byrd Machine"; the "People's Ticket" had to avoid direct challenges to Prieur and employ the same conservative rhetoric. To avoid charges of trying to build their own machine, they promised that, if elected, they would retire in 1950.[10]

The campaign's final day featured a big June 10 parade of blacks, conducted by Grand Marshall James E. Smith, with floats and four bands. Starting at Water Street and Princess Anne Road at 7:00 P.M., marchers wound along Church, Fenchurch, Freemason, Brambleton, and Monticello avenues and Olney Road, reminding blacks to vote the next day. Even so, Victor Ashe was to receive fewer than three thousand votes (no doubt nearly all of them black) and Norfolk blacks had to suffer more years of taxation without representation.[11]

The *Virginian-Pilot*, assured that the result depended on style more than substance, forecast a light turnout even though the campaign had been the liveliest in years. It did not appear "that anything truly fundamental is at stake," frenzied "last-minute campaign literature, notwithstanding."[12] But style, in the form of aggressive new candidates challenging safe mediocrities, might be a suitable substitute for substance, especially if the challenge reflected the mood of an impatient electorate.

Political revolution is often heralded by street barricades and guillotines, but that of 1946 stole quietly in like the fog over Wide Water Street. Even the spectacle of an astonishing 17,000 voters on June 11, far more than in the Roosevelt–Dewey contest of 1944, failed to show editor Lenoir Chambers that he had missed anything fundamental. The *Pilot* conceded that the election signaled "the democratic process redeemed from lethargy to action." But the winners, the writer predicted, would soon learn the difference between "managing law, gravel and automobile businesses . . . and running a city government." There would be ample time to repent of those words in later years.[13]

The idea that businessmen, now a council majority, could run a city effectively was that of Smith-Douglas fertilizer magnate Oscar F. Smith, who felt that the heads of energetic Community Fund drives and volunteer groups might perform as well in political office. The Community Fund, inaugurated in 1923, was weakly supported until Charles L. Kaufman, W. S. Royster, and C. Wiley Grandy led a successful 1939 drive and Smith himself later joined the team. After that, a high profile on the fund and similar service groups was seen as important to those with political ambition, an obligation owed by civic leaders.[14]

Cooke (the new mayor), Darden (elected mayor in 1948), and Twohy seemed bent at first on proving Smith wrong. They let council meetings run on for up to six hours to hear everyone with a gripe, went to Smithfield to sniff Swift and Company pig pens and packing houses to see if they smelled bad (Swift was considering a Norfolk plant), and generally carried on like the eager amateurs they were. But they hired Schenectady, New York's city manager Charles A. Harrell, reputedly the nation's best, and gradually got the hang of their new jobs.[15]

Harrell, given a free hand, put business leaders on all boards and commissions, including many new ones, and brought in platoons of professionals and consultants, enabling him to circumvent city hall at every step. The council created a Negro Advisory Committee to avail itself of input, especially in redevelopment and housing, from the likes of P. B. Young Sr. and Jr., Rev. Richard Bowling, and J. Eugene Diggs. (Roosevelt's "black cabinet" seemed to be the model.) A major new tool of the reformers was Virginia's 1946 Redevelopment Act, which let private firms participate in redevelopment projects.[16]

Reformers who feared entrenched bureaucracies such as the police cheered when Captain of Detectives Claude Straylor, during a temporary absence of the police chief, raided "protected" gambling and numbers dens; inquiry showed that over half the police force was taking bribes and payoffs. The policemen charged with corruption were acquitted, but the council seized the chance to reorganize the department under a new chief, A. Leroy Simms, a former marine general. Reformers could proceed more confidently to design new building codes, health and safety ordinances, and the nation's first minimum housing code.[17]

By the end of 1946 the new administration had bought Berkley Bridge to make it toll-free and found funds to hire forty more policemen (including the first six blacks) to deal with what some were calling a crime-wave in Norfolk. There would be thirty-one new police (301 in all) the following year. Meanwhile, progress was made toward a new water treatment plant, a modernized bus system, and new connecting links for the downtown area.[18]

True to their threat to increase "certain levies," the council raised the assessed value of all buildings and some land and increased the tax rate. Meanwhile, many older city employees were retired under a pension plan and new blood was brought in. In the summer of 1946 the city resumed control of its disheveled municipal airport, used in the war years by the army air force, and made plans to rehabilitate it.[19]

The reformers were only warming to the task. Departments of public safety and public health (the latter under Dr. John Huff, rated one of the country's best health officers) were soon in existence, and food-service laws were tightened. (Selling contaminated food became punishable by fines and up to six months in jail.) Teachers got a 7 percent raise and operating costs for city schools (with over twenty thousand students) increased by 50 percent. Contracts were let in 1949 for a $23 million Norfolk–Portsmouth tunnel, which opened in 1952, as did a new Berkley Bridge as part of the bridge-tunnel connection. Each initiative was borne along by solid newspaper support and, despite some discontent, popular approval.[20]

Nothing in the new regime equalled the drive of the Norfolk Redevelopment and Housing Authority. This was a 1946 outgrowth of the Norfolk Housing Authority, created in 1940 to clear slums but diverted to defense housing. Under Chairman Charles L. Kaufman, a corporate lawyer with ties to financial institutions, the NRHA tackled Norfolk's basic social problems. Slums covered one-twentieth of the city, contained one-seventh of its population, and registered two-thirds of its rapes, and one-third or more of its fires, assaults, robberies, larcenies, homicides, and tuberculosis cases. Most slum housing was rental property meant for single families but subdivided into rooms or apartments, each likely to have one or more families sharing bathrooms and other facilities, if any.[21]

Standing conspicuously near key business areas and flanking main thoroughfares, slums absorbed almost half the cost of city services but paid for barely a fourth. They choked the central downtown business district, constricting trade. The city council in 1948 used $25,000 for a study of slum removal and NRHA hired planning consultant Charles K. Agle to make a block-by-block study of downtown and recommend action. He found that all major highways ended a mile or more from the central business area and fed traffic into a maze of narrow streets descended from ancient cowpaths and carriage ways. Accessibility, parking, and ease of movement could only be achieved by massive slum clearance and redevelopment.[22]

The situation was most critical in Brambleton. A white area with black slum housing on two sides, some of its residents resisted as blacks in the postwar years began crossing Corprew Avenue, the traditional racial dividing line, into Brambleton housing. A series of ugly incidents led to the appointment of biracial committees which, however, found no solutions. Virtually no city housing had been built for blacks in some fifteen years while the black population had soared.[23]

Kaufman got help from the Women's Council for Inter-racial Cooperation (WCIC), which had long been studying and publicizing slum conditions, for a house-to-house survey in target areas to determine family sizes, incomes, rents, and other data. Under Mrs. G. W. C. Brown, its chairperson, the WCIC used 128 volunteers in teams under Mrs. Thelma Bryant, Mrs. W. S. Jones, Mrs. Nora B. Diggs, and Rev. W. P. Wise. Horrors they found included a Cumberland Street family of five living in one room and a Nicholson Street bedroom with a gap in the ceiling over the bed "through which rain poured." A memorable interviewee was a ten-year-old: "I hope they'll change the name of the street so I won't have to remember where I once lived."[24]

The NRHA's application for funds under the 1949 Federal Housing Act was the first in the nation and the first granted. "Project Number One" was to clear the dilapidated forty-seven-block black slum bounded by Brambleton and Monticello avenues, Broad Creek Road, and Lincoln Street, and replace it with the Young Park and Tidewater Park developments. Meanwhile, some two thousand families were moved to new two-story brick buildings in Roberts Park, Chesterfield Heights, Campostella, and Ballentine Boulevard. To the 3,300 public housing units built by the old NHA would now be added two thousand more. New housing codes requiring at least one window per room, inside running water, and so forth would protect older middle-class areas such as Ghent, Riverview, Fairmont Park, Brambleton, and Winona from deterioration.[25]

Removal of slum housing also made land available for new schools, playgrounds, streets, and highways. New land for light industry would attract to Norfolk firms that might reduce city dependence on the navy, which, for all its benefits, paid no real, personal, or other local taxes.[26]

The first slum building was demolished on December 11, 1951. By 1956 NRHA had erected over 3,400 low-rent apartments in Tidewater Park and started the final three hundred-odd units of Project Number One. Young Park became a community of 752 modern apartments with fire and police stations and a school. The minimum housing codes had resulted in the rehabilitation of over one thousand dwellings and demolition of sixty-two others outside the slum areas. Redevelopment spinoffs included many new private investments, expansions, and rehabilitations. A second project, focusing on ninety-eight acres of Atlantic City slums, soon began.[27]

Casting about for ways to broaden the city's economic base, the council in 1948 created the Norfolk Port Authority. The pressing need was to bring in more general cargo, the port's coal and other bulk products yielding small revenue in comparison with other merchandise. Publicity campaigns, including its new magazine, *World Trade,* helped the Port Authority introduce shippers to Norfolk's possibilities; in 1950 it was also given control of the municipal airport. The city went into the parking business in 1950 by purchasing and equipping five lots.[28]

By the end of the 1940s a blueprint existed for a gigantic overhaul of decrepit downtown and waterfront areas. Intracoastal shipping having declined as refrigerated freight cars took Florida, Texas, and California produce to large urban markets, the waterfront was a purgatory of rotting wharves and abandoned warehouses. The main retail district had retreated two blocks north and spawned an infestation of honky-tonks and cheap commercial outlets where narrow streets bottlenecked traffic to a snail's pace. City planners dreamed improbably of tearing down the whole unsavory mess and starting over.[29]

Blueprints called for downtown commercial strips to yield to a huge cultural center between the Norfolk (now Chrysler) Museum and a new Center Theater/Civic Auditorium complex. A main library would rise at the area's center, the Confederate Monument moving to a nearby minipark. Offices of civic and charitable organizations might occupy adjacent sites, maybe corporate headquarters of major businesses, even a "consulate row" of NATO trade delegations. There should be a major convention hotel, a municipal aquarium or naval museum, sidewalk cafes, restaurants, and parks. All this would blend with existing Georgian and Federal period houses on Ghent and Freemason streets and Smith Creek's Hague Yacht Basin with its waterfront park, bridges, and footpaths. It would make downtown the focus of municipal activity, a compelling attraction to tourists and visitors.[30]

Meanwhile, the waterfront would be transformed with sea walls, an amphitheater, parks, and promenades. A big Port Authority concrete pier, with cafes and specialty shops, would accommodate the largest ships afloat. A big new quay would have a small-boat marina, travel agencies, seafood vendors, restaurants, and so on.[31] In 1946 the city planning commission, now with a full-time staff, had made a study of the need for annexations for planned development. A 1948 report showed less than one-fifth of the city's land undeveloped, a ratio far less than most cities of comparable size. With Norfolk certifiably overcrowded, hired annexation experts proposed that the city's size be doubled. Tanner's Creek district and twenty-five square miles of mostly open land east of it in Princess Anne should be taken in, besides twelve square miles of the industry-heavy Washington district south of the eastern branch (Portlock and Money Point). Norfolk, it was assumed, must eventually front the Atlantic Ocean. Moreover, the annexations must occur before urbanization undermined planning options and made them too expensive.[32]

This was a vision of growth beyond anything Norfolk had known and an expense that must undercut improvements needed within the existing boundaries. But the logic of annexation seemed so compelling that the council decided to take much of the proposed area anyhow. Norfolk County, facing loss to the city of tax revenues, set up a howl and South Norfolk moved to annex the Washington district to itself. Almost at once, the council came up against the state supreme court, which ruled that Norfolk must take in the Tanner's Creek area, already fully urbanized, before proceeding against Princess Anne. That threw everything off schedule, but the council moved aggressively toward its goals.[33]

By June 1950 the *Virginian-Pilot* had surrendered. The vision and energy of the city council over the past four years was undeniable; its accomplishments surpassed all expectations. The year 1946, the paper conceded, had seen "a political revolution." Cooke, Darden, and Twohy, smitten by barrages of conservative criticism, held to their promise not to run again, but the programs they had generated seemed certain to continue.[34]

Perhaps the greatest surprise in the postwar years was the reversal of the situation after World War I: the engine of the city's wartime growth continued pumping with hardly a cough. The menace of Soviet power and acquisitive thrust meant that the navy had to remain at wartime strength. Norfolk, like Charleston in its favorable climate for year-round operations and central position in the Atlantic defense line, found itself the beneficiary of military and other federal activity in peace as it had been in war. Housing and other facilities designed for destruction at the war's end were now deemed essential for the indeterminate future.[35]

Private enterprise took its cue from international events. The Norfolk and Western Railway in 1946 announced plans to spend $6 million on its local port facilities, Ford reopened its Newton Park plant, and the United States Gypsum Company ordered a big plant in Berkley. Soon, Sears and

Roebuck began work on a huge new store on Twenty-first Street to replace that on Freemason, and Norfolk and Southern took options on one thousand acres in Princess Anne for its McGinnis Industrial Center to lure more manufacturers to the area. In April 1950 WTAR TV brought the area its first television broadcasts and the end of the year saw forty thousand sets of talking furniture installed in the vicinity.[36]

Changes in American lifestyles were reflected in Norfolk, which was unaware of the extent of its own contributions to the new modes. The habit of eating on the run, for example, owed something to Fred Phillips, a deputy constable in 1946, who in 1908 suggested to a peanut-butter firm, Bosman and Lohman (at Norfolk and Western's Granby Street crossing), that it market its product between crackers. The company let him hire four women to give door-to-door samples of peanut-butter sandwiches. The response led the company to assign him its New Jersey territory, where consumers thought peanuts grew above ground like grapes. But they liked his sandwiches and National Biscuit Company soon sent Phillips an order for thirty thousand, placing the little sandwich in the big time.[37]

Peanut butter itself, first concocted in St. Louis in 1890, owed much to Robert I. Bosman and Julius G. Lohman, the first to make and distribute it nationally. They founded their company on Commercial Place in 1891 to manufacture candy and other confections, but began making peanut butter with a sausage grinder as soon as they heard about it. Their product, marketed as "Nut-Let," became the "best known brand in the world." Bosman and Lohman made tons at a time at the Granby Street factory they occupied in 1902. Bosman and Lohman discontinued operation in the 1920s, leaving the field to Skippy in Portsmouth and Planter's in Suffolk, among others.[38]

A year before Fred Phillips dreamed up cracker sandwiches, Abe Doumar, a Lebanese immigrant peddling Holy Land souvenirs at the St. Louis Exposition, suggested to a waffle vendor that he shape waffles into cones and fill them with ice cream. The treat was at once popular, and Doumar soon opened his own ice cream cone stand at Coney Island. He put one up at the Jamestown Exposition in 1907 and did so well that he opened another at Ocean View, later moving his family from New Jersey to Norfolk. (On a day in 1925, Doumar's Ocean View stands sold a tongue-chilling 22,600 cones.) Abe's brother George opened a shop on Monticello Avenue in 1934 where, at this writing, Al or one of his kin still makes two hundred cones each evening in one of Abe's orginal waffle machines.[39]

Norfolk's strong musical tradition was enriched when Conductor Edgar Schenkman, a graduate of the Juilliard School of Music, in 1948 took charge of the symphony orchestra and civic chorus, the groups merging in 1949. From amateurs giving three performances a year, the symphony was converted into a semiprofessional group offering jointly with the chorus eleven annual performances, three of them for children. Former navy bandmaster I. E. Feldman in 1946 formed the Feldman Chamber Music Society, which gave an annual concert series. William and Mary's Norfolk division three years later began its Opera Workshop.[40]

A study of library facilities in 1958 found Norfolk "one of the most underprivileged cities in the United States" in that respect. It had about one-third of the library system of most cities its size. The study proposed spending $2.5 million for a downtown main library and three branches in new areas besides better placement of three other branches. Costs seemed prohibitive, but a $500,000 gift by Miss Bessie Kirn allowed work to begin in 1960 on a modern main library at City Hall Avenue and Bank Street and a new Ocean View branch.[41]

Meanwhile, Frederic Huette, superintendent of the city's parks and forestry, enhanced Norfolk's reputation for its lovely flowers. Having already embellished Lafayette Park and the Azalea Gardens, Huette in 1947 cleared more land at the latter and planted it with azaleas, rhododendrons, daffodils, and camellias along new miles of trails. In 1950 the League of Virginia Municipalities recognized him for outstanding work in beautifying Norfolk. In April 1954 the first International Azalea Festival drew thousands of spectators to the garden for the events, including the crowning of a queen of the Azalea Court.[42]

That the New Era in city government had yet to solve many of Norfolk's problems was brought home in a July 1949 *Saturday Evening Post* article. The writer thought Charles Harrel an astute city manager and Port Authority leader E. O. Jewell (lured from New Orleans) a top-notch official. Harrell got deserved credit for improving water and street lights, building and fire-prevention codes, and a tough licensing policy aimed at "quickie" hotels and speakeasies. Norfolkians were generally polite and their climate pleasant. Some residential areas even bespoke "an American Venice of neat houses edging on creeks and inlets."[43]

But the writer slammed Norfolk's "too-easy social conscience." East Main's honky-tonks bred the nation's highest rate of venereal disease; the three-mile-square black slum district had "ragged tenements ranged along rutted streets and muddy sidewalks" with "outdoor privies, one to four families or more." White slums around the coal yards were little better. There were few parks or theaters. A later issue carried letters from Norfolk castigating the *Post*'s failure to mention Granby Street's beauty or the quality housing occupied by many blacks. But Mrs. A. F. McKinney, who had moved to Norfolk three years earlier, claimed to have seen "through the mists of tradition and priggism which have strangled the growth of this town."[44]

A new trio of councilmen, the "Harmony Ticket," with W. Fred Duckworth, formerly the Ford plant manager, as mayor, in 1950 succeeded the 1946 reformers and reinforced the positive initiatives of its predecessors. Duckworth was to serve six terms as mayor, during which epoch no councilman ever voted against an NRHA proposal. The new council wanted a juvenile detention center, a water bond issue, the rebuilding of twenty-one thoroughfares into major highways fed by wide collector streets, and new taxes on cigarettes and utilities.[45] Its plans for the future, evolving rapidly, soon embraced much else besides.

The early years of the Duckworth administration (its council in 1951 expanded to seven) coincided with the Korean War, which broke out in 1950 and brought further infusions of defense spending. In 1952, when Supreme Allied Command Atlantic offices opened, Norfolk became headquarters of the first peacetime international navy. The reconditioning of the aircraft carrier *Lake Champlain* and battleship *Kentucky* at the naval shipyard and an air defense center at Dam Neck were among the new military projects, though Norfolk was not subjected to the human and material inundation that accompanied World War II. In 1951 General MacArthur, commander of United Nations forces in Korea, visited Berkley for a dedication of the Hardy home, a memorial to his mother.[46]

Seaborne traffic became so heavy that the navy did more damage to itself than the Koreans and Red Chinese could. Even in 1948 the dreadful swamping of a launch from the carrier *Kearsarge* cost the lives of thirty sailors returning from liberty to their ship off Old Point Comfort. Five died in 1951 when a seaplane tender collided with a collier off Cape Henry and five more the next year when a navy transport and a Texaco tanker rammed one another in the same waters. In the interim, the navy suffered its worst peacetime disaster when the minesweeper *Hobson*, a few days out of Norfolk, hit the carrier *Wasp* in midocean, with the loss of 146 crewmen of the former. There was also a high number of groundings and other marine mishaps in the area during 1952.[47]

Among the leading commercial ventures of the Duckworth years were a large VEPCO plant at Gilmerton in 1951, Esso Standard Oil's 1954 plan for a refinery of over eight hundred acres in Portsmouth, Cargill, Inc.'s 1956 decision to put a 2.1 million-bushel grain elevator in South Norfolk, and Colonial Stores' announcement of a $5 million operations center for Broad Creek Village. In August of the latter year, a record eight hundred commercial ships entered Hampton Roads. The Hampton Roads Maritime Association at year's end exclaimed that "Never before . . . has there been as much business, as many new and expanded facilities and services, as many ships loading and unloading, or sailing to as many ports, or as many people earning a living in maritime activities."[48]

The annexation of the Tanner's Creek district climaxed in 1954, Norfolk being required to pay the county $8 million in compensation and spend $2 million more on Tanner's Creek improvements. To win over reluctant Tanner's Creekers, the city set up a Public Relations Institute, sent speakers to public meetings, and published a semimonthly paper, *Residents of Tomorrow,* to peal the benefits of annexation. Tanner's Creek population swelled Norfolk to 290,000 and an area of over 121 square miles, making it, as of January 1, 1955, Virginia's largest city. But planners turned promptly to annexing thirty-three square miles of Princess Anne (almost all of the Kempsville district).[49]

As Norfolkians looked ahead to the Kempsville expansion, they conceived an urban goliath formed by joining a Greater Norfolk with Portsmouth and even Newport News into one of America's great cities. Opposition within the city and protests from Princess Anne County seemed only the sort of obstacles so often overcome before. Small voices must not deter the locomotive of destiny.

But the annexation court turned a sour glare on Norfolk's application, dragged the issue out to 1959, and finally let the city take only thirteen and a half square miles (less than a third of what it sought)—an area that was already developed. The annexation cost the city another $3 million and left the ratio of developed to undeveloped city land worse than when the annexation program began in the 1940s. It was a mortal blow to the Grand Design. On January 1, 1963 little Virginia Beach merged with Princess Anne County to create a metropolis of 255 square miles, forming what is now Virginia Beach; South Norfolk merged with Norfolk County to create the new city of Chesapeake. Norfolk City's fifty square miles were walled off from expansion in any direction. The Chesapeake Bay Big Apple was not to be.[50]

Some major Norfolk needs were being addressed by the general assembly and the military. In 1956 the army drew plans for a hurricane sea wall to protect downtown from flooding while the legislature approved a second

Norfolk–Portsmouth tunnel and a physical link between the eastern shore and the South Hampton Roads mainland. Work had also begun on a three-and-a-half-mile bridge-tunnel across Hampton Roads from Hampton to Willoughby.[51]

A general assembly grant in 1952 gave the Norfolk division of the College of William and Mary funds for a new library, opened in 1959 (with a fine arts building in 1960), to make possible a four-year program. Enrollment, spurred by the "G. I. Bill," had surged after the war and now approached five thousand. The school awarded its first four-year degrees in June 1956 and, four years later, the legal path was cleared for it to become an independent school. Norfolk Polytechnic Institute (now Norfolk State University), also a four-year school, moved its 1,800 students in 1955 to its new campus on Corprew Avenue.[52]

That Norfolk, along with eight other American cities, in 1957 was awarded a "Community Home Achievement Award" by *Look* magazine was welcome recognition but might be dismissed as a ploy to sell magazines. Two years later, however, *Newsweek* carried a less ostentatious notice of Norfolk as a place where, "In the coming decade, even the sailors are certain to pipe a happier tune." Norfolk, it appeared, was on its way to becoming "the Manhattan of the South [dare we hope?] once the new Chesapeake Bay Bridge-Tunnel has been built." Its housing and redevelopment program, the bridge-tunnels to Portsmouth and Hampton, were seen as handsome achievements for a city that had been "called many things in its frowsy past, . . . most of them unprintable."[53]

As the city eyed suspiciously the rose petals strewn in her path, Colgate Darden was invited to Springfield, Massachusetts, in late 1959 to argue Norfolk's worthiness to receive the National Municipal League's (and *Look*'s) All-American City Award. Darden, governor in the years of Norfolk's "worst war town" image, accepted the challenge and spoke of his adopted city's late rebirth as "the most remarkable thing [Jamestown, Williamsburg, and Yorktown, hold your breath!] to have happened in Virginia." His adopted city boasted a vigorous public housing program, an outstanding medical center, a new Golden Triangle Motor Hotel and Maritime Tower Building (part of a major downtown redevelopment), and such laudable citizen initiatives as a successful drive for funds to raise faculty pay at William and Mary's Norfolk division.[54]

There were twenty-two finalists, but Norfolk learned on February 4, 1960, that it was one of eleven winners, the only other in the South being Winston-Salem. Three Virginia cities (Petersburg, Richmond, and Roanoke) had won the honor in the past decade. The awards jury praised the new civic and medical centers and industrial park as monuments to a city reborn. Special notice was paid to "the mighty citizen effort" to eliminate blight by tearing down 326 acres of decrepit housing and relocating five thousand families, as well as attacks on tuberculosis and organized vice. Clearly, the source of most of the gains was the splendid work of the Norfolk Redevelopment and Housing Authority.[55]

The All-American Award reflected completion of NRHA's Projects I and II, the first for 190 acres of slum clearance for low-rent housing, wider streets, boulevards, and controlled business and industrial development. Project II, launched in 1956, aimed to replace the two-thirds of Atlantic City's housing considered substandard with apartment buildings overlooking garden plots and the water. A waterfront expressway was planned, along with a medical arts complex comprised of the Municipal Public Health Civic Center, King's Daughters Hospital for children, and Medical Office Tower around an expanded Norfolk General Hospital. Broad Creek Village's "demountable" World War II housing had been torn down to make room for the 468-acre Norfolk industrial park. The rebuilt municipal airport was dedicated in May 1951.[56]

Newspapers called attention to NRHA Director Charles Kaufman and Executive Director Lawrence A. Cox, as deserving praise for the city's national prestige. Buried in the glowing reports were the self-effacing words of Chamber of Commerce Chairman Pretlow Darden, whose vision and energy helped initiate the renaissance fourteen years earlier: "It was hard work and cooperative efforts of the citizenry that made it possible."[57]

The year 1960 seemed to many Norfolkians a watershed in the long and tempestuous history of their maritime city, a beginning, at least, of liberation from decades of ill-fortune and scathing rebuke. A bond issue was approved in February, assuring a second Elizabeth River tunnel, its opening scheduled for early 1963. (The bridge-tunnel to Hampton had been in use since late 1957.) Historian Marvin Schlegel, in 1960 updating the Wertenbaker city history of 1930, sang of a coming decade that might unite southside cities and counties, and a 1970s that could "mould both sides of Hampton Roads into a single harmonious community."[58]

Acceptance of the All-American City award was attended by more pomp and circumstance than officials had time to think through carefully. A ceremony was held at city hall on February 4; Mayor Duckworth made the announcement and a blue and white award flag, to fly all year, was hoisted at the Plume Street entrance, the city council beaming from the steps. On

March 3 an official award luncheon at the city arena was attended by over 1,200 people. The arena was decorated in red, white, and blue bunting, with shields of all eleven winning cities decked in greenery behind the head table. The Navy's CinClant band played, *Look's* publisher made commendatory remarks, and Duckworth hoped the award would "only be the starting point for making Norfolk a better place to live."[59]

An even more obvious starting point was outside the window as the mayor spoke. Oddly out of harmony with the self-congratulatory proceedings were several black members of the Congress of Racial Equality picketing on the sidewalk. One, attorney Joseph A. Jordan, a crippled war veteran, carried a sign declaring that "Discrimination and Segregation are not All-American."[60]

Inquiries revealed that forty-one blacks had signed a protest that invitations to the award luncheon excluded blacks. Last-minute arrangements put two blacks, including Rev. Eugene Brown, on the guest list and opened the ceremony to the public, but the protesters called for a black boycott of the proceedings. Black real estate and insurance man Harry A. Reid applied to City Manager Thomas F. Maxwell for a picketing permit for five to ten people and was denied. Maxwell offered lamely that the luncheon, sponsored by the Chamber of Commerce, was a private affair for civic club members. The question why hung heavily unanswered.[61]

It was not just indignation at being left out that prompted the protests. Norfolk had won its award despite a traumatic showdown with the monster of school integration. Little progress had been made in uprooting the old fences of racial separation; NRHA's low-income houses were as isolated from white communities as the hovels of old. Among other disreputable incidents, the Coronado section had been the scene in 1954 of a racially motivated bombing.[62] Norfolk's blacks, like the students staging a "sit-in" at Woolworth's lunch-counter in Greensboro, North Carolina, as the All-American awards were presented, were, at long last, fed up. In fact, Duckworth's unprecedented political strength and tenure were already doomed.

CHAPTER 25

A Sojourn in the Byrd-Cage

POSSIBLY no body of public officials ever faced a seemingly more impossible situation. U.S. District Court Judge Walter E. Hoffman's order of June 7, 1958, directed Norfolk's school board to assign 151 black applicants to all-white schools for the coming year. But state laws, passed two years before, required any school with both black and white students, whether voluntarily or by court order, to be closed and removed from the public school system.[1] What was needed was the knowing wink, the symbolic gesture, that was customary from authorities in such crises. But Hoffman failed to signify how his order was to be avoided.

Chairman Paul T. Schweitzer and three of the five other school board members reflected Norfolk's strong desire to keep the schools open; they thrashed around for a way out of the impasse and seemed in a few weeks to find one. Rigidly applying guidelines adopted earlier in the summer, the board on August 18 rejected all 151 applicants. The reasons given included concern for the pupils' health and safety, their social adaptability, and their place of residence.[2] This gave Hoffman a face-saving excuse to rescind his order on the high ground of concern for the children's welfare and so provide reassurance that he knew how the game was played.

Hoffman, still unaware, it seemed, of what was needed, rejected the ploy. He demanded that the board review its findings and report to him by August 29, though agreeing that applicants might be assigned to white schools nearest their homes. The board on the final morning reluctantly admitted to six white junior and senior high schools seventeen black applicants who met every defensible qualification. It asked that the court defer the admissions until September 1959, by which time the Supreme Court might have reconsidered its own position. Hoffman refused, as did the Fourth Circuit Court of Appeals on September 27.[3]

Norfolk's last hope was flexibility from Richmond or else its white high schools must close. But Governor J. Lindsey Almond Jr. was in no mood or

A suit on behalf of these seventeen applicants finally opened Norfolk's public schools to blacks in 1959 after a period of "massive resistance" to integration. (Courtesy of The First Baptist Church, Norfolk, Va.)

position to be flexible. He had championed segregated schools as attorney general and the Byrd machine's 1957 gubernatorial candidate. His victory was seen as a mandate for the state's official policy of massive resistance to integrated schools. Guided by Richmond editor James J. Kilpatrick and the ghost of John C. Calhoun, Byrdmen exhumed an old notion that states in certain circumstances could exercise sovereignty against the federal government to prevent encroachment on constitutionally reserved state powers.[4]

The signal that Norfolk would not be spared came on September 8, 1958, when Almond closed Warren County's schools, where other black students sought transfer to white institutions. Like Charlottesville, Norfolk had postponed school opening in the hope of rescue, but Charlotteville schools closed on September 19. Eight days later the axe fell: six white Norfolk schools were closed—Maury, Granby, and Norview high schools, Northside, Blair, and Norview junior highs. Fifty other city schools with some forty thousand students were unaffected, but ten thousand white students were evicted, by far the largest number of any Virginia system.[5]

The situation abounded in irony and contradiction. By Virginia standards, Norfolk was cosmopolitan, with fifty thousand naval personnel in port at any given time, its businesspeople inclined to cooperate with the federal government on which the local economy depended. The Norfolk Ministers' Association and Ministers' Fellowship were interracial, as were some twenty boards devoted to education, health, and religion. The Catholic schools had integrated without incident in the mid-1950s. But Norfolk's workforce was drawn heavily from Southside and North Carolina counties, where resistance to integration was intense. Seashore State Park, a wooded area on the bay to the northeast, had been closed for four years owing to a legal standoff between integrationists and segregationists.[6]

The Byrd organization had less support in Norfolk than in Virginia as a whole and the city would favor Kennedy liberalism in 1960 when Nixon carried the state. The Charlottesville, Warren County, and Norfolk school closings came in opposition to local majority feeling and to satisfy segregationists elsewhere. Black schools stayed open, no whites having applied to enroll in them.[7]

Some Norfolk school officials had been on a collision course with the Byrd machine since 1954, when School Superintendent J. J. Brewbaker proposed "an intellectual rather than an emotional" response to the Supreme Court's *Brown v. Board of Education* ruling. Given state intransigence, however, Brewbaker and the school board resisted NAACP calls to plan for an early end to segregation. The NAACP itself found its opposition to state policy impeded by state laws restricting its activity. But the Norfolk NAACP and its president, Rev. John Henderson, in October 1958 filed suit in behalf of the seventeen blacks denied admission to white schools.[8]

Norfolk was deeply divided. A voice for open schools was Dr. Forrest White's Norfolk Committee for Public Schools (NCPS), formed in September, which was kept all-white to retain legitimacy with the white community. Besides letters and petitions to officials, the NCPS in October filed its own suit against the governor on behalf of white realtor Ellis James, whose daughter was a locked-out Maury student, and others. Teachers, through the Norfolk Education Association, called loudly for reopening, as did the Women's Council for Interracial Cooperation and numerous ministers. The Junior Chamber of Commerce mustered a bare majority in favor of reopening.[9]

Norfolk also had a chapter (since 1955) of the Defenders of State Sovereignty and Individual Liberties (DSSIL), a name by which racism sustained itself in an era when its more blatant expressions were socially unacceptable. DSSIL President James G. Martin IV saw in integration a Red plot to mongrelize Americans and split them into warring factions. It was a threat to be taken as seriously as the Red aim to fluoridate drinking water and surrender American sovereignty to the United Nations. DSSIL came down hard on the school board for assigning blacks to white schools against state law. In the same camp was the Norfolk Council of PTAs, led by W. I. McKendree, a charter member of DSSIL.[10]

Leola Beckett and other black parents, with NAACP support, had in 1956 filed suit against the Norfolk school board. They sought admission of their children to white schools by attacking the state's Pupil Placement Act under which a state placement board routinely rejected black applicants to white schools. Judge Hoffman declared the placement act unconstitutional in its effects, but Attorney General Almond replied that Virginia would observe its terms until appeals were exhausted. This gained the state some two years of delay. Black Norfolk parents also brought the 1958 suit under which Hoffman ordered blacks placed in white schools.[11]

With their high schools padlocked, white parents scrounged for alternatives and prayed that colleges and universities might be willing to stretch accreditation and entrance standards. DISSL set up a Tidewater Educational Foundation (TEF) to create private classes for unschooled students, but found its effort resisted by those who saw in it a scheme to undermine public education. TEF President Martin made a call on October 3 for volunteer teachers but was unable to secure the services of any of Norfolk's 450 locked-out teachers. Still, TEF found outside teachers and enrolled 270 students in its classes.[12]

Part of the educational void that fall was filled by teachers who, unwilling for so many students to miss graduating, formed tutorial groups in churches and wherever space was found. South Norfolk's Oscar Smith High held night classes for 950; others were accommodated by nearby communities or left their homes for classes elsewhere. Vivian Mason, a community activist and first of her race in modern times to serve on the school board, created a tutoring group for the seventeen displaced black students. Teachers, still under state contract, continued to draw salaries, but fees were charged for transportation and materials or costs were met in other ways. Football schedules were retained, the closed schools playing full slates, though bands performed without uniforms, which were locked in gymnasiums.[13]

Despite makeshifts, over 2,700 children were unaccounted for and presumably ended their educations in the spring of 1958. Some could not afford private schools, did not live within commuting distance of tutoring groups, or opted for alternatives such as marriage, jobs, or military service. Even those with alternative schooling usually found it a poor substitute for the opportunities and activities they had known in public schools.[14]

Norfolk could gain attention by winning national awards but never so much as when things went badly. Newshounds descended on the city to ask people how they felt about school closings, and broke the news globally that they did not much like it. After in-depth research, *Life* and CBS learned that many Norfolk whites did not want to go to school with blacks. *The New York Times Magazine, Boston Sunday Globe,* and *Time* joined in.[15] Only a still graver crisis in the schools of Little Rock, Arkansas, seemed to prevent Norfolk's inundation by reporters vying frantically with one another to belabor the obvious and obviate the laborious.

What these forays did not reveal was a way out of the trouble. Neither the federal government nor Almond's administration gave any indication of yielding. Norfolk, twitching forlornly between the Potomac rock and Richmond's hard place, watched helplessly as its public schools disintegrated before its eyes. The first city in Virginia to have public schools—and possessor of the state's largest school system—seemed to be on its way to becoming perhaps the first to lose its schools. The city council, it soon appeared, was anxious to facilitate precisely that outcome.[16]

Mayor W. Fred Duckworth, now head of his own powerful political machine, could be blamed for the agony as much as anyone. A man of high managerial and political skills, he had by the mid-1950s seen the NRHA's ambitious initial redevelopment program through to successful conclusion. He also found it a superb instrument for enhancing his control through NRHA power to determine which structures to demolish or exempt, decide the acquisition value of targeted property, depress the worth of property considered for demolition, dispose of cleared lands, and apply leverage with local banks and lending institutions. For example, the National Bank of Commerce (now Sovran), a preserve of many financial leaders, was a major beneficiary of NHRA investment funds.[17]

By 1956 Duckworth, discarding plans of reformist predecessors for a downtown cultural center, contrived his own second phase of NRHA goals. It included a dramatic Project II to clear 135 acres in Atlantic City to expand Norfolk General Hospital and provide new highways and tunnels, and thirty-seven Lambert's Point acres for the growth of what is now Old Dominion University. Also, some 2,600 Broad Creek houses would be demolished for a Tidewater Drive light industrial park. Scarcely were the plans announced than NRHA came up with a scheme to rip out two hundred acres of the city's oldest part, including the East Main honky-tonk district, for wider streets, parking, modern commercial development, and other uses.[18]

The package of projects was twice the scope of those of any other American city and ten times larger than Project I; it would raze some five hundred commercial buildings and displace more than twenty thousand people. It would create many new jobs, attract business and industry, eradicate many delapidated structures, give employment to armies of professionals, bring in vast new funding, and wipe out many sources of the old sin-city image. Few public critics of the mayor's dictatorial rule remained, but no doubt many of those were won over by the breadth and rapid initiation of his program.[19]

Elements of the black community, led by Joseph A. Jordan and J. Madison Grant, detected a hidden agenda in NRHA's bold projects. Atlantic City redevelopment would spare Ghent, home of many wealthy families, from contamination by doomed black middle-class and ghetto neighbors; a Lambert's Point project meant a buffer between working-class neighborhoods and Larchmont and Edgewater elites. No public housing would be built for the uprooted thousands, though help was available to relocate families. Most painful was the abolition of deeply rooted community ties and institutions. Redevelopment gurus, preoccupied with large, impressive edifices, looked less to such needs than to a city hall, public safety building, Kirn Memorial Library, Treasure Island at the Azalea Gardens, Courts Building, and financial centers.[20]

Communities where blacks had begun to acquire homes and white flight was occurring were hardest hit by NRHA bulldozers. It could be argued that the new projects aimed at clear separation between white and black communities to forestall court-ordered integration. (The preservation of segregated housing was an obvious goal.) Some also suspected an intention through redevelopment to rid the city of its poor. In areas where, owing to their proximity, whites and blacks might be assigned to the same schools, school buildings were earmarked for demolition or other uses, or surrounding communities were engineered into single-race districts.[21]

It was a glaring shortcoming of Duckworth's administration that the mayor allowed himself to earn the antipathy of much of black Norfolk. His commissions and committees had no blacks in policy-making roles except as recreation commission advisors; his police force had no blacks above the rank of patrolman. In June 1958, when black leaders asked him to appoint a biracial committee to forestall growing racial ill-will, the mayor uttered a coarse racist rejoinder that shocked reporters and others who heard it. The incident helped unite blacks in opposing him and redouble their effort to integrate the public schools.[22]

As the school crisis wallowed to a climax in the late 1950s, some observers of the powerful redevelopment impetus espied another impending crisis: the decimation of the city's material heritage. As clusters of buildings fell, revered architectural relics went with them. Cobblestoned streets, elegant

Federal-era townhouses, and landmark monuments stood directly in the paths of wrecking crews. The 1960s might see the last physical links with the past smashed and downtown Norfolk made over into a gleaming facade of glass, steel, and concrete towers. Nothing might remain to suggest that the city had not descended full-blown from the sky from the 1940s, a place with no discernible past. A similar razing had happened in 1776 when war swept the colonial town away; now the remnants of Federal and Victorian Norfolk were threatened and, as before, by friends rather than enemies.

Even Norfolkians with slight regard for emblems of yore could appreciate that a rootless city, an Elizabeth River Levittown, might hold little allure for tourists. If bright young engineers from distant places meant Waterside Drive to bisect cobblestoned portions of Freemason and Bute, then maybe the plan should be reconsidered. But it was only in May 1963 that concerned citizens formed the Norfolk Historic Foundation and began trying to save what was left of the city's heritage. Much that deserved sparing was already gone, but the foundation gained clout from membership in the National Trust for Historic Preservation, whose trustees included Norfolk's influential Henry Clay Hofheimer.[23]

Under President Barron F. Black, the foundation set out to acquire and restore the Willoughby–Baylor House, built by William Willoughby in the 1790s at Freemason and Cumberland. The first building on the site was Freemason's Hall—hence the street's name—where Dunmore and his lady were feted at a ball in 1774. The Moses Myers House farther along Freemason was under the wing of the Museum of Arts and Sciences and safe from redevelopers. Through the National Trust, Norfolk profitted from the experience of such cities as Savannah, Richmond, and Charleston, all embarked on their own preservation programs.[24]

Although Lawrence M. Cox, the NRHA executive director, had the power of eminent domain to devour virtually anything in his course, he proved to be an ally of the preservationists. The proposed route of Waterside Drive had already been diverted for preservation purposes, and the landmark customs house and juvenile court building were spared. There was reason to hope that the Whittle, Armand-Archer, and Oliver S. Glisson houses on Duke Street, among others, might be saved by the wave of citizen activism.[25]

Special circumstances saved the city hall-courthouse, where the city council had met before moving in 1918 to the Norfolk Armory. Built in 1851, it was converted in 1962 by New York architects William and Geoffrey Platt and Norfolk's Finley F. Ferguson into a city-owned memorial to General MacArthur. The general came to Norfolk in May 1963 to dedicate it as a "museum-memorial-mausoleum" and, as the *Pilot* put it, "a tourist attraction of the first rank for Virginia's largest city." When MacArthur died in April 1964, his remains were interred beside a space intended for his widow in a crypt under the rotunda. The rotunda's walls held panels depicting his military exploits and extracts from his speeches. Throughout the building were displays of personal and military memorabilia.[26]

The general's mother, Mary Pinckney Hardy MacArthur, was born in the Riveredge section of Berkley where he too, would have been born but for the transfer of his parents, General and Mrs. Arthur MacArthur, to Little Rock just before their son's birth in 1880. (A Norfolk paper reported his birth as occurring "while his parents were away," a remarkable beginning for a remarkable man.) As in life, MacArthur remained controversial in death. Many letters to local editors complained of the costs and seemliness of the memorial, though others warmly endorsed it. The Jean MacArthur Research Center, housing the general's papers, a theater, and a gift shop, was later erected on MacArthur Square.[27]

Lingering in limbo were such structures as old Fort Norfolk by the river at the south end of Colley Avenue. The original fort was an earthwork built in 1794. The present brick structure was erected about 1810 by the Army Corps of Engineers, but had never inflicted injury on an enemy. In 1923 it became the corps' district headquarters but survived in the 1980s only as a storage facility, its arched entrance, guardhouse, and tiny dungeon the artifacts of purposes long forgotten, its future hanging on some brainstorm of adaptive restoration or commercial development.[28]

Norfolk's new interest in preserving its past reflected a more general hope of retaining humane and livable qualities in a city sprawling upward and outward at an almost frightening pace. What was trumpeted as an "art boom," as measured in the number of area art shows, paintings sold through galleries and outdoor shows, and regional and national prizes won by local painters, had begun in the 1950s. The birth of the phenomenon was concurrent with the coming of Charles Sibley to Norfolk in 1955 as head of the art department at Old Dominion College. In subsequent years, Sibley nurtured whatever talent he could find, built an excellent art faculty, and in many ways fostered local interest in art.[29]

An example of this interest was the Boardwalk Art Show, which began as a small Virginia Beach affair in 1956 but soon became a major Tidewater event with a mile of paintings by more than three hundred artists. The Norfolk Arts Festival, inaugurated in 1961, developed simultaneously into an important month-long showing, while shopping centers throughout the area held their own weekend shows through much of the year. Leading artists of the era included, besides Sibley, A. B. Jackson of the Norfolk division of Virginia State College art department, and Walter Thrift.[30]

In 1965 the Norfolk Little Theatre opened its first summer season and gave forty-two performances of four plays. They included *The Snow Queen* for children, *The Thurber Carnival,* and *The Knack* by Ann Jellicoe. The Little Theatre began in 1959 as a workshop for experimental plays; the Little Creek Players was composed of service personnel and their families. Norfolkians also enjoyed access to Paul Green's outdoor dramas: Williamsburg's *Common Glory,* Roanoke Island's *Lost Colony,* and, in 1958 and 1959, *The Confederacy,* in an unlikely Virginia Beach setting.[31]

Sports fans had turned Norfolk's annual October "Oyster Bowl" football game (intially for high schools) into a major attraction. The 1965 game was preceded by a morning parade of four thousand, including service and high school bands, the William and Mary Queens Guards, Shriners, floats, flag-carrying girls, motorcycle police, and others, sweeping down Bank Street and City Hall Avenue to Granby Street. Professional football had had a dismal introduction in 1954, when a Philadelphia–Baltimore game drew only a small crowd to Foreman Field. In 1960, however, with televised pro games creating a mass audience, the Redskins and Eagles met on the same field before twenty thousand spectators.[32]

The city in 1965 gained its own pro football team, the Neptunes (the name Gobs was proposed and, happily, rejected) of the Continental League. This helped compensate for the 1955 departure of the Tars pro baseball team, Piedmont League pennant-winners from 1951 through 1954 and cradle for such Yankee careers as those of Yogi Berra, Phil Rizzuto, and Whitey Ford. But it meant that backers had to try to find jobs for thirty-eight pro players, who had to work by day and practice by night, their salaries being minimal. An initial game against Hartford's Charter Oaks was lost, 21–17, by the Neptunes and the league soon collapsed. More successful was something touted by promoter Joe Murnick as professional wrestling, which involved a great deal of grunting and grimacing but little else to qualify it as a sport.[33]

Another Norfolk flourished around the three-story, red-brick Plaza Hotel at Church and Eighteenth, a favorite with entertainers of "the Chitlin' Circuit": musical greats such as Louis Armstrong, Nat "King" Cole, Count Basie, Billy Eckstine, Cab Calloway, and Ella Fitzgerald. Proprietress Bonnie McEachin was by 1955 the Nationwide Hotel Association's "Hotel

Woman of the Year." She threw big annual Valentine's Day parties for children and sent busloads of underprivileged to the circus. The Plaza, long since closed, burned in 1980. In its prime it was favored for formal dances, Mother's Day outings, and other festive occasions; its celebrated clientele were wildly cheered at such places as the Breezy Point Officers' Club and Norfolk Municipal Arena though denied lodgings at the Monticello, Commodore Maury, or other well-known hostelries.[34]

A few blocks away, Frank Guida, self-styled "Latin from Manhattan," was recording on his LeGrand label a group known as "The Church Street Five." Their drummer, Emmett "Nabs" Shields, and his "double bass drum lick" introduced what was first called "the Norfolk Sound" and, later, after being purportedly adopted by an obscure English group called the "Beatles," "the Liverpool Sound," a beat that altered rock 'n roll's history. Gary Anderson, later internationally famous as Gary U.S. Bonds, one of the most successful LeGrand artists, sent tunes like "New Orleans" and "Quarter to Three" to the top of national charts.[35]

Norfolk redevelopers roared into the 1960s with all the furious energy they had showed in the previous decade. Since the first slum-clearing in 1951, the face of downtown had been transformed. The goal now, by tackling remaining pockets, was to make Norfolk the first American city entirely to rejuvenate its central business district. It meant a face-lifting and maybe canopied sidewalks for a nine-block "retail core" of variety shops, department stores, and so on bounded north by Charlotte Street and south by City Hall Avenue, between Boush Street and Monticello Avenue.[36]

By 1965 redevelopment had cleared over one thousand acres of slums (and many perfectly sound structures) and, in its early phase, put up over five thousand public housing apartments. Skyscrapers were being erected for the Virginia National and Seaboard Citizens National banks on redeveloped downtown property. A new Brambleton Avenue connected eastern to western Norfolk, and Waterside Drive was under construction. If Downtown Norfolk Association President Kurt Rosenbach, realtor Hunter A. Hogan, and others had their way, part of Market Street would be a pedestrian plaza for downtown ceremonies, promotions, and so on. Boosters foresaw a million people living in the seven-city Hampton Roads area by the mid-1980s, and area beaches yearly drawing hundreds of thousands of vacationers.[37]

A burning issue was how large to make the coliseum planned for a fourteen-acre tract fronting Brambleton Avenue at Charlotte Street. Consultants in 1965 recommended a facility of five to eight thousand seats, which many thought too small. Mayor Roy B. Martin Jr. wanted up to 11,000 seats, and Old Dominion Athletic Director Bud Metheny, anticipating big-time basketball at his school, was sure nothing less than 12,000 would suffice. Advocates of the larger building argued that Norfolk had lost chances to host trade shows, circuses, ice extravaganzas, and other spectacles because it offered no suitable accommodation.[38]

The whole Hampton Roads area was also on a binge of high-rise apartment construction. Norfolk had many choice locations and Pembroke Towers, opened in 1962, was the first to soar twelve stories upward from its site on the Hague, the tallest previous apartment buildings being eight stories. Soon afterward, ground was broken for the Hague Apartments opposite Pembroke Towers, and Lafayette Towers on Delaware Avenue. Virginia Beach meanwhile watched its Virginian rise on Atlantic Avenue and Portsmouth its Crawford Place on Crawford Street. Such quarters were affordable and attractive to those in upper income brackets who disdained or could no longer handle the cares of homeowning. The high-rise lifestyle also offered social amenities and services often unavailable to those in separate residences.[39]

The last vestige of Norfolk's physicial isolation disappeared with the opening of the $140 million Chesapeake Bay Bridge-Tunnel in April 1964. (Norfolk's "Midtown" tunnel to Portsmouth opened in 1962.) Planners foresaw the extension of the heavily urbanized Northeast, for better or worse, down Delmarva Peninsula to draw the Hampton Roads megalopolis into a sprawling "Boswash" already stretching from the Potomac to southern New Hampshire. The 17.6-mile engineering marvel, involving four manmade islands and two tunnels under a pair of bay ship-channels, completed a process begun with the opening of the James River Bridge in 1928. There was even talk of a third Elizabeth River tunnel, a second under Hampton Roads, and a branch tunnel off the bay bridge to Hampton.[40]

Redevelopment brought about desirable downtown social changes apart from blotting out honky-tonks and ghettoes of the poor. By early 1963 skid-row "smoke-hounds," once prevalent in weed-filled lots, old warehouses, and deserted residences, seemed to have vanished. These were derelicts who, unable to afford whiskey or wine by the bottle, strained denatured alcohol from twenty-cent cans of liquid heat through a rag or sock and mixed it with soda or fruit juice for a potent "high." People were known to die or go blind from the concoction. One such unfortunate, known to police as "Snake Man," habitually carried a pet snake coiled about his waist or under his hat. Deprived of their haunts by urban renewal, "smoke-hounds" did not vanish but merely deployed to other run-down areas in East Ghent, Berkley, and Lamberts Point.[41]

Only slowly in the 1960s did realization dawn that, apart from its manipulation to perpetuate segregation, redevelopment might be guilty of technical misjudgments. James McNally's 1965 letter to the *Virginian-Pilot* reflected growing critical reaction to what was afoot. He noted that downtown business, especially along Granby and to the west, had fallen steeply. Automobiles took shoppers to peripheral shopping centers, while public transport declined in variety and efficiency. Redevelopment had moved many residents from easy access to downtown business; new high-rises had not taken up the slack. The city government's core was the new civic center at the foot of St. Paul's Boulevard, an inconvenient walking distance for government employees to Granby Street.[42]

Professional critics discerned in redevelopment a proliferation of large buildings of haphazard design on ill-chosen sites. The "auditorium and sports arena . . . float in isolated splendor on an elevated plaza" overlooking a motel, a bus station, and piles of bricks, "sterile arenas . . . walled off from . . . the community by arterial roads and concrete pods." New barrier highways defeated the urban core's "natural interaction"; slum clearance destroyed the city's "historic scale and texture . . . , leaving the surviving buildings alone in a wasteland where the street signs were the only other markers." Redevelopment (like the slums it destroyed) cut Norfolk into self-contained pockets, hurting downtown business and, perhaps, any genuine sense of community.[43] The next steps in urban renewal had to include remedies for its mistakes.

In the meantime, the school crisis had led to sharp alteration in the character of the city's political leadership. Mayor Duckworth and the city council, with Clerk of Courts William Prieur, Senator Byrd's Norfolk viceroy, sided with the forces of massive resistance and were ready, in late 1958, to cut off funding for black high schools to "spread the burden" of closed schools. But the action threatened to divert attention from downtown renewal projects, considered by leading citizens vital to Norfolk's future, and delay their commencement. Elements of the old "People's Party" began to stir restlessly with desire to restore the coalition of the late 1940s and return leadership to those unwilling to exalt the segregation issue over basic economic goals.[44]

Businesspeople worried about the navy, many of whose families were affected by school closings. Few navy families could afford private schools but many were trapped in Norfolk for their tours of duty. It was not surprising that the morale of navy personnel declined during the fall, some joining the Norfolk Committee for Public Schools, others seeking transfer to different stations. Business leaders feared that the navy's patience might be strained to the point of moving certain operations elsewhere. It was also noticed that new businesses were bypassing Norfolk to locate in North Carolina, where schools remained open.[45]

Duckworth and the council insisted that overwhelming public opinion opposed desegregation; Governor Almond in 1957 had received the largest percentage of Norfolk votes of any candidate in over half a century. Blame for the school closings, the mayor felt, rested squarely on the shoulders of ungrateful blacks who attacked what he called "the best city in Virginia in regard to its colored population." Blacks, he added with a startling want of tact and relevance, made up 75 percent of the city's jail population but paid less than 5 percent of its taxes.[46]

Parents and others put pressure on the city council, through letters, petitions, and personal appearances, to find some way to reopen the schools. In response, the council in late 1958 called for a referendum on whether to petition the governor to reopen the schools on an integrated basis. In doing so, the sponsors expected the proposal's defeat and sought to ensure that outcome by wording the ballot to warn that reopened schools would mean substantial tuition payments by parents to replace state funds. With only 21,000 voting—an astonishing show of apathy over so basic an issue—the proposal to petition the governor was defeated by a margin of three to two. (Some perhaps felt that the referendum was, at best, a symbolic gesture.)[47]

Virginian-Pilot editor Lenoir Chambers kept up a staccato sniper-fire against massive resistance in general and the council's malignly worded referendum in particular. Steps to close black schools seemed to him "little and mean in spirit and dictatorial in action." Segregationists brutally attacked his stand, but Chambers won the 1959 Pulitzer Prize for his uncompromising editorials on the school issue. (The sister *Ledger-Dispatch*, on the other hand, supported massive resistance and assailed the federal government's integrationist stance.) In 1959 Chambers also published his two-volume biography of Stonewall Jackson. His and Joseph E. Shank's graceful history of a century of Norfolk newspapers, *Salt Water and Printer's Ink*, appeared in 1967.[48]

The city council, giddy with the success of its referendum, now severely overreached itself. On November 25 it moved to eliminate funding for all of the city's black high schools and their seven thousand students. Councilman Roy Martin's dissenting vote was the first breach of council unanimity in

Duckworth's eight and a half years as mayor. The council's action generated a firestorm of protest; even Governor Almond called it "a vicious and retaliatory blow against the Negro race." But on January 19 (Robert E. Lee's birthday) the federal district court and the Virginia supreme court handed down decisions in the cases of *James v. Almond* and *Harrison v. Day* (the Norfolk NAACP suit), respectively, both ruling Virginia's massive-resistance policy unconstitutional.[49]

Many fence-straddlers may have been influenced by Edward R. Murrow's CBS documentary, "The Lost Class of '59," broadcast on the night of January 21. Although carefully nonjudgmental, it allowed many Norfolk viewers for the first time to see their plight as it was viewed elsewhere around the country. Norfolkians squirmed at what seemed to be their status as pariahs, their city a den of extremists who drowned out the thin, small voice of moderation.[50]

Even now the city council maneuvered to find a way to resist integration, but the January 26 issue of the *Virginian-Pilot* carried what proved to be the coup de grace against the council's attitude. It was a declaration, bearing one hundred signatures of leading business and professional men, that, while preferring segregated schools, they strongly favored open schools to closed ones; they urged the council to effect reopening "as promptly as possible." Accompanying editorials in both the *Pilot* and the segregationist *Ledger-Dispatch* endorsed the statement. The principal recruiters for the petition included Pretlow Darden, NRHA Director Charles Kaufman, and Frank Batten, publisher of both papers. Next day a similar statement by one hundred younger civic leaders appeared. Duckworth faced a full-scale insurrection.[51]

On February 2, 1959, the six white high schools reopened after eight months, with the seventeen black students in attendance. Plainclothes policemen stood sentinel at and near the schools to handle violence but, to the city's lasting credit, none occurred; it was an eerily calm conclusion to one of the most difficult half-years Norfolk had ever endured. Returning to classes were 6,868 of the "Lost Class of '59" out of the original ten thousand. Meanwhile, Almond called the general assembly into special session and began backing away from massive resistance. Desegregation in Norfolk was extended in September 1959 to an elementary school and five more black students, a tokenism that belied the transformation of the legal-judicial landscape over the preceding year.[52]

It was fortunate for the future of Virginia's race relations and public education that Norfolk was a primary target of the forces of massive resistance.

The unusual makeup of the city's population, its strong ties to the federal government, especially the navy, a business community alive to the danger massive resistance posed for redevelopment and economic well-being, and other factors, made this a dangerous place for social reactionaries to experiment. Public school teachers, especially, displayed considerable character in responding to the emergency and, when parents seemed to grow complacent over private schooling, in announcing that tutoring groups would end by January 1, 1959, if the high schools had not reopened.[53]

The crisis brought the revival of the coalition of businesspersons, blacks, and politicians that inaugurated redevelopment in the 1940s. Duckworth declined to run again, and the 1962 city elections saw business progressives, supported by the newspapers and west-side precincts that had backed the old "People's Ticket" and "Committee of 100," win decisive majorities. Billy Prieur remained secure at the clerk's office but found it politic to reach accommodation with the new leaders. Meanwhile, the Norfolk Committee for Public Schools in the 1959 general assembly elections backed two successful candidates for the Senate and six for the House. This election saw the advent into public life of Henry Howell, destined to be a key figure in the city and state affairs for years to come.[54] There would be no more tilting at integration windmills; the city had trouble enough of other kinds.

CHAPTER 26

The Greening of Norfolk

I T WAS NOT unlike a first encounter with some lost tribe which, after centuries of isolation, is discovered through the persistence of intrepid explorers. Inevitably, there was a rush of scholars to the haunts of the tribesmen to study them in their natural habitat. Soon came the *papparazzi* for photos of outlandish specimens, and journalists to chronicle curiosities of manner, speech, dress, and religion. There was a ripple of excitement in the art and fashion worlds in adapting for commercial exploitation styles peculiar to the tribe, as well as a gaggle of articles and master's theses tracing the roots of the language, myths, beliefs, and political structures of this intriguing people.

Surprisingly, the teenagers (*Adolescens americanus*) had lived in Norfolk unnoticed, it seemed, from the 1680s or before. Over many generations, they had been misidentified as a part either of the tribe of children or that of adults and had gone unclassified as an altogether separate group. Their discovery in the 1960s came as a shock, the intrusion of an alien element into traditional patterns. The public must now accustom itself to sections of newspapers, radio and television programs, devoted to the group's exotic ways. Worse still, teenagers were scarcely found before analysts pointed to profound influences they were having on society at large.

Teenage dress, for example, might be primitive, but it made its undeniable mark. "Do Teen Spenders," asked the *Virginian-Pilot* in 1968, "Set Tidewater Fashion Pace?" The answer was not yet, but trends were clear. Retailers knew that 37 percent of Norfolk–Portsmouth's population was under eighteen (with 27,752 teenage females), many with almost unlimited use of charge cards and spending a larger proportion of available funds on clothes than their parents. Those in college came home with a yen for what was popular on campus, though perhaps a season or two behind New York and London; miniskirts and body shifts, the rage elsewhere, only reached Norfolk as the 1970s began. Others wanted what they saw in movies or magazines. In August and September 1967 area teenagers spent over $6 million on clothes and accessories.[1]

Clothing stores paid keen attention to teenage tastes, but what did it signify for adults? Norman Goodwin, buyer for the Tree House, told the *Pilot* that Norfolkians in their late twenties or thirties were "afraid to admit they're looking at teens for fashion but they are. They want to look young and sharp especially in their dressy and casual wear." The Virginia Beach surfing crowd was the major trend-setter for the area's casual and summerwear and swimsuits.[2] Few adults realized the extent to which teenyboppers influenced what stores carried; in fact, they were taking over.

Teenage economic clout was not confined to clothing and accessory shops. In 1965 a new institution, the coffeehouse, blossomed in Norfolk alleyways. Youth thronged to these places to sip coffee and cider in dark, mysterious surroundings, and to listen to folk, jazz, and other types of music, to hear mandolins, dulcimers, banjos, autoharps, and guitars (electric guitars were discouraged because they drowned out folk singers). At some coffeehouses, like The Folk Ghetto on West Freemason, poetry reading was in vogue for a mostly college and high school clientele. Here, candles lit tiny tables covered with red cloth, and girls (often enough, boys as well) wore their hair long and straight. Even the attic in Colley Avenue's Lutheran Church had such a place, called, of course, The Attic.[3]

Some three thousand teenagers squeezed daily into pulsating dance emporia called discotheques, which began to appear around 1964—the Ebb Tide and Jolly Roger at Ocean View, the Peppermint Beach Club and Top Hat at Virginia Beach. Soon came the Beachcomber at the naval base entrance, the Congo, Peppermint Lounge, and others at Seaside and elsewhere, reverberating to The Big Beat. This rite consisted of a "hypnotic, repetitive, thumping explosion" of rock and roll, arms and hips twisting wildly, partners often separated by wide intervals. The movements had names like the Jerk, Monkey, Stomp, Slop, Bird, and Twist. ABC board rules banned the go-go girls and special lighting of true discotheques, but many patrons came during daylight hours to dance barefoot in bathing suits.[4]

Disco cacophony and caterwauling were unable to still tribal yearnings for orgiastic celebration; summer and fall brought huge rock and roll festivals. Some 250 teenage rock and roll bands bespread the *Virginian-Pilot* circulation area (west to Southampton County, south to Hyde County, North Carolina) and the paper in 1966 sponsored a festival that attracted thousands from both states and featured groups in age categories of seventeen to twenty-three and thirteen to sixteen. Bedlam reigned at the new Scope in July 1972 with the Rolling Stones and Mick Jagger, "A vision in skin-tight, purple, sequined jump suit, with ratty brown hair and darting eyes." Columnist Lawrence Maddry stared agape at "teens in jeans and bare belly buttons . . . squirming in time" while Mick "pranced with mincing, mocking movement of his lean, skinny flanks."[5]

Students of teenage myths and religious beliefs found them to range from unreflective orthodoxy to the woozy outer fringes of metaphysical speculation. A house in Granby Street's 300 block was headquarters for the Children of God, already under fire by the early 1970s, when it arrived from the West Coast, for allegedly kidnapping and brainwashing its members. The proximity of Hugh Lynn Cayce (son of deceased psychic Edgar Cayce) and his Association for Research and Enlightenment, Inc. at Virginia Beach helped make local teenagers and many adults susceptible to trendy prattle about recalling former lives. Psychic Jeane Dixon drew a capacity crowd when she appeared at the Norfolk Arena in 1967 to lull the skeptical and cull the gullible.[6]

If some teenagers led bizarre and meaningless lives, others were role models of wholesome traditionalism. Norfolk's Debbie Shelton in the spring of 1970 won the title of Miss Virginia before sashaying across a Miami Beach stage to victory as Miss United States, and Sallye Anne Austin two years later carried off the title of Miss Black Teenage International Beauty Pageant. Austin, a Lake Taylor High sophomore, was a member of the Norfolk Civic Ballet, Shelton an Old Dominion University senior. Shirley Thompson, of North Shore Road, graduated from singing in *H. M. S. Pinafore* and other Norfolk productions to mezzo-soprano roles in *Carmen* and *Il Trovatore* for the Heidelberg Opera Company.[7]

Teenagers were more liable than others in the social order to take up causes. In 1963 some two thousand Booker T. Washington High students marched to protest overcrowded and "unbearable conditions" in the school. Hundreds participated in Earth Day activities at Old Dominion in 1970 to show concern for the deteriorating Hampton Roads environment. Enthusiastic crowds heard speakers on air and water pollution, erosion, and other ecological topics before discarding cold-drink cans and paper cups along grassless shortcuts to their dorms. Thousands took part in the May 1971 Walk Against Hunger, coordinated by Maury's sixteen-year-old Esther Anten and Granby's eighteen-year-old Mickey Garrison.[8]

Teenage zeal for causes and such lighter fare as Mick, ESP, and the Slop may have blinded analysts to a darker side of youthful concerns. Readers of underground campus literature might have noted attitudes far more menacing to the established order than the craze for rock and roll or the fleeting allure of coffeehouses. At Old Dominion, for example, campus radicals published *Brown Shoes,* a saucy sheet that waged guerrilla warfare against the school administration, city police, "welfare bureaucrats," and authority figures in general. At Norfolk State College in 1969 a professor came under student fire for assigning papers on a *U.S. News and World Report* article purporting to show that blacks were incapable of conceptual reasoning.[9]

Not only in the newly recognized teenage subsociety but among adults as well there was a climate of spiritual and, less often, intellectual experimenting and groping. Beyond the stained glass and silver service of mainline churches was a sprawling spiritual world of ragged little congregations where a dozen or so gathered regularly for a kind of communion unavailable elsewhere. They called themselves Mt. Olive Apostles Church of Faith, Jesus Christ Charity Faith Temple of Apostles, Emanuel Temple, Jerusalem Holy Church, Holy Temple of Apostolic Faith, and so on. They occupied converted pool halls, barber shops, and beer taverns, and were known collectively as "storefront churches."[10]

Such groups were found in the 1960s and later in Ghent, along Princess Anne Road and Church Street, and elsewhere, sometimes outnumbering regular churches. Some had women ministers, a practice discouraged by older denominations. They tended to have short life spans, dying here, reemerging there, shifting from site to site, ministering always to those who felt alien or unwelcome in the comfortable solemnity of older churches. Their communicants also included a few like Larry Cherry, a former Norfolk State College student, who told a reporter in 1966 that Emanuel Temple on Church Street brought him a peace and joy he found nowhere else: "The Holy Ghost presents itself there and thrills our souls. It is a feeling like no other in the world."[11]

The year 1960 saw the death of the colorful and charismatic Bishop C. M. "Daddy" Grace, who had lived for some years in Norfolk but presided over a spiritual empire of 350 churches across the country. Those in Norfolk were on Church and Freemason streets and Bowden's Ferry Road. Claiming to be a native of Lisbon, he first appeared in Norfolk in 1926, the year he opened his first church in Charlotte. By the 1950s he was nationally known and enormously successful, able to erect an apartment house, Grace Village Apartments, on East Princess Anne Road, where he had a top-floor residence. He also had an eighty-five-room mansion in Los Angeles, a coffee plantation in Brazil, an egg hatchery in Cuba, and other holdings. His version of Christianity was unblushingly upbeat, with ample room for brass bands and colorful parades.[12]

"Sweet Daddy," as he was known to some who thought him the Messiah or even God, was said to have ten thousand Norfolk followers at the height of his career. But his empire went into steep decline after his death and, by 1965, only one of his Norfolk churches remained—a big red, white, and blue edifice on Olney Road where only a few dozen members attended with regularity.[13]

What "Daddy" Grace lacked was TV, a medium pioneered in the area by Rev. M. G. "Pat" Robertson, son of former Virginia Senator A. Willis Robertson. In 1959 Robertson bought a defunct Portsmouth country-and-western station for his "faith-keyed" programming. He parlayed a $3.00 commercial checking account into a multimillion-dollar enterprise. Robertson became one of the most successful of a new breed of hat-passing tele-vangelists; by 1967 he was offering a full schedule of UHF programs on Channel 27 and radio station WXRI, including the "Jim and Tammy Show" for children. By now his Christian Broadcasting Network planned to buy a Bogota, Colombia station and produce programs for showing worldwide.[14] It was only the beginning.

A vibrant mainline church was the Annunciation Greek Orthodox, which in 1971 celebrated its sixtieth year in Norfolk. Tidewater had some three thousand citizens of Greek descent, nearly all Greek Orthodox and many active in a dozen Greek organizations, including the Hellenic Woman's Club, Greek American Civic League, and American Hellenic Educational and Progressive Association. Norfolk's Greek community traced its origin to the year 1900, when John Gretes and the George Christopouloses opened a Main Street shoe store, the first of what became a three-state chain. Later, concessions run by Pericles Boogades inaugurated the Ocean View Amusement Park and Christopolous opened Virginia's first movie theater, the Eagle, on Main Street.[15]

Norfolk had little that might be called a "hippie" community, but small groups of teenagers and older companions were scattered about in the cheap housing of East Ghent and other slums. These were part of a major problem Norfolk's redevelopers only began to face squarely in the late 1960s. So far, the focus of the expensive redevelopment programs had been bricks and mortar. As slum-dwellers vacated downtown areas ahead of the bulldozers, many moved into old or substandard housing in Ghent, Berkley, Park Place, and elsewhere.[16] Slums were not so much eradicated as simply pushed farther back from downtown.

Ghent was a middle- and upper-class residential area developed in the 1890s, with Botetourt Street, Orapax Avenue, Princess Anne Road, and Mowbray Arch as its borders. Work began in 1899 on a new area of Ghent, including Stockley Gardens, where Colley Creek once ran. Nestled across Smith Creek (renamed the Hague) from Norfolk's business center, it was a pleasant walk or trolley ride for professional men to downtown offices and for their wives to the best stores and markets. But the last major project there had been the Norfolk Museum of Arts and Sciences in 1933, after which parts went into slow decline; well-to-do families moved farther out and the Victorian houses were divided into apartments. To the east, a middle-class East Ghent emerged. It also deteriorated during and after World War II, though at a more rapid rate.[17]

Redevelopment leaders came to realize what was happening to East Ghent and at length sought ways to arrest or reverse the process. In 1963 a federally sponsored "war on poverty" program, the Southeastern Tidewater Opportunity Project (STOP), began looking into the problem, but mostly limited its service to encouraging local initiative. It was not until 1967, following a Norfolk visit by Housing and Urban Development Secretary Robert C. Weaver, that a formidable alliance was arranged between federal and local forces and coordination introduced into the work of social service agencies. As a result, East Ghent became part of the federal Model Cities Program, and sizable sums became available for the human as well as physical renewal of the area.[18]

By this time East Ghent was a basket-case of unpainted houses, dark and ruptured streets, curtainless windows, garbage-strewn sidewalks, broken glass, and poor black children playing in grassless yards. Projected redevelopment hastened the decay. The promise of the East Ghent Project, as the Model Cities effort there was known, was that ramshackle houses would be demolished (beginning in 1970) and replaced with a healthier mix of lower-, middle-, and luxury-class housing. This might repair much of the area's human damage and give redeveloped downtown some of the consumers and workforce routed by great office complexes and thoroughfares.[19]

That was the promise. By late 1971 East Ghenters complained that, with demolition well underway, no housing was yet started for the evicted. The *Ledger-Star* in 1973 explained that new homes were not erected for the thousand East Ghent families already displaced because "extra care . . . has gone into planning the new community." But the windows in that explanation kept out none of the cold and the roof failed to keep out the rain; a long time would pass before East Ghent partook of Model Cityhood, and many were forced to thrash about in the interim as best they could. The older West Ghent area, meanwhile, enjoyed something of a renaissance in chic regentrification as preservationists moved into some of the grand old homes and put them in mint condition.[20]

Redevelopers were bombarded with complaints of similar problems elsewhere. The lower end of Church Street had been streamlined into a downtown plaza, civic center, and St. Paul's Boulevard. But the street's upper portion, containing the heart of the black business community, steadily decayed. Businesspeople there complained that it was "dirty, dull, and uninteresting," that the city must share the blame because it allowed inadequate police, street cleaning, and lighting. Loafers and toughs congregated in the Church Street area; burglaries, muggings, and vandalism kept shoppers away. Massive clearance and rebuilding were not needed, but help to upgrade and renew the district's appeal to clients. As with Granby Street, however, Church Street was succumbing to new shopping centers.[21]

A Church Street Business and Professional Association was formed in 1965 to find solutions. Consultants proposed more off-street parking, landscaping, and removing overhead signs. The association looked to city hall for help. In 1966 the papers reported the city laying plans for Church Street. A *Ledger-Star* item in 1973 noted that the city "stands generally ready to join in soundly-based improvements for which there is a demonstrated need." Soon, a "major plan" to revitalize Church Street was "in the works." By 1975 the city council had plans "to assist revitalizing" Church Street business—and the two-term Nixon presidency had come and gone.[22]

Sometimes the whole redevelopment program seemed to come temporarily unglued. In 1973 it was reported that property values on downtown Granby had dropped sharply in the previous five years. In the six blocks from Brambleton Avenue to Main Street, fourteen business locations were vacant and more of the 152 remaining likely to become so. Shoppers found dirty sidewalks, battered trash cans, derelicts, and beggars. Some saw the solution in turning Granby into a traffic-less mall, an idea later tried and abandoned. Louis B. Fine, owner of several of the properties, thought things would improve "as soon as the Housing Authority gives Granby Street as much consideration as is given Church Street."[23]

Granby could not compete with the sixty-five shopping centers in the South Hampton Roads area, including the sprawling Military Circle complex near new Virginia Beach Expressway (opened in 1967) intersection with I-64. A West Virginia sailor, after a brief sojourn, took home news that the downtown shopping area was "a tiny little section where millions of traffic-snarled roads come together in one mammoth mess." Traffic on the Chesapeake Bay Bridge-Tunnel was below projected estimates; 1972 Census figures showed Norfolk's population down by 25,000 in two years.[24]

Even so, a nineteen-story Seaboard Citizens National Bank Building had lately gone up downtown. Ground was broken in 1973 for the $12.3 million Omni Hotel; its designer, Maurice D. Alpert, soon announced a big shopping and entertainment complex, modeled on Copehhagen's International Gardens, nearby. NRHA had always known that long delays would be necessary to insure the best use of available land. Still led in the late 1960s by Charles L. Kaufman, it had for a quarter-century enjoyed a remarkable continuity of personnel and purpose. The tenure of Vice Chair James E. Etheridge ("Father of the Oyster Bowl") also went back to the 1940s, as did that of Pretlow Darden; it remained Kaufman's aim to make Norfolk "one of the nation's first slum-free cities."[25]

Equally stable in leadership and aim was the Port Authority, since 1960 known as the Norfolk Port and Industrial Authority (NPIA). NPIA pushed energetically in the 1960s to develop Norfolk International Terminals (once the army terminal) into a modern container facility to accommodate the container ships that were revolutionizing the shipping industry. (A Portsmouth facility at Pinner's Point threatened to become a major rival.) It also operated the expanding Norfolk airport and some buildings in the industrial park, which it rented to private firms. Its general manager, James N. Crumbley, had come from New Orleans with the first general manager, Edward O. Jewell, as had Jewell's immediate successor, Michael M. Mora. Even Crumbley's secretary, Mrs. Catherine Cuykendall, had been with the NPIA since 1948.[26]

Commercial flights from the Norfolk municipal airport by 1967 numbered fifty-two daily with seven hundred thousand passengers a year, about half of them military. Despite a major expansion of facilities in 1959 and a new terminal in 1964, passengers often lined up from the ticket counters back to the wall and drank coffee standing up in the coffeeshop for want of enough tables. A freight terminal, new roads, and expanded parking were planned, though existing runways, according to airport manager Charles P. Mangum Jr., were adequate for another decade or so. The airport's accessibility was much enhanced when the Virginia Beach Expressway opened.[27]

Another in Norfolk's array of authorities was the Norfolk Area Medical Center Authority, created in 1964 and first chaired by Dr. Mason C. Andrews, a Norfolk native. A medical tower with office space for eighty doctors had opened at Norfolk General Hospital in 1961, the region's first full-time medical research laboratory in 1967. These were seen as steps toward an Eastern Virginia School of Medicine, the state's third such institution. The facilities would attract top-flight researchers and specialists, adding immeasurably to Norfolk's importance and prestige as a center of medicine.[28]

The original proposal for a medical school had come in a 1959 civic address by Lawrence Cox, though doctors as early as 1812 or before envisioned such a school. A national shortage of physicians and interns lent urgency to the prospect, but a study showed that Norfolk had the second-highest ratio of people-per-doctor of the nation's fifty largest cities.[29]

Dr. John S. Thiemeyer, president of the Norfolk County Medical Society (NCMS), in 1960 called for a feasibility study, an idea that won Mayor Duckworth's support and Medical Society action in 1961. Mason Andrews, Thiemeyer's NCMS successor, had by now taken on the project as a personal crusade. Funds were raised from city, state, federal, and private sources, the latter including $1.2 million from Mr. and Mrs. Sidney Lewis of Richmond, large grants from the Oscar Smith Memorial Fund, Virginia National Bank, and Landmark Communications. What was called "the greatest challenge this community ever tackled" became a reality in 1973.[30]

The Museum of Arts and Sciences, opened in Ghent in 1933, was for thirty-five years chiefly a repository of Tidewater historical artifacts and a few pieces of prized artwork, including Renoir's oil sketch, *Trees on the Bank of a River*. But in 1968 Mayor Roy Martin got a call from Mrs. Walter P. (Jean Outland) Chrysler Jr., a Berkley native and Martin's former classmate at Maury, about a permanent home for the Chrysler art collection, then in cramped quarters in Provincetown, Massachusetts, and a New York City warehouse. After some discussion, it was agreed that the collection would go to the Museum of Arts and Sciences, and that its name would be changed to The Chrysler Museum. Norfolk would provide $1 million for a new museum wing and maintenance.[31]

This was an art bonanza such as few cities possessed and thrust the Chrysler to the front rank of American museums. Chrysler, son of the automotive tycoon, was said to own the nation's second largest collection of glasswork besides a huge number of paintings, a total of over 25,000 objects valued at $60 million. Although Chrysler released the artpieces in small numbers for tax purposes, the museum ultimately held over 85 percent of his collection. (Much was lost at his death as he was about to reword his will to convert the loan to a gift.) Norfolk gained the Chryslers as residents and, in Mrs. Chrysler, an active patron of art and productions of the Virginia Opera Association. (A museum board chairperson who resented renaming the museum was replaced by a businessman representing the city power structure.)[32]

The Chrysler gift led to naming the theater, opened in 1972 near Scope Coliseum, the Chrysler Theater. Its 2,500-seat auditorium did for stage shows what Scope did for sporting events, ice capades, and circuses. Here could be staged *Hello Dolly!* and *The Sound of Music* (or the Virginia Opera's *Lucia di Lammermoor* and *Barber of Seville*), shows barely performable in the old center. State-of-the-art acoustics and red, gold, and teak decor enhanced the pleasure of attendance. There were ten office or meeting rooms, a dressing room-lounge for receptions or prima donnas, a three hundred-seat rehearsal hall, main and side lobbies, and a hall for dances and formal gatherings. The new structures gave downtown Norfolk a pair of magnets to recapture the lost clientele of previous years.[33]

The Norfolk Symphony, by now in its second century, made bold strides under the leadership of Russell Stanger, who became its conductor in 1966 and, within a decade, saw its budget increase from about $90,000 to almost $250,000. With the city's population constantly in flux and no large industries whose generosity might be regularly tested, the Symphony Opera, Little Theater, and other artistic institutions and groups depended on such devoted supporters as Ruth and Pierre Schmitz, Alan Hofheimer, and others. The 1976 Festival of the Arts in July and August offered a cornucopia of plays and films, art and craft shows, dance performances, music, and other attractions.[34]

Even without the new theater and coliseum, Norfolkians were exposed to a wide range of cultural opportunities, apart from those of neighboring cities. In 1968 the area gained its fifth dinner theater (at Lake Wright Motor Lodge), and concerts were offered by Old Dominion College and the Norfolk Community Concert series. Over sixty thousand attended the city park 1967 summer arts festival; guest performers that year ranged from Van Cliburn, Victoria de los Angeles, Jose Greco, and the Czech Philharmonic Orchestra, to popular offerings such as Ferrante and Teicher, Fred Waring, Johnny Mathis, and the Peter, Paul, and Mary trio.[35]

Norfolk's sons and daughters who made their mark in the world of high culture included black artists Lorraine Graves, a product of the Academy of Tidewater Ballet and ballerina with Arthur Mitchell's Dance Theater of Harlem. Terri Tompkins of Norfolk performed with the same company. Charles Holland, who quit Booker T. Washington High School and at nineteen went to Europe, became a leading tenor with L'Opera Comique de Paris, the Nederlandsche Opera in Amsterdam, and Oslo's Norske Opera, among others. He had an emotional return to Norfolk in 1983 to sing with the Virginia Philharmonic. His race had barred him from working with American companies; as Holland put it, "the tenor gets the girl."[36]

Norfolk's shimmering prosperity was symbolized by the Ford assembly plant on Springfield Avenue. Repurchased from the navy in 1946, the seventy-three-acre facility built 3 million vehicles between 1925 and 1974. Converted in the latter year from cars to trucks, it began a multimillion-dollar expansion and by 1977 employed over 2,500 people with a payroll over $58 million. More typical was the James G. Gill's Company factory on West Twenty-second Street, whose forty-five workers processed fifteen tons of coffee a day. One of the country's few remaining regional coffee roasters, it was founded in 1902 when Gill put a coffee roaster in his Water Street wholesale grocery. It had remained a family business ever since.[37]

To bury its dead for the next six decades, Norfolk in 1971 acquired land for the forty-four-acre Riverside Cemetery, its seventh public graveyard. Others were Cedar Grove in 1824 on what is now Princess Anne Road, Elmwood in 1853 (its west end reserved for blacks and called West Point) on the same road, the Hebrew Cemetery at Princess Anne and Tidewater Drive in 1857, Forest Lawn at the Bunting Farm on Granby in 1906, Magnolia, and Calvary (north of Roberts Park) in 1911.[38]

Overseeing this multidimensional growth and change was the coterie of businesspeople and financiers who resumed power after the Duckworth years. In 1971 Norfolk gained stature in Richmond with the election of its own Henry Howell as lieutenant-governor. (A populist who eagerly took on "Big Boys" such as the Virginia Electric and Power Company, Howell soon made enemies among the state's more conservative leaders and was to lose three campaigns for governor.) The council responded to the growing clamor of blacks for political entitlement by naming black leaders to boards and commissions while declining to put them on the administration ticket in councilmanic elections.[39]

Enemies as well as friends mourned the death of former mayor Fred Duckworth when he was shot to death near his home on March 3, 1973. A member of the Chesapeake Bay Bridge-Tunnel Commission, board chairman at Cavalier Ford and the MacArthur Memorial (his brainchild), Duckworth left his Riverfront home around 6:30 in the evening for his usual walk, made a telephone call at a booth on West Little Creek Road, and was shot six times as he returned home along Major Avenue. The identity and motive of his assailant were never learned.[40]

The distinction of becoming the first black to breech the city council

During the post–World War II decades, Mrs. Evelyn T. Butts and Joseph A. Jordan, Jr., were extremely active and effective in civil rights issues, community development activities, and other key roles in the city. (Courtesy of *The Virginian-Pilot*)

fortress was that of attorney Joseph A. Jordan Jr. in 1968. Four years earlier Jordan had brought the historic suit ending the poll tax; he was to crown his career in 1977, after a period as vice mayor, with a seat on Norfolk's general district court. (John Charles Thomas, a Norfolk native and graduate of Maury High, in 1983 would become the first black on the state supreme court.) In 1969 Dr. William P. Robinson, head of Norfolk State University's political science department, was elected to the House of Delegates (where he was one of two blacks and the first to represent Norfolk in the twentieth century).[41]

Women, too, fought their way into the city's inner political circles in the 1960s. Mrs. Evelyn T. Butts, a powerful black voice on the city's Democratic Committee as forty-second precinct representative, won her party's highest state service award in 1981. Betty Howell, wife of Lieutenant Governor Henry Howell, in 1974 became Norfolk's first city councilwoman, bringing to city politics a brand of populism not unlike that of her husband.[42]

Norfolk gained stature as an educational center with the 1966 opening of Virginia Wesleyan College on a three hundred-acre site astraddle the Norfolk-Virginia Beach boundary near Landsdale Traffic Circle. It was the first of four "Academic Villages," such as Jefferson had planned for the University of Virginia, which were eventually to comprise the Virginia Wesleyan campus, students living, working, eating, studying, and playing under single roofs.[43]

Undergraduates were concerned by many things, but none more than the military draft. Clarence E. Perry III of Norfolk State's ROTC Pershing Rifles drill team, felt strongly that none "should duck the draft." In a burst of fatalistic patriotism, he told the *Virginian-Pilot* in 1966 that "You're going to have to go one day anyway, so you may as well make the best of it." Shelton Baise, senior history major at Old Dominion, was sure the draft was unfair, often interrupting educations. Some local teenagers were said to rally to the national emergency by inhaling cigarettes soaked in iodine to cause temporary spots on their lungs and insure draft-board rejection. Dean of Student Affairs G. William Whitehurst complained that ODU lost a hundred students a term to the draft, which fouled up planning committees.[44]

Negative attitudes toward the draft led to a protest by some ODU students in February 1967. Several belonged to the school's chapter of Students for a Democratic Society (SDS), the occasion being a campus visit by Dow Chemical Company recruiters, who were greeted by raw eggs and heckling for Dow's role in making napalm. A March 10 faculty censoring of the protesters was welcomed by SDS as helping to raise its esprit de corps.

But freshman Lynn Adams could not find that protesters had "a good logical reason to disagree" with Dow's agents. An SDS "newsletter" on the issue was promptly banned by the Student Activities Committee for two "objectionable words" from an e. e. cummings poem, raising cries of "political censorship" even from the faculty senate.[45]

Teenage impatience with their elders, local and national, poured out in a tumult of fear and anger in May 1970 after the killing of four antiwar demonstrators (eleven more were injured) by National Guardsmen at Ohio's Kent State University. If foes of the war and draft needed martyrs to galvanize adherents, they must now make the most of it. On May 5, the day after the shootings, 250 students marched to the office of ODU President James L. Bugg Jr. as a peaceful "expression of revulsion"; the Student Government Association (SGA) called for a memorial service in honor of the dead students. The campus Americans for Democratic Action demanded President Nixon's impeachment for sending American troops into neutral Cambodia (announced on April 30).[46]

Meanwhile, about thirty Virginia Wesleyan students held silent vigil on the dining hall steps as students and faculty circulated a petition for Nixon and the Congress to reconsider the Cambodian affair. On May 7 about four hundred students at Norfolk State called for a boycott of classes on May 18, and the SGA endorsed it. By the next day, some two thousand (about half the student body) had voted to boycott. SGA President J. Anthony Sharp, a Vietnam veteran with an Air Medal for thirty combat missions, called the war an "indecency" and said the boycott should last until the war ended and Black Panther leader Bobby Seale was freed from jail. On May 14 patrolmen killed two more students at Mississippi's Jackson State College.[47]

From mute obscurity, teenagers emerged as a potent force in shaping foreign policy and perceptions of the administration's credibility. The radical blaze roared on across campuses, sucking in other issues. Lawrence Maddry's *Pilot* column told of ODU students selling "Strike" T-shirts bearing red clenched fists to promote a twenty-four-hour class boycott, a sign asking students and faculty to wear black clothes or armbands. Forums were scheduled on campus police, Kent State, ROTC, and other concerns. At NSC, Nixon was burned in pin-striped effigy; protesters burst into classes to slam students' books shut, erase blackboards, and shout, "Classes are cancelled. We're striking." But the strike's main target, most said, was white racism. Campus sessions were held on the Black Panthers and the scheduled integration of Crestwood, Booker T. Washington, and other area black schools.[48]

The teenage voice was less than monolithic. Robert R. Brunner Jr. of

ODU felt that "most students are apathetic and don't really care" about protesters, that the National Guard at Kent State "could do nothing but react." He condemned a vote by the Campus Americans for Democratic Action against the ROTC, and thought such attitudes might also be turned against, among others, the business department for being materialistic and the engineering department for aiding military technology. Vincent G. Connery of Virginia Wesleyan did not especially agree with protesters but thought the "silent majority" were "just scared, that's all" and opposed the demonstrators for the wrong reason.[49]

Teenage attention spans proved mercifully (or exasperatingly) short. Despite the ruckus of 1970, calm returned to city campuses within a year or so. Music station WGH's Teen Panel found local youth wrapped "in their own personal concerns and [not] excited about much else that happens around the world." Mark Feldman of Willard Junior High thought boys were mostly interested in sports; Beni Partin of Rosemont revealed that "girls are concerned about boys." Northside's Mark A. Hubal and Rosemont's Linda Ridgwell were named the Optimist Club of Suburban Norfolk's outstanding junior citizens of 1971; President Donald Beamon commended them as "good young people, the ones who obey the law, the quiet ones who never cause trouble."[50]

On the whole, the teenagers seemed to vanish as mysteriously as they had appeared in the 1960s. The *Pilot's* bimonthly *Action* magazine section, addressed to teenagers and their interests, faded to a single page en route to early death. Teenagers appeared to retreat into the rain forests of acquiescence, the caves of conformity. But their brief efflorescence would be discussed for many years afterward, and tales of their curious habits and beliefs would be passed down from generation to generation.

Republican candidate G. William Whitehurst carried the second district congressional race in 1970; Nixon and Agnew won a landslide victory in 1972, triumphing handily in Norfolk and the state. Nixon, traveling in 1972 to China and Russia, seemed to be reshaping the world order in ways favorable to American interests. Sixteen-year-old Sheila Graham Smith of Lake Taylor High, self-styled "superconservative" and the state's Outstanding Teenage Republican of 1971, acknowledged that she "idolizes Vice President Spiro Agnew because he 'tells it like it is.'"[51] Charles A. Reich's 1970 best-seller, *The Greening of America,* lauding the virtues of the "youth culture," already seemed rather a quaint period piece of no enduring value.

Yet the implied epitaph for teenage radicals was perhaps misleading and premature. By late 1974 Agnew was a disgraced outcast for tax evasion as governor of Maryland, and Nixon had been cursed and hounded into permanent political exile over his role in Watergate; the United States had quit the Vietnam War in defeat. Eighteen-year-olds were in 1971 granted the right to vote, a welcome alternative to demonstrations as a means of influencing governmental policy; the draft was ended. If teenage radicals could be set down as essentially wrong-headed in action, it was a judgment that need not apply to their instincts.

CHAPTER 27

Dreams, Schemes, and Nightmares

OWING in part to the recent return of many Gulf War veterans, Norfolk's July Fourth celebration in 1991 had about it a heightened sense of patriotic good cheer. Quick and almost bloodless victory had cleansed for America's military most, if not all, the stain left by the Vietnam War. The collapse of European communism made Americans feel more secure from nuclear obliteration than at any time since the early phases of the Cold War more than four decades before. As the Ninth Annual Fourth of July Great American Picnic and Norfolk Victory Party began, the city recognized that there had not been as much to celebrate for almost half a century.[1]

Its fate long linked with that of the military, notably its naval arm, Norfolk felt the surge of patriotic exultation more than most cities. July 4 meant more in 1991 than striking up martial airs, setting off fireworks, and holding a Main Street parade. To give the day a panache in keeping with the occasion, it was arranged that the new destroyer *Arleigh Burke*, lately launched at Bath, Maine, would be commissioned at a Norfolk ceremony. Up to one hundred thousand people were expected for the formalities, followed by a Town Point Park picnic, fireworks, and other festivities in honor of men and women of "Operation Desert Storm."[2]

Inclement weather cut attendance figures drastically, but those on hand saw the grand old navy town's waterfront in its glory. The *Arleigh Burke*, lashed to the Town Point Park bulkhead, was the most advanced destroyer ever built, a thing of dazzling capabilities. Its 550-foot length was driven at high speed through the roughest seas by a 100,000–horsepower engine, almost twice as powerful as that of a World War II destroyer. Its Aegis armaments system, a computerized marvel, could track up to a hundred targets at a time and fire the right kind of missile to destroy each. Its "Gatling Gun" could deliver three thousand rounds a minute at close targets; Harpoon missiles and torpedoes could race toward distant enemy ships and submarines,

This state-of-the-art destroyer, the USS *Arleigh Burke*, symbolizing Norfolk's close partnership with the navy, was christened at the city docks on July 4, 1991. (Official U.S.
Navy photograph)

and Tomahawk missiles could roar off at targets up to a hundred miles away.
The ship's first skipper, Commander John G. Morgan Jr., was a University
of Virginia graduate.[3]

The waterfront scene, with guided tours of the destroyer, was visual am-
brosia for ship-lovers. Not far off lay the huge carrier *Theodore Roosevelt* and
its battle group, just home from the Persian Gulf. Nearby Otter Berth held
the regal Soviet *Kruzenschtern;* the ship was sixty-five years old and the
world's second largest sailing vessel. Its crew of sixty-two could set more
than 36,500 square feet of canvas to the wind. It was greeted that morning
at Hampton Roads Bridge-Tunnel by a flotilla of pleasure boats and welcomed at noon by Mayor Joseph Leafe and the Virginia Symphony's brass
quintet. She carried 116 cadets, some perchance descendants of the Russian
seamen who had descended on Norfolk in 1877.[4]

The passage of 114 years since the visit of *Svetlana* and her escorts had
made for vast changes in both visitors and hosts. Gone were the Gilded Age
aristocrats and gentry, replaced by space age technocrats. Gone were the
thunder of cannon salutes, the rounds of lavish dinners and balls. Yet the
great-grandsons retained at least the animal needs that weeks at sea engen-

der; the *Kruzenschtern* was scarcely dockside before her cadets issued a blanket invitation for women between the ages of seventeen and twenty to a shipboard disco party at 8:30 P.M. Those who attended, despite downpours that pelted the canopy, thought the Russians were less stiff and danced better than their American counterparts.[5]

At the morning commissioning, special guests included the ship's eighty-nine-year-old namesake admiral, World War II hero Arleigh "31-knot" Burke, Secretary of Defense and featured speaker Dick Cheney, Admiral Frank B. Kelso, chief of naval operations, and others. (Burke, three times chief of naval operations, was reportedly the first living person to have a U.S. warship named in his honor.) The party and fireworks featured music by the U.S. Atlantic Fleet Band, the Armed Forces School of Music Facility Ensemble, and a local group, "Savannah."[6]

Amid the sounds of revelry arose discordant notes, not least a Norfolk Catholic worker group holding a service at the corner of Boush and Charlotte streets to mourn the loss of life on all sides in the Gulf War and repent American preparations for future wars. Commissioning speakers avoided mention of Representative John D. Dingell's (D-Mich.) letter to Secretary Cheney, released the day before, alleging design flaws in the $864 million ship. But it remained for Cheney himself to play the role of party-poop. With rumors afloat that he would deliver a major policy statement, he announced that the fleet was to be cut from 550 to 440 ships.[7] It was a revelation that sent shudders across Hampton Roads.

Twenty-four years earlier, in 1967, Norfolk had celebrated the golden anniversary of its naval base. The *Virginian-Pilot,* stressing the navy's importance to the city, observed that day that "Norfolk and the Navy are a single community . . . and a harmonious one, in which each element of the partnership upholds the other."[8] Norfolk, however, was the dependent partner; it might not be able to survive without a conspicuous naval presence. Any reduction of the navy was bound to affect the city and its people adversely—and this in a time of national economic recession.

Statistics made the point. By 1983 Norfolk was homeport for 130 of the navy's 438 ships, including 6 of the 14 aircraft carriers. The Oceana Naval Air Station was one of the world's busiest airfields, with a takeoff or landing every 3 minutes. The military employed 98,000 personnel in the area, besides 40,000 civilian workers; the navy "family" locally amounted to 450,000 people. Newport News Shipbuilding, where nuclear vessels were built, was Virginia's largest private employer. Norfolk alone had 225 navy command billets and 67 shore-based activities. The naval base was the world's largest, sprawling over 3,400 acres. The city's leaders liked to boast—with consider-able justice—that Norfolk was the "Naval Capital of the World."[9]

Throw a rock in South Hampton Roads, and you were apt to hit the military. In Norfolk were the Little Creek Amphibious Base and the Atlantic fleet headquarters compound with its NATO command. Skip your rock and it might strike Langley Air Force Base (Tactical Air Command headquar-ters), Fort Monroe and its Army Training and Doctrine Command, Fort Eustis, or Camp Peary. There were also the navy yard in Portsmouth, the NASA research facility in Hampton, the Yorktown Naval Weapons Station, and many other installations.[10]

The navy was everywhere, into everything. Many of the city's public school teachers and hospital nurses were navy spouses. The Community Fund and other civic efforts depended heavily on navy support, and the service was a key part of the Azalea Festival, Harborfest, Norfolk Tour, and similar events. Service personnel retired in Norfolk to be near PXs and other facilities available to veterans and their families. The navy had played a key role in edging Norfolk toward desegregation and reopening the schools in 1958. The churches were keenly conscious of their debt to navy support, Catholics alone having doubled the number of their Norfolk par-ishes since World War II.[11]

It was hard to imagine Norfolk without sailors. Following East Main's sanitizing in the 1950s, sailors shifted to "the Strip" at the end of Hampton Boulevard just outside naval base gates one and two. From 4:00 in the after-noon until after midnight in the 1960s and early 1970s, the Strip was a rol-licking bazaar of loud music, insistent prostitutes, massage parlors, and sudsy bacchanalia. From here an inebriated Tar might navigate back to his ship without the embarrassment of a pilot. But the navy in 1975 began buy-ing up the property for such mundane uses as an air-cargo terminal, piers, and a dispensary. Soon the Strip was gone.[12]

Some looked to Ocean View Amusement Park as a recreational alterna-tive, savoring with their dates the mysteries of the tunnel of love and the gut-curdling joy of the roller coaster. But by 1978 restless developers were eyeing the park's mile-long bayshore for resort hotels and shopping centers. Soon it, too, was gone; the celebrated chute-the-chute, star of the film *Roll-er-Coaster,* was burned in 1979 (after efforts to blow it up failed) for a scene in another movie, *Amusement Park.*[13] Again the sailors slunk away toward wherever neon beckoned, but the glimmer was faint and came, alas, from afar.

The navy's presence made Norfolk a focus of uninvited interest from the

Soviet Union. Despite easy access of the navy to the city and vice-versa, not until 1982 did a Norfolk sailor become the first person prosecuted for espionage in the area since World War II. Brian P. Horton advertised his treachery in calls and a letter to the Soviet Embassy, offering data from his post as fleet intelligence center analyst in the nuclear-strike planning branch. He was lucky to get only a short prison term.[14] (But his efforts quailed before the relentless perfidy of John A. Walker.)

The death of the Strip and the amusement park put many others besides sailors to the task of occupying their time in fulfilling ways. On May 13, 1980, according to the *Pilot*, 41 persons committed larcenies and one a murder, 2 stole cars, and 1,235 called the public library's 15 branches with questions. Over 1,800 bought hamburgers at the Military Circle McDonald's and 471, mostly different people, were admitted to the area's 12 hospitals. Another 211 had cases heard at Norfolk's Traffic Court, 34 were born, 7 died, and 2,732 went to the Lafayette Park Zoo. Trailways and Greyhound buses took away 684 and brought 709, but 125 more passengers arrived at International Airport than departed, almost evening things up.[15] A city so devoted to libraries, the zoo, and hamburgers could not be all bad.

Most would have benefited more, however, in the *Pilot*'s view, from a steak dinner at the Colony House Restaurant in Colley Village Shopping Center, observing how guard Tom Collins at the federal building used the plate glass windows for surreptitious girl-watching, or ogling foam-rubber sculpture at Chrysler Museum. These, besides the basso-profundo voice of WVEC-TV weatherman Joe Foulkes, and other small joys, were cited as "some good things" about living in Norfolk. But probably few sailors saw in such joys recompense for the loss of Peggy, the blonde tassel-specialist at Lovey's Bar on the Strip.[16]

To the Strip denizen who asked the *Pilot* gloomily in 1975, "What is there to do? For real, what is there to do?" answers might be found at Scope arena or Metropolitan Park baseball bleachers. Scope was home that year to the Virginia Squires, a professional basketball team, and the Tidewater Sharks, pro ice hockey, on both of which it was losing money; the latter sold only about 1,200 tickets a game and was playing on very thin ice. (The Admirals, a later ice hockey team, was a big success.) The Norfolk Tides, a New York Mets' Triple-A franchise that moved from Portsmouth in 1970, did well in their six thousand-seat Northampton Boulevard stadium. Older fans recalled Yogi Berra catching for the Norfolk Tars and other major league heroes playing in Norfolk early in their careers.[17]

The Reagan military buildup of the 1980s brought Hampton Roads more jobs, people, homes, shopping places, and income. The city's economy through 1988 was prosperous and in some ways spectacular.[18] It was a time when dreams came true, though the finance company would one day want its money back at 16 percent.

A city being torn down and replaced could dream for itself a future in which fairies touched wands to the tops of skyscrapers, turning concrete to gold. Some dreamed of viable sports franchises. Others fancied a lovely Norfolk Gardens recreation area on City Hall Avenue opposite Kirn Library or, like Norfolk State professors Jesse Pendleton and Brinston Collins, a permanent berth near the Omni for the retired ocean liner *United States.* Oceanographer Jacques Cousteau, after talking Long Beach, California, into a Cousteau museum and permanent berth for the *Queen Mary,* a $50 million flop, envisioned a Norfolk waterfront with Cousteau Society administrative offices and another museum. Some termed it a nightmare and vowed to resist.[19]

A dream fulfilled was the sparkling Waterside marketplace that opened in June 1983 with the crack of a bottle of confetti by Virginia's first lady, Lynda Johnson Robb, and red, white, and blue balloons lofted from thirty tugboats. The complex had 122 retail outlets, including restaurants, fast-food stands, specialty shops, kiosks, and pushcarts. In an opening-day address, Mayor Vincent J. Thomas predicted Waterside would reestablish Norfolk's historic connection with its waterfront, build a tax base, produce jobs, strengthen Norfolk's role as the hub of Hampton Roads, and create spinoff development. Developer James W. Rouse wagered that Norfolk had "never done anything that will increase its revenues as much over the next 30 years as it has in building Waterside."[20]

Norfolk's Ron Mack, on the other hand, thought redevelopers had foisted off another alabaster pachyderm on taxpayers, as he told the *Virginian-Pilot.* First had come Scope, which had proved unable to keep a basketball team or a series of ice hockey teams. Then came "rejuvenated" downtown, now little more than a "showplace for prostitutes." After that had come the city's acquisition of Ocean View, which would "give Norfolk the public beach we need," but did not. And now came Waterside, another oversold trip to the public money-trough. Maybe, he implied icily, it was time to let taxpayers spend some of their own money.[21]

Roger and Judith Carr of Massachusetts dreamt of a baby despite removal of Judith's fallopian tubes after a tubal pregnancy. On December 28, 1981, their dream came true when Dr. Mason Andrews delivered Elizabeth Carr by caesarean section at Norfolk General Hospital. She was America's first "test-tube baby," crowning the work of the in vitro fertilization clinic started in 1978 at Eastern Virginia Medical School (EVMS) by Drs. Howard and Georgeanna Jones. It vaulted the fledgling school from relative obscurity to world leadership in the field, greatly enhancing its own and Norfolk's international prestige. It also created ethical conundrums and furious debate, but the clinic, unfazed, by mid–May 1992 was responsible for birthing 1,045 in vitro babies.[22]

Young Park's Pernell "Sweetpea" Whitaker dreamed of winning the Olympic gold medal lightweight boxing championship, and did so in 1984 in Los Angeles. His vision probably did not include being married in the boxing ring, but he did that, too, when, in late 1985 he wed Rovonda Anthony after scheduled fights at the Pavilion in Virginia Beach, the first such wedding on record. In between, he relished "Sweetpea Whitaker Day" in August 1984, when admirers had a flag ceremony at Town Point Park, with a band, parade, and speeches. Lorene Stokes in 1983 realized her dream of becoming the first black Azalea Queen.[23]

By 1983 EVMS had evolved from a first small graduating class in 1976 into a major medical center. It had some one thousand employees, had trained over six hundred doctors, and spurred the area's economy as well as health care. Its microsurgical research center had nationally recognized plastic surgery and urology faculties, besides other EVMS researchers in cancer, heart disease, arteriosclerosis, spinal surgery, and infertility. The Eastern Virginia (formerly Norfolk) Medical Center Authority, parent of EVMS, had also launched the Eastern Virginia Graduate School of Medicine, Community Mental Health Center and Psychiatric Institute, and Center for Communication Disorders.[24]

Prince Ellis's dream came to him one 1916 morning in Concord, North Carolina. It moved him to build his One-Man Black Cat Rattlesnake Can Band, later a Norfolk tourist attraction. The "Can Band" was a mad hybrid of two-by-fours, planks, bolts, five-gallon drum, hinges, rotary-saw blade, sixteen frying pans, cymbal, coffee pots, tin washboard, and incidentals. It had fifteen wooden dancing figures, and, when activated by a foot-pedal, approximated a sixteen-piece band. For years Ellis had it on a platform in the trunk of his Oldsmobile, playing at fairs, weddings, and other gatherings. When reached at his Wood Street home by Ferrum College's Blue Ridge Institute in 1977 about a recording, Ellis, down and out at seventy-six, admitted that he had burned it the night before to keep warm.[25]

The Blue Ridge Institute was luckier with Oscar "Sonny" Walker. Known for decades along Granby Street, Walker, blind since age three, was the beneficiary of a musical education at Hampton's School for the Deaf and Blind. A stocky figure in dark glasses, who crept with a silver-headed cane along the sidewalk in six-inch steps, Walker accepted contributions for the gospel songs he rendered in a rich bass-baritone. He also sang with the chancel choir at Rev. John L. White's First Calvary Baptist Church when recorded by the institute in 1977.[26]

Women often dreamt of running the front office, though few were yet seen in top management. Laura Kierstead, who sharpened pencils for the Chesapeake and Potomac Telephone Company in the 1940s, was a district traffic manager in 1975 to whom 506 operators and clerks reported. Helen "Ginny" Goode in the same years rose from bank messenger to vice president of Virginia National Bank, the only female among its seventy vice presidents. Bettie Myers, starting as a clerk in Rose's toiletries, in 1975 became manager of Rose's latest and largest store in Virginia Beach, the only woman among 265 store managers. Their consensus was that women scaled such heights by overcoming their socialization against taking risks—and working three times harder than men.[27]

Norfolk's blacks, dreaming more bountifully than ever before, made impressive gains. Herman Valentine, a shoeshine boy in the 1940s, by the late 1970s headed, in the sixteen-story Maritime Tower on the same street, a computer store with annual sales of over $50 million. Rosa Alexander rose from picking cotton to become the head of A&B Janitorial Service in 1979, with 280 employees and millions in contracts. Veronica Moody's Walking Tall, Ltd. clothing stores occupied locations at military circle shoppes and Lynnhaven Mall, and Bishop L. E. Willis owned a twenty-three-station broadcasting empire carrying his daily "Crusade for Christ" show, music, and other religious programming.[28]

The 1950s dream of a desegregated school system as a step toward a truly integrated society receded in the 1980s under the Reagan administration. Earlier policies requiring massive busing to offset segregated housing burdened Norfolk with moving 29,000 students 1.7 million miles a year at a cost of over $4 million. Sociologist David Armor's 1982 study concluded that Norfolk schools had suffered substantial "white flight" to private and surburban schools, and that busing had measurably negative effects on education. Reagan's Justice Department opposed mandated busing for integration, but it came as a shock in 1983 when the Norfolk school board revealed its intention to seek the Justice Department's help in ending cross-town busing for elementary schools.[29]

Many whites as well as blacks feared a return to segregated schools with disparities in allocating public funds. A rally at St. John's AME Church in early 1983 began mapping strategy to block the school board plan by means of protests, boycotts, and legal challenges. Much of Norfolk's segregated housing pattern was said to be rooted in NRHA building strategies from the 1950s. In effect, white-dominated city government, in helping create black neighborhoods, made busing the obvious means to integrate schools, and now made that an excuse for largely segregated ones.[30]

Opponents labored essentially in vain; federal courts upheld the school board request in 1984 and 1985. The next year saw ten all-black elementary schools, though blacks made up but 58 percent of all students. After-school "multicultural" classes in music, snorkeling, and so forth, meant to foster interracial contact, were up to 86 percent black, though few were so disproportionate. The Supreme Court's 1954 ruling that segregated schools were inherently unfair was lost in jesuitical distinctions between de facto and de jure. The 1990 Census, showing all-white neighborhoods down since 1980 from twenty-two to thirteen, gave cause for hope, but those virtually all-black remained as numerous.[31]

Other dreamers clung to the idea of a Hampton Roads supercity. When the 1980 Census showed over a million people living on the margins of Hampton Roads, the U.S. Chamber of Commerce consolidated this statistically as a major metropolitan area, making it eligible for larger chunks of federal funds. It created one of the country's thirty largest metropolitan areas. Three years later, a New York commercial surveyor cited this as the fourth best place in the nation in which to locate a business. A needed step would be completion of a superhighway linking all of Hampton Roads. It could utilize an interstate link through a proposed Newport News–Suffolk tunnel, meet I-64 to sweep south of Portsmouth, cross I-264 east of downtown Norfolk, and return to the peninsula via the Hampton Roads Bridge-Tunnel.[32]

Whatever developers and redevelopers conceived was likely to be challenged by diverse groups as Norfolk grew more cosmopolitan in makeup. Anna Mah and her family celebrated the advent of the year 4675 (February 18, 1977) at Ying's Chinese-American Restaurant on North Military Highway. Many of Tidewater's five hundred or so Chinese families observed the day by staying up until New Year's sunrise, keeping front porch lights on all night and observing other traditional practices. Members of the Chinese community sent around to Chinese businesses two men in a lion's costume to collect money deposited for "the lion" mounted atop high sticks and to leave the message "Gung Hoy Fet Toy"—prosperity in the new year.[33]

Owing to war in Vietnam, Norfolk gained a sizable Vietnamese community. Some three hundred Vietnamese refugees reached Tidewater in the latter half of 1975 alone. Sponsors like Norfolk's Lorraine and Roy Hudson helped refugees such as Kim and Thinh Le find jobs and housing, but the newcomers found it hard to adjust to the cold weather and often had to live for extended periods in tiny apartments. But many had worked for the American military in Vietnam and brought skills that gained them ready employment in Norfolk. Churches were frequent sponsors of individuals and families, many of whom had escaped from South Vietnam by boat, leaving all they owned, as the Viet Cong swept in.[34]

Some three hundred Latin American families lived in Tidewater by the mid-1970s, representing at least fourteen countries; many of them were refugee Cubans. A Hispanic-American Club on Tidewater Drive helped them adjust to new lives, but many, such as Dr. Elio Ladada of Norfolk General Hospital, and Dr. José G. Simón, associate professor of languages at Old Dominion (both Cubans), needed little aid, though often arriving empty-handed. Others, like Puerto Rican J. Uriel Quinones, came mainly for broader economic opportunities. Their presence meant, among other things, a more frequent exposure of Norfolkians to such cultural benefits as the guitar music of Carlos Montoya, New York's Spanish Theater Repertory Company, Andalucian flamenco dancers, and others.[35]

Besides gains from immigration, Hampton Roads enjoyed the fruits of foreign investment. Some sixty foreign manufacturers came in the 1970s, including the Mercedes-Benz plant in Hampton, and Spain's Banca March, which in 1979 became the biggest stockholder in the Bank of Virginia. Most of these firms chose Virginia Beach or Chesapeake over crowded Norfolk, but were important to all of Hampton Roads; they usually cited local port facilities as the area's most attractive economic feature.[36]

Ballast for the international miscellany was provided, in part, by Norfolk's old families: Seldens, Grandys, Myerses, Taylors, Tylers, and others. In 1980 Janet Fauntleroy Taylor still lived in the Stockley Gardens house built by her father, Walter H. Taylor III, where she was born seventy-five years before. The Taylors had lately revived a tradition of Christmas reunion for descendants of Richard and Elizabeth Calvert Taylor (great-great-great-great-granddaughter of Adam and Sarah Thorowgood), who founded the dynasty in the late eighteenth century. Her gallery of family portraits reminded visitors of the generations of businessmen, lawyers, doctors, politicians, bankers, and soldiers the family has given the community.[37]

Some of these families traced their heritage to Berkley (formerly Powder Point and Washington Point), the old village at the fork of the Elizabeth River's eastern and southern branches. By the 1960s Berkley, a community of about 3,500 people, was 98 percent black and plagued by decay. Once a prosperous complex of shipyards, an iron foundry, lumber mills, and box factories, it was annexed by Norfolk in 1906. When fire (in 1922) and Prohibition destroyed the Garrett Winery and dwindling forests chased off box factories and lumber mills, Berkley went into decline. Well-to-do residents fled across the river to Norfolk and rented out their substantial Berkley homes, which were subdivided into apartments that received little attention from landlords.[38]

Then came a small miracle. Enterprising Berkleyites in the depths of the 1930s formed the Beacon Light Civic League (BLCL) to try to arrest the blight. In 1939 BLCL appealed to city hall for street improvements, but the war put such hopes on hold. Refining its organization during the war years, the league renewed its addresses to the city council in 1945, seeking help for street damage by heavy trucks and drainage problems. Its appeals brought street lights and repairs, better traffic control, and other action. Close attention to Berkley's needs taught BLCL how bureaucracies could be made to yield benefits.[39]

Beacon Light led voter registration drives, raised funds for worthy causes, sponsored musical programs, backed the Montgomery bus boycott and 1958 school desegregation suit, held cleanups, and recruited citizens and businesses. By the 1960s BLCL, nearly all-black and led by Horace Downing, Edith Jones, George Banks, and others, was Norfolk's oldest continuous civic league.[40]

Beacon Light saw in 1966 that the new federal Model Cities Act, mandating community involvement in plans to improve urban slums, was tailor-made for its peculiar blend of raging need and community activism. Norfolk was ready to apply for a Model Cities grant for five neighborhoods even before enabling legislation passed. A result was the construction of Bell-Diamond Manor, 128 units of federally subsidized housing that was a landmark in community initiative.[41]

Model Cities funds went on to refurbish an abandoned building as a social, health, and educational center. In 1969 Berkley was the first community to approach the NRHA for a housing project. Plans emerged for 128 new townhouse and garden apartments and eight single-family dwellings. By the early 1970s Norfolk's $5 million Model Cities' budget was attracting members of the city establishment to its boards; neighborhood involvement began to wane. But Berkley was an inspiring example of a community shaping its own future rather than being molded by others.[42]

By 1980 NRHA had used millions of Model Cities funds to help Berkley renovate some ninety-five buildings, a start in reversing decades of neglect. But the city council and NRHA found themselves in a race with drug lords for Berkley's soul. Already in May 1972 the race had resulted in a front-page tragedy. Norfolk policeman L. W. "Kit" Hurst Jr. (son of the narcotics squad's chief), leading a 3:00 A.M. Lancaster Street drug-bust, was shot and killed by an occupant, Mrs. Lillian Jones Davidson. The Davidsons, a respected elderly couple, had been mistakenly fingered by a tipster. Mrs. Davidson was not prosecuted.[43]

Berkley's interaction with the city government cast new light on the past thirty-five years of Norfolk's political evolution. A 1973 analysis suggested that city government was guided by "a small group of relatively wealthy businessmen, many of them unknown to the general public," who set city priorities. They operated through formal and informal links with a larger group of subordinate leaders who implemented programs. The mayor's office was crucial, owing to its vested authority and "interaction with the 15 most powerful men" in the city. The NRHA had by the mid-1970s, however, lost much of its independence; federal funds did not go directly to the agency but were channeled through city hall.[44]

Typical in the analyst's view was the idea to build Norfolk's convention center, which came from a phone call by NRHA's director to Mayor Roy Martin and a quick decision, without action by any municipal body, to apply for federal funds. Yet the project involved $30 to $50 million and major downtown changes. It was possible, as when black protestors surrounded city hall to force reversal of a decision to replace Booker T. Washington High with a renamed school some miles distant, for citizens to affect directly the governing process. But ordinary mortals were rarely so vehement. In day-to-day matters, it appeared that the Virginia National Bank and other elite outposts not only had disproportionate influence with city hall but could also tongue-tie local newspapers.[45]

The analyst concluded, however, that Norfolk's council-manager government, "widely recognized as one of the most efficient and honest in the nation," had enabled the city to avoid the financial and social chaos faced by other cities, while keeping tax rates relatively low. Norfolk, for better or worse, was governed by a "beneficent oligarchy" not unlike some other cities.[46]

The navy's presence meant many benefits but might also become Norfolk's worst menace. Chief Warrant Officer John A. Walker's dream was to
save the family business, pay his debts, maybe set a little aside for the kids'
education. A career man, he had served his country as a communications
specialist for twelve years.[47]

Walker went to Washington in 1967 and struck a deal at the Soviet Embassy. For $4,000 a month and bonuses, he turned into a spy-nest his job at
Atlantic fleet operations headquarters off Terminal Boulevard. He dropped
stolen data at points around Washington, and picked up cash at others. The
superpowers were not going to war and the Russians would give no secrets
to North Korea, so no one would be hurt.[48]

The Soviets told him not to throw cash around but those desk-jockeys
were not school drop-outs with a police record and saddled with a wife and
four kids. If John's three-bedroom Norfolk apartment had a doorman and
wall-to-wall, who could fault him? He bought a twenty-four-foot sailboat,
the *Dirty Old Man,* that drew chicks like "Jimi-Jet" Thomas, an Old Dominion co-ed.[49]

John's horizons expanded. At Norfolk he was on a two-man team responsible for firing Polaris missiles in case of war. For $1 million he could neglect
to transmit firing orders and abort all the Atlantic fleet's nuclear missiles.
The Soviets, reserving their cash for services rendered rather than promised, declined.[50]

In 1968 he was deployed to California, where he recruited a drinking
buddy, navy radio instructor Jerry Whitworth. After John returned to Norfolk in 1974, Jerry sent packets of data and film in return for hefty payments.
John retired from the navy in 1976 and divorced his wife Barbara, but remained the conduit for secrets Whitworth copied at various duty stations.
His earnings went mostly to high living—a brown and burnt-orange Grum-
man Tiger, eighteen-foot sailboat and trailer, Chrysler New Yorker, investments in the Caribbean, Florida, and on the North Carolina coast, and so
on.[51]

In 1978 the Soviets began flying John to Vienna twice a year for deliveries
and discussions. They began paying in lump sums of up to $200,000. John
took work with the Norfolk office of Wackenhut, a security firm, and courses
at Thomas Nelson Community College to help in the job. He traded the
sailboat for a houseboat, the *JAWS* (his initials), threw parties, and entertained girls.[52]

In 1980 he and a co-worker formed Confidential Reports, a Kempsville
firm offering businesses protection from industrial spies. He also formed a

company to cover his spy earnings and recruited his older brother Arthur, a retired naval officer, for spying. Art joined the VSE Corporation, a Chesapeake defense contractor, and provided navy ship specifications and other secrets. In 1983 John's son Michael, a navy enlistee, joined the team. It was John's pride that he had built perhaps the most effective spy-ring in American history and provided the Soviets with over a million mostly top-secret documents.[53]

John's greed was his undoing. On leaving the navy, he told Barbara he had quit spying and cut off her alimony. In 1984, when she demanded $10,000 so she could go back to school, he refused. She told her daughter-in-law: "I'm going to fix him."[54]

The spy network began to crumble. Worried over getting caught, Whitworth sent the FBI a letter signed "RUS" mentioning the spy-ring and proposing contact if assured, by *Los Angeles Times* ads, of immunity from prosecution. The FBI's ads tried to lure him in without such an offer but had so far failed when Barbara called its Boston office, wanting to talk. An agent visited her but decided she was unreliable. When nothing happened, she persuaded her daughter Laura to back up her story. The agent met Laura but felt he was wasting time. In early 1985 he relayed the case routinely to Washington, which routinely notified the Norfolk FBI office.[55]

Agents Joseph R. Wolfinger and Robert W. Hunter took an interest. They bugged John's phone and tailed him when he left his 8524 Old Ocean View Road home about noon on May 19. He took evasive action, doubling back and so on, but saw none of the six cars staked out nearby. Reassured, he headed out Route 64 to Washington to make a drop for the Soviets.[56]

He was soon leading forty-one agents in twenty vehicles and an airplane, all of whom contrived to lose him on a Maryland road, but sky agents soon spotted the minivan on the same road. Augmented fleets of cars resumed surveillance. He set his 7-Up-can signal by the road for the Soviets to leave his money and drove off. FBI men promptly removed it. Around 8:00 P.M., a Malibu with Soviet diplomatic plates came by, saw no 7-Up can, and left. But John went to the drop-site and put his packet of 129 documents behind a telephone pole. It was quickly retrieved by the FBI. Puzzled to find no money where it should be, John went to a Rockville motel and was arrested around 3:00 A.M.[57]

Michael, Arthur, and Whitworth were also arrested. At their 1986 sentencing, Arthur got life, Michael twenty-five years, and John two life terms plus one hundred years; serving the terms concurrently, he would be eligible for freedom in ten years. National interest led to a 1989 CBS miniseries,

"Family of Spies," and a "60 Minutes" segment in 1990. His property was auctioned to help pay $200,000 in IRS taxes on his seventeen-year earnings as a spy.[58]

Damage wrought by the ring cannot be fully assessed. *Family of Spies*, Pete Earley's 1988 book, cites instances when the ring's data may have been critical. A cryptographic machine, codes for which Walker stole, was seized on the USS *Pueblo* spy-ship off North Korea, perhaps on KGB orders. The subsequent sinking of the Norfolk-based nuclear sub *Scorpion* led to suspicion that spies may have betrayed its location.[59] If there was cause to rejoice, it was that Walker's dream had not become civilization's nightmare.

CHAPTER 28

Chesapeake at Bay

A T 6:00 A.M. on July 18, 1989, Pennsylvania dairy farmer James Van Blarcom began machine-milking his 65 cows. Within 90 minutes, as the final squirts of his 390 gallons were collected, he also had an odoriferous start toward 1,000 gallons of manure he would accumulate that day.

Van Blarcom's manure, pushed from stalls by a scraper, gurgled into a 4-feet deep trench that guided it to a storage pond. From there, it would empty into a branch of the Susquehanna River. Oozing into the river, it would blend with average daily deposits of 16,400 pounds of Quaker State cow-droppings. By year's end, the river, from this source, would convey 30,000 tons of potentially deadly nitrogen, 1,600 tons of phosphorus, to the Chesapeake Bay.[1]

Fifty miles southwest of Van Blarcom's farm, Anne Arundel County, Maryland, that Monday registered 78 more boats, South Hampton Roads another 72. Anne Arundel's 28,639 boats, their toilets served by one pump-station, made that day's contribution to a million gallons of raw sewage entering the bay. (We need not estimate the swimmers, surfers, skiers, boaters, and fishermen who dispensed with toilets altogether.) At Cape Charles, another 150 miles southeast, 140,000 gallons of waste wound leisurely through the sewage system to the bay to commingle with 4 million gallons discharged by 5,000 bay-area treatment plants.

Chesapeake Bay was not just a five-state septic tank. Fifteen outfalls at Norshipco's Berkley plant, sixteen at its Brambleton and Southern yards, excreted daily into the Elizabeth River. Included were grease, oil, iron, and phosphates, sometimes toxic levels of copper, lead, silver, zinc, and organic compounds. Fifty more self-monitoring industries added rivulets of exotic gunk.[2]

An average daily traffic of nine naval vessels entered or left Hampton Roads, each periodically disgorging ballast and bilge tank slops. On 100 or more commercial vessels using the bay, engineers this day flushed out water laced with diesel fuel, tossed poisonous lantern batteries overboard, forgot to close oil hatches. In August a ruptured oil barge would spill 159,000 gallons into the bay. There were 270 more vessels known that year to have spilled a total of 66,000 gallons, many undetected.[3]

At Norfolk naval station, rain on July 17 flushed pollution into Willoughby Bay from 121 storm sewers. (In February the base released toxic amounts of phenol, a compound for disinfectants and paint; in May a Sewell's Point pipe emitted cyanide 20 times above fatal concentrations.) The naval base violated its discharge permits 35 times in 1988. Little Creek Amphibious Base that month pumped 230,000 gallons of raw sewage into its harbor, and Norfolk Naval Air Station released almost 100,000 gallons of fuel.

Every shower washed hazardous metals from Norfolk streets, the lead alone (from paint, auto exhausts, etc.) ten times more than from all the bay's sewage plants, twenty times that of its factories. Street sediments, oil, grease, and lawn fertilizers worked their way into oyster beds, smothered underwater grasses, and poisoned fish. During the year, Norfolk released into its air, water, and land over a thousand tons of chemicals.[4]

As Exxon and Texaco pondered deep-water rigs to hunt for oil at the bay's mouth, nuclear wastes passed through Hampton Roads for trucking to South Carolina. Norfolk naval base's thirty-one nuclear ships created ten thousand cubic feet of such wastes a year, a figure matched by Norfolk Naval Shipyard and exceeded by Newport News Shipbuilding. Newport News had built fifty nuclear submarines. Many nuclear-powered vessels were refueled or scrapped locally each year. No major accident had as yet been reported.[5]

Besides its role as lavatory for thousands of miles of streams and rivers, the Chesapeake was seen by some as a sink for airborne soot, exhaust, and dust. Scientists guessed (mistakenly) that a third of the bay's nitrogen was from acid rain. There were large pesticide residues, cancer-causing PCBs (once used in electrical transformers), PAHs (combustion by-products of autos, shipyards, and chemical plants), cadmium, copper, and nickel. Each day brought over five billion gallons of industrial waste, hydrocarbons, heavy metals, and other such matter. A Hopewell firm no longer poured cancer-causing Kepone into the James River; it didn't need to—the stuff was virtually permanent.[6]

If the Chesapeake was the most dramatic victim of the offal of modern life, it was not unique. Most of Norfolk's forty thousand pre-1950 homes were coated inside and out at least in part with lead paint, a cause of learning disabilities, kidney problems, and even death, in children. Norfolk Southern installed a sprinkler system to hold down coal dust at its Lambert's Point piers, but malfunctions still blanketed Ghent, generating loud complaints.[7]

July 18 also witnessed, at serene Windmill Point in Lancaster County, work on eight of the forty condominiums being built there. The builder chose trees for clearing and kept watch over another sixty-nine houses and seventy-eight condos going up at a forested plot on Wilton Creek in Middlesex. More than 230 people bought lots or moved into homes in the bay's watershed on July 18. The 1990 Census put Norfolk's population at 266,000; the next three decades were expected to add 2.2 million to the 13 million already living in the bay's drainage area. Each toilet-flush sent six gallons of excremental water into the bay, a shower nine gallons a minute, a bath fifty gallons, all full of potentially lethal microorganisms.[8]

At each lunch and dinner, thousands of fish and shellfish from this estuarial witches' vat were relished by grateful diners. People bathed and frolicked in these waters, perchance made love in them. One could conjure up a nightmare future when only dripping swamp-things inhabited the region, roaming desolate beaches in search of edible flotsam. It might come to pass unless efforts to restore the bay and its tributaries became far more resourceful.

The complexity of the bay's problems showed forcibly that no solution could be piecemeal. Realistic programs of preservation or renewal had to involve coordination among many local and several state governments in partnership with Washington. They must impose cooperation on agencies and institutions neither well-equipped nor well-disposed toward it. Ideally, a Chesapeake Bay Authority, like TVA, might ultimately have to take the matter in hand.

There might have been a moment in the era of moon travel and Great Society rhetoric when that approach seemed possible. The year 1966 saw creation of what became the Chesapeake Bay Foundation as a step toward intergovernmental and interagency action. By the 1980s it had Richmond, Annapolis, and Harrisburg offices with seventy-five employees. It proposed and reviewed laws, fostered educational programs, pursued litigation, and recommended action. By the late 1980s signs indicated some positive benefits.[9]

Leaders in the bay's southern region became gradually aware that there were other problems than those of the bay waters demanding regional rather than local approaches. Some supposed that the merging phenomenon of the 1960s—communities with each other or with counties—might spawn a

Hampton Roads megacity. Individual localities might, as in New York City, become boroughs working in harmony to address common concerns.[10]

Regionalists pointed out that the Hampton Roads area embraced a million and a half people—a quarter of all Virginians. Its Richmond legislators—eight of forty senators, twenty of one hundred representatives—could be far more effective cooperating than competing with one another. Northern Virginia had what the *Pilot* called "a steamroller" delegation, especially effective in gaining support for its proposals. A *Pilot* supplement, "Discovering Hampton Roads," regularly plugged existing examples of regional togetherness and the need for more. By the 1990s there were six regional agencies—planning districts, sewer and garbage, mass-transit, and so forth. Jail overcrowding, tourism, pollution, and other problems seemed to demand a regional approach.[11]

"Imagine," intoned the ever-hopeful *Pilot*, "one city with more than a million residents, with a unified water system, one economic development program and one delegation voting as a bloc in the . . . legislature, and it becomes obvious why serious men and women entertained thoughts of a regional merger." But some discerned in the megacity a "Greater Norfolk" giving banking and business interests the power once sought by annexation and other means.[12]

Issues like transportation clearly would go unresolved in a climate of intercity squabbling. As Chesapeake, Virginia Beach, Newport News, Hampton, Suffolk, and Portsmouth grew, their residents, like Norfolk's, sought better access to, around, and through each other's communities. But the costs of what was needed seemed beyond the means of federal or state governments. A legislative subcommittee's 1990 public meeting at Christopher Newport College on Hampton Roads' transportation needs helped focus the issue. One side wanted a regional financing authority with the option of using tolls, gas surcharges, and other means to raise funds. Others saw in this "unelected, unaccountable bureaucrats" able to undercut electoral processes.[13]

The 1990s began with forty interstate and sixty-seven urban projects planned or in progress for southeastern Virginia. They included a Midtown Norfolk-Portsmouth Tunnel with a connector to Port Norfolk Bridge. For clogged Virginia Beach Expressway, interchanges, widenings, and flyovers were scheduled. Used by ten million vehicles in 1968, this route carried over sixty million in 1989, and on a hot summer day up to 180,000. A proposed light rail line from downtown Norfolk to Virginia Beach was challenged, among other reasons, because bus riders had dropped by half in the 1980s. A public wedded to private transportation was not ready to consider alternatives. A second Berkley Bridge span in 1991 permitted rapid transit through at least one old bottleneck.[14]

A 1990 *Places Rated Almanac,* ranking urban areas for indices of "livability" such as crime, health care, arts and recreation, cost of living, education, transportation, and job outlook, placed Hampton Roads thirty-third of 333, a gain from fortieth in 1991. *Money* magazine's 1990 ranking of America's 300 best places to live dropped Hampton Roads from 122 to 128. (It grew more livable even as it became a less inviting place to live!) A 1991 national survey ranked Norfolk's metropolitan area twenty-second as a place to do business, a drop from fourth in 1990. *World Trade* magazine rated it one of the ten best American cities for international companies.[15] It was all food for thought, but probably not much.

A national recession in 1990 signaled that the Hampton Roads party might be over, especially for developers and builders. Miller and Rhoads closed all its department stores, six of them in Hampton Roads. Norfolk-based Colonna's Shipyard, 111 years old, filed for bankruptcy. As the slump deepened, FX electronics closed two of five Hampton Roads stores, work stopped on a fourteen-story One Bank Street office tower, the Ford plant had recurrent shutdowns owing to weak sales; other closings and cuts occurred. One culprit was overbuilding—in factories, offices, homes, nearly everything. A 1991 merger of Sovran Bank with North Carolina National Bank into NationsBank betokened a restructuring that could cost Norfolk many white-collar jobs and headquarters prestige. (It soon appeared, however, that jobs might be gained by consolidating NationsBank credit-card operations.)[16]

The city hall–NRHA juggernaut plowed on under its executive director, David H. Rice, though with more modest funding and expectations, even as development tides ebbed. In late 1989 the City Council voted over $1 million to design a flashy National Maritime Center, called "Nauticus," on the waterfront at the foot of Main Street. A riverfront baseball stadium for the Tidewater Tides was also in the works.[17]

Scope, once billed as "the jewel in Norfolk's crown," turned an anemic twenty years old in 1991. In its hey-day it hosted Presley, Sinatra, the Rolling Stones, conventions of the Worldwide Church of God, and a kaleidoscope of other events and attractions. Consigned now to the periphery of downtown development, it had no profitable years after 1976. Even so, the drawing power of the Hampton Roads Admirals ice hockey team, anticipations of future trade shows, and other prospects gave hope that Scope might return to its glory days and fulfill its planners' goals.[18]

A twenty-three-story Marriott convention hotel on downtown Main Street also had critics. The 405-room hotel with a 150-seat pub opened in 1991, providing five hundred new jobs. The year brought to town only three conventions, but ample space might mean that Norfolk was more often considered by convention planners. To make sure, the city launched a direct-mail campaign to lure more conventions.[19]

More sweeping debunkers like Hunter A. Hogan Jr. and Kenneth H. Rossen decried as "monumental errors" the "so-called Norfolk International Airport," Scope, snake-bitten Granby Mall, and "the chase after Jacques Cousteau." The latter criticism arose from $1.2 million spent to plan a Cousteau Ocean Center (Nauticus's progenitor) before it was scuttled in 1986. (The Cousteau Society's international headquarters was on Ghent's West Twenty-first Street.) It could be argued, however, that city hall–NRHA projects succeeded more often than not and that the new additions to the city gave benefits that compensated for any deficiencies. In 1991 NRHA won the Urban Land Institute's Special Award for excellence for developing the affluent Ghent Square neighborhood.[20]

Private and public development enhanced NRHA's downtown enterprises. One was the $13.5 million addition to the Chrysler Museum in 1990, providing fifty thousand square feet of new courtyard and exhibit space. (It opened soon after Walter Chrysler's death.) The historic Wheat Building at Main and Atlantic, once scheduled to be demolished, was renovated and renamed the Life Building by a new owner, Life Savings National Bank. Attorney Peter G. Decker Jr.'s Decker I and II buildings on Granby and East Plume streets were renovations meant to "breathe new life into the downtown Granby Street corridor" by encouraging others to follow his lead.[21]

NRHA Executive Director Rice felt his organization had enjoyed major success in slum-removal, house-building, and finding money for "a framework for rebuilding the city." Granby Street seemed to be its main failure; most agreed that Military Circle's enclosed shopping mall syphoned off much Granby business, as did Waterside and other shopping areas. Redevelopers in 1976 sought to arrest Granby's decline by closing it to traffic, creating a pedestrian mall; ten more years of decline led to its reopening. The closing of Woolworth's Granby store in 1989 followed by six months the bankruptcy of Smith and Welton's department store.[22]

City hall in 1989 hired the Urban Land Institute (ULI) to make proposals for downtown redevelopment and in November approved a version of ULI's plan. It called for changing one-way Boush Street to a two-way extension of Waterside Drive and more high-density residential units between Boush Street and the river. Nauticus would be completed; Norfolk Center Theater and Arena would be renovated as an opera house and performing-arts center. Whether any of this would help Granby Street was uncertain. ULI proposals for Ocean View redevelopment bore fruit in 1991 when the city targeted the rundown East Ocean View area. Besides buying and clearing deteriorated property, the city planned Ocean View Park on West Ocean View Avenue, street beautification, and other improvements.[23]

An NRHA success story was Huntersville. Once a showplace of black culture and pride between Virginia Beach Boulevard and the Norfolk Southern tracks, it was dessicated by the 1970s. Drug lords controlled the streets, families huddled twelve to a room, houses had plastic for windows. NRHA began buying property there in 1980 and spent over $10 million building, demolishing, and renovating structures. Complementary private initiatives included Bea Jennings's Olde Huntersville Development Corporation. Starting in 1984, her group focused on housing for low- and moderate-income families, fostering beautification and humanitarian projects. She was featured in *Newsweek* magazine as "an American hero."[24]

Brambleton was sliding into oblivion. Many houses were dilapidated beyond repair and flanked by vacant lots that functioned as open-air drug markets. By late 1990 NRHA mulled a "housing conservation plan" for central Brambleton and redevelopment of the southern part. But more might depend on the Brambleton Civic League and the Episcopal Church-sponsored Plumb Line Ministries, which aimed to restore traditional family orientation. Recovering local control and building affordable low-income housing were seen as essential to halt the blight. Neighboring Norfolk State University had a new outreach center to promote better ties with its neighborhood.[25]

A 1990 *Virginian-Pilot* poll tried to gauge Hampton Roads racial attitudes and found them more positive than expected. Almost 80 percent of 1,218 people queried thought antiblack feeling was the same or less than five years before. Over half of both thought antiwhite feeling was the same or less. More than three-fourths of the whites and two-thirds of the blacks lived in integrated neighborhoods.[26]

Clearly, racism was no longer publicly acceptable, but interviews indicated that it lived on in subtle ways. Some of each race still chose withdrawal, as far as practicable, from the other. Many whites lived in segregated communities, or nearly so, and belonged to white-only clubs and organizations. Some blacks joined the Nation of Islam's Mosque No. 57 on Colonial Avenue or some other serving about eight hundred Muslims. Bishop Walter "Sweet Daddy" McCullough nurtured his Church Street United House of Prayer into a vehicle for community rejuvenation before his death in 1991. He had some three million followers in 132 cities.[27]

A riot by vacationing black college students and others at the Virginia Beach "Greekfest" on Labor Day weekend in 1989 sparked fears of collapsing race relations. When police launched an antidrug crackdown in the spring of 1991, ugly confrontations occurred with blacks on Spruce Street, at Northside Park, and in Diggs Town, none of them drug-related. Blacks complained of police overreaction, such as the use of an incapacitating spray. Low-income neighborhoods ringing downtown—Diggs Town, Berkley, East Ocean View—were high-crime zones with a booming gun-trade. (Norfolk's sixty-seventh 1991 murder, recorded on October 2, was a city record.) A race-related melee at Waterside in June added further tension, but there seemed to be no clear pattern of racial ill-will.[28]

Many more blacks than ever found success in the American mainstream. Norfolk had 2,800 black-owned businesses as the 1990s began. Most were small but some, like Herman Valentine's Systems Management American Corporation (SMA), grossed millions yearly. In 1991, however, SMA—by then one of the nation's largest black-owned firms—pleaded guilty to tax evasion and defrauding the government on a navy contract and was fined $500,000. Valentine was not charged with criminal conduct, but three vice presidents and other SMA officers were convicted.[29]

Native son Leroy R. Hassell, a Harvard Law graduate, was named to Virginia's supreme court in 1989, the second black in its history. He replaced retiring black justice John Charles Thomas, also of Norfolk. In 1984 Dr. Yvonne Miller became the first Norfolk black woman in the state House of Delegates and, four years later, the first in the state senate. Pernell "Sweetpea" Whitaker, former Olympic boxing champ, became the world lightweight champion in 1989.[30]

Blacks were disappointed by a plan to erect a monument to Dr. Martin Luther King Jr. on the traffic circle at Brambleton Avenue and Church Street. A 150-foot obelisk with relief sculptures of King at its base was designed in 1975. From January 1990, when fund-raising head Rosa Alexander had put a contribution thermometer at the site, only $63,000 of a needed $400,000 had been raised. There was little prospect that the monument would rise in this century. A city decision to take over renovation of the old

Wells Theater from the Virginia Stage Company raised hope that something might be done for Church Street's crumbling Attucks Theater.[31]

From 1983 a suit had been working its way through the federal courts that had wide implications for Norfolk's city government. The suit, *Herbert M. Collins Sr. v. City of Norfolk*, alleged that the seventy-five-year-old councilmanic election system was unfair to blacks. Under the system, each voter could vote for all seven city council seats. Collins held that this effectively diluted the black vote, making it hard for blacks to win seats. On August 19, 1989, city papers headlined the announcement that the Fourth U.S. Circuit Court of Appeals had condemned the system. The court demanded its replacement by a system of wards.[32]

In a ward system, the city, as of old, would be divided into districts of roughly equal numbers of voters; each ward would elect only its own council member. Blacks, comprising some 35 percent of the population, theoretically would elect more members (there were two in 1989). Heretofore, black candidates won only by allying with "Westside" business interests; five members lived within a mile of one another near the Lafayette River's mouth. Black success came only on white terms. A ward system would allow blacks to run and vote on their own terms, and would likely undercut the tradition of near-unanimity in council decisions. Ward delegates, each with his or her own priorities, were almost certain to enliven elections with horse-trading and disputation.[33]

Wards would probably cost the white business community some influence, threatening a traditional business/black alliance and giving business-oriented candidates fewer black votes. Eastside white votes would no longer go automatically to business candidates. This might yield larger voter turnouts (barely 18,000 had voted in 1990 city elections). Formation in 1991 of grassroots community groups—the Northside Coalition for Government in the Sunshine, the Common Sense Coalition of Norfolk—augured a trend likely to grow with the ward system. The *Virginian-Pilot* sided with those who foresaw councils ignoring the needs of the city as a whole (Marriott Hotels, Watersides) for narrowly selfish ends. Wards were likely to enhance the role of black activists unable to get white support.[34]

City hall's ward plan of March 1991 had to pass muster with the U.S. Department of Justice. Critics felt they discerned in it features whereby the council's status quo would be preserved. It embodied five wards (some 52,000 people each), two with slim black majorities, three with larger white majorities. There would also be both a black and a white "superward." The first, 62 percent black, would encompass east and south sides and mostly

A *Virginian-Pilot* photographer in a helicopter caught these biplanes in formation over downtown Norfolk in April 1991. (Courtesy of Bill Tiernan, *The Virginian-Pilot and The Ledger-Star*)

black Park Place and Lambert's Point. The second, 79 percent white, covered the city north of Little Creek Road and elite West Side areas. It would let up to five incumbents be reelected; the council, as before, would choose the mayor. Most foes of the plan wanted a simple geographical system of seven to nine wards.[35]

The gauging of political issues in racial terms seemed destined to continue far into the next century. Many immigrants made their homes in the area in the 1980s, but Hampton Roads lacked the employment base to attract great numbers and the city's racial subdivisions remained markedly black or white. Some immigrants owed their presence to the navy's increasingly cosmopolitan character. Groups of Hispanics and native Americans could be found around the naval base. Filipinos, favored by a 1946 treaty that let them immigrate after service in the navy, had long outnumbered other immigrants. The 4,450 Filipinos counted by the 1990 Census exceeded all other Asian groups combined. But Norfolk also had over 600 Chinese natives, 338 East Indians, 277 Japanese, and 257 Koreans, besides Thais, Cambodians, Laotians, and others.[36]

Asians ranged from occupants of corporate suites to crabmeat pickers in waterfront fish houses, and tended to cluster in certain places. Downtown had neighborhoods of Vietnamese and Cambodians in the fishing industry, some on their own boats. Others, in the suburbs, were agents of Japanese goliaths like Canon, Mitsubishi, and Sumitomo, besides smaller firms. A "Little Manila" flourished in Coleman Place near the Norfolk industrial park, where many Filipinos worked. There was a Greek-American Festival each spring, a Chinese Community Association with its own center on Newtown Road, Roma Lodge 254 of the Sons of Italy, a Tidewater Scottish Festival, and other national groups and observances.[37]

Hispanics, led by Puerto Ricans and Mexicans, numbered nearly seven thousand in 1990. They were mainstays of the Catholic Church, whose Knights of Columbus celebrated its ninetieth anniversary in 1988. The Irish, more assimilated and less unified than in Boston or New York, clung to a sense of community through the Irish-American Society and Ancient Order of Hibernians. Irish and British Festivals at Waterside helped fan the embers of their heritage. The 20 percent growth of Hampton Roads' Jews in the 1980s arose from a Sunbelt shift that brought other northerners. Some seventy-five, however, were recently settled Russians.[38]

Hampton Roads Jews, twenty thousand strong, found themselves touched by the 1991 Gulf War, as did the tiny local Arab community. Iraqi Scud missile attacks on Israel endangered relatives and friends of many Norfolk Jews. A prolonged ravaging of Kuwait and Iraq touched directly the lives of sons and daughters of both in Hampton Roads. But the Gulf War, like others in which America took part, deeply concerned all walks and nationalities.[39]

Hampton Roads was second only to Washington, D.C., in its share of defense spending. While average American families paid about $3,000 a year to support the military, those in Hampton Roads *gained* almost $15,000 each. So commercial and personal despair attended the departure of ships, planes, and personnel in late 1990 and early 1991, rapture their return a few months later. The war gave brief promise of reviving the sluggish local economy as the carrier *Theodore Roosevelt* steamed home for $40 million in repairs, the *America* for $30 million, the *John F. Kennedy* for $25 million. Other nuclear-powered ships, thirteen amphibious ships, many cruisers, frigates, and oilers returned for refueling, maintenance, or repair. There was a gladsome spectacle of sailors crowding malls and auto showrooms to spend accumulated pay. "Whatever I see, I buy," a *Kennedy* crewman told a reporter, and Lynnhaven Mall merchants glowed in patriotic welcome.[40] But gains were soon offset by military cuts occasioned by the Cold War's end.

The long-term outlook for defense-related industries was, in fact, dismal. The Gulf War had little impact on government plans to close many military bases and cut military spending. Norfolk suffered no loss of installations in a list earmarked for eventual shutdown and even expected gains by the shifting of personnel from closing facilities elsewhere. (The naval air research facility was eventually shut down.) But the navy would likely lose about one-sixth of its ships, including some stationed at Norfolk. The city was likely to lose the headquarters of some of Virginia's largest financial institutions. National recession forced Norfolk to freeze salaries, reduce services, postpone building projects, and raise certain taxes in fiscal 1991–92.[41]

Still, optimists might hail the fact that the Hampton Roads channel, deepened in 1988 from forty-five to fifty feet, tempted bulk shippers, who increasingly dominated maritime transport. This was especially so in the case of coal. Central Appalachia's coal, from the world's oldest deposits, burns hotter and cleaner than most others. As clean-air standards grew more stringent, this coal could soon become the fuel of choice for many countries. Anticipating this, Norfolk Southern had expanded the capacity of its Lambert's Point pier, while CSX and other coal-carrying railroads invested in new fleets of coal hoppers. Each added ton handled paid $18.00 to local harbor pilots, tugboat crews, coal piers, and other port services.[42]

The Port of Norfolk, more accessible to cargo ships by a day's sailing than Baltimore, lured shippers from the Maryland port at a rate sufficient to have moved a record 37,000-plus containers in January 1990. A single shipper, Taiwan's Yang Ming Line, found it could save $1 million a year by using Hampton Roads instead of Baltimore. Revenues of the Virginia International Terminals, Inc., the nonprofit agency operating Hampton Roads' state-owned docks, were well above projections and growing.[43]

A U.S. Department of Commerce forecast in 1990, soon found to be too optimistic, showed Hampton Roads gaining 177,000 people and 116,000 jobs in the next decade. Per capita income would not rise dramatically, forecasters conceded, owing to the low-paying, tourism-related, and service jobs of most area workers. Hampton Roads should retain its rank among metropolitan areas but not overtake any ahead of it.[44] This outlook, of course, depended on imponderables beyond the scope of economic science. Chief among them, perhaps, looms the future of the great, life-giving bay.

No long-term prophecy could omit the impact of the bay's deterioration. Scores of groups and agencies formed or were directed during the 1970s and 1980s to focus on aspects of the problem. The bay's appalling condition is a catalyst for environmentalists in many areas of concern. Governors

Robb and Baliles made environmental protection a key goal of their 1980s administrations, the general assembly enacting laws to complement federal initiatives. A massive study issued in 1983 by the U.S. Environmental Protection Agency documented the Chesapeake's slow demise from pollutants, toxic industrial chemicals, boom-time development, and nutrients from farms and sewage plants.[45]

Baliles persuaded the assembly to create a cabinet secretary to oversee state environmental agencies and backed bills to ban phosphates and restrict TBT, a toxic boat paint. Discharge permits grew more restrictive as the water board acquired a computerized system to spot chronic polluters. Most municipal sewage plants came into compliance with federal clean-water laws. A pollution control board regulated toxic emissions from plants; a pesticide control board oversaw safety in the use of farm and household chemicals. In 1989 Virginia became the first state with land-use rules to protect the bay from development and farm pollution.[46]

Simultaneously, two hundred government officials at a Growth Management Forum in Williamsburg agreed that land-use regulation must take precedence over policing sewers and smokestacks. (A 1988 law initiated regulation of land use on the bay and its tributaries.) Growth in the next three decades was expected to deplete productive farm and woodlands and waterfronts, as well as create demands for more roads, sewers, landfills, electricity, and water.[47]

By 1990 the Elizabeth River, its industries and other polluters a principal enemy of the bay, was the focus of teams of state water control board "river watchers" seeking to minimize pollution's impact. They were part of a cleanup, begun in 1988, known as the Elizabeth River Initiative. The Craney Island fuel storage facility was one of sixty-eight allowed to discharge limited amounts of pollutants into the river. All are required to submit monthly, some additional quarterly, reports on discharges. Boat patrols scour the shoreline for illegal or unusual sources of pollutants, and mobile toxic laboratories do spot-monitoring at shoreline points. Danger points such as the Craney Island Fuel Terminal, where reusable oil is removed from forty million gallons of navy bilge and ballast water yearly, get special attention.[48]

Navy "oil patrol" teams daily check the bay for spills. They try to prevent harmful discharges from nineteen navy and marine installations in the bay watershed that have drains, sewer plants, and hazardous-waste dumps. The naval air station tries to stop fuel leaks but, pumping over four million gallons a year into ships and planes, cannot hope to eradicate them. (In 1991 the navy promised to make Norfolk nuclear-free within a year.) A local volunteer group of scuba buffs, U.S. Conservation Divers, devotes a day a month to dredging junk from lakes, rivers, and bays.[49]

The fate of Norfolk area wetlands is a special concern of environmentalists. Twelve generations of settlers have worked to fill in creeks, ponds, marshes, and bogs to create dry surfaces. The health department has led efforts to destroy the breeding grounds of mosquitoes; NRHA and other developers up to the 1970s used wetlands for landfills when tearing down houses and ripping up streets.[50] These efforts were crowned with success; many square miles of land were secured from the ravages of marsh cordgrass, fiddler crabs, diamondback terrapins, clapper rails, great egrets, blue herons, ducks, geese, and other wildlife. Now, soaring condominiums, concrete abutments, and parking lots festoon lands once given up to blue crabs and periwinkles.

In the early 1980s Norfolk retained seven hundred acres of saltwater wetlands, mostly along the Elizabeth and Lafayette rivers. People of vision saw profitable excuses to pave it over. At about this time, however, developers began to hear the bad news about why nature built these scruffy bogs. Marsh plants, it seems, absorb large amounts of the nutrients so damaging to local waters. Moreover, the death of cordgrass initiates the marine life food-chain. Bacteria break it down into components that feed microscopic phytoplankton, which are eaten by zooplankton, the sustenance of small fish eaten by big fish.[51]

The Chesapeake no doubt once had more wetlands than it needed. But almost four centuries of occupation by the offspring of the European Renaissance squeezed the wetlands sponge to the point that it no longer served its purposes. Nor was there any substitute: most Chesapeake wildlife was doomed unless remaining wetlands were preserved, perhaps increased.

At least dimly recognizing this, Norfolk in 1982 created a wetlands board, a seven-member panel responsible for protecting saltwater marshes and beachfronts along 144 miles of estuary shore and bayfront. Ten years earlier, the federal government had enacted the Coastal Zone Management Act, a step toward wetlands preservation. Only vigilance can prevent filling in creeks and ponds with broken concrete, wood, and dirt.[52]

In 1988 came the Chesapeake Bay Preservation Act, requiring changes in zoning and land-use law to protect the bay, wetlands, and tributaries. It covered waterfront development in ninety-eight cities, towns, and counties. In Norfolk, it affected 6,500 acres, or about a fifth of the city's land. Developers must have fifty- to one hundred-foot buffers of trees, grass, and shrubs between houses and shoreline wetlands. They must plant vegetation or build drainage systems to filter pollution from rainwater before it reaches the shore, and replace destroyed wetlands with new ones. These and other rules may prove troublesome to developers and homeowners, sometimes needlessly so. But environmentalists take comfort from the knowledge that their actions have begun to strike a balance between the legitimate claims of nature and development.[53]

It will take years of study and testing before anyone can say whether this belated concern for ecology will halt or reverse the processes of environmental decay. Some predict that the success of either developmental or environmental activists will spell the doom of the other. But the threat to the Chesapeake has stirred fears in ordinary people that no amount of theoretical speculation could achieve. If nothing else, the environmentalism of the past quarter-century has resulted in a vast amount of data on what is wrong and how to deal with it. The counterattack is underway and there is cause for optimism that the bay can be saved, though it may take many years to achieve that goal.

To that extent, the great, sprawling old Bahía de Santa Maria, the bay of the Chesapeians, has performed a splendid service for the contiguous states of America in general, and for Norfolk in particular. It has became a great laboratory for testing remedies vitally needed from ocean to ocean. It has performed such services, in war and peace, for many centuries. God willing and man cooperating, it will continue doing so for many to come.

CHAPTER 29

Xanadu—If Kublai Can

In Xanadu did Kublai Khan
A Stately Pleasure Dome Decree,
Where Alph the Sacred River Ran,
Through Caverns Measureless to Man,
Down to a Sunless Sea.
—SAMUEL TAYLOR COLERIDGE, "Xanadu"

ONE MAY assume that the busy city council on December 17, 1991, took no time to note and relish the symbolic implications of its major action of the day. Certainly its commitment to sell $40 million in bonds to finance an enormous "whazzit" on the Norfolk waterfront, to be known as Nauticus, was a significant act.[1] But only the readers of portents and omens could truly treasure the moment's metaphorical overtones.

For one thing, there was the portentous date. It was on this fateful December day, eighty-eight years before, that Orville Wright had been wafted aloft from the sand seventy miles south of Norfolk on mankind's first airplane flight. Like Nauticus, the launching of the "Wright Flyer" was fraught with breathtaking elements of faith and danger, a bold venture into alien realms. As omens go, the Wrights' success was auspicious for the council.

A more ominous and instructive precedent was Norfolk's decision in 1907 to have the Jamestown Exposition at Sewell's Point. Hoping for fifteen million visitors, they settled for fewer than three million and a humiliating receivership, much of its debt unpayable. Like the exposition's sponsors, the backers of Nauticus relied on favorable but controversial projections.

There was also a suggestive literary parallel. Nauticus called to mind Samuel Taylor Coleridge's lines 194 years earlier on a Mongol emperor's desire for a riverside palace. The council could not, like Coleridge, claim a drug-induced dream as its inspiration—though critics were ready to swear this was the case. The $40 million must somehow be wrestled loose from an economy deep in recession and defended from predictably aggressive efforts by shocked taxpayers to throttle the whole idea.

And what would $40 million, with $12 million more in anticipated donations, buy? Well, it would be something with the lordly title of the National Maritime Center. Jutting ostentatiously into the river from the foot of Main Street, it would be formed roughly in the shape of a huge ship. At its scheduled 1993 opening, it would have three levels of exhibit halls. They would feature shipbuilding, marine biology, commerce, laboratories, navigation, a new and enlarged Hampton Roads Naval Museum, shops, a restaurant, and a theater. Into this Epcot on the Chesapeake, the council persuaded itself, would throng a million visitors a year, their tickets paying most of the cost.[2]

That was not all. Hand-in-hand with the maritime center, a $15 million baseball stadium was planned for "Bessie's Place," an abandoned farmers' market on the industrial waterfront east of Berkley Bridge. Here a minor league baseball team would draw fans from throughout Hampton Roads and beyond, the parent New York Mets organization repaying the city over a period of twenty years.[3]

The folly seemed clear to many taxpayers. Twelve days after the Nauticus action, the *Virginian-Pilot* helpfully called the toll of the economic calamities of 1991. In January federal regulators seized TrustBank's twelve Hampton Roads branches, calling them "unsafe and unsound." In February the area's forty Tinee Giant convenience stores went bankrupt. In March it was the Norfolk-based Royster Company's fifty fertilizer outlets, in May Smith and Welton's department store chain. Then the navy's *Seawolf* submarine contract was awarded to Groton, Connecticut, over Newport News. The Gulf War's end brought a momentary splurge by returning servicemen that summer, then a deeper slump as auto and mall sales dwindled and companies laid off workers.[4]

In these alarming circumstances, it was the Jamestown expo precedent that seemed most pertinent. If continuing bad news was needed to hold the council suspect, it came quickly. In early 1992 Hofheimer's, Inc., Norfolk's 107-year-old shoe retailer, filed for bankruptcy, its debts almost four times its assets. Its collapse closely followed those of many old and respected stores—Thalhimers, Smith and Welton, Miller and Rhoads, The Famous. Ames would follow in October. Hampton Roads in 1992 experienced a record 5,273 bankruptcies.[5]

Many businesses that had so far avoided bankruptcy were in trouble. Norshipco, its shipyard South Hampton Roads' largest, laid off one-third of its workers that year owing to military cuts that cancelled contracts. Waterside, the showpiece marketplace, had trouble paying debts and cast about for relief; a critic groused that the market and its associated Festevents were "rip-offs" that only made Granby Mall "darker and unfriendlier than ever."[6]

Ill-omens gathered like fishhawks above a trawler's net. A 1992 survey of hotel value, based on such indices as occupancy and average room rates in the nation's largest markets, ranked Norfolk dead last. The real estate value of the city's hotels had dropped by 55 percent in the preceding five years, almost one-third of that in 1991. The problem was national but more serious in Norfolk than anywhere else. By September 1992, despite signs of incipient national recovery, the Hampton Roads economy, according to wage and job data, was still headed downward. Cuts at Newport News Shipbuilding had cost four thousand area jobs in the preceding year.[7]

Experts conceded that the prognosis was not good. Although the recession was two years old, some feared it was only half over, if that. Navy contracts in the area had dropped by nearly $200 million in three years and were expected to continue to decline. Since 1990 Norfolk's homeport fleet of 147 vessels had been reduced by a dozen and would drop further before 1993, each ship representing a big local payroll.[8] The left-right punch of a weak economy and military retrenchment was a double whammy aimed at Norfolk's livelihood, a dizzying blow to its self-confidence.

The declining economy meant smaller increases than predicted in tax collections and other city revenues. Besides efforts to manage public funds more efficiently, shortfalls led to more than five hundred jobs being culled from the city payroll from 1987 to 1992. Despite increases in various taxes and fees in the 1992–93 budget, the library and some other departments suffered cuts. Tidewater Regional Transit by mid-1992 was cutting bus routes and seeking other ways to make up for a seven-year decline in fares and riders and an expected drop in federal and state support.[9]

The trouble was not only economic. The state department of education in 1992 reported Hampton Roads students less proficient in reading, taking fewer challenging courses, and more apt to drop out than their counterparts in northern Virginia's more affluent districts. Many blacks remained bitter over the abandonment of cross-town busing in 1986 and the city council's recent refusal to name a fourth black to the seven-member school board, though the system's students were mostly black.[10]

Still more worrisome was rising crime. *Atlantic Monthly* magazine's lead article in January 1993 traced the history of a semiautomatic handgun with which Norfolk's Nicholas Elliott killed a Virginia Beach teacher, injured another, and fired at two more. Aided by permissive state gun laws, an older friend, and an obliging salesman, the fifteen-year-old bought his weapon at an Isle of Wight gunshop. Interstate I-95 from Norfolk to New York had the nickname "Iron Road" in token of its extensive traffic in illegal guns. (New York's stiffer gun laws made Virginia and the Carolinas prime sources of Gotham's light artillery.)[11]

Guns turned parts of Norfolk into war-zones. Despite the expenditure of $16 million for two decades of redevelopment and rehabilitation, Park Place and contiguous areas along upper Colley Avenue had lately fallen prey to drug-traffickers and resulting spasms of shooting and other violence. The addition of a police substation and more patrols was said to bring at least temporary improvement, but few thought that better law enforcement reached to the heart of the problem. The six-square-mile area had some 8,800 residents, but one-fifth of its houses were vacant and many had been demolished. Joblessness was pervasive, and many who could were leaving. Park Place suffered from a social anomie that went beyond economics.[12]

Park Place had no monopoly on crime, random violence, and poverty. At Sentara Hospital's shock-trauma center, only car injuries outnumbered gun injuries, the latter rising from 10 percent of all injuries in 1987 to 23 percent in 1991. From gloomy crack-alleys, gun violence spilled over into playgrounds, classrooms, and shopping malls.[13] The death toll, it might be said, inhibited the emergence of a National Victims Association to lobby legislators in behalf of rights of those at whom guns were fired.

In these circumstances, it was not surprising that an angry constituency assailed city council action on Nauticus and the baseball stadium as wreckless and insensitive. A citizens' group led by Ballentine Boulevard grocer Herbert M. Collins, victor in the fight against the councilmanic election system, petitioned to force the council to reconsider or submit its plans to public referendum. The petitioners argued that the maritime center, "world-class" though it might be, would not draw nearly as many visitors as projected, that the ball park, if built at all, should be on I-64 where it might better attract regional support. A serious shortfall of visitors and fans would have long-term adverse effects on city finances and, inevitably, taxes.[14]

There was a malodorous cook's broth of other daunting challenges, direct and indirect, as 1991 wallowed to a close. It was not immediately noted, however, that the unfolding months after December of that year produced subtle alterations of economic and other patterns that cast the Nauticus and stadium issues in a different light. Most obvious was the state supreme court's denial in late 1992 of the petition for a referendum on Nauticus and the ball park.[15] These projects, for good or ill, could proceed without the threat of a citizens' revolt. It was a burden lifted from the council's shoulders, though no endorsement of its wisdom.

A key question in Hampton Roads at the Cold War's end was whether local business could wean itself from dependency on the military and find other profitable avenues. Analysts pointed out that this dependency on the federal government had, in fact, long been receding. In 1969 almost half the employment in Hampton Roads was defense-related; by 1992 diversification reduced the proportion to just over a quarter.[16] The lesson seemed to be that Norfolk could learn, if it must, to prosper from peace as it had for so long from war. It seemed possible that the Wright brothers' precedent, after all, might be more relevant than that of the 1907 exposition.

If the need was for local firms to diversify more rapidly, some were demonstrating how. Norshipco, whose main revenue had long come from military orders, was finding that its facilities were in escalating demand by the booming cruise-ship industry. The company, under its president, Charles E. Eure, in 1992 already handled maintenance and refurbishing for 60 percent of Miami's Caribbean cruise ships; it was positioning itself to compete aggressively with Scandivavian and German shipyards. Colonna's Shipyard, a waterfront fixture for 117 years, went into bankruptcy in 1990 but bounced back nicely by 1992 under the leadership of a new president, James Herndon.[17]

The signals, mixed but generally upbeat, tended toward enhancement of the city council's IQ or confirmation of its dumb luck—the choice was open. For every old business that went under, others came in or expanded. Farm Fresh Inc., for example, in early 1993 revealed that it would open six Rack & Sack warehouse-groceries in Hampton Roads. The five-acre Church Street Crossing Center, opened in January 1992, indicated that even inner-city investment was still a viable business option.[18]

Even in the depths of recession, ships reached Port Norfolk at a rate of three thousand a year, their cargoes handled by 13,000 workers, their owners paying tugboats, harbor and docking pilots, cargo checkers, mechanics, freight forwarders, steamship agents, and others, besides the repair yards. A big ship might spend $150,000 a visit. The end of the Cold War meant that ships of former communist-bloc nations now used Norfolk's facilities, adding considerably to the port's business. Hampton Roads from 1990 had been the nation's busiest port, handling over seventy million tons of cargo a year. Port officials planned development of a 283-acre site north of Norfolk International Terminals, doubling the terminal's capacity over the next fifteen to twenty years.[19]

The high hopes of Barry Bishop, president of the Downtown Norfolk Council, rested on reviving old buildings along Granby Street and other shabby corridors. The *Virginian-Pilot*, its offices adjacent to Granby's dessicated east end, lent itself eagerly to downtown boosterism. New "yuppie" enterprises—coffeeshops, restaurants, antique and art stores—complemented plans to convert old structures to educational and city-government uses, including a mini-city hall in the old Rices Nachmans store at Granby and Freemason streets. The Center Theater in 1992 began a $10 million renovation into Harrison Opera House. The old Attucks Theatre on Church Street, occupied from the 1950s by a clothing store, was ticketed for renovation as a regional focal point for black history and culture.[20] Many projects took shape in worn-out or neglected neighborhoods.

Foes of the supposed overbuilding of Hampton Roads hotels had to contend with data showing that occupancy in Norfolk's largest hotels rose by nearly one-fourth in the first quarter of 1992 over the same period in 1991; hotel revenues had increased by over a third. The Marriott's connection with Omni via Waterside was seen as the main reason why Norfolk and Virginia Beach gained a 1997 Kiwanis International Convention, which might bring 15,000 delegates and $8 million in business. The 1992 National Hurricane Convention in Norfolk was over 50 percent better-attended than its previous meetings in Houston and Miami. Waterside Marketplace, facing foreclosure, was saved in early 1992 by refinancing arrangements on its mortgage.[21]

In short, neither recession nor the vagaries of world politics affected Norfolk's special geographic advantages. In peacetime as in war, Hampton Roads remained one of the world's great seaports. Painful adjustment would doubtless continue, but there was reason to believe that it could be made without serious disruption of Norfolk's economy. There were indications by 1993 that Norfolk, after a period of the shakes, was recovering its self-confidence.

Progress in linking Norfolk to other markets seemed likely to help sustain recovery. North Carolina agreed to transform US Route 17 into part of a 119-mile expressway from Raleigh to Norfolk. Virginia would reciprocate with work on its southeastern stretch of Route 17 and state route 194, bringing expressway traffic to Norfolk via 464. The highway, expected by the year 2002, would create new jobs and a sprawling city-suburb in parts of South

Hampton Roads adjacent to North Carolina. Meanwhile, a parallel span would be built on the Chesapeake Bay Bridge-Tunnel, though squeezing traffic through existing tunnels. The result would be a considerable increase in the seven thousand vehicles using the route daily. Within South Hampton Roads, new high-occupancy-vehicle lanes were expected to ease rush-hour congestion.[22]

A further source of optimism was the march of higher education. Norfolk State University's president, Dr. Harrison B. Williams, anticipated his school's first doctoral programs, an expanded library, and a performing arts center. The new Ph.D.s, if funded by the state, would presumably increase black faculty in state-aided colleges from an anemic 7 percent. Old Dominion University, under President James D. Koch, emerged in the 1990s as a leading oceanographic center, sending its experts on world-girdling expeditions to study marine life, circulation and temperature variations of ocean water, and global climate changes. Plans were made for a Granby Street campus for Tidewater Community College by 1995. Supporters of the idea saw yet another chance to revitalize this downtrodden sector.[23]

All three schools became partners in an ambitious plan to create a joint campus off Princess Anne Road in Virginia Beach. It was anticipated that up to six thousand students would be served at the facility by the century's end. The two universities were already cooperating in rented Virginia Beach quarters and their Tri-Cities Center in Portsmouth and were contemplating a similar operation in Chesapeake. Promoters of South Hampton Roads nourished a vision that added prestige in higher education would make the area more attractive to new business and industry.[24]

With annual tourism more important as an industry, changes at Norfolk Botanical Gardens, under superintendent Peter G. Frederick, were highly promising. Late 1992 brought an anonymous gift of $1 million in matching funds and a prospect of transforming them into one of the nation's leading public gardens. The money would pay for a visitors' reception and orientation center with a gift shop and plant market. But this was one part of a master plan by which the gardens were to raise over $10 million for a conservatory with a tropical rain forest. An education building, children's garden, cafe and terraces, and other additions were included in the twenty-year project.[25]

Norfolk was by now a respected city of medicine. When Jones Institute for Reproductive Medicine dedicated its $12.5 million facility on Mother's Day-eve 1992, hundreds of the 1,045 in vitro babies it had helped birth were on hand. With major support from the U.S. Agency for International

Development, the institute was researching the prevention of birth defects through genetic diagnosis, providing menopausal hormone-replacement therapy, and training over seventy doctors a year in reproductive medicine. In its two decades, the institute had helped put Eastern Virginia Medical School on the international health-care map. A coalition—the Medical College of Hampton Roads—involving Sentara Health System, Children's Hospital of The King's Daughters, DePaul, Blue Cross, and Blue Shield would soon offer free medical care to the children of Norfolk's working poor.[26]

A reflection of medicine's prestige was the choice of Dr. Mason C. Andrews as mayor in 1992. Andrews was co-founder of the medical school and had persuaded Drs. Howard and Georgeanna Jones to move to Norfolk from Baltimore. He was also a veteran city councilman and an activist in public affairs. The new mayor quickly reaffirmed his image by promoting a long list of his priorities. They included more housing, a regional shopping complex east of Granby Street, crime control, revitalization of Park Place, and downtown historic sculpture and markers to display Norfolk's cultural heritage. Broadly, he aimed "to get the greatest number of people feeling a sense of possession and belonging and pride" in their city. That the council unanimously chose him as mayor gave promise of a team effort by city leaders.[27]

By 1993 Park Place began taking its problems in hand in the resolve of community leaders, including L. G. Bond, Rev. Frank Guns, Thelma Harrison, and Carlos A. Howard, to curb the area's murder rate. In other categories, crime there had already been reduced from earlier levels. At the request of local businesses, the city council appointed a task force to improve small-business opportunities.[28] These and other initiatives bore promise of bringing Park Place into the mainstream of community revival pioneered in Berkley and elsewhere.

There were similar stirrings in Ocean View. The April 1992 opening of six-acre bayfront Ocean View Park fulfilled a million-dollar investment by the city in a troubled neighborhood. After the demise of its famous amusement park, the area became a rendezvous point for gangs, prostitutes, and drug-pushers. Seven civic leagues in the area, aided by NRHA and the Greater Norfolk Corporation, launched a major revitalization program. In 1990 part of the old amusement park became a housing development, Pinewell-by-the-Bay, joining Nansemond-by-the-Bay condominiums, which occupied another part. By 1993 NRHA was sponsoring an East

Ocean View thrust to encourage new single-family homes, a park and school, and the rebuilding of streets.[29]

If 1991, with eighty-six homicides, was Norfolk's "most murderous year ever," 1992 saw a drop not only in murder (to seventy-nine) but most other categories of serious crime. Community activism and police crackdowns helped reduce auto thefts, robberies, aggravated assaults, burglaries, and larcenies. Efforts to save Chesapeake Bay were rewarded with sharp reductions (by banning phosphate in laundry detergents) in phosphorus dumped into it and a modest reduction in nitrogen from treatment plants and industries. Early payoffs included reappearance of underwater grasses in depleted areas and record numbers of rockfish in the bay.[30]

Norfolk's struggle was manifested in announcements in 1992 that the opening of Nauticus would be delayed to the spring of 1994 and that the baseball stadium's cost had gone up by over $2 million. On the other hand, General Colin Powell, head of the Joint Chiefs of Staff, proposed consolidations of the military that could make Norfolk a veritable "shadow Pentagon." His plan would make Norfolk the seat of the commander-in-chief of all troop-training in the United States. The new command might also be responsible for American roles in UN peacekeeping missions and oversight of the military in disaster relief. The choice of Norfolk would reinforce the importance of Hampton Roads by bringing more senior-level officials to the area.[31]

Those who viewed Festevents as a "rip-off" of taxpayers were challenged by that organization's response that the city provides only about one-eighth of the cost of such celebrations; the rest comes from funds and services donated by the corporate community. While contributing much to a sense of municipal "bonding," it was argued, Festevents raises over $250,000 a year for local charities and other worthy causes. Festevents sponsors the great majority of 375 festival programs registered with the Hampton Roads Festival Association; most of these take place in Norfolk.[32]

Many citizens by 1992 could applaud the sentiments of Cathy Coleman of Holly Avenue, a Norfolk resident of twenty years standing. In a *Virginian-Pilot* letter, she told of having witnessed Norfolk's change in two decades from "a sleepy Navy town to a vibrant, competitive waterfront city that has capitalized on its assets, a city that has been recognized nationally for its quality of life and its metamorphosis." Much of that transformation, she felt, was owed to much-maligned Scope and Waterside and to such ambitious initiatives as Nauticus and the baseball stadium, Harbor Park, which opened in April 1993. The change could not have occurred "if we had not enjoyed visionary leadership willing to take the calculated risk of making informed investments in the city's future."[33]

The year 1993 opened with declarations that "the worst is over," and the recession was in retreat. Retailing in Hampton Roads was "better than expected." There was "a good, solid growth rate." "Housing, Public Works Will Fuel Rally," read a headline; Hampton Roads "Factories Could Be Recovery's Surprise," sang another. Tourism was up and "Experts Foresee a Steady Recovery."[34] Much of this was unvarnished boosterism and there were many caveats, but the overall mood was spryly upbeat. Many things conspired to make the city council's brashness seem clairvoyant.

The voyage of the *Ceilidh* incarnated something of the city's indomitable spirit. To enter the "America 500," a commemorative event in which boats would retrace Columbus's route to America, Norfolk's John Callander in 1989 bought the thirty-five-foot sailboat *Ceilidh* (pronounced *kay-lee*). After refurbishing it with the aid of the Lively Point Sailing Club, Callander, head of ODU's Virginia Beach graduate center, and Portsmouth navigator Bob Scott, set out in June 1992 for the Azores. ODU faculty member Bob Lucking, Chesapeake's Jim Hodges, and *Virginian-Pilot* staffer Ronald Speer also took turns navigating the boat from the Azores to Palos, Spain, then back via Madeira and the Canaries to San Salvador in the Bahamas. The often-grueling voyage of over eight thousand miles, outlasting Atlantic gales and a near-miss by a tornado–like waterspout, was successfully completed on December 19.[35]

Future generations might also draw their inspiration from the career of former seamstress Evelyn T. Butts, whose death the city mourned in March 1993. A Norfolk native, Butts distinguished herself by mounting a court challenge against Virginia's poll tax—*Butts v. Harrison*—and winning a landmark victory. She had been a leader in many community initiatives, including the revitalization of Oakwood and other sections. She served terms as chairperson of the Democratic Party's second district and of Concerned Citizens of Norfolk. In 1975 she became the first black woman appointed as a commissioner of Norfolk, a post she held until she retired in 1987. In addition, she had been for eight years a member of the state's board of housing and community development.[36]

In their landmark decisions to build Nauticus and a stadium for the renamed Norfolk Tides, city leaders steered a perilous course mapped for them by four centuries of history. Walled in by neighbors, its life-giving bay in mortal danger, global currents running against its traditional interests, its infrastructure at risk, national and regional economies stagnating, Norfolk made a costly wager on what seemed to many an unpromising future. Rather than hunker down to await more persuasively favorable signs, the city pushed ahead in the faith that the economy was stronger than it appeared, that times must soon be better, and that bold initiatives could help make them so. The actions harked back to the decision in 1680 to erect a town on the swampy eastern side of the Elizabeth River rather than the higher ground on the other side. It was Norfolk's time-honored way.

Even the urban walls that enclosed Norfolk, stifling its territorial enlargement, gradually changed to bridges linking the city more solidly with its Hampton Roads neighbors. Regionalism was still obstructed by local fears and suspicions, but the logic of cooperation—in crime control, traffic, tourism, and an increasing array of urban issues—waged vigorous war with localism. Time seemed to soften Norfolk's old yearning for dominance and deepen the self-confidence of neighboring cities.

Born amid seventeenth-century tempests, plagues, rebellions, pirates, and wars, the river village learned in infancy to thrive on adversity. Ravaged in the eighteenth century by pestilence and war, occupied repeatedly by foes, the town suffered the most thorough obliteration of any in American history—and scrambled back to pulsating life. Scourged in the nineteenth century by plague and fire, victimized by Richmond politics and economic cataclysms, besieged and trampled under the boots of enemy armies, the city clawed its way up from each setback to a greater prosperity than before. The raging demons of the twentieth century were met and vanquished by Norfolk's invincible will to persevere and prosper.

Judged by historical precedent, the city council's expensive decisions of 1991 were neither right nor wrong but foreordained. Time's ravages have not rescinded nature's decree that a great port city must stand at the mouth of the Elizabeth River, whatever vicissitudes befall it. This would probably be so even if man had bent all his efforts to prevent it—which, often enough, he has seemed to do. (Indeed, it can be said that Norfolk, early and late, has suffered perhaps more at the hands of friends than enemies.) No matter: walls have not retained nor disasters overwhelmed it. The Big Oyster still produces her glistening pearls. Norfolk's history proclaims her the Invincible City.

NOTES

CVSP   *Calendar of Virginia State Papers*
LNCA   *Lower Norfolk County Antiquary*
NCHR   *North Carolina Historical Review*
VMHB   *Virginia Magazine of History and Biography*
WMQ   *William and Mary Quarterly*

CHAPTER 1

1. Carl Bridenbaugh, *Early Americans* (New York, 1981), p. 7; Helen C. Rountree, *Pocahontas's People: The Powhatan Indians of Virginia through Four Centuries* (Norman, Okla., 1990), p. 15; Paul E. Hoffman, *A New Andalucia and a Way to the Orient: The American Southeast during the Sixteenth Century* (Baton Rouge, La., 1990), pp. 183–84; Clifford M. Lewis and Albert J. Loomie, *The Spanish Jesuit Mission in Virginia, 1570–1572* (Chapel Hill, N.C., 1953), p. 15.

2. Hoffman, *New Andalucia*, pp. 183–84; Bridenbaugh, *Early Americans*, pp. 7–8.

3. Hoffman, *New Andalucia*, pp. 183–84; Bridenbaugh, *Early Americans*, p. 7; Rountree, *Pocahontas's People*, p. 15; Charlotte M. Gradie, "Spanish Jesuits in Virginia: The Mission That Failed," *VMHB* 96 (1988): 142.

4. Hoffman, *New Andalucia*, p. 184; Lewis and Loomie, *Spanish Jesuit Mission*, pp. 20–21.

5. David B. Quinn, *North America from Earliest Discovery to First Settlement: The Norse Voyages to 1612* (New York, 1977), pp. 146–240; Quinn, *England and the Discovery of America, 1481–1620* (New York, 1974), pp. 139–247; Samuel Eliot Morison, *The European Discovery of America: The Northern Voyages A.D. 500–1600* (New York, 1971), p. 235; David B. and Alison M. Quinn, *The First Colonists: Documents on the Planting of the First English Settlements in North America, 1584–1590* (Raleigh, N.C., 1982), pp. 6, 9, 27; Paul E. Hoffman, *Spain and the Roanoke Voyages* (Raleigh, N.C., 1987), pp. 3–5.

6. Gradie, "Spanish Jesuits in Virginia," p. 135.

7. Bridenbaugh, *Early Americans*, p. 8.

8. Hoffman, *New Andalucia*, p. 186; Bridenbaugh, *Early Americans*, p. 9.

9. Hoffman, *New Andalucia*, p. 186; L. A. Vigneras, "A Spanish Discovery of North Carolina in 1566," *NCHR* 46 (1969): 308–407; Bridenbaugh, *Early Americans*, pp. 10–11; Gradie, "Spanish Jesuits in Virginia," p. 136.

10. Hoffman, *New Andalucia*, pp. 186, 245; Vigneras, "Spanish Discovery of North Carolina," pp. 406–7.

11. Bridenbaugh, *Early Americans,* pp. 11–12; Lewis and Loomie, *Spanish Jesuit Mission,* pp. 24–25.

12. Gradie, "Spanish Jesuits in Virginia," p. 141; Bridenbaugh, *Early Americans,* p. 12; Lewis and Loomie, *Spanish Jesuit Mission,* pp. 24–28; Rountree, *Pocahontas's People,* p. 16; Hoffman, *New Andalucia,* pp. 261–62.

13. Hoffman, *New Andalucia,* p. 262; Lewis and Loomie, *Spanish Jesuit Mission,* p. 89.

14. Hoffman, *New Andalucia,* p. 263; Lewis and Loomie, *Spanish Jesuit Mission,* pp. 39–43; William Jack Hranicky, "Spanish Influences on Pre-Colonial Virginia," *Quarterly Bulletin, Archaeological Society of Virginia* 33 (1978): 164–67; Rountree, *Pocahontas's People,* p. 16.

15. Bridenbaugh, *Early Americans,* p. 13.

16. Gradie, "Spanish Jesuits in Virginia," p. 144; Lewis and Loomie, *Spanish Jesuit Mission,* pp. 89–90.

17. Lewis and Loomie, *Spanish Jesuit Mission,* p. 92.

18. Rountree, *Pocahontas's People,* p. 16.

19. Lewis and Loomie, *Spanish Jesuit Mission,* p. 43; Helen C. Rountree, *The Powhatan Indians of Virginia: Their Traditional Culture* (Norman, Okla., 1989), pp. 58–62.

20. Rountree, *Powhatan Indians,* pp. 88–89.

21. Ibid., p. 79.

22. Ibid., pp. 80–84.

23. Ibid., p. 84.

24. Lewis and Loomie, *Spanish Jesuit Mission,* p. 181.

25. Ibid., pp. 44–45.

26. Bridenbaugh, *Early Americans,* pp. 13–14; Lewis and Loomie, *Spanish Jesuit Mission,* pp. 44–45, 180–81; Rountree, *Pocahontas's People,* pp. 16–17.

27. Lewis and Loomie, *Spanish Jesuit Mission,* p. 45; Rountree, *Pocahontas's People,* p. 16.

28. Lewis and Loomie, *Spanish Jesuit Mission,* p. 46.

29. Hoffman, *New Andalucia,* p. 264; Lewis and Loomie, *Spanish Jesuit Mission,* pp. 46–47; Rountree, *Pocahontas's People,* p. 17.

30. Hoffman, *New Andalucia,* p. 264; Lewis and Loomie, *Spanish Jesuit Mission,* pp. 46–47.

31. Gradie, "Spanish Jesuits in Virginia," p. 146.

32. Hoffman, *New Andalucia,* p. 264; Lewis and Loomie, *Spanish Jesuit Mission,* pp. 49–50; Rountree, *Pocahontas's People,* p. 17.

33. Hoffman, *New Andalucia,* p. 264; Rountree, *Pocahontas's People,* p. 17.

34. Hoffman, *New Andalucia,* p. 264; Lewis and Loomie, *Spanish Jesuit Mission,* pp. 51–52; Rountree, *Pocahontas's People,* p. 17.

35. Lewis and Loomie, *Spanish Jesuit Mission,* pp. 52–53; Rountree, *Pocahontas's People,* p. 17.

36. Hoffman, *New Andalucia,* p. 264; Lewis and Loomie, *Spanish Jesuit Mission,* pp. 52–53.

37. Lewis and Loomie, *Spanish Jesuit Mission,* p. 53.

38. Ibid., pp. 54–55; Rountree, *Pocahontas's People,* pp. 17–18.

39. Lewis and Loomie, *Spanish Jesuit Mission,* p. 56.

40. Gradie, "Spanish Jesuits in Virginia," p. 154.

Notes

41. Hranicky, "Spanish Influences on Pre-Colonial Virginia," p. 161.

42. Lewis and Loomie, *Spanish Jesuit Mission*, p. 161.

CHAPTER 2

1. David B. and Alison M. Quinn, *The First Colonists: Documents on the First Planting of the English Settlements in North America, 1584–1590* (Raleigh, N.C., 1982), p. 26.

2. Ibid., pp. 12, 17, 32.

3. Ibid., pp. 28, 31.

4. Ibid., pp. 26, 27.

5. Ibid., pp. 27–28.

6. Ibid., p. 31.

7. David B. Quinn, *Set Fair for Roanoke: Voyages and Colonies, 1584–1606* (Chapel Hill, N.C., 1985), p. 54.

8. Quinn and Quinn, *First Colonists*, pp. 27–28.

9. Ibid., pp. 32–33.

10. Ibid., pp. 25, 32–33, 39; Paul Hulton, *America 1585: The Complete Drawings of John White* (Chapel Hill, N.C., 1984), pp. 86, 183.

11. Quinn and Quinn, *First Colonists*, pp. 37–42.

12. Ibid., pp. 42–45.

13. Ibid., p. 33.

14. Ibid., pp. 25, 27.

15. David B. Quinn, *North America from Earliest Discovery to First Settlements* (New York, 1977), p. 339; Quinn and Quinn, *First Colonists*, p. 93.

16. Quinn and Quinn, *First Colonists*, p. 97.

17. Ibid., pp. 102–4.

18. Ibid., pp. 103, 126.

19. Ibid., pp. 125–28.

20. Ibid., pp. 36–37.

21. Quinn, *Set Fair for Roanoke*, pp. 307–9.

22. Quinn, *England and the Discovery of America, 1481–1620* (London, 1974), pp. 423–29.

23. Ibid., pp. 419–31.

24. Ibid., pp. 482–88.

25. Ibid., pp. 486–88.

26. Edmund S. Morgan, *American Slavery, American Freedom: The Ordeal of Colonial Virginia* (New York, 1975), p. 71.

27. Quinn and Quinn, *First Colonists*, p. 9.

28. Quinn, *Set Fair for Roanoke*, p. 362.

29. David B. Quinn, ed., "Observations Gathered out of 'a Discourse of the Plantation of the Southern Colony in Virginia by the English, 1606.' Written by that honorable gentleman, Master George Percy" (Charlottesville, Va., 1967), p. 8; Quinn, *First Colonists*, pp. 7, 9.

30. Quinn, *First Colonists*, pp. 8–10.

31. Ibid., p. 31.

32. Ibid., p. 32.

33. Quinn, *Set Fair for Roanoke,* p. 364.

34. Quinn and Quinn, *First Colonists,* pp. 25, 28; Quinn, *England and the Discovery of America,* pp. 256–57.

35. Quinn, *Set Fair for Roanoke,* p. 364.

36. Quinn and Quinn, *First Colonists,* pp. 25, 38; Quinn, *England and the Discovery of America,* pp. 256–57.

37. Hranicky, "Spanish Influences on Pre-Colonial Virginia," p. 161; Carl Bridenbaugh, *Jamestown 1544–1699* (New York, 1980), pp. 10–33; Rountree, *Pocahontas's People,* pp. 18–19.

38. Bridenbaugh, *Jamestown 1544–1699,* p. 19.

39. Nancy O. Lurie, "Indian Cultural Adjustment to European Civilization," in James M. Smith, ed., *Seventeenth Century America: Essays in Colonial History* (Chapel Hill, N.C., 1959), pp. 43–44.

40. Ibid., pp. 46–47.

41. Quinn, *Set Fair for Roanoke,* pp. 367–68.

42. Ibid., pp. 362–68.

43. Ibid., p. 367.

44. See, e.g., Alice Granbery Walter, ed., *Book 'B' Lower Norfolk County, Virginia, 2 November 1646–15 January 1651/2* (n.p., 1978), p. 294 (Oct. 20, 1645).

45. J. Leitch Wright Jr., *The Only Land They Knew: The Tragic Story of the American Indians in the Old South* (New York, 1982), p. 79; Rountree, *Pocahontas's People,* pp. 21–22.

CHAPTER 3

1. Wilson Miles Cary, "Lower Norfolk County Records 1636–1646," *VMHB* 39 (1931): 240.

2. Ibid.

3. Norfolk County Minute Book B, ms. in Norfolk County Courthouse, Great Bridge, Va., p. 53a (Nov. 10, 1647).

4. Walter, *Minute Book B,* p. 48 (July 13, 1647).

5. Ibid.

6. Ibid.

7. Ibid.

8. Ibid., p. 48 (Aug. 16, 1647).

9. Ibid.

10. Ibid., p. 37 (Mar. 5, 1647).

11. Ibid., p. 53 (Nov. 10, 1647).

12. Ibid., p. 53a (Dec. 15, 1647).

13. Kate Mason Rowland, "The Offley Family," *VMHB* 12 (1905–6): 201–2.

14. Phyllis W. Francis, "Some Lineal Descendants of Captain Adam Thorowgood (1602–1640), Lynnhaven Parish, Princess Anne County, Virginia," *Virginia Genealogist* 16 (1972): 4–5.

15. Nell Marion Nugent, ed., *Cavaliers and Pioneers: Abstracts of Virginia Land Patents and Grants, 1623–1666* (Baltimore, Md., 1979), p. 22; Mary D. B. McCurdy, "The Townleys and Warners of Virginia and Their English Connections," *VMHB* 81 (1973): 320.

Notes

16. Georgia D. Wardlaw, *The Old and Quaint in Virginia* (Richmond, Va., 1939), pp. 222–23.

17. Francis, "Descendants of Captain Adam Thorowgood," p. 7; Nugent, *Cavaliers and Pioneers*, p. 22.

18. Alice G. Walter, comp., *Captain Thomas Willoughby 1601–1647 of England, Barbados and Lower Norfolk County, Virginia. Some of His Descendants 1601–1800* (n.p., 1983), p. 26.

19. Nugent, *Grants, 1623–1666*, p. 22.

20. Francis, "Descendants of Captain Adam Thorowgood," pp. 5–6. The site of the six-room frame Thorowgood house was evidently found in 1955 by archaeologist Floyd Painter. The existing "Adam Thorowgood House" in Lynnhaven is from a later generation. See Florence K. Turner, *Gateway to the New World: A History of Princess Anne County, Virginia 1607–1824* (Easley, S.C., 1984), p. 35.

21. See, e.g., Edmund Ruffin, *Agricultural, Geological and Descriptive Sketches of Lower North Carolina and the Similar Adjacent Lands of Virginia* (Raleigh, N.C., 1861), pp. 91–92; Hugh T. Lefler, ed., *A New Voyage to Carolina by John Lawson* (Chapel Hill, N.C., 1967), pp. 69–70; *Virginian-Pilot* (Norfolk), Sept. 1, 1989.

22. Nugent, *Grants, 1623–1666*, pp. 71, 79, 80; "St. Botolph's Grimston: Visit of Members of Eastern Shore Chapel May 21st 1989. Our American Connections," St. Botolph's church bulletin, Grimston, 1989.

23. George C. Mason, "The Colonial Churches of Norfolk County, Virginia," *WMQ*, 2d ser., no. 21 (1941): 139.

24. Walter, *Captain Thomas Willoughby*, pp. 24–29; Rogers Dey Whichard, *The History of Lower Tidewater Virginia*, 2 vols. (New York, 1959), 1:18.

25. Francis, "Descendants of Captain Adam Thorowgood," p. 6.

26. Nugent, *Grants, 1623–1666*, p. 27; John G. Herndon, "The Reverend William Wilkinson of England, Virginia, and Maryland," *VMHB* 57 (1949): 316–21; Whichard, *Lower Tidewater*, 1:229; Francis, "Descendants of Captain Adam Thorowgood," p. 7.

27. Cary, "Lower Norfolk County Records," p. 2 (May 15, 1637).

28. Ibid., p. 19 (Mar. 4, 1638).

29. Ibid., p. 135 (Aug. 3, 1640).

30. Ibid.

31. Francis, "Descendants of Captain Adam Thorowgood," p. 7; Wardlaw, *Old and Quaint in Virginia*, pp. 222–23.

32. Frederick W. Gookins, *Daniel Gookin 1612–1687, Assistant and Major General of the Massachusetts Bay Colony* (Chicago, Ill., 1912), p. 57.

33. Ibid., pp. 67–68.

34. Ibid., pp. 73–198.

35. Walter, *Minute Book B*, p. 82 (June 15, 1648); Philip A. Bruce, *Institutional History of Virginia in the Seventeenth Century*, 2 vols. (New York, 1910), 1:149–50, 160, 166, 201, 221. See Mason, "Colonial Churches of Norfolk County," pp. 140–42; George C. Mason, "The Colonial Churches of Lynnhaven Parish, Princess Anne County, Virginia," *WMQ*, 2d ser., no. 18 (1938): 270–71. See also Bruce, *Institutional History*, 1:210, 257–58; Walter, *Minute Book B*, p. 74a (May 29, 1648); John B. Boddie, *Seventeenth Century Isle of Wight County Virginia* (Baltimore, Md., 1938), p. 59.

36. Walter, *Minute Book B*, p. 59a (Dec. 16, 1647); J. Henry Lee, "Certificates of Head

Rights in the County Court of Lower Norfolk County," *New England Historical and Genealogical Register* 47 (1893): 82–83. See also William L. Shea, *The Virginia Militia in the Seventeenth Century* (Baton Rouge, La., 1983), p. 52.

37. Shea, *Virginia Militia,* pp. 62–63; Lea, "Certificates of Head Rights in the County Court of Lower Norfolk County," pp. 82–83.

38. Boddie, *Seventeenth Century Isle of Wight,* p. 98; Bruce, *Institutional History,* 2:82–83.

39. Bruce, *Institutional History,* 2:255.

40. Ibid., 2:82–83.

41. Gookin, *Daniel Gookin,* pp. 57–58.

42. See, e.g., Walter, *Minute Book B,* p. 8a (Nov. 16, 1646), p. 33a (Apr. 26, 1647), p. 51c (Aug. 16, 1647); Lower Norfolk County Minute Book B, p. 209 (Dec. 15, 1643), p. 248 (June 16, 1643), p. 255 (June 1645), p. 257 (Aug. 1645), p. 258 (Aug. 1645), p. 264 (Aug. 1645); Paul Wilstach, *Tidewater Virginia* (Indianapolis, Ind., 1929), p. 105; "Notes from the York County Records, Court Held Sept. 24, 1646," *VMHB* 17 (1909): 109; Nugent, *Grants, 1623–1666,* pp. 136, 143, 145.

43. Walter, *Minute Book B,* p. 41a (June 15, 1647); Warren M. Billings, ed., *The Old Dominion in the Seventeenth Century: A Documentary History of Virginia, 1606–1689* (Chapel Hill, N.C., 1975), pp. 90–91.

44. Walter, *Minute Book B,* p. 53a (Dec. 15, 1647), p. 63 (Jan. 20, 1648).

45. W. G. Stanard, "Abstracts of Virginia Land Patents," *VMHB* 1 (1893): 85–86.

46. Nora Miller Turman and Mark C. Lewis, "Inventory of the Estate of Argoll Yeardley of Northampton County, Virginia, in 1655," *VMHB* 70 (1962): 410; Susie M. Ames, *County Court Records of Accomack-Northampton Virginia 1640–1645* (Charlottesville, Va., 1973), p. 176.

47. Ames, *County Court Records of Accomack-Northampton,* p. 301.

48. Gary Parks, indexer, *Genealogies of Virginia Families from Tyler's Quarterly Historical and Genealogical Magazine,* 4 vols. (Baltimore, Md., 1981), 4:557–58.

49. Ames, *County Court Records of Accomack-Northampton,* p. 238; Clara Ann Bowler, "Carted Whores and White Shrouded Apologies," *VMHB* 85 (1977): 418; Turman and Lewis, "Inventory of the Estate of Argoll Yeardley," p. 410.

50. Morgan, *American Slavery, American Freedom,* p. 16; Walter, *Minute Book B,* p. 186 (Oct. 3, 1651).

51. Walter, *Minute Book B,* p. 458 (Nov. 11, 1653); John R. Pagan, "Dutch Maritime and Commercial Activity in Mid-Seventeenth Century Virginia," *VMHB* 90 (1982): 485–95.

52. Pagan, "Dutch Maritime and Commercial Activity," p. 489; Walter, *Minute Book B,* p. 61 (Jan. 20, 1648).

53. "Letter Extracted from the County Record Books 1. Lower Norfolk County, formed in 1637 from Elizabeth City County," *VMHB* 35 (1927): 50–51; Beverly C. Fleet, "Lower Norfolk County 1651–1654," in Fleet, *Virginia Colonial Abstracts,* 4 vols. (Baltimore, Md., 1988), 3:435 (Nov. 10, 1652).

54. Stanard, "Abstracts of Virginia Land Patents," p. 86.

55. "Francis Yeardley's Narrative of Excursions into Carolina, 1654," in Alexander S. Salley, ed., *Narratives of Early Carolina, 1650–1708* (New York, 1911), p. 25.

56. Ibid., pp. 25–26.

57. Ibid., p. 26.

58. Ibid.

59. Ibid.

60. "Francis Yeardley's Narrative," p. 26; Fleet, "Lower Norfolk County," p. 467 (Apr. 18, 1654); Fleet, "Lower Norfolk County," p. 458 (Dec. 12, 1653).

61. Fleet, "Lower Norfolk County," p. 466 (Mar. 22, 1654); "Francis Yeardley's Narrative," p. 27; Christian F. Feest, "North Carolina Algonquians," in Bruce E. Trigger, ed., *Northeast,* in William C. Sturtevant, gen. ed., *Handboook of North American Indians,* 15 vols. (Washington, D.C., 1978), 15:271–88.

62. "Francis Yeardley's Narrative," p. 28.

63. Ibid.

64. Ibid., pp. 25–29.

65. Ibid., pp. 28–29. See also Charles E. Hatch Jr., "Mulberry Trees and Silkworms: Sericulture in Early Virginia," *VMHB* 65 (1957): 53.

66. Turman and Lewis, "Inventory of the Estate of Argoll Yeardley," p. 412; Whichard, *Lower Tidewater,* 1:263.

67. William S. Powell, "Carolina and the Incomparable Roanoke: Explorations and Attempted Settlements, 1620–1663," *NCHR* 51 (1974): 20; LNC Minute Book D, p. 85 (Aug. 17, 1657).

68. "Letter from County Record Books," p. 7; Francis, "Adam Thorowgood," p. 9.

69. Norfolk County Wills and Deeds, Book D (1656–66), Aug. 15, 1661.

CHAPTER 4

1. Philip A. Bruce, *Economic History of Virginia in the Seventeenth Century,* 2 vols. (New York, 1935), 2:522–65.

2. Ibid., pp. 522–23, 539–40.

3. John C. Rainbolt, "The Absence of Towns in Seventeenth-Century Virginia," *Journal of Southern History* 35 (1969): 343–47.

4. Whichard, *Lower Tidewater,* 1:255.

5. Morgan, *American Slavery, American Freedom,* pp. 187–89.

6. Ibid., p. 189.

7. Richard L. Morton, *Colonial Virginia,* 2 vols. (Chapel Hill, N.C., 1960), 1:192.

8. Morton, *Colonial Virginia,* 1:228–29; "The Indians of Southern Virginia, 1650–1711: Depositions in the Virginia and North Carolina Boundary Case," [Part I], *VMHB* 7 (1900–1901): 345–47.

9. Morgan, *American Slavery, American Freedom,* p. 242; Morton, *Colonial Virginia,* 1:193–94.

10. Morgan, *American Slavery, American Freedom,* pp. 196–98, 240–42.

11. Ibid., p. 241; Morton, *Colonial Virginia,* 1:193–94.

12. William S. Powell, ed., *Ye Countie of Albemarle in Carolina: A Collection of Documents 1664–1675* (Raleigh, N.C., 1958), p. 62; Morton, *Colonial Virginia,* 1:193; Morgan, *American Slavery, American Freedom,* p. 242.

13. Powell, *Ye Countie of Albemarle,* pp. 62–63; Morgan, *American Slavery, American Freedom,* p. 243; Whichard, *Lower Tidewater,* 1:279.

14. Morgan, *American Slavery, American Freedom*, pp. 242–43; Morton, *Colonial Virginia*, 1:215–17.

15. Morgan, *American Slavery, American Freedom*, p. 246.

16. Ibid., pp. 238–39; Walter, *Minute Book B*, pp. 50, 135.

17. LNC Minute Book C, p. 63; Morgan, *American Slavery, American Freedom*, p. 153; Cary, "NC Records 1636–1646," *VMHB* 39 (1931): 249; Morgan, *American Slavery, American Freedom*, p. 154.

18. Cary, "LNC Records," p. 9; Walter, *Minute Book B*, p. 453; F. Roy Johnson, *The Algonquians*, 2 vols. (Murfreesboro, N.C., 1972), 2:172–84; William L. Saunders, ed., *The Colonial Records of North Carolina*, 10 vols. (Raleigh, N.C., 1886–90), 1:226.

19. Walter, *Minute Book B*, pp. 50, 90, 115a.

20. Lea, "Certificates of Head Rights in the County Court of Lower Norfolk," p. 68.

21. Billings, *Old Dominion in the Seventeenth Century*, pp. 157, 161.

22. Morgan, *American Slavery, American Freedom*, pp. 162, 164, 193.

23. Thomas C. Parramore, "The Tuscarora Ascendancy," *NCHR* 59 (1982): 307–26; Anita H. Rutman, "Still Planting the Seeds of Hope: The Recent Literature of the Early Chesapeake Region," *VMHB* 95 (1987): 10.

24. Bruce, *Institutional History*, 1:231, 235, 240.

25. Ibid., p. 250.

26. Morgan, *American Slavery, American Freedom*, pp. 215–34, 237; Cary, "LNC Records," p. 10.

27. Morton, *Colonial Virginia*, 1:228–30.

28. Whichard, *Lower Tidewater*, 1:259; John D. Neville, *Bacon's Rebellion: Abstracts of Materials in the Colonial Records Project* (n.p., n.d.), p. 81.

29. Hugh F. Rankin, *Upheaval in Albemarle: The Story of Culpeper's Rebellion 1675–1689* (Raleigh, N.C., 1962), pp. 43–44.

30. Neville, *Bacon's Rebellion*, pp. 363–64.

31. Morgan, *American Slavery, American Freedom*, pp. 284–85.

32. Whichard, *Lower Tidewater*, 1:256–57, 331; Bruce, *Virginia in the Seventeenth Century*, p. 160.

33. Whichard, *Lower Tidewater*, 1:246, 249; Morgan, *American Slavery, American Freedom*, p. 151.

34. Whichard, *Lower Tidewater*, 1:260–62.

35. Ibid., 1:366–67.

36. Morgan, *American Slavery, American Freedom*, pp. 280–82.

37. Ibid., pp. 283–85; Whichard, *Lower Tidewater*, 1:257.

38. Morgan, *American Slavery, American Freedom*, p. 285.

39. Whichard, *Lower Tidewater*, 1:325–29.

40. Thomas J. Wertenbaker and Marvin W. Schlegel, *Norfolk: Historic Southern Port* (Durham, N.C., 1962), pp. 4–5.

41. Whichard, *Lower Tidewater*, 1:330–39.

42. Morgan, *American Slavery, American Freedom*, pp. 182, 184.

43. Bruce, *Economic History of Virginia*, 1:372, 486; Wertenbaker and Schlegel, *Norfolk*, pp. 29–30.

44. Whichard, *Lower Tidewater*, 1:279–359.

45. Ibid., 1:285–86, 334, 335.
46. Ibid., 1:335–36.

CHAPTER 5

1. Donald G. Shomette, *Pirates on the Chesapeake* (Centreville, Md., 1985), pp. 60–61, 93; H. R. McIlwaine et al., eds., *Executive Journals of the Council of Colonial Virginia*, 6 vols. (Richmond, Va., 1925–66), 1:170–71, 194–95.

2. McIlwaine, *Executive Journals*, 1:163–82, 235–36.

3. Ibid., 1:177–82.

4. Ibid., 1:178–79.

5. Ibid., 1:179.

6. Ibid.

7. Bruce, *Institutional History*, 1:510–11.

8. Judith McGhan, ed., *Genealogies of Virginia Families from the William and Mary College Quarterly Historical Magazine* (Baltimore, Md., 1982), p. 170; W. G. Stanard, "Abstracts of Virginia Land Patents," *VMHB* 4 (1903): 82.

9. Edward W. Jones, ed., "Witchcraft in Virginia," *WMQ*, 2d ser., no. 2 (1922): 58–59.

10. *Lower Norfolk County Antiquary*, 5:56.

11. "Papers Relating to the Administration of Governor Nicholson and to the Founding of William and Mary College," *VMHB* 7 (1906): 170; Samuel A. Ashe et al., eds., *Biographical History of North Carolina: From Colonial Times to the Present*, 8 vols. (Greensboro, N.C., 1905–17), 2:369; John J. Cadbury, ed., *The Journal of George Fox* (Cambridge, 1952), pp. 646–47.

12. Ashe, *Biographical History of North Carolina*, 2:372; J. Bryan Grimes, ed., *Abstract of North Carolina Wills Compiled from Original and Recorded Wills in the Office of the Secretary of State* (Raleigh, N.C., 1910), p. 295.

13. Shomette, *Pirates on the Chesapeake*, p. 38.

14. Ibid., pp. 93–94.

15. Lefler and Powell, *Colonial North Carolina*, p. 82.

16. Shomette, *Pirates on the Chesapeake*, pp. 77–78; McIlwaine, *Executive Journals*, 1:107–9.

17. Morton, *Colonial Virginia*, 1:347–48.

18. Shomette, *Pirates on the Chesapeake*, pp. 100–102.

19. Ibid., pp. 103–7.

20. Ibid., pp. 107–10.

21. Ibid., p. 128.

22. McIlwaine, *Executive Journals*, 1:154, 256; William K. Boyd, *Histories of the Dividing Line betwixt Virginia and North Carolina* (New York, 1967), p. 39.

23. Whichard, *Lower Tidewater*, 1:339–41.

24. Ibid., p. 345; Norfolk County Deed Book 9 (1710–17), Part 1, pp. 79, 91, 109, 193 (June 21, 1717), ms. in Norfolk County Courthouse, Chesapeake, Va.

25. Norfolk County Deed Book 9, p. 164.

26. "Pitch and Tar in Virginia, 1704," *WMQ*, 2d. ser., no. 3 (1923): 209–10; Shomette, *Pirates on the Chesapeake*, p. 131.

27. Wertenbaker and Schlegel, *Norfolk*, p. 36.

28. R. A. Brock, ed., *Documents, Chiefly Unpublished, Relating to the Huguenot Emigration to Virginia* (Baltimore, Md., 1979), pp. 6–7.

29. Whichard, *Lower Tidewater*, 1:253–54, 292, 298.

30. Ibid., 1:337, 340, 354, 356; McIlwaine, *Executive Journals*, 2:16, 42, 59, 73, 106, 115, 122; Norfolk County Deed Book 9, p. 82.

31. Elizabeth D. Coleman, "The Witchcraft Delusion Rejected," *Virginia Cavacade* 6 (1956–57): 28–34; William S. Price Jr., ed., *North Carolina Higher-Court Records 1702–1708* (Raleigh, N.C., 1974, *The Colonial Records of North Carolina* [2d ser.]), 4:96, 280–81, 296.

32. McIlwaine, *Executive Journals*, 2:105; Norfolk County Deed Book 6 (1695–1703), pp. 173–74; "Miscellaneous Colonial Documents from the Originals in the Virginia State Archives," *VMHB* 16 (1910): 76.

33. Shomette, *Pirates on the Chesapeake*, pp. 129–30.

34. Whichard, *Lower Tidewater*, 1:45; Shomette, *Pirates on the Chesapeake*, p. 133.

35. Shomette, *Pirates on the Chesapeake*, pp. 133–34.

36. Whichard, *Lower Tidewater*, 2:61–62; McIlwaine, *Executive Journals*, 2:70; Shomette, *Pirates on the Chesapeake*, pp. 135, 149–51.

37. McIlwaine, *Executive Journals*, 2:94; Shomette, *Pirates on the Chesapeake*, pp. 157–70.

38. Shomette, *Pirates on the Chesapeake*, pp. 170–77.

39. Ibid., pp. 188–89.

40. Morton, *Colonial Virginia*, 2:461; Shomette, *Pirates on the Chesapeake*, pp. 194–207.

41. Shomette, *Pirates on the Chesapeake*, pp. 198–216.

42. Ibid., pp. 240–42.

43. Byrd, *Histories of the Dividing Line*, pp. 37–38.

44. Ibid., p. 36.

45. Ibid.

46. Ibid.

47. Ibid., pp. 38–39.

48. Ibid., p. 38.

49. Wertenbaker and Schlegel, *Norfolk*, pp. 33–34.

50. Byrd, *Histories of the Dividing Line*, pp. 37–41; Whichard, *Lower Tidewater*, 1:349; Wertenbaker and Schlegel, *Norfolk*, p. 11.

51. Wertenbaker and Schlegel, *Norfolk*, pp. 34–35.

52. Norfolk County Book 9, pp. 51, 69, 91–92, 195, 217; Norfolk County Deed Book 10 (Feb. 19, 1719–Aug. 18, 1722), p. 10.

53. G. McLaren Bryden, "The Virginia Clergy," *VMHB* 32 (1924): 322–23.

Notes

CHAPTER 6

1. Brent Tarter, *The Order Book and Related Papers of the Common Hall of the Borough of Norfolk, Virginia, 1736–1798* (Richmond, Va., 1979), pp. 46, 47, 49.

2. Ibid., pp. 50, 51, 52–53.

3. Ibid., pp. 57–58, 63.

4. Ibid., pp. 63, 65.

5. *Virginia Gazette*, Oct. 20, 1738; Tarter, *Order Book*, pp. 60–61.

6. Tarter, *Order Book*, pp. 60, 69.

7. Ibid., pp. 88, 90; *Virginia Gazette* (Rind), Sept. 1, 1768.

8. Robert McColley, *Slavery in Jeffersonian Virginia* (Urbana, Ill., 1964), pp. 12–13; Wertenbaker and Schlegel, *Norfolk*, p. 43.

9. John E. Selby, *The Revolution in Virginia, 1775–1783* (Williamsburg, Va., 1988), p. 31; Wertenbaker and Schlegel, *Norfolk*, p. 44.

10. Jacob M. Price, "The Rise of Glasgow in the Chesapeake Tobacco Trade, 1707–1775," *WMQ*, 3d ser., no. 11 (1954): 187–89; Wertenbaker and Schlegel, *Norfolk*, pp. 44–46; Whichard, *Lower Tidewater*, 1:362, 363; Tarter, *Order Book*, p. 46; *Virginia Gazette*, July 31, 1746.

11. Whichard, *Lower Tidewater*, 1:353–54.

12. Tarter, *Order Book*, pp. 35–41.

13. Ibid., pp. 35–36, 73–74; Whichard, *Lower Tidewater*, 1:379.

14. Tarter, *Order Book*, pp. 7–8, 39, 40, 44.

15. *Norfolk Herald*, Jan. 7, 1835.

16. Ibid.; *Virginian-Pilot*, Nov. 23, 1975.

17. Whichard, *Lower Tidewater*, 1:351–52, 406–7; Thomas C. Parramore, *Launching the Craft: The First Half-Century of Freemasonry in North Carolina* (Raleigh, N.C., 1975), pp. 6–41.

18. *Virginia Gazette*, July 31, 1746.

19. Ibid.

20. Hugh F. Rankin, "Criminal Trial Proceedings in the General Court of Colonial Virginia," *VMHB* 72 (1964): 65–66; Tarter, *Order Book*, p. 89.

21. Tarter, *Order Book*, p. 101.

22. Ibid., pp. 103–4; Whichard, *Lower Tidewater*, 1:380–82.

23. Margaret E. Parker to James Parker, Aug. 22, 1760, in Parker Family Papers, ms. copy at Foundation Library, Williamsburg; Whichard, *Lower Tidewater*, 1:154; *Virginian-Pilot*, Feb. 18, 1990.

24. "A French Traveller in the Colonies, 1765," *American Historical Review* 26 (1920–21): 739.

25. *Norfolk Herald*, Jan. 7, 1835; "French Traveller in the Colonies," p. 743.

26. Whichard, *Lower Tidewater*, 1:383–90.

27. *Day-Book* (Norfolk), Sept. 18, 1860.

28. "French Traveller in the Colonies," pp. 739, 740, 744.

29. George Reese, ed., *The Official Papers of Francis Fauquier, Lieutenant Governor of Virginia, 1758–1786*, 3 vols. (Charlottesville, Va., 1967), 2:1500–1501.

30. Whichard, *Lower Tidewater*, 1:392–93; Wertenbaker and Schlegel, *Norfolk*, pp. 23–24.

31. Whichard, *Lower Tidewater,* 1:392–94; Wertenbaker and Schlegel, *Norfolk,* p. 24; *Virginia Gazette* (Purdie), Mar. 21, 1766, July 11, 1771.

32. *Virginia Gazette* (Purdie and Dixon), June 6, 1766, Jan. 2, 1772.

33. *Virginia Gazette* (Purdie and Dixon), Dec. 17, 1767; Feb. 4, Sept. 29, 1768; John S. Watterson, *Thomas Burke, Restless Revolutionary* (Washington, D.C., 1980), pp. 7–12, 220–21.

34. Pauline Maier, "Popular Uprisings and Civil Authority in Eighteenth-Century Virginia," *WMQ,* 3d ser., no. 30 (1973): 17–18; Edward A. Smyth, "Mob Violence in Prerevolutionary Norfolk, Virginia" (M.A. thesis, Old Dominion University, 1975), p. 9.

35. Maier, "Popular Uprisings," pp. 8, 18; Smyth, "Mob Violence," pp. 10–11; Wertenbaker and Schlegel, *Norfolk,* p. 69; William Maxwell Read, "My Mother," *Lower Norfolk County Antiquary* 2 (1897): 97.

36. Captain William Smith to Jeremiah Morgan, Apr. 3, 1766, *WMQ,* 1st ser., no. 21 (1912–13): 167.

37. Jesse Lemisch, "Jack Tar in the Streets: Merchant Seamen and the Politics of Revolutionary America," *WMQ,* 3d ser., no. 25 (1968): 391; Wertenbaker and Schlegel, *Norfolk,* p. 17; Reese, *Official Papers of Francis Fauquier,* 3:1500–1502.

38. *Virginia Gazette* (Purdie and Dixon), Oct. 20, 1768.

39. *Virginia Gazette* (Rind), Aug. 25, 1768; *Virginia Gazette* (Purdie and Dixon), Jan. 9, 1772; Patrick Henderson, "Smallpox and Patriotism: The Norfolk Riots, 1768–1769," *VMHB* 73 (1965): 413–14; Frank L. Dewey, "Thomas Jefferson's Law Practice: The Norfolk Anti-Inoculation Riots," *VMHB* 91 (1983): 39–40.

40. *Virginia Gazette* (Rind), Aug. 25, 1768.

41. Ibid.

42. Ibid.

43. Ibid.

44. Ibid.; James Parker to Charles Steuart, Apr., 27, 1769, Charles Steuart Papers, fol. 19, National Library of Scotland, Edinburgh (ms. copy in Foundation Library, Williamsburg).

45. *Virginia Gazette* (Rind), Aug. 25, 1768; *Virginia Gazette* (Purdie and Dixon), Sept. 1, 1768.

46. *Virginia Gazette* (Purdie and Dixon), Sept. 29, 1768; *Virginia Gazette* (Rind), Aug. 25, 1768; Sept. 1, 1768; Charles Steuart to James Parker, July 8, 1768, Parker Family Papers.

47. *Virginia Gazette* (Rind), Aug. 25, 1768.

48. *Virginia Gazette* (Rind), Aug. 25, 1768; Dewey, "Thomas Jefferson's Law Practice," p. 42.

49. *Virginia Gazette* (Purdie and Dixon), Sept. 29, 1768.

50. Dewey, "Thomas Jefferson's Law Practice," p. 39.

51. Ibid., p. 43; Henderson, "Smallpox and Patriotism," pp. 418–20; *Virginia Gazette* (Purdie and Dixon), Jan. 9, 1772.

52. Dewey, "Thomas Jefferson's Law Practice," pp. 42–43.

53. Wertenbaker and Schlegel, *Norfolk,* p. 13; Dewey, "Thomas Jefferson's Law Practice," pp. 52–53.

54. *Norfolk and Portsmouth Herald (Norfolk),* Jan. 7, 1835; Adele Hast, *Loyalism in Revo-*

lutionary Virginia: The Norfolk Area and the Eastern Shore (Ann Arbor, Mich., 1982); Henderson, "Smallpox and Patriotism," pp. 420–24; Wertenbaker and Schlegel, *Norfolk*, p. 52.

55. Dewey, "Thomas Jefferson's Law Practice," pp. 49–50; Henderson, "Smallpox and Patriotism," pp. 422–24.

56. Tommy L. Bogger, "The Slave and Free Black Community in Norfolk 1775–1860" (Ph.D. diss., University of Virginia, 1976), pp. 11–12.

57. *Virginia Gazette* (Rind), Aug. 25, 1768.

58. Wertenbaker and Schlegel, *Norfolk*, pp. 17, 49; Reese, *Official Papers of Francis Fauquier*, 3:1501; Captain William Smith to Jeremiah Morgan, Apr. 3, 1766, *WMQ*, 1st ser., no. 21 (1912–13): 167.

59. Tarter, *Order Book*, pp. 165, 166, 168–71, 172, 173.

CHAPTER 7

1. Wertenbaker and Schlegel, *Norfolk*, pp. 50–51.

2. Ibid., p. 50.

3. Ibid., p. 51.

4. Selby, *Revolution in Virginia*, p. 55.

5. Wertenbaker and Schlegel, *Norfolk*, p. 53.

6. Selby, *Revolution in Virginia*, p. 58.

7. William J. Schreeven and Robert L. Scribner, comps., Robert L. Scribner, ed., *Revolutionary Virginia: The Road to Independence*, vol. 5: *The Clash of Arms and the Fourth Convention, 1775–1776. A Documentary Record*, 7 vols. (Charlottesville, Va., 1979), p. 12; Selby, *Revolution in Virginia*, pp. 58–59; Lord Dunmore to Earl of Dartmouth, Oct. 5, 1775, C. O. 5/1353, fols. 300–302, Public Record Office. Material cited from the Public Record Office may be found on microfilm in the Virginia Colonial Records Project, Foundation Library, Williamsburg.

8. Selby, *Revolution in Virginia*, p. 59.

9. Tarter, *Order Book*, p. 191.

10. Maxwell, "My Mother," 96; Wertenbaker and Schlegel, *Norfolk*, p. 49.

11. Maxwell, "My Mother," pp. 97, 98.

12. Ibid., pp. 62, 98.

13. Ibid., pp. 24–26.

14. Ibid., pp. 98–99.

15. *Virginia Gazette, or Norfolk Intelligencer* (Norfolk), Aug. 18, 1774.

16. Maxwell, "My Mother," pp. 32, 56–60.

17. Ibid., pp. 26–27, 97–98.

18. James Parker to Charles Steuart, Oct. 9, 1775, fol. 112, Steuart Papers; Selby, *Revolution in Virginia*, p. 67.

19. Dunmore to Lord Dartmouth, Oct. 22, 1775, fols. 310–11, C. O. 5/1353; Selby, *Revolution in Virginia*, p. 63; James Parker to Charles Steuart, Oct. 18, 1775, Steuart Papers.

20. Selby, *Revolution in Virginia*, p. 66.

21. Dunmore to Lord Dartmouth, Dec. 6, 1775, fol. 321, C. O. 5/1353; Selby, *Rev-*

olution in Virginia, p. 64; Bogger, "Slave and Free Black Community in Norfolk," pp. 23–24.

22. Selby, *Revolution in Virginia,* p. 69.

23. Ibid.

24. Wertenbaker and Schlegel, *Norfolk,* p. 55.

25. Maxwell, "My Mother," pp. 81, 132.

26. Ibid., pp. 134–37.

27. Dunmore to Dartmouth, Dec. 6, 1775, fol. 321, C. O. 5/1353; Selby, *Revolution in Virginia,* p. 70.

28. Dunmore to Dartmouth, Dec. 6, 1775; Selby, *Revolution in Virginia,* pp. 70–72.

29. Dunmore to Dartmouth, Dec. 6, 1775; Selby, *Revolution in Virginia,* p. 73.

30. Dunmore to Dartmouth, Dec. 6, 1775; Selby, *Revolution in Virginia,* p. 73.

31. Luther P. Jackson, "Virginia Negro Soldiers and Seamen in the American Revolution," *Journal of Negro History* 27 (1942): 273; Selby, *Revolution in Virginia,* pp. 73, 74; Maxwell, "My Mother," p. 138.

32. Selby, *Revolution in Virginia,* p. 74.

33. Wertenbaker and Schlegel, *Norfolk,* pp. 60–61.

34. Maxwell, "My Mother," p. 79; Selby, *Revolution in Virginia,* p. 82.

35. Maxwell, "My Mother," p. 80; Dunmore to Lord Dartmouth, Jan. 4, 1776, fol. 321, C. O. 5/1353; Selby, *Revolution in Virginia,* p. 82.

36. Selby, *Revolution in Virginia,* p. 83.

37. Wertenbaker and Schlegel, *Norfolk,* p. 62; Maxwell, "My Mother," p. 80.

38. Selby, *Revolution in Virginia,* p. 84. See also William F. Ainsley Jr., "Changing Land Use in Downtown Norfolk, Virginia, 1680–1930" (Ph.D. diss., University of North Carolina, 1977), p. 68.

39. Selby, *Revolution in Virginia,* p. 80.

40. Ibid., pp. 104–6.

41. Carmeline V. Zimmer, "Selected Letters from the Parker Family Papers: The Correspondence of Margaret Parker" (M.A. thesis, Old Dominion University, 1969), pp. 22–24.

42. Ibid., p. 25.

43. Ibid., pp. 21–22.

44. Hast, *Loyalism in Revolutionary Virginia,* pp. 73–74.

45. Zimmer, "Parker Family Papers," pp. 61, 64–65.

46. Ibid., pp. 66–68.

47. Ibid., p. 36.

48. James Parker to Margaret Parker, Mar. 8, 1776, James Parker Papers.

49. Zimmer, "Parker Family Papers," p. 62.

50. Ibid., p. 63.

51. Ibid., p. 67.

52. Wertenbaker and Schlegel, *Norfolk,* p. 71; Hast, *Loyalism in Revolutionary Virginia,* p. 97.

53. Hast, *Loyalism in Revolutionary Virginia,* p. 118.

54. Jacob Ellegood to Charles Steuart, Oct. 16, 1781, ms. 5032, fols. 194–95, Steuart Papers.

55. Ibid.

Notes

56. Hast, *Loyalism in Revolutionary Virginia*, p. 106.

57. Ibid., pp. 109–14.

58. Ibid., p. 117.

59. Ibid., pp. 92, 117; Wertenbaker and Schlegel, *Norfolk*, pp. 69–70.

60. Patrick Parker to James Parker, Jan. 10, 1783, James Parker Papers; Hast, *Loyalism in Revolutionary Virginia*, p. 92; Wertenbaker and Schlegel, *Norfolk*, p. 74.

61. Patrick Parker to James Parker, Jan. 10, 1783, James Parker Papers; James Parker to Margaret Parker, Feb. 5, 1784; Zimmer, "Parker Family Papers," pp. 120–21.

62. Bogger, "Slave and Free Black Community in Norfolk," pp. 29–31.

63. Maxwell, "My Mother," pp. 79–80.

64. Margaret Parker to James Parker, Feb. 19, 1777, July 8, 1783, James Parker Papers; Zimmer, "Parker Family Papers," p. 101.

CHAPTER 8

1. *Virginia Chronicle* (Norfolk), July 12, 1792.

2. Frances S. Childs, *French Refugee Life in the United States, 1790–1800: An American Chapter of the French Revolution* (Baltimore, Md., 1940), p. 15.

3. Kenneth and Anna M. Roberts, eds. and trans., *Moreau de St. Mery's American Journey (1793–1798)* (Garden City, N.Y., 1947), p. 51; Isaac Weld, *Travels Through the States of North America and the Provinces of Upper and Lower Canada, during the Years 1795, 1796, and 1797* (London, 1800), p. 131; Althea de Puech Parham, ed. and trans., *My Odyssey: Experiences of a Young Refugee from Two Revolutions by a Creole of Saint Domingue* (Baton Rouge, La., 1959), p. 99; *Daily Advertiser* (New York), July 23, 1793.

4. Childs, *French Refugee Life*, pp. 86–87; Palmer, *CVSP*, 6:437, 447; *Virginia Chronicle*, Nov. 2, 1793.

5. Tarter, *Order Book*, p. 338; Roberts, *Moreau de St. Mery's American Journey*, pp. 50, 56; *Virginia Chronicle*, July 13, Aug. 24, 1793.

6. Parham, *My Odyssey*, p. 99.

7. *Virginia Chronicle*, Aug. 31, 1793; Roberts, *Moreau de St. Mery's American Journey*, pp. 56, 61; Palmer, *CVSP*, 10:277–78.

8. *Virginia Chronicle*, Oct. 19, 1793, Feb. 8, 1794; *American Gazette and Norfolk and Portsmouth Advertiser* (Norfolk), Sept. 1, 1795; Roberts, *Moreau de St. Mery's American Journey*, p. 54; Wertenbaker and Schlegel, *Norfolk*, pp. 88–89.

9. La Rochefoucault Liancourt, *Travels through the United States of America, the Country of the Iroquois, and Upper Canada, in the Years 1795, 1796, and 1797*, 2 vols. (London, 1799), 2:11; *Daily Advertiser* (New York), Aug. 9, 1793.

10. *Virginia Herald, and Fredericksburg Advertiser* (Fredericksburg), Feb. 7, June 8, 1793.

11. Childs, *French Refugee Life*, pp. 9–15.

12. Ibid., p. 82; *Virginia Herald Fredericksburg Advertiser*, July 25, 1793.

13. *Virginia Herald Fredericksburg Advertiser*, July 25, Aug. 8, 1793; *Virginia Chronicle*, Nov. 2, 1793; *Independent Gazeteer* (Philadelphia), Nov. 30, 1793.

14. *Virginia Chronicle*, July 3, Aug. 7, 1794.

15. *Virginia Gazette* (Dixon), Oct. 11, 1776; "Letters from Virginia, 1774–1791," *The*

Magazine of History 3 (Apr. 1906): 215; Douglas Robertson, ed., *An Englishman in America* (Toronto, 1933), p. 4; "Virginia in 1785," *Virginia Historical Magazine* 23 (1915): 407.

16. Edward C. Carter II, ed., *The Virginia Journals of Benjamin Henry Latrobe 1795–1798* (New Haven, Conn., 1977), p. 75; Anne Ritson, *A Poetical Picture of America: Virginia: Social Life and Customs* (London, 1809), p. 103.

17. Weld, *Travels,* p. 131; Ainsley, "Changing Land Use in Downtown Norfolk," p. 73.

18. La Rochefoucault, *Travels,* 2:6; Roberts, *Moreau de St. Mery's American Journey,* p. 47.

19. Mary C. Chrysostomides, "The Effect of the Revolution on Norfolk Politics" (M.A. thesis, Old Dominion University, 1986), pp. 58, 80–83.

20. Tarter, *Order Book,* pp. 343, 351.

21. Carter, *Virginia Journals of Benjamin Henry Latrobe,* p. 75; Tarter, *Order Book, passim.*

22. Peter C. Stewart, "Elizabeth River Commerce during the Revolutionary Era," in Richard A. Rutyna and Peter C. Stewart, eds., *Virginia in the American Revolution: A Collection of Essays* (Norfolk, Va., 1977), pp. 61–72.

23. Stewart, "Elizabeth River Commerce," p. 71; La Rochefoucault, *Travels,* 2:10.

24. La Rochefoucault, *Travels,* 2:13; Roberts, *Moreau de St. Mery's American Journey,* p. 52; *Virginia Herald Fredericksburg Advertiser,* July 12, 1792.

25. *Virginia Herald Fredericksburg Advertiser,* July 12, 1792; Wertenbaker and Schlegel, *Norfolk,* pp. 117–18; *Norfolk and Portsmouth Chronicle* (Norfolk), July 10, 1790; *Charleston Morning Post and Daily Advertiser,* Dec. 19, 1786.

26. *Virginia Herald Fredericksburg Advertiser,* July 12, 1792.

27. Suzanne K. Sherman, "Show Goes on in Norfolk," *Virginian-Pilot,* Mar. 19, 1950; *Virginia Chronicle,* July 6, 1793, July 10, 1794.

28. *Virginia Chronicle,* May 5, 1794; *Epitome of the Times* (Norfolk), Oct. 2, 1801; Wertenbaker and Schlegel, *Norfolk,* p. 121; Sherman, "Show Goes on in Norfolk"; A. G. Roeber, "A New England Woman's Perspective on Norfolk, Virginia, 1801–1802: Excerpts from the Diary of Ruth Henshaw Bascom," *Proceedings of the American Antiquarian Society* 88 (1979): 290, 306; *Virginia Chronicle,* July 6, 1793.

29. *Virginia Chronicle,* May 5, July 10, 1794; *Epitome of the Times,* Oct. 2, 1800; Wertenbaker and Schlegel, *Norfolk,* p. 121.

30. Francis Baily, *Journal of a Tour in Unsettled Parts of North America in 1796 & 1797* (London, 1856), p. 21; Order Book No. 6 (1792–95), p. 58, ms. in Circuit Court Clerk's Office, Norfolk; Roeber, "New England Woman's Perspective on Norfolk," pp. 293, 294, 296, 303, 310, 318–19; *Virginia Chronicle,* Jan. 26, 1793.

31. Tarter, *Order Book,* p. 283; *Virginia Chronicle,* June 16, 19, July 3, 1794; Wertenbaker and Schlegel, *Norfolk,* p. 90; *Epitome of the Times,* May 15, 1801.

32. Roberts, *Moreau de St. Mery's American Journey,* p. 58; Roeber, "New England Woman's Perspective on Norfolk," p. 310.

33. Carter, *Virginia Journals of Benjamin Henry Latrobe,* pp. 75, 82–83; Roberts, *Moreau de St. Mery's American Journey,* pp. 47–49; Wertenbaker and Schlegel, *Norfolk,* pp. 136–37; Roeber, "New England Woman's Perspective on Norfolk," pp. 285, 293, 297, 302, 308–9, 311.

34. Roberts, *Moreau de St. Mery's American Journey,* pp. 47, 62, 65–66; La Rochefou-

Notes

cault, *Travels*, 2:14; Carter, *Virginia Journals of Benjamin Henry Latrobe*, pp. 79–80; Ainsley, "Changing Land Use in Downtown Norfolk," p. 76.

35. Carter, *Virginia Journals of Benjamin Henry Latrobe*, p. 79; Roberts, *Moreau de St. Mery's American Journey*, pp. 55–56; Baily, *Journal of a Tour*, p. 22.

36. Roberts, *Moreau de St. Mery's American Journey*, p. 62; La Rochefoucault, *Travels*, 2:7, 14; Weld, *Travels*, pp. 136–37; Ainsley, "Changing Land Use in Downtown Norfolk," p. 74.

37. Bogger, "Slave and Free Black Community in Norfolk," pp. 42, 53.

38. Roberts, *Moreau de St. Mery's American Journey*, pp. 60, 66; La Rochefoucault, *Travels*, 2:15.

39. Roeber, "New England Woman's Perspective on Norfolk," p. 289; Wertenbaker and Schlegel, *Norfolk*, p. 188; *American Gazette and Norfolk and Portsmouth Advertiser*, Sept. 1, 1795, Oct. 18, 1797.

40. Wertenbaker and Schlegel, *Norfolk*, p. 188.

41. Ibid., p. 128; Roeber, "New England Woman's Perspective on Norfolk," p. 311; Ainsley, "Changing Land Use in Downtown Norfolk," p. 74.

42. *Virginia Chronicle*, Feb. 22, Mar. 1, 1794; *Independent Gazeteer* (Philadelphia), Feb. 5, 1794.

43. *Independent Gazeteer*, Sept. 9, 24, 1794; *Virginia Chronicle*, Apr. 5, 1794.

44. Roberts, *Moreau de St. Mery's American Journal*, pp. 58–59; Hugh Blair Grigsby, "A Chapter in the History of Norfolk—The Great Mob of 1796," *The Monthly Visitor* 1 (1871): 37–40. Grigsby tentatively dates the event in 1796, but the circumstances seem to conform to an incident Moreau de St. Mery mentions as occurring in April 1794. The victim was probably merchant George Logan.

45. Roberts, *Moreau de St. Mery's American Journal*, pp. 58–59.

46. Childs, *French Refugee Life*, pp. 187–88.

47. Carter, *Virginia Journals of Benjamin Henry Latrobe*, p. 445; Chrysostomides, "Effect of the Revolution on Norfolk Politics," p. 66.

48. Jedidiah Morse, *A Sermon Exhibiting the Present Dangers, and Consequent Duties of the Citizens of the United States. Delivered at Charles-Town, April 15, 1799* (Charlestown, Mass., 1799), pp. 12–50; *Epitome of the Times*, May 15, 1801.

49. Morse, *Sermon*, pp. 37–45; *Epitome of the Times*, May 15, 1801.

50. *Norfolk Weekly Journal; and Country Intelligencer* (Norfolk), Apr. 4, 1798.

51. Charles William Janson, *The Stranger in America 1793–1801* (New York, 1935), pp. 349–51.

52. Ibid., p. 351.

53. Thomas Fairfax, *Journey from Virginia to Salem Massachusetts 1799* (London, 1936), pp. 4–5.

54. Weld, *Travels*, p. 175; *Day-Book*, July 27, Aug. 14, 1860; Roeber, "New England Woman's Perspective on Norfolk," pp. 282, 294, 300, 301, 302, 306, 313, 314, 321, 323.

55. *Virginian* (Norfolk), Jan. 31, 1866.

CHAPTER 9

1. John Cowper to James Monroe, Apr. 17, 1802; George McIntosh to Monroe, May 5, 1802, mss. in Executive Papers, Virginia State Library and Archives, Richmond.

2. Cowper to Monroe, Apr. 17, 1802, Flournoy, *CVSP,* 10:293; McIntosh to Monroe, May 5, 1802, Executive Papers; Bertram Wyatt-Brown, *Southern Honor: Ethics and Behavior in the Old South* (New York, 1982), p. 430.

3. Cowper to Monroe, Apr. 27, May 18, 1802 (enclosing a transcript of Jeremiah's trial), Executive Papers; Roeber, "New England Woman's Perspective on Norfolk," p. 307.

4. Cowper to Monroe, Executive Papers, May 18, 1802.

5. Wertenbaker and Schlegel, *Norfolk,* p. 127.

6. McIntosh to Monroe, May 5, 1802, Executive Papers; Wyatt-Brown, *Southern Honor,* p. 428.

7. Confession of Jeremiah, dated May 2, 1802, in Thomas Newton to Monroe, May 7, 1802, Executive Papers; *Russell's Boston Gazette* (Boston), June 24, 1802.

8. Transcript of Jeremiah's trial record, May 1802, Executive Papers.

9. McIntosh to Monroe, May 5, 1802, Executive Papers.

10. Ibid.

11. Jeremiah's letter, May 2, 1802, in Cowper to Monroe, May 18, 1802, Executive Papers.

12. McIntosh to Monroe, May 5, 1802, with enclosures, Executive Papers; Wyatt-Brown, *Southern Honor,* p. 428.

13. Newton to Monroe, May 7, 1802, Executive Papers.

14. Cowper to Monroe, May 18, 1802, Executive Papers.

15. Council Journal, 1801–3, p. 241, ms. in Virginia State Library and Archives.

16. Flournoy, *CVSP,* 9:271, 280–81.

17. See, e.g., John A. Robertson to Monroe, Jan. 15, 1802, Executive Papers.

18. *Virginia Herald Fredericksburg Advertiser,* May 5, 1792; *Epitome of the Times,* Oct. 2, 1800; Bogger, "Slave and Free Black Community," pp. 114–17.

19. *Norfolk and Portsmouth Journal,* Dec. 17, 1788; *American Gazette* (Norfolk), Jan. 31, 1798.

20. *Virginia Chronicle and Norfolk and Portsmouth General Advertiser* (Norfolk), Aug. 24, 1793.

21. Bogger, "Slave and Free Black Community," p. 113; *Norfolk Herald* (Norfolk), Jan. 15, 1801.

22. Cowper to Monroe, Mar. 11, 1802, Executive Papers; Roeber, "New England Woman's Perspective on Norfolk," p. 306.

23. Thomas Mathews to Monroe, Mar. 10, 1802, Executive Papers; Monroe to Cowper, May 11, 1802, Flournoy, *CVSP,* 9:281.

24. Cowper to Monroe, May 20, 1802, with enclosures, Executive Papers.

25. See, e.g., *Norfolk Herald,* May 13, 1802; Ainsley, "Changing Land Use in Downtown Norfolk," p. 91.

26. Norfolk City Deed Book 9 (1804–5), p. 267 (Jan. 1, 1803); Bogger, "Slave and Free Black Community," pp. 47, 126.

27. Ibid., pp. 54, 57–58, 127.

28. Ibid., pp. 167, 170–71, 172, 204.

29. Ibid., pp. 62–69, 170–73, 179.

30. Ibid., pp. 180–201, 205.

31. Ibid., pp. 223–26; Cassandra L. Newby, "'The World Was All Before Them': A

Study of the Black Community in Norfolk, Virginia, 1861–1884" (Ph.D. diss., College of William and Mary, 1992), pp. 279–81.

32. *Norfolk Public Gazette & Public Ledger* (Norfolk), May 24, 1805.

33. Bogger, "Slave and Free Black Community," pp. 111–12, 169–70.

34. Ibid., p. 181.

35. Ibid., p. 168.

36. Ibid., pp. 113, 167–68, 202.

37. *Gazette of the United States* (Philadelphia), Apr. 27, 1802; Newton to Monroe, May 14, 1802, Executive Papers.

38. "Court vs. Ned," transcript accompanying Newton to Monroe, May 14, 1802; McIntosh to Monroe, May 19, 1802, and enclosures, Executive Papers.

39. McIntosh to Monroe, May 19, 1802, and enclosures, Executive Papers.

40. Ibid.; Wyatt-Brown, *Southern Honor*, pp. 428–29.

41. Cowper to Monroe, June 1, 1802, Executive Papers; Roeber, "New England Woman's Perspective on Norfolk," p. 316.

42. McIntosh to Monroe, May 19, 1802, Executive Papers; Thomas C. Parramore, "Conspiracy and Revivalism in 1802," *Negro History Bulletin* 43 (Apr.–June 1980): 28–31.

43. *Norfolk Herald,* Jan. 15, 1801.

44. McIntosh to Henry A. Wise, Dec. 22, 1856, Executive Papers; *Petersburg Intelligencer* (Petersburg), Aug. 25, 1802.

45. *Pennsylvania Gazette* (Philadelphia), June 23, 1802.

46. William Newsum to Monroe, May 19, 1802, Executive Papers.

47. Bogger, "Slave and Free Black Community," pp. 122–23; Thomas C. Parramore, "Aborted Takeoff: A Critique of 'Fly Across the River,'" *NCHR* 48 (Apr. 1991): 111–21.

CHAPTER 10

1. John C. Emmerson Jr., *The Chesapeake Affair of 1807* (n.p., 1954), p. 12.

2. Ibid., p. 19.

3. Ibid., p. 20.

4. Ibid.; Charles B. Cross Jr., *The Chesapeake: Biography of a Ship* (n.p., 1968), p. 51.

5. Ibid.

6. Emmerson, *Chesapeake Affair,* p. 115.

7. Cross, *Chesapeake,* pp. 51, 53.

8. Ibid., pp. 45–46; Emmerson, *Chesapeake Affair,* pp. 17–18.

9. Emmerson, *Chesapeake Affair,* p. 17.

10. *Ledger* (Norfolk), June 24, 1807; Edwin M. Gaines, "The Chesapeake Affair," *VMHB* 44 (1956): 134.

11. Cross, *Chesapeake,* pp. 19–21.

12. Ibid., pp. 21–24; *Norfolk Herald,* May 24, 1800.

13. *Norfolk Gazette and Public Ledger,* June 24, 1807.

14. Ibid.

15. Ibid., July 6, 1807.

16. Ibid.

17. Emmerson, *Chesapeake Affair,* pp. 46–50.

18. Ibid., pp. 35–42, 60–63.

19. Cross, *Chesapeake,* p. 59.

20. Wertenbaker and Schlegel, *Norfolk,* pp. 98–99.

21. Ibid., pp. 96, 98–99.

22. *Petersburg Intelligencer,* Apr. 16, 1805.

23. Peter C. Stewart, "The Commercial History of Hampton Roads, Virginia, 1815–1860" (Ph.D. diss., University of Virginia, 1967), p. 16; Wertenbaker and Schlegel, *Norfolk,* p. 96.

24. Thomas Costa and Peter C. Stewart, "The Life and Legacy of Moses Myers: Merchant of Norfolk, Virginia," pp. 17–18, 48–91, unpublished biography of Moses Myers in possession of Peter C. Stewart; Carter, *Virginia Journals of Benjamin Henry Latrobe,* pp. 79–80.

25. *Norfolk Gazette and Public Ledger,* Oct. 23, 1804.

26. Costa and Stewart, "Life and Legacy of Moses Myers," pp. 31, 79; William F. Carson, "Norfolk and Anglo-American Relations, 1805–1815" (M.A. thesis, Old Dominion University, 1965), pp. 4–5.

27. Whichard, *Lower Tidewater,* 1:437, 440–41, 449.

28. Wertenbaker and Schlegel, *Norfolk,* pp. 128, 131.

29. *Norfolk and Portsmouth Chronicle* (Norfolk), June 2, 1792; Wertenbaker and Schlegel, *Norfolk,* p. 136.

30. Costa and Stewart, "Life and Legacy of Moses Myers," pp. 30, 33, 36, 42, 44–45; Wertenbaker and Schlegel, *Norfolk,* p. 121; *Norfolk Herald,* Feb. 8, May 17, 1811; Ainsley, "Changing Land Use in Downtown Norfolk," p. 93.

31. *Norfolk Gazette and Public Ledger,* Sept. 25, Nov. 22, 1805, July 3, 1807; *Norfolk Herald,* May 29, 1811.

32. *Norfolk Herald,* Feb. 8, May 13, 1811, Mar. 25, 1812; Costa and Stewart, "Life and Legacy of Moses Myers," p. 45.

33. *Norfolk Herald,* Apr. 27, June 21, 1807, May 31, 1811, Aug. 31, 1812; *Norfolk Gazette and Public Ledger,* May 16, 1806; *Petersburg Intelligencer,* Feb. 21, 1804.

34. *Norfolk Herald,* Mar. 8, 1811.

35. *Norfolk Gazette and Public Ledger,* Sept. 12, 1806; Ritson, *Poetical Picture of America,* pp. 80–81.

36. Hugh Blair Grigsby, *Discourse on the Life and Character of the Hon. Littleton Waller Tazewell* (Norfolk, Va., 1860), pp. 22–23, 40; *Norfolk Herald,* June 12, 1800, July 19, 1803; Whichard, *Lower Tidewater,* 1:452, 453.

37. Costa and Stewart, "Life and Legacy of Moses Myers," pp. 133–34.

38. *Norfolk Herald,* Sept. 30, 1812; Costa and Stewart, "Life and Legacy of Moses Myers," p. 41.

39. Carson, "Norfolk and Anglo-American Relations," pp. 24–31.

40. Ibid., pp. 31, 36, 46.

41. Ibid., pp. 51–52.

42. Wertenbaker and Schlegel, *Norfolk,* p. 105; Carson, "Norfolk and Anglo-American Relations," pp. 74–75.

43. Wertenbaker and Schlegel, *Norfolk,* p. 107.

44. Carson, "Norfolk and Anglo-American Relations," pp. 7–11.

45. Ibid., p. 103.

46. Ibid., pp. 98–99.

Notes

47. Ibid., pp. 105–6, 109.

48. Wertenbaker and Schlegel, *Norfolk*, p. 111; John M. Hallahan, *The Battle of Craney Island: A Matter of Credit* (Portsmouth, Va., 1986), pp. 42–43.

49. Carson, "Norfolk and Anglo-American Relations," pp. 124–25.

50. Ibid., pp. 134–35; Wertenbaker and Schlegel, *Norfolk*, p. 110.

51. Wertenbaker and Schlegel, *Norfolk*, p. 112; Fitzgerald Flournoy, "A Virginia Boy during the War of 1812," *VMHB* 46 (1958): 428; Hallahan, *Battle of Craney Island*, pp. 62–66.

52. Wertenbaker and Schlegel, *Norfolk*, p. 113; Hallahan, *Battle of Craney Island*, pp. 67–71.

53. Wertenbaker and Schlegel, *Norfolk*, pp. 113–14.

54. Ibid., p. 115.

55. Cross, *Chesapeake*, p. 58; *Norfolk Herald*, Feb. 20, 1845.

CHAPTER 11

1. Alexander C. Brown, *The Dismal Swamp Canal* (Chesapeake, Va., 1967), pp. 31–38.

2. Ibid., p. 39.

3. *Norfolk Herald*, Dec. 6, 1811; Peter C. Stewart, "The Romantic vs. the Real: A History of the Great Dismal Swamp," p. 115, unpublished ms. in possession of its author.

4. Brown, *Dismal Swamp Canal*, p. 49; Hustings Court Order Book No. 21 (1815–17), p. 117, ms. in Norfolk Circuit Court Clerk's Office.

5. *American Beacon* (Norfolk), June 9, 1818.

6. Brown, *Dismal Swamp Canal*, pp. 54–55.

7. Wertenbaker and Schlegel, *Norfolk*, pp. 145–48.

8. Ibid., pp. 153–54.

9. Ibid., pp. 157–58.

10. *American Beacon*, May 2, 1829.

11. Wertenbaker and Schlegel, *Norfolk*, p. 161; Philip M. Rice, "The Early Development of the Roanoke Waterway—A Study in Interstate Relations," *NCHR* 31 (1954): 50–64.

12. Brown, *Dismal Swamp Canal*, p. 57; Whichard, *Lower Tidewater*, 1:194.

13. See, e.g., John F. D. Smyth, *A Tour of the United States of America*, 2 vols. (New York, 1968), 2:100–101, 236–37; Johann David Schoepf, *Travels in the Confederation 1783–1784*, trans. and ed. Alfred J. Morrison, 2 vols. (New York, 1968), 2:99; Hubert J. Davis, *The Great Dismal Swamp: Its History, Folklore and Science* (Murfreesboro, N.C., 1971), *passim*.

14. Lord John Russell, ed., *Memoirs, Journal, and Correspondence of Thomas Moore*, 6 vols. (London, 1853), 1:138–41; Hubert J. Davis, *Myths and Legends of Great Dismal Swamp* (Murfreesboro, N.C., 1981), pp. 19–21.

15. Brown, *Dismal Swamp Canal*, pp. 39, 70–71; Andrew Nicol, "The Peat Soils of Scotland Compared with the Juniper Soil of the Dismal Swamp," *Farmer's Register* 3 (1837): 528–29.

16. Wertenbaker and Schlegel, *Norfolk*, p. 120; Whichard, *Lower Tidewater*, 1:453;

Anne N. Royall, *The Black Book; or a Continuation of Travels in the United States*, 3 vols. (Washington, D.C., 1828), 1:254.

17. Royall, *Black Book*, 1:258–59.

18. *Norfolk Herald*, July 26, 1811; Hervey Allen, *Israfel: The Life and Times of Edgar Allan Poe*, 2 vols. (New York, 1926), 1:14; George H. Tucker, "Early Norfolk Theatres," clipping in John C. Emmerson Jr., ed., "Norfolk & Portsmouth Cultural 1795–1869," typescript, 1969, in Sargeant Room, Kirn Library, Norfolk; James R. Hines, "Musical Activity in Norfolk, Virginia, 1680–1973" (Ph.D. diss., University of North Carolina, 1974), p. 157; Wertenbaker and Schlegel, *Norfolk*, p. 118; *American Beacon* (Norfolk), Nov. 13, 1817.

19. Russell, *Memoirs, Journal, and Correspondence of Thomas Moore*, 1:138; Hines, "Musical Activity in Norfolk," p. 42.

20. Hines, "Musical Activity in Norfolk," pp. 34–37, 56–59, 157.

21. Ibid., pp. 39, 59, 80, 160–62.

22. Ibid., pp. 68–69, 80, 92.

23. Ibid., p. 80; *American Beacon*, Dec. 16, 1817, Oct. 29, 1825, Mar. 10, 1829.

24. Wertenbaker and Schlegel, *Norfolk*, pp. 122–23; *American Beacon*, Oct. 22, 26, 1824.

25. Wertenbaker and Schlegel, *Norfolk*, pp. 122–23; *American Beacon*, Oct. 22, 1824.

26. Wertenbaker and Schlegel, *Norfolk*, p. 122; *American Beacon*, Oct. 18, 22, 1824.

27. *Landmark* (Norfolk), Mar. 22, 1882.

28. Wertenbaker and Schlegel, *Norfolk*, pp. 128–29; *American Beacon*, May 2, 1822, Aug. 3, 1826, Mar. 10, 1827, Nov. 4, 1833; Whichard, *Lower Tidewater*, 1:431–32; Ainsley, "Changing Land Use in Downtown Norfolk," p. 91.

29. Anne N. Royall, *Mrs. Royall's Southern Tour; or Second Series of the Black Book*, 3 vols. (Washington, D.C., 1830–31), 1:28, 30.

30. Ibid., pp. 254–56.

31. Ibid., p. 256.

32. *American Beacon*, Dec. 10, 16, 1817, Jan. 22, June 20, 1818, Mar. 16, 30, Nov. 22, 23, 1822, Apr. 29, 1825, Feb. 18, 1829, Apr. 29, 1833.

33. Record of the Common Council No. 4 (Nov. 5, 1817–June 11, 1827), pp. 3, 144, ms. volume in City Clerk's Office, Norfolk; *American Beacon*, Jan. 22, Mar. 10, 1818, Feb. 19, 1824; Hustings Court Order Book No. 21, p. 133; Hustings Court Order Book No. 22, ms. in City Clerk's Office, Norfolk, p. 192.

34. Record of the Common Council No. 4, pp. 126, 204; *American Beacon*, July 11, 1818; Tommy L. Bogger, "The Darker Side of Freedom: Free Blacks in Norfolk, Virginia, 1790–1860," p. 55, unpublished ms. in possession of the author.

35. Bogger, "Darker Side of Freedom," pp. 39–42.

36. Ibid., pp. 42–44.

37. Ibid., pp. 44–47; P. J. Staudenraus, *The African Colonization Movement 1816–1865* (New York, 1961), pp. 92, 96–97, 109, 154, 241.

38. *Virginian-Pilot*, May 26, 1991.

39. Bogger, "Darker Side of Freedom," pp. 40–41, 46–51.

40. Moses Grandy, *Narrative of the Life of Moses Grandy, Formerly a Slave in the United States of America* (Boston, Mass., 1844), *passim*.

41. Ibid., pp. 27–36.

42. Stewart, "Commercial History of Hampton Roads," pp. 21–23, 26–28.

43. Ibid., pp. 25–26, 29; *American Beacon*, May 10, 1834.

44. Brown, *Dismal Swamp Canal*, pp. 49–51, 56–57.

45. Rice, "Early Development of the Roanoke Waterway," pp. 56–61.

46. Brown, *Dismal Swamp Canal*, pp. 56–65; Wertenbaker and Schlegel, *Norfolk*, pp. 161–62.

47. Brown, *Dismal Swamp Canal*, pp. 66–75.

48. Wertenbaker and Schlegel, *Norfolk*, pp. 162–63.

49. *American Beacon*, Aug. 6, Sept. 17, 1829, Jan. 29, 1830, Feb. 20, 1835.

50. Wertenbaker and Schlegel, *Norfolk*, pp. 164, 165; *Virginian-Pilot*, Feb. 3, 1993.

51. Wertenbaker and Schlegel, *Norfolk*, p. 163.

52. *Milton* (N.C.) *Gazette*, July 31, 1830.

Chapter 12

1. *Norfolk Herald*, Oct. 6, 1834, July 29, 1835.

2. *American Beacon*, Aug. 9, 1834, July 28, 1835; *Virginian-Pilot*, July 13, 1986.

3. *American Beacon*, June 22, Aug. 9, 11, 1834.

4. *Norfolk Herald*, July 29, 1835; William P. Meyer, "The Rives Affair: The Study of a Southeast Virginia Railroad Controversy, 1830–1846" (M.A. thesis, Old Dominion University, 1969), pp. 22, 36–37; *American Beacon*, July 21, 1835.

5. Stewart, "Commercial History of Hampton Roads," pp. 69–70; Peter C. Stewart, "Railroads and Urban Rivalries in Antebellum Eastern Virginia," *VMHB* 81 (1973): 5.

6. Stewart, "Railroads and Urban Rivalries," p. 6; Meyer, "Rives Affair," p. 35.

7. Wertenbaker and Schlegel, *Norfolk*, p. 169.

8. Stewart, "Railroads and Urban Rivalries," p. 7.

9. Wertenbaker and Schlegel, *Norfolk*, pp. 171–72.

10. Stewart, "Railroads and Urban Rivalries," p. 7.

11. *American Beacon*, Sept. 29, 1840; *Norfolk Herald*, Dec. 13, 1837.

12. Wertenbaker and Schlegel, *Norfolk*, p. 171; Meyer, "Rives Affair," p. 38.

13. "Leaves from the Southwest and Cuba," *Knickerbocker, or New York Monthly Magazine* 8 (1836): 45; Meyer, "Rives Affair," pp. 28–29.

14. Charles W. Turner, "The Early Railroad Movement in Virginia," *VMHB* 55 (1947): 356; Thomas C. Parramore, *Southampton County: A History* (Charlottesville, VA., 1978), p. 125.

15. *American Beacon*, Aug. 26, 1831; Deborah Shea, ed., "Spreading Terror and Destruction Wherever They Have Been: A Norfolk Woman's Account of the Southampton Slave Insurrection," *VMHB* 95 (1987): 72.

16. Shea, "Spreading Terror and Destruction," p. 69; *American Beacon*, Aug. 26, 1831; *Norfolk Herald*, Aug. 26, 1831; *Virginian-Pilot*, Aug. 29, 1965.

17. Parramore, *Southampton County*, pp. 93–96.

18. Norma Lois Peterson, *Littleton Waller Tazewell* (Charlottesville, Va., 1983), p. 195.

19. Peterson, *Littleton Waller Tazewell*, p. 243; Bogger, "Darker Side of Freedom," p. 192.

20. Willard B. Gatewood Jr., *Free Man of Color: The Autobiography of Willis Augustus Hodges* (Knoxville, Tenn., 1982), pp. 25–26.

21. Ibid., pp. 26–27.

22. *American Beacon*, May 19, 1845.

23. Ibid.

24. Peterson, *Littleton Waller Tazewell*, pp. 213–16.

25. Bogger, "Darker Side of Freedom," pp. 137–39.

26. Ibid., pp. 140–49.

27. *Norfolk Herald*, Jan. 3, 1845; H. W. Burton, *The History of Norfolk, Virginia* (Norfolk, Va., 1877), p. 10.

28. Burton, *History of Norfolk*, p. 10; *American Beacon*, Aug. 20, 1853; Ainsley, "Changing Land Use in Downtown Norfolk," p. 95.

29. *American Beacon*, June 3, 1839; James Silk Buckingham, *The Slave States of America*, 2 vols. (London, 1842), 1:455.

30. *American Beacon*, Dec. 7, 12, 1833; Burton, *History of Norfolk*, p. 9; Forrest, *Historical and Descriptive Sketches of Norfolk*, pp. 211–12; Ainsley, "Changing Land Use in Downtown Norfolk," p. 92.

31. *Virginian-Pilot*, June 4, 1989.

32. See, e.g., *American Beacon*, Jan. 2, Sept. 10, 1834, Apr. 7, 1835; Forrest, *Historical and Descriptive Sketches*, pp. 200–216; *American Beacon* (Norfolk), Aug. 20, 1838.

33. Buckingham, *Slave States*, 1:454, 456.

34. Ibid., 1:452–54.

35. Ibid., 1:487–88.

36. Ibid., 1:487; *American Beacon*, Aug. 5, 1835.

37. Costa and Stewart, "Life and Legacy of Moses Myers," pp. 171–75.

38. Buckingham, *Slave States*, 1:480–81.

39. *American Beacon*, Dec. 7, 1835.

40. Ibid., July 31, 1840.

41. Ibid., May 25, 1840.

42. Stewart, "Commercial History of Hampton Roads," pp. 21–22; *American Beacon*, July 20, 1839, Mar. 3, 1840.

43. *American Beacon*, Mar. 3, Aug. 1, 1840.

44. Ibid., Mar. 3, 1840, May 4, 1844.

45. Stewart, "Commercial History of Hampton Roads," pp. 44–47; Wertenbaker and Schlegel, *Norfolk*, p. 285; *Virginian*, Aug. 5, 1879.

46. Stewart, "Commercial History of Hampton Roads," pp. 44–47.

47. *American Beacon*, July 13, 1835.

48. Wertenbaker and Schlegel, *Norfolk*, pp. 166–87; *American Beacon*, Feb. 4, 1840.

49. *American Beacon*, June 25, 1834, June 23, 1835; Bogger, "Slave and Free Black Community in Norfolk," p. 181.

50. Stewart, "Railroads and Urban Rivalries," pp. 8–9; Walter Gwynn, *Reply of the President of the Portsmouth and Roanoke Rail Road Company to the Address of Capt. Francis E. Rives to the Public* (Norfolk, Va., 1844), pp. 14–17; Meyer, "Rives Affair," p. 34.

51. Gwynn, *Reply of the President*, p. 15.

52. Ibid., pp. 15–16; Meyer, "Rives Affair," p. 52.

53. Gwynn, *Reply of the President*, pp. 16–17; "Opinion of the Supreme Court of

Notes

North Carolina in the Case of the State of North Carolina v. Francis E. Rives—December Term, 1844," *American Law Magazine* 4 (July 1845): 263–65; Meyer, "Rives Affair," pp. 97–101.

54. *American Beacon,* May 8, 1849; Meyer, "Rives Affair," p. 27; Wertenbaker and Schlegel, *Norfolk,* pp. 166, 176–77.

55. *Norfolk Herald,* Mar. 6, 1852.

CHAPTER 13

1. Diary of William Lamb, July 23, Aug. 1–2, 1855, ms. in William Lamb Diaries and Letters, 1855–1909, Swem Library, College of William and Mary, Williamsburg, Va.; William S. Forrest, *The Great Pestilence in Virginia; Being an Historical Account of the Origin, General Character, and Ravages of the Yellow Fever in Norfolk and Portsmouth in 1855* (New York, 1856), p. 27.

2. Allen D. Alberti, "Yellow Fever Epidemic in Norfolk and Portsmouth" (M.A. thesis, Old Dominion University, 1971), p. 24; Wertenbaker and Schlegel, *Norfolk,* p. 191.

3. Alberti, "Yellow Fever Epidemic," pp. 19, 21; Forrest, *Great Pestilence,* pp. 11–12.

4. Alberti, "Yellow Fever Epidemic," p. 25; Diary of William Lamb, July 30, 1855; David R. Goldfield, "Yellow Fever in Norfolk 1855," *Virginia Cavalcade* 23 (1973–74): 38.

5. Alberti, "Yellow Fever Epidemic," pp. 23–26.

6. Diary of William Lamb, Aug. 3–4, 1855.

7. Forrest, *Great Pestilence,* p. 39.

8. Alberti, "Yellow Fever Epidemic," p. 26.

9. Forrest, *Great Pestilence,* pp. 47–48; Alberti, "Yellow Fever Epidemic," pp. 38–43.

10. Alberti, "Yellow Fever Epidemic," p. 30; Forrest, *Great Pestilence,* p. 80.

11. Forrest, *Great Pestilence,* p. 55; David R. Goldfield, *Urban Growth in the Age of Sectionalism: Virginia, 1847–1861* (Baton Rouge, La., 1977), p. 155.

12. Forrest, *Great Pestilence,* p. 85; Wertenbaker and Schlegel, *Norfolk,* p. 194.

13. Dr. Samuel Selden, "The City of Pestilence," *Virginian,* Jan. 19, 1866.

14. Forrest, *Great Pestilence,* pp. 88, 91, 106; Alberti, "Yellow Fever Epidemic," pp. 30–31.

15. Diary of William Lamb, Sept. 6, 1855.

16. Forrest, *Great Pestilence,* p. 55; Diary of William Lamb, July 30, 1855.

17. W. Darrell Overdyke, *The Know-Nothing Party in the South* (Baton Rouge, La., 1950), pp. 45–54; *American Beacon,* Mar. 22, Apr. 27, May 24, 1855; Wertenbaker and Schlegel, *Norfolk,* pp. 199–200.

18. T. R. Turner, "1855 Gubernatorial Campaign in Virginia" (M.A. thesis, University of Virginia, 1967), p. 134; *American Beacon,* Feb. 1, June 26, 1855.

19. *American Beacon,* Feb. 19, Feb. 20, Mar. 5, 1855; *Virginian-Pilot,* Jan. 30, 1906; *Norfolk Herald,* May 28, 1859.

20. Joseph F. Magri, *The Catholic Church in the City and Diocese of Richmond* (Richmond, Va., 1906), p. 54; *Southern Argus* (Norfolk), June 26, 1856, June 26, 1857; *Virginian-Pilot,* Mar. 11, 1990.

21. Goldfield, *Urban Growth in the Age of Sectionalism,* p. 10.

22. Ibid., p. 101.

NOTES

23. *American Beacon*, Apr. 24, Oct. 2, 1852, Mar. 23, 1853; *Southern Argus*, July 25, 1854; Goldfield, *Urban Growth in the Age of Sectionalism*, p. 145; Ainsley, "Changing Land Use in Downtown Norfolk," p. 94.

24. *American Beacon*, July 7, 1848, Jan. 3, 1852, June 13, 1853; Goldfield, "Yellow Fever in Norfolk 1855," p. 36.

25. *American Beacon*, Jan. 5, Feb. 8, 1848; *Southern Argus*, Sept. 23, 1854; Bogger, "Slave and Free Black Community in Norfolk," pp. 172–73.

26. *American Beacon*, June 29, 1848, Dec. 5, 1851, Dec. 23, 1852; Forrest, *Historical and Descriptive Sketches*, pp. 421–23.

27. *American Beacon*, July 7, Aug. 10, Sept. 1, 12, 18, 1852.

28. Bogger, "Slave and Free Black Community in Norfolk," pp. 252–60.

29. *Southern Argus*, Oct. 24, 29, 31, 1850, Nov. 24, 1858.

30. Bogger, "Slave and Free Black Community in Norfolk," pp. 177–79; Bogger, "Darker Side of Freedom," pp. 223–28.

31. Newby, "'The World Was All Before Them,'" pp. 241–46.

32. Ibid., pp. 278–82.

33. Ibid., pp. 284–85.

34. Goldfield, *Urban Growth in the Age of Sectionalism*, pp. 123, 167; *Southern Argus*, July 25, Aug. 23, 26, 1854.

35. Bogger, "Slave and Free Black Community in Norfolk," pp. 217–21, 229–30; Newby, "'The World Was All Before Them,'" pp. 188–91.

36. Newby, "'The World Was All Before Them,'" pp. 80–82.

37. Goldfield, *Urban Growth in the Age of Sectionalism*, pp. 160–62.

38. Wertenbaker and Schlegel, *Norfolk*, p. 133; *Virginian-Pilot*, Aug. 6, 1989.

39. *Southern Argus*, June 14, 1854.

40. Goldfield, *Urban Growth in the Age of Sectionalism*, pp. 25–26, 48–54, 107; *Southern Argus*, Oct. 24–26, 1854.

41. Goldfield, *Urban Growth in the Age of Sectionalism*, p. 51.

42. Forrest, *Historical and Descriptive Sketches*, p. 27.

43. Ibid., pp. 331–38.

44. Goldfield, *Urban Growth in the Age of Sectionalism*, pp. 10–11, 184–91, 202–3.

45. Wertenbaker and Schlegel, *Norfolk*, pp. 167–73, 180–85; *Southern Argus*, May 9, Aug. 15, 1854; Goldfield, "Yellow Fever in Norfolk," p. 36.

46. Frederick Law Olmstead, *A Journey in the Seaboard Slave States in the Years 1853–1854 with Remarks on Their Economy*, 2 vols. (New York, 1904), 1:150–51.

47. Olmstead, *Journey in the Seaboard Slave States*, 1:151, 156.

48. *American Beacon*, Jan. 10, 1854.

49. *Southern Argus*, June 22, 1854.

50. Ibid., May 4, June 22, 1854; Forrest, *Historical and Descriptive Sketches*, pp. 398–403; *American Beacon*, Jan. 10, 1848.

51. Forrest, *Historical and Descriptive Sketches*, pp. 352–82.

52. *Southern Argus*, Aug. 7, 1854.

53. Ibid., Aug. 7, 10, 1854; Ainsley, "Changing Land Use in Downtown Norfolk," pp. 102–4.

54. Ainsley, "Changing Land Use in Downtown Norfolk," pp. 101–2.

Notes

55. Kenneth H. Schwartz, "Ben Butler and the Occupation of Norfolk: 1862–1865, A Reappraisal" (M.A. thesis, Old Dominion University, 1972), p. 9.

56. Alberti, "Yellow Fever Epidemic," p. 32.

57. *Southern Argus*, Nov. 6, 1854; Alberti, "Yellow Fever Epidemic," p. 27.

58. Alberti, "Yellow Fever Epidemic," pp. 46, 48, 50; Forrest, *Great Pestilence*, p. 47.

59. Wertenbaker and Schlegel, *Norfolk*, p. 195.

60. Forrest, *Great Pestilence*, p. 53; Alberti, "Yellow Fever Epidemic," pp. 49–51.

61. Forrest, *Great Pestilence*, p. 250; Alberti, "Yellow Fever Epidemic," pp. 53, 58–59.

62. Alberti, "Yellow Fever Epidemic," pp. 34, 36.

63. Todd L. Savitt, *Medicine and Slavery: The Diseases and Health Care of Blacks in Antebellum Virginia* (Urbana, Ill., 1978), pp. 241–45.

64. Diary of William Lamb, July 30, Aug. 9, 1855; Alberti, "Yellow Fever Epidemic," p. 18.

65. *Virginian-Pilot*, Jan. 27, 1991.

66. Goldfield, *Urban Growth in the Age of Sectionalism*, pp. 159–60, 167, 238.

67. Ibid., pp. 195, 197, 206, 214, 229, 241.

68. Goldfield, "Yellow Fever Epidemic of 1855," pp. 38–39; Goldfield, *Urban Growth in the Age of Sectionalism*, p. 214.

CHAPTER 14

1. R. W. Daly, *How the Merrimac Won: The Strategic Story of the CSS Virginia* (New York, 1957), pp. 28–29.

2. *New York Herald*, Mar. 14, 1862; A. A. Hoehling, *Thunder at Hampton Roads* (Englewood Cliffs, N. J., 1976), pp. 101, 105, 106.

3. Wertenbaker and Schlegel, *Norfolk*, p. 213; Hoehling, *Thunder at Hampton Roads*, pp. 103, 104.

4. *Day-Book* (Norfolk), Mar. 10, 1862.

5. Hoehling, *Thunder at Hampton Roads*, pp. 10, 103–4.

6. Ibid., pp. 107–8; Daly, *How the Merrimac Won*, p. 109.

7. Hoehling, *Thunder at Hampton Roads*, p. 122.

8. Ibid., p. 109.

9. *Day-Book*, Mar. 10, 1862; Daly, *How the Merrimac Won*, pp. 109–11.

10. Daly, *How the Merrimac Won*, pp. 114–15, 119.

11. Ibid., pp. 108, 118; Hoehling, *Thunder at Hampton Roads*, pp. 121–22, 128.

12. Hoehling, *Thunder at Hampton Roads*, pp. 123–25.

13. Daly, *How the Merrimac Won*, pp. 113–14, 117–18; Hoehling, *Thunder at Hampton Roads*, pp. 127, 150.

14. Hoehling, *Thunder at Hampton Roads*, p. 150.

15. *Day-Book*, Aug. 4, 6, 1860.

16. Ibid., May 3, 4, 1860.

17. Ibid., Oct. 9, 10, 12, Dec. 1, 1860.

18. Ibid., Nov. 7, 1860.

19. Bogger, "Darker Side of Freedom," pp. 102–36.

20. *Day-Book*, Nov. 17, Dec. 1, 1860.

21. Ibid., Aug. 17, 1860.

22. Ollinger Crenshaw, "The Knights of the Golden Circle: The Career of George Bickley," *American Historical Review* 47 (1941): 23–50; *Day-Book*, July 30, 1860.

23. *Day-Book*, Oct. 30, Dec. 8, 1860.

24. Burton, *History of Norfolk*, p. 58; *Norfolk Dispatch* (Norfolk), Nov. 26, 1903; William H. Stewart, ed., *History of Norfolk County, Virginia, and Representative Citizens* (Chicago, Ill., 1902), p. 610.

25. Wertenbaker and Schlegel, *Norfolk*, pp. 201–4.

26. *Day-Book*, Dec. 4, 1860; Wertenbaker and Schlegel, *Norfolk*, pp. 205–6.

27. Daly, *How the Merrimac Won*, p. 6.

28. Kenneth H. Schwartz, "Ben Butler and the Occupation of Norfolk: 1862–1865, A Reappraisal" (M.A. thesis, Old Dominion University, 1972), pp. 4–6; W. A. Swanberg, *First Blood: The Story of Fort Sumter* (New York, 1957), p. 297.

29. Wertenbaker and Schlegel, *Norfolk*, pp. 207–8.

30. Daly, *How the Merrimac Won*, pp. 8–9, 13.

31. Ibid., pp. 13–14.

32. Schwartz, "Ben Butler and the Occupation of Norfolk," p. 4; Bogger, "Slave and Free Black Community in Norfolk," p. 285; Wertenbaker and Schlegel, *Norfolk*, pp. 208–9; Newby, "'The World Was All Before Them,'" p. 19.

33. Wertenbaker and Schlegel, *Norfolk*, p. 209; William S. and Addie S. Hoole, eds., *Confederate Norfolk: The Letters of a Virginia Lady to the Mobile Register, 1861–1862* (University, Ala., 1984), *passim; Daily Express* (Petersburg), Sept. 20, 1861; "Norfolk and Her Traducers," clipping from *Day-Book*, Aug. 27, 1861, in Virginia Gordan Scrapbooks, Sargeant Room, Kirn Library, Norfolk.

34. Undated clippings from "J.T.M." and "Young Guards," *Day-Book* (Norfolk) in Virginia Gordan Scrapbooks.

35. *Daily Express*, Dec. 7, 9, 1861, Jan. 3, 1862.

36. See, e.g., "Loroque," in *Daily Express*, Sept. 12, 1861.

37. Burton, *History of Norfolk*, pp. 58, 61; Schwartz, "Ben Butler and the Occupation of Norfolk," pp. 7–9; Wertenbaker and Schlegel, *Norfolk*, p. 210.

38. Wertenbaker and Schlegel, *Norfolk*, pp. 210–11.

39. Daly, *How the Merrimac Won*, pp. 88–89.

40. Gideon Wells, Aug. 17, 1872, to _____, ms. in Portsmouth Public Library, Portsmouth, Va.

41. Hoehling, *Thunder at Hampton Roads*, pp. 38–41; Daly, *How the Merrimac Won*, pp. 25–29.

42. Wertenbaker and Schlegel, *Norfolk*, p. 216; Hoehling, *Thunder at Hampton Roads*, pp. 56–57; Daly, *How the Merrimac Won*, pp. 28–29.

43. Hoehling, *Thunder at Hampton Roads*, p. 153.

44. Ibid., pp. 153–54.

45. Wertenbaker and Schlegel, *Norfolk*, p. 215; Daly, *How the Merrimac Won*, p. 121; Hoehling, *Thunder at Hampton Roads*, pp. 155–57.

46. Hoehling, *Thunder at Hampton Roads*, pp. 157–59.

47. Ibid., pp. 157–61.

48. Ibid., pp. 163–64.

49. Ibid., pp. 165–66.

Notes

50. Ibid., pp. 167, 171; Daly, *How the Merrimac Won,* pp. 126–27; Wertenbaker and Schlegel, *Norfolk,* p. 216.

51. *Daily Express,* Mar. 11, 1862.

52. Ibid., Mar. 13, Apr. 8, 25, 1862.

53. Daly, *How the Merrimac Won,* pp. 145–65.

54. Wertenbaker and Schlegel, *Norfolk,* pp. 216–17.

55. Hoehling, *Thunder at Hampton Roads,* pp. 179–81.

56. Carl Sandburg, *Abraham Lincoln: The Prairie Years and the War Years* (New York, 1954), pp. 294–95.

57. Wertenbaker and Schlegel, *Norfolk,* p. 217; Burton, *History of Norfolk,* pp. 79–80.

58. Newby, "'The World Was All Before Them,'" pp. 30, 31.

59. Wertenbaker and Schlegel, *Norfolk,* p. 218.

60. Daly, *How the Merrimac Won,* pp. 178–80; Hoehling, *Thunder at Hampton Roads,* pp. 182–83; undated article from *Inquirer* (Philadelphia) in Virginia Gordan Scrapbooks.

61. Sandburg, *Abraham Lincoln,* p. 295.

CHAPTER 15

1. Ervin L. Jordan Jr., "A Painful Case: The Wright-Sanborn Incident in Norfolk, Virginia, July–October, 1863" (M.A. thesis, Old Dominion University, 1979), pp. 10, 24–26, 61, 66–68.

2. Ibid., p. 8.

3. Ibid., pp. 7, 11.

4. Ibid., pp. 24–26.

5. Ibid., pp. 25–26.

6. Ibid., pp. 6–7; Wertenbaker and Schlegel, *Norfolk,* p. 221.

7. Jordan, "Painful Case," pp. 12–14.

8. Ibid., pp. 16–18.

9. Ibid., p. 22.

10. Ibid., pp. 27–28.

11. Ibid., pp. 29–30.

12. R. N. Scott et al., eds., *The War of the Rebellion: A Compilation of the Official Records of the Union and Confederate Armies,* 70 vols. (Washington, D.C., 1880–1901), ser. 2, 6:187.

13. Jordan, "Painful Case," p. 32.

14. Schwartz, "Ben Butler and the Occupation of Norfolk," pp. 18–23, 36.

15. Ibid., pp. 19–22; Ludwell H. Johnson III, "Blockade or Trade Monopoly? John A. Dix and the Union Occupation of Norfolk," *VMHB* 93 (1985): 54–56; Newby, "'The World Was All Before Them,'" p. 86.

16. Bogger, "Slave and Free Black Community in Norfolk," pp. 290, 306–9; Michael E. Hucles, "Postbellum Black Economic Development: The Case of Norfolk, Virginia, 1860–1890" (Ph.D. diss., Purdue University, 1990), pp. 42–43.

17. Hucles, "Postbellum Urban Black Economic Development," pp. 43–47; Newby, "'The World Was All Before Them,'" pp. 40, 88.

18. Newby, "'The World Was All Before Them,'" p. 87.

19. Schwartz, "Ben Butler and the Occupation of Norfolk," pp. 26–29; Johnson, "Blockade or Trade Monopoly?" pp. 56–75; Hucles, "Postbellum Urban Black Economic Development," p. 59; Newby, "'The World Was All Before Them,'" pp. 90–91.

20. Schwartz, "Ben Butler and the Occupation of Norfolk," pp. 31–32, 35–38.

21. George Neville to Nellie Newman, June 7, Aug., 1862, mss. in Neville–Newman Correspondence, Accession numbers 1291 and 2024, University Archives, University of Virginia, Charlottesville.

22. Wertenbaker and Schlegel, *Norfolk,* p. 228.

23. Schwartz, "Ben Butler and the Occupation of Norfolk," pp. 40–45.

24. McPherson, *Battle Cry of Freedom,* pp. 551–52.

25. Schwartz, "Ben Butler and the Occupation of Norfolk," pp. 47–49, 52.

26. Ibid., p. 77.

27. Johnson, "Blockade or Trade Monopoly?" pp. 56–78.

28. Ibid., pp. 75–78; Schwartz, "Ben Butler and the Occupation of Norfolk," pp. 69–71.

29. Schwartz, "Ben Butler and the Occupation of Norfolk," pp. 73–79; Wertenbaker and Schlegel, *Norfolk,* pp. 223–24.

30. Schwartz, "Ben Butler and the Occupation of Norfolk," pp. 84–85.

31. Ibid., pp. 79–81, 83–84.

32. Ibid., pp. 81–83.

33. Ibid., pp. 84–85; Newby, "'The World Was All Before Them,'" pp. 66–67.

34. Schwartz, "Ben Butler and the Occupation of Norfolk," pp. 87–89; Newby, "'The World Was All Before Them,'" p. 85.

35. Newby, "'The World Was All Before Them,'" pp. 100–104.

36. McPherson, *Battle Cry of Freedom,* p. 564; William Paquette, "Lower Tidewater's Black Volunteers," in Jane H. Kobelski, ed., *Readings in Black and White: Lower Tidewater Virginia* (Portsmouth, Va., 1982), pp. 17–21; Hucles, "Postbellum Black Economic Development," pp. 54–55; Newby, "'The World Was All Before Them,'" pp. 52–57.

37. Newby, "'The World Was All Before Them,'" p. 52.

38. Wertenbaker and Schlegel, *Norfolk,* p. 220; Schwartz, "Ben Butler and the Occupation of Norfolk," pp. 92–94, 119; Newby, "'The World Was All Before Them,'" p. 43.

39. Newby, "'The World Was All Before Them,'" p. 72.

40. Schwartz, "Ben Butler and the Occupation of Norfolk," pp. 29–30, 98–100.

41. Ibid., pp. 101–9.

42. *New Regime* (Norfolk), Jan. 6, 1865.

43. Ibid., Mar. 17, 31, Sept. 18, 1864, Jan. 1, 1865.

44. Ibid., Mar. 18, 1864.

45. Newby, "'The World Was All Before Them,'" pp. 286–88.

46. Jordan, "Painful Case," pp. 33–38.

47. Ibid., pp. 38–39.

48. Ibid., pp. 40–42.

49. Ibid., pp. 42–44.

50. Ibid., p. 45.

51. Ibid., pp. 46–48.

52. Wertenbaker and Schlegel, *Norfolk,* p. 221; Jordan, "Painful Case," pp. 48–49.

Notes

53. Jordan, "Painful Case," pp. 49–51.

54. Ibid., pp. 51–52.

55. A. P. Morse, "The Capture of the 'Maple Leaf,'" *Southern Magazine* 9 (1871): 302–9.

56. Haas, "Civil War Diary of Captain Julius Giesecke," *passim.*

57. Morse, "Capture of the 'Maple Leaf,'" *passim.*

58. *Daily Richmond Examiner* (Richmond), June 15, 23, 1863.

59. Johnson, "Blockade or Trade Monopoly?" pp. 77–78; Schwartz, "Ben Butler and the Occupation of Norfolk," pp. 55–72.

60. Schwartz, "Ben Butler and the Occupation of Norfolk," pp. 72–73, 113, 125–30.

61. Wertenbaker and Schlegel, *Norfolk,* pp. 229–30.

62. Ibid., pp. 229–31.

CHAPTER 16

1. John H. Moore, "The Norfolk Riot 16 April 1866," *VMHB* 90 (1982): 157.

2. Ibid., pp. 157–59; Newby, "'The World Was All Before Them,'" p. 160.

3. Moore, "Norfolk Riot," p. 158; Newby, "'The World Was All Before Them,'" pp. 163–64.

4. U.S. Congress, House Executive Document No. 72, XI, Thirty-ninth Cong., Second sess., 1866 (Washington, D.C., 1867), 14–66; Moore, "Norfolk Riot," p. 158; Wertenbaker and Schlegel, *Norfolk,* pp. 234–35.

5. Moore, "Norfolk Riot," p. 158.

6. Ibid.; Newby, "'The World Was All Before Them,'" p. 166.

7. Moore, "Norfolk Riot," p. 163; Newby, "'The World Was All Before Them,'" pp. 168–69.

8. *Day-Book,* Apr. 17, 1866.

9. Moore, "Norfolk Riot," p. 162.

10. Joseph P. Hanrahan, "Politics, Political Parties, and Voter Participation in Tidewater Virginia during Reconstruction, 1865–1900" (Ph.D. diss., Michigan State University, 1973), pp. 72–77.

11. Bogger, "Slave and Free Black Community in Norfolk," pp. 316, 320; Earl Lewis, *In Their Own Interests: Race, Class, and Power in Twentieth-Century Norfolk, Virginia* (Berkeley, Calif., 1991), p. 10.

12. Whiteman, "Equal Suffrage in Norfolk, Virginia," pp. 11–12; Bogger, "Slave and Free Black Community in Norfolk 1775–1865," pp. 312–13; Newby, "'The World Was All Before Them,'" pp. 140–41.

13. Whiteman, "Equal Suffrage in Norfolk, Virginia," pp. 14–15.

14. Whiteman, "Equal Suffrage in Norfolk, Virginia," p. 15; George Tucker, "Ex-Slave: Wilson's Career Spanned Sailor, Soldier, Editor Roles," *Virginian-Pilot,* Feb. 19, 1989; Hucles, "Postbellum Urban Black Economic Development," p. 78.

15. *Virginian,* Jan. 23, 1866.

16. Ibid., Mar. 22, 1866; Wertenbaker and Schlegel, *Norfolk,* pp. 253–54.

17. Hucles, "Postbellum Urban Black Economic Development," pp. 81–82; *Post* (Norfolk), June 26, 29, July 7, 1865; Newby, "'The World Was All Before Them,'" pp. 133–34.

18. Moore, "Norfolk Riot," *passim,* p. 163.

19. See, e.g., Wertenbaker and Schlegel, *Norfolk,* pp. 233–35; *Journal* (Norfolk), Jan. 1, 2, 1866; *Day-Book,* Jan. 20, 1866; *Virginian,* Dec. 18, 1865, Jan. 8, 1866.

20. *Virginian,* Mar. 28, 1866.

21. Ibid.

22. Ibid.

23. Ibid., Jan. 24, 1866.

24. Ibid., Jan. 23, 25, 26, 1866.

25. Newby, "'The World Was All Before Them,'" pp. 305–7.

26. *Virginian,* Dec. 27, 1865, June 11, July 8, 1867; Hucles, "Postbellum Urban Black Economic Development," p. 229; Wertenbaker and Schlegel, *Norfolk,* p. 265.

27. *Virginian,* Dec. 29, 1866, June 10, 22, 29, 1867, May 28, July 7, 1869.

28. Ibid., Aug. 9, 1867, June 5, Aug. 25, 1870, May 20, June 7, 1873.

29. Ibid., Apr. 18, 1871.

30. Diary of William Lamb, Dec. 30, 1869; Burton, *History of Norfolk,* p. 146.

31. Joseph E. Shank, "Shank's Raw Materials on the History of Norfolk–Portsmouth Newspapers," typescript, 7 vols., in Sargeant Room, Kirn Library, Norfolk, 2:432.

32. Diary of William Lamb, Jan. 14, Feb. 24, Mar. 16, June 4, 30, 1866; Diary "B" (July 1–Sept. 9, 1866) for Lamb's shipwreck.

33. Diary of William Lamb, Oct. 15, Nov. 13, Dec. 20, 1866, Jan. 4, Mar. 11, May 30, Nov. 4, 1867.

34. Wertenbaker and Schlegel, *Norfolk,* pp. 272–73; Diary of William Lamb, Mar. 16, 1866.

35. Wertenbaker and Schlegel, *Norfolk,* pp. 271–78.

36. Diary of William Lamb, July 12–20, 1870, Feb. 16, 1872; Wertenbaker and Schlegel, *Norfolk,* p. 277.

37. Wertenbaker and Schlegel, *Norfolk,* p. 272.

38. F. Roy Johnson, *The Peanut Story* (Murfreesboro, N.C., 1964), pp. 93–101; Wertenbaker and Schlegel, *Norfolk,* p. 285; Ainsley, "Changing Land Use in Downtown Norfolk," pp. 114–15.

39. Wertenbaker and Schlegel, *Norfolk,* pp. 260, 261; *Virginian,* Mar. 21, 1866.

40. *Virginian,* June 2, 5, 7, 13, 1871, Apr. 4, May 17, 1873.

41. Wertenbaker and Schlegel, *Norfolk,* pp. 247–51; Ainsley, "Changing Land Use in Downtown Norfolk," p. 111.

42. Wertenbaker and Schlegel, *Norfolk,* pp. 251–52.

43. Diary of William Lamb, June 25, Dec. 3, 1868, Mar. 3, July 2, 1869.

44. Emanuel Meyer, "Walter Herron Taylor and His Era" (M.A. thesis, Old Dominion University, 1984), *passim;* Newby, "'The World Was All Before Them,'" pp. 294–300.

45. Newby, "'The World Was All Before Them,'" pp. 293–94.

46. Ibid., pp. 193–212; Hucles, "Postbellum Urban Black Economic Development," pp. 172–74, 179.

47. Newby, "'The World Was All Before Them,'" p. 212.

48. Jack P. Maddex, *The Virginia Conservatives 1867–1879* (Chapel Hill, N.C., 1970), pp. 204–8; Newby, "'The World Was All Before Them,'" p. 212.

49. Hucles, "Postbellum Urban Black Economic Development," pp. 119, 158–59; *Virginian-Pilot*, Feb. 11, 1990.

50. Hucles, "Postbellum Urban Black Economic Development," pp. 91–102.

51. Tucker, "Ex-Slave"; Whiteman, "Equal Suffrage in Norfolk, Virginia,'" p. 7; Lewis, *In Their Own Interests*, p. 23; Newby, "'The World Was All Before Them,'" p. 152.

52. Wertenbaker and Schlegel, *Norfolk*, p. 235.

53. Ibid.

54. Burton, *History of Norfolk*, p. 114; Bogger, "Slave and Free Black Community in Norfolk," p. 348.

55. *Virginian*, Oct. 21, 1971; Wertenbaker and Schlegel, *Norfolk*, p. 236.

56. *Journal*, July 8, 1869; Newby, "'The World Was All Before Them,'" p. 264.

57. Burton, *History of Norfolk*, p. 134; Hucles, "Postbellum Urban Black Economic Development," pp. 167–68.

58. Bogger, "Slave and Free Black Community in Norfolk," p. 324; Lewis, *In Their Own Interests*, p. 15.

59. Burton, *History of Norfolk*, p. 134; Hanrahan, "Politics, Political Parties, and Voter Participation," pp. 108, 167.

60. Hanrahan, "Politics, Political Parties, and Voter Participation," pp. 223–25, 271, 278–79.

61. Bogger, "Slave and Free Black Community in Norfolk," p. 348; *Virginian*, May 23, 1873.

CHAPTER 17

1. *Landmark*, Jan. 14, 18, 26, 1877.

2. *Virginian*, Jan. 14, 19, 1877.

3. *Landmark*, Jan. 23, 1877.

4. Ibid., Jan. 23, 24, 25, 27, 1877; *Virginian*, Feb. 3, 1877.

5. *Landmark*, Feb. 8, 1877.

6. Ibid., Jan. 25, Feb. 9, 1877; *Virginian*, Feb. 9, 1877.

7. *Landmark*, Feb. 9, 1877.

8. Ibid., Feb. 9, 11, 14, 1877.

9. *Virginian*, Sept. 10, 1882.

10. Ibid., Sept. 10, 1882.

11. Ibid.

12. Ibid.

13. Ibid.

14. Ibid.

15. James T. Moore, *Two Paths to the New South: The Virginia Debt Controversy, 1870–1883* (Lexington, Ky., 1974), pp. 83–92.

16. *Virginian*, Sept. 14, 1882; Diary of William Lamb, Jan. 1, July 13, 1881.

17. Moore, *Two Paths to the New South*, pp. 69–82; Lenoir Chambers, Joseph E. Shank, and Harold Sugg, *Salt Water and Printer's Ink: Norfolk and Its Newspapers, 1865–1965* (Chapel Hill, N.C., 1967), pp. 146–47; Diary of William Lamb, June 17, 1880.

18. Diary of William Lamb, July 19, 20, Sept. 28, Dec. 15, 1880, June 30, Nov. 9, 22, 1881, Jan. 24, 1882; Chambers et al., *Salt Water and Printer's Ink*, p. 147.

19. *Landmark*, Feb. 16, 21, Mar. 4, 7, 1882; *Public Ledger* (Norfolk), Apr. 13, 1882; Moore, *Two Paths to the New South*, pp. 93–94.

20. Diary of William Lamb, Dec. 12, 13, 1880; *Virginian*, Dec. 6, 1882; Chambers et al., *Salt Water and Printer's Ink*, pp. 146–47.

21. James S. Kitterman Jr., "Reformers and Bosses in the Progressive Era: The Changing Face of Norfolk Politics, 1890–1920" (M.A. thesis, Old Dominion University, 1971), pp. 40–41; Diary of William Lamb, May 5, Oct. 11, 1880, Mar. 11, 1882.

22. M. Glennan, "A Review of a Reply to a Paper Which Included the Sketch of Two Lives" (Norfolk, 1883), p. 1; Moore, *Two Paths to the New South*, p. 116.

23. Diary of William Lamb, Dec. 6, 1880; Moore, *Two Paths to the New South*, p. 116.

24. Hucles, "Postbellum Urban Black Economic Development," pp. 208–14; Newby, "'The World Was All Before Them,'" pp. 232, 271

25. *Landmark*, Feb. 4, 1877, July 14, 1885.

26. *Virginian*, Sept. 27, 1877, Sept. 28, 1881, Sept. 9, 1882, Mar. 6, 1894; *Landmark*, Sept. 19, 1879; Wertenbaker and Schlegel, *Norfolk*, pp. 295–96.

27. *Virginian*, Apr. 19, 20, 1888; *News and Observer* (Raleigh, N.C.), May 31, 1925.

28. *Virginian*, Apr. 19, 1888; *News and Observer*, May 31, 1925.

29. *Public Ledger*, Feb. 2, 1877.

30. *Post*, June 22, 1865; George I. Nowitzky, *Norfolk* (Norfolk, Va., 1888), pp. 58–59.

31. David L. Jackson, "There Were Some Taverns in the Town," *Virginian-Pilot*, Apr. 17, 1968, Nov. 26, 1989.

32. Nowitzky, *Norfolk*, pp. 34–42; *Public Ledger*, Oct. 4, 1886.

33. *Virginian*, May 24, 1879; *Landmark*, Sept. 13, 1881; Samuel R. Borum, *Norfolk and Its Environs* (Norfolk, Va., 1896), p. 27.

34. *Virginian*, Jan. 14, 17, Feb. 18, Mar. 4, 1877, Aug. 5, 1879; David G. Stevens Jr., "The Temperance Movement in Norfolk, Virginia, 1880–1916" (M.A. thesis, Old Dominion University, 1968), p. 17.

35. *Landmark*, Feb. 6, 1877; Henry S. Rorer, *History of Norfolk Public Schools 1681–1968* (n.p., 1968), pp. 17–20, 83; Hucles, "Postbellum Urban Black Economic Development," pp. 160–61, 225; Newby, "'The World Was All Before Them,'" pp. 225–30.

36. Wertenbaker and Schlegel, *Norfolk*, pp. 264, 377; *Virginian-Pilot*, Oct. 30, 1966.

37. Donna Dashiell Mayer, "A Higher Education: The Norfolk College for Young Ladies, 1879–1899," *Virginia Cavalcade* 43 (Winter 1994): 100–111.

38. *Virginian-Pilot*, May 10, 1987.

39. Ibid., Oct. 17, 1965, Oct. 30, 1966.

40. Diary of William Lamb, Feb. 28, 1881; *Public Ledger*, May 12, 1884; *Virginian*, Mar. 27, 1880; Wertenbaker and Schlegel, *Norfolk*, p. 260.

41. *Virginian*, Jan. 21, 1877, Aug. 5, 1879, Jan. 28, 1880.

42. Wertenbaker and Schlegel, *Norfolk*, pp. 272–76, 282.

43. Hucles, "Postbellum Urban Black Economic Development," pp. 174–79, 196.

44. Ibid., pp. 187–88, 239.

45. Ibid., p. 194.

46. William E. Spriggs, "The Virginia Colored Farmers' Alliance: A Case Study of Race and Class Identity," *Journal of Negro History* 94 (Summer 1979): 194–96.

47. *Landmark*, Jan. 26, 27, 1877; *Virginian*, Jan. 14, Feb. 3, 1877.

48. *Landmark*, Jan. 30, Feb. 6, 15, 18, 1877; *Virginian*, Mar. 6, 1877.

49. *Virginian*, Mar. 6, 1877; *Public Ledger*, Feb. 11, 1877.

50. *Public Ledger*, Feb. 2, 1877.

51. Glennan, "Review of a Reply," *passim;* Moore, *Two Paths to the New South,* pp. 109–18; Hucles, "Postbellum Urban Black Economic Development," p. 216.

52. *Landmark*, Mar. 26, 27, 1884.

53. Ibid., Mar. 27, 1884.

54. Moore, *Two Paths to the New South,* pp. 114–18.

55. *Virginian*, July 2, 1886.

56. Ibid., Dec. 6, 1882, Aug. 1, 1888; Kitterman, "Reformers and Bosses," p. 48.

57. Moore, *Two Paths to the New South,* p. 86; Diary of William Lamb, July 3, 1880, Sept. 14, Oct. 5, 1881.

58. *Virginian*, May 27, 1882; Luther P. Jackson, *Negro Office-holders in Virginia, 1865–1895* (Norfolk, Va., 1945), p. 83; Hucles, "Postbellum Urban Black Economic Development," pp. 167–68.

59. Newby, "'The World Was All Before Them,'" pp. 265–72.

60. Lewis, *In Their Own Interests,* p. 24; Newby, "'The World Was All Before Them,'" p. 232.

61. Newby, "'The World Was All Before Them,'" p. 307.

62. Ibid., pp. 308–9.

63. *Public Ledger*, Jan. 20, 1881.

CHAPTER 18

1. *Public Ledger*, Dec. 14, 15, 1892, Feb. 23, 1893.

2. *Virginian-Pilot*, Dec. 2, 1900; *Virginian*, May 20, 1894; *Norfolk Dispatch* (Norfolk), Dec. 5, 1900.

3. *Public Ledger*, June 7, 1894.

4. Ibid., Nov. 12, 18, 1892.

5. Ibid., Nov. 2, 1892, Jan. 6, Feb. 23, 1893.

6. Ibid., Dec. 10, 1892, Mar. 24, Apr. 4, 1893; *Landmark*, May 7, 25, 1893.

7. *Landmark*, Apr. 27, 28, 29, 1894; C. Clifford Boocks, "Experiment in Municipal Reform: The Prohibition Party in Norfolk Politics, 1892–1896" (M.A. thesis, Old Dominion University, 1967), pp. 37–38.

8. *Landmark*, Apr. 29, 1894; *Virginian*, Feb. 12, 1891, May 24, 1894.

9. *Landmark*, Apr. 28, 29, 1894.

10. *Virginian*, Apr. 13, 29, May 1, 1894; Boocks, "Experiment in Municipal Reform," p. 41.

11. *Landmark*, Apr. 15, 1894; Kitterman, "Reformers and Bosses," pp. 48–52.

12. *Virginian*, Apr. 27, May 1, 1894; *Landmark*, Apr. 27, 1894.

13. Boocks, "Experiment in Municipal Reform," pp. 48–50; Kitterman, "Reformers and Bosses," p. 53.

14. Boocks, "Experiment in Municipal Reform," pp. 11–13; Kitterman, "Reformers and Bosses," pp. 38–39.

15. Kitterman, "Reformers and Bosses," pp. 29–47; on Trehy, see *Virginian-Pilot*, "20th Century Edition," June 1900.

16. Jackson, "There Were Some Taverns in the Town."

17. Kitterman, "Reformers and Bosses," pp. 11–27.

18. David G. Stevens Jr., "The Temperance Movement in Norfolk, Virginia, 1880–1916" (M.A. thesis, Old Dominion University, 1968), *passim*.

19. Stevens, "Temperance Movement in Norfolk," pp. 40, 50–51.

20. *Landmark*, Apr. 28, 1894; *Public Ledger*, Oct. 1, 1892; *Virginian-Pilot*, May 28, 1902.

21. *Public Ledger*, Oct. 25, Nov. 26, 1892; *Landmark*, Jan. 29, 1899; Shank, "Shank's Raw Materials," 4:1168.

22. *Norfolk Dispatch*, Mar. 24, June 22, 1899; Stevens, "Temperance Movement in Norfolk," p. 40.

23. *Public Ledger*, Apr. 30, May 1, 3, 21, 1894; *Landmark*, June 1, 1894; Wertenbaker and Schlegel, *Norfolk*, p. 255.

24. *Public Ledger*, Mar. 18, 22, 1893.

25. Ibid., July 12, 1893, Sept. 14, 1897; *Virginian*, Mar. 9, 1890, Sept. 8, 1892.

26. See, e.g., *Public Ledger*, Oct. 29, Nov. 3, 1892; *Norfolk Dispatch*, Aug. 22, 31, 1899.

27. *Landmark*, Dec. 6, 1898, Feb. 10, 1899; *Norfolk Dispatch*, June 28, 1899; Jackson, "There Were Some Taverns in the Town."

28. *Public Ledger*, Nov. 26, 1892; *Landmark*, Nov. 12, 1898.

29. *Public Ledger*, July 31, 1893.

30. *Ledger-Dispatch* (Norfolk), Jan. 23, 1937; Thomas C. Parramore, *Cradle of the Colony* (Edenton, N.C., 1967), p. 85. *Nowitzky's Monthly* (later *Nowitzky's Quarterly*) appeared first in October 1884, but seems to have lapsed from 1885 until 1895, when its second volume, then entitled *Nowitzky's Monthly and Travelers' Guide*, appeared.

31. Jackson, "There Were Some Taverns in the Town."

32. *Virginian*, Apr. 27, 1893; *Public Ledger*, Oct. 11, 14, 1892, Apr. 17, 18, 20, 21, 22, 24, 1893.

33. *Public Ledger*, Aug. 22, 1891; *Landmark*, Nov. 20, 1891; Wertenbaker and Schlegel, *Norfolk*, p. 292.

34. Wertenbaker and Schlegel, *Norfolk*, p. 293; *Landmark*, Oct. 18, Dec. 2, 1893.

35. Wertenbaker and Schlegel, *Norfolk*, p. 290; *Virginian-Pilot*, June 28, 1900; *Norfolk Dispatch*, June 28, 1900; Jackson, "There Were Some Taverns in the Town."

36. *Virginian*, Apr. 1, 1892; *Public Ledger*, May 2, 1894; *Landmark*, Dec. 25, 1901; Stewart, *History of Norfolk County*, p. 467.

37. *Landmark*, Nov. 6, 7, 1898; Chambers et al., *Salt Water and Printer's Ink*, pp. 207–8; Stewart, *History of Norfolk County*, p. 473.

38. Kitterman, "Reformers and Bosses," pp. 55–56; Boocks, "Experiment in Municipal Reform," pp. 91–96, 123–29.

39. Boocks, "Experiment in Municipal Reform," pp. 93–94, 96–99.

40. *Public Ledger*, Oct. 5, Nov. 16, 24, 1892, May 18, 1893; Lewis, *In Their Own Interests*, p. 16.

41. Boocks, "Experiment in Municipal Reform," pp. 80–81, appendix E, pp. 141–43.

42. Boocks, "Experiment in Municipal Reform," pp. 76–77, 82–84.

43. Chambers et al., *Salt Water and Printer's Ink*, pp. 164–84.

44. Ibid., pp. 162–63.

45. Boocks, "Experiment in Municipal Reform," pp. 74–76, 79–81, 85–90.

46. Ibid., pp. 102–11, 116–18; *Landmark*, Nov. 14, 1894.

47. Kitterman, "Reformers and Bosses," pp. 59–60, 67.

48. Andrew Buni, *The Negro in Virginia Politics, 1902–1965* (Charlottesville, Va., 1967), pp. 16–25.

49. Ibid., pp. 10–11.

50. Kitterman, "Reformers and Bosses," p. 91.

CHAPTER 19

1. *Landmark*, Apr. 27, June 6, 1907; Charles R. Keiley, ed., *The Official Blue Book of the Jamestown Ter-Centennial Exposition* (Norfolk, Va., 1909), pp. 708, 733, 739, 757, 773.

2. *Landmark*, Apr. 30, May 8, 1907.

3. "Where Independence Was Born," *Jamestown Magazine* 1 (Sept. 1906): 49–52; "A Faithful Old Spring," *Jamestown Magazine* 1 (Sept. 1906): 22.

4. Keiley, *Official Blue Book*, pp. 726, 775–78.

5. Albert Hess, "Big Attendance at 1907 Ter-Centennial," *Jamestown Magazine* 1 (July 1906): 4; Keiley, *Official Blue Book*, pp. 29–33, 46.

6. Keiley, *Official Blue Book*, pp. 70–81, 112–14.

7. Ibid., pp. 726–29, 757–59; *Ledger-Dispatch*, Aug. 27, 1907; *Virginian-Pilot*, Aug. 31, 1907.

8. Keiley, *Official Blue Book*, pp. 704–9, 730–44, 759; *Landmark*, May 1, June 4, 1907; Chambers et al., *Salt Water and Printer's Ink*, p. 267.

9. *Landmark*, Apr. 27, 1907.

10. Ibid., Apr. 23, 24, 30, May 4, 1907.

11. *Dispatch*, Apr. 13, 1905; *Ledger-Dispatch*, Feb. 22, Mar. 19, 1906.

12. *Landmark*, May 30, 1907; *Virginian-Pilot*, Aug. 19, 1906.

13. Shank, "Shank's Raw Materials," 5:1563; Chambers et al., *Salt Water and Printer's Ink*, p. 259; *Virginian-Pilot*, Jan. 1, 1907, Feb. 4, 1910; *Ledger-Dispatch*, Mar. 12, 1910.

14. Wertenbaker and Schlegel, *Norfolk*, p. 293; *Virginian-Pilot*, July 24, 1910.

15. *Landmark*, Feb. 14, June 9, 1902; Chambers et al., *Salt Water and Printer's Ink*, p. 253.

16. Wertenbaker and Schlegel, *Norfolk*, p. 294; *Landmark*, Nov. 12, 1911.

17. *Dispatch*, May 25, 1903, Sept. 19, 1904; *Ledger-Dispatch*, Jan. 18, 1908; *Landmark*, Dec. 11, 1910; Carl Abbott, "Norfolk in the New Century: The Jamestown Exposition and Urban Boosterism," *VMHB* 85 (1977): 89.

18. Interview with Dr. Proctor by Dr. Tommy L. Bogger, 1990, transcript in Norfolk State University Archives.

19. Interview with Dr. Capps by Dr. Tommy L. Bogger, 1989, transcript in Norfolk State University Archives.

20. Ibid.

21. *Public-Ledger*, May 25, 1904, Mar. 9, 1906; *Virginian-Pilot*, Sept. 10, 1911.

22. Chambers et al., *Salt Water and Printer's Ink*, p. 229; Henry L. Suggs, *P. B. Young*,

Newspaperman: Race, Politics, and Journalism in the New South, 1910–1962 (Charlottesville, Va., 1988), *passim; Landmark,* Dec. 24, 1911; *Virginian-Pilot,* Dec. 28, 1989.

23. Irwin M. Berent, "A History of Tidewater Jewry," *Renewal* 3 (Sept. 4, 1986): 17–20.

24. Ibid., pp. 20–23, 93, 99.

25. *Landmark,* Jan. 24, 1909; Wertenbaker and Schlegel, *Norfolk,* pp. 282–83, 285.

26. *Virginian-Pilot,* Oct. 16, 1908, July 29, 1911; *Landmark,* May 27, 1904, Dec. 2, 1910, July 8, 1911.

27. *Virginian-Pilot,* May 10, Dec. 18, 1903; Chambers et al., *Salt Water and Printer's Ink,* pp. 239–47.

28. *Virginian-Pilot,* Jan. 7, 1990.

29. *Landmark,* Apr. 28, May 22, 23, June 8, 1907; *Virginian-Pilot,* Nov. 15, 1910; Keiley, *Official Blue Book,* pp. 762–65.

30. *Virginian-Pilot,* Sept. 7, 1986.

31. Kitterman, "Reformers and Bosses," pp. 67–84.

32. Ibid., pp. 85–96.

33. Ibid., pp. 97–113.

34. Ibid., pp. 114–18.

35. Ibid., pp. 117–28.

36. Keiley, *Official Blue Book,* pp. 171–73, 184, 190–93, 214, 250, 440.

37. Ibid., pp. 153–333, 216, 261–65.

38. Ibid., pp. 444–46; Wertenbaker and Schlegel, *Norfolk,* p. 298.

39. Keiley, *Official Blue Book,* pp. 153–333, 335–79, 381–89.

40. Ibid., pp. 463–99, 517–678, 569, 599, 675–78.

41. Ibid., pp. 153–333; *Landmark,* May 3, 29, June 2, 1907.

42. Keiley, *Official Blue Book,* pp. 679–88, 749; *Landmark,* June 7, 1907.

43. *Landmark,* May 4, 16, 19, 1907.

44. Keiley, *Official Blue Book,* pp. 153–333.

45. *Virginian-Pilot,* Apr. 13, 1905; Lucy R. Wise, "Romantic Sewell's Point," *Jamestown Magazine* 1 (Oct. 1906): 25; "Faithful Old Spring," p. 22.

46. Keiley, *Official Blue Book,* frontispiece (John Smith statue), pp. 165–66, 205–8; *Landmark,* Apr. 26, 27, May 9, 1907.

47. Keiley, *Official Blue Book,* pp. 463–511.

48. Willard Homan, "An Early Virginia Witch," *Jamestown Magazine* 1 (Sept. 1906): 47–48; A. S. Skelton, "The First University in America," *Jamestown Magazine* 1 (Oct. 1906): 15; Charles F. Stansbury, "Historic Yorktown," *Jamestown Magazine* 1 (Nov. 1906): 11–15; Emily P. Christian, "Historic Williamsburg," *Jamestown Magazine* 1 (Dec. 1906): 39–42.

49. See, e.g., "The Only Up-to-Date Summer Resort on the Atlantic Ocean," *Jamestown Magazine* 2 (Sept. 1907): 20–21; Abbott Morris, "Norfolk," *Jamestown Magazine* 1 (Oct. 1906): 41–42; J. W. Hough, "Norfolk from a Real Estate Point of View," *Jamestown Magazine* 1 (Sept. 1906): 41–42.

50. "Jamestown Exposition in Brief," *Jamestown Magazine* 2 (Sept. 1907): 47; Chambers et al., *Salt Water and Printer's Ink,* p. 268; *Virginian-Pilot,* Oct. 19, 1907; *Ledger-Dispatch,* Dec. 2, 1907.

51. *Ledger-Dispatch,* Nov. 8, Dec. 27, 1907.

52. *Landmark*, Apr. 9, 1909.

53. *Ledger-Dispatch*, Jan. 1, 1913.

CHAPTER 20

1. *Virginian-Pilot*, Apr. 1, 1917.

2. Ibid.

3. Ibid., Apr. 6, 7, 17, 1917.

4. Ibid., Apr. 6, 8, 1917.

5. Ibid., Apr. 7, 10, 18, 1917.

6. Ibid., Apr. 10, 24, 1917.

7. Ibid., Apr. 13, 18, 1917.

8. Theodore A. Curtin, "A Marriage of Convenience: Norfolk and the Navy, 1917–1967" (M.A. thesis, Old Dominion University, 1969), pp. 11, 13, 20, 31, 35; author's interview with Mrs. Barbara P. Wool, Sept. 1, 1990.

9. Curtin, "Marriage of Convenience," pp. 34–35; Chambers et al., *Salt Water and Printer's Ink*, p. 288.

10. Stephen P. Nasca, "Norfolk in the First World War" (M.A. thesis, Old Dominion University, 1979), pp. 9, 17–18, 26–27.

11. Ibid., p. 20; Wertenbaker and Schlegel, *Norfolk*, p. 308.

12. Wertenbaker and Schlegel, *Norfolk*, pp. 308–9.

13. *Virginian-Pilot*, July 12, 1914; Wertenbaker and Schlegel, *Norfolk*, p. 310.

14. *Virginian-Pilot*, Apr. 9, 1989.

15. *Ledger-Dispatch*, May 8, 9, 13, 1916.

16. *Virginian-Pilot*, July 5, 1914.

17. Ibid., July 9, 1914; *Ledger-Dispatch*, May 5, 12, 1916.

18. *Landmark*, Mar. 28, 1915.

19. *Ledger-Dispatch*, May 14, 1916; *Virginian-Pilot*, Apr. 16, 1917.

20. *Ledger-Dispatch*, June 20, 1915.

21. Wertenbaker and Schlegel, *Norfolk*, pp. 300–301; Nasca, "Norfolk in the First World War," pp. 5, 51, 55; Lewis, *In Their Own Interests*, p. 48.

22. James R. Short, "Meet Me at Pender's," *Virginia Cavalcade* 3 (1953–54): 44–47.

23. W. Edwin Hemphill, "It Gingered Them Up but They Let It Down: The Story of a Soft Drink That Had a Hard Life," *Virginia Cavalcade* 4 (1954–55): 39–42.

24. *Virginian-Pilot*, July 7, 11, 17, 31, Aug. 3, 1914.

25. *Journal and Guide* (Norfolk), Oct. 21, 1916, Jan. 6, Mar. 17, 1917; Lewis, *In Their Own Interests*, p. 44.

26. Suggs, *P. B. Young*, pp. 23–24.

27. Irwin M. Berent, "A History of Norfolk Jewry," *UJF Virginia News* 3 (Sept. 28, 1986): 47–49; *Virginian-Pilot*, May 15, 1921.

28. *Ledger-Dispatch*, Nov. 13, 1913; *Virginian-Pilot*, Apr. 24, July 1, Aug., 9, 1914, Apr. 7, 1917.

29. Kitterman, "Reformers and Bosses," pp. 128–30.

30. Ibid., pp. 130–32.

31. Chambers et al., *Salt Water and Printer's Ink*, p. 304; Kitterman, "Reformers and Bosses," pp. 133–35.

32. Kitterman, "Reformers and Bosses," pp. 134–38; Chambers et al., *Salt Water and Printer's Ink*, p. 305; Wertenbaker and Schlegel, *Norfolk*, pp. 318–19.

33. Peter C. Stewart, "Norfolk in Nineteen Nineteen," typescript in possession of its author, pp. 1–2.

34. Stewart, "Norfolk in Nineteen Nineteen," pp. 2–5.

35. Wertenbaker and Schlegel, *Norfolk*, pp. 304–5.

36. Nasca, "Norfolk in the First World War," p. 55.

37. Ibid.

38. Lewis, *In Their Own Interests*, pp. 52–53.

39. Ibid., pp. 52–58.

40. Nasca, "Norfolk in the First World War," pp. 47, 52, 56–57.

41. Chambers et al., *Salt Water and Printer's Ink*, pp. 301–2; Curtin, "Marriage of Convenience," pp. 44–45.

42. Nasca, "Norfolk in the First World War," pp. 64–67, 79–81.

43. Curtin, "Marriage of Convenience," pp. 41–42; Chambers et al., *Salt Water and Printer's Ink*, p. 297.

44. Curtin, "Marriage of Convenience," pp. 1–3, 52.

45. Ibid., pp. 44–45, 55–56; Nasca, "Norfolk in the First World War," pp. 89–90; Chambers et al., *Salt Water and Printer's Ink*, pp. 298–99.

46. Curtin, "Marriage of Convenience," pp. 46–54.

47. Wertenbaker and Schlegel, *Norfolk*, pp. 302–3, 310–17; Nasca, "Norfolk in the First World War," pp. 33–45.

48. Stewart, "Norfolk in Nineteen Nineteen," pp. 16–17.

49. Nasca, "Norfolk in the First World War," p. 87; Kitterman, "Reformers and Bosses," p. 128.

50. *Virginian-Pilot*, Apr. 19, 1917.

51. Stewart, "Norfolk in Nineteen Nineteen," pp. 32–33.

52. Ibid., pp. 37–38.

53. Ibid., pp. 46–47.

54. Nasca, "Norfolk in World War I," pp. 94–96; *Virginian-Pilot*, May 7, 1921.

55. Nasca, "Norfolk in World War I," pp. 93–94.

CHAPTER 21

1. Newspaper clipping in Leon Nowitzky Scrapbook No. 2, Jan. 1, 1923, July 6, 1926, in possession of Richard B. Nowitzky, Norfolk.

2. Ibid., Jan. 2, 1923.

3. Ibid., Jan. 4, 1923.

4. Ibid., Jan. 12, 31, Feb. 3, 10, 1923.

5. Ibid., Feb. 10, 1923.

6. Ibid., Feb. 9, 15, 21, 1923.

7. Scrapbook No. 4, Apr. 18, 1948, Aug. 12, 1950.

8. Scrapbook No. 2, July 29, 1924, July 3, 1927, undated clipping from *Norfolk Post* entitled "Cap Shots."

Notes

9. Ibid., Dec. 20, 1925, Mar. 23, June 1, 1926, Mar. 3, 1929.

10. Ibid., Oct. 16, 1926, June 2, 1932; Scrapbook No. 4, June 2, 1948, Aug. 12, 1950.

11. Scrapbook No. 2, Jan. 9, 15, 25, Feb. 22, 23, 1923.

12. Ibid., Oct. 14, 1933.

13. Scrapbook No. 1, Mar. 10, 12, 1919 and two clippings marked "March 1919" on same pages, Dec. 18, 1930, Jan. 19, Apr. 29, 1933.

14. Scrapbook No. 2, Feb. 12, Mar. 16, 1925.

15. Nancy B. Cuthbert, "Norfolk and the K.K.K. in the Nineteen Twenties" (M.A. thesis, Old Dominion University, 1965), pp. 61–62.

16. Ibid., pp. 62, 65, 71–75.

17. Ibid., pp. 75–77.

18. Ibid., pp. 78–87.

19. Ibid., pp. 88–90.

20. Pearl _____ to John Wesley Carr, Nov. 9, 1928, ms. in John Wesley Carr Papers, South Carolina Historical Society, Charleston.

21. *Virginian-Pilot*, Jan. 1, 1926.

22. *Ledger-Dispatch*, May 13, 21, 1926.

23. *Virginian-Pilot*, Nov. 24, 28, 1920.

24. *Ledger-Dispatch*, Dec. 9, 10, 11, 12, 13, 1924.

25. Shank, "Shank's Raw Materials," 6:2154–55.

26. *Ledger-Dispatch*, Dec. 16, 1921; *Virginian-Pilot*, Aug. 29, Sept. 12, 1920; Lewis, *In Their Own Interests*, p. 38.

27. *Ledger-Dispatch*, Aug. 4, 1923, Aug. 5, 1925, July 30, 1927.

28. *Virginian-Pilot*, Aug. 29, 1950, Jan. 26, 1982.

29. David Grafton, "Peggy Hopkins Joyce, Inc.," *Forbes* Oct. 23, 1989, pp. 69–70; *Virginian-Pilot*, June 9, 1921.

30. Grafton, "Peggy Hopkins Joyce, Inc.," pp. 69–70; *Virginian-Pilot*, June 13, 1957.

31. *Ledger-Dispatch*, Aug. 1, 1925; *Virginian-Pilot*, Jan. 1, 1926.

32. Ibid., Aug. 27, 1922, Oct. 31, 1926.

33. Ibid., Oct. 31, Nov. 11, 14, 1926.

34. Ibid., Nov. 22, 25, 1926.

35. Ibid., Feb. 22, 1920; *Ledger-Dispatch*, Oct. 15, 1923, Sept. 20, 1948.

36. *Virginian-Pilot*, Aug. 18, Sept. 16, 1920; Wertenbaker and Schlegel, *Norfolk*, p. 327.

37. Wertenbaker and Schlegel, *Norfolk*, pp. 322–23; *Ledger-Dispatch*, July 10, Oct. 7, 1922

38. Wertenbaker and Schlegel, *Norfolk*, pp. 319–23.

39. Chambers et al., *Salt Water and Printer's Ink*, pp. 308–9; *Ledger-Dispatch*, Mar. 4, 1919.

40. *Ledger-Dispatch*, May 3, 1919, June 28, Nov. 17, 1923, Nov. 7, 1925; *Virginian-Pilot*, Sept. 5, 1919, Jan. 1, July 13, 1926; *Journal and Guide*, Jan. 18, 1921.

41. *Virginian-Pilot*, Nov. 27, 1990.

42. Lewis, *In Their Own Interests*, pp. 58–60.

43. Ibid., pp. 69–71.

44. Ibid., pp. 72–74.

45. Ibid., pp. 77–79.

46. Ibid., pp. 80–86.

47. *Virginian-Pilot*, Jan. 1, 1926; Suggs, *P. B. Young*, pp. 48–49.

48. Suggs, *P. B. Young*, pp. 44–58.

49. *Journal and Guide*, Feb. 9, 1923.

50. Berent, "History of Tidewater Jewry (Part III)," pp. 10, 14–20, 54.

51. Scrapbook No. 4, Apr. 18, 1948, Aug. 12, 1950; author's interview with Richard B. Nowitzky, Leon's grandson, Sept. 15, 1990.

52. *Sunday News* (Norfolk), Aug. 11, 1946.

53. Ibid.

54. Ibid.

55. Ibid.

56. Ibid.

57. Ibid.

58. Ibid.

59. Ibid.

60. Ibid.

61. Scrapbook No. 4, Apr. 18, 1943, Apr. 18, 1948, Aug. 12, 1950.

CHAPTER 22

1. Norma C. Fields, "Blacks in Norfolk Virginia during the 1930's" (M.A. thesis, Old Dominion University, 1979), pp. 46–47.

2. Ibid., p. 47; Earl Lewis, "Aline E. Black & Melvin O. Alston *vs.* The City of Norfolk 1939–1940: Equalizing the Pay of Black Teachers," *University of Michigan Center for Afroamerican and African Studies* 6 (1990): 7–9.

3. Fields, "Blacks in Norfolk Virginia during the 1930's," pp. 4, 44.

4. Ibid., p. 46; Lewis, "Equalizing the Pay of Black Teachers," pp. 8–9.

5. Lewis, "Equalizing the Pay of Black Teachers," pp. 9–10; Fields, "Blacks in Norfolk Virginia during the 1930's," pp. 47–48.

6. Lewis, "Equalizing the Pay of Black Teachers," p. 10; *Virginian-Pilot*, June 26, 1939.

7. *Virginian-Pilot*, June 26, 1939.

8. Ibid.

9. Ibid., June 27, 1939.

10. Ibid., June 28, 1939.

11. Lewis, "Equalizing the Pay of Black Teachers," p. 8.

12. Ibid., pp. 10–11.

13. Wertenbaker and Schlegel, *Norfolk*, pp. 329–43.

14. *Virginian-Pilot*, Dec. 25, 1930; Chambers et al., *Salt Water and Printer's Ink*, pp. 352, 361–62; *Ledger-Dispatch*, Feb. 10, 1934; Wertenbaker and Schlegel, *Norfolk*, p. 329.

15. Mattie B. Patterson, "Poverty and Private Charity in Norfolk during the Depression Years 1929–1933" (M.A. thesis, Old Dominion College, 1969), pp. 46, 67–72.

16. Neil Sheehan, *A Bright and Shining Lie: John Paul Vann and America in Vietnam* (New York, 1988), pp. 400–401.

17. Ibid., pp. 400–405.

18. Ibid., pp. 404–408, *passim.*

19. *Virginian-Pilot,* Sept. 1, 1935.

20. Ibid., Sept. 30, 1935.

21. Ibid., Oct. 29, 1989.

22. Patterson, "Poverty and Private Charity in Norfolk," pp. 3–7, 64–93, 151.

23. Chambers et al., *Salt Water and Printer's Ink,* pp. 360–62.

24. Lewis, *In Their Own Interests,* pp. 122–23.

25. Ibid., pp. 128–30; Fields, "Blacks in Norfolk Virginia during the 1930's," pp. 3, 80–86.

26. Lewis, *In Their Own Interests,* pp. 132–33.

27. Ibid., pp. 143–51.

28. Ibid., pp. 144–46.

29. Wertenbaker and Schlegel, *Norfolk,* pp. 339–40, 348; Patterson, "Poverty and Private Charity in Norfolk," pp. 351–52.

30. Wertenbaker and Schlegel, *Norfolk,* p. 338.

31. *Virginian-Pilot,* Jan. 1, 1929; Wertenbaker and Schlegel, *Norfolk,* p. 339; *Ledger-Dispatch* (Norfolk), Mar. 25, 1938.

32. *Ledger-Dispatch,* Sept. 1, Oct. 21, 1931, Apr. 13, 1933; *Virginian-Pilot,* July 13, 1930, Jan. 13, Dec. 18, 1932, Apr. 8, 1938.

33. *Virginian-Pilot,* Oct. 31, 1930, Apr. 8, 1938; *Ledger-Dispatch,* Apr. 14, 1933.

34. Chambers et al., *Salt Water and Printer's Ink,* pp. 365–66; Robert C. McClelland, *Annals of the College of William and Mary in Norfolk* (Norfolk, Va., 1955), pp. 1–8; Wertenbaker and Schlegel, *Norfolk,* pp. 385–86.

35. *Virginian-Pilot,* Oct. 15, 1939, Nov. 18, 1956; Wertenbaker and Schlegel, *Norfolk,* pp. 340, 342.

36. Dorothy E. Hansell, "The Norfolk Botanical Garden," *The Garden Journal* 13 (1963): 18–20; Wertenbaker and Schlegel, *Norfolk,* pp. 342, 345; *Journal and Guide,* Jan. 12, 1938.

37. Hines, "Musical Activity in Norfolk, Virginia," pp. 661–66; *Virginian-Pilot,* Jan. 1, 1931.

38. Wertenbaker and Schlegel, *Norfolk, passim.*

39. *Ledger-Dispatch,* Dec. 31, 1929, Jan. 4, 1935; *Virginian-Pilot,* Aug. 31, 1930, Apr. 6, 1933.

40. *Ledger-Dispatch,* Oct. 4, 1933; Shank, "Shanks' Raw Materials," 6 (1919–1931): 2324; *Ledger-Dispatch,* Feb. 14, 20, 1934; *Virginian-Pilot,* Sept. 10, 1934.

41. *Virginian-Pilot,* Jan. 9, 1932, Nov. 9, 23, 1938, Jan. 1, 1939; *Ledger-Dispatch,* Sept. 11, 1935, May 4, Nov. 19, 21, 1938.

42. *Ledger-Dispatch,* June 8, 9, 1931, Aug. 21, 1933; *Virginian-Pilot,* Mar. 1, 1932, Aug. 23, 31, 1933.

43. Fields, "Blacks in Norfolk Virginia during the 1930's," pp. 6, 16, 29–32.

44. Fields, "Blacks in Norfolk Virginia during the 1930's," pp. 2, 5, 53; *Journal and Guide,* Feb. 5, Oct. 14, 1938.

45. Fields, "Blacks in Norfolk Virginia during the 1930's," pp. 10–14.

46. Lewis, *In Their Own Interests,* pp. 86–87, 147.

47. Fields, "Blacks in Norfolk Virginia during the 1930's," pp. 34, 65–70.

48. Ibid., pp. 35, 38, 88.

49. Ibid., pp. 36–38; Lewis, "Equalizing the Pay of Black Teachers," pp. 10–11.
50. Fields, "Blacks in Norfolk Virginia during the 1930's," p. 55.
51. Lewis, "Equalizing the Pay of Black Teachers," p. 11.
52. Ibid., pp. 11–12.
53. Ibid., pp. 12–13.
54. Ibid.

CHAPTER 23

1. Walter Davenport, "Norfolk Night," *Collier's Weekly,* Mar. 28, 1942, pp. 17–18.
2. Ibid.
3. Ibid., pp. 28, 30; J. Blan Van Urk, "Norfolk—Our Worst War Town," *American Mercury* 56 (1943): 148.
4. Marvin W. Schlegel, *Conscripted City: Norfolk in World War II* (Norfolk, Va., 1951), pp. 277–78; *Virginian-Pilot,* Mar. 2, 1944.
5. Van Urk, "Norfolk—Our Worst War Town," p. 148; Davenport, "Norfolk Night," p. 28; Schlegel, *Conscripted City,* pp. 145, 322–23.
6. Van Urk, "Norfolk—Our Worst War Town," pp. 145–46.
7. Ibid., p. 144.
8. Ibid., pp. 144–46; Schlegel, *Conscripted City,* p. 328.
9. Van Urk, "Norfolk—Our Worst War Town," pp. 146–47.
10. Ibid., pp. 147–48; Schlegel, *Conscripted City,* p. 333.
11. Davenport, "Norfolk Night," pp. 17, 28–30; Chambers et al., *Salt Water and Printer's Ink,* p. 371; Schlegel, *Conscripted City,* pp. 187–89.
12. Van Urk, "Norfolk—Our Worst War Town," pp. 144–51.
13. Ibid., p. 151; Davenport, "Norfolk Night," p. 17.
14. *Virginian-Pilot,* Mar. 2, 3, 4, 1944.
15. Ibid., Mar. 22, 1942.
16. Schlegel, *Conscripted City,* p. 10; Lewis, *In Their Own Interests,* p. 169.
17. Schlegel, *Conscripted City,* pp. 12–13, 20, 155, 348.
18. Ibid., pp. 14–19, 31; Lewis, *In Their Own Interests,* pp. 171–72.
19. Schlegel, *Conscripted City,* pp. 18, 32–34.
20. Ibid., pp. 78–83.
21. Ibid., pp. 31–32, 39–40, 59, 60, 156.
22. Charles F. Marsh, ed., *The Hampton Roads Communities in World War II* (Chapel Hill, N.C., 1951), pp. 75–90; Chambers et al., *Salt Water and Printer's Ink,* p. 372.
23. Wertenbaker and Schlegel, *Norfolk,* p. 349; Schlegel, *Conscripted City,* pp. 34–38, 63–65.
24. Lewis, *In Their Own Interests,* pp. 176–81.
25. Ibid., pp. 182–90.
26. Schlegel, *Conscripted City,* pp. 125–26.
27. Ibid., pp. 127–29.
28. Ibid., pp. 65, 91–92, 177–78.
29. Ibid., pp. 36–38, 157.
30. *Virginian-Pilot,* Dec. 17, 1991.
31. Wertenbaker and Schlegel, *Norfolk,* p. 359; Schlegel, *Conscripted City,* pp. 191–92.

32. Schlegel, *Conscripted City*, pp. 59, 64, 176, 231, 255.

33. *Virginian-Pilot*, Aug. 20, 1942; Schlegel, *Conscripted City*, pp. 193–95; Lewis, *In Their Own Interests*, p. 191.

34. Suggs, *P. B. Young*, pp. 119–21, 126.

35. Ibid., pp. 126–28, 131; Schlegel, *Conscripted City*, pp. 14–15.

36. Lewis, *In Their Own Interests*, pp. 195–97.

37. Schlegel, *Conscripted City*, pp. 5, 63–64, 93–97, 157–58, 252–53.

38. Schlegel, *Conscripted City*, pp. 92–93, 97–99, 252–53, 312–13.

39. Wertenbaker and Schlegel, *Norfolk*, p. 356; Schlegel, *Conscripted City*, pp. 210–11.

40. Schlegel, *Conscripted City*, pp. 111–13, 178–79, 235–38, 241–49; Marsh, *Hampton Roads Communities in World War II*, p. 159.

41. Chambers et al., *Salt Water and Printer's Ink*, p. 373; Schlegel, *Conscripted City*, pp. 49–50, 72, 134, 137–40, 170, 227–28, 258–59; Wertenbaker and Schlegel, *Norfolk*, p. 359.

42. Schlegel, *Conscripted City*, pp. 194, 326; Wertenbaker and Schlegel, *Norfolk*, p. 359.

43. Schlegel, *Conscripted City*, pp. 274–75.

44. Ibid., pp. 275–76.

45. Ibid., pp. 277–78.

46. Ibid., pp. 322–24.

47. *Virginian-Pilot*, Sept. 22, 1943, Mar. 2, 3, 4, 1944; Schlegel, *Conscripted City*, pp. 323–26.

48. Schlegel, *Conscripted City*, pp. 325–26

49. Ibid., pp. 326–28.

50. Ibid., p. 330.

51. Ibid., pp. 331–34.

52. Ibid., pp. 334–36.

53. Ibid., pp. 100–101, 158, 199–200, 311–12, 320–21; *Virginian-Pilot*, Dec. 15, 1991.

54. Schlegel, *Conscripted City*, pp. 231–32, 254, 311–13, 316–17, 359.

55. *Virginian-Pilot*, Aug. 1, 1965.

56. Marsh, *Hampton Roads Communities in World War II*, p. 75.

57. *Virginian-Pilot*, Nov. 3, 1981.

CHAPTER 24

1. *Virginian-Pilot*, Mar. 17, Apr. 12, 1946, Feb. 11, 1990; *Journal and Guide*, Mar. 9, 1974.

2. Ibid., Mar. 17, May 13, 1946.

3. Ibid., May 13, 1946.

4. Ibid., May 21, 1946.

5. Ibid., Mar. 17, 1946.

6. Ibid., Mar. 31, 1946; Chambers et al., *Salt Water and Printer's Ink*, pp. 376–77.

7. *Virginian-Pilot*, Mar. 31, Apr. 5, 1946.

8. Ibid.

9. Forrest R. White, "School Desegregation and Urban Renewal in Norfolk, 1950–1959" (Ph.D. diss., Old Dominion University, 1991), pp. 54–58.

10. Ibid., pp. 54–69.

11. *Virginian-Pilot,* May 21, June 13, 1946.

12. Ibid., June 10, 12, 1946.

13. *Virginian-Pilot,* June 13, 1946; Chambers et al., *Salt Water and Printer's Ink,* pp. 376–77.

14. Chambers et al., *Salt Water and Printer's Ink,* pp. 377–78: *Virginian-Pilot,* Sept. 24, 1961.

15. Chambers et al., *Salt Water and Printer's Ink,* pp. 377–78.

16. Forrest R. White, interview with Dr. Tommy L. Bogger, Apr. 13, 1990; *Virginian-Pilot,* Apr. 11, 1964; White, "School Desegregation and Urban Renewal," p. 70.

17. White, "School Desegregation and Urban Renewal," pp. 71–74; Shank, "Shank's Raw Materials," 7:2531, 2552; Chambers et al., *Salt Water and Printer's Ink,* pp. 378–79.

18. Shank, "Shank's Raw Materials," 7:2531, 2552; Chambers et al., *Salt Water and Printer's Ink,* pp. 378–79; White, "School Desegregation and Urban Renewal," pp. 73–74.

19. Shank, "Shank's Raw Materials," 7:2531.

20. Ibid., 7:2531, 2532; *Virginian-Pilot,* Jan. 1, 1947, Apr. 27, May 23, 1952.

21. Wertenbaker and Schlegel, *Norfolk,* pp. 370–37; White, "School Desegregation and Urban Renewal," pp. 78–80.

22. *This Is It,* pamphlet of Norfolk Housing and Redevelopment Authority, May 1946, p. 4; "The Norfolk Story: Official Annual Report of the City of Norfolk," *Virginian-Pilot,* July 23, 1949, Jan. 29, 1956; White, "School Desegregation and Urban Renewal," pp. 80–81.

23. White, "School Desegregation and Urban Renewal," pp. 79–80.

24. "Report by Mrs. Charles Lovitt at Membership Meeting, Women's Council for Interracial Cooperation, October, 1949," ms. in Women's Council for Inter-Racial Cooperation Papers, 22 (Oct. 1949), Norfolk State University Archives.

25. Wertenbaker and Schlegel, *Norfolk,* pp. 370–71; White, "School Desegregation and Urban Renewal," pp. 74–80.

26. White, "School Desegregation and Urban Renewal," pp. 90–91.

27. "The Norfolk Story," *Virginian-Pilot,* Jan. 29, 1956; White, "School Desegregation and Urban Renewal," p. 101.

28. Wertenbaker and Schlegel, *Norfolk,* p. 368; Shank, "Shank's Raw Materials," 7:2559.

29. White, "School Desegregation and Urban Renewal," pp. 191–92.

30. Ibid., pp. 192–95.

31. Ibid., pp. 195–97.

32. Wertenbaker and Schlegel, *Norfolk,* pp. 362–63.

33. Ibid., pp. 363–65.

34. *Virginian-Pilot,* June 14, 1950; Wertenbaker and Schlegel, *Norfolk,* p. 362.

35. Wertenbaker and Schlegel, *Norfolk,* p. 362.

36. Shank, "Shank's Raw Materials," 7:2531, 2543, 2551, 2559.

37. *Virginian-Pilot,* June 3, 1946.

38. Ibid., Mar. 4, 1990.

39. Carl Cahill, "This Virginia: Doumar," *The Commonwealth,* p. 28, undated reprint furnished to author by Mr. Al Doumar.

40. Wertenbaker and Schlegel, *Norfolk,* pp. 381–82.

41. Ibid., pp. 384–85.

Notes

42. Ibid., pp. 382–83.
43. Richard Tregaskis, "Norfolk," *Saturday Evening Post,* July 9, 1949, pp. 32–33, 73.
44. Ibid., pp. 33, 73.
45. Wertenbaker and Schlegel, *Norfolk,* p. 362; *Virginian-Pilot,* Apr. 11, 1964.
46. Shank, "Shank's Raw Materials," 7:2559.
47. Ibid., 7:2549, 2560, 2563, 2569.
48. Ibid., 7:2561; *Virginian-Pilot,* May 17, Sept. 1, Dec. 22, 1956.
49. Wertenbaker and Schlegel, *Norfolk,* p. 364; *Virginian-Pilot,* Jan. 1, 1955.
50. Wertenbaker and Schlegel, *Norfolk,* pp. 364–65; Ruby Nell Isom, "The Beacon Light Civic League: A Study of the Functioning of a Community Organization" (Ph.D. diss., University of North Carolina, 1973), p. 27.
51. *Virginian-Pilot,* Feb. 28, Mar. 5, Nov. 26, 1956.
52. Wertenbaker and Schlegel, *Norfolk,* pp. 385–87.
53. *Virginian-Pilot,* Feb. 5, 1960.
54. Ibid., Nov. 21, 1959.
55. *Ledger-Dispatch,* Feb. 4, 1960.
56. Wertenbaker and Schlegel, *Norfolk,* pp. 372–75; Shank, "Shank's Raw Materials," 7:2560.
57. *Journal and Guide,* Feb. 13, 1960; *Virginian-Pilot,* Feb. 5, 1960.
58. Wertenbaker and Schlegel, *Norfolk,* pp. 366–67.
59. *Virginian-Pilot,* Mar. 4, 1960.
60. Ibid., Feb. 5, Mar. 4, 1960.
61. Ibid., Mar. 2, 4, 1960; *Ledger-Dispatch,* Mar. 3, 1960; Wertenbaker and Schlegel, *Norfolk,* pp. 373–75.
62. *Virginian-Pilot,* Aug. 5, 1954.

CHAPTER 25

1. Nancy P. Ford, "The Peaceful Resolution of Norfolk's Integration Crisis of 1958 and 1959" (M.A. thesis, Old Dominion University, 1979), pp. 17–18, 28.
2. Ibid., pp. 28–30; Chambers et al., *Salt Water and Printer's Ink,* p. 385.
3. Ford, "Peaceful Resolution of Norfolk's Integration Crisis," pp. 30–31; Wertenbaker and Schlegel, *Norfolk,* p. 387.
4. Ford, "Peaceful Resolution of Norfolk's Integration Crisis," pp. 15, 20–21.
5. Ibid., pp. 22–23, 31–32, 38; Chambers et al., *Salt Water and Printer's Ink,* p. 385.
6. Jane Reif, *Crisis in Norfolk* (Richmond, Va., 1960), p. 1; Ford, "Peaceful Resolution of Norfolk's Integration Crisis," pp. 3–4, 23.
7. Reif, *Crisis in Norfolk,* pp. 1–2; Ford, "Peaceful Resolution of Norfolk's Integration Crisis," pp. 3–4.
8. Ford, "Peaceful Resolution of Norfolk's Integration Crisis," pp. 24–27, 60.
9. Ibid., pp. 47–55; Reif, *Crisis in Norfolk,* pp. 4–6.
10. Ford, "Peaceful Resolution of Norfolk's Integration Crisis," pp. 35, 51–52, 56–57; Reif, *Crisis in Norfolk,* pp. 10–11.
11. Ford, "Peaceful Resolution of Norfolk's Integration Crisis," pp. 27–28.
12. Ibid., pp. 35–37; Wertenbaker and Schlegel, *Norfolk,* p. 388.

13. Ford, "Peaceful Resolution of Norfolk's Integration Crisis," pp. 33–35, 60; Wertenbaker and Schlegel, *Norfolk*, pp. 388–89.

14. Ford, "Peaceful Resolution of Norfolk's Integration Crisis," pp. 34, 38.

15. Wertenbaker and Schlegel, *Norfolk*, p. 389; Reif, *Crisis in Norfolk*, p. 22.

16. Ford, "Peaceful Resolution of Norfolk's Integration Crisis," pp. 39–40.

17. White, "School Desegregation and Urban Renewal," pp. 242–48.

18. Ibid., pp. 207–13.

19. Ibid., pp. 183, 191–99, 212.

20. Ibid., pp. 210, 238, 253–54; *Virginian-Pilot*, Dec. 3, 1967.

21. White, "School Desegregation and Urban Renewal," pp. 253–83; *Virginian-Pilot*, Oct. 7, 1979.

22. White, "School Desegregation and Urban Renewal," pp. 122–40, 284–303.

23. *Virginian-Pilot*, May 31, June 21, 1964.

24. Ibid., May 31, 1964.

25. Ibid., May 31, June 21, 1964.

26. Ibid., Jan. 19, 1963, Apr. 12, 1964.

27. Ibid., Jan. 19, 1963; Edward J. Boone Jr., "History of the General Douglas MacArthur Memorial," typescript in Jean MacArthur Research Center, Norfolk.

28. *Virginian-Pilot*, Jan. 30, 1991.

29. Ibid., Apr. 11, 1964.

30. Ibid., Apr. 11, 1964, Aug. 1, 1965.

31. Ibid., Aug. 1, 1965; Wertenbaker and Schlegel, *Norfolk*, p. 382.

32. *Virginian-Pilot*, Aug. 8, Oct. 31, 1965.

33. Ibid., Aug. 8, 1965, Jan. 2, 1991.

34. Ibid., Dec. 8, 1980, Apr. 9, 1990.

35. Ibid., Sept. 18, 1990.

36. Ibid., Sept. 28, 1965.

37. Ibid., Apr. 11, 1964, Sept. 28, 1965.

38. Ibid., Oct. 24, 1965.

39. Ibid., May 31, 1964.

40. Ibid., Apr. 11, 1964.

41. Ibid., Feb. 2, 1964.

42. Ibid., Oct. 3, 1965.

43. Carl Abbott, *The New Urban America: Growth and Politics in Sunbelt Cities* (Chapel Hill, N.C., 1981), p. 154.

44. Reif, *Crisis in Norfolk*, p. 16; Abbott, *New Urban America*, pp. 127–29.

45. Ford, "Peaceful Resolution of Norfolk's Integration Crisis," pp. 55–56; Reif, *Crisis in Norfolk*, pp. 10–12.

46. Ford, "Peaceful Resolution of Norfolk's Integration Crisis," pp. 39–40; Reif, *Crisis in Norfolk*, p. 16; Abbott, *New Urban America*, p. 130.

47. Ford, "Peaceful Resolution of Norfolk's Integration Crisis," pp. 40–41; Reif, *Crisis in Norfolk*, pp. 17–18.

48. David Pace, "Lenoir Chambers Opposes Massive Resistance," *VMHB* 82 (1974): *passim;* Chambers et al., *Salt Water and Printer's Ink*, p. 388.

49. Reif, *Crisis in Norfolk*, p. 18; Ford, "Peaceful Resolution of Norfolk's Integration Crisis," p. 41; White, "School Desegregation and Urban Renewal," p. 387.

50. White, "School Desegregation and Urban Renewal," p. 399.

51. Reif, *Crisis in Norfolk,* pp. 13–14; Ford, "Peaceful Resolution of Norfolk's Integration Crisis," pp. 55–56.

52. Reif, *Crisis in Norfolk,* p. 25; Ford, "Peaceful Resolution of Norfolk's Integration Crisis," pp. 69–70.

53. Reif, *Crisis in Norfolk,* pp. 6–7; Ford, "Peaceful Resolution of Norfolk's Integration Crisis," pp. 50–51.

54. Abbott, *New Urban America,* pp. 131–32; White, "School Desegregation and Urban Renewal," pp. 440–41.

CHAPTER 26

1. *Virginian-Pilot,* Jan. 23, 1968.
2. Ibid.
3. Ibid., Nov. 19, 1966, Feb. 24, 1968.
4. Ibid., Aug. 13, 1966.
5. Ibid., Aug. 13, 1966, July 8, 1972.
6. Ibid., Nov. 19, 1967, July 9, 1972.
7. Ibid., May 17, 1970, July 8, 1972.
8. Ibid., May 10, June 8, 1970, Mar. 6, 1971.
9. "Hassle at N.S.C.," *Brown Shoes* 1 (Apr.–May 1969): 4; "We Ain't Marching Anymore," *Brown Shoes* 1 (n.d.): 4.
10. *Virginian-Pilot,* Aug. 14, 1966.
11. Ibid., Aug. 14, 1966, Feb. 25, 1968.
12. Ibid., Jan. 13, 17, 1965.
13. Ibid., Jan. 17, 1965.
14. Ibid., May 7, 1967.
15. Ibid., Mar. 14, 1971.
16. Ibid., Sept. 19, 1965, Nov. 26, 1967.
17. Ibid., May 21, 1980.
18. Ibid., Sept. 19, 1965, Mar. 26, 1967.
19. Ibid., Mar. 1, 1964.
20. Ibid., Nov. 30, 1971; *Ledger-Star,* Apr. 7, 1973.
21. *Ledger-Star,* Mar. 22, 1965, Feb. 5, June 28, 1966.
22. Ibid., Mar. 22, 1965, Dec. 7, 1965, July 6, 1966, Dec. 11, 1973; *Virginian-Pilot,* Aug. 25, 1967, May 29, 1968; *New Journal and Guide* (Norfolk), June 21, 1975; Lawrence H. Coleman, ed., "A Decade of Decay during the Brick-and-Mortar Administration" (n.d., n.p.), *passim.*
23. *Virginian Pilot,* Aug. 9, 1973.
24. Ibid., Apr. 16, 1967, Feb. 18, 25, 1968, Aug. 19, 26, 1973.
25. Ibid., June 26, Nov. 6, 1966, Sept. 23, 1973.
26. Ibid., Dec. 10, 1967.
27. Ibid., Jan. 1, 1967.
28. Ibid., Jan. 26, 1967, Jan. 7, 1973; Dr. Mason Andrews, "Remarks for Fund Raising Dinner January 15, 1970," ms. in Medical Center Papers, in possession of Dr. An-

drews; John P. Flemming IV, "The Emergence of a Medical School in Hampton Roads" (Ph.D. diss., Old Dominion University, 1988), pp. 92, 166.

29. Flemming, "Emergence of a Medical School in Hampton Roads," pp. 8, 92; Frank Batten to C. Mason Andrews, Nov. 20, 1961, personal files of Dr. Andrews.

30. Flemming, "Emergence of a Medical School in Hampton Roads," pp. 109, 166; *Virginian-Pilot,* Jan. 28, 1970.

31. *Virginian-Pilot,* Feb. 20, 1966, Dec. 3, 1967; *Washington* (D.C.) *Post,* Feb. 26, 1989.

32. *Virginian-Pilot,* Feb. 20, 1966; Isom, "Beacon Light Civic League", p. 72.

33. *Virginian-Pilot,* Feb. 14, 1971, May 16, 1976.

34. Ibid., May 16, 29, 1976.

35. Ibid., Feb. 25, 1968.

36. *Ledger-Dispatch,* Aug. 4, 1983; "Terri Tompkins on way to fame as N. Y. dancer," undated, unidentified clipping, dated Nov. 11, 1987, in Sargeant Room biographical files, Kirn Memorial Library, Norfolk.

37. *Virginian-Pilot,* Dec. 21, 1975, May 16, 30, 1976.

38. Ibid., Feb. 2, 1975, July 16, 1978.

39. Isom, "Beacon Light Civic League," pp. 26–27; *Virginian-Pilot,* May 30, 1981, Apr. 1, 1990.

40. *Virginian-Pilot,* Mar. 25, 1973.

41. Ibid., Apr. 12, June 12, 1983; *Ledger-Star,* Mar. 11, 1969.

42. *Virginian-Pilot,* Nov. 4, 1971, Apr. 18, 1984.

43. Ibid., Sept. 11, 1966.

44. Ibid., Mar. 11, 1970.

45. Ibid., May 6, 1970.

46. Ibid., May 5, 6, 1970.

47. Ibid., May 9, 1970.

48. Ibid., May 16, 22, 31, June 13, 1970.

49. Ibid., May 30, 1970.

50. Ibid., Feb. 20, 1971.

51. Ibid.

CHAPTER 27

1. *Ledger-Star,* July 5, 1991.

2. *Virginian-Pilot,* July 3, 1991.

3. Ibid., July 3, 4, 1991; *Ledger-Star,* July 4, 1991.

4. *Virginian-Pilot,* July 4, 1991.

5. Ibid., July 6, 1991.

6. Ibid., July 3, 1991.

7. *Ledger-Star,* July 5, 1991; *Virginian-Pilot,* July 3, 1991.

8. *Daily Press/Times Herald* (Newport News–Hampton), Apr. 16, 1985; Curtin, "Marriage of Convenience," pp. 171–72, 182.

9. Jane H. Sobie, "The Navy in Norfolk," *Ladycom Magazine,* Oct. 1983, p. 36, clipping in files of Sargeant Room, Kirn Memorial Library; Curtin, "Marriage of Convenience," p. 183.

Notes

10. *Daily Press/Times Herald*, Apr. 16, 1985.
11. Curtin, "Marriage of Convenience," pp. 148–72.
12. *Virginian-Pilot*, Jan. 19, 1975.
13. Ibid., June 20, 1979, Sept. 13, 1981.
14. *Daily Press/Times Herald*, Apr. 8, 1985.
15. *Virginian-Pilot*, May 25, 1980.
16. Ibid., May 16, 1976.
17. Ibid., Jan. 19, Nov. 16, 1975, Mar. 13, 1977, July 23, 1978.
18. Ibid., Dec. 31, 1989, Oct. 3, 1990.
19. Ibid., Sept. 12, 1976, Aug. 10, 1980.
20. *Ledger-Star*, June 1, 1983; *Virginian-Pilot*, June 2, 1983.
21. *Virginian-Pilot*, June 2, 1983.
22. *Ledger-Star*, May 11, Dec. 28, 1981; *Virginian-Pilot*, May 14, 1992.
23. *Ledger-Star*, Aug. 23, 1984; *Virginian-Pilot*, May 1, 1983, June 20, 1990.
24. *Virginian-Pilot*, Jan. 30, 1983.
25. Ibid., Feb. 27, 1977.
26. Ibid.
27. Ibid., Jan. 19, 1975.
28. Ibid., Sept. 16, Dec. 13, 1981, Apr. 15, 1984, Apr. 15, 1989.
29. Ibid., July 11, Dec. 26, 1982, Feb. 20, 1983.
30. Ibid., Sept. 7, 1986, May 10, July 12, 1987, Feb. 28, 1991.
31. Ibid., May 10, 1987.
32. Ibid., Sept. 16, Dec. 13, 1981, Apr. 15, 1984, Apr. 15, 1989.
33. Ibid., Feb. 20, May 8, 1977.
34. Ibid., Nov. 23, 1975.
35. Ibid., Sept. 12, 1976.
36. Ibid., May 25, 1980.
37. Ibid., Jan. 13, 1980.
38. Ibid., May 25, 27, 1972.
39. Isom, "Beacon Light Civic League," pp. 30–35.
40. Ibid., pp. 36–39.
41. Ibid., pp. 44–45.
42. Ibid., pp. 21, 29, 45–47.
43. *Virginian-Pilot*, May 25, 27, 1972.
44. Isom, "Beacon Light Civic League," pp. 74–75; *Virginian-Pilot*, July 29, 1990.
45. Ibid., pp. 71, 75–78.
46. Ibid., pp. 79–80.
47. Pete Earley, *Family of Spies: Inside the Walker Spy Ring* (Toronto, 1988), pp. 53, 56–61.
48. Ibid., pp. 58, 62–65, 69.
49. Ibid., pp. 73, 78, 83–85, 92–93.
50. Ibid., pp. 86–87.
51. Ibid., pp. 138, 143, 148; *Virginian-Pilot*, May 21, 1985, Dec. 11, 1986.
52. Earley, *Family of Spies*, pp. 158–62, 168–69, 191–94, 204.
53. Ibid., pp. 73, 201–11, 262–65; *Virginian-Pilot*, May 21, 1985.
54. Earley, *Family of Spies*, pp. 91, 142–43, 276.

55. Ibid., pp. 271–72, 279–83.

56. Ibid., pp. 302–3, 306–10, 320–23.

57. Ibid., pp. 324–27.

58. Ibid., pp. 358–59, 363; *Virginian-Pilot,* May 21, 23, 1985, Dec. 11, 1986, Mar. 24, 1990; *Ledger-Star,* Mar. 26, 1990.

59. Earley, *Family of Spies,* pp. 72, 73, 75–76.

CHAPTER 28

1. *Virginian-Pilot,* Aug. 6, 1989.

2. Ibid.

3. Ibid.

4. Ibid., Aug. 6, 1989, Feb. 28, 1991.

5. Ibid., Aug. 6, 1989, July 17, 1990.

6. Ibid., July 11, 17, Aug. 6, 1990.

7. Ibid., July 11, Aug. 5, 1990.

8. Ibid., Aug. 6, 1989, July 17, 1990.

9. Ibid., Aug. 6, 1989.

10. Ibid., May 1, 1983.

11. Ibid., Aug. 5, 1989.

12. Ibid., May 1, 1983, Feb. 27, Sept. 10, 1989.

13. Ibid., Sept. 22, 1990.

14. Ibid., Feb. 11, June 21, July 6, 1990, Jan. 15, June 26, 1991.

15. Ibid., Oct. 26, 1989, Aug. 23, Oct. 3, 1990, Dec. 8, 1991.

16. Ibid., Dec. 30, 1990, Nov. 22, 1991.

17. Ibid., Nov. 8, 1989, Jan. 8, Mar. 3, Dec. 15, 1991.

18. Ibid., Nov. 10, 1991.

19. Ibid., May 8, 1990, Nov. 17, 1991.

20. Ibid., Aug. 12, 30, Sept. 7, 1990, Nov. 25, 1991.

21. *Virginian-Pilot, Downtowner* (Norfolk), Nov., 1990.

22. *Virginian-Pilot,* Mar. 27, 1989, July 29, 1990, May 25, 1991.

23. Ibid., July 8, 1989, Feb. 16, 1991.

24. Ibid., Feb. 8, 1991.

25. Ibid., Nov. 18, 1990.

26. Ibid., Mar. 18, 1990.

27. Ibid., Jan. 7, 1990, Mar. 26, 1991.

28. Ibid., June 16, Oct. 3, Dec. 17, 1991.

29. Ibid., June 11, 1991.

30. Ibid., May 1, 1983, Mar. 15, 1988, Oct. 29, Dec. 18, 1989, June 16, 1991; Biographical clipping File, 1984, 1988, Sargeant Room, Kirn Library, Norfolk.

31. *Virginian-Pilot,* Sept. 16, 1990.

32. Ibid., Aug. 19, 1990, July 1, 1991.

33. Ibid., June 1, 1990, Mar. 24, 1991

34. Ibid., Aug. 22, 1989, June 1, 1990, Sept. 1, 1991.

35. Ibid., Mar. 24, 1991.

36. Ibid., June 9, 1991.

Notes

37. Ibid., Dec. 10, 1990, *Discover Hampton Roads* (Norfolk), Aug. 2, 1989.
38. *Virginian-Pilot,* July 11, 1982, Nov. 20, 1983, Aug. 20, Dec. 13, 1990, Apr. 10, 1991.
39. Ibid., Jan. 28, 1991.
40. Ibid., Aug. 19, 1990, Mar. 3, 31, Aug. 16, 1991.
41. Ibid., Mar. 11, Dec. 15, 1991.
42. Ibid., Feb. 22, 1989, Apr. 23, 1990.
43. Ibid., Feb. 5, 1989, Feb. 23, 1990.
44. Ibid., Oct. 12, 1990.
45. Ibid., Aug. 6, 1989.
46. Ibid., Aug. 6, 1989, Apr. 22, 1990.
47. Ibid., Aug. 6, 1989.
48. Ibid.
49. Ibid., Aug. 6, 1989, Nov. 10, 1991.
50. Ibid., Aug. 6, 1989.
51. Ibid.
52. Ibid.
53. Ibid., Dec. 15, 1991.

CHAPTER 29

1. *Virginian-Pilot,* Dec. 18, 1991.
2. Ibid., Dec. 15, 18, 1991.
3. Ibid., July 8, 1992.
4. Ibid., Dec. 29, 1991.
5. Ibid., Mar. 12, Dec. 27, 1992.
6. Ibid., Apr. 16, 1992.
7. Ibid., Sept. 3, Oct. 7, 1992.
8. Ibid., Jan. 20, Aug. 16, 1992, Jan. 6, 1993.
9. Ibid., July 9, May 10, 1992.
10. Ibid., May 28, 1992, Jan. 17, 1993.
11. Erik Larson, "The Story of a Gun," *Atlantic Monthly* Jan. 1993, pp. 48–78.
12. *Virginian-Pilot,* Sept. 20, 24, 1992.
13. Ibid., Jan. 6, 1993.
14. Ibid., Feb. 18, May 27, Oct. 11, 1992.
15. Ibid., Nov. 7, 1992.
16. Ibid., June 22, Oct. 22, 1992.
17. Ibid., Apr. 13, July 2, Nov. 2, 1992.
18. Ibid., Nov. 16, 1992, Jan. 7, 1993.
19. Ibid., Oct. 6, 1991, June 22, 1992.
20. Ibid., May 6, Nov. 16, 29, 1992, Jan. 13, 1993.
21. Ibid., May 13, July 14, 1992.
22. Ibid., Aug. 2, Dec. 23, 26, 1992.
23. Ibid., July 20, Sept. 28, Nov. 11, 1992.
24. Ibid., Sept. 2, Sept. 9, 1992.

25. Ibid., Apr. 26, Dec. 16, 1992.
26. Ibid., May 14, July 12, Dec. 23, 1992.
27. Ibid., July 2, Dec. 31, 1992.
28. Ibid., Sept. 20, Dec. 31, 1992, Feb. 8, 1993.
29. Ibid., Apr. 20, Nov. 6, Dec. 30, 1992.
30. Ibid., Mar. 11, 1992, Jan. 2, 1993.
31. Ibid., July 8, Sept. 4, 1992, Jan. 1, 1993.
32. Ibid., Apr. 22, 1992.
33. Ibid., Sept. 1, 1992.
34. Ibid., Jan. 11, 1993.
35. Ibid., Dec. 20, 1992.
36. Ibid., Mar. 17, 20, 1993.

INDEX

Index

Index

Index

Index

Index

Index

Index

Index